MW00451348

Myths and Legends
of the Eastern Front

Myths and Legends of the Eastern Front

Reassessing the Great Patriotic War 1941–1945

Boris V. Sokolov

Edited and translated by
Richard W. Harrison

Pen & Sword
MILITARY

First published in Great Britain in 2019 by
PEN & SWORD MILITARY

An imprint of
Pen & Sword Books Ltd
Yorkshire – Philadelphia

ISBN 978-1-52674-226-1

Typeset in 11/13 point MinionPro

Printed and bound by TJ International

Pen & Sword Books Ltd incorporates the Imprints of Aviation, Atlas, Family History, Fiction, Maritime, Military, Discovery, Politics, History, Archaeology, Select, Wharncliffe Local History, Wharncliffe True Crime, Military Classics, Wharncliffe Transport, Leo Cooper, The Praetorian Press, Remember When, White Owl, Seaforth Publishing and Frontline Publishing.

For a complete list of Pen & Sword titles please contact
PEN & SWORD BOOKS LIMITED
47 Church Street, Barnsley, South Yorkshire, S70 2AS, England
E-mail: enquiries@pen-and-sword.co.uk
Website: www.pen-and-sword.co.uk
                                     Or
PEN & SWORD BOOKS
1950 Lawrence Rd, Havertown, PA 19083, USA
E-mail: Uspen-and-sword@casematepublishers.com
Website: www.penandswordbooks.com

Contents

Translator's Introduction

The study contains a number of terms that may not be readily understandable to the casual reader of military history. Therefore, I have adopted a number of conventions designed to ease this task. For example, major Soviet field formations (i.e., Western Front) are spelled out in full, as are similar German formations (i.e., Army Group South). Soviet armies are designated using the shortened form (i.e., 38th Army). German armies, on the other hand, are spelled out in full (i.e., Eighteenth Army). In the same vein, Soviet corps are designated by Arabic numerals (1st Guards Cavalry Corps), while the same German units are denoted by Roman numerals (e.g., VII Army Corps). Smaller units (divisions, brigades, etc.) on both sides are denoted by Arabic numerals only (7th Guards Cavalry Division, 255th Infantry Division, etc.).

Given the large number of units appearing here, I have adopted certain other conventions in order to better distinguish them. For example, Soviet armoured units are called tank corps, brigades, etc., while the corresponding German units are denoted by the popular term *panzer*. Likewise, Soviet infantry units are designated by the term rifle, while the corresponding German units are simply referred to as infantry.

Elsewhere, a *front* is a Soviet wartime military organization roughly corresponding to an American army group. Throughout the narrative the reader will encounter such names as the Western Front and Soutwestern fronts, etc. To avoid confusion with the more commonly understood meaning of the term front (i.e., the front line), italics will be used to denote an unnamed *front*.

The work subscribes to no particular transliteration scheme, because no entirely satisfactory one exists. I have adopted a mixed system that uses the Latin letters ya and yu to denote their Cyrillic counterparts, as opposed to the ia and iu employed by the Library of Congress, which tends to distort proper pronunciation. Conversely, I have retained the Library of Congress's ii ending (i.e., Tukhachevskii), as opposed to the commonly used y ending. I have also retained the apostrophe to denote the Cyrillic soft sign.

The work contains endnotes by the author. They have been supplemented by a number of appropriately identified editor's notes, which have been inserted as an explanatory guide for a number of terms that might not be readily understandable to the foreign reader.

Preface

The famous American historian Anne Applebaum rightly believes that in modern Russia 'the ruling class considers itself the heir of the Soviet system'.[1] As a result, the Great Patriotic War is becoming the centre of a Russian-Soviet identity and in a variant only slightly updated from the Soviet myth. It is only this period of twentieth-century history that up until now has remained a positive historical myth. Victory in the Great Patriotic War is the sole event of the last century, in the positive perception of which the overwhelming majority of Russian citizens are united. This is the single component part of the Russian national idea that the current powers can offer to the people. And for the sake of preserving this idea, which is almost the single foundation of the Russian identity, practically the entire period of the Second World War has to be shifted beyond the bounds of historical science, leaving it exclusively within the power of political mythology.

The history of the Great Patriotic War is viewed only as a weapon of political propaganda. Only those events are taken which may be interpreted in a heroic key, not excluding, for example, the tragic events of the war's beginning. However, in history there is not only the heroic and tragic, but the low, foul, criminal, and shameful as well. When such themes have to be addressed, they only mention them and, as far as possible, try to justify the actions of the Red Army, the Soviet people, Stalin, and other Soviet leaders. After all, respect for the traditions of preceding generations in Russia is first of all respect for totalitarian and authoritarian traditions, insofar there were almost no others in the history of Russia and the USSR.

The main component parts of the great heroic myth of the Great Patriotic War, which remains to this day, are as follows:

1. Soviet foreign policy during 1939–41 was not expansionist and was directed exclusively at securing its own security: the USSR was not preparing to attack Germany.
2. The Red Army's losses in the war were comparable in size to those of the *Wehrmacht*; in 1941–2 Soviet losses were greater than the Germans', and in 1943–5, when the Red Army had learned how to fight, the Germans

lost more than the Soviet forces, not only in captured, but in killed as well, so that on average the irreplaceable losses of both sides during the war were almost equal to each other.

3. The Soviet Union made the decisive contribution to the victory over Nazi Germany and was capable of winning even without the aid of the Western Allies.

All of these myths are quite easy to refute in an objective study of the history of 1939–45. The basic conclusions of this book boil down to the following: Stalin's Soviet Union could fight and win only at the price of great losses. In principle, it could not be otherwise.

The Red Army fought much worse than the *Wehrmacht* throughout the war.[2] Thus even at the end of 1944 and in 1945, given a more or less bearable correlation of forces, the German forces inflicted tactical defeats on the Soviet troops, although this did not have any influence on the overall strategic situation, which was unfavorable for Germany.

The USSR's 'decisive contribution' to the victory over Germany manifested itself only in the enormous size of Soviet irreplaceable losses, which exceeded the losses of all the war's other participants taken together. However, this is a highly doubtful subject for pride, in that it is the consequence of the Stalinist strategy of 'burying them with corpses'. Yes, the German ground forces really did suffer the greatest losses on the Soviet-German front. However, the decisive role in the war of this or that country can only be determined according to the principle of whether this or that country could have won without the participation of its allies. The Soviet Union, as we are convinced, could not have won without the support of the British Empire and the USA. And could the Western Allies have won if the Red Army had suffered a heavy defeat in 1942 or 1944? Yes, they could have, but only by employing the atomic bomb against Germany.

Stalin and his generals and marshals simply buried the enemy with corpses. They did not know how to fight otherwise. Stalin did not need a professional army in which he saw a threat to his absolute power. The Soviet dictator preferred a poorly trained militia that would bury the enemy with corpses.

The Soviet Union during the Second World War was neither an economically advanced country nor an innocent victim of aggression. And for the Soviet peoples the great victory was only a great tragedy. To admit to this is extremely difficult for the Russian sense of consciousness, insofar as Russians, as well as the other Soviet peoples, were single-mindedly taught the opposite over the course of several decades.

And without the help of the Western Allies, who not only delivered critically vitally strategic materials, fuel and munitions to the USSR, but who destroyed the main part of the *Luftwaffe* and the Germany navy, and who during the final year of the war diverted upon themselves up to 40 per cent of the German ground forces, the Red Army would not have won.[3] It is not by accident that the *Wehrmacht* began to suffer the greatest losses on the Eastern Front precisely during the last year of the war, following the Alied landing in Normandy, when the Germans began to be catastrophically short of men for waging war on two fronts and the Soviet superiority in men and materiel became truly overwhelming. This factor of overwhelming superiority annulled the circumstance that the quality of the Soviet armed forces during 1941–5, contrary to widespread opinion, not only did not improve, but quite the opposite, became continually worse. The cadre Red Army, which had been more or less trained to fight, had been practically completely destroyed before the end of 1941. The last cadre formations, which were transferred from Siberia and the Far East, perished at the very end of 1941 and the beginning of 1942. They were replaced by a militia, which they hardly trained to fight before the very end of the war. A similar worsening of the quality of the rank and file took place among the Germans, but significantly more slowly, so that the *Wehrmacht*'s irreplaceable losses were of an order less than in the Red Army. And it was namely following the landing in Normandy that the correlation of Soviet and German losses significantly worsened, although all the way up to Nazi Germany's capitulation it remained in favour of the Germans. It is simply that from the second half of 1944, aside from the establishment of Soviet air superiority and the overwhelming Soviet superiority in tanks, the Red Army's superiority in ground forces became even more overwhelming – seven to eight times in the combat units. The Germans could no longer withstand such pressure.

There is still another important conclusion, which one must take into account in studying the history of the Second World War, which is that Stalin was an equal architect of the Second World War alongside Hitler. One could not have planned and realized this enormous tragedy in the history of mankind without the other. The essential difference between them was that Hitler emerged among the vanquished, while Stalin emerged among the victors, and thus was able to impose upon the global community his picture of the war, at least on the Eastern Front, and this picture was only slightly modernized by his successors and remains dominant in both Russian historical science and Russian society. In accordance with this concept, the Soviet Union in 1939–40 did not carry out any expansionist plans and did not seek to attack Germany, and that all annexations that arose from the Molotov-Ribbentrop Pact were carried out exclusively for supporting its security and repelling a future German invasion.[4] It is also necessary to keep in mind that many Soviet feats, which were forcefully circulated by Soviet propaganda in the war and postwar years, either had no place in reality or were in no way performed in the way they were written about in Soviet books and newspapers.

However, these and other tenets are now being declared in Russia a falsification of history, harmful to Russian interests. In reality, the powers that be are reestablishing through forcible means the Soviet picture of the war, moreover in the harshest Stalinist variant. Against all facts, Stalinist foreign policy and the Stalinist manner of waging war are being fully justified. And a flawed picture of the history of the Great Patriotic War only facilitates Russia's cultural and political isolation.

The subject of Soviet military crimes, carried out by the Red Army both during the concluding stage of the Great Patriotic War in the countries of Eastern Europe and in Germany, as well as in Asian countries during the brief Soviet-Japanese War, remains absolutely taboo.[5] At the same time, this unattractive part of the war's history is also important for the comprehension of the history of the Great Patriotic War and the recognition of the fact that in this regard the people also have reason to repent.

Three kinds of documents most accurately reflect the real operational situation in the USSR during the years of the Great Patriotic War. These are, first of all, the wire conversations of the *Stavka* of the Supreme Commander-in-Chief with the commanders of the *fronts* and armies and with the *Stavka* representatives at the *front* headquarters.[6] Stalin often conducted these conversations himself from Moscow, or he entrusted them to the chief of the General Staff. Iosif Vissarionovich did not mince words and demanded that they report the entire truth to him, while the commanders were afraid to lie to him to his face. As regards reports and operational summaries, which the commanders at various levels dispatched upward, from company to *front*, these reports were first of all designed to justify the actions of their authors, to cover up mistakes and miscalculations, to underestimate their own losses and to inordinately exaggerate the enemy's losses, while as the information reached the higher headquarters these tendencies manifested themselves even more noticeably. They often failed to communicate the abandonment of important inhabited locales for days at a time in the hope that they would still be able to win them back, the scale of enemy breakthroughs was minimized, while, just the opposite, one's own successes were exaggerated. As a result, the *Stavka* lacked an objective picture of what was happening at the front, where at times the situation would radically change in mere hours and it was unable to adopt the correct decisions. Thus, from the beginning of the war the General

Staff sent its representatives to the *front* and army headquarters (in 1943 they even appeared in corps and even some division headquarters). Their chief task was to inform the General Staff and the *Stavka* of the true state of affairs. Although the General Staff's representatives did not directly bear responsibility for the course and outcome of combat operations, they answered with their head for the veracity of the reports sent up the chain of command. Thus, their information was sufficiently objective. However, the overwhelming majority of these reports remain classified and unpublished. Besides this, Stalin judged the situation at the front by the reports of the special sections (from 1943 these were known as SMERSH military counterintelligence sections).[7] They were obliged to report not only about the fight against spies and diversionists, but about the overall situation at the front as well. And in those parts dealing with combat operations these reports are, for the most part, truthful, insofar as the SMERSH workers bore no responsibility for the course of combat operations. However, when they wrote about purely 'Chekist' affairs, then these reports at times remind one of the tales of Scheherazade, although quite sad ones.[8] The SMERSH workers, in order to fulfill the plan for catching spies, often arrested and shot completely innocent people.

The special section reports are mainly stored either in the *Stavka* files, or in the FSB archives, and for the most part are not accessible to researchers.[9] Materials of the special commissions for the investigation of certain of the Red Army's major failures, which were created by a decision of the *Stavka* (Stalin, to be exact) and the GKO also have great importance for studying the history of the Great Patriotic War.[10] Some of these were gathering dust in the Russian State Archive of Socio-Political History and to one degree or another are available to researchers. Others, as before, are stored in the Presidential Archive, which is practically closed to historians, including documents of the Molotov commission, which investigated the circumstances of the Western Front's disaster in October 1941, and the Malenkov commission, which studied the circumstances of the Soviet forces' failure during the tank battle at Prokhorovka in July 1943.[11] The Presidential Archive and the General Staff's Military Memorial Centre evidently also contain the main documents of the *Stavka* of the VGK, only a small portion of which may be found in the Russian State Archive of Socio-Political History. And without the operational planning documents it is impossible to judge just how effectively they were carried out and to what extent they achieved their assigned objectives. Here we often have to rely on the memoirs by generals and marshals, from whom it is difficult to expect objectivity, as they are interested parties.

For some reason it is believed that it is impossible to hide historical truth in the archives, as if important information is so often repeated that even the opening of a part and, even more so, the majority of archival holdings allow researchers, given a bit of skill and experience, to get hold of the necessary information. Yes and no. If one is speaking of social history, about researching the state of the economy, society and everyday life, and even the mores of various strata of society, not excluding the highest ruling circles, then such work requires great masses of documents and generalizations garnered on the basis of their study. Here the secrecy of these documents truly, in principle, cannot hinder the researcher and fundamentally influence the conclusions drawn.

However, it is quite a different situation when considering more traditional political history, with which history began as a science. After quantitative methods achieved significant successes in history, the most scientific parts of historical science began to be considered, economic, socio-economic and social history, not only in Russia, but in the world at large. Political history, to which the entire historical process was once reduced, and which as early as the second half of the nineteenth century was unconditionally the 'queen' of the historical sciences, is today, if not in exile, at least playing second fiddle. It is no longer fashionable and political history has begun to be viewed as a sort of intertwining and collision of subjective wills, behind which we can discern no kind of clear regularities, as well as a collection of these and other examples, which are employed for various reasons for substantiating these or other ideological, historical, political, philosophical, or ethical concepts, or for the purpose of adapting them to modern political needs. But the belittling of political history can be seen as completely pointless. After all, it also has its regularities, although of course it lacks postulated Marxist laws. However, we really will not find regularities either in economic or social history. And attempts to find certain regularities in the events of political history are not only worth it, but very necessary in order to understand many processes taking place in the social and economic sphere. For political decisions most decidedly influence them and to understand why this or that political decision is adopted, why one political force replaces another and which decisions are characteristic to a greater degree to one or another political forces, it is necessary to properly familiarize oneself with the socio-economic problems of history and contemporaneity.

No small amount of this book about the Eastern Front during the Second World War is devoted to quantitative indices of human losses, troop strengths and data on the production of various types of industrial and agricultural items, although political and purely military history is not neglected either.

One should emphasize that in no other country do they call the Second World War either Great or Patriotic, nor do they block out the years of their participation in the Second World War into a separate war. In the USA, for example, no one would ever take it upon themsleves to speak of some sort of Great American War from 7 December 1941 to 2 September 1945. And in order that the war always remains in Russia Great and Patriotic, it must be preserved in the social consciousness in the form of a great heroic myth. And the gradual constricting of access to Soviet archives is required, first of all, to preserve just this myth. Sometimes this myth leads to absurdity. For example, in all honesty, it is not clear which is correct – 'Leningrad, the hero-city' or 'Saint Petersburg, the hero-city'. In essence, both of these word combinations sound absurd. In the first case, it transpires that we are speaking of a city that has not existed on the map since 1991. In the second case, we are speaking of a real and existing city, which was, however, not known by this name during that period when the events took place, in connection with which it received the title of hero-city.

During the conduct of his research, the moral evaluation of the object of his study should not worry the researcher, whether we are speaking of history or physics. Of course, it does not occur to anyone to think about a moral evaluation of physics. No one will assess an atom or electron from the point of view of morality. But the thought of the moral appraisal of the object of his study occurs to the historian almost all the time. And it is very difficult for him to step back from the positive or negative evaluation of this or that historical event or historical figure accepted in society, and this influences in a most negative way the objectivity of his study. At the same time, a moral consideration of events and personages, of course, can and should be given, but only upon completing the research, according to its results.

Stalin was the same kind of dictator and aggressor as Hitler. And the Red Army, just like the *Wehrmacht*, seized foreign territories, even before the German attack. And in 1944–5, when the Red Army entered Eastern Europe, while liberating its peoples from the Nazi yoke, it either once again annexed these territories, or imposed puppet communist regimes there. However, the *Wehrmacht*, in liberating Soviet territory from communist power, established there the Nazis' 'new order', transforming them into German colonies. The only difference was that Stalin ended up in the camp of the victors and Hitler completely lost the war.

Chapter 1

The Origins of the Second World War

The Role of Hitler and Stalin in its Outbreak. The Soviet Occupation of Eastern Poland, the Baltic States, Bessarabia, and Northern Bukovina. The 'Winter War' with Finland

Having signed the Non-Aggression Pact on 23 August 1939 and the corresponding secret protocols to it, Stalin and Hitler embarked upon the path of unleashing the Second World War. Actually, the USSR entered the war on 17 September 1939, when the Red Army, without a declaration of war, invaded Polish territory and occupied Western Ukraine, Western Belorussia and the Vilnius corridor. The Soviet Union entered the war as an aggressor. The occupation of the Baltic States, Bessarabia and Northern Bukovina, and the attack on Finland were also acts of aggression.

Winston Churchill thus evaluated the Molotov-Ribbentrop Pact and the secret protocols to it:

> only totalitarian despotism in both countries could have faced the odium of such an unnatural act. It is a question whether Hitler or Stalin loathed it most. Both were aware that it could only be a temporary expedient. The antagonisms between the two empires and systems were mortal. Stalin no doubt felt that Hitler would be a less deadly foe to Russia after a year of war with the Western Powers. Hitler followed his method of 'One at a time.' [. . .]
>
> On the Soviet side it must be said that their vital need was to hold the deployment positions of the German armies as far to the west as possible so as to give the Russians more time for assembling their forces from all parts of their immense empire. They had burnt in their minds the disasters which had come upon their armies in 1914, when they had hurled themselves forward to attack the Germans while still themselves only partly mobilised. But now

their frontiers lay far to the east of those of the previous war. They must be in occupation of the Baltic States and a large part of Poland by force or fraud before they were attacked. If their policy was cold-blooded, it was also at the moment realistic in a high degree. [...]

This treaty was to last ten years, and if not denounced by either side one year before the expiration of that period, would be automatically extended for another five years. There was much jubi-lation and many toasts around the conference table. Stalin sponta-neously proposed the toast of the Fuhrer, as follows, 'I know how much the German Nation loves its Fuhrer, I should therefore like to drink his health.' A moral may be drawn from all this, which is of homely simplicity – 'Honesty is the best policy.' [...] Crafty men and statesmen will be shown misled by all their elaborate calculations. But this is the signal instance. Only twenty-two months were to pass before Stalin and the Russian nation in its scores of millions were to pay a frightful forfeit. If a government has no moral scruples, it often seems to gain great advantages and liberties of action, but 'All comes out even at the end of the day, and all will come out yet more even when all the days are ended'.[1]

The war was viewed by the armies and peoples of all the belligerent states as a patriotic war, that is, a war in defence of one's homeland, regardless of whether they had to fight on their own or someone else's territory. Thus, it is more correct to speak of the Second World War and not of a patriotic war of this or that people. And who was the aggressor and who was the victim was determined by the policy of the governments of the corresponding states. The undisputed aggressors were Germany, the USSR, Italy, Hungary, Japan, and Siam (Thailand). The just as undisputed victims of aggression, if one picks only the period of the Second World War, remain Poland, France, Belgium, Holland, Luxembourg, Denmark, Norway, Great Britain, the USA, China (the Japanese attacked the latter as early as 1937), Lithuania, Latvia, and Esto-nia. And some peoples were aggressors and victims. The first among these were the Finns. In 1939 they became the victim of Soviet aggression and in 1941 fought against the USSR together with Hitler in order to return the lands seized following the 'Winter War'.[2] One may understand the Finns, but the fact that they fought against one aggressor in alliance with another aggressor made them participants in aggression. Romania, from which Stalin in 1940 seized Bessarabia and Northern Bukovina, was in the same situation, which roused Romania to a joint campaign with Hitler against the USSR.[3] However, the Ukrainians also appear as victims and as part of the aggressor's army, although because they lacked their own state they can in no way be viewed as participants in aggression, either Soviet or German. In 1939 those Ukrainians who lived in Poland became victims of German and Soviet aggression. However, the majority of Ukrainians were part of the Red Army, which seized Eastern Poland, the Baltic States, Bessarabia, and Northern Bukovina, and then unsuccessfully tried to seize all of Finland. The same sort of duality was characteristic of all the Soviet peoples, not excluding the Russian people. Having become the victim of German aggression, they at the same time carried out aggression against other peoples as part of the Red Army and the Soviet punitive organs. They try not to speak of this in contemporary Russia, presenting the USSR as the main victim of German aggression and the Russian people the main author of victory.

If one objectively compares the Soviet and Nazi regimes, then they have much more in common than what separates them. The domination of one dictator, one party and one ideology, imposed on the entire population of a country. The complete absence of any kind of democratic freedoms. Cruel repressions against the political enemies of the regime and all who are suspected of political disloyalty, as well as against all those national and social groups of the population declared as inferior. An aggressive foreign policy, directed at the achievement of hegemony in Europe. All of these points of contact are sufficient to ponder; was the victory of such a regime in the Second World War really so good, and is there anything here to celebrate? There were also differences between the regimes, although the points of contact are more important for us here. In evaluating Soviet policy during 1939–41, one cannot help but recognize its aggressive character, which was expressed, in particular, in the attack on Finland and the occupation and annexation of the three Baltic countries. Russian diplomats still do not employ the word 'occupation' in their conversations with their colleagues from these countries, preferring to speak of the 'peaceful attachment' of Lithuania, Latvia, and Estonia to the USSR. And Russian historians, or at least those who work in the official structures of the Russian Academy of Sciences, are strictly forbidden to employ the term 'occupation' in regard to Soviet actions in the Baltic States, about which some of them honestly admitted in striving for an objective evaluation of the events of 1939–41. At the same time, if one compares the introduction of Soviet forces into the Baltic States and their subsequent attachment to the Soviet Union with the German 'peaceful occupation' (without combat operations) of Austria, Czechoslovakia, Denmark, and Luxembourg, then it transpires that there are no practical differences between them. It is interesting that in the joint Russian-German textbook, *The History of Germany*, which was published in 2008, it is directly stated that 'On 12 March 1938 German troops occupied Austria. A true terror was unleashed within the country against all political enemies.' And here it is emphasized that following these events 'the term *Anschluss* acquired the meaning of the forcible seizure of territory'.[4] If one inserts in the place of Austria one of the Baltic States, and 'March 1938' with 'June 1940,' then one doesn't even have to change the phrase about terror against political opponents.

Of course, there were differences between the Soviet and Nazi totalitarian systems, although it's impossible to say that they were ones of principle and touched upon their attitude toward the values of European civilization. Nazism stressed more the racial principle, and communism the class principle. In cases of necessity, however, Hitler carried out repressions of communists and social democrats, or, for example, Catholics, while Stalin repressed entire 'punished peoples,' struggled against 'rootless cosmopolitans' and during the Great Terror executed representatives of 'particularly unreliable' nationalities, for example, Germans and Poles in the course of the NKVD's 'national operations'.[5] And if one is to speak of the closeness to European civilization, then even under Hitler Germany remained significantly closer to its standards. Nazi totalitarianism did not destroy the market economy and private property and did not introduce such harsh limitations, as in the USSR, on the activity of Christian churches. From the point of view of the quality of armaments production, military equipment and the armed forces' level of military training, Germany was significantly superior to the Soviet Union and in this sphere, undoubtedly, relied on the achievements of European civilization in military affairs. In this regard, czarist Russia was sufficiently backward, which manifested itself in the First World War. But practically everything that Nazi Germany was charged with at Nuremberg could also be laid at the feet of the Soviet Union of that time.[6]

At first the population of the territories occupied by Stalin did not exhibit any sort of hostility toward the Soviet forces. However, several months of the 'communist paradise', with its forcible collectivization, the shuttering of churches, a consumer goods deficit, and repressions against the intelligentsia and representatives of the propertied classes radically changed the situation.[7] For example, in Northern Bukovina many sought to run away to Romania, and not only Romanians, but ethnic Ukrainians as well, although they came up against Soviet border guards on their way. On 1 April 1941 the first secretary of the Ukrainian Communist Party, Nikita Khrushchev, reported to Stalin:[8]

> Part of the peasants from the four closest villages in the Chernovtsy Oblast's Glibokoe District left for the district centre of Glybokoe with the demand that they be sent to Romania. The crowd numbered about a thousand people, predominantly men. In the middle

of the day on 1 April the crowd entered the village of Glybokoe and went up to the NKVD district building, while many carried crosses and a single white banner (which, the participants of this procession explained, was supposed to symbolise their peaceful intentions). The following sign was glued to one of the crosses: 'Behold, brothers, these are the same crosses that the Red Army soldiers broke.' The crowd's participants were not seen to have any weapons. After they explained to them at the district NKVD building the illegality of such a gathering and demanded that the people disperse, the crowd melted away . . . The chief of the State Security Administration ordered the arrest of the instigators, which was done today at night.

Two days ago several groups of peasants came to the district executive building in the Storozhinets border district with the same demand. It transpired that they had been instigated by kulaks and Guardists [members of the 'Iron Guard' fascist organization, B.S.].[9] The identified instigators in the Storozhinets district have been arrested . . .

At about 7 p.m. a crowd of 500–600 people in the Glybokoe area attempted to break through to Romania. The border guards opened fire. As a result, according to preliminary data, about 50 people were killed and wounded, and the remainder ran away. No one broke through over the border.

Iosif Vissarionovich was quite satisfied by the fact that no one ran away to Romania, but on 2 April he criticized Nikita Sergeevich a little in a comradely fashion: 'Overall, it is clear from your message that your work in the frontier areas is going very poorly. One can, of course, shoot at people, but shooting is not the main method of our work.'[10] In this instance it's sufficient to arrest the 'instigators', and then perhaps you don't need to shoot anyone. On the whole, however, the task facing Khrushchev and his subordinates was a very difficult one. It was necessary to convince the Ukrainian and Romanian peasants that in 'boyar' Romania, where landowners in the usual sense of the word were no more, and where the state took only the smaller part of the harvest, it was harder to make a living than under the Soviets, when they took almost the entire harvest.

The Russian historians Lev Lopukhovskii and Boris Kavalerchik admit:

Despite all the attempts to more broadly inculcate German methods of training and German tactics into the Red Army, the results achieved were somewhat different than in the *Reichswehr*.[11] The difference between the two armies was too great and in the human material from which they were created, and in their equipment, and in their living conditions and work. In his summary report on his study in Germany, Uborevich wrote about this sufficiently frankly:[12] 'German specialists, including the military ones, stand immeasurably above us.' None the less, the positive effect on the RKKA from the prewar Soviet-German military cooperation is difficult to overestimate.[13]

Stalin, as did Hitler, wanted to create a multi-million combat-effective army in a short time. At the same time, the USSR, unlike Germany, was not constricted by any limitations imposed by the Treaty of Versailles, and in 1935, when Hitler set about to openly remilitarize Germany, the Red Army already numbered 930,000 men, equipped with tanks and heavy artillery, and combat aircraft and submarines, that is, everything that Hitler still lacked.[14] During 1930–3 9,224 aircraft and 7,865 tanks and tankettes were built in the USSR. The *Reichswehr* at the time numbered 240,000 men, and by the end of 1933 it disposed of eight training tanks without turrets.[15]

However, having maintained right up until 1941 a quantitative advantage in men and weapons and not being too inferior to the main potential enemy in the quality of armaments and combat equipment, the Red Army could not compare with the *Wehrmacht* in the quality of combat training of its troops and commanders and therefore lost the main battles in the first year of the war.

It should be noted that the Red Army grew even more rapidly than the *Wehrmacht*. During 1935–8 its strength rose almost four times, to 3.5 million men. However, at the same time the level of training, both of individual soldiers and commanders, as well as of entire units and formations, fell considerably because of the low quality of the NCO contingent and commanders at the platoon – company – battalion level.

The difference in the educational level of the two countries' population also told. In 1939 only 7.7 per cent of Soviet citizens had completed seven or more grades, while only 0.7 per cent had a higher education. However, for men of draft age, 16–59 years, these indices were twice as high, 15 per cent and 1.7 per cen respectively. In Germany there existed practically universal secondary education. On the eve of the war only a little more than 7 per cent of the Red Army's commanders had a higher military education, while among the Germans this index was closer to 100 per cent.[16]

The Germans had a significant superiority not only in general, but in functional, literacy among the rank and file of the armed forces. Thus, for example, in the *Wehrmacht* the repair of tanks and other damaged equipment was organized far better. In the Soviet Union they failed altogether to devote appropriate attention to the training of draftees, and in the beginning of the war they utterly amazed the Germans with their 'know-how' of sending completely untrained reinforcements into battle.

There was a strategic theory in the Soviet Union analogous to the theory of the modernized *blitzkrieg* – the theory of the deep offensive operation, which was developed by Vladimir Triandafillov and Konstantin Kalinovskii.[17] This theory also called for the broad employment of mechanized units and armoured equipment, supported by aviation. However, as opposed to the German theory, the Soviet one in practice devoted clearly insufficient attention to the problems of cooperation of the various combat arms, as well as to all-round training and the rear support of a strategic operation. In the first Soviet armoured formations – brigades, as opposed to the German tank divisions, there was no infantry and very little artillery, which rendered them incapable of operating independently. It was planned to simply attach them to the rifle divisions and corps, which would limit the tank units' mobility and reduce them to being employed primarily as direct infantry support tanks. However, taking into account the level of training for the Soviet tank troops and the tank commanders, it's possible that this form of employment would have been the best. But at the beginning of the Second World War, under the influence of the German tank formations' victories in France, mechanized corps were formed in the USSR, and subsequently tank armies, which were designated for independent operations, primarily for developing the success while breaking through the enemy's defence. However, the effectiveness of their operations compared with that of the Germans' tank formations was low, while their equipment losses were too high.

An important role was played by the fact that the Germans' tank units were far better than the Soviet ones, being equipped with radios, which were also of a higher quality. By the close of 1942 all of the German tanks were outfitted with proper radios, while radio receivers predominated among the Soviet tanks. And the level of training for the German tank crews was completely beyond comparison with that of the Soviet crews and remained such until the end of the war.

Hitler could have been stopped as late as 1938, if the Western powers had exhibited firmness and demonstrated a true readiness to fight. But in 1939, when the Polish crisis began, no amount of firmness could have stopped Hitler, who had embarked on a course of achieving world dominance and a world war.

Emboldened by his success at Munich, on 14 March 1939 Hitler forced the president of Czechoslovakia, Emil Hacha, under the threat of war, to agree to the annexation of the Czech lands to Germany as a protectorate.[18] The Western powers could in no way justify aggression as the realization of the Germans' right to self determination and issued guarantees of territorial integrity to the next potential victim of German aggression – Poland. On 21 March 1939 Ribbentrop presented the Polish ambassador with an ultimatum to transfer to Germany Danzig and an extraterritorial highway and railroad in the 'Polish corridor', linking East Prussia with the major part of the Reich. Insofar as Poland rejected the ultimatum, Hitler began to prepare for a world war. He believed that the powers, having given guarantees to Poland this time, would fight. The German press began a propaganda campaign about the supposed 'ethnic cleansing' of Germans in Poland, which had supposedly caused a flood of refugees, but no proof of this was offered either at that moment or after the occupation of Poland. And so in order to create an excuse for the war, a provocation was arranged at Gleiwitz. As a result,120 SS men, dressed in Polish military uniforms and speaking Polish, attacked a radio station in Gleiwitz, in German Upper Silesia and, upon capturing the transmitter, called upon the local Polish population to rise up. To make it convincing, several corpses of concentration camp prisoners, who were dressed in Polish uniforms, were left by the radio station building.

The idea for such a provocation proved infectious. Stalin already had a ready plan for occupying Finland, and in order to secure a pretext for an attack, arranged a provocation near the frontier village of Manaila on 26 November 1939. Seven artillery rounds were fired against the Red Army's positions, and according to the official version four men were killed and nine wounded. However, in his memoirs Khrushchev admitted that the bombardment was carried out on Stalin's orders. The Russian historian Pavel Aptekar has found in the archives documents from the 68th Rifle Regiment, which was stationed in the Manaila area, which show that during the 25–9 November period the regiment suffered no losses among the rank and file.[19] Stalin here proved to be more humane than Hitler and did not kill anyone. And when the USSR attacked Finland and the question was being discussed in the League of Nations, they declared in Moscow that they were not fighting against anyone, but quite the opposite, and lived in peace and friendship with the Finnish Democratic Republic, against which it not only had no territorial claims, but on the contrary, was preparing to cede significant territory in Soviet Karelia. The government of the FDR was created on Stalin's orders in the village of Terioki, which had been occupied by Soviet forces, and was headed by Otto Kuusinen, a secretary of the Comintern.[20] To be sure, the trick with the FDR did not work out and the Soviet Union was nevertheless excluded from the League of Nations as an aggressor.

Stalin was in no way prepared to conclude a military alliance with Great Britain and the USA in the summer of 1939, as such an alliance could have prevented the Second World War, and Stalin was not interested in this. He conducted the negotiations with British and French delegations in Moscow only in order to make Hitler more conciliatory as regards Soviet territorial demands.

Did the Poles have a chance of withstanding the German and Soviet aggression? Here we can only enter the sphere of alternative history. Let's imagine that Jozef Pilsudski had not died in 1935, but had lived to at least the end of 1946.[21] In principle there is nothing unlikely in this. Pilsudski would have been 79 years old. He could not have prevented the Molotov-Ribbentrop Pact and the partition of Poland, just as he could not have forced France and Great Britain to undertake an immediate offensive on the Western Front. Both London and Paris were aware of the secret partition of Poland between Stalin and Hitler, while the French army was neither morally nor materially prepared for an offensive. But here Pilsudski, possessing no small amount of military and political talent, could easily not only have guessed that such a partition had been agreed on, but also chosen the most rational defensive tactic against the two enemies – Germany and the USSR. While leaving powerful garrisons in a number of fortresses, such as Poznan, Warsaw, Brest, and L'vov, and perhaps some others as well, the Polish army's main forces should have been concentrated on a small bridgehead near the Romanian frontier, establishing their main defensive line along the Dnestr River and the Slovak border, which ran along the Carpathian Mountains. Then the garrisons of the fortresses might have held out a few weeks, while the main forces could have held out a month-and-a-half to two months. The *Wehrmacht* and the Red Army would have suffered significantly higher casualties in frontal attacks against the Polish army's main forces defending along a short front and with a high operational density of forces, and while storming the fortresses, than was the case in the actual Polish campaign. The Polish army's main forces, having fired off all of their ammunition, would have been interned, along with the Pilsudski government, in Romania. Then the number of interned Polish servicemen would have been higher by an order than the actual number of Poles interned in the autumn of 1939 in Hungary, Romania, Lithuania, and Latvia. The majority of Poles would probably have been able to reach France from Romania together with Pilsudski, and far fewer Polish officers would have fallen into Soviet captivity and been executed at Katyn'.[22] A far more numerous Polish army would have been recreated in France than was actually the case in the spring of 1940 and London and Paris would have been forced to take it into account as an important ally, particularly after France dropped out of the war and the Polish army was evacuated to the British Isles. Pilsudski also enjoyed far greater international authority than Wladyslaw Sikorski, Stanislav Mikolajczyk and the other leaders of the Polish government in exile.[23] Given such a turn of events, there would have been a greater chance that Great Britain and the USA would have more decisively supported the Polish government in its conflict with Stalin due to Katyn' and he would have had a much more difficult time in forming a Polish government and army controlled by the USSR. Thus the Poles would have had a definite chance of preserving an independent Poland after the war. However, once again, this could only have taken place in an alternative reality.

In regard to the Second World War, it is often said that Stalin's chief mistake was in concluding the non-aggression pact with Germany. In this manner he not only opened the path to the Second World War, but also created conditions for Germany's surprise attack on the USSR. However, this was a crime, but not a mistake, and the Soviet dictator was never embarrassed by such crimes. Stalin was working hard so that the Second World War would begin with Germany against Poland and its Western Allies. The non-aggression pact would open the path to the Second World War and would pit Hitler against the Anglo-French coalition and give the Red Army a convenient jumping-off place for a subsequent attack on Germany. Stalin foresaw the rapid collapse of Poland, which he was 'fraternally' preparing to partition with Hitler and which was fixed in the secret supplementary protocol to the Molotov-Ribbentrop Pact. The treaty on friendship and borders with Germany is often referred to as Stalin's mistake. However, from the point of view of Stalin's policy, there was no mistake. The treaty not only concluded, thanks to the secret supplementary protocols to this treaty, the delineation of spheres of interest in Eastern Europe, but also gave Hitler to understand that he could freely attack France without fear for his rear in the East. He himself was preparing to knife Germany in the back at that moment when the *Wehrmacht*, as he hoped, got bogged down at the Maginot Line. Here Stalin really did make a mistake, having underestimated the *Wehrmacht's* combat capability and overestimated the French troops' combat capability and toughness. So, Stalin was not a professional military man and the majority of his errors concern military affairs. In particular, he overestimated the combat capability and readiness of the Red Army, which got stuck at the Mannerheim Line, which was far less powerful than the Maginot Line.[24] Thus in March 1940 a compromise peace had to be quickly concluded with Finland, in order to have the opportunity to throw the Red Army's main forces toward the Soviet-German demarcation line. Otherwise, the war with Finland could have dragged on until summer following the onset of the spring thaw.

In the same way, Stalin overestimated the Red Army's combat capability and underestimated the *Wehrmacht's* combat capability. Thus he trained his troops only for the offensive, and not for defence. And because of this, Stalin did not expect a German attack in 1941 and the Red Army suffered very heavy defeats. If it had adhered to defensive tactics and employed its tank formations in a more dispersed fashion, its losses would probably have been less and its defeats less disastrous. However, Stalin was sure that, possessing a significant superiority in men, tanks and aircraft, the Soviet forces could quickly crush the enemy and place the greater part of Europe under their control. At the same time, he failed to take into account the troops' severe shortages in communications equipment and, what is still more important, the significantly lower level of training both of the command and the rank and file, particularly in the navy, air force and tank troops, compared with the *Wehrmacht*. This circumstance predetermined the fact that victory was achieved at a very dear price and that the war stretched out a lengthy four years.

Stalin sincerely believed that the Soviet Union had caught up with the capitalist West in terms of the level of economic development, which meant that the Red Army could not be weaker than the German army. If only for this reason, he could not adopt defensive tactics. On the other hand, Stalin understood that a prolonged defence, as the experience of the First World War showed, demoralizes the troops and may lead to revolution.

In spite of the military defeats of 1941–2, in political terms Stalin, having unleashed the Second World War, won it, having acquired, thanks to the military political situation that took shape in 1941, British and American allies, which guaranteed the final victory.

The Russian historian Andrei Smirnov proves that the level of the Soviet forces' combat training and that of the command was quite low both in the first half of the 1930s, as well as during 1939–41 and was significantly inferior to the chief potential enemy – the *Wehrmacht*. The repressions of 1937–8 did not have any kind of material influence on these indices. One may contest this conclusion only in the sense that as a result of the repressions the troops' lack of faith in their commanders increased and the fear of the commanders to make independent decisions increased, although they were not particularly distinguished earlier by a propensity for independence. Smirnov also points out that the Red Army's backwardness vis-à-vis the German army was conditioned by a number of features inherited by the Red Army from the Russian imperial army, particularly the great predominance of theoretical knowledge over practical knowledge, by the low functional literacy of the soldiers and officers, and the inability to train the soldiers to do what would be realistically required in war. It is possible that the reasons for this lie in the deep feudal hierarchy of both pre-revolutionary Russian and Soviet (and post-Soviet as well) society. The mass of the people was not accustomed to independent actions and did not particularly strive to acquire practical skills, which meant significantly less than one's place in the social hierarchy, which for the most part was not dependent upon practical achievements. And following the Great Terror there were no major changes for the better in the Red Army's level of combat training all the way up to the beginning of the Great Patriotic War, and this revealed itself most negatively in the size of Soviet military losses.[25]

In Smirnov's evaluation, by the middle of 1937 the level of the Red Army's combat training could be rated at between two and three on five-point scale and in 1940 it had, at best, only inched toward a three. Smirnov ties the chief reasons for the low level of combat training in the Red Army to the fact that they did not train soldiers and commanders for the conditions of actual combat, but for the collision with a relatively weak enemy, probably from those of the small border states or a German army limited by the conditions of the Treaty of Versailles. He emphasizes that:

> The famous theory of the deep operation and the concept of the deep battle, which were developed by Soviet military theoreticians, really did reflect the nature and demands of modern war, but the RKKA was not in a condition to realize this theory and concept in practice and inculcate it even at the end of the epoch of Tukhachevskii, Yakir and Uborevich (that is, by the middle of 1937).[26] The reason for this was the poor training of those who were to put these military theories into practice–the commanders, staffs and troops.

The main part of the command element lacked the desire for decisive manoeuvre, for operations against the enemy's flank and rear, and the display of initiative, which was, in Smirnov's opinion, the result of the overall weakness of the army's operational-tactical thinking. Also, commanders from the battalion level upwards did not know how to organize cooperation among the various combat arms. Many commanders at the tactical level were not possessed of any kind of tactical thinking. The overwhelming majority of commanders poorly controlled their troops. As Smirnov notes:

> It's not accidental that cooperation between the combat arms during 1935 through the first half of 1937, if it was achieved, occurred only in the opening stage of the battle or operation, and when the altered situation demanded the organization of cooperation once again, it disappeared. The commanders and staffs were not capable of once again carrying out the work of organizing cooperation in an intense situation and with tight deadlines.

It should be noted that the same thing happened, unfortunately, in the years of the Great Patriotic War.

Another obstacle to success was the poor level of troop training. As Smirnov emphasizes, the lone RKKA infantryman

> did not have the necessary training either in entrenching, masking, or in observing the battlefield, nor in choosing a firing position, nor in making rushes and crawling, nor in throwing himself into the attack, and was completely untrained to throw a grenade or in using the bayonet. He knew how to 'handle' a rifle and machine gun to the extent that he could shoot at the second or third level on a scale of one to five; as a rule, he could not find a target independently and quite often he reduced his gun to a state of technical disuse due to corrosion in the gun barrel . . . The mechanic-drivers in the tanks had little experience in driving, even by the middle of 1937, and did not know how to drive their combat vehicles in realistic field conditions, but only level ground at the tank training centre!

Smirnov further quotes Marshal Budennyi's brilliant words, which were uttered at a session of the defence commissar's military council on 21 November 1937: 'At times we wander around on a great operational-strategic scale, but how will we conduct operations if the company is no good, the platoon is no good, or the squad is no good?'[27] What can one say? Semyon Mikhailovich was not quite as stupid as we are accustomed to think.

The same situation prevailed in the other combat arms. Numerous similar examples are put forth in a monograph which cites papers and reports on the troops' condition. When comparing the level of the RKKA's training with that of the armies of the likely enemies, the author sums up the situation as follows: 'Of course, in the quantitative sense, neither the *Reichswehr*, nor the *Wehrmacht* which grew out of it after 1935, ever surpassed the Red Army.' However, as regards 'quality', as early as 1931, B.S. Gorbachev, who headed the military-educational establishments in the Moscow Military District and who had been to Germany, wrote that: 'The Germans have mastered their equipment and manage it incomparably better than we do.'[28] And following the transformation of the *Wehrmacht* into a mass army, the training of the individual soldier and the subunit remained considerably higher than in the Red Army. Colonel A.I. Starunin, the chief of the first section of the RKKA's intelligence directorate, reported on this, observing the *Wehrmacht's* manoeuvres in September 1938. He noted that 'the training of the individual soldier is good, particularly with instruments and with guns', while the infantry 'in the offensive operated in dispersed order, and its bunching up, which was noted in previous maneuvers, was not observed'. The Japanese army's level of training was inferior to that of the German army, but nevertheless according to the majority of parameters, its level of combat training was higher than in the RKKA. As Major V.I. Polozkov, who was studying with the Japanese tank troops in 1936, reported, 'The Japanese tank officer is well trained in waging general combat, knows infantry tactics and the terrain, and understands the situation', although at the same time 'he does understand cooperation with other combat arms as well' and is not at his best in organizing the battle of his tanks with other tanks. Also, according to Tukhachevskii, the Japanese officers knew how to organize 'good cooperation of the infantry and artillery and constantly remembered the necessity to look after the flanks and the boundaries with neighbors', and also that 'they are little taken with the methodology of battle, subordinating everything to bravery and initiative'. Certainly, as Smirnov notes, 'The Japanese infantry continued to attack in close formation, which European armies had renounced as early as 1917, as too vulnerable to the fire of the modern defence. However, the reason was not in the poor training of the individual soldier, but in the outdated tenets of their manuals'. Here one should add that the main focus for Japan was still the navy and those army units which were supposed to operate in conjunction with the fleet. The Red Army attacked in close formation during the Great Patriotic War as a result of the low level of troop training. As regards the Polish army, it is very difficult to compare it with the Red Army, insofar as in the 1930s the Polish armed forces evolved significantly. As early as the beginning of the 1930s the operational-tactical thinking of the Polish officers was not practically distinguished from the thinking of Soviet commanders, which manoeuvres demonstrated. However, in Smirnov's opinion, as early as 1937 the superiority in this regard was obviously in favour of the Polish side. And the training of the Polish artillery officers was better than that of the Soviet officers as early as the beginning of the 1930s. Smirnov reaches the logical conclusion that

> the training of the combined-arms and infantry commanders, which was obviously superior to what the Soviets, in conjunction with the unconditionally better (as the result of their superiority in the art of firing and in the tactical training of the commanders of the artillery regiments) training of the artillery commanders allows us to conclude that during 1935 through the first half of 1937 the command element of the Polish army, in terms of its training, on the whole was superior to that of their Soviet colleagues.

From this the overall conclusion reached is that 'the training of the "pre-repression" Red Army was not simply low, but that it was lower than that of its likely enemies – the Germans, Japanese and the Poles'.

Smirnov sees one of the most important reasons for this state of affairs in the revolution of 1917. As a result of the revolution, 'Insofar as it was possible, they did not allow representatives of the intelligentsia into the "Workers'-Peasants'" army; they began to renounce this policy of "social racism" only in 1933 and fully renounced it only in 1936.' This policy resulted in a low educational level among the command element. The author also sees one of the reasons behind the low level of combat training in the Bolsheviks' struggle against the army's 'caste' character and in the extermination of the 'soldierly and purely military spirit'. They tried to inculcate the command element with:

> the idea of the secondary nature of professional obligations com-
> pared to social and political activity and, in the final analysis, facil-
> itated the development among the command element of that same
> lack of responsibility and failure to manifest the necessary demands
> on oneself and one's subordinates, that is it facilitated the command
> element's sloppy attitude toward combat training, and therefore the
> weakness in combat training.

The junior command element and the rank and file were corrupted by the liberal tenets of the combat manuals, which did not call for the unconditional fulfillment of orders and the 'widespread practice of persuasion and requests instead of orders and commands'. It is interesting, as Smirnov observes, that 'as opposed to the arguments of Soviet historiography, up until 1936 army communists and *Komsomol* members repeatedly proved to be disciplined no better, but worse than non-party members'.[29] Smirnov also notes the influence of objective factors, which were not directly dependent upon the revolution of 1917. Among these are the rapid growth in the size of the Red Army during the 1930s, the state's limited financial opportunities and the peculiarities of the Russian mentality. Here one must make the reservation that the state's limited financial opportunities actually did lead to a situation in which too few funds were put into training the soldiers and commanders. However, of much greater significance is the mentality of Stalin and his generals, who preferred to put greater resources in the quantitative growth of armaments, combat equipment and the rank and file, and not into increasing the quality of its training. Also significant was the fact that Stalin saw the threat of 'Bonapartism' in a highly professional army and thus preferred to deal with what was essentially a poorly trained and numerous militia force.

As Smirnov shows, the transfer of commanders with little experience to high posts began in the Red Army long before the repressions:

> In 1933 more commanders were promoted and transferred in the RKKA than in the notorious year of 1937, when the army was also one and a half times larger in size. There were also more such transfers in 1936 than in 1937, and even before the beginning of the mass repressions lieutenants (who also had often not passed through commanding a platoon or half-company) had come to comprise the main mass of commanders of the Red Army's rifle companies, while junior commanders had begun to head the rifle regiments' heavy artillery companies in such an important RKKA group of forces as the Special Red Banner Far Eastern Army (OKDVA)![30]

By the start of the Second World War all of the division and regimental commanders in the German army had service experience as officers in the First World War. At the same time, one could literally count on the fingers of one hand the former czarist officers. This circumstance significantly lowered the Red Army's combat capability in comparison with the *Wehrmacht*.

The Red Army's weakness arose from the peculiarities of the Soviet totalitarian system, which to a significant degree had been created by Stalin and for which he is completely responsible. Among these are the repressions, the cruel collectivization campaign, the contempt for human life and the habit of acting by rote and on command. Stalin did not need a professional army, in which he saw a threat to his own unlimited power, but a massive and poorly trained host, in essence a people's militia, which could only be victorious at a high price in blood.

It should be stressed that the seizure of Lithuania, Latvia, and Estonia by the Soviet Union was a typical 'peaceful occupation', when no armed resistance was offered to it. In the same way Germany occupied Austria, the Czech lands, Denmark, and Luxembourg without a single shot being fired, while these actions are defined completely legally as an occupation in the verdict of the Nuremberg tribunal.

As is known, the governments of Lithuania, Latvia, and Estonia did not resist Soviet aggression. They accepted the ultimatums and allowed Soviet forces to enter their territory in October 1939. After this there could be no hint of any kind of armed resistance to the Soviet ultimatums in June 1940. One could have resisted in the autumn of 1939. Let us imagine, nonetheless, that the governments of the Baltic States had decided to oppose Soviet expansion with force. Would they have had any chances of success?

Lithuania, Latvia, and Estonia should have united with each other and with Finland in order to oppose the USSR. The armies of the Baltic States taken together numbered about 60,000 men in peacetime. In order to attempt to withstand the Soviet Union, they would have had to carry out a mobilization as early as the *Wehrmacht's* and the Red Army's Polish campaign. However, there were not even the necessary stores of firearms in order to arm the mobilized forces in Lithuania, Latvia, and Estonia, not to mention heavy weapons. There was not even any kind of developed military industry there. However, in the event of the conclusion of an alliance with Finland, one could hope to receive at least part of the necessary arms from Finland, as well as from Sweden. And then they would have had the real opportunity of withstanding the Red Army in October 1939. Of course, there was a definite difference between Finland and the Baltic States. In Finland a democratic regime remained, while in Lithuania, Latvia, and Estonia there existed soft, but nonetheless authoritarian, regimes. Perhaps this explains the fact that Kaunas, Riga, and Tallinn did not resist Stalinist aggression, hoping to come to an agreement with the Soviet dictator about preserving if only a formal independence, as was the case with Mongolia. But there unconditionally dominated among the population of the three Baltic republics the desire to preserve their full-blooded national independence and the readiness, should there be a corresponding call from their governments, to defend it with armed force. It should be noted that the one Estonian and two Latvian SS divisions, which fought in 1943–5 on Germany's side, displayed a high degree of combat capability, which exceeded the combat capability of the Red Army.[31] When in the second half of 1944 the Latvians of the 19th SS Division had to fight against the Red Army's 43rd Guards Rifle Latvian Division, the correlation of killed was five to one in favour of those who fought on the German side.[32] Let's allow that in 1939 the combat capability of the Baltic States' armies was lower than the combat capability of the Baltic States' SS divisions, which had gone through German training. But this training, in any case, was not lower than in the Red Army. Finland's army was many times superior to the Red Army in combat capability, although it was inferior to it in numbers and the amount of combat equipment.

If in October 1939 a bloc of Lithuania, Latvia, Estonia, and Finland had opposed the USSR the further course of events would have depended on Stalin. He might have launched his main attack either against the Baltic States, or against Finland. In the first instance, it is unlikely that the three Baltic States would have been able to hold out, taking into account the fact that they would have had to defend with their small armies a very extended front, along which there were practically no fortifications, if only comparable with the Mannerheim Line, particularly from the direction of Eastern

Poland, which had been occupied by the Red Army. Thus in this case the occupation of Lithuania, Latvia, and Estonia by the Red Army their loss of independence would have been inevitable. The Finnish army, due to the small number of tanks and aircraft, could not have attacked Leningrad to distract significant forces from the Red Army from the Baltic States. However, it is just as likely that Stalin would have launched his first blow against Finland. It can be concluded, using the experience of both the Winter and Great Patriotic wars, that in general he preferred to strike a major blow by the strongest grouping of his troops against the strongest grouping of enemy troops. Perhaps the Soviet leader was afraid that if he struck with his main forces against the weakest grouping of an enemy, the latter, in turn, could manage to defeat the weaker grouping of the Soviet troops with its strongest group. Therefore, it is possible that given a choice between the Baltic States and Finland Stalin would have taken Finland as the object of the first strike. He colossally underestimated the Finnish army's combat capability and calculated that he could deal with Finland in two weeks. And while the Red Army was bogged down along the Mannerheim Line, the Baltic States would have had a chance to complete their mobilization and withstand those limited Soviet forces which would have been allotted against them. In this scenario, Lithuania, Latvia, and Estonia would have had a pretty good chance, as did Finland, to hold on until March 1940 and then conclude the same kind of compromise peace as the Moscow Peace Treaty, ceding part of their territory but retaining their independence.[33] In view of the major German offensive in the West, Stalin would not have risked continuing the war with the Baltic States and Finland. And following the defeat of Germany in 1945, Lithuania, Latvia and Estonia would have remained in the Soviet sphere of influence with the establishment of communist regimes there, according to the example of Poland and Czechoslovakia, but would have had the chance to retain a formal independence. One could rate the Baltic States' chances of retaining their independence in the event of armed resistance as 50:50 in the autumn of 1939.

Creating alternative scenarios for the Second World War is a very popular exercise. Dozens of books have been written on this topic, both academically popular and literature. Dozens of computer games have been devised. Films have been shot, the most famous of which are Quentin Tarantino's *Inglorious Basterds* and Christopher Menaul's *Fatherland*. The latter is an adaptation of the novel of the same name by the British journalist and writer Robert Harris, which appeared in 1992, not long after the collapse of the USSR. In the literary works devoted to the victory of Hitler's Reich during the Second World War, one sees the predominance of fantasies which dispense entirely with real facts, while, as a rule, in historical works of the alternative genre only those facts are taken into account which could buttress the alternative scenario put forward by the author, while inconvenient facts are ignored.

In Harris' *Fatherland* Hitler wins a military victory over the Soviet Union in 1942 and throws back the remnants of the Red Army well beyond the Ural Mountains, where they wage a guerilla war for decades against the victors similar to the one conducted by Chiang Kai-shek's army for eight years against the Japanese.[34] Harris has the Second World War ending with Hitler's conquest of Great Britain, while the USA, having finished off Japan with the help of atomic bombs, achieves hegemony in the Asian-Pacific theatre. Only two superpowers – Germany and the USA – remain on the planet.

Harris, in order to create his alternative history, needed to retain the atomic bombing of Japan and conjecture Hitler's victory over Great Britain. However, in the case where the Second World War had continued without the Eastern Front, the Americans would not have bothered to waste their limited atomic supplies on Japan. They would have accumulated their atomic bombs and, according to Harris, would have inflicted them on Berlin and other major German cities some time in the middle of 1946, all the more so because, according to Harris, Iceland would have been under American control, from which bombers could reach Germany. And the USA had more than enough aircraft carriers. The Second World War would have ended with this. The USA was ahead of Germany in the field of nuclear weapons by approximately two-and-a-half years and the USSR's participation in the war on Germany's side would in no way have shortened this gap. Quite the opposite, those resources which Great Britain and the USA spent on aiding the USSR would have, in this case, been used to build up the strategic bombardment of Germany, which could have slowed the development of the realization of the German atomic project even further. Germany would nevertheless have been unable to catch up with the USA in aircraft construction and naval weapons, even if it had reoriented its entire industry to the *Luftwaffe's* and navy's needs.

If, nonetheless, the unrealizable alternative could be realized approximately, as in Robert Harris' *Fatherland*, and Germany had won the Second World War, they would be observing the seventieth anniversary of the Great Victory in the Third Reich in just about the same way as in Putin's Russia today, but only as if in a mirror. Of course, Hitler would no longer be alive, having died in the 1960s, and at the latest, in the 1970s. It doubtful that Goring, who was only four years younger than the führer, would have outlived him by much.[35] It's likely that they would have been succeeded by younger and more pragmatic Nazis, like Speer and Schellenberg, who were not directly linked to the mass extermination of innocent victims.[36] By 2015 the successors to Speer and Schellenberg would be in power. They would probably have transformed the Third Reich into a more or less soft totalitarian dictatorship of the Brezhnev type, without the mass extermination or confinement to concentration camps of the racially or psychologically inferior population and dissidents.[37] It is not possible to say if they would call the Second World War the Great Patriotic War in the Nazi Germany of the twenty-first century, or if other names would be in circulation, such as the Great German War, the Great War for the Triumph of the German Race, the Great War of Liberation, or something else. But they would probably extol the genius of Hitler, who saved Europe from both Bolshevik and Anglo-Saxon hegemony and united the Europeans in a fraternal European Union led by Germany. The Second World War would be viewed as a defensive struggle on Germany's part and the Jews, Anglo-Saxon plutocrats and the Bolsheviks declared its chief instigators, as would be the Polish nationalists. All of these groups only dreamed about how they would attack Germany and divide it up. The Polish provocation at Gleiwitz and Warsaw's intention of raising a revolt in Upper Silesia (in the same way as, according to the Stalinist version, the Soviet-Finnish War arose because of the Finnish provocation in Mainila and Helsinki's plans to create a Greater Finland at the expense of Soviet Karelia and the Northern Urals) would have been declared the reason for the Polish-German War. It would be maintained that the Soviet peoples joyfully met their German liberators from the Bolshevik yoke. As for the Jews, there would be no extermination, no matter how revisionist historians, writing for American-Zionist money, engaged in slander. Among the Jewish population of Europe there was an extremely large number of Anglo-American and Bolshevik spies. Thus, due to security concerns, it was necessary to deport the Jewish population to remote areas and to isolated ghettos, where they would be unable to carry out their hostile activity. There were anti-Semitic excesses at the local level, which were the fault of the local chiefs, who were not able to restrain popular anger. During the war there was a shortage of food from time to time. But 6 million supposedly exterminated Jews – that's just enemy propaganda fairy tales. After all, not a few Jews now live in territories controlled by Germany. The victory in the war was the greatest achievement of the German people, led by their führer Adolph Hitler and the party. It was to the credit of the *Wehrmacht* – the most capable and mighty armed forces of modern times. The Second World War was the greatest event not only in German history, but in world history. Thanks to the victory in the war, Germany became, together with the USA, one of the two world superpowers, which even enemies respect and fear. And the collapse of the Third Reich would be a real catastrophe for the world.

It will be attempted here, as far as possible, to take into account all the main facts relating to the waging of the war and to trace how they could have influenced its course in the case of an alternative scenario being realized from a particular time and which relies only on possible and real variations of the development of events.

It would seem that the enormous inequality in the human and economic potential of the nations of the anti-Hitler coalition and Germany and its allies would from the beginning exclude Hitler's victory. However, upon closer examination, this is not as simple and straightforward as it seems. If the experts predicted the rapid defeat of Poland, then the equally rapid collapse of France proved to be a complete surprise. The Western Allies were unable to help Poland for two reasons. First of all, the French army could be ready for an offensive not earlier than the war's third week, due to its mobilization and concentration schedule, when the fate of the Polish army had already been decided. Secondly, they were aware in London and Paris of the secret protocol to the Molotov-Ribbentrop Pact and guessed that the Red Army would soon invade Poland. And this made Warsaw's situation hopeless, so even an offensive on the Western Front could not have saved the Poles.

No one expected a similar catastrophe to befall France. The correlation of the number of troops and combat equipment was approximately equal. Given this situation, a renewal of a positional war seemed inevitable, as was the case in 1914. However, such a scenario did not at all suit Hitler, who needed a quick victory and not a war of attrition, which would be fatal for Germany. And he defeated France, thanks to the more effective tactics of the German forces and the extremely low combat capability of the French and also the Belgian and Dutch forces. The lack of desire of the French political and military elite to fight to the end, in which regard its attitude completely coincided with the main mass of the French population, which did not wish to die not only for Danzig, but for Paris as well, also played a role.

In connection with the French campaign of 1940, one may espy an alternative scenario applicable to the events in Dunkirk. More than a thousand pages of text have been written on the subject of what would have happened if the British Expeditionary Force had been unable to evacuate from Dunkirk.[38] There exists the widespread opinion that Hitler practically offered the British a 'golden bridge' by halting the offensive by the German tank units. However, in reality, the 'halt order' in no way influenced the circumstances of the Allies' evacuation from Dunkirk. This is what the British military historian and theoretician of mechanized forces John Fuller writes about the counterattack by British tanks on 22 May south of Arras: 'the 1st Army Tank Brigade did well, its heavily armoured "I" tanks coming as a complete surprise to the Germans.'[39] As a result, on 24 May Hitler halted the offensive by Guderian's tanks 25km from Dunkirk. However, he did this on the recommendation of the commander of Army Group A, Colonel General Gerd von Rundstedt, who was concerned by the large tank losses and the necessity of allowing the tank units to rest.[40] Also, on 23 May the commander of the French 4th Tank Division, Charles de Gaulle, launched his counterblow near Abbeville.[41] However, the British, in terms of winning additional time for an evacuation, did not profit from the halting of the German tanks as at this moment the retreat of the British forces had also halted. As Fuller writes, only on 26 May, when 'there was no hope of the French armies south of the Somme attacking northwards, Lord Gort was ordered to save what he could of his army by withdrawing it to the coast'.[42] And it was on this day that the German offensive on Dunkirk was renewed. Prior to this, the British army had been reinforced by the 3rd Tank Brigade, so that at that moment there lived only the hope that the Dunkirk bridgehead could be retained, but that a counterblow could be launched from it to meet the French. The 3rd Tank Brigade was excessive to cover a withdrawal, as the existing two tank brigades would have been sufficient. Thus they had to leave even more armoured equipment on the shore. If it is assumed that there had been no 'halt order' from Hitler, Heinz Guderian's XIX Motorized Corps would have already broken into Dunkirk by the close of 24 May.[43] But then Lord John Gort would have received orders to withdraw on that very day, and not on 26 May. The German tank troops would not have been able to hold Dunkirk, towards which the entire British Expeditionary Corps was heading. The Germans probably would have carried out some kind of destruction of the port, but it is unlikely that this would have been sufficient to foil the evacuation. And they would have suffered additional losses in armoured equipment. Thus the absence of a 'halt order' could not have materially influenced the schedule and capacity of the British evacuation.

It should be noted that in the same year of 1940 the British were already waging a successful manoeuvre war against the Italians in North Africa. The British army was a professional one and the officers who served in it were trained to operate independently just as their German colleagues. All the more so, as the British soldiers were primarily designated for operations in the colonies, where the great distances and the absence of reliable communications often forced commanders to operate at their own risk. This explains to a great exent the relatively successful actions of the British troops in France and during the evacuation from Dunkirk.

Yet another group of alternative scenarios is tied to the possibility of the *Wehrmacht's* landing in the British Isles. It is precisely with the success of this landing that all the other alternative variations for the development of events and which lead to Germany's victory in the Second World War are linked. The first is that the German troops should have attempted to land in Britain immediately following the evacuation of British troops from Dunkirk, as *Luftwaffe* Field Marshal Albert Kesselring declared.[44] He wrote: 'Nothing ventured, nothing gained! . . .' and 'their still available bomber forces could be held in check by flak alone . . .' and 'The British fighter forces could be dissipated, softened up and destroyed by appropriate tactics . . .' .[45] Kesselring placed great hope on the self-propelled Siebel ferries, parachute troops, and transport aviation.[46] However, taking into account all the facts known today, a landing immediately following Dunkirk, at the end of June or in July, would have been doomed to failure. Kesselring himself admits that 'Even in the autumn of 1939, when the offensive against the west was already determined there is positive proof that our preparations never envisioned an invasion of England.'[47] No one assumed then that the question of a landing on the British Isles would so quickly become a part of the agenda. And the Germans found it very difficult to concentrate beforehand in their own ports hundreds of ships for a future movement to the as-yet uncaptured ports along the English Channel. In reality, they were only able to concentrate the necessary tonnage for Operation 'Sea Lion' in August, while they were forced to employ even river vessels.[48] The *Luftwaffe* was only able to restore its losses incurred during the course of the French campaign in July. Since they were unable to disrupt the evacuation from Dunkirk, it was all the more difficult to think that they would be able to defend the landing vessels in the ports and at sea from attacks by British aviation and the fleet. The German fleet, following major losses in the Norwegian operation, had by the completion of the French campaign only 48 submarines, 1 heavy cruiser, 4 destroyers and 3 torpedo cutters combat-ready. Such paltry forces, even with the return to duty of ships within the coming months, would not have been able to defend an armada of invasion ships against attacks by the British fleet, even had the *Luftwaffe*, by some kind of miracle, gained air superiority over the English Channel. Thus, even during the most unfavourable time for Britain, the Germans had no chance of carrying out a successful landing on the British Isles. And there was even less chance of success subsequently, once the USA openly entered the war. All the scenarios involving a successfully accomplished Operation 'Sea Lion' could not have been realized in principle, as their inability to be realized did not depend on the adoption of these or other decisions by the belligerents. One may consider as realistic only that alternative which issues from other military and political decisions adopted by the leaders of the chief powers in reality.

Chapter 2

Stalin's and Hitler's Plans to Attack Each Other

Both dictators fully understood the inevitability of a collision between the USSR and Germany. Following the conclusion of the Molotov-Ribbentrop Pact, Stalin did not trust Hitler and did not doubt that the latter would attack him and wanted to forestall such an assualt. In the very same way, Hitler did not trust Stalin and did not doubt that the latter would attack him and prepared to strike first. The difference lay only in the fact that Hitler could not attack the USSR earlier than 1941 because he first had to deal with Poland and France. Stalin fully allowed for an assault against Germany in 1940, hoping that having begun a general offensive in France, Hitler would get bogged down along the Maginot Line.[1] Linked to this idea was the fact that as early as the end of February 1940, even before the conclusion of the war with Finland, Germany was named the chief enemy in Soviet naval plans.[2] Also, the demobilization of the Red Army soldiers called up for the Finnish War was delayed until 1 July 1940, while simultaneously the concentration of Soviet forces was taking place along the Soviet-German demarcation line in Poland.[3] The decision hurriedly adopted in March 1940 to execute the Polish officers, which was carried out in April and the first half of May in Katyn' and in other places, may also be explained by the preparation for an attack against Germany. After all, the Polish officers, for quite understandable reasons, felt no sympathy for the USSR. And in case of war between the USSR and Germany, they would have to be freed and transferred to the Polish government in exile in Paris for the formation of a new Polish army not under the control of the USSR. Stalin did not desire such an army, which is why he hurried the execution of the Poles. But France let him down and collapsed after only three weeks, and Stalin decided to postpone the attack until 1941.

As early as 1943 the Roosevelt administration did not doubt one bit that the crime against humanity perpetrated at Katyn' was the work of Stalin, and not Hitler. The British Foreign Office came to a similar conclusion. As early as May 1943, a group of American and British prisoners of war was transported by the Germans to the Katyn' forest against their will. There they came to the unambiguous conclusion that the execution of the captured Polish officers had been carried out by the Soviets, as the clothes of the dead (springtime clothes, although the Germans captured this area in the summer) pointed to this, and the absence of any kind of documents on the bodies dated later than the spring of 1940, and, what was most important, the very logic of the enemy's actions: the Germans, who had by this time a very poor reputation for carrying out crimes against humanity, would never have risked publicly ascribing the victims of the mass burial in Katyn' to the Soviet side if the German *Einsatzgruppen* had actually disposed of the Poles.[4] Two American prisoners of war, Captain Donald Stuart and Lieutenant Colonel John Van Fleet, managed through a secret communications channel (probably through representatives of the Red Cross) to pass on corresponding thoughts to US army intelligence. They laid particular stress on the fact that the uniforms and footwear of the dead was new and had not had time to get worn, because they had been taken captive in September 1939, when, if one accepts the Soviet version, the Polish officers had to have spent two years in Soviet captivity before their execution by the Germans. The German version left the Poles only seven months in captivity. Besides this, Churchill sent Roosevelt a highly detailed report by his assistant, Owen O'Malley, who maintained contact with the Polish government in exile. According to O'Malley, the Polish government's data 'leaves in great doubt the veracity of Russia's assertions as to its innocence regarding the events in Katyn''.[5] However, the Roosevelt administration preferred to support Stalin's position, fearing the break-up of the anti-Hitler coalition. It's another question as to how realistic these fears were. Of course, history does not have the subjunctive mood, but if we objectively analyze the situation during the spring and summer of 1943, when German troops stood near Kursk and on the Taman' peninsula, fears of the possibility of a Soviet-German separate peace appear exaggerated. Stalin, realizing that the Red Army's combat capability depended to a critical degree on Lend-Lease deliveries, would not likely have risked concluding a separate peace with Hitler.[6] After all, he, no less than Great Britain and the USA, feared Nazi Germany, which in the event of a halt to combat activities on the Eastern Front, would have had the opportunity to significantly increase its military potential. On the other hand, if Great Britain and the USA had supported the position of their ally, the Polish government in exile in London, regarding the Katyn' question (and the Poles did not doubt that the crime had been committed by Stalin), it is possible that the tragedy of the Warsaw uprising could have been avoided and that following the end of the war there would have remained the chance of forcing the Soviet Union to recognize the establishment in Poland of a democratic government.[7] However, Roosevelt and Churchill feared most the reaction of public opinion in their own countries. If the Soviet responsibility for Katyn' had been publicly admitted, this would mean that the USA and Great Britain were allies of a regime just as criminal as the Hitlerite one. Besides this, in 1943 both the American and British leaders still hoped for cooperation with Stalin in the postwar establishment of peace and were obviously not ready for a subsequent confrontation with him.

However, what is even more amazing, as declassified documents demonstrate, even in their secret correspondence during the Cold War following 1945, the representatives of the American government never laid direct responsibility for Katyn' on the Soviet Union, explaining this by the absence of undisputed evidence. This continued all the way up to Gorbachev's admission in 1990 of Soviet responsibility for Katyn'.[8] At the same time, irrefutable proof did exist and it had been presented sufficiently long ago. As early as 1952 hearings on Katyn' were held in the American Congress, where, among others, the evidence offered by Stuart and Van Fleet was heard. However, other documents served as decisive corroboration. These were lists, which had been compiled in the spring of 1940, by those Polish officers who remained alive and who were being held in the camp at Kozel'sk and whose comrades were later found in the Katyn' forest. They were listed by name and who among the officers were removed from the camp and on what day. It later transpired that those officers who had been taken on the same day from the camp were later found in the same graves.[9] The Germans could not have shot the Poles in the same groups in which they were taken out of the camp by NKVD officers. Thus this proof is decisive and indisputable. But the American government preferred not to pay attention to this, just as it did regarding the proposal by the participants of the hearing in 1947 to create a special international tribunal to try the perpetrators of the Katyn' crime. It is possible that in Washington and in other Western capitals they were afraid that an open accusation by the American government that the government of the Soviet Union had killed the Polish officers might make the Cold War 'hotter'. It is probable these fears were in vain.

The unearthing of the Katyn' crime by the Germans did not only not cause Stalin any great unpleasantness, as Goebbels expected, but, on the contrary, it was used by the Soviet dictator to his own advantage.[10] Having accused the Sikorski government of cooperating with the international commission created by the Germans to investigate the Katyn' crime, Moscow broke off diplomatic relations with it. After this, an important obstacle on Stalin's path to forming a pro-communist power structure in Poland (the future Polish Committee for National Liberation, or the Lublin Committee) and pro-Soviet military formations (the Polish army's two field armies) disappeared.

If there is only circumstantial evidence of Stalin's plans to attack Germany in 1940, then there is direct evidence of the preparation of such an attack in 1941. On the plan for the Red Army's deployment in the west, which was adopted on 11 March 1941, there is the resolution by the deputy chief of the General Staff, Lieuenant General Vatutin: 'Begin the offensive on 12.06.'[11]

It's interesting that in 1941 Vatutin only appears in the visitor's book for Stalin's Kremlin office before the war on 2 and 25 January, 19 and 24 May, and also 3, 6, 9, and 17 June.[12] However, and what is very significant, on 11 March 1941, when it's most likely that the corresponding strategic deployment plan was being examined, there were no visitors at all to the Kremlin office, just as there were none on 18 September 1940 (the day of the preceding strategic deployment plan and the plan for a new attack on Finland).[13] But it is well known that Stalin received his subordinates not only in his Kremlin office, but also at his 'nearby' dacha in Kuntsevo, and (more rarely) at his Kremlin apartment. There was no registration of visitors at his dacha and apartment, which guaranteed even greater secrecy.

That is why one may fully allow for the possibility that Vatutin was at Stalin's dacha namely on 11 March 1941 and that it was there that he received instructions regarding a possible date for an attack on Germany. Iosif Vissarionovich likely simply added three months to 11 March and arrived at the date of 12 June. But due to the low carrying capacity of the Soviet railroads, the deadline of 12 June was not met. They did not have time to concentrate all the supplies and equipment, and the attack on Germany was shifted to July. Evidence of this is a Politburo decree of 4 June 1941 on the formation by 1 July 1941 of the Central Asian Military District's 238th Rifle Division, which was 'formed from rank and file of Polish nationality and those knowing the Polish language'.[14]

It is interesting that in the middle of October 1940 that Beria, while discussing with Lieutenant Colonel Berling, Colonel Gorczynski, Lieutenant Colonel Bukaenski, and Lieutenant Colonel Gorczynski the forthcoming formation of the Polish division, replied to Berling's request to free the Polish officers needed to form the division that as regards them 'We committed a big mistake'.[15] From this account one may conclude that, first of all, Beria was against the execution of the Polish officers and was willing to limit himself to their deportation to the Asian part of the USSR and that, secondly, the matter of forming a Polish division was being discussed as early as October 1940.

It should be emphasized that as early as 26 October 1939, exactly a month before the Soviet provocation in Mainila, K.Ye. Voroshilov issued an order for the formation of the 106th Special Rifle Corps, made up of the USSR's Finnish and Karelian population.[16] On 23 November the newly formed corps was renamed the 1st Mountain Rifle Corps and upon the beginning of the Soviet-Finnish War was immediately dispatched to the front and named the 1st Rifle Corps of the Finnish People's Army, nominally subordinated to the Finnish puppet government of O. Kuusinen. Certainly, there were few Finns in the corps, although it had a very international coloration, including inhabitants of Central Asia. The author's late stepfather recalled that when units of the corps marched through Leningrad they cursed fluently in Russian, without any kind of Finnish accent. This corps did not win any laurels on the battlefields and was manned for the most part by Russians and the representatives of other Soviet nationalities, who lacked any kind of association with Finland.[17]

The hurried formation of the Polish division would have been useful to Stalin only if he had been preparing to wage military operations on Polish territory in the near future and to establish in Warsaw a puppet pro-Soviet government. Stalin's correspondence with Beria on the formation of this division from Soviet citizens and 'reliable' Poles among the prisoners of war took place at least from the beginning of November 1940. Undoubtedly, the formation of the Polish division was a very powerful provocation in relation to Germany, as it directly violated the secret protocol to the Soviet-German treaty on friendship and borders of 28 September 1939, according to which both sides were obliged to oppose the rebirth of the Polish state. In the event of Germany's attack, there would have been no particular use for a Polish division because in the beginning combat operations would have been conducted on Soviet territory. In this case they could have begun the formation of a Polish division right after a German attack. If the USSR was preparing to attack Germany, then the Red Army would have to immediately invade Polish territory. They should have begun to form a Polish division not long before the beginning of an invasion so that German intelligence would not find out about it. Since they decided to form the division by 1 July, this means that Stalin at that moment was thinking about beginning the war with Germany at the start of July.

Stalin was sure that Hitler would not attack the USSR in 1941, but would try to finish off Great Britain. The Soviet dictator had an exaggerated notion of the Germans' abilities to make a landing on the British Isles and was preparing to strike at that moment when, as he thought, the *Wehrmacht's* main forces would be concentrated in the West for a landing in Great Britain. Hitler also allowed for the possibility that Stalin could attack him as early as 1941, and thus hurried to carry out Operation 'Barbarossa'.[18] But even if Stalin had managed to strike first, the Red Army, which was inferior by an order of magnitude to the *Wehrmacht* as regards combat capability, would nevertheless have suffered just as serious defeat in 1941 as actually happened. Stalin, as was Hitler, was focused on a *blitzkrieg* and calculated on defeating the *Wehrmacht's* within forty days.[19] This, in any event, was called for in the plan for a preemptive attack, which was drawn up in the middle of May 1941.[20] Stalin had an excessively high opinion of the Red Army's combat capabilities and believed that a Soviet division was at least the equal of a *Wehrmacht* division, while 'Stalin's falcons' could fight it out on equal terms with the *Luftwaffe's* aces. But all of this was far removed from reality.

In the middle of May there appeared the plan for a preemptive blow, which was drawn up by Vatutin and Vasilevskii on orders from people's defence commissar Timoshenko and chief of the General Staff Zhukov, who undoubtedly received corresponding instructions from Stalin.[21] According to this plan, which was dated no later than 15 May 1941, the Soviet forces were to make their main attack along the southwestern direction and as early as the thirtieth day of the operation reach the front Ostroleka–Narew River–Lowicz–Lodz–Kreuzberg–Oppeln–Olomouc.[22] The first one to publish this text in full (with the exception of a number of still-classified supplements) in German was V.D. Danilov.[23] 'The subsequent strategic goal' was to be 'an offensive from the Katowice–Cracow area to the north or northwest', during the course of which it was planned 'to defeat the major forces of the center and northern wing of the German front and to occupy the territory of former Poland and East Prussia. The immediate objective is to defeat the German army east of the Vistula River and along the Cracow axis, to reach the Narew and Vistula rivers and to capture the Katowice area.' A supporting attack was to be made by the Western Front's left wing towards Warsaw and Deblin, in order to assist the Southwestern Front in defeating the enemy's Lublin group of forces. However, this offensive was to begin only on the operation's thirtieth day. Before this time only an active defence was planned along the Western Front, as well as the others, with the exception of the Southwestern Front. This was probably linked to the fact that they wanted to put all of their men and materiel into the Southwestern Front's attack. In all likelihood there was not enough fuel and munitions for a second offensive along the Western Front. Thus it worked out that during the first month of the war the Red Army was not to carry out even supporting or demonstration offensives along the other directions. The Germans would have immediately determined the direction of the main Soviet attack and would have launched a powerful counterblow from the north into the flank and rear of the attackers.

Timoshenko and Zhukov thought that the main German group of forces (100 of 180 divisions that were to be deployed in the East) would be concentrated along the southwestern direction, 'to the south of the line Brest–Deblin, for launching the main attack in the direction of Kovel', Rovno and

Kiev'. A total of 152 RKKA divisions were to operate against this group of forces. Then by a vigorous offensive to the Baltic the Soviet forces were to cut off the *Wehrmacht's* forces in Poland and East Prussia from Germany.

In reality, the *Wehrmacht* was to launch its main attack along the central direction. Thus the Soviet forces, even had they begun the war first, would in no way have been able to defeat the *Wehrmacht's* main forces, but quite the opposite; they would have been subjected to a powerful flanking attack. But the level of the Red Army's combat training would not have increased one bit just because the Soviet forces attacked first. The *Luftwaffe*, even having been subjected to a surprise attack, would nonetheless have won air superiority within two to three days. But it's unlikely that the attack would have been such a surprise for the Germans as it proved to be for the Red Army on 22 June. The German planes would have rapidly slowed down the pace of the Soviet forces' advance. The clumsy organizational structure of the Soviet tank formations would have played a negative role. The mechanized corps numbered 1,000 tanks each, but the small number of radios within them would have rendered them practically uncontrollable. Because of this and because of the numerous breakdowns in equipment, which nobody had any idea how to repair, the Soviet columns would have become easy prey for the *Luftwaffe*. It should be noted that the Soviet pilots' level of combat training on 22 June 1941 was higher than at any other period of the war. On this day the *Luftwaffe* suffered its greatest one-day losses for the entire Soviet-German war, although there were subsequently days, for example, at the beginning of the Battle of Kursk, when the *Luftwaffe* employed even more planes against Soviet forces than on the day of the attack against the USSR. It's likely that the average level of training for the Soviet tank troops, as well as for the infantry, was at that moment higher than it subsequently was, as on the first day of the war cadre troops and commanders who had served a year and more accounted for the maximum share of the Red Army's strength. But, as with the tank troops, the experience of the cadre specialists was lessened in value by the preponderance of inexperienced draftees in the tank troops, which was a consequence of the rushed growth in the number and strength of the tank formations in 1940–1, as well as the shortcomings of the Soviet armoured forces' organizational structure. In any case, one may assume that in the event of a Soviet attack the main mass of the Southwestern Front's forces would have been encircled somewhere in southern Poland and the neighbouring areas of Western Ukraine. It's likely that they would have shot the *front* commander, Colonel General Mikhail Kirponos, for the defeat, and not the commander of the Western Front, General Dmitrii Pavlov, as actually happened (if, of course, Kirponos had been able to break out of the encirclement without being killed or captured).[24] Further on, the course of the war would have been approximately the same as it was in 1941 and the German forces would still have been halted in front of Moscow. The Soviet attack against Germany would have become theoretically possible if the *Wehrmacht's* Balkan campaign had become much extended.[25]

The Polish division, the formation of which was to have been completed by 1 July, was necessary only for an attack against Germany. But it still had to be transported to the West from Kazakhstan, where it was being formed. This information gives the approximate date for the beginning of the offensive – the second ten-day period of July.

It's entirely excluded that Timoshenko and Zhukov possessed the courage to prepare such an extremely serious document as a plan for a preemptive attack on Germany without Stalin's direct sanction. The example of Tukhachevskii and his other colleagues, who were shot in 1937–8, was still very much in their minds. There's no way the RKKA's new leadership wanted to end up at 'Tukhachevskii's headquarters'. It's another matter entirely that Zhukov, even in a private conversation after the war, was unable to admit that Stalin really planned to attack Hitler. In this event, the entire Soviet conception of the Great Patriotic War would have collapsed.

As Mark Solonin believes:

> From January through June 1941, the scenario of the operational 'games' undergoes very noticeable changes: the number of forces for the 'easterners' becomes fewer and fewer and their missions and successes less and less ambitious. From an offensive on Budapest to counterblow around Vil'nius and Bialystok . . . The evaluation of the combat capability of one's own forces remains unchangeably high . . . Given a numerical equality with the enemy, the Red Army successfully attacks, slowly, to be sure, advancing 'only' ten kilometers per day, but it attacks. Given a twofold numerical superiority over the enemy, the 'easterners' smash the 'westerners' to smithereens. Given the enemy's twofold numerical superiority, the 'easterners' stubbornly defend, going over at times to a mobile defence. The 'westerners' are able to break through the 'easterners'' front only having a three-four or fivefold numerical superiority in infantry and an overwhelming one in tanks; however, in these cases a breakthrough does not signify 'the beginning of the catastrophe,' but an inevitable and immediate crushing counterblow by the Red Army along a neighboring and inevitably weakened sector of the enemy's front.[26]

Solonin also notes that during the prewar war games and staff rides the theme of 'the *front* and armies' defensive operation in conditions of an offensive by major enemy forces against a background of our forces' uncompleted concentration; the conduct of a counterblow with the forcing of a river obstacle' was usually played out.[27] And the researcher's careful assumption sounds thus: 'The contours of the front line on the maps of the "May game" clearly show . . . that the Germans launched the first blow, advanced 50–100 kilometers into Soviet territory and, only after this do they encircle and defeat them in three "cauldrons" – near Alytus, Lublin and Kamenets-Podol'sk . . .'

Stalin really did disagree with the authors of the May 'Considerations' (that is, with Vasilevskii, Vatutin, Zhukov, and Timoshenko). Stalin did not only 'reject' but proposed an alternative variation. It was just this variation that was verified during the course of the strategic 'war game' on 20–1 May.

Let's assume that the scenario for the beginning of the war (for argument's sake, we'll call it 'Stalin's variation',) consisted of the following: the Red Army begins and during the first fifteen days completes its strategic deployment, and that the deployment, on the whole, is carried out within the confines of the plan drawn up during August 1940–May 1941. At some point (either during the deployment, or in the first days following its completion, but more likely the former rather than the latter), in Hitler's headquarters, they make the quite predictable decision for such a situation ('Under no circumstances surrender the initiative to the Soviet command, to preempt the enemy and attack the Red Army at that moment when it will be deploying'). And then, after this, there takes place everything that we see today on the slightly yellowed maps of the 'May game'. Why and for what reason did it occur to Stalin to give Hitler the doubtful honour of violating the Soviet-German Non-Aggression Treaty (while at the same time losing the serious tactical advantages of the first blow)? Perhaps because, not having absorbed the bitter experience of December 1939 (the unsuccessful attempt to 'liberate Finland from the White Finnish and Mannerheim bands'), he had come to understand that the main thing for victory in war is 'noble fury' and in order for it to 'boil up like a wave' it makes sense to accord the right of the first shot to the enemy.[28]

It is likely that Solonin's hypothesis is mistaken, for the following reasons. The May plan for a preemptive attack was the real plan for the deployment of troops, which was gradually carried out all the way up to 22 June 1941, when it ceased to make sense. The war games, the documents of which not just four people were familiar with, as was the case with the May 'Considerations', but at a minimum tens of executors, are mere sketches. According to the results of these games, certain corrections were made to the plan, although it rarely changed in a significant way. As no other later plan, different from the May plan for a preemptive attack, has yet been found, it can only be concluded that it remained in force. And according to this plan, as is known, it was planned to keep the German forces from Soviet territory and to attack first. These are how the specific tasks were formulated:

  a). to launch the main attack with the forces of the Southwestern Front in the direction of Cracow and Katowice and to cut Germany off from her southern allies;

  b). to launch a supporting attack by the left wing of the Western Front in the direction of Warsaw and Deblin, for the purpose of tying down the Warsaw group of forces and capturing Warsaw, as well as to support the Southwestern Front in defeating the Lublin group of forces;

  c). to carry out an active defence against Finland, East Prussia, Hungary, and Romania and be ready to launch an attack against Romania under favorable conditions. However, even the Western Front, according to this plan, was supposed to first defend and only later attack toward Warsaw. The following describes its activities: 'The Western Front . . . Mission: to firmly secure the Lida and Bialystok axes by means of a stubborn defence along the front Druskienniki–Ostroleka;

  d). with the start of the offensive by the armies of the Southwestern Front, it is to defeat the Warsaw group of forces with an attack by the *front's* left wing in the direction of Warsaw and Siedlce and capture Warsaw and, in conjunction with the Southwestern Front defeat the Lublin–Radom enemy group of forces, to reach the Vistula River and capture Radom with mobile units.[29]

Thus the war was to begin with an offensive by the Southwestern Front in the direction of Cracow and Katowice. The remaining *fronts* were to defend at the start of the war. Timoshenko and Zhukov evidently assumed that the enemy, having gone over to the offensive along the other fronts, would attempt to distract Soviet forces from the southwestern direction. In those games, the various administrative materials of which have been published by Solonin, events develop in accordance with the May plan. The forces of the future Western and Northwestern fronts at first defend, and then launch counterblows. Timoshenko and Zhukov probably feared that the enemy might attempt to cut off the Bialystok salient, which is why at first it was planned to repulse possible German attacks from the northwest and then, when the Southwestern Front had completely defeated the enemy by the thirtieth day, to go over to the offensive towards Warsaw and Siedlce. Of course, the executors, who were not privy to all the details of the plan for the start of the war, were at a loss to understand, as Solonin well showed, why the German troops, who were attacking in depth into Soviet territory, suddenly and unexpectedly halted. But Timoshenko, Zhukov, and the other generals familiar with the May plan believed with reason that once the Southwestern Front's success became clear the German command would be forced to halt the offensive and throw forces from the other fronts against the Southwestern Front. It would have been another matter altogether, if the Red Army had managed to really preempt the *Wehrmacht* and strike first; then the German command would probably have acted otherwise. That is, approximately how it acted during the Soviet offensive on Khar'kov in May 1942. Then the Army Group South command allowed the Southwestern Front's forces to approach sufficiently close to Khar'kov along the German Sixth Army's front and then launched an attack by Kleist's group against the Southern Front along the base of the Barvenkovo salient and surrounded the attacking group of forces.[30] As opposed to what they thought in the Soviet General Staff, the Germans' most significant forces in the summer of 1941 were not in Army Group South, but in Army Group Centre. And in the event of the beginning of an offensive by the Soviet Southwestern Front, it is most likely that the German command would not have attempted to invade Lithuania and Belorussia with the forces of Army Group Centre but, while limiting itself to a defence along the border against the Western Front and allowing the main forces of the Southwestern Front to invade southern Poland, would have concentrated Army Group Centre's main forces for a counterblow from the north for the purpose of destroying the Southwestern Front's forces. And only following the fulfillment of this mission could one expect an invasion by all three German army groups into Soviet territory. The Red Army command, believing that an attack towards Cracow and Katowice would rout the Germans' main forces along the Eastern Front, did not expect counterblows from the north against its shock group of forces, hoping that the Western and Northwestern fronts would safely tie down the enemy forces opposing them, which would have only eased the Germans' task.

Solonin managed to find war game materials for a number of military districts, but not the most powerful one – the Kiev Military District; this can be simply explained. The war game materials for the future Southwestern Front probably remain classified 'secret'. To all appearances, there was also the ritual phrase that the German forces had invaded Soviet territory. However, in all likelihood, they began to play out the actual course of combat operations only from that moment when the Soviet forces, having thrown the enemy back to the frontier, shifted combat operations to Polish territory. And there is nothing surprising that during the war games that were carried out in the military districts, all the Soviet forces proved to be fully mobilized, and the planes ready for immediate take-off for battle. Since the Kiev Military District was supposed to begin the war, then the remaining districts were also to be fully ready for war, although they were to resolve only defensive tasks during the first days of the war.

It's opportune to mention that the opinion is widely held that as the May plan for a preventive attack is a manuscript with a significant number of corrections, it could not be presented to Stalin in that form. However, the crux of the matter lies in the special secrecy of the document, which was drawn up as a single copy. Vasilevskii or Vatutin would need an entire day to rewrite it from scratch, and time was of the essence. All the more so, they could have easily communicated the text of the document to Stalin orally. And they probably showed him maps and tables listing men and materiel as supplements to the plan. Even some of Stalin's or somebody else's resolutions could have remained on the maps. But these maps have not yet been published.

As is clear, Solonin came to the correct conclusion that during the course of the war games the Soviet command significantly exaggerated its own forces' combat capabilities. But this is what proves that Timoshenko, Zhukov, and Stalin were not so much afraid of the *Wehrmacht* and counted on defeating it in the course of two offensive operations. As they believed, even given a numerical equality of forces, the Red Army could easily attack at the rate of 10km per day and easily destroy the enemy with a two-fold superiority, then what was there to be afraid of? First we'll destroy the Germans' main forces in the southwest, then we'll occupy the Upper Silesian and Moravian industrial areas and, with an attack to the north and in conjunction with the Western and Northwestern fronts, we'll destroy the remaining German forces in Poland and East Prussia. And after this, Germany may freely capitulate. Such evaluations of their combat capability could not be propaganda, as all of the war games were conducted on this basis, as were the calculations regarding the timetables for combat operations.

The reality of war, as we know, was much gloomier, as the *Wehrmacht* was head and shoulders above the Red Army in terms of combat capability. In 1941–2 the Germans attacked successfully, advancing 30–40km per day, against an overall Soviet superiority in men and materiel, concentrating sufficient forces for an offensive at the decisive points. And beginning with 1943, when the Soviet superiority had increased significantly, the Germans successfully defended against a force of Soviet men and materiel two to three times greater. It was only from the middle of 1944, following the Allied landing in Normandy, when the Soviet superiority in men in combat units reached nearly seven times and was even more significant in combat equipment, was the Red Army able to encircle and quite rapidly destroy major enemy groups of forces, although it suffered considerable losses in doing so. But the knowledge that the *Wehrmacht* was stronger than the Red Army, if it entered the head of Stalin and his generals, came no earlier than the middle of the war. And in 1941 the Soviet forces were doomed to defeat, regardless of who managed to begin the war first.

Parts of the 15 May plan were being carried out on the eve of the war. For example, the call-up of 793,000 men began at the end of May 1941, under the guise of 'major training assemblies' (BUS). Four armies and a rifle corps from the high command reserve began to move toward the Dnepr and Western Dvina rivers from the middle of May. Troops were moving up to within 20–80km from the state border in the border military districts. The concentration was to have been completed between 1 and 10 July 1941. The transfer of several air divisions to the west began in the middle of June from the Trans-Baikal and Far East. And from the middle of May there began large-scale measures for the rear support of offensive operations, the concentration of reserves of equipment, armaments, munitions, food, forage, and fuels and lubricants, and the creation of a hospital base.[31]

All the way up to the beginning of the war, Stalin, as did Hitler during the first stages of the preparation for Barbarossa, maximally masked the concentration of forces and did not cut back on civilian traffic on the railroads. However, during the final preparatory stages, Stalin could order civilian traffic to be reduced to a minimum and thus speed up the concentration of forces and the necessary supplies. In this case, one could hope to complete the concentration, if not by the middle of July, then by the beginning of August. In any event, Stalin prepared to attack Hitler only when the concentration of the first-echelon troops and the means designated for them had been achieved.

If the war in the Balkans had become prolonged and Hitler had been forced once again to move the beginning of 'Barbarossa', Stalin theoretically had the opportunity to preempt him and realize the May plan. But this would have led to the same kind of disaster that in reality struck the Red Army on 22 June.

And even at that moment when the German dictator attacked the Soviet one, Stalin in no way ceased to be the aggressor. After all, if Stalin had been the first to attack Hitler, the powers of the anti-Hitler coalition would not have ceased as a result of this to regard Germany as an aggressor and were ready to render the Soviet Union all manner of help. This explains the Allies' subsequent policy in 1943–5 in regard to Poland, the Baltic States, and other countries and peoples of Eastern Europe, where communist totalitarian regimes were established on Soviet bayonets. When the Soviet-German war began, the

Estonians, Lithuanians, and Latvians and a significant part of the inhabitants of Ukraine and Belorussia waited for Hitler as a liberator. On the other side of the border, the Poles, Czechs and the millions of Jews that had not yet been exterminated in the ghettos of Poland, looked on the Red Army as a liberator. But Hitler, as is known, was not planning to liberate anyone and did not take advantage of the opportunity to attract the peoples of the USSR as his allies. However, Stalin was ill-suited for the role of liberator, having made the peoples of Eastern Europe either a part of the USSR or its disenfranchised satellites and ruthlessly dealt with the supporters of the Polish government in exile. German soldiers brought probable death to the Jews and Gypsies, the status of slaves for the non-Aryan peoples, and the role of satellites for those Aryan peoples among the population of the Soviet Union which, at the beginning of the war, they numbered the Estonians, Latvians, Cossacks, and the peoples of the Caucasus and Turkestan. During the later years of the war and after Soviet forces brought death and repressions in the liberated territories to the representatives of the well-to-do ('exploiting') classes, government workers, officers, police, and national intelligentsia.

Following the war, the leaders of the OKW, Wilhelm Keitel and Alfred Jodl, testified that Hitler believed that Stalin might attack him in the near future.[32] For example, Jodl, in an interrogation on 17 June 1945, declared: 'There existed the political opinion that the situation would become complicated in the event of Russia's attack against us. And insofar as sooner or later war with her was inevitable, then it was better for us to choose the time for an attack.'[33] The former chief of foreign intelligence of the Reich Main Security Office (RSHA), Walter Schellenberg, maintained in his memoirs that in April 1941 the head of the RSHA, Reinhardt Heydrich, told him the following: 'Russia's preparations are so tremendous that at any moment Stalin could exploit any commitment of our forces that we may make in Africa or in the West; which means he'd be able to forestall any future action we may be planning against him . . . in other words, that Stalin will soon be ready to join battle with us.'[34] During his interrogation of 18 June 1945, W. Keitel testified:

> I cannot say what kind of political plans Hitler had, but as regards the preparations for war in the East I evaluated the situation strictly from a military point of view; the General Staff possessed informa-tion that beginning in the early spring of 1941 the Soviet Union had begun a massive concentration of its forces in the border areas, which testified to the preparation by the USSR, if not of the open-ing of military operations, then at least to exerting open military pressure on German foreign policy . . . All of the preparatory meas-ures carried out by us up to the spring of 1941 had the character of

defensive preparations in the event of an attack by the Red Army. Thus to a certain extent one may call the entire war in the East a preventive one. Of course, in preparing these measures, we decided to choose a more effective means, namely to preempt Soviet Russia's attack and by an unexpected blow rout her armed forces. By the spring of 1941 I had come to the definite opinion that the heavy concentration of Russian forces and their subsequent attack on Germany could place us in an extremely critical situation in the strategic and economic sense. Our two flank bases – East Prussia and Upper Silesia – which stuck out to the east, were under particular threat. Our attack was the direct consequence of that threat.[35]

Field Marshal G. von Rundstedt told his chief of staff, G. Blumentritt, that:[36]

In 1941 the news was spreading that the Russians intended to attack not only Germany, but the whole of Europe! Hitler pointed to the massive Soviet armaments, the higher number of divisions and the war in Finland. He took the view that the Russians could only be making such great preparations to launch a sudden attack on Germany. He recalled Lenin, who had proclaimed that the aim of Soviet ideology was world revolution, which could only be attained by force. Hence the feverish building up of the Red Army. Hitler said, however, that he would not wait until the Russians were ready, but that he would anticipate this danger from the east in defence of Germany and Europe. He expected the Russian attack to come in 1941.[37]

Of course, all of this postwar evidence comes from people with an interest in justifying aggression against the USSR. However, one shouldn't doubt that Hitler was sure that Stalin would attack Germany to the exact same degree that Stalin had no doubt of Hitler's analogous intentions regarding the Soviet Union. Characteristically, Zhukov, in a fragment from his memoirs that did not make it into the edition published during his life, recalled:

I remember how once, in reply to my report that the Germans had strengthened their aerial, agent and ground intelligence, I.V. Stalin said: 'They're afraid of us. I'll tell you in secret that our ambassador had a serious personal conversation with Hitler and the he told him in confidence': 'Please don't worry when you receive information about the concentration of our troops in Poland. Our troops will be undergoing a great amount of retraining for particularly important assignments in the West.'[38]

Thus it turns out that Stalin did not doubt that Hitler should be afraid of the concentration of Soviet forces, but at the same time he was sure that Germany would not attack the USSR in 1941.

Those pronouncements of Stalin, such as during a speech before the higher command element on the occasion of the end of the war with Finland, or the address before the graduates of the military academies on 5 May 1941, which belittle the merits of the German army and exaggerate the RKKA's successes, are declared to be propaganda directed at raising the soldiers' martial spirit. However, it was a quite dangerous matter to disorient the higher command element as regards the real combat capability of the main potential enemy's army. Those pronouncements confirming Stalin's fear of Hitler are not authentic pronouncements by Stalin himself, but postwar testimonials by Marshal Zhukov and others of Stalin's comrades-in-arms. However, in no way, not even in the most intimate conversation, could they admit that the Soviet Union was planning to attack Germany. And one can easily allow that both Stalin and his generals truly underestimated the *Wehrmacht's* power, believing that there were no fewer hidden shortcomings in the German army than in the Red Army and that during the course of a war against the Red Army these would certainly manifest themselves.

The *Wehrmacht's* superiority over the Red Army, which was evident in the level of training of the troops and command element, and which was especially overwhelming in the air force and tank troops, the Germans' significantly better provisioning with communications equipment, and the far higher level of cooperation between the combat arms guaranteed a German victory in 1941, no matter what the Red Army did. It would have been defeated not only in the event it landed the first blow on 12 June, but even if they had chosen the most dangerous variation, from the German point of view, of waging combat operations, which was linked to the timely withdrawal of their main forces to the line of the Dnepr and Western Dvina rivers long before the possible beginning of the war, while leaving only weak covering units to the west of this line.

However, victory in 1941 did not save the *Wehrmacht*. A subsequent prolonged war was inevitable, in which Stalin had the capability of throwing into the furnace of war countless numbers of untrained but practically limitless human reinforcements to a certain death, the endless Russian expanses and the durability of a totalitarian regime, and the aid of the Western Allies. All of this guaranteed final victory, although in 1941 Stalin really did not have the choice of a good strategy, although he probably did not realize this, in that he rated the Red Army's combat capability too highly.

According to all available evidence, Stalin expected Hitler's attack in 1942, but not in 1941, insofar as he believed that the latter would first attempt to finish the war against Great Britain. And there is no evidence that Stalin was undertaking any kind of defensive measures against a possible German attack. The Red Army was oriented only towards the offensive. Defensive operations at the strategic level, inevitable in the event of a German attack, were not even played out at the *front* or army level. Hitler allowed for a Soviet attack as early as 1941. According to the testimony by the General Inspector of Tank Troops, Heinz Guderian, Hitler admitted to him that the visit to Berlin by the head of the Soviet government in November 1940 and the expansionist demands put forth by him finally convinced Hitler as to the inevitability of war with Russia:[39]

In Berlin Molotov put forth the following claims:

1. Finland was to be regarded as belonging within the Soviets' sphere of interest.
2. An agreement was to be made concerning the future of Poland.
3. Soviet interests in Romania and Bulgaria must be recognized.
4. Soviet interests in the Dardanelles must also be acknowledged.

After Molotov had returned to Moscow, the Russians restated these demands in more precise form, in writing.

Hitler was highly incensed by the Russian claims and expressed his displeasure at length during the Berlin conversations, while simply ignoring the subsequent Russian note. The conclusion he drew from Molotov's visit and its results was a belief that war with the Soviet Union must sooner or later be inevitable. He was to describe to me repeatedly the course that the Berlin conference took; I have given his version here. It is true that he never talked to me about this matter before 1943, but later on he did so several times and always in exactly the same terms. I have no reason to believe that what he said to me was not a repetition of his opinions at the time in question.[40]

Both Stalin and Hitler would sooner or later have attacked each other, as both dictators strived toward undisputed hegemony in Europe. But the timing of the attack depended on concrete and sufficiently chance circumstances, which also determined which of the dictators, would manage to preempt the other. Hitler did not exclude a Soviet preventive attack in Romania. Thus Hitler created a powerful group of forces there, which at first had a defensive mission, and strengthened the Ploesti oil region with anti-aircraft guns. However, Hitler was not carrying out defensive measures along the main directions of the future Eastern Front. He probably thought that in certain conditions, in which the *Wehrmacht's* main forces were already concentrated for an attack on the USSR, they would be able to defeat the enemy, either in meeting battles (as actually happened in the tank meeting battle in the Dubno–Lutsk–Rovno area during 23–30 June 1941), or by attacking the flank and rear of the attackers.

And if Stalin had actually attacked Germany first, then no one in the world, except for Hitler's allies, would have condemned him. Quite the opposite, Great Britain, as before, feared a German landing on the British Isles, while the USA, having adopted the Lend-Lease law and which was being drawn deeper and deeper into the world war, very much hoped for a collision between the USSR and Germany as a surefire means for bringing victory in the war nearer, and even encouraged Stalin to launch a preventive blow, reporting to him on the concentration of German troops at the Soviet borders. They were ready to forgive him, if only for a time, the short-lived alliance with Hitler, the stab in the back against fighting Poland, the aggression against Finland, and the occupation of the Baltic States, as well as Bessarabia and Northern Bukovina.

Even while the May plan for a preventive attack was being compiled, the initial deadline for the attack of 12 June was not being met. The concentration of troops and the necessary supplies was running late and by the beginning of June the Red Army could have begun an offensive at the earliest only in the middle of July, sometime during the period 6–15 July. In order for this attack to have taken place earlier than the beginning of Operation 'Barbarossa', it was essential that the anti-German coup in Yugoslavia, which made it necessary to throw major forces against Yugoslavia into the operation in the Balkans, take place not on 27 March 1941, but ten days later than was actually the case, already following the beginning of the German forces' military operations against Greece. If the Yugoslav army had come to the assistance of the Greeks, the Germans would have had to attempt to carry out a regrouping during the course of military operations already underway, in order to launch an attack against Yugoslavia and the Balkan campaign might have stretched out three more weeks in comparison with the real timetable for its completion. Then the time for the beginning of carrying out Operation 'Barbarossa' might have been moved from Sunday, 22 June, to Sunday, 13 or 20 July. And Stalin would have had the opportunity to strike first.

Except that the results would have been exactly the same as during the conduct of 'Barbarossa'. As the main group of German forces would not have come under the principal attack by Soviet forces, it is more than likely that the German command would have launched an attack from the north against the attacking forces of the Soviet Southwestern Front. And the latter would probably have gotten into the same 'cauldron' in which the troops of this *front* ended up around Kiev in September 1941. Only this cauldron would have been somewhere in southern Poland at the end of July or the beginning of August 1941. There could be no other outcome, in that the combat capability of the *Wehrmacht* and the Red Army differed by an order of magnitude, and this correlation did not practically depend upon which of the sides was attacking and which was defending. According to this development of events, German troops would have invaded Soviet territory not earlier than August. They probably would have created several other successful 'cauldrons', although probably not in those places where 'cauldrons' were formed following the beginning of 22 June in the course of realizing the real Operation 'Barbarossa'. However, the Germans still would not have had time to take Moscow before the beginning of the autumn rains in the second half of October 1941. Further on, the course of the war would have been exactly the same as was the real course of the Great Patriotic War.

Vasilevskii recalled that in reviewing plans for deploying the Red Army and equally secret documents, Stalin would issue instructions only orally.[41] Even if this thesis is accepted unconditionally, it mustn't be doubted that some of Stalin's instructions, particularly those that were large in volume and contained concrete numbers, surnames, and names, had to be summarized by his subordinate generals and marshals. Not too long ago, for example, there was published a summary of Stalin's instructions made by Molotov before the November trip to Berlin.[42] It's quite possible that someday it will be possible to examine a summary of Stalin's instructions regarding the forthcoming war with Germany, handwritten by Timoshenko or Zhukov. Actually, one may assume that the almost complete absence of direct and documented instructions by Stalin to the leadership of the defence commissariat in the final pre-war months may be explained by the immediate action of three factors. First of all, Stalin really could, due to considerations of secrecy, as well as not wishing to bear responsibility before the court of history in the event his instructions proved to be mistaken, try to issue orders on such a delicate question as preparations for war predominantly in oral form. Secondly, surviving papers with Stalin's signature and summaries of his instructions, made by the executors, may still be in secret storage and remain inaccessible to researchers. Thirdly, a part of the most incriminating documents for Stalin, linked to the preparations for an attack on Germany, could have been destroyed both during and after the war, for example, during the second half of October 1941, when, having destroyed three Soviet *fronts* around Vyaz'ma and Bryansk, the *Wehrmacht* was rushing toward Moscow, while the Council of Peoples' Commissars and the embassies were being evacuated to Kuibyshev. That the latter assumption may correspond to the truth is proven on examination of Stalin's archive. On viewing the folder with communications from the foreign press for 1941, which they brought Stalin and upon which he often wrote quite eloquent resolutions, there is a note from Zhukov to Stalin, marked 'secret', on the official paper of the chief of the General Staff, and dated 16 April 1941.[43] It reads: 'Comrade Poskryobyshev. I am returning to you page 12 of the TASS Service Bulletin of 14.4.41, which was given to me personally by comrade STALIN.'[44] Stalin undoubtedly handed over this TASS document on the evening of 14 April, when Zhukov was in Stalin's Kremlin office. On this paper, under the title 'The United Press Correspondent on New Methods of War in the Balkans and North Africa (A Radio Intercept)', the following was reported:

> Vichy, 14 April (TASS).[45] According to reports by the correspondent from the United Press Agency, French circles declare that 1) at present large German aircraft are being employed in eastern Libya for the transfer of high-speed light tanks [this and the text further on was underlined by Stalin, B.S.]. This enabled the German and Italian units to carry out several isolated raids in the direction of Khartoum. The aircraft transport the tanks hundreds of miles across the desert, the passage through which of tanks is made difficult by the dunes, as well as the necessity of having an enormous amount of fuel. In connection with this tactic, at the present time a threat has arisen to such positions which were formerly considered defended by hundreds of miles of desert.

The correspondent of the French newspaper *Paris Soir*, located on the Italian front, reports that the Germans are employing in the Balkans 2) a new secret weapon – mines, launched by tanks. The tank has an embrasure, through which large mines are launched forward, for destroying enemy positions, as well as obstacles from sandbags and small concrete warehouses. Further on the correspondent reports that:

> 3) the Germans are also employing against the Yugoslavs and Greeks specially trained parachutists, armed with flamethrowers. They are dressed in asbestos uniforms. Following their landing, the parachutists immediately surge to the nearest fortified positions and train their flamethrowers against the apertures designated for machine guns, or artillery pieces, and thus fill the blockhouse with death-dealing fire, which strikes those soldiers located inside.

What's interesting is that on the page containing this TASS communiqué there remains a map, drawn by Stalin, which likely reflects the movement of the second strategic echelon's divisions to the West.[46]

One is struck by the fact that the descriptions of all three new types of German weapons in the reporting of the French press are absolute disinformation, quite possibly issuing from the German special services. The Germans did not transport any kind of light tanks through the desert and did not undertake any kind of offensive against Khartoum. They transported tanks to Libya not by plane, but by sea transport. In the description by the correspondent from *Paris Soir*, the German tanks appear to be analogues of heavy mortars or mortars capable of destroying even permanent concrete fortifications. In actuality, German mine-laying tanks and mine sweepers were usually employed for the rapid laying of mine obstacles and blowing up the enemy's minefields; moreover, in 1941 their employment was only experimental. And they were only slightly modernized PzKpfw1 tanks, which were already out of date by the start of the Second World War.[47] Thus it would be very difficult to call them a new weapon. Nor did the Germans have any paratroop-flamethrowers, all the more so dressed in exotic asbestos uniforms. Actually, the *Wehrmacht's* flamethrowers wore grey protective leather uniforms, but they used them very rarely in order not to stand out on the battlefield. The German command was seeking to disinform its current and future enemies regarding its tactics and intentions and to focus their attention on the airborne forces, which were actually playing quite a modest role but, as they feared in London and Moscow, could play an important part in a landing on the British Isles. In this way it was planned to distract attention from the tank formations that were to become the main strike force for 'Barbarossa' and which did not have to be transported through the air in order to end up deep in the Soviet rear. Perhaps it was under the influence of such reporting that Soviet commanders in the first months of the war imagined that they saw German parachutists, including those with tanks.

Stalin attached such great significance to a 'journalistic false report', which he swallowed whole, that he personally passed on a report from Vichy to the chief of the General Staff. Stalin himself probably had quite a distorted picture of the *Wehrmacht* and was hardly capable of adequately evaluating the correlation of forces of the Germans and Soviets.

The incident with the report from Vichy also proves that Stalin passed on to the leaders of the Red Army information about military affairs that he received and which he considered important for them and that these actions left documented traces in the archives.

What is still more interesting is that following Zhukov's note, dated 16 April, there is the TASS report of 13 November 1941 'On Romanian Atrocities in Odessa', which was published in *Pravda* three days later. Of course, it's impossible to imagine that from 16 April to 13 November Stalin did not receive any TASS reports, which of themselves did not contain any secrets and thus did not find a place in his archive. Part of them, representing responses to the TASS declaration of 9 May 1941, which sought to refute rumors regarding the transfer of Soviet troops to the West, is located in other files in Stalin's archive.[48] However, the fact that TASS reports for two-and-a-half prewar months and the first four-and-a-half wartime months were removed and most likely placed in another file, allows one to assume that at the end of October or the beginning of November these papers could have been thoroughly cleaned up, removing the pages with Stalin's most dangerous resolutions, which under no circumstances were to fall into the hands of the Germans.

The preparation of staffs, commanders and the troops for war with an enemy like Germany was not a joking matter. However, there is no proof that Stalin fully realized the difficulties of such an undertaking. According to the testimony of then-people's commissar of the navy, N.G. Kuznetsov:[49]

> I.V. Stalin imagined our armed forces' combat capability to be higher than it actually was. While precisely knowing the number of the latest aircraft, which had been stationed by his order on border airfields, he believed that they could at any minute take off upon receiving the alarm and deliver a fitting rebuff to the enemy. He was simply blown away by the news that our planes had not had the time to take off, but perished right there on the airfields.[50]

And the same Kuznetsov further testifies:

> When the world war flared up in Europe, the Main Naval Staff and I sought to more actively learn what our tasks were in the event of war. I can now maintain responsibly that we had no serious plans drawn up. There were plans for deploying the troops, which were classified to such a degree that they were not actually put into practice . . . The liberation of Bessarabia in the summer of 1940 also took place without any kind of planning, preparation and coordination by all of the armed forces. I recall how as already at the last minute I was told that within a few days definite actions would be taken on land against Romania and that the Black Sea Fleet should be ready to act in the event of serious resistance. There was nothing for me to do but, having quickly issued instructions, to go to Sevastopol' and to personally discuss everything with the fleet commander and then travel by destroyer to Odessa for personal communications with Timoshenko and other army commanders there.[51]

Lopukhovskii and Kavalerchik cite the order to the Baltic Military District, which was issued a week before the start of the war, where on the experience of troop exercises it was established that the gathering of the rank and file of the formations and units as the result of an alert and their occupation of defensive structures and lines was carried out much more slowly than was called for by the plan.[52] However, there is no information that the military district commanders reported to Stalin about this situation, which was quite distinct from the plans that existed only on paper. Thus one should not consider as uncontroversial the opinion that Stalin realized that he had no chance of launching a surprise attack and thus gain a decisive advantage at the beginning of the war, and therefore he did not prepare to attack first.[53]

The executors at the local level well understood that they would be unable to bring the Red Army up to full strength according to the schedule called for by the plan. However, it is by no means a fact that Stalin grasped this. It's more than likely that he did not, just as Timoshenko and Zhukov did not understand. Otherwise, they would not have ordered the launching of poorly prepared counterblows with decisive goals during the first days of the war. All the more so, it was no secret to Stalin or his generals that the German army had been fully mobilized and was being maintained accordingly at wartime strength. This means that they were working on the basis of defeating a fully mobilized and deployed German army. For example, in the plan for the preventive attack of 15 May 1941, it is stated openly: 'Taking into account the fact that at present Germany maintains a fully mobilized army, with deployed rear services, it has the opportunity to forestall us in deploying an to launch a surprise attack.' At the same time, it was considered necessary 'to in no way give up the initiative to the German command, to preempt the enemy in deployment and to attack the German army at that moment, when it will be deploying and has not yet had time to organize the cooperation of the combat arms'.[54]

This means that Zhukov and Timoshenko, and probably Stalin, with their prompting, at that moment considered it possible to complete the mobilization and deployment of the Soviet forces before the likely German attack, which, as they thought, would not occur before Hitler crushed Great Britain.

Lopukhovskii and Kavalerchik's thesis, which was widely present in Soviet historiography, that Stalin did everything he could so as not to irritate Hitler in hopes of preventing or putting off a German attack, does not seem to correspond with reality. If this was actually so, then Stalin should have accepted the proposal made by Hitler to Molotov regarding the USSR's adherence to the Tripartite Pact on German terms and to put forward his own demands to consign Bulgaria and Turkey to the Soviet sphere of influence and to annex Finland to the USSR.[55] It will probably never be known if Hitler would have renounced carrying out 'Barbarossa' in 1941 if Stalin had agreed to adhere to the Tripartite Pact without reservations, or whether the proposal itself was a means to lull Soviet vigilance in order to carry out the attack. During his interrogation, Keitel maintained that Molotov's visit to Berlin was of key significance in the decision to attack the USSR:

> Following these negotiations, I was informed that the Soviet Union put forward a number of absolutely unrealizable conditions in regard to Romania, Finland and the Baltic States. One may consider the question of war with the Soviet Union to have been decided from this time. At the same time, one must understand that the threat of an attack by the Red Army had become clear for Germany.[56]

However, one is more receptive to the idea that even the acceptance by Stalin of the German conditions for the USSR's adherence to the Tripartite Pact would not have prevented a German attack and that the very proposals regarding the adherence to the German–Italian–Japanese alliance were made simply to lull the Soviet leader into a false sense of security. And if Stalin had truly feared a German attack in 1941 he would never have concluded on 5 April 1941 a treaty of friendship and non-aggression with Yugoslavia, immediately after the military coup that overthrew the pro-German government in that country and on the eve of the *Wehrmacht's* invasion of Yugoslav territory.

The disposition of the Soviet forces by the time of the German invasion favoured the realization of the German plan, according to which the Red Army's main forces were to be defeated west of the Western Dvina and Dnepr rivers. Stalin and his generals actually accepted battle west of this line. It's clear that the optimal course of action for the Soviet command would have been a rapid withdrawal of these forces behind the Dnepr and Western Dvina. However, there is no proof that there existed such a plan for Stalin and his generals, or even a sketch of one. And no one sought to act accordingly during the first days of the war.

Stalin and his generals were preparing for an offensive war. But they did this quite incoherently. The decision to form the mechanized corps and their subsequent increase to twenty-nine was poorly thought out. After all, compared to the former tank corps, the number of tanks in the mechanized corps grew by a factor of two, while the amount of communications equipment did not increase. At the same time, the tank corps somehow managed to even fall behind the cavalry during the Polish campaign, thus demonstrating the complete lack of control over them. The new mechanized corps were becoming even more uncontrollable, which sharply reduced their combat capability. There was also a shortage of experienced tank troops in the Red Army.

In order to prevent the premature shortening of the tanks' lifespan, very little time and very few tanks were set aside for training the tank troops. The same picture existed in the air force, where due to economizing on fuel the pilots were allotted almost no flying time in combat aircraft.

It is thought that the Red Army was not ready for war in 1941, but would have been prepared for war in 1942. Actually, it was never ready for war. After all, all of Soviet life, and not just the economy, was premised upon the continuous increase of quantity at the expense of quality. Even if the war had not begun in 1941, the factories would have continued to increase the output of tanks and aircraft. It would have been necessary to form new mechanized corps and air regiments and to dispatch thousands of new tank troops and pilots there. At the same time, the resources allotted to the training of a single pilot or tank driver would have been reduced even more, which means that the combat capability of the armoured forces and air force would only have declined. Given the nature of the country's military construction, the Red Army would never have been able to prepare itself well for war. It is no accident that in 1945 the *Wehrmacht* was superior to the Red Army at the tactical level, which did not save it from an overall defeat.

And it is doubtful that Stalin was so naïve as to hope to postpone war, if he believed that Hitler had made the decision to begin it. It is also doubtful that the Soviet leader believed that Hitler could not attack just like that and that an attack must be preceded by some kind of political demands, on the basis of which negotiations could be begun and during which period he would have time to complete the mobilization and deployment of the Red Army. After all, Stalin well understood that if necessary one can come up with an excuse for a war quite easily, as did Hitler in attacking Poland and which he himself did in attacking Finland. After all, Hitler invaded Denmark, Norway, Belgium, Holland, and Luxembourg during the war without any kind of negotiations. There was no basis for thinking that some kind of prior political demands would be presented in the event of an attack on the USSR. All the more so, such demands were actually presented to Molotov during his November visit to Berlin, but no real negotiations followed from this. Stalin's behaviour is probably explained by the fact that up until the last moment he believed that Hitler would not attack the USSR in 1941, but would attempt to land on the British Isles.

According to the May plan, the overwhelming majority of the Soviet military districts was supposed to carry out defensive tasks in the beginning of the war. And in the May plan for a preventive attack there was an item in which they were supposed 'to fully force the construction and armament of the fortified areas, to begin the construction of fortified areas along the rear line Ostashkov–Pechep, and to plan the construction of new fortified areas in 1942 along the border with Hungary, as well as to continue the construction of fortified areas along the old state boundary'. Simultaneously, it was required 'to organize a secure defence and covering of the state boundary, employing for this all the troops of the border military districts and almost all of the aviation designated for deployment in the West', while it was demanded that plans for covering the state boundary were to be drawn up by 1 June 1941.[57] These measures were evidently meant to disinform the enemy as to the Soviets' true intentions.

Goebbels' article 'Crete as an Example', which appeared in the official Nazi newspaper *Volkischer Beobachter* on 13 June 1941, was a disinformation action designed to convince world opinion that the *Wehrmacht* was about to land on the British Isles. The newspaper run, as is known, was immediately confiscated by the censorship, but calculating that the embassies in Berlin, as well as foreign subscribers, would receive their copies. At the same time, the TASS declaration, which was first transmitted by radio on the evening of 13 June, was a reaction to the publication of Goebbels' article. This is just how the Reich Minister for Propaganda himself saw it, noting in his diary that: 'It seems the Russians don't suspect a thing.' On 14 Goebbels noted with satisfaction the opinion of British and world mass communications that 'our deployment against Russia is pure bluff, with the aid of which we are counting on masking our preparations for an invasion of Great Britian'.[58] Stalin tried to determine by the expected German reaction to the TASS declaration if Hitler was really preparing to subdue Great Britain and whether or not the article was a cover for the preparation of a landing operation. But the German response, or rather the absence of any kind of official reaction, was a continuation of the previous game. After all, if the concentration of German forces in the East was only a cover for the forthcoming landing on the British Isles, then the German reaction to the TASS declaration would have been the same – silence, in order to create on the British side the conviction that the Germans' actual intention was to invade Russia. This is how Stalin at first evaluated all of these events and took no measures for raising the troops' readiness to repel a possible attack, while continuing preparations for his own invasion of Poland, Germany, and Romania.

Stalin decided that Hitler was really preparing to finish with the British Empire and that the troops were concentrating in the East only for the purpose of masking this intention. Thus the Soviet leader continued to prepare to invade Western Europe. And only after 18 June, when they had already ceased masking the concentration according to Operation 'Barbarossa' and tank and motorized formations moved up to the border and aircraft arrived at the border airfields, did he really begin to be concerned, but it was too late, particularly as they only began to put the Soviet forces into combat readiness during the fateful night of 22 June, while they were head and shoulders inferior to the *Wehrmacht*.

As early as the September 1940 plan for deploying the Red Army, two variations for launching the main Soviet attack were prepared – north and south of the Pripyat' River. However, during the operational-strategic war games conducted by the RKKA's higher command element on 2–6 and 8–11 January 1941, it transpired that the permanent fortifications in East Prussia were an obstacle that would be difficult to overcome for the attacking Soviet forces and thus preference was given to the alernative of deploying the Red Army's main forces south of the Pripyat' River for launching an attack in the southwestern direction.

The 'Westerners' carried out an attack during the course of both war games, but the actions to repel the 'aggression' were not played out at all. Moreover, the early period of the war was completely ignored. The prearranged scenario of the conflict assumed that during the first week or two of combat operations the 'Westerners', in conjunction with their allies, without having completed their deployment, carried out an attack against the 'Easterners' and were able to advance into their territory to a depth of 50–120km. Then the 'Easterners' would launch powerful counterblows and throw the forces of the 'Westerners' back to their starting positions and shift combat operations to the enemy's territory. Only the offensive operations by the 'Easterners' were played out during the war games.

In essence, the war games did not even begin from the moment when the Soviet forces launched a counteroffensive, but only when they had already reached the line of the state border, having thrown the enemy out of their territory.[59] If Stalin had truly feared a German attack, then defensive battles for repelling an attack should have been played out in the war games before anything, as well as the first period of the counteroffensive by the 'Easterners', when it was still taking place on Soviet territory. The real scenario of the war games leads one to think that the initial data for the attack by the 'Westerners' against the 'Easterners' was nothing but a genuflection towards the propaganda stereotype, according to which the Red Army would not begin the war first, but was to respond with 'an attack against an attack'. In reality, only the Red Army's invasion of the territory of Germany and its allies was played out during the course of the war games.

In June 1941 the western military districts and the high command had in reserve mechanized corps that were the least outfitted with armoured equipment. If one takes, for example, the German forces' group before the beginning of Operation 'Citadel', they had in reserve the XXIV Panzer Corps, which was the weakest in tanks, having only 118 tanks in 2 divisions, while in the remaining 15 tank divisions and 2 tank brigades there were 2,121 tanks, with an average of 125 tanks per division, even more than they had overall in the reserve tank corps.[60] At Kursk the Germans tried to put all their strength into the first blow and thus left the weakest corps in reserve. Since the Soviet command in 1941 actually planned a powerful first strike against Germany, then it was quite logical to leave in reserve those mechanized corps least supplied with tanks, calculating that it would still be possible to reinforce them with equipment at the moment when they would have to be committed into the fighting for developing the success.

Characteristically, the plans for covering the border military districts that were presented to the General Staff at the end of May and beginning of June 1941 contained primarily defensive tasks. Only for the Kiev Military District, as was the case in the May plan, did it call for: 'Under favorable conditions, all defending troops and the armies' reserves in the district are to be ready, upon instructions from the High Command, to launch vigorous attacks to defeat the enemy's groups of forces and to shift combat operations to his territory and to seize favorable lines.'[61] It should be noted that the actions of the Kiev and other military districts were played out in just this way at the beginning of the war. As early as 23 June they launched counterblows for the purpose of defeating the invading German groups of forces and shifting combat operations on to enemy territory. As is known, nothing good came of these counterblows. If Stalin, and also Timoshenko and Zhukov, even following the surprise German attack, considered it possible to assign their forces offensive missions with such decisive goals, then the idea that they were preparing to begin an offensive operation against Germany, which was supposed to prove a surprise for the enemy and take place in more favourable conditions for the Soviet forces than those which arose following the German attack, appears quite logical. At the same time, the troops in the Soviet covering armies were supposed to occupy the permanent and field fortifications along the border even before the beginning of combat operations. This circumstance may be explained either first by the unbounded stupidity of Stalin, Timoshenko, and Zhukov, who on the basis of the experience of the first two years of the Second World War still failed to understand that should Hitler decide to attack the USSR then there would be no threatening period at all. Secondly, by Stalin's intention to choose the time for beginning the war himself, after which the Red Army would conduct defensive operations along the greater part of the contact line between the Soviet and German forces, while along the southwestern direction it would go over to a decisive offensive for the purpose of routing the enemy, thus carrying out the May plan for launching a preemptive attack. Furthermore, Soviet intelligence overestimated by a factor of 1½:2 the strength of German forces that could be deployed against the Soviet Union. One may assume that this overestimation was done by the military in order, on the one hand, to convince Stalin to concentrate the maximum number of men and materiel in the West and, on the other hand, to justify possible failures by citing the fact that the enemy was too strong.

The headquarters of the border military districts received orders 'to prepare rear defensive lines and draw up a plan for creating anti-tank obstacles throughout the entire depth and a plan for mining important sites'.[62] But such instructions may be viewed as conscious large-scale disinformation, analogous to the wide-ranging German measures for preparing an invasion of the British Isles, which were actively conducted by the Germans in 1941 for the purpose of masking the preparations for an attack on the Soviet Union. All the more so, since the troops of the western military districts were more positioned in offensive rather than in defensive groups of forces, although by 22 June 1941 they were neither ready to defend nor attack, which, by the way, was noted by Manstein in his memoirs.[63]

According to Lopukhovskii and Kavalerchik, the *Wehrmacht* in the East disposed of 3,811 tanks and 290 assault guns, including the armoured equipment from the 2nd and 5th panzer divisions, transferred to the Eastern Front only in September.[64] By the beginning of June 1941 the Soviet Union had 23,078 tanks and 2,376 tankettes, including 16,150 vehicles in the western border districts and in the 4 reserve armies designated for operations in the west.[65] It should be noted that the German Pz1 tanks, which are also counted among the German tank strength, should be called, employing Soviet terminology, tankettes.

Following the beginning of the secret mobilization, Stalin could hope to significantly raise the level of the Red Army's provisioning with automobile transport, which on the eve of the war stood at only 36 per cent of wartime norms. According to other data, only 68 per cent of the required auto mobile transport was available, as Ya.N. Fedorenko, chief of the Main Auto-Armoured Administration, assumed.[66] This should have been sufficient to outfit the first-echelon divisions and later on Stalin could hope for a rich haul of German and other Western European motor vehicles. However, as a result, Stalin did not make use of captured German equipment, nor did Hitler take advantage of captured Soviet equipment, of which he was short of, in order to take Moscow.

Chapter 3

The 1941 Campaign

Why the Blitzkrieg Failed

On 22 June 1941 the two most absolute and most ruthless totalitarian dictatorships in Europe, the Nazi and the Soviet, entered into a fatal struggle. And when they say that Hitler's greatest mistake was his decision to attack the USSR, they are either being less than honest or are in all conscience mistaken, repeating the Soviet wartime and postwar propaganda thesis. It's apropos to mention that this thesis is still popular among Western historians and political scientists. Actually, Hitler fully recognized just how risky the enterprise he was undertaking was. Both he and the German generals feared the endless Russian spaces and the seemingly bottomless human resources of the USSR. The führer understood that if following the defeat of the Soviet cadre army in the west Stalin did not halt his resistance, then the German army's situation in Russia would become very difficult and Germany's loss of the war, as a whole, practically inevitable. It is not accidental that on 30 May 1941 Hitler told his friend, the representative of the Ministry of Foreign Affairs, Walter Hewell:[1] '*Barbarossa* is a risk, just like everything else, and if it is unsuccessful then everything is lost any way. But if it had been successful, then a situation would have arisen that probably would have forced Great Britain to conclude peace.'[2]

If one wants to speak about Hitler's mistake, then it was not in the attack on the USSR, but in unleashing, together with Stalin, the Second World War. It's not for nothing that the führer pointed out in a conversation with Hewell that the Second World War was an extremely risky undertaking. But he strove for world domination and was determined not to retreat, operating according to the principle of triumph or perish.

The Ukrainians' illusions regarding Hitler the liberator were dispersed very quickly, as early as 12 July 1941, when in L'vov the Ukrainian government, created by Stepan Bandera and Yaroslav Stetsko, was dispersed and they were themselves imprisoned in a concentration camp.[3] The Polish government in exile, headed by Wladyslaw Sikorski, entertained illusions about the possibility of cooperating with Stalin, at a minimum until the opening of the graves in Katyn' and the breaking off of diplomatic relations with Moscow in

April 1943. And among the successors to Sikorski, who tragically perished during this time, such illusions did not completely disappear until August 1944, when the Soviet dictator's refusal to support the Warsaw uprising, the repressions carried out against the soldiers of the Armia Krajowa, and the creation of a puppet pro-Soviet government left no doubts as to the future Stalin had prepared for a Poland liberated from the Germans.[4]

Up until the evening of 21 June 1941 Stalin did not believe that Hitler was about to attack and did not undertake any measures to repel such a strike. Thus the measures being taken to move Soviet forces to the borders were not taking place to repel the coming German attack, but to prepare Stalin's own attack.

At the beginning of the Great Patriotic War the Red Army was at its most combat-capable in comparison with all other periods during 1941–5. At this point military personnel who had managed to serve a year and more and who had managed to learn at least something comprised its greater part. As early as the end of 1941 practically untrained militia began to predominate in the Red Army. Many Soviet commanders in 1942 and later unsuccessfully asked Stalin to send them well-trained soldiers, both as reinforcements and as new divisions. But these could be had nowhere. They hardly had time to train new draftees, insofar as the front demanded that the huge losses be replenished. In essence, these draftees had little to distinguish themselves from militia in terms of their level of training. The few soldiers among those who returned to the front after being wounded simply drowned in the mass of such militia.

The serious decline in the quality of Soviet pilot training may be illustrated by the following example. On 22 June 1941, the day of the attack on the Soviet Union, the *Luftwaffe* suffered 78 irreplaceable (60 per cent and higher degree of damage) aircraft losses, including 61 due to combat reasons. Another 89 aircraft were damaged, including 50 in battle.[5] On 5 July 1943, on the first day of the Battle of Kursk, when the Germans committed into the battle as many aircraft as on the day they attacked the USSR, the *Luftwaffe's* combat irreplaceable losses comprised 26 aircraft against 176 Soviet.[6] Stalin's falcons had begun to fight significantly worse than during the first days of the war. This is hardly surprising. There were considerably more experienced pilots in the Red Army Air Force in June 1941 than in July 1943. But what can be said about the infantry?

Few of the soldiers and commanders of 1941 lived to the victorious year of 1945, due to the huge irreplaceable losses. The victories of the Soviet forces in 1944–5 were achieved in the first place not because the Red Army had become more powerful and proficient, but because the *Wehrmacht* had become weaker.

There were fewer experienced soldiers and commanders in the German army, due to the large losses. Besides this, a significant portion of men and materiel in the final years of the war had to be diverted to the struggle with Great Britain and the USA.

The defence of the fortress of Brest, which lasted from 22–9 June 1941, while one of the defence's leaders, Major Pyotr Gavrilov, was captured only on 23 July, is an example of the pretty effective actions of the cadre Soviet military personnel. However, the drawing out of the fortress's defence for up to thirty-two days, as some Russian historians assume, is hardly justified, because active combat operations had completely halted by 29 June. The prolonged defence of the fortress became possible thanks to a mistake by the commander of the German 45th Infantry Division. Hoping that a powerful artillery preparation had accomplished its mission and that part of the Russians had either been killed or run away, General Fritz Schlieper threw in only a single battalion to occupy the fortress. But at that moment there remained in the fortress only half of the garrison, the rest having been able to abandon it at the beginning of the war (for the most part, these troops were captured), more than 4,000 soldiers and commanders, even if they had been taken by surprise still in possession of several guns and machine guns and located in casemates, for the destruction of which heavy artillery was required. The Germans lost 300 men killed alone on the first day in the Brest fortress. The *Wehrmacht* never suffered such losses on the Eastern Front as on that day. In all, according to Schlieper's account of 8 July, the division lost 453 men killed before the end of June, which accounted for 5 per cent of the Germans' irreplaceable losses in the East, and 668 wounded and took 7,223 prisoners. According to the list of the 45th Division's losses, 475 of the division's military personnel perished before the end of June (it is possible one soldier was left out), of which 5 died before 22 June, 2 perished far from Brest, and 1 drowned in a river on 30 June. Of this number, about thirty soldiers also perished in the fighting in Brest itself and to the east of the city, and ten fell victim to 'friendly fire'. Besides this, one soldier was killed and six wounded from the 201st Assault Gun Battalion's 3rd Battery. Thus, according to the calculations of the German historian Christian Hanser, approximately 429 Germans perished or died from their wounds directly in the fighting for the fortress, that is, even fewer than in Schlieper's report. According to Hanser's calculations on the basis of the list of losses and daily reports on losses, the 45th Infantry Division lost during 22–7 June 378 killed and 49 who died from their wounds at a later point. It's possible that another two soldiers perished in the fortress, because the date and place of their deaths have not been determined. Of this number, 370 soldiers died or were fatally wounded during 22–4 June. From this it follows that the intensive fighting in the fortress ceased after as little as three days. Another nineteen men perished on 25 June and twelve on 26 June. After this irreplaceable losses did not rise above ten. Hanser calculates the number of Soviet prisoners as between 6,713 and 7,779 men. He arrives at the conclusion based on the high degree of reliability of the figures contained in Schlieper's report. Hanser believes that approximately 440 prisoners were taken on 22 June in Brest itself, but he is not sure whether they form part of the 7,223 prisoners listed by Schlieper. The main mass of prisoners was taken during 22–6 June. After 29 June there was only one armed incident in which a single German soldier from the 502nd Security Battalion was wounded and a single Soviet officer captured – most likely Major Gavrilov. From 5 July the 502nd Security Battalion performed police functions in Brest and a total of 133 men were in the fortress. By this time the resistance of the surviving defenders of the fortress had long since ceased. Before 28 June about 2,000 corpses of Red Army soldiers had been found in the vicinity of the fortress. It's possible that this number subsequently increased to 2,400. It's likely that a certain number of Red Army corpses were not located in the ruins and casemates of the fortress, but the number of undiscovered corpses could not be as high as 9,000, as the German researcher C. Hartmann assumed.[7] It seems that the most realistic evaluation of the losses among the defenders of the Brest fortress is 3,000 killed. In this case, the correlation of losses killed would be 7:1, which is 2.4 times more favourable for the Soviet side than the average correlation for the period June 1941–May 1944. The reason for this being the relatively high degree of training among the fortress's defenders, as well as the fact that the Germans had to storm fortified positions.

The defenders of the fortress also made a mistake. Their commanders suffered from an *idée fixe* that they had to attempt to break out of the fortress in order to link up with the main forces, although as early as the second day it became clear that the front had fallen back far to the east. As a result of the break-out attempts, the besieged suffered heavy losses in killed and captured, while inflicting almost no losses on the Germans, who held all the exits from the fortress under fire. If a strictly defensive form of action had been adopted, upon which Captain Ivan Zubachev unsuccessfully insisted, then it's possible that the defenders would have managed to extend organized resistance by a week or two, But it turned out that the Germans required only eight days to suppress all centres of resistance.

At the very start of the war five Soviet *fronts*, Southern, Southwestern, Western, Northwestern, and Northern, faced the German army groups South, Centre, and North, as well as the independent army 'Norway'. Practically each army group was faced by a *front*. Only Army Group South was faced by two *fronts*, the Southwestern and Southern, although this was quite justified, in that at the beginning of the war this army group operated along two directions, from southern Poland and Romania. But subsequently, as the number of Soviet divisions and armies grew, the number of *fronts* began to increase markedly, and as early as August 1941 a single Soviet *front* opposed one German army. Such an abundance of *fronts* created its own problems of command and control, and as early as July 1941 they began to create the high commands of the strategic directions, which existed, with breaks, all the way up to the summer of 1942. Each strategic direction unified two or three *fronts*, operating most often against one German army group. But this structure proved ineffective. The commander-in-chief of a strategic direction did not have his own, separate staff and usually commanded the most powerful *front* of the strategic direction. However, first of all, he often made decisions in favour of 'his' *front*, and secondly, in actual practice the headquarters of one *front* could not control the operations of the other *fronts*, as it had enough worries of its own. Thus the high commands of the strategic directions were inferior in operational capabilities to the German army groups, which had full-blooded headquarters. Beside this, following the heavy losses of the summer of 1941, the corps' level of command was effectively disbanded on the pretext of the lack of staff cadres. As a result, an army headquarters at times had to control tens of divisions and brigades, which forced them to create improvised operational groups, which had no true headquarters apparatus. This circumstance also lowered the controllability of the Soviet forces and the quality of operational planning. The corps level began to be reformed only in 1943.

In place of the high commands of the strategic directions, Stalin came up with the idea of the institution of *Stavka* representatives. They differed from the former commanders-in-chief of the strategic directions in that they not only did not have their own special staff, but did not command any *fronts*, thus lacking a corresponding *front* headquarters staff at their disposal. The role of the *Stavka* representatives came down to advising and issuing commands to the *front* commander and, sometimes, to the army commanders. Naturally, as regards command and control they were inferior to the commanders of the German army groups, with their fully fledged staffs.

In launching its main attack against the Western Front, which was weaker than the Southwestern Front, the German command split the Soviet defence line, created a broad breakthrough along the central direction, and made it more difficult for the Soviet *fronts* to coordinate their activities. Instead of quickly withdrawing the fronts to the line of fortifications along the old boundary, Stalin, Timoshenko, and Zhukov carried out counterblows with mechanized corps along the entire front. They sought to put into practice the 15 May 1941 offensive plan in the southwestern direction. But everything ended in defeat.

The Soviet Southwestern Front's main armoured forces were defeated in a tank engagement in the Dubno–Lutsk–Rovno area during 23–30 June 1941. The 1st Panzer Group's panzer divisions were enough to do this. Nor did the Soviet T-34 tank's superiority over the existing German tanks help matters.[8] The Germans put up 728 of their tanks and 71 assault guns against 3,128 Soviet tanks. By 30 June the Southwestern Front's forces that took part in the counteroffensive had lost 2,648 tanks, about two-thirds of what they had at the start of the war, and nearly all of these were irreplaceable losses. The German forces lost only 260 tanks and assault guns, only an insignificant part irreplaceably. The Soviet mechanized corps entered the fighting in an uncoordinated fashion, without interaction with the infantry, artillery, and air force. The *Luftwaffe*, taking advantage of the superiority of its tactics, the quality of its aircraft and the training level of its pilots, immediately gained air superiority. By 9 July Soviet losses had reached 3,464 vehicles and there were almost no Soviet tanks left in line. As early as the evening of 26 June Kirponos realized the futility of continuing the offensive and approached the General Staff for permission to pull the mechanized corps out of the fighting and to organize a withdrawal to new defensive positions. However, Zhukov, who had just returned to Moscow, forbade this. As a result, the senseless counterblows continued. The Southwestern Front suffered heavy losses and still failed to hold the L'vov salient. The German tanks broke through the Stalin Line along the old state border on the heels of the retreating Soviet forces and as early as 10 July occupied Zhitomir.[9] And along the central sector of the front Guderian's tanks broke into Smolensk on 15 July.

In the middle of August 1941, following the completion of the Battle of Smolensk, there arises the possibility of alternative scenarios for the Second World War and immediately after. There is the widespread opinion, which was first put forth by a number of German generals, including Guderian, that if Hitler had not halted Army Group Centre's offensive on Moscow and had not dispatched in his 21 August directive part of its forces to the south in order to defeat the Southwestern Front and to seize Kiev and left-bank Ukraine, then the *Wehrmacht* could have captured the Soviet capital before the start of the autumn rains and thus won the war with Russia. In his 21 August directive to the army high command, Hitler demanded that:

> The most important task before the onset of winter is not the capture of Moscow, but the capture of the Crimea, the industrial and coal regions of the Donets River and the blocking of the Russians' oil

transport routes from the Caucasus . . . The seizure of the Crimean peninsula has great importance for securing the delivery of oil from Romania. It is necessary, even to commit our motorized formations into the fighting, to strive to quickly force the Dnepr and attack the Crimea before the enemy is able to bring up fresh forces.[10]

In the middle of August 1941 Guderian and many other German generals believed that the offensive on Moscow should be continued. However, the *Wehrmacht* was nevertheless not ready for an immediate offensive on Moscow. Even the army high command (OKH), which supported the idea of continuing the offensive on Moscow, according to the draft of a directive on 18 August, proposed beginning the offensive on the Soviet capital only in the beginning of September.[11] At the same time, such an offensive would have been conducted with significantly smaller forces than the actual offensive on Moscow within the confines of Operation 'Typhoon' at the end of September/ beginning of October.[12] In August it was planned to throw against Moscow 42 infantry and 12 tank and mechanized divisions, including only 2 panzer groups (minus the Fourth Panzer Group's main forces which were fighting around Leningrad), out of 4. In October 3 out of 4 panzer groups attacked here, for a total of 72 divisions, including 22 tank and motorized divisions. At the beginning of September Army Group Centre would have been opposed by the forces of the recently formed Reserve Front, which had begun its offensive against the Yel'nya salient and which had not yet been weakened by heavy losses in the course of this offensive. Also, the Western Front would not have been reduced by losses incurred in local offensive operations in the first half of September, and the Bryansk Front would not yet have been in a position to sustain heavy losses in unsuccessful attempts to defeat the German Second Panzer Group. Besides this, the Southwestern Front, which was still quite combat-capable at that point, in the event of a German offensive on Moscow, could have either launched a counterblow against Army Group South's flank, or transferred part of its forces for the immediate defence of Moscow. In order to repel this counterblow and defeat the armies taking part in it, the Germans would have had to turn part of their forces from the Moscow direction and lose a certain amount of time. In the same way, they would have had to expend forces and time in order to grind down the Southwestern Front's divisions if they had been thrown directly into the defence of the capital. More likely, the Soviet losses would have been even less in such a turn of events than they lost in reality in the two gigantic cauldrons in the areas of Kiev and Vyaz'ma– Bryansk. And in any case, the Germans would have had no chance to take Moscow before the middle of October, that is, before the autumn rains. This means that further on the war would have unfolded in the same way that it actually did.

As a result of the Second Army's and Second Panzer Group's turn to the south, the Southwestern Front's main forces were encircled and destroyed in the Kiev 'cauldron.' The German forces occupied Kiev. And at the end of September they were prepared for an offensive on Moscow.

From the very beginning of the war, the Red Army suffered irreplaceable losses exceeding those of the *Wehrmacht* by an order of magnitude. However, with the first publication in 1993 of the collection *The Seal of Secrecy Removed* (*Grif Sekretnosti Snyat*), as was the case in all succeeding editions of this collection, the Russian official figures for the Red Army's irreplaceable losses in the Great Patriotic War are understated by an average of three times. This concerns those instances when Soviet forces had to fight against the armies of Germany's allies, which, with the exception of the Finnish army, were significantly inferior in combat capability to the *Wehrmacht*.

Let's take, for example, the defence of Odessa by the Independent Maritime Army, from 5 August–16 October 1941. The official figures for Soviet losses in this operation, where the Red Army's foe was the Romanian army, are 16,578 killed and missing in action and 24,690 wounded and sick.[13] It is known, however, that during the course of the battle for Odessa the Romanian army took about 16,000 prisoners.[14] The Romanian army lost 1,246 in prisoners during this fighting.[15] Total Romanian losses in the Odessa area numbered 17,729 killed and died from wounds and diseases, 63,345 wounded, and 11,471 missing in action.[16] Taking into account the fact that only 1,246 Romanian soldiers and officers were captured, the remaining 10,225 missing in action should be considered as having perished. Then the overall number of Romanian military personnel lost during the siege of Odessa may be calculated at 27,954 men, 63,345 wounded, and 1,246 captured, giving a total of 92,545 men.

It is highly unlikely that during the more than two months of fighting the defenders of Odessa lost only 578 killed. According to a report by Vice-Admiral F.S. Oktyabr'skii to Stalin on 23 August 1941, the forces of the Odessa defensive area lost daily an average of 800–1,000 men.[17] As a result, the overall losses for the 72 days of the defence may be calculated at 64,800 men, which is 23,532 men higher than the official number. According to testimony by K.M. Simonov, he found data in a document that the Maritime Army lost 33,367 men wounded from 12 August–15 October, which was 1.35 times greater than the official figure.[18] The irreplaceable losses may then be calculated at 31,400 killed and missing in action and the number killed at 15,400 men. It should be noted that this evaluation was close to that done by Romanian and British historians on the basis of Romanian documents and prisoner testimony. Mark Axworthy and his Romanian co-authors, Cornel Scafes and Cristian Craciunoiu, calculate Soviet losses during the siege of Odessa at 60,000 men.[19] The correlation of overall losses is then 1.43:1 in favour of the Red Army, with irreplaceable losses 1.08:1 in favour of the Romanian army, which is due to the large number of Soviet prisoners. Figures close to the 16,578 killed and missing in action were repeated in the recently released book by A.S. Yunovidov, *The Defence of Odessa*. Here a more detailed structure of losses is given, as well as their breakdown by divisions. It transpires that 4,397 men were killed, 9,747 were missing in action, 336 were captured, 24,218 were wounded, 450 were ill, and 1,279 were put out of action for other reasons.[20] The overall losses of 40,427 men are even 841 men lower than in the book *Russia and the USSR in the Wars of the XX Century* (*Rossiya i SSSR v Voinakh XX Veka*), possibly because A.S. Yunovidov did not take the fleet's losses into account.

Apropos of this, the 1,279 men who were out of action for other reasons are most likely irreplaceable losses and include victims of disease, accidents, suicides, and military tribunals, as well as, possibly, those who died from their wounds. Thus the overall number of prisoners, according to Soviet official data, could not exceed 10,083 men. However, 5.5 wounded to 1 man killed is unlikely. If it is assumed that the correlation between killed and wounded is 1:3, then the number of those killed should be about 8,100 men and the number of prisoners would then not be more than 6,400 men.

It is clear from A.S. Yunovidov's book that a composite rifle regiment, an independent reserve rifle battalion, and the Odessa Rifle Division (in reality, militia) were formed in Odessa but did not arrive in Sevastopol'. A.S. Yunovidov's writes that this division, 'despite its name of "Odessa", was actually formed from units from the eastern defensive sector and was only reinforced by residents from Odessa'.[21] Subsequently, on 11 September, this division, which had been reinforced by 5,000 Odessa militiamen, was reformed into the 421st Rifle Division. It's likely that the division's losses before its reformation into a regular rifle division, alongside the earlier losses of the units that comprised it, were not taken into account either by Krivosheev or Yunovidov, nor were the losses of the 3rd Marine Infantry Regiment, which is absent from Yunovidov's listing of losses, but which appears in Sevastopol' with 1,525 men. Also, besides this unit, the 1st Marine Infantry Regiment, with a strength of about 1,300 men, took part in the defence of Odessa, as well as the 2nd Marine Infantry Regiment, with a strength of about 700 men. Their losses and fate are not mentioned at all in A.S. Yunovidov's book. However, they were included within the Odessa Rifle Division, as were five battalions from the Tiraspol' Fortified Area, the 26th NKVD Regiment, the 64th Independent Machine Gun Battalion, a battalion from the 249th Convoy Regiment, the 136th Reserve Regiment's 1st Battalion, the 25th Rifle Division's 54th Rifle Regiment, and two anti-tank battalions. On 30 August 5,000 reinforcements were delivered by sea to the division, which was still known simply as the Odessa Division.[22] Most likely, the losses of all the remaining divisions and units, particularly regarding missing in action, were also undercounted. In Odessa, during the defence of the city, a total of 29 units were formed, including 1 division, 1 regiment, 4 independent battalions, 9 independent companies, 3 detachments, and 3 armoured trains.[23]

Many Odessa natives preferred to desert and surrender. It is not by accident that A.S. Yunovidov notes that 'reports on the low combat qualities of the Odessa residents were even sent to Mekhlis (then the chief of the GlavPUR).[24] A report from the manpower section of the Maritime Army headquarters, which was compiled in March 1942, notes the 'high combat qualities of the reinforcements that have arrived with the replacement companies from the North Caucasus Military District', while at the same time among the reinforcements called up from the city of Odessa 'there proved to be no few people who displayed cowardice, desertion and who surrendered'. Thus on 11 October all of the Odessa-born Red Army soldiers who had been recalled from their units were evacuated from Odessa, a day before the order to evacuate was issued to the unit commanders.[25] However, as early as the beginning of October the Romanian troops were distributing information through loudspeakers and leaflets about the Soviet forces' imminent abandonment of Odessa, so that many Odessa residents could desert in time and surrender to the Romanians. The strength of the formations evacuated from Odessa leads one to think about the undercounting of losses. For example, the 25th Rifle Division, which lost 10,960 men, numbered 9,838 men. This yields an overall strength of the division (together with reinforcements) of 20,798 men, which significantly exceeds authorized strength and leads one to assume it received reinforcements. This is all the more so, as the division transferred one of its rifle regiments and other elements to the 421st Rifle Division, and this loss was then made up in reinforcements. The same picture exists in the 95th Rifle Division, where against the background of losses of 16,674 men its strength in Sevastopol' was equal to 8,947 men, which was approximately 5,500 less than authorized strength. And the 421st Rifle Division, which lost 3,483 men, arrived in Sevastopol with 6,998 rank and file. This yields an initial strength of 10,481 men, which is lower than the prewar authorized strength. According to authorized strength table No. 04/400 of 5 April 1941, the strength of a rifle division was 14,483 men. The 421st Rifle Division was about 4,000 men under strength compared to its authorized strength. Even though a new authorized strength table, No. 04/600, of 10,859 men, was introduced on 29 July 1941, it's unlikely that they had managed to find this out in Odessa.[26] One may assume that the 421st Rifle Division's losses are given only for the period from 11 September–16 October 1941, while the losses for its predecessor, the Odessa Rifle Division (1st Odessa Rifle Division from 1 September), and the units comprising it were probably not counted for the period 8 August– 10 September. And these were probably greater than during the period from 11 September–16 October. If at the end of August the division received 5,000 reinforcements, it is unlikely that the losses for August were less than this amount. The 2nd Cavalry Division's losses of 4,475 men, given its strength of 2,008 men in Sevastopol' prompts one to think about the undercounting of losses, insofar as according to the authorized strength for 22 June 1941 the division should have contained 9,240 men.[27] The 2nd Cavalry Division's strength in Sevastopol' proved to be 2,800 less than authorized strength. Finally, the 157th Rifle Division, which lost a total of 806 men in Odessa, is not listed in Sevastopol' at all. At the same time, this division was transferred to Odessa at fully authorized strength (about 14,500 men, and 12,600 men according to Romanian estimates) during 15–20 September, while another 15,000 in reinforcements arrived with it.[28] The 157th Rifle Division played the main role in the counterblow of 22 September, while its 633rd Rifle Regiment relieved units of the 421st Rifle Division during the attack's preparation. As the regiment's veterans recalled, 'There were few Red Army soldiers and sailors in the relieved subunits, but a lot of civilians, including women.' In Yunovidov's book there are no data about the 157th Rifle Division's strength, because it was evacuated from Odessa first. As early as 10 October it was transferred to Perekop as part of the 51st Independent Army.[29] Most likely, the data on its losses in Odessa were understated significantly. Of importance here is also the testimony about the presence of civilians, including women, within the ranks of the 421st Rifle Division. Most likely this was a situation in which people were called up directly into their units and the losses among such draftees were particularly high and were particularly poorly recorded. Among the 3,939 losses from various units, including 1,252 missing in action, in all likelihood this includes losses by rear units whose strength in Sevastopol' amounted to 9,797 men, and combat support units, numbering 8,824 men in Sevastopol'.

One should also take into account the fact that no less than 20,000 reinforcements were delivered to the troops of the Odessa defensive area from the North Caucasus Military District and that there were probably mobilized, as a minimum, the same number of civilians, taking into account that no less than 13,700 of them ended up in Romanian captivity, a few thousand were evacuated, and some number were killed and wounded. Besides this, the shortage of forces in the 2nd Cavalry and the 95th and 421st rifle divisions, compared to their authorized strength, can be determined to be 12,300 men. One may assume that the figure of 5,500 men above authorized strength came about due to the transfer of approximately this number of troops to the future 421st Rifle Division. Then the overall excess of true losses over the official ones may be determined as 52,300, even without the likely undercounting of the 157th Rifle Division's losses. Of this number we should subtract, as a minimum, 5,000 Odessa draftees-militiamen, who were employed during the initial formation of the future 421st Rifle Division. In this case, the overall excess of losses over the official numbers will be 47,300 men, and the overall real losses at 88,600 men. If this evaluation of Soviet losses during the battle for Odessa is closer to the truth, then they are almost equal to the Romanian ones. Then the correlation of overall losses will be only 1.04:1 in favour of the Red Army. On the whole, as the research shows, the correlation of losses killed in the Red Army's battles with Romanian forces was close to 1:1.[30]

The siege of Leningrad by the German and Finnish forces of the Soviets' 'northern capital' lasted much longer than the siege of Odessa. The city, which before the war numbered 2,900,000 people, ended up being blockaded for 872 days. Behind these figures stand one of the greatest tragedies of the Second World War. During the blockade, it is believed, no less than 1,000,000 civilian residents of Leningrad died. According to data from the city commission for establishing and investigating the atrocities committed by the German-Fascist aggressors, 16,747 Leningraders died from artillery fire and bombings, while another 632,253 succumbed to hunger and disease.[31] However, one should take into account the fact that many Leningraders died following their evacuation and in the first weeks or months on the 'mainland', weakened by dystrophia. Besides this, by no means could all the deaths be registered. People were often buried not at the cemeteries, but in city gardens and parks, without any kind of registration. And the fact that the official figure of 650,000 is a round one is indicative of its approximate and estimated character. Only a small number of Leningraders became victims of artillery fire or aerial bombings. In the main, they perished by the hand of an invisible enemy – hunger.

And what were the military losses in the Battle of Leningrad? The German Eighteenth Army, which was conducting the blockade of the city, during the period from the middle of September 1941 to the end of January 1944, when the operation to lift the blockade was completed, lost 58,051 men killed and

9,940 missing in action.[32] It can be estimated, on average, during the war the correlation of losses in men killed between the *Wehrmacht* and the Red Army was 10:1 in favour of the Germans. Taking into account the fact that a portion of those Germans missing in action should be assigned to the killed category, the Red Army's losses killed during the Battle of Leningrad may be estimated at a minimum of 600,000. However, according to the author's calculations, during the period from 22 June 1941–31 May 1944, which completely embraces the blockade of Leningrad, the correlations of losses killed was even more favourable for the *Wehrmacht* and was 16.6:1. If one accepts this ratio for calculating, then the number of killed Soviet soldiers in the Battle of Leningrad may be estimated at 1,000,000, and when taking into account those who died from their wounds and diseases, a minimum of 1,100,000 men. Thus the number of killed Red Army soldiers and sailors in the fighting for Leningrad is approximately equal to the number of victims among the civilian population and the overall number of those who perished exceeds 2 million people.

Here are some typical examples of the correlation of losses in the battle for Leningrad. During the period of 17–20 September 1941 the 54th Independent Army, while trying to break through the blockade of Leningrad, in the words of its commander, Marshal G.I. Kulik, lost 10,000 men killed and wounded.[33] During 11–20 September the opposing German Sixteenth Army lost 7,222 men.[34] But it fought against the same 54th Army during the period from 11–16 September as well, and also during the entire ten-day period against the Northwestern Front and part of the Leningrad Front's forces.

On 8–9 October, during the unsuccessful counteroffensive at Uritsk, the Soviet forces fighting against units of the 58th Infantry Division lost, according to German estimates, 1,369 killed and 294 captured.[35] In the ten-day period from 1–10 October the entire German Eighteenth Army lost only 758 killed and 48 missing in action.[36]

During the fighting to the south of Leningrad the Soviet troops sought unsuccessfully to win back Demyansk. The 26th Stalin Rifle Division, which was not only a cadre unit, but an elite one as well, and which entered the fighting for the first time and did not have any previous losses, lost 655 killed, 3,128 wounded, and 356 missing in action in the fighting during 24–6 September.[37] The entire German Sixteenth Army, out of which only a single infantry regiment from an SS division (*Totenkopf*), supported by artillery and engineers, fought against the 26th Rifle Division, lost during 21–30 September 1941 1,355 killed, 4,871 wounded, and 200 missing in action.[38] This is 1.6 times more wounded and 1.5 times killed and missing in action than one Soviet division during the course of three days. It transpires that in terms of combat capability the single cadre and elite 26th Rifle Division was not superior to newly minted and essentially militia divisions. During 24–6 September the losses of the SS *Totenkopf* Division amounted to 91 killed, 21 missing in action, and 336 wounded.[39] This was 9.3 times less than the losses of the 26th Rifle Division and nine times less than its irreplaceable losses. However, the *Totenkopf* Division had to fight against not only the 26th Rifle Division, but also against the 182nd and 254th rifle divisions, the 8th Tank Brigade, the 46th Independent Motorcycle Regiment, and some other units. The *Totenkopf* Division's losses for 24–30 September amounted to 250 killed, 68 missing in action, and 786 wounded.[40] This accounts for 20.5 per cent of the irreplaceable losses and 16.1 per cent of the wounded for the German Sixteenth Army during 21–30 September.

The chief of the Main Political Administration of the Workers'-Peasants Fleet, Army Commissar Second Class Ivan Rogov wrote on 5 October 1941 to the secretary of the VKP(b) Central Committee, Georgii Malenkov:[41]

> The chief of the political administration of the Baltic Fleet issued on 28.9.41 directive No. 110/s, in which the following is noted: 'To explain to the entire rank and file of the ships and units that all families of Red Navy sailors, Red Army soldiers and commanders who have gone over to the enemy, or who have surrendered to the enemy, will be immediately shot as families of turncoats and traitors to the Motherland, as will all defectors who have surrendered to the enemy upon their return from captivity.'
>
> I immediately enquired of the Baltic Fleet's political administration on the basis of what instructions the directive was issued, which contradicted the instructions contained in the *Stavka* of the Red Army high command order No. 270.[42]
>
> The member of the military council of the Red Banner Baltic Fleet, comrade SMIRNOV and the chief of the Red Banner Baltic Fleet's political administration, comrade LEBEDEV, report in their telegram of 4.10.41 that directive No. 110/s was compiled on the basis of coded telegram No. 4976, by the commander of the Leningrad Front, comrade Zhukov, which contained the following:
>
> 'Explain to the entire rank and file that all families of those who have surrendered to the enemy will be shot and that they will also be shot upon returning from captivity.'
>
> The Peoples' Commissar of the Navy, comrade KUZNETSOV, and I did not know that paragraph two of *Stavka* order No. 270 had been changed.

> I consider that coded telegram No. 4976 by the Leningrad Front command to be in contradiction to the instructions contained in order No. 270 by the *Stavka* of the Red Army high command.[43]

It is not known if they had time to shoot anybody in accordance with the sinister order No. 4976 during those few days when Zhukov commanded the Leningrad Front before he was hurriedly summoned back to Moscow following the German breakthrough near Vyaz'ma. The order, of course, was primarily for propaganda effect. The Red Army soldiers' families were either in the rear or in occupied territory and Zhukov's power did not reach that far. It is doubtful that they would have found in such a short time the families of prisoners in the front zone. But they could easily have shot ten or so Red Army soldiers suspected of having been prisoners as a warning. Zhukov's order was finally revoked in February 1942, but it's doubtful that anyone recalled it after Zhukov's departure. It is unlikely that this 'cannibalistic' order in any way raised the combat capability of the Leningrad Front's forces.

But Malenkov did not cancel Zhukov's order then in October. He probably simply had no time for this in conditions in which German tanks were racing toward Moscow and the main forces of the three *fronts* defending Moscow had ended up in 'cauldrons'.

Could all of these sacrifices been avoided? At one time, this question, which was raised during a radio broadcast on 'Moscow Echo' as to whether Leningrad should have been surrendered in order to reduce the victims among the civilian population, aroused a hailstorm of indignant telephone calls and threats to bring the author of the question to court on charges of insulting the memory of the fallen. But let's look at this alternative dispassionately, and relying on fact let's try to understand would could have happened if in September 1941 German forces had occupied Leningrad. According to a directive by the chief of staff of the German navy on 22 September 1941, entitled 'The Future of the City of Petersburg', 'The fuhrer has decided to erase the city of Petersburg from the face of the earth. Following the defeat of Soviet Russia, the further existence of this major inhabited locale does not present any interest.' In the same directive, it was noted:

> If requests are made to surrender as the result of the situation in the city, they will be rejected, because the problems connected with the population's residence in the city and supplying it with food cannot and must not be decided by us. In this war, which is being waged for the right to exist, we have no interest in the maintenance of even a part of the population.[44]

What can one say? These are barbaric intentions. But this could have been carried out only following the USSR's defeat and the ending of the war. The Germans would not have taken it upon themselves to destroy the city in wartime conditions; quite the opposite, they would have tried to employ it in the interest of waging the war. They acted the same way with other captured major Soviet cities, such as Kiev, Khar'kov and Dnepropetrovsk. The Germans would have used the port of Leningrad for maritime transport and Leningrad's heavy industrial factories for repairing weapons and military equipment and, possibly for the production of munitions. Much would have depended on how much the port, docks, and factories had been destroyed by German shelling and bombing and, in particular, by Soviet troops in case they abandoned the city. But in any case, the Germans would have tried to at least partially restore the work of the port, docks, and factories. An occupation administration would also have been created in the city, as well as police from the local population. Besides this, the factories would have been working to supply the occupation services and the troops and workers and administrators in the port and factories. A few hundred-thousand workers and members of their families might have remained in the city. The occupation administration would have provided them with rations ensuring survival. The Germans would only have begun blowing up the city in the event that the *Wehrmacht* was forced to abandon Leningrad. But here everything depended on how much time and explosives the German engineers had. They would first of all have tried to blow up the bridges and port buildings, and the rest as well as they could.

It's possible that there would have been fewer victims among the Leningraders in the event of the timely abandonment of the city by the Red Army than in the conditions of the blockade. But then the city would have had to have been abandoned as early as the end of August or beginning of September 1941, a few months before the onset of the cold weather. If following the German breakthrough of the Luga defensive line in the middle of August 1941, when the encirclement of Leningrad became a realistic prospect (the Germans did not plan to take the city by storming then, fearing large, by their standards, losses), Stalin would have made the decision to abandon the city, while simultaneously evacuating from it at least part of the residents and industry, this might possibly redounded to the benefit of the Red Army and the Leningraders themselves. Up until the that moment when the blockade ring actually closed, there remained more than three weeks and one could have carried out the evacuation and withdrawal of the troops in relative order. The Germans, as is known, evacuated the population of the Leningrad suburbs captured by them to the Baltic States (not only the able-bodied, but also old people and children; the author had the opportunity of speaking with the descendants of these evacuees in Estonia and Latvia), who were thus saved them from death by hunger, although those they were not able to evacuate in time died just as they did in blockaded Leningrad. Of course, the Germans would not have been able to evacuate the entire population of Leningrad. The fate of other major Soviet cities such as Kiev, Khar'kov, and Stalingrad would have awaited it. In Leningrad there would have remained only those who were needed for servicing the transportation infrastructure (the railroads and port), those industrial concerns that the Germans would have begun to use for military needs (particularly for the repair of military equipment) and the city administration. The Germans would not have turned over Leningrad to the Finns before the end of the war. Part of the residents would have been evacuated to the Baltic States and, possibly, to Belorussia, having in mind their employment primarily in agriculture, as well as for possible shipment to the Reich for work in industry. The Germans would have offered the remaining city residents the chance to survive as best they could, by moving to a rural area, or dying. But insofar as this would have occurred in the beginning of September, they would have had a better chance of survival than in the first blockade winter. All Jews who had not managed to evacuate or escape from Leningrad would undoubtedly have been shot. As regards the remainder of the population, in conditions of German occupation, which would most likely have continued until the beginning of 1944, and which was nobody's idea of fun, hundreds of thousands of Leningraders who had abandoned the city would probably have died from hunger or repressions, but the number of those who perished would nevertheless have been less than actually proved to be the case in the actual conditions of the blockade from hunger, bombings, and shelling.

Of course, in the event Leningrad had been abandoned, the Baltic Fleet would have perished. The ships would most likely have been blown up, while part of the guns would have been removed for use on land. But even if all of the Baltic Fleet's ships and submarines had fallen into German hands undamaged, this would not in any way have influenced the outcome of the war. The Germans would have had no way able of employing Soviet surface ships. It's not for nothing that in January 1943 Hitler was reviewing the possibility of sending all the German surface ships to the scrap yard because of their uselessness and gave up this idea only because the operation for utilizing these ships would have swallowed up too many resources. It's very difficult to imagine Doenitz's submariners employing Soviet submarines for any purpose other than target practice.[45] These vessels were too inferior in quality to the German ones. In reality, the Soviet Baltic Fleet, both during the blockade and following its lifting, had practically no effect on German shipments in the

Baltic and, during the last year of the war, when it would have seemed to have complete superiority in the Baltic Sea, it was unable to in any way seriously hinder the maritime evacuation of German troops and population. Of course, in the event of the loss of the Baltic Fleet, there would not have occurred the famous attack by Aleksandr Marinesko, which, one might add, had only very limited military significance.[46] On the whole, the Germans' efforts spent combating the Baltic Fleet were quite small and they could have in no way influenced the course of the Battle of the Atlantic.

Leningrad's industry during the war was engaged almost exclusively in the repair of combat equipment and weaponry. Besides this, if Leningrad had been abandoned in a systematic way, then even more equipment and workers could have been evacuated, which would have increased the output of weaponry and equipment in the Ural Mountains and other areas in the eastern part of the country. So, to repeat, if one steps back from the moral factor, which is difficult to evaluate, from the strictly military point of view, the abandonment of Leningrad no later than the beginning of September 1941 would have reduced losses and possibly, if only by a little, have brought victory nearer. All the more so, as the surrender of Leningrad would have essentially resulted in Finland's exit from the war and would have freed up part of the forces which the Leningrad Front was forced to hold against the Finns along the Karelian isthmus in the real conditions of the war.

But Stalin had no plans to abandon Leningrad in August or the beginning of September. It should also be noted that the surrender of Leningrad would have had a colossal demoralizing effect on the Red Army and the entire country. It's unlikely that the Red Army's losses in attempts to liberate Leningrad would have been less than in its attempts to break through the blockade. On the basis of the moral factor above all – the symbolic importance of Leningrad as the city of Lenin and the cradle of the revolution and the negative influence of its loss on the fighting spirit of the army and people – Stalin at that moment was not preparing to surrender Leningrad, also because he underestimated the seriousness of the situation the Red Army was in. It was for this same reason that he refused to surrender Kiev, which led to a disaster for the Southwestern Front.

Later, however, during the German offensive on Moscow, Stalin had the idea of surrendering Leningrad. These are the instructions he sent on the night of 22–3 October 1941 to the commander of the Leningrad Front, General Ivan Fedyuninskii, and the members of the *front's* military council, the leaders of the Leningrad communists, Andrei Zhdanov and Aleksei Kuznetsov.[47]

> Judging from your slow actions, one may come to the conclusion
> that you have not yet realized the critical situation which the troops

of the Leningrad Front are in. If you don't break through the front and do not restore secure communications with the 54th Army, which links you with the rear of the country, within the next few days all of your forces will be captured. The restoration of this link is necessary not only for supplying the Leningrad Front's forces, but especially for giving the Leningrad Front's forces a way out to withdraw to the east in order to avoid capture, if it is necessary to surrender Leningrad. Keep in mind that Moscow is in a critical situation and that it is not in a position to assist you with new forces. Either you will break through the front within the next two to three days and give our forces an opportunity to fall back to the east in the event of the impossibility of holding Leningrad, or you will be taken prisoner.

We demand decisive and rapid actions from you.

Concentrate eight or ten divisions and break through to the east. This is necessary in the event Leningrad is held, and in the event of surrendering Leningrad. The army is more important for you. We demand decisive actions from you. Stalin.[48]

At that moment, the German armies, having destroyed the main forces of three Soviet *fronts* in the 'cauldrons' around Vyaz'ma and Bryansk, were surging towards Moscow. And Stalin thought that by abandoning Leningrad he might be able to save the capital. At the same time, the fate of the civilian population did not worry him in the least, which expressed itself in a characteristic phrase: 'For us the army is more important.' But if the plan for abandoning Leningrad had been realized, it would have led not to saving Moscow, but to a real disaster. The Leningraders' fate would then have been even sadder than during the blockade. In this case, the Germans would have occupied Leningrad sometime in the beginning of November, when the frosts had already arrived. It is worth noting that the highest mortality rates in the Leningrad suburbs captured by the Germans were precisely in November, before the surviving residents were evacuated to the occupied Baltic States in December. Thus it is unlikely that the number of victims among the civilian population according to such a scenario would have been less than they proved to be during the continuation of the siege of Leningrad.

However, in the military sense, the breakthrough of the blockade and the subsequent withdrawal of the Leningrad Front's forces to the 'mainland' would have been no less catastrophic. It is necessary to stress that in the subsequent fighting to break through the blockade the correlation of losses with those of the Germans was probably the most unfavourable for the Red Army during the entire war. For example, near Nevskaya Dubrovka on 9 November 1941 the 1st Shock Communist Regiment, which had been formed mostly from Leningraders, lost 1,000 men (the remainder perished or were wounded the following day[49]) out of 1,500. Let's compare: the German Eighteenth Army, which was carrying out the blockade of Leningrad, both along the internal and external front, and which at the time numbered 18 divisions, lost only 878 men, including 164 killed and 20 missing in action during the ten-day period from 1–10 November.[50] But if it they had managed to break through the enemy ring and begin a withdrawal, then the troops of the Leningrad Front would have had to try and get out through a narrow corridor completely enfiladed by the enemy. They would have ended up in approximately the same situation in which the 2nd Shock Army of General Vlasov, of tragic fame, found itself in the spring and summer of 1942 in the swamps of the Volkhov River.[51] His army was almost completely destroyed in an attempt to break out of encirclement. The same fate would undoubtedly have befallen the troops of the Leningrad Front if they had attempted to abandon the city along a narrow corridor. And it this case it would not only have been impossible to employ them to save Moscow, but quite the opposite; the German command could have transferred the greater part of the freed-up divisions of the Eighteenth Army for seizing the Soviet capital, which could have enabled the *Wehrmacht* to take Moscow. Here, as they say, when there's no happiness, then unhappiness lent a hand. They were unable to break through the blockade in the autumn of 1941 and the matter of abandoning Leningrad was removed from the agenda.

Chapter 4

The Battle of Moscow

Victory or Defeat for the Red Army?

At the end of September and beginning of October the Soviet forces along the western direction were very poorly led. There were three *fronts* here – the Western, Reserve and Bryansk – the commanders of which failed to practically coordinate their operations with each other. Nor did the *Stavka*, led by Stalin, carry out such vitally necessary coordination. What was even worse was the fact that the forces of the Western and Reserve fronts were arranged in alternating fashion, which meant that the majority of the Reserve Front's armies, which were the Western Front's second echelon, were not subordinated to the commander of the latter, which made the waging of defensive fighting more difficult. Due to the shortage of radio communications equipment and combat experience, the army and *front* commanders relied more on wire communications and officers sent directly to the troops. However, wire communications were often broken in combat conditions and the officers were not able to find the headquarters, which frequently changed their location because the enemy had broken through the front and they had to fall back rapidly.

The organization of the command and control of the troops covering the Moscow direction also left a great deal to be desired. The three *fronts* contained sixteen armies, to which were subordinated in turn ninety-five divisions and thirteen tank brigades.[1] There were on average little more than seven divisions and about one tank brigade per army headquarters. This was one-and-a-half to two times more than in a single German army corps, which numbered three to five divisions. Following the disastrous defeats of the first months of the war the corps level was eliminated. On the other hand, there were several times as many armies in the Red Army than in the *Wehrmacht*. Three field armies and three tank groups subordinated to them advanced on Moscow in October 1941. All of these were united in a single Army Group Centre. Accordingly, the opposing Soviet forces' optimal structure would have been one *front*, three to four armies and sixteen corps headquarters. And the number of divisions could have been reduced in order not to overload the corps headquarters. After all, the Soviets had fewer communications means than the Germans. Thus they should have had fewer divisions, but of a relatively larger size, in order to reduce the overall number of divisions and therefore increase the amount of radio equipment available for their headquarters. But, unfortunately, the Soviet *Stavka* acted in exactly the opposite manner. Following the heavy losses of the first weeks of war, the authorized strength of the divisions was reduced from the prewar 14,483 men to 10,858 on 29 July 1941. And this was at the same time that the authorized strength of a German infantry division was 16,859.[2] If the Soviet rifle divisions had had an authorized strength approximately equal to the German infantry divisions and if the Soviet tank brigades had been deployed into divisions, like the Germans, that is, reinforced with motorized infantry and artillery (according to the number of tanks, two Soviet tank brigades at that time were approximately equal to a single German panzer division), then they would have had along the Moscow direction about sixty-one rifle, motorized rifle, and tank divisions, for which sixteen corps headquarters, organized into four armies, would have been quite enough. In this case, the command system would probably have been more streamlined and decisions adopted and transmitted to the units and formations more rapidly. But in practice a completely different organizational strategy was employed in the Red Army. A passion for gigantomania, which was characteristic of the Soviet system, predominated. Let there be a larger number of divisions – it'll look more imposing. Let there be armies instead of corps. First of all, there'll be a few more generals' positions with more stars. Second of all, if necessary, its easier for the army commander to approach the *front* commander and even the *Stavka* itself, despite the fact that the confusion in troop control will increase due to this. In the final year of the war Hitler suffered from a desire to form new divisions instead of reinforcing the existing ones. It's possible that this helped him to underrate in his own consciousness the scope of the defeats that the *Wehrmacht* was suffering. The Red Army's leadership suffered from a similar passion throughout the entire war.

The directive to assume the defensive along the Western direction was issued by the *Stavka* of the VGK only on 27 September 1941, and within three days the Second Panzer Group began its offensive against the Bryansk Front, which before this had been unsuccessfully attempting to defeat it. There was no possibility of preparing a defence in three days. The situation was no better along the Western and Reserve fronts, which before this had been attacking during the course of one-and-a-half to two months and had not had time to prepare a long-term defence.

As early as 21 September 1941 von Bock wrote in his diary: 'From the east the Russians continue to press Guderian's Second Panzer Group. The 29th Motorized Division (Fremerey) along the sector near Novgorod-Severskii faces units of 8–9 Russian divisions.'[3] The fighting along this sector of the front continued the following day. Certainly, along the other sectors of the army group's front, he confidently noted as early as 20 September that the enemy was obviously going over to the defensive. But two weeks proved to be insufficient in order to properly prepare to repel an enemy offensive. All the more so, as some kind of local attacks nevertheless continued. In particular, on 23 September, Halder noted the 'insignificant enemy attacks' along the army group's front.[4] In the opinion of M. Khodorenok and B. Nevzorov,

> the 16th, 19th, 22nd, 24th, 29th and 43rd armies' formations were even attacking in the last ten days of September, General Yermakov's group throughout the entire second half of the month, and the 13th Army essentially spent the entire month attacking. This pulled the troops from organizing a deeply-echeloned defence and prevented us from creating defensive groups of forces and, in the final analysis, led to great losses among the rank and file. For example, Yermakov's group lost 4,913 men killed, wounded and missing in action on 27 September alone.[5]

The former deputy chief of staff of the Bryansk Front, General L.M. Sandalov, admitted in his memoirs: 'The fact that Yermakov's group chiefly waged offensive battles in the second half of September and paid little attention to questions of defence weakened the front's left-flank forces and brought the enemy enormous advantages.'[6] Just the opposite, the former commander of the Bryansk Front, Marshal A.I. Yeremenko, maintained in his memoirs: 'In summing up in brief the results of the of the Bryansk Front's forces during the period from 14 August through 30 September 1941, one should say that as a result of the counterblows and counterattacks by the front's forces, particularly the counterblow in the Trubchevsk area, the Hitlerites suffered significant losses, which weakened the strength of their shock groups of forces.'[7] He notes, however, that the forces of Yermakov's group and the 13th Army received orders to go over to the defensive only on 28 September.[8]

It was only on 25 September, as Halder noted in his diary, that the construction of fortifications by the enemy was recorded along the front of Army Group South.[9] At the same time, the commander of the Western Front, General I.S. Konev, believed that the Germans would attack along the most direct route – along the Smolensk road.[10] The main fortifications were being built there. The Germans, however, launched attacks north and south of the road. It's possible that the testimony of a captured German pilot influenced Konev's decision. On 26 September the commander of the Western Front reported to Stalin and Shaposhnikov that according to interrogation materials of a captured pilot 'The enemy is preparing for an offensive in the direction of Moscow, with the main group of forces along the Vyaz'ma–Moscow highway.'[11]

Operation 'Typhoon', which the *Wehrmacht* began on 30 September and 2 October 1941, having unleashed an offensive against the Bryansk, Western and Reserve fronts, was supposed to victoriously complete the blitzkrieg with the capture of Moscow. This, as Hitler and his generals hoped, would lead to the collapse of Soviet resistance and enable them to leave a minimum of men and materiel in the East in order to concentrate on the fight against Great Britain. At first everything seemed to be proceeding smoothly and Hitler was aided in no small way by Stalin and his generals. The two sides' forces were approximately equal, but the grouping and the poor troop control of the three Soviet *fronts* doomed them to a serious defeat. The rank and file strength of Army Group Centre at the beginning of October was 1,183,693 men (minus the *Luftwaffe* and those units directly subordinated to the army group headquarters). They had about 1,700 tanks.[12] They were opposed by the forces of three Soviet *fronts*, which had 1,252,591 men, 849 tanks, 5,637 guns, 4,961 mortars, and 62,651 vehicles and tractors along an approximately 730km front.[13] The German researcher based his information on Soviet data, which are obviously understated, at least concerning tanks, because the Germans captured 1,242 of them in the Vyaz'ma and Bryansk cauldrons, while a certain number of tanks were able to get out of the encirclement. It's possible that the 849 tanks represent the number of vehicles ready for combat by the beginning of October. Also, the data that there were 486 tanks in the RKKA's units in the Western Front's defensive zone against the *Wehrmacht*'s 591, and correspondingly 4,028 and 5,651 guns and mortars, also proves that there were no less than 1,242 Soviet tanks.[14] Otherwise, it works out that the Western Front had more than 57 per cent of all the tanks in the three *fronts* along the western direction.

By 1 October Soviet aviation disposed of 1,368 aircraft around Moscow, including 578 bombers, 708 fighters, 36 assault aircraft, and 46 reconnaissance planes against the *Luftwaffe*'s 1,320 planes, including 720 bombers, 420 fighters, 40 assault aircraft, and 140 reconnaissance planes. Thus the *Luftwaffe* enjoyed a numerical superiority in bombers and Soviet aviation in fighters.[15]

The forces of the Western Front's 22nd, 29th, 30th, 19th, 16th, and 20th armies occupied defensive positions along the main, Moscow direction in a zone 340km in width from Lake Seliger to Yel'nya. The Reserve Front's 24th and 43rd armies were defending the line from Yel'nya to the Roslavl'– Kirov railroad in a zone up to 100km in width, and the Reserve Front's 31st, 49th, 32nd, and 33rd armies occupied positions in the rear of the Western Front along a zone 300km wide along the line Ostashkov–Selizharovo–east of Dorogobuzh. The Bryansk Front's forces (50th, 3rd, and 13th armies, and

Major General Yermakov's operational group; commander Colonel General Yeremenko) covered the Bryansk–Kaluga and Sevsk–Orel–Tula axes; the forward edge of their defence was 290km wide and ran along the line Snopot'–Pochep–Pogar–Glukhov.[16]

The mistake was in the placement of four of the Western and Reserve fronts' armies along the rear defensive line. Following the breakthrough of the defence, they were unable to either launch a counterblow or to delay the enemy's advance and were defeated. It would have been better to have employed them to hold the main defensive zone.

The Western Front command and the *Stavka* of the Supreme High Command incorrectly determined the most likely direction of the enemy attack, believing that it would be launched along the Smolensk–Moscow highway. At the same time, the data available in the *fronts'* headquarters and the *Stavka* on the grouping of the German forces would have enabled them to determine that the enemy would launch his main attacks along the flanks in order to encircle the Soviet forces defending along the approaches to Moscow.

The resulting correlation of forces would have enabled the Red Army to successfully defend, but only on the condition that it could coordinate the actions of all of the defending forces along the Moscow direction and allocate them correctly. There was an average of 1,650 men, 14.2 guns and mortars (including 8 guns), 1.65 tanks, and 1.3 aircraft per km of defensive front. Taking into account that a significant part of the defensive zone passed through forested areas and swamps that were difficult to navigate, it was possible to significantly increase the troops' density by concentrating the forces along the most dangerous axes that German tanks could traverse. However, as the troops of the three *fronts* had been conducting offensive operations right up until the final third of September, there was practically no time left for regrouping. By way of comparison, the Germans in Normandy in June 1944 had a density of less than three guns and one tank per km of front, and nevertheless they managed to hold the front against the Allies' Normandy beachhead for nearly two months.[17]

On 24 September 1941 the chief of the German General Staff, General F. Halder, located with the headquarters of Army Group Centre in Smolensk, together with the commander-in-chief of the army, Field Marshal W. von Brauchitsch, wrote in his diary: 'Von Bock reported that he wants to attack along Guderian's front on 30.9, and on 2.10 along the other sectors. In any event, there must be no more than a 48-hour gap between these two phases of the offensive.'[18] Field Marshal von Bock, the commander of Army Group Centre, himself noted in his diary on the same day:

At the meeting of the army and tank group commanders in his [Brauchitsch, B.S.] presence, nothing new was heard, with the exception that Guderian had been allowed to attack as early as 30 September. I would prefer if he got a bit of a head start, because he is still quite far from the right flank along which the main attack will be launched and one may expect results from the tanks' operations only 4–5 days following the beginning of the operation. The other commanders will be ready only by 2 October, and only Hoth (Third Panzer Group) proposes 3 October.[19]

Actually, such a spreading out by two days of the time for the start of the offensive along different axes allowed them to hope that the Soviet reserves would first of all be thrown into repelling Guderian's attack, which would make it easier to conduct an offensive along the main axis. This too told of the poor organization of the three Soviet *fronts*. In practice, the *Stavka*, which, however, had to devote attention to all the strategic directions, carried this out and thus was catastrophically late in making decisions to repel 'Typhoon'.

On 2 October the chief of the German General Staff noted with satisfaction in his diary:

The army' group's main forces have gone over to the offensive (Typhoon) and are advancing successfully. Guderian believes that his formations have broken through the enemy's defence throughout the entire depth. The formations of Guderian's group, which are operating in the center, are vigorously attacking toward Orel. The Second Army has been engaged in stubborn fighting in forcing the Desna River. It managed to force the river and throw the enemy back approximately five kilometers. The Fourth Panzer Group has scattered the enemy's resisting groups and has advanced 15 kilometers into the depth. The Fourth Army's forces are attacking successfully along the entire front and have advanced on an average of 6–12 kilometers. Hoth's panzer army and the Ninth Army are attacking quite successfully, having advanced up to 20 kilometers in depth. The command of the armies and panzer groups, as was the case on 22.6, give different answers as to whether the enemy was intending to wage a stubborn defence or not. Only along those sectors where the enemy had rear defensive positions, that is facing the Fourth and Ninth armies, could one assume with confidence beforehand that he was preparing for a defence. One might think that he intended to hold his positions along the remaining sectors as well, but as a result of the significant decline in his forces' combat capability; he was quickly crushed by our units. However, following this, despite his hurried withdrawal along individual sectors of the front, we see no evidence of a planned and deep withdrawal. The enemy's groups which have become bogged down in the large forested areas between our attack wedges will show us before long that the enemy was not preparing to pull back.[20]

And as early as 4 October Halder was noting with satisfaction in his diary:

Operation Typhoon is developing in an almost classical manner. Guderian's panzer group, while attacking through Orel, has reached Mtsensk, without encountering any kind of resistance. Hoepner's panzer group has energetically broken through the enemy's defence and has reached Mozhaisk.[21] Hoth's panzer group has reached Kholm, having thus reached the upper course of the Dnepr, while in the north it has advanced as far as Belyi. The enemy continues everywhere to hold the sectors of the front not under attack, as a result of which one can foresee the deep encirclement of these enemy groups.[22]

The reason for the encirclement of such a large number of Soviet divisions was their unfortunate defensive dispositions, as a result of which many sectors were weakly covered. It was precisely these sectors that the German tank groups attacked. And the order to withdraw came quite late. It was received only on 5 October, but as early as 7 October Guderian's and Hoth's panzer groups closed the ring around Vyaz'ma. And it was only on 12 October that all of the forces operating along the western direction were united under the command of the newly appointed commander of the Western Front, G.K. Zhukov.

As M. Khodorenok and B. Nevzorov note, 'Seven army headquarters (out of 15), 64 divisions (out of 95), 11 tank brigades (out of 13), and 50 High Command Reserve artillery regiments (out of 64) were encircled along the central sector of the Soviet-German front. These formations and units formed part of 13 armies and one operational group.'[23] A report by the German command on the results of the battle of Vyaz'ma lists 663,000 prisoners, 1,242 captured Soviet tanks, and 5,412 guns.[24] Overall Soviet losses were 959,200 men, including 855,100 irreplaceably and 104,100 wounded. The Germans' Army Group Centre lost 145,000 killed, wounded, and missing in action.[25] Army Group Centre's losses for October amounted to 62,870 men killed, missing in action, and wounded, including 16,225 irreplaceably.[26]

A total of 85,000 men managed to get out of the Vyaz'ma cauldron and about 23,000 from the one around Bryansk. To this figure should be added the 98,000 men from the 29th and 33rd armies, who avoided encirclement, Yermakov's group, and the 22nd Army, only one division of which was encircled.[27]

On the whole, one can state that the reasons for the rapid defeat of the Soviet forces around Bryansk and Vyaz'ma in October 1941 were as follows: the poor preparation of defensive lines because the assumption of the defensive by the Western, Bryansk and Reserve fronts was carried out too late; the poor coordination of the operations by the three Soviet *fronts* along the western direction, which essentially lacked a unified leadership; the incorrect determination of the direction of the German troops' main attack; the belated authorization to withdraw; the rapid loss of command and control of the Soviet forces by their commanders following the breakthrough of the front. The fault for this lies with both the *Stavka* and the *front* commands.

The only correct decision by Konev on the evening of 1 October would have been the immediate beginning of a rapid withdrawal by the *front's* main forces to the Vyaz'ma defensive line along with the simultaneous reinforcement of the forces along the threatened axes. Then it would have been theoretically possible to avoid the disaster. But even if Konev had risked beginning an immediate withdrawal without Stalin's order, he nevertheless could not have realistically carried it out. Within a day or two the *Stavka*, upon discovering the unsanctioned withdrawal, would most likely have turned the retreating troops around, which would only have increased the muddle. And Ivan Stepanovich would surely have been removed from his post and most likely shot, just like his predecessor, Dmitrii Grigor'evich Pavlov, having made him the chief culprit in the Vyaz'ma disaster. The Red Army's shortcomings were of a systemic character and were in many ways inherited from as far back as the czarist army. Under this system the actions of a few talented commanders were not able to change anything.

There is one more longstanding failing of the Soviet system – the practice of enhancing reality in reports to one's superiors and to justify one's own actions (or inactions) at any price. During Stalin's time a failure in bureaucratic fiction could result in the threat of death. And, as a consequence, in an initial report the scale of the German breakthrough was understated, insofar as the generals still calculated on restoring the situation through counterblows and would forget to inform the *front* headquarters about the abandoned towns and stations. And the *front* commanders and the *Stavka* were late in making the decision to withdraw. Then, once the scale of the German successes became clear, the opposite tack was taken and in Soviet reports the enemy's strength was significantly exaggerated in order to justify one's own defeat. All of this made the adoption of correct decisions by the *front* commanders and the

Stavka more difficult. Also, fearing to repeat the fate of General D.G. Pavlov, who was shot along with a group of generals for the Western Front's failure at the beginning of the war, the commanders would reluctantly pull back forces from sectors of the *front* not under attack, which only made the Germans' task of creating a gigantic cauldron all the easier.

Purely theoretically, in conditions of poor communications and the coordination of operations, it would have been wiser to construct the defence in a single echelon. After all, the second-echelon armies actually did not have time to take part in the repulse of the German offensive and the majority of them perished in the encirclement. Thus if the density of the defence had been increased by the addition of second echelons, the Germans would have expended more time and forces on the breakthrough and a significant part of the Soviet forces would probably have managed to avoid encirclement. But neither Stalin nor his generals and marshals wanted to admit even to themselves that the *Wehrmacht* stood head and shoulders above the Red Army then as regards the level of operational-tactical skill and in order to successfully fight it one would have to adopt the tactics of the weakest against the strongest.

During course of the battle of Vyaz'ma the commanders of the Soviet *fronts*, having rapidly lost communications with the troops, headed out to those armies which, as they thought, had been subjected to the enemy's main attacks, abandoning their headquarters at their previous locations. The same thing happened to a lot of army commanders. As a result, the troops received contradictory orders from both the commanders and from their headquarters, as well as from the *Stavka*. The commanders searched for their headquarters and the headquarters for their commanders, while the *Stavka* searched for both of them. All the Soviet countermeasures were hopelessly late. There were almost no Soviet forces between the German advance units and Moscow. Germans reconnaissance elements reached the outskirts of the capital.

But the *Wehrmacht* had invaded the USSR with only a three-month supply of fuel, which ran out by the middle of October. Food, fuel, and munitions had to be brought up in order to continue the offensive, but the muddy conditions interfered with this. At the same time, the encircled group of forces, headed by the commander of the 19th Army, General Mikhail Lukin and which held on until 20 October, was tying down up to fourteen German divisions.[28]

Perhaps the optimal variant for those encircled would have been not to attempt to immediately break out, but to adopt an all-round defence and, while being supplied by air, wait for help from without, while drawing upon themselves the maximum number of enemy forces. However, this option should be considered in theory only. Soviet generals and commanders were not taught to wage an all-round defence before the war, because, as it was believed, the Red Army would only attack. All of the airfields in the cauldrons were very quickly lost and not a single one of the encircled groups of forces even tried to create a long-term defence.

It should be stressed that as a rule, when getting into an encirclement, the Soviet forces did not adopt an all-round defence and without fail sought to break out of the encirclement. At the same time, the break-out has to succeed within a week because after that time the command would lose control over the encircled forces and the fuel and munitions would run out, insofar as the Soviet air force was unable to organize a fully fledged 'air bridge' into the cauldrons. At best, the cargos were thrown out of the aircraft and only occasionally actually reached their destination.

The rainy weather that began in the second half of October prevented the *Wehrmacht* from immediately developing the offensive on Moscow and employing its advantage in troop mobility. The Germans were then unable to immediately reach Moscow, which at that moment was very weakly defended. It should be noted that there was no military secret at all that in the second half of October the rainy season begins in central Russia and that the great majority of Russian roads could in no way be compared with European highways. The German command knew about this, but had no opportunity to influence the situation. Theoretically, one could have shifted all of Army Group Centre's supply and, partially, the transfer of forces to transport aviation. But in practice the *Luftwaffe* had neither a sufficient number of aircraft nor fuel. Moreover, there were too many days when the weather did not allow for flying. Moreover, during the rainy season, the Germans could attack only along the main roads. The *Wehrmacht* overcame the Mozhaisk defensive line by the end of October, but it was not able to renew the general offensive on Moscow until 16 November, when the frosts froze the ground and the rainy season came to an end. During this time, reserves, which were sufficient not only for a successful defence but for a counteroffensive, were brought up to the Western and Kalinin fronts. Zhukov was able to create a sufficiently sturdy defence along the approaches to the capital from the surviving forces and those transferred from the east. From 18 October forty divisions moved up to Moscow from the areas of the Volga River, the Ural Mountains, and Siberia. They were later joined by divisions from the Far East.

The breakthrough of the Mozhaisk defensive line during 7–25 October 1941 was reflected most of all in the memoirs and diaries of the German generals and field marshals representing the command of Army Group Centre, the panzer groups, and the air force.

On 7 November the commander-in-chief of the army, Field Marshal Walter von Brauchstitsch, demanded that the offensive by Hoth's Third Panzer Group along the Ninth Army's northern wing develop to the north for the purpose of destroying the Russian forces facing the left flank of Army Group Centre and the right flank of Army Group North. The commander-in-chief of Army Group Centre, Field Marshal Fedor von Bock, had a different opinion and noted in his diary: 'As regards the offensive by the Third Panzer Group to the north, I am not entirely in agreement with it. Perhaps I am wrong and that a powerful attack launched to the north will weaken the enemy's resistance in other sectors, including the central one.'[29] This turn to the north is sometimes considered one of the reasons that the Germans did not take Moscow. At the same time, they forget that had there not been a German offensive along the Ninth Army's northern flank, then the Soviet forces operating in the area of the boundary between army groups North and Centre would likely have been shifted immediately to the defence of Moscow.

As early as 8 October 1941 von Bock wrote in his diary:

> Because I am not certain Kluge has fully realized the necessity of the immediate shifting of the LVII Panzer Corps to the east, I telephoned his chief of staff and repeated that it is extremely important for us to reach Maloyaroslavets and Mozhaisk before the enemy and thus we should speed things up.[30] Besides, it is necessary for us to organize deep reconnaissance along the Moscow direction.[31]

However, on the following day the field marshal was forced to note: 'The LVII Panzer Corps (Kuntzen), which was supposed to attack through Maloyaroslavets, "has gotten bogged down" due to the blown up bridges and has practically failed to advance over the Izver' River to the east. The *Das Reich* SS Division [the *Das Reich* SS Division, commanded by Hausser, had been attached to Guderian's panzer group] has captured Gzhatsk after heavy fighting.'[32]

On 10 October von Bock wrote in his diary that 'The Fourth Army's eastern front is moving in fighting over the Ugra and Izver' rivers to the northeast. The *Das Reich* SS Division has run into the enemy's fierce resistance in its sector.'[33] On 11 October the LVII Panzer Corps captured Medyn'. On 13 October Hitler ordered that Moscow be encircled along the line of the rail ring road and forbade German troops to enter Moscow, fearing heavy losses in street fighting (von Bock insisted on an encirclement along a less lengthy perimeter, maintaining that he did not have enough troops for such a broad encirclement). But as early as 14 October the commander of Army Group Centre noted with concern:

> Similar to what we had after Smolensk, they are condemning the army group to a dispersal of force and an offensive along several

different axes, thus weakening its offensive along the axis of the main attack . . . Due to the roads, which are drowning in the mud, and the Russians' increasing resistance, only a limited advance can be observed along the Fourth Army's eastern front.[34]

On 16 October von Bock stated that the Fourth Army 'is moving extremely slowly due to the horrible road conditions'.[35] On 18 October the capture of Mozhaisk and Maloyaroslavets by the Fourth Army's forces was not cause for particular optimism on his part, insofar as 'whether we are able to take advantage of these successes depends predominantly on the weather', and that the

distribution by sectors of the divisions that have become entangled in the fighting in the area of the Vyaz'ma 'cauldron' is taking up a lot of the Fourth Army's time, insofar as several of the roads available for the movement of transport and which lead to the east, are blocked by the attacking panzer groups' tanks and armoured transports. There are still no infantry units whatever between the Moscow highway and the northern boundary of the Fourth Army's zone of responsibility. In order to somehow secure and support the troops' advance in the general direction of Moscow, I have ordered that the road leading from the south toward Kalinin be cleared and that it be used for transferring the corps from the Ninth Army's right flank to Volokolamsk for the purpose of its subsequent attachment to the Fourth Army.[36]

On 19 October von Bock stated: 'The army group's forces are gradually beginning to get bogged down in the mud and swamps'.[37] Von Bock said the main cause of the difficulties with supplying the troops was that 'the bridges along the way to the front have been blown up and the delivery of food and military supplies is being carried out along alternate routes over roads that have been completely destroyed and which are awash in mud, the majority of which are completely impassable to auto transport'.[38] On 20 October he wrote that 'In the Fourth Army's sector only a limited advance can be noted, and that only in some places. I hope that the army's affairs will go better when the infantry corps catch up to the motorized units.'[39] And on the following day he emphasized in particular: 'The Russians bother us a lot less than the slush and mud.'[40] On 25 October, the day Volokolamsk was captured, von Bock basically admits that the offensive on Moscow had failed: 'The division of the army group and the terrible weather conditions were to a significant degree the reason why the pace of our troops' advance has sharply declined. As a result of this, the Russians received additional time to strengthen their defence and reinforce their worn-out divisions. Moreover, the developed railroad net around Moscow still remains in their hands. This is very bad!'[41] Even the capture of Volokolamsk by the Fourth Army's V Corps, which was noted by von Bock in his diary on 27 October, failed to render his evaluation of the situation more optimistic. Von Bock understood that his army group would still have to halt because of the rainy weather, despite the fact that the Mozhaisk fortified line, the last one before Moscow, had already been pierced.

The former commander of the SS *Das Reich* Division, Paul Hausser, recalled that having completed the encirclement along the Smolensk–Moscow highway in the Gzhatsk area, the *Das Reich* Division turned to the east:

> To the east, in the Borodino area, the positions before Moscow were especially well fortified. On 13 and 14 October along this sector the division, together with the 10th Panzer Division, attacked the enemy, during which time the division commander was wounded and was unable to continue in command [on 14 October Hausser lost an eye in the fighting, B.S.]. Then the axis of the offensive was turned to the north, toward Ruza. Beginning on 27 October, the autumn slush paralyzed the movement of the panzer and motorized units. They were tied down in positions north of Ruza and up until the middle of November were forced to defend themselves as they were.[42]

Hausser also quotes excerpts from the diary of an enlisted man in an anti-tank-gun crew in the *Das Reich* Division:

> 15.10.1941. The most important key position before Moscow has been pierced. It's been snowing non-stop all day. It's impossible to imagine how our infantry is fighting in such snow and in such cold. The long-range batteries are covering our ranks with heavy fire. The Bryansk and Vyaz'ma cauldrons have been almost already destroyed.
>
> 16.10.1941. The attacks continue. Our division is melting away before our eyes. But our strength of will still remains our armour-piercing weapon.[43]

On 16 and 17 October the *Das Reich* SS and 10th Panzer divisions lost 280 men in wounded alone. During the breakthrough of the Mozhaisk defensive line, from 9–21 October, the Fourth Panzer Group captured 40,360 prisoners and destroyed and captured 179 tanks and 475 guns of various calibres.[44] However, at the price of these losses, the Soviet forces were able to detain the Germans on the Mozhaisk defensive line until the onset of the rainy weather.

The Germans were preparing to outflank Moscow from the north and south, in order to force the Soviet forces to fall back under the threat of being encircled and in order to avoid prolonged street fighting. As a result, some German generals and historians have put forth the opinion that instead of an attempt to encircle Moscow, it would have been better to attack it frontally. But the later experience of Stalingrad shows that the Germans would not have been able to seize Moscow, a much larger city than Stalingrad, and that the gathering winter would have made the withdrawal of Army Group Centre to winter quarters inevitable.

The valour of the defenders of Moscow and the arrival of reserves from the depth of the country foiled the plan for 'Typhoon' and prevented the Germans from capturing the capital. The *Wehrmacht's* insufficient preparations for winter were not the most significant factor here. The former commander of the Third Panzer Group, H. Hoth, noted in his memoirs that:

> On 14 October the Third Panzer Group captured Kalinin. But after this the enemy's ally appeared, which managed to do that which, despite all kinds of sacrifices, the Russian command was unable to achieve. It was not the Russian winter but the autumn rains that put an end to the German offensive. It rained day and night, it rained non-stop, alternating with snow. The roads became waterlogged and movement halted. The shortage of munitions, fuels and lubricants and food defined the tactical and operational situation of the following three weeks.

Hoth asks the question: 'Did the German command have a basis, following the conclusion of the battles around Bryansk and Vyaz'ma, to count on a successful continuation of the operations to encircle Moscow in the middle of October?' And he answers in the negative:

> We should have taken account of the weather during the preceding weeks and expected the further worsening of the roads. Under such conditions, the rapid conduct of operations proved to be impossible. And it was namely rapid actions that were needed, so that the enemy did not recover from the heavy defeat that had been inflicted on him. We also had to act rapidly because we could not stretch out the conduct of operations until winter, which had already arrived. To be sure, in the rear they had carried out certain preparations for a winter campaign: warm clothing, blankets, medicines against frostbite, and stoves, etc., had been stockpiled, but all of this was far away from the troops and the supply situation was becoming more

difficult as we moved further from the final railheads. The delivery of supplies became dependent on the condition of the dirt roads.[45]

Incidentally, this statement contradicts the widely circulated opinion that the German army was completely unprepared for a winter campaign and did not have sufficient reserves of suitable clothing and other equipment necessary for the conditions. The problem was not its absence, but the impossibility of bringing all of this forward to the troops on time and in sufficient quantities. For example, according to the note in Halder's diary of 5 November 1941, there were no problems with winter clothing in Finland, where the roads were good: 'In the report from Finland it states that the troops are exhausted, but that good quality winter clothing is there in sufficient supply.'[46]

Hoth believed that there was little chance of encircling Moscow from the south and north, given the condition of the German panzer troops and the transfer of Soviet reinforcements from Siberia and the Far East. In Hoth's opinion, following the elimination of the 'cauldrons' around Vyaz'ma and Bryansk, the German army should have halted and renounced the capture of Moscow in 1941:

> It would have been easier to explain the situation in the upper courses of the Volga, Don, Dnepr and Western Dvina rivers as wise self limitation than the subsequent defeat on the approaches to Moscow. After all, this defeat restored the Red Army's moral spirit and gave a mighty impulse to the Russians' national feelings and to a colossal degree strengthened faith in the leadership's strength, and these factors in no way help to force the enemy to enter into peace talks.[47]

Strictly speaking, peace talks in October 1941 were hardly likely. At that time Hitler was ready to accept only unconditional capitulation and would not have concluded a compromise peace. Stalin also understood that Hitler was not ready to make concessions, while he himself had not lost faith in ultimate victory. The inclination to compromise arose in Hitler only when, following the breakthrough of the Mozhaisk defensive line, the first German offensive on Moscow petered out, while the second offensive, which began on 15–16 November, developed too slowly and did not promise great successes. On 19 November, according to an entry in Halder's diary, the führer declared to him: 'On the whole, one may expect that both hostile groups of countries, not being in a condition to destroy each other, will arrive at a compromise agreement.'[48] But the anti-Hitler coalition was not thinking about any sort of compromise peace at that moment.

The former chief of staff of the Fourth Army, Gunther Blumentritt agreed with Hoth and stated:

> We knew, of course, that the rainy season was waiting for us – we had read about it in books. But the reality exceeded our worst fears. The rainy weather began in the middle of October, during the fighting in the Vyaz'ma area, and increased uninterruptedly until the middle of November. It's impossible to tell what the Russian rainy season is to someone who has never encountered it. Only a few paved roads have been built in this corner of the world. The entire territory of the country is covered with impassable and viscous mud.
>
> The infantryman slides on the roads made slippery by water. It's necessary to harness a lot of horses in order to drag the guns. All the wheeled vehicles are submerged in the viscous mud. Even tractors move with great difficulty. Many heavy guns became bogged down on the roads and thus were not employed in the Battle of Moscow. Tanks and other tracked vehicles were often swallowed up by the mud. Now it is not difficult to imagine to what tension our tired and exhausted troops were subjected to.[49]

Albert Kesselring, the former commander of the *Luftwaffe's* Second Air Fleet, which was supporting Army Group Centre, wrote in his memoirs:

> The extremely unfavorable weather conditions hindered our aviation's ability to render assistance to the ground forces from the air; rain and snow fell and the roads, which were already deeply rutted wrecked even more the heavy four-wheel drive trucks; as a result, movement along the roads was made more difficult, and by 5 October ceased almost entirely. Attempts to move the aircraft by towing them with the aid of the anti-aircraft gunners' tractors proved unsuccessful, insofar as the towing chains could not withstand the strain. When difficulties arose with supplying the troops with food products, the *Luftwaffe* had to drop food to a number of units in the Second Panzer Army by air. The physical and emotional strain exceeded all allowable limits. One should also add that the army units' equipment was not adapted to combat activities in winter . . . At the same time, I was convinced that Hoepner and Guderian would not have had great trouble in simply pushing their tanks forward to get as far as Moscow and maybe even further. But the gods, having sent the rain, disposed otherwise; the Russians got the opportunity to create a thin defensive line to the west of Moscow

and to suffuse it with their last reserves, consisting of workers and cadets from military schools. They fought heroically and halted the offensive of our troops who had nearly lost their mobility.[50]

Here the field marshal honestly confesses that he had not expected such rainy weather as he saw in Russian in the middle of October 1941. In the same way, the other German generals did not expect that the rainy weather would almost completely paralyze the movement of transportation.

In Kesselring's opinion,

> Following the battle in the Bryansk and Vyaz'ma area, one could only notice the enemy's movements in the encirclement zone in individual cases; the concentration of the best Siberian divisions had not been fixed or was not evaluated as such. We were dealing with small, isolated centers of resistance; the enemy disposed of a large number of small, permanent firing structures, which were scattered here and there, and it was extremely difficult for our pilots, who were flying at high speeds, to detect and destroy them, especially in bad weather.[51]

Heinz Guderian, whose Second Panzer Army was trying to break through the weakest southern sector of the Mozhaisk defensive line, wrote in his memoirs:

> The OKH was of the opinion that these satisfactory developments now made possible the further prosecution of the offensive for Moscow. The intention was to prevent the Russians from establishing fresh defensive positions to the west of Moscow. The OKH proposed that Second Panzer Army should continue to advance through Tula and seize the Oka crossings between Kolomna and Serpukhov – undoubtedly a very large objective. This was to correspond to a similar move by Panzer Group 3 to the north of Moscow. The commander-in-chief of the army found Army Group Centre to be in full agreement with this plan of his.
>
> On 8 October I flew along the line of our 'road' from Sevsk over Dmitrovsk to Orel, where I found my command vehicles which I had previously sent on ahead. The state of the traffic along the 'road' as far as Kromy was appalling.

Guderian admits that:

> The Russians attacked us frontally with infantry, while they sent their tanks in, in mass formation, against our flanks. They were

learning. The bitterness of the fighting was gradually telling on both our officers and our men. Gen. von Geyer brought up once again the urgent need for winter clothing of all sorts. In particular there was a serious shortage of boots, shirts and socks . . .

The next few weeks were dominated by the mud. Wheeled vehicles could only advance with the help of tracked vehicles. These latter, having to perform tasks for which they were not intended, rapidly wore out. Since chains and couplings for the towing of vehicles were lacking, bundles of rope were dropped from airplanes to the immobilised vehicles. The supplying of hundreds of such vehicles and their crews now had to be done by the air force. Preparations made for the winter were utterly inadequate. For weeks we had been requesting anti-freeze for the water coolers of our engines; we saw as little of this as we did of winter clothing for the troops. This lack of warm clothes was, in the difficult months ahead, to provide the greatest problem and caused the greatest suffering to our soldiers – and it would have been the easiest to avoid of all our difficulties . . .

Not only we but also Army Group South, with the exception of First Panzer Army, were now bogged down. Sixth Army succeeded in capturing Bogodukhov to the northwest of Khar'kov. To our north XIII Army Corps took Kaluga. Panzer Group 3 seized Staritsa and went on towards Kalinin.

The OKH issued instructions for the encirclement of Moscow but these never reached us.[52]

Typically, German authors, not only in their memoirs but also in their diaries, which were maintained during the course of combat operations, in describing the breakthrough of the Mozhaisk defensive line, pay much more attention to the rainy weather than to the resistance of the Soviet troops. One might explain such a difference in emphasis in the memoirs by the desire to justify in hindsight their defeat around Moscow. However, when the diaries were being written their authors did not yet doubt the triumph of German arms, but nevertheless devoted a lot more attention to the weather than to the enemy's resistance. Some of them, in particular Hoth, reached the conclusion that following the formation of the Vyaz'ma and Bryansk cauldrons they should have halted and waited out the rainy weather, which actually meant the renunciation of an attempt to seize Moscow in 1941. It should be noted that the *Wehrmacht's* possible November offensive on the capital would have encountered far more Soviet forces, having been strengthened by the transfer of reinforcements and sitting behind the much-improved Mozhaisk defensive line. In these conditions, most likely the German command would not have ventured a new offensive on Moscow in 1941. If such an assault had nevertheless been undertaken, then, in all likelihood, it would have ended in failure as early as the stage of breaking through the Mozhaisk defensive line and the German forces would not have been able to reach the Moscow suburbs at the end of November. In this case, the German troops would have met the summer of 1942 in approximately the same positions as was actually the case. But they would not have experienced that defeat which they suffered during the course of the Soviet counteroffensive around Moscow, which began on 5–6 December 1941. It's difficult to say whether Stalin would have undertaken a large-scale counteroffensive around Moscow if the German forces had halted in front of the Mozhaisk defensive line and renounced their attack on Moscow. It's quite likely that the counteroffensive would have been undertaken, as we know that Stalin stubbornly attacked the Rzhev–Vyaz'ma salient throughout 1942. However, it would most likely have ended in failure and could have been concluded relatively quickly. The *Wehrmacht* would not then have experienced the bitterness of a major retreat from the gates of Moscow and would not have lost a large amount of heavy weaponry, combat equipment and auto transport. All of this had to be abandoned because of a shortage of fuel and good roads. On the other hand, the correlation of losses in this case, to all appearances, would have been more favourable for the Red Army than actually proved to be the case in the course of the Soviet counteroffensive around Moscow. It is impossible to arrive at a correlation of irreplaceable losses for the sides for December 1941. However, it is equal to 24.9:1 in January, 22.6:1 in February, 34.7:1 in March, and 28.5:1 in April, in each case in favour of the *Wehrmacht*.[53] These are record indices for the entire war. If a large-scale Soviet counteroffensive had not been undertaken in December 1941–April 1942, the Red Army would not have suffered such heavy losses. The Germans, in their turn, would have sustained far fewer losses in weapons, combat equipment, and auto transport, in that many vehicles, tanks, and guns had to be abandoned during the retreat, which was carried out under pressure from Soviet forces. However, the temporary exhaustion of the Red Army's human resources was more important for the German offensive of May–June 1942, as the German losses in weaponry and equipment did not become an obstacle for the *Wehrmacht's* new general offensive. Thus one should not claim that the alternative method of operations for the *Wehrmacht* – the renunciation of the offensive on Moscow following the rout of the Soviet forces around Vyaz'ma and Bryansk – would have yielded better results for the Germans. In any event, from the point of view of the correlation of irreplaceable losses in people, those actions that the German command undertook in October–November 1941 proved to be optimal.

By the end of November the German offensive on Moscow had burned itself out. The chief of the German General Staff, Franz Halder, noted in his diary on 29 November the opinion of the commander of Army Group Centre, Field Marshal Fedor von Bock, that 'If the ongoing offensive on Moscow does not enjoy success . . . then Moscow will become a second Verdun, that is the battle will turn into a bitter, frontal abattoir'.[54] The *Wehrmacht* was spent. And the Red Army had the opportunity to commit fresh forces into the fighting and on 5–6 December went over to a counteroffensive against Army Group Centre's flank groups of forces, which were attempting to take Moscow. The Soviet forces numbered about 1,100,000 men. The Germans had approximately the same number of officers and men. As a result of the Soviet counteroffensive, the enemy was thrown back 100–250km from Moscow. The Moscow, Tula, and Ryazan' oblasts were completely liberated, as well as a number of districts in the Kalinin, Smolensk, and Orel oblasts. However, the Soviet forces did not manage to encircle any kind of major German forces and defeat, as had been planned, Army Group Centre and eliminate the Rzhev–Vyaz'ma salient, the struggle for which continued for an entire year following the conclusion of the Battle of Moscow. In the opinion of Marshal Konstantin Rokossovskii, who commanded the 16th Army during the Battle of Moscow, the offensive should have been halted at the end of December 1941, with the capture of the Volokolamsk line, in that further on the Germans had prepared positions, the breakthrough of which should have been carefully organized as early as the spring-summer campaign, having accumulated men and materiel.[55] However, Stalin, both during the counteroffensive around Moscow, and during other offensive operations, continued to attack until his troops were completely exhausted, while hoping to wear out the enemy, although the successes achieved at the later stages in no way corresponded to the huge losses.[56] As a result of the counteroffensive around Moscow, it was not the Germans who were completely exhausted, but the Soviet forces, which predetermined the Red Army's failures during the spring-summer 1942 campaign.

The strategic significance of the Soviet victory around Moscow was that the plan for a 'lightning war' against the USSR collapsed. The Soviet Union stood firm and now a prolonged war along several fronts awaited Germany, in which the superiority in resources of the anti-Hitler coalition made the Germans' defeat inevitable. Army Group Centre was thrown back 150–200km from Moscow.

The Red Army achieved victory around Moscow at a very high price. The Battle of Moscow, one of the decisive battles of the Second World War, lasted from 30 September 1941 to 20 April 1942. There is various information on Army Group Centre's losses in this battle. The German historian Klaus Reinhardt, in his book *The Turning Point at Moscow*, cites the following data on overall losses by month: 25,000 men during 1–7 October, 23,000 during 8–16 October, 40,000 during 17 October–15 November, 41,000 during 16–30 November, 104,000 during 1–31 December, 145,000 during 1–31 January, 109,000 during 1–28 February, and 80,000 during 1–31 March. Overall losses were 796,000 men, for which there were only 331,000 replacements. Thus the overall strength of Army Group Centre decreased by 465,000 men due to losses not made up for.[57]

According to a document from the headquarters of Army Group Centre of 16 April 1942, combat losses for the period from 1 January to 31 March 1942 were 173,764 men, including 40,089 killed, 13,685 missing in action and 119,990 wounded.[58] According to Reinhardt's data, during this period the overall losses for Army Group Centre were 334,000 men or 160,000 more. The 16 April 1942 document does not contain data on the Second Army's losses, although it is impossible to imagine that it lost nearly as many men as the other five armies – two field and three panzer. Evidently, the difference arose chiefly due to non-combat losses, particularly cases of frostbite and the evacuation of the sick. Typically, the level of overall losses rises significantly, more than twice as much, during the winter months of 1941–2 and even in March the figure remains almost twice as high as in November. Here the significant increase in the number of frostbite cases and sick in the winter months plays a role.

According to the notes in F. Halder's diary, during the period from 31 December 1941 to 31 January 1942, German losses on the Eastern Front were 87,082, including 18,074 killed and 7,175 missing in action. The Red Army's irreplaceable losses (in killed and missing in action) in January 1942 were 628,000 men, which yields a loss correlation of 24.9:1. During the period from 31 January to 28 February 1942 German losses in the East were 87,651 men, including 18,776 killed and 4,355 missing in action. Soviet losses in February were 523,000 men and were 22.6 times the Germans' irreplaceable losses.

During the period from 1–31 March 1942 German losses on the Eastern Front were 102,194 men, including 12,808 killed and 5,217 missing in action. Soviet losses in March 1942 were 625,000 men killed and missing in action. This yields a record correlation of 34.7:1. In April, when the offensive began to die down, but the Soviet forces were still suffering very few losses in prisoners of war, the German losses were 60,005 men, including 12,690 killed and 2,573 missing in action. Soviet losses during this month were 435,000 killed and missing in action. This yields a correlation of 28.5:1.

These figures correspond to the data put forth in the German reports. For example, in the summary report of 14 April 1942 by the commander of the IX Army Corps, General Hans Schmidt, to the headquarters of the Fourth Panzer Army on the fighting along the corps' left flank:

> The enemy's attacks, which were conducted from 4.3.42 by seven rifle divisions and seven rifle and two tank brigades against the 252nd Infantry Division's northern flank and against the 35th Infantry Division's front for the purpose of capturing Gzhatsk, were beaten off. The enemy lost 800 prisoners in this fighting.
>
> His losses in killed, according to prisoner testimony, and according to our calculations, amount to more than 20,000 men. 36 enemy tanks were destroyed.
>
> Taking into account the favorable conditions for the enemy, one may expect that this sector of the corps (the automobile road, the main railroad and the old mail road) will remain, as before, the axis of the main attack.
>
> During the course of the fighting, from the moment we occupied winter positions, our losses were:
>
> A). killed [and wounded – this word was left out in the Russian translation, which repeated a widespread mistake by Soviet translators during the war of translating the word combination 'blood losses' (*Die blutigen Verluste*) as 'killed' instead of 'killed and wounded']–127 officers and 5,649 NCOs and enlisted men.
> B). Losses from severe frostbite and serious illnesses are more than 3,200 officers, NCOs and enlisted men.
> C). Aside from the temporary decline in combat effectiveness, brought about by the cold, light cases of frostbite and freezing, the corps' overall losses since the time it occupied winter positions are 9,000 officers, NCOs and enlisted men.
>
> Of the 27 infantry battalions of the corps' divisions, 24 are now engaged in heavy fighting ... of which 12, along with new reinforcements, have been committed into the fighting a second time.
>
> Another 3 battalions, 3 engineer battalions and 2 reconnaissance battalions (sometimes for a second time), which are not part of the corps, were committed. Some battalions have suffered up to 90% overall losses.
>
> From the time we occupied our winter position [the withdrawal of Army Group Centre's forces by 20 January 1942 to the line

Yukhnov–Gzhatsk–Zubtsov–Rzhev], the following reinforcements have arrived at the corps: 6,547 officers, NCOs and enlisted men. If these reinforcements cover the latest losses only by 2/3, then in infantry alone, if one takes as a starting point the new wartime organization (three infantry regiments of two battalions each), as a result of previous losses there is a shortage of 10,000 unfilled slots.

The corps' sector now stretches along a 46.5-kilometer front. The corps' existing combat strength is about 9,300 men. Thus there are 156 men per kilometer, or one man per 6.4 meters of front. These figures show not only the weakness of the front, but also the difficulty of creating a defence in depth and the creation of any kind of reserves.[59]

It should be noted that the German estimation of Soviet losses along the IX Army Corps' front at more than 20,000 killed during the period from 4 March–13 April 1942 appears to be sufficiently realistic. The number of killed in March for the entire Red Army was probably about 600,000 men and about 175,500 for 13 days in April. Total losses may be estimated at 756,000 men for the period from 4 March–13 April, then the losses of the Soviet forces fighting the German IX Corps (7 rifle divisions, 7 rifle battalions, and 7 tank battalions) account for about 2.6 per cent of all of the Red Army's losses in killed during the period in question. This takes into account the fact that on 1 April 1942 the active army contained 293 rifle divisions, 102 rifle brigades, 8 ski-rifle brigades, 5 independent rifle regiments, 12 fortified areas, 7 airborne brigades, 34 cavalry divisions, 1 independent cavalry regiment, and 184 independent ski battalions, 55 tank brigades, and four motorized rifle brigades.[60] Seven divisions make up 2.4 per cent of all rifle divisions, 7 rifle brigades yield 6.9 per cent of all rifle brigades, and 2 tank brigades account for 3.6 per cent of all tank brigades. However, given the absence in the group of forces of airborne, ski and cavalry units and motorized rifle brigades, its average strength, by all appearances, is from 2–3 per cent of the overall strength of the army at the front, which completely corresponds to the group of forces' share of irreplaceable losses of 2.6 per cent.

The IX Corps' losses of 5,776 killed and wounded should be counted from 21 January 1942, when the German forces around Moscow took up their winter positions, having halted their withdrawal, up until 13 April 1942. During this period the Fourth Panzer Army, to which the corps was subordinated, lost 4,090 killed and 864 missing in action, for a total of 5,954 irreplaceable losses, as well as 12,980 wounded. Overall losses were 18,934 men. Irreplaceable losses accounted for 31.4 per cent of overall losses. Of this number there were 2,386 killed and 453 missing in action, for a total of 2,839 irreplaceable losses, and 6,716 wounded from 1 March to 20 April. Overall losses were 9,555 men, or 50.5 per cent of overall losses since 21 January. Irreplaceable losses accounted for 29.7 per cent.[61] If it is assumed that that the missing in action are equivalent to killed in action, then the IX Army Corps accounts for 30.5 per cent of the Fourth Panzer Army's losses in the final report. Having assumed that during the period from 1 March to 20 April that the share of irreplaceable losses for the corps is the same as in the army, that is 50.5 per cent, then during this period the IX Army Corps should have lost 2,917 men. If it is assumed that the share of irreplaceable losses in the corps was the same as in the Fourth Panzer Army during this period, then they may be estimated at 866 men. This is 23 times less than that of the Red Army units attacking the IX Army Corps.

According to data from the Russian historian M.M. Khodorenok, the Soviet forces' losses along the Moscow direction amounted in October to 855,100 killed and captured and 104,100 wounded (most likely, the majority of wounded were captured).[62] It's likely that among the irreplaceable losses were those encircled troops who were captured but who were later liberated by the Red Army. Their overall number is estimated at 939,700 men during 1941–2. Taking into account the fact that during this period about 5,500,000 men were captured by the Germans, then something in the order of 118,000 encircled troops could have been in Army Group Centre's attack zone in October. Then the overall number of Red Army soldiers killed can be estimated at 48,100 men. This figure is probably understated, in that among those encircled there could have been those who actually escaped from captivity. We may assume that this number could be up to one-third of the overall number of those surrounded. In this case, the overall number of killed may be estimated at 87,000 men. The Red Army's overall irreplaceable losses along the Moscow direction in October may be estimated at 816,000, minus those encircled soldiers who were not captured.

Data on the *Wehrmacht's* irreplaceable losses from October 1941 to April 1942 are found in the diary of the chief of staff of the German army, General Franz Halder, but they relate to the entire Soviet-German front and not only to Army Group Centre. During the period from 30 September to 16 November 1941 German losses totalled 158,548 men, including 33,044 killed, 5,412 missing in action, and 120,092 wounded. One should note that during this period it was unlikely that the losses from frostbite had already appeared, or that there was data on those evacuated due to illness. Thus K. Reinhardt's figures for October–November 1941, which relate to Army Group Centre's overall losses, may, without major error, be taken as equal to the losses for killed, wounded, and missing in action. During the period from

30 September to 15 November they amounted to 88,000 men, or 55.5 per cent of the losses along all the fronts. If it is assumed that the share of killed and missing in action among Army Group Centre's losses was approximately the same as for the losses among all the German ground forces in the East, then the overall number of killed and missing in action in Army Group Centre during the period from 1 October to 15 November may be estimated at 21,400 men. One may also assume that during the period from the middle of October to the middle of November, that is, before the beginning of the final German offensive on Moscow, the main mass of losses, up to three-quarters, occurred during the second half of October, as during the first half of November the front was quiet. Then the number of killed and missing in action in Army Group Centre in October may be estimated at 19,000 men. The correlation of Soviet and German losses along the Moscow direction in October 1941 proves to be 42.9:1 in favour of the Germans. If it is assumed that the German losses of 19,000 men is composed almost entirely of killed, then the correlation of losses killed proves to be close to 4.6:1, also in favour of the Germans. Clearly this correlation is low, in that Soviet losses in killed in October, which were suffered during the German breakthrough of the Mozhaisk defensive line, which was outside the zone of the Vyaz'ma–Bryansk encirclement, were not taken into account. If it is assumed that they were at least not less than the losses in killed in the Vyaz'ma and Bryansk cauldrons, then the overall number of Red Army soldiers killed in October comes to no less than 174,000, and the correlation of losses killed increases to 9.2:1.

Accurate data on Soviet losses in November and December 1941 are missing. In 1993 the famous military historian and adviser to the Russian president, D.A. Volkogonov, published data on the Red Army's irreplaceable losses for 1942, broken up by month. In January they were 435,000 killed and missing in action.[63] As any kind of reliable data on the Red Army's losses during the Battle of Moscow is absent, then it makes sense to compare only the size of the Soviet and German losses.

It's more complex to define Soviet losses around Moscow in November and December 1941. These will be estimated as follows. Let's assume that Army Group Centre's losses in November and December, as was the case in October, accounted for 55.5 per cent of all German losses in the East. According to Halder's diary, the losses for the army in the East from 6 November to 31 December amounted to 144,795 men, including 28,539 killed, 7,022 missing in action, and 109,234 wounded. Then Army Group Centre would have suffered about 19,700 killed and missing in action. Let's take the correlation of losses killed of 9.2:1, established for October, and take it as applying to all irreplaceable losses in November and December. Then the Soviet forces' irreplaceable losses in the Battle of Moscow in November and December may be estimated at 181,000 men. It is not excluded that they are understated, particularly as regards December, when during the Red Army's counteroffensive the correlation of irreplaceable losses was probably closer to what it was in January–March 1942, all the more so as the Germans had almost no losses in men captured.

It is estimated that the Red Army's total losses during the Battle of Moscow were 3,182,000 killed and captured. It should be stressed that the overwhelming majority of those captured around Vyaz'ma and Bryansk did not survive the winter of 1941–2. It is estimated that the *Wehrmacht's* total losses around Moscow were 118,000 men. The correlation of irreplaceable losses is thus 27:1 in favour of the Germans.

The correlation of losses looked as follows in some of the divisions. It completely confirms the overall figures and proves that the correlation of the sides' losses in killed in the Battle of Moscow, as was the case in other battles that took place at the end of 1941 and beginning of 1942, was of a different order. On 1 November 1941 the 154th Rifle Division around Tula suffered 106 irreplaceable losses – 88 killed and 18 missing in action.[64] Guderian's Second Panzer Group, which was opposite, suffered only three times as many irreplaceable losses during the period from 1–10 November – 323 men, with 237 killed and 86 missing in action.[65] During the first ten days the Second Panzer Group was engaged in both defensive and offensive fighting.

To the south, in the area of the Severskii Donets River, A.V. Gorbatov's 226th Rifle Division, which was part of the 21st Army, lost 21 killed, 25 missing in action, and 89 wounded during the fighting on 28 November.[66] The losses of the opposing German Sixth Army for the ten-day period from 21–30 November 1941 proved to be not much higher – 58 killed, 32 missing in action, and 173 wounded.[67] This yields a correlation of 2:1 in irreplaceable losses and 1.9:1 in wounded in favour of the Soviet division. However, it must be taken into account that the German Sixth Army numbered some fifteen divisions, which were engaged in fighting, and not only on 28 November.

The same 226th Rifle Division lost 10 killed, 18 missing in action, and 39 wounded in the fighting on 5 December.[68] This time its losses proved to be comparable with the losses of the entire German Sixth Army for the period from 1–10 December – 59 killed, 12 missing in action, and 136 wounded.[69] As for missing in action, the division even won that competition, having lost one-and-a-half times more than the army. The correlation of irreplaceable losses was 2.5:1 and 3.5:1 in wounded in favour of the division.

The German Sixth Army's contest in losses with the 226th Rifle Division continued in March 1942, although the division was now part of the

38th Army. During this month the division lost more than 3,000 men killed and wounded.[70] The German Sixth Army lost during this time 1,690 killed and 5,432 wounded, which yields a total of 7,122 men, or 2.4 times the division's losses. This correlation would most likely have been equal if there had been a possibility of taking into account Soviet losses in missing in action. The German Sixth Army lost only 308 men missing in action in March 1942.[71] It's quite possible that in March the 226th Rifle Division's losses in missing in action even exceeded this figure. It should be noted that at this time three Soviet armies – 21st, 38th, and 6th – were fighting against the German Sixth Army. There are absolutely no grounds to suppose that the 226th Rifle Division's losses were greater than the losses of the other Soviet divisions fighting against the German Sixth Army in March 1942.

The German Second Panzer Army's losses in January–March 1942 in killed, wounded, and missing in action may be estimated at one-fifth of the losses of Army Group Centre's remaining 5 armies, or 34,760 men, with all of Army Group Centre's combat losses at 212,500 men, including 64,500 killed and missing in action. According to Halder's diary, the German army's losses in the East during the period from 1 January–31 March 1942 were 276,927 men, including 49,831 killed, 201,624 wounded, and 16,647 missing in action. Of the 66,478 killed and missing in action during this period, Army Group Centre accounted for 64,500 men, or 96.7 per cent. If it is assumed that the same percentage of Soviet irreplaceable losses for this period occurred during the Battle of Moscow, then these may be estimated at 1,717,400 men. Here killed predominate, because compared with October 1941, there were relatively few captured. The correlation of irreplaceable losses is 26.6:1 in favour of the Germans. One may assume that approximately the same correlation of irreplaceable losses along the Moscow direction was unchanged in April 1942. German losses in April 1942, according to Halder's diary, were 60,005 men, including 12,680 killed, 2,573 missing in action, and 44,752 wounded. Of the 15,253 killed and missing in action, Army Group Centre seemingly accounts for 14,750 men. Soviet losses in killed and missing in action in this month may be estimated at 420,600 men. One should take into account that the correlation of losses of 26.6:1 is somewhat exaggerated in favour of the Germans, insofar as Volkogonov's data includes air force and national air defence losses, as well as, possibly, those wounded who died in rear-area hospitals, while Halder's data does not include losses by the *Luftwaffe* and those who died from their wounds. However, it's not likely that this factor materially changes the overall correlation of irreplaceable losses.

The fact that the volume of Soviet irreplaceable losses during the course of the Moscow counteroffensive, which began in December and which grew into an offensive along all the fronts, was enormous, which is testified to by those few surviving veterans, who personally took part in the attacks. For example, Guards Captain A.I. Shumilin, the former commander of a rifle company, recalled: 'Not just one hundred thousand soldiers and thousands of junior officers passed through the division. Of these thousands, only a few remained alive.' He recalls one of his 119th Rifle Division's battles on the Kalinin Front during the counteroffensive around Moscow:

> On the night of 10–11 December 1941 we reached the Mar'ino area and lay down along the jumping off position in the snow before the village. We were told that following two shots from a 45mm gun we were to rise up and move on the village. It was already getting light. There were no shots. I asked by telephone what the matter was and was ordered to wait a bit. The Germans rolled out anti-aircraft batteries for firing over open sights and began firing on the soldiers lying in the snow. Everyone who ran off was blown to pieces at the same moment. The snowy field was covered with bloody corpses, bits of meat, blood and splattered guts. Out of 800 men only two got out by evening. Interesting, does there exist a list of the rank and file for 11 December 1941? After all, no one of the staff officers saw this massacre. All of these participants disappeared wherever they could with the first shot from the anti-aircraft guns. They didn't even know that they were firing on the soldiers with anti-aircraft guns.[72]

And this is how it was viewed from the German side. Heinrich Happe, a doctor with the 3rd Battalion/18th Regiment/6th Infantry Division, which repulsed a Soviet attack on 27 December 1941 in the village of Shchitnikovo, in the Kalinin Oblast's Staritsa District, wrote in his memoirs:

> There were about a thousand Russians and two hundred of us. The machine guns along the road brought down their fire on the thinned-out woods, from which this terrible enemy wave would roll down on us. Many Russians fell, cut down by these bursts; a larger number of them nevertheless broke through and came right under fire from our automatic rifles and rifles. In the bright moonlight, plus rocket flares, the storm of our aimed fire personified death itself, and as a result the Russians faltered and began to fall back.
>
>   Our superbly trained and prepared artillery spotter directed this fire precisely into that sector of the woods where the Russians were retreating . . .

This slaughter lasted for five and a half hours until the Russians grew tired of it and fell back, while attempting to drag some of their wounded back.

But more than a hundred of them nevertheless remained on the bloodied snow right in front of the houses we were defending. Our losses were four killed and six wounded.

The following morning we discovered a significant number of dead Russians still in the woods. These were mostly wounded, who had been abandoned by their comrades during the retreat. More than a hundred of them, who were not in a condition to crawl back to their positions because of their wounds, froze to death. Regrouping their forces, the Russians attacked us again and again, but each time were halted and thrown back by defensive fire from our machine guns, automatic rifles and rifle. Nor did our light artillery weapons and mortars, of course, play the second fiddle here.[73]

It should be noted that Haape wrote his memoirs on the basis of diary entries and that because of his position he was the one who was responsible for keeping tabs on his battalion's losses. If he estimated the Russian losses accurately, then it means that no less than 200 Soviet soldiers were killed attacking, without artillery support along terrain previously registered by the Germans, versus 4 Germans killed.

The 10th Army's 323rd Rifle Division along the Western Front lost 3,060 men, including 496 killed, 1,200 missing in action, 1,294 wounded, and 70 ill in 3 days of offensive fighting, from 17–19 December 1941.[74] As the division was attacking, the overwhelming majority of those missing in action should be added to the number of those killed. The German Second Panzer Army, which was opposing the Soviet 10th Army during the period from 11–20 December, lost only 295 killed, 123 missing in action, and 1,324 wounded.[75] This yields a correlation of irreplaceable losses for a German army (418) and a Soviet division (1,696) of 4.1:1 in favour of the Germans. At the same time, one must take into account that the 10th Army included seven rifle and two cavalry divisions, not counting army reinforcement units, and that all of them, as was the case with the 323rd Rifle Division, suffered significant losses not only during 17–19 December, but also during the 11–16 December period. For example, in the fighting on 11 December, during the course of its turn to the south toward the town of Yepifan' and the inhabited locale of Lupishki, the 323rd Rifle Division lost 78 men killed, 153 wounded, and up to 200 missing in action. And during 17–19 December the 323rd Rifle Division, along with the 10th Army's other divisions, was successfully attacking, by Soviet standards, the German defensive line along the Upa River. And by the time of its arrival at the next line, the

Plava River, the 323rd Rifle Division was by no means the most battered of the 10th Army's divisions, which were fully up to strength before the start of the Moscow counteroffensive. There remained 7,613 men in the 323rd Rifle Division, while in the neighbouring 326th only 6,238 were left.[76] Taking this into account, the irreplaceable losses for the entire 10th Army for the 10-day period could have exceeded the 323rd Rifle Division's losses in 3 days of fighting by 20 to 25 times, and the irreplaceable losses of the opposing German forces by 80 to 100 times.

Taking the example of the same 323rd Rifle Division, one is persuaded of just how incomplete was the individual (nominal) account of irreplaceable losses in the Red Army. According to the division report, the 10th Army's (Western Front) 323rd Rifle Division during three days of fighting (17–19 December 1941) lost 3,060 men, including 496 killed, 1,200 missing in action, 1,294 wounded, and 70 men ill.[77] However, in the nominal reports on losses, which included only killed who died during this period, there are only 90 men, that is, 18.1 per cent of the number of those killed and only 5.3 per cent of the overall number of irreplaceable losses.[78] Aleksandr Shumilin, the former company commander, attests: 'We suffered heavy losses and would then receive new reinforcements. New people would appear each week in the company. Could you really remember their surnames in this human flood? You often don't recognize your own soldiers!'[79] This is why the nominal account was so incomplete. The German Second Panzer Army, which was opposing the 323rd Rifle Division from 11–20 December 1941, lost only 295 killed, 123 missing in action, and 1,324 wounded.[80]

During the course of the Battle of Moscow the Red Army's 413th Rifle Division lost 2,052 men killed and missing in action in the fighting around Tula from 2–11 November 1941.[81] During the period from 1–20 November the entire German Second Panzer Army lost only 597 killed and missing in action.[82] The 1st Guards Cavalry Corps also lost 1,478 men around Tula during the period from 8–14 December 1941.[83] The German Second Panzer Army's losses from 1–20 December totaled 587 killed and missing in action.[84] On 14 December the 1089th Rifle Regiment's 3rd Battalion lost 150 men killed.[85] The irreplaceable losses for the entire German Second Panzer Army for the period from 11–20 December were only 2.8 times more – 418 men.[86]

During the fighting for the Warsaw highway from 9–22 February 1942, the 413th Rifle Division lost 1,761 men killed and missing in action.[87] The opposing German Fourth Army lost from 1–28 February 3,882 men killed and missing in action, or 2.2 times more, while the army included 14 divisions and they were involved in fighting throughout February.[88]

During 5–6 March 1942 the 385th Rifle Division irreplaceably lost 828 men in the area of Zaitsev hill.[89] Its opponent – the German Fourth Army – lost 1,137 killed and missing in action from 1–10 March, or 309 men more.[90]

During 29–30 March 1942 the 116th Rifle Division lost 704 men killed near the Warsaw highway.[91] The opposing German Fourth Army lost 628 men killed and 156 missing in action from 21–31 March.[92] Here the 239th Rifle Division lost from 5–25 April 1942 9,923 killed and missing in action.[93] This exceeds by exactly five times the irreplaceable losses of the German Fourth Army for April 1942, which numbered 1,974 men.[94] This example completely illustrated the fanciful quality of the official figures for losses, according to which during the Rzhev–Vyaz'ma operation, which lasted from 8 January–20 April 1942, the Western and Kalinin fronts irreplaceably lost 272,329 men.[95] It works out that one division during an incomplete month suffered 3.6 per cent, or about one-thirtieth of the overall number of irreplaceable losses of two *fronts* over three-and-a-half months. At the same time, at the beginning of the operation both *fronts* had 95 divisions and 46 brigades, while during the operation another 29 divisions and 33 brigades were committed. If it is assumed that each formation took part, on average, in the fighting for at least a month and, for the sake of argument, take two brigades as being equal to a division, it works out that if each division irreplaceably lost, on average, per month as many men as the 239th Rifle Division in April, then the overall losses of the two *fronts* during the operation may be estimated at 1,630,600 men. Army Group Centre, from 1 January–30 April 1942, lost 43,629 men killed and missing in action.[96] Of course, the strength of Soviet divisions varied. The 239th Rifle Division evidently was at full strength at the beginning of April and probably managed to receive reinforcements during the fighting. Many divisions and brigades could have had a smaller strength. But this factor is to some degree compensated for by the condition that each formation took part in the fighting only by month. After all, there were divisions and brigades which took part in the fighting for two and for all three-and-a-half months.

The 56th Army's 13th Rifle Division lost 638 men on 27 January 1942 in the fighting for the inhabited locale of Novoselovskii, in the Rostov Oblast', while the opposing German First Panzer Army lost only 562 men from 21–31 January.[97]

Loking at the north, there the 376th Rifle Division, in the offensive fighting along the Volkhov River from 30 December 1941 to 24 January 1942, when it was pulled out of the line, lost 15,000 men killed, wounded, and missing in action. During this time the division was pulled out for replenishing and received 12,000 reinforcements.[98] The authorized strength of a rifle division was established in August 1941 at 11,447 men, of which by 1 January 1942 there remained a total of 10,530 in the 376th Rifle Division, which leads one to assume that the division's true losses were approximately 5,000 more than listed in its 'History' (15,000). By comparison, the German Eighteenth Army, which was opposing four armies (4th, 59th, 2nd Shock, and 52nd) of the Volkhov Front and the Leningrad Front's 54th Army, lost only 9,475 men from 1 January–31 January 1942, including 2,381 irreplaceably. Moreover, only part of this army was operating along the Volkhov River, while the other part was facing the Leningrad Front's main forces. Certainly, active combat operations were not being waged around Leningrad at this time. Even if the losses during the last ten days of December – 3,705 men, including 739 irreplaceably – are added to this, it means that the Eighteenth Army suffered only 13,180 men killed, wounded, and missing in action, which is even lower than the officially recognized losses of the 376th Rifle Division for the same period.[99] There were more than forty divisions within the five Soviet armies, as well as a significant number of brigades and other independent units. One may assume that, by taking into account reinforcements, about 1,000,000 men fought against part of the German Eighteenth Army's forces during the period from the last ten days of December 1941 to the end of January 1942.

The naval infantry brigades, which were poorly trained for fighting on land, also suffered huge losses. For example, the 76th Naval Infantry Brigade, which formed part of the 56th Army in the fighting along the Mius River, lost from 8–10 March 1942 1,632 men killed, wounded, and missing in action.[100] The opposing German First Panzer Army lost 596 men killed, 1,804 wounded ,and 140 missing in action, for a total of 2,540 men in the first 10 days of March, which was only 1.6 times more than the losses of the 76th Naval Infantry Brigade in 3 days of fighting.[101]

Its neighbour, the 68th Naval Infantry Brigade, which was also attacking during the Taganrog operation, lost 639 men killed and 1,893 wounded and missing in action, or 2,532 men, from 8–17 March.[102] The Germans' First Panzer Army lost 238 men killed, 747 wounded, and 10 missing in action during the second 10 days of March 1942. In all, this army lost 3,535 men during the first 20 days of March 1942, while the losses of the 2 Soviet naval infantry brigades for, correspondingly, 3 and 10 days of fighting amounted to 4,164 men, that is, 1.2 times more. As G.K. Puzhaev notes:

> On 8 March, the first day of the offensive, 772 men were killed and 1,728 soldiers and officers wounded, according to the army head-quarters. There were many cases of frostbite. If you calculate the losses for that day according to data from the units and formations, then the number of killed and wounded greatly exceeded the given figures . . . There existed a practice in the army that reports were often corrected as they went from bottom to top and our losses were understated and the enemy's were exaggerated.[103]

One may agree with this conclusion. On 1 March 1942 the 56th Army included four rifle divisions, two rifle brigades, one fortified area, and one independent rifle regiment, as well as a number of artillery and other specialized units.[104] By the start of the offensive the 56th Army was additionally reinforced by the 3rd Guards Rifle Corps, consisting of one rifle division, three brigades of naval infantry, and one rifle brigade, as well as one tank brigade.[105] During the first twenty days of March one rifle brigade remained in reserve and took no part in the fighting. Four rifle divisions, four rifle, and one tank brigade formed the shock group, which suffered the main part of the losses. The remaining formations waged holding actions. If the 76th Naval Infantry Brigade alone lost 1,312 men on 8 March, then the 56th Army's remaining 11 formations, not counting the fortified area, the independent rifle regiment, and the 102nd Rifle Brigade, which took no part in combat operations during the first 20 days of March, remaining in the 3rd Guards Rifle Corps' reserve, are responsible for a total of 188 losses, which is completely unrealistic.[106] On 8 March 1942 the 30th Rifle Division's 71st Rifle Regiment alone lost 100 men killed and more than 200 wounded.[107]

If it is assumed that during the first 20 days of March each of the 56th Army's formations suffered losses no less than that of the 68th Naval Infantry Brigade for the period from 8–17 March and at the same time take the fortified area, the independent rifle regiment, and the tank brigade as one formation, then it may be estimated that the 56th Army's overall losses were 27,900 men, of which no less than 7,000 alone were killed. During this period the German First Panzer Army lost 3,535 men, including 834 killed. According to overall losses, the correlation is 7.9:1 and 8.4:1 in killed in favour of the Germans. However, if the correlation according to irreplaceable losses, taking into account those missing in action, of which the overwhelming majority were Soviet, as they were attacking, should in this case be consigned to those killed, then the actual correlation will be even more favourable for the German side. After all, in the period under examination the German First Panzer Army lost only 150 men missing in action. According to the data from an operational report by the headquarters of the 3rd Guards Rifle Corps at 19:00 on 9 March, during the fighting on 8–9 March the 76th Naval Infantry Brigade lost 138 men killed and 1,381 wounded, and the 2nd Guards Rifle Division 118 killed, 309 wounded, and 194 missing in action. The division also lost two damaged 76mm guns and seventeen horses killed and eleven wounded. The 63rd Tank Brigade lost six men killed and eleven wounded. Three KV tanks were burned and five knocked out.[108] As the report noted, 'There was no information on the remaining units. Losses are being elaborated.'[109]

One should not doubt that in the remaining units, and this includes two naval infantry brigades, the losses were no less than in the 76th Naval Infantry Brigade. For example, during 9–10 March the 81st Naval Infantry Brigade lost 2,350 men.[110] And the 76th Naval Infantry Brigade probably had large losses among the missing in action. Otherwise, it appears that there were ten wounded for each man killed – a correlation highly unlikely for the Red Army and for the Second World War as a whole. By the way, the total of killed and missing in action in the 2nd Guards Rifle Division – 312 men – even exceeds the number of wounded – 309 men. And this division alone lost 1.3 times more in two days of fighting than did the entire German First Panzer Army in twenty days. Obviously, the 76th Naval Infantry Brigade's losses of 1,638 men for 8–10 March have been given without taking into account the missing in action and have been reduced, at a minimum, by one-and-a-half times. If it is assumed that in the 68th Naval Infantry Brigade's losses for the period from 8–17 March the number of wounded is approximately equal to the number of killed, as was the case with the 3rd Guards Rifle Division, then the number of missing in action in this brigade may be estimated at 627 men for this period. If the losses in missing in action for the remaining formations were approximately the same, then the 56th Army's overall losses for the first twenty days of March 1942 may be estimated at 6,900 men. Then the correlation of irreplaceable losses will be 14.1:1 in favour of the Germans.

According to V.I. Afanasenko's estimate, the losses for the 56th Army's shock group during the period from 8 March–10 March amounted to more than 5,000 killed and about 10,000 wounded and frostbitten. According to his data, the 81st Naval Infantry Brigade lost 2,350 men killed and wounded during 15–16 March, and the 68th Naval Infantry Brigade 2,629 killed and wounded during 14–16 March.[111] Evidently the losses of the two brigades were even larger, if the missing in action are counted.

During the Taganrog offensive operation, from 8 March to 2 April 1942, the 2nd Guards Rifle Division's losses, according to the summary report, are estimated at 5,738 killed, wounded, and missing in action. The enemy's losses during the Taganrog operation, according to the latest estimate by the Southern Front headquarters, were 17 captured and 1,555 killed.[112] This estimate seems close to the truth, although somewhat exaggerated. The German First Panzer Army's losses for March 1942 were 941 killed and 169 missing in action. Another 93 men killed, 344 wounded, and 1 missing in action were lost in the first 10 days of April.[113] If the 17 men captured from the number of missing in action are subtracted, then the overall number of killed may be estimated at 1,186 men, which is only 1.3 times less than the estimate of the Southern Front's headquarters. If it is assumed that at the final stage of the Taganrog operation from 21 March to 2 April the same correlation of losses in killed was maintained as at the beginning of the operation, then Soviet losses in killed for the entire Taganrog operation may be placed at 16,700 men. The overall losses probably exceeded 30,000 men.

And here's an instance in which a single Soviet battalion suffered losses in one day comparable to the opposing German army for ten days. According to the former operational representative of the special section of the 12th Rifle Brigade's 3rd Rifle Battalion (51st Army), L.G. Ivanov, on 9 April, during the unsuccessful assault against the Ak-Monai positions, this battalion lost about 600 men killed and wounded.[114] The German Eleventh Army, which was opposite the battalion, lost 175 men killed, 719 wounded, and 20 missing in action, for a total of 914 men, during the period from 1–10 April 1942, which is only 1.5 times less than the losses of the 12th Rifle Brigade's 3rd Rifle Battalion for the single day of 9 April.[115] One may assume that about half of the 3rd Battalion's losses were irreplaceable ones. It would then exceed the losses of the Eleventh Army's German divisions suffered for the ten days. There were also Romanian units in the German Eleventh Army, but in this case their losses do not have great importance, insofar as the 12th Rifle Brigade attacked the positions of the German forces. There were eighty-one battalions in the Eleventh Army's nine German divisions. These divisions had to repel the Soviet offensive on the Kerch' peninsula, not only on 9 April, but also on 3, 4, and 10 April. Besides this, the troops besieging Sevastopol' were fighting as well. According to Ivanov, their brigade was a regular one and even enjoyed deserved fame along the entire front.

In practice, the training level for the regular cadre units was practically just as low as for the militia units.

The most striking thing about the Battle of Moscow is probably that the *Wehrmacht* command did not commit any material mistakes, but nevertheless lost. Many German generals following the war reproached Hitler for not beginning the offensive as early as August, preferring to first destroy the Kiev group of Soviet forces. However, an August offensive would not have led to a German victory. In this case, the Soviet Southwestern Front would either have been employed for an offensive against the flank of Army Group Centre, or a significant part of its forces would have been transferred to the Moscow direction. In either case, the Germans would have had to destroy this group of forces and realistically the offensive on Moscow could have begun no earlier than October, and probably with the same results as in the course of Operation 'Typhoon'. The German command also could have foregone launching a new offensive on Moscow in mid-November and pulled back its forces to winter quarters. This would have enabled them to avoid the significant losses in equipment which Army Group Centre suffered during the course of the Soviet counteroffensive. Then they had to abandon a lot of tanks, automobiles, and artillery pieces due to a lack of fuel and the difficulties of moving along the winter roads. But, in principle, the renunciation of an offensive on Moscow would have nevertheless meant the factual collapse of the *blitzkrieg*. The Soviet totalitarian regime proved to be in a position as early as the first year of the war to mobilize more resources, particularly human ones, than Nazi Germany and to preserve control of its armies and government even during the most severe defeats. This enabled them to halt the *blitzkrieg*, the collapse of which conformed to objective reality.

Zhukov puts forth hair-raising data on the losses among the tank troops. According to the data in G.K. Zhukov's order of 19 February 1942, by the beginning of the December counteroffensive the Western Front had 709 tanks in 9 tank brigades. By 15 February there remained 153 machines in action. There were 586 losses, including 322 irreplaceably.[116] Incidentally, the total losses and those remaining in line do not equal 709, but 739 machines. Either Georgii Konstantinovich made a counting error, or during the course of the offensive the brigades received a reinforcement of thirty new tanks. By way of comparison, the entire German army in the East lost 951 tanks in December 1941 and January 1942, or 1.6 times more than the Western Front's 9 brigades.[117]

As for the *Luftwaffe*, according to available data, irreplaceable losses due to combat in 1941 in the East were 2,093 machines of all types, including 267 non-combat aircraft. Another 1,362 aircraft, including 473 bombers and 413 fighters, were damaged in combat. Non-combat losses amounted to 382 destroyed and damaged machines.[118] In 1941 the Soviet air force lost irreplaceably 17,900 combat aircraft (not counting reconnaissance planes), including 10,300 machines lost in combat.[119] During the Moscow defensive battle irreplaceable losses from combat causes alone were 293 aircraft.[120] If it is assumed that in the Moscow defensive battle the share of irreplaceable combat losses of the *Luftwaffe's* combat aircraft of all losses in the East in 1941 was approximately the same as the Red Army Air Force, then German irreplaceable combat losses during the conduct of Operation 'Typhoon' may be estimated at twenty-eight machines. However, during the offensive on Moscow the *Luftwaffe's* losses proved to be considerably higher. According to German data, the *Luftwaffe's* 51st Fighter Squadron lost (destroyed and damaged) 14 machines from 22–31 October, while the entire Second Air Fleet lost 105 machines from 2–10 October, of which no less than 29 were lost irreplaceably due to combat. Another 11 machines were missing in action, while 19 aircraft were irreplaceably lost due to non-combat reasons.

Even taking into account the fact that the data here refers to the period of the most intensive fighting in the air, it is obvious that the *Luftwaffe's* irreplaceable losses were significantly greater than the calculated figure. During the course of the offensive on Moscow, the *Luftwaffe's* losses were relatively greater than the average for the campaign in the East in 1941.[121]

On 7 November 1941 Hitler admitted during a meeting with the leadership that the seizure of the Caucasus and, most likely, the central area along with Moscow, would have to be moved to 1942. As early as 19 November he was saying that the war would end with a compromise peace. Taking this into account, there was no sense or possibility of throwing all forces into the Eastern Front. To completely expose France, Norway, and the Balkans could not be done. In this case, the threat of a British landing would increase, and the position of the French government under Petain might change for the worse for Germany.[122] Rommel had two German panzer divisions in North Africa.[123] There was no way these could be removed from there, as this would mean turning over North Africa to the British. Another two panzer divisions were in the OKH reserve, primarily in the event of a British landing across the English Channel or in the Balkans. When this threat had passed, both divisions were transferred to the Eastern Front in October and took part in Operation 'Typhoon'. And even if Hitler had risked setting aside another fifteen to twenty divisions, this could have taken place no earlier than the end of September when, according to weather conditions, the threat of a landing across the Channel would have vanished. But these divisions were actually transferred to the Eastern Front at the end of 1941 and the beginning of 1942, but they made no difference and only helped to halt the Soviet counteroffensive.

During the Battle of Moscow for the first time the Stalinist strategy of burying the enemy with corpses brought about a strategic success. For the first time since the beginning of the campaign in Russia, the German army was forced to undertake a full-scale retreat. The plan for a 'lightning war' against the USSR had been foiled. Stalin hoped that his strategy would subsequently bring only victories and counted on concluding the war in 1942.

Chapter 5

The Battles for Stalingrad and the Caucasus

Did Hitler Have an Alternative?

Another alternative development of events is linked to the course of the fighting in 1942, which in the final analysis led to the destruction of Friedrich Paulus's army in Stalingrad.[1] It's common to blame Stalin for the fact that in the summer of this year he expected the Germans' main attack not in the south, but along the Moscow direction. Actually, however, it was precisely a German campaign against Moscow that presented the greatest danger to the Red Army. Only German troops would have taken part in this campaign from the Rzhev or Vyaz'ma bridgeheads, which occupied a flanking position vis-à-vis the Western and Kalinin fronts' forces. Thus, given the concentration of a sufficient amount of men and materiel, there would have been a very good chance of encircling and destroying a significant part of the Soviet forces defending along the western direction and to occupy a comparatively short front line 100–50km east of Moscow. In this case, the likelihood of Leningrad's fall and the destruction of a significant part of the Leningrad Front's forces would also have been high. In this case, the Germans would most likely have limited themselves to seizing the Taman' peninsula and Rostov in the south. In choosing such a strategy the Germans would be seeking to destroy significant Soviet forces and shortening the front line. Only with such a strategy did the *Wehrmacht* have even a minimal chance of significantly weakening Soviet resistance.

The German Operation 'Blau' called for seizing the Baku oilfields and reaching the Volga River. The prerequisite for the successful achievement of this plan was the defeat of the Southwestern and Southern fronts' main forces before the Germans reached the line of the Don River along the entire length of the front from Voronezh to Rostov. This, as is known, did not happen, which to a great degree predetermined the German forces' campaign all the way to Stalingrad in the hope of grinding up the Soviet troops' main forces in the battle for this city. Stalingrad initially was not among the priority goals of Plan *Blau*. It was assumed that following the German forces' arrival in the great bend of the Don River, they would be able, with the aid of the *Luftwaffe*, to fully put Stalingrad out of commission as an industrial and transportation centre. It was planned to seize the city later, only following the capture of Baku, when the quick weakening of Soviet resistance could be expected. In principle, one may allow that if Plan *Blau* had not been altered by the addition of the campaign to seize the Western Caucasus for the purpose of taking the Black Sea ports, and if the operations to encircle the Soviet forces during its opening phase had been better carried out, with the emphasis namely on encircling and destroying and not the seizure of this or that city, then it would have been possible to eliminate the Soviet troops' main forces west of the Don River. If the forces of Germany and its satellites had limited themselves to a campaign against Maikop and Baku, having taken up a defensive position along the Don River without attempting to attack Stalingrad, then the opportunity for them to take the Baku oilfields would have arisen as early as September. But this would not have led to the collapse of Soviet resistance. Then the Red Army would have retained the Volga River area and the Western Caucasus and would not have suffered the heavy losses while defending Stalingrad they actually did.

It's impossible to say for sure if the Germans would have managed to take Baku, even if they had renounced the offensive on Stalingrad. After all, in this case the Soviet command could have thrown into the defence of the Caucasian passes those forces that it actually ground down while defending Stalingrad.

Having been deprived of Baku, the USSR would have begun to receive oil and oil-related products from Iran, which the *Wehrmacht* lacked the strength to seize. And the Americans would have generously shared their oil. Thus the weakening of the Red Army would have lasted half a year, or a year at most, and because of this the Second World War in Europe would have lasted another half year. The USSR's dependence on the Allies would have increased. In any event, as Solonin has well shown, the USSR was already heavily reliant on Lend-Lease deliveries, particularly as regards aviation fuel, aluminum, explosives, and machine tools. If it is said that the Soviets would have won anyway without the Allies by fighting another year or year-and-a-half, this is fantasy. They would not have had the manpower for such a prolonged war. The correlation of Soviet and German losses and the fact that usually the losses of Soviet divisions are compared with those of German armies illustrates this well.

Even had the Germans in 1942 by some kind of miracle managed to seize Stalingrad and the Caucasus, and then Moscow, with Soviet resistance significantly weakened, this would have led neither to the Red Army completely ceasing to resist nor Germany's victory in the Second World War. In this case, a semi-partisan war would have continued in the East similar to the one Chiang Kai-shek's government was waging against the Japanese in China and which, following the loss of the major cities, was based in Chungking.

Kuibyshev or Sverdlovsk (now Yekaterinburg) could have become the Soviet Chungking. Taking into account that Stalin would still have disposed of the industrial bases in the Urals, the Volga area, and Siberia, as well as small oil deposits beyond the Volga, as well as Lend-Lease deliveries over the Far Eastern and possibly the northern and Iranian routes, Soviet resistance would have remained sufficiently serious and required the presence in the East of up to sixty to seventy divisions. But even such a favourable development of events would not have brought Hitler victory in the Second World War. Germany's economic potential was not comparable with that of the USA and Great Britain.

On the other hand, the defeat of the USSR would have helped Hitler little in his struggle with Great Britain and the USA. It was difficult to reorient industry to the needs of the air force and navy, nor can Germany's industrial opportunities be compared with those of American industry. For the *Wehrmacht* a landing on the British Isles would nonetheless have remained an unattainable dream.

And the war would then have ended in the autumn of 1945 or, at worst, at the beginning of 1946 with the atomic bombardment of German cities by the Americans. The Americans would not have put off an atomic bombardment, insofar as they did not know that the Germans were behind them in developing an atomic bomb by two-and-a-half years. It's likely that if the Americans had carried out the atomic bombing of Germany, Hitler probably would not have surrendered after just two bombs, as was the case with the Japanese government. It's possible that it would have been necessary to drop ten to twelve bombs on Germany and turn all of the major German cities into radioactive ruins. Then it's possible that there would have been no German economic miracle following the war and that France and Italy would have played the role of the chief states of the European Union following the war. Incidentally, if the Allies had not landed in Normandy in June 1944 but had postponed the landing until 1945, then they would not have succeeded in defeating Germany before the autumn of 1945 and the atomic bomb scenario would have become timely.

But the Soviet Union's geopolitical situation in this case would have been completely different. Stalin would then have been in the kind of condition Chiang Kai-shek was in at the end of the war. In the best case, the Soviet Union would have remained within the boundaries that existed as of 1 September 1939. It is not impossible that in such a scenario the USSR would have fallen apart and the processes that began in 1991 would have begun in 1946.

Both Stalin and the former commander of the Western Front, Georgii Zhukov, understood all the advantages of a German offensive on Moscow. Thus they repeatedly attacked the Rzhev and Vyaz'ma bridgeheads, attempting to defeat Army Group Centre. Quite the opposite, in the south, in the event of an advance on Stalingrad and the Caucasus, the length of the front line more than doubled. The Germans' single hope for success was linked to an attempt to encircle and destroy the Soviet troops' main forces close to the old front line, in the areas of Rostov-on-Don and Voronezh. Then one might have achieved the offensive's stated goals, while counting on meeting weak resistance by the Red Army. However, the commanders of the Southwestern and Southern fronts, Semyon Timoshenko and Rodion Malinovskii, who had learned from the bitter experience of the Khar'kov disaster, were able to pull back their forces, which cost them their commands and brought about Stalin's famous order No. 227.[2] However, as a result of this, a sufficient number of Soviet troops fell back to the foothills of the Caucasus, and to Stalingrad and Voronezh, in order, upon being reinforced with reserves, to hold the Germans, although with heavy losses. The *Wehrmacht* was forced in the south to rely to a greater degree on the Romanian, Hungarian, and Italian troops, who were much less combat-capable than the Germans.

It is of interest that in the evaluation of the American secretary of war in the event of a Soviet capitulation during the second half of 1942, the Western Allies would have had to form a 700–900 division army with an overall strength of 25 million men, in order to defeat the Axis powers in Europe.[3] The Austro-Czech historian Denis Havlat quite justly calls these figures fantastic, in that the USA was not able to mobilize for the armed forces more than 10 per cent of the population, that is, 13.5 million men, otherwise they would have been forced to curtail industrial production.[4] More than likely, these numerical calculations had only propaganda value, in order to convince the opposition in Congress of the necessity of increasing Lend-Lease deliveries to the USSR. Realistically, in the event of a Soviet capitulation the Allies would have put the emphasis on an air war, and naval blockade, and the gradual increase of the ground forces along all the fronts.

The final opportunity for realizing alternative scenarios for the Second World War arose in the summer of 1942 during the *Wehrmacht's* conduct of Operation '*Blau*' – the plan for an offensive along the southern wing of the Eastern Front, which called for the seizure of the Baku oilfields and the army's arrival at the Volga. Here the seizure of the Baku oilfields, as well as those of Maikop and Groznyi, was considered the main goal, in order to deprive the Soviet Union of its chief sources of oil and oil products and thus decisively undermine its capabilities of resistance. A prerequisite for the successful accomplishment of this plan was the defeat of the Southwestern and Southern fronts' main forces before the Germans reached the line of the Don River along its entire length from Voronezh to Rostov. This, as is known, did not happen, which to a great degree predetermined the German forces' campaign all the way to Stalingrad in hopes of grinding up the Soviet troops' main forces in the battle for this city. Stalingrad initially was not among the main goals of Plan *Blau*. It was assumed that following the German forces' arrival in the great bend of the Don River, they would be able, with the aid of the *Luftwaffe*, to fully put Stalingrad out of commission as an industrial and transportation centre. It was planned to seize the city later, only following the capture of Baku, when the sharp weakening of Soviet resistance could be expected. In principle, one may allow that if Plan *Blau* had not been altered by the addition of the campaign to seize the Western Caucasus in order to gain the Black Sea ports, and if the operations to encircle the Soviet forces during its opening phase had been better carried out, with the emphasis namely on encircling and destroying and not the seizure of this or that city, then it would have been possible to eliminate the Soviet troops' main forces west of the Don River. If the forces of Germany and its allies had limited themselves to a campaign against Maikop and Baku, having taken up a defensive position along the Don River without attempting to mount an attack on Stalingrad, then the opportunity of taking the Baku oilfields by the Germans would have arisen as early as September. However, it is impossible to say with confidence that Germany and its allies would have had the strength for this. But would this have resulted in a material weakening of the Soviets' power of resistance? The facts, as they are known today, lead one to question this.

One should not doubt that the Baku oilfields, as was the case with the Maikop oilfields, which actually were seized by the Germans, would have been completely destroyed by the Soviets during their retreat. And all of the oil-refining plants would also probably have been completely wrecked or evacuated. In these conditions, even if the Germans had managed to partially restore oil extraction, as they did in Maikop, it would have been impossible to send the extracted oil to Central Europe or to Romania for refining, just as it would have been impossible to attempt to restore the oil refineries in Baku. After all, a single rail spur through Rostov-on-Don tied the southern wing of the Eastern Front with Europe. It would have made no sense to burden it with crude oil or oil-refining equipment, as this would have threatened troop supply. But Hitler's main goal was not so much to seize additional sources of fuel for Germany as it was to deprive the Soviet Union of its main sources of fuel for its tanks, aircraft, and auto transport. But this task would not have been resolved even by the capture of Baku. After all, the deliveries of aviation fuel through Lend-Lease, which took place from August 1941 to September 1945 accounted for 57 per cent of Soviet aviation fuel production from July 1941 to September 1945. But taking into account the fact that 97 per cent of the imported fuel had an octane level of 99 and higher and that the USSR was desperately short of 78-level octane fuel, the role of the Lend-Lease deliveries was even more critical. The Soviets mixed imported fuel with their own in order to raise its octane level. The role of foreign imports was significantly lower as regards gasoline for automobiles – only 2.8 per cent of Soviet wartime production.[5] But one should not doubt that if the Germans had seized Baku the Americans, Canadians, and British would have done everything in order to increase the delivery of fuel to the USSR. This includes the employment of Iranian oil deposits and the major oil-refining plant in Abadan. Besides this, there were oil deposits in northern Iran as well, in the Soviet occupation zone. The Germans had no plans for a campaign against Iran, where Soviet, British, and American forces were stationed and to where the Soviet group of forces from the Eastern Caucasus would have retreated, due to their obvious lack of resources for such a large-scale undertaking. One may assume that in the event the Germans had seized Baku they would have first of all attempted to defeat Soviet forces in the Western Caucasus in order to eliminate the Black Sea Fleet and to shorten the already lengthy front line. But even if this had succeeded and the remnants of the Soviet group of forces in Georgia and Armenia had also fallen back into Iran, it nevertheless would not have brought about an end to the war. It would seem that the Germans would not have been able to begin an advance to the lower Volga or on Moscow earlier than the spring of 1943; moreover, without the guarantee that the offensive would be successful. After all, by this time Allied deliveries would have partially compensated for the absence of Baku oil. And the Red Army would have restored its combat capability. All the more so as according to this scenario only the Soviet forces in the Caucasus would have been routed, while the group of forces between the Don and the Volga, along with the arriving reserves, would have suffered significantly fewer losses than was actually the case. An alternative scenario could only prolong the war and lead to the atomic bombing of Germany. Thus one can say that having undertaken a mistaken, from the point of view of strategy, campaign against Stalingrad, Hitler saved Germany from the horrors of atomic bombings and the Soviet forces, having held on to Stalingrad and the Caucasus, were also fighting in order to spare the German people a nuclear nightmare. For this today's Germans should be thankful to the Russians.

Before the start of Operation *Blau*, the German troops routed the Soviet forces on the Kerch' peninsula and around Khar'kov and carried out the storming of Sevastopol'. The *Wehrmacht* suffered large losses in killed and wounded during the storming.

The German losses during the second storming of Sevastopol' from the beginning of June to 3 July 1942 inclusively amounted to 4,337 killed, 1,591 missing in action, and 21,977 wounded. Romanian losses were 1,597 killed, 277 missing in action, and 6,580 wounded. There were 95,000 men captured by the German-Romanian forces.[6] According to other data, the German Eleventh Army's losses from 1 June to 10 July 1942 were 4,598 killed, 1,280 missing in action, and 22,071 wounded.[7] Earlier, from 1 to 20 May, when the Eleventh Army destroyed the forces of the Crimean Front on the Kerch' peninsula, its losses were 1,289 killed, 342 missing in action, and 5,708 wounded.[8] There were 1,228 men of the command element and party nomenklatura evacuated from Sevastopol'.[9] According to the account presented by Oktyabr'skii and Kulakov on 9 July 1942 to the General Staff, the overall number of troops in the Sevastopol' defensive area was 130,125 men; irreplaceable losses numbered 31,068 men; 17,894 wounded were evacuated before 28 June; 1,207 died in field hospitals.[10] In June the 138th and 142nd rifle brigades (5,323 and 3,915 men respectively) were delivered by sea and 2,674 men as reinforcements.[11] One may estimate Soviet losses in killed, adding to the number of troops in the Sevastopol' defensive area the reinforcements received up until the fall of the fortress, and subtracting from the resulting figure the evacuated wounded and those who died from their wounds, as well as those who were evacuated during the final days of the defence of Sevastopol' and the number of those who became prisoners. One arrives at the figure of approximately 26,700. It is not impossible that the number of those killed was understated by several thousand men due to those mobilized directly into units from among the inhabitants of Sevastopol' after 1 June 1942, which probably significantly increases the number of wounded and dead after 28 June. As Yefim Kel'ner notes, 'The repulse of the third storming required the mobilization for the front of almost everyone who could carry a weapon . . . During the particularly tense June battles the city's entire *Komsomol* organization declared itself mobilized and took up arms.'[12] During the final days of the defence of Sevastopol' even women were called up into the army. During a meeting of the city defence committee on 15 June 1942 the following resolution was adopted: 'To oblige the district committees of the VKP(b) and the VLKSM to undertake mass agitation work in the city's factories and shelters to call up women into the ranks of the Red Army and fleet.' No fewer than 225 women were called up, and another several hundred women were mobilized for work in the hospitals. By 18 June 15 combat detachments of workers and employees numbering 1,800 people were also formed.[13]

If one assumes that all German and Romanian missing in action were killed, and assuming that the number of killed on the Soviet side in the struggle against the Romanian forces is approximately equal to the number of killed on the Romanian side, it works out that in the struggle with the Germans the losses of the Sevastopol' defensive area in killed were 24,800 men. This yields a correlation of 4.2:1 in favour of the Germans. By taking into account a few thousand called up directly into the units, this correlation may increase, although unlikely to exceed 5:1. From 21 May to 3 July Soviet losses in wounded were 55,289 men.[14] The correlation between killed and wounded in the Maritime Army also proves to be closer to the classic 1:3 and is 2.1:1 during the second storming of Sevastopol'. It's probable that the correlation of losses during the final storming of Sevastopol' is the most favourable for the Red Army for the entire period of 1941–2. Taking this into account, the best strategy for the Red Army would have been a defence along previously constructed defensive positions with a quantity of reinforced concrete and armoured pillboxes. The Germans would break through the usual defence with pillboxes, losing in killed 15–20 times fewer than the Red Army. The second storming of Sevastopol' was practically the only case during the war when an entire Soviet army defended in such conditions in a separate theatre of military activities and along a very narrow front. If such tactics had been adopted along the 'Stalin Line' in 1941 and its timely occupation by a significant number of field troops and this line had been equipped predominantly with artillery and not machine guns, then the German losses in killed and wounded would have increased and the Soviet losses would have decreased. It's another matter when a continuous line of fortifications is absent. The fortified areas could be bypassed and the troops defending them could be surrounded, as happened, for example, with the Kiev fortified area. It would have been more expedient to spend resources on reinforcing the fortified areas instead of creating the unwieldy mechanized corps, which were destroyed during the first two months of the war, not having inflicted serious losses on the enemy. The creation of highly manoeuvrable tank-mechanized troops required highly professional soldiers and officers, of which there were none in the Red Army. If one takes all of the Soviet forces' irreplaceable losses during the course of the final storming of Sevastopol' (minus those who died from their wounds and from non-combat losses), then they are greater than those of the German-Romanian forces by 15.6 times.

Taking into account the Eleventh Army's very heavy losses in the storming of Sevastopol', the question naturally arises whether the city-fortress should have been assaulted. Perhaps it would have been better to limit themselves to continuing the siege of Sevastopol', leaving against it only that group of forces which remained there before May 1942, wearing out the city's defenders with artillery shelling and air strikes, and to immediately throw the divisions freed up following the rout of the Crimean Front against the Taman' peninsula. Demoralized by the defeat on the Kerch' peninsula, the Soviet forces would not likely have put up serious resistance. Manstein would have had a realistic chance to seize Novorossiisk and Tuapse would have been subject to attack by the *Luftwaffe*. In these conditions, it would hardly have been possible to continue supplying Sevastopol' or to organize its evacuation and the city's defenders would have been forced to capitulate no later than August–September, if only due to the lack of food. On the other hand, the Soviet command would have been forced to weaken the Southern Front due to the threat from Taman' on the very eve of the Germans' general offensive according to Plan *Blau*.

It should be noted that the Eleventh Army's losses during the final assault on Sevastopol' were three times more than during the rout of the Crimean Front in May. Moreover, there were 2.5 times as many Soviet troops on the Kerch' peninsula as in Sevastopol'. This means that the soldiers in Sevastopol' fought 7.5 times more effectively than those of the Crimean Front on the Kerch' peninsula. The fact that the backbone of the Sevastopol' garrison consisted of approximately 30,000 soldiers and commanders from the Maritime Army, which already had the experience of a successful two-month defence of Odessa played an important role. Also, the garrison of Sevastopol' suffered almost no losses during the five-month breathing space between the two assaults and the soldiers, who were honing their knowledge of military science, were learning and gaining experience, particularly that of defensive fighting. The Crimean Front's forces consisted, for the most part, of raw recruits, insufficiently trained and, at best, having the experience of the police action in Iran. And from the moment they landed on the Kerch' peninsula they only attacked and suffered heavy losses, which prevented them from preserving cadres of experienced soldiers. The main thing was that they completely lacked experience of defensive fighting, which led to tragic consequences during Manstein's May offensive. Also, Petrov and Oktyabr'skii, for all their not very appealing moral qualities, were nevertheless somewhat better commanders than Kozlov and Mekhlis.[15]

It should be stressed that it was namely the leaders of the Sevastopol' defensive area that initiated their own evacuation, without troops. On the morning of 30 June F.S. Oktyabr'skii and N.M. Kulakov dispatched the following report:

> To comrades Kuznetsov, Budennyi and Isakov.[16] The enemy has broken in from the northern side to the Korabel'naya area. Combat

consists of street fighting. The remaining troops are extremely tired and clearly exhibiting apathy. The number of troops leaving their posts has increased sharply, although the majority continues to fight heroically. The enemy has sharply increased pressure through air and tanks, taking into account the sharp decline in our firepower; one must consider that in such a situation we will hold out for a maximum of two to three days. Proceeding from the concrete situation, I request that you authorize me to evacuate by 'Douglas' aircraft on the night of 30.6-1.7.1942 200–250 responsible party workers and commanders to the Caucasus, as well as, if it is possible, to myself abandon Sevastopol', leaving behind my deputy, Major General Petrov.[17]

Budennyi immediately transmitted this dispatch to the *Stavka*, adding on his own the following:

1. The Sevastopol' defensive area no longer has prepared lines for further defence. 2. As a result of exhaustion, the troop's combat capability has declined. 3. We cannot offer immediate aid from sea or air. All the ships breaking into and out of Sevastopol' are subjected to heavy bombardment from the air and torpedo attacks from launches and submarines. [. . .] Taking into account the planned operation No. 170457 [the landing on the Kerch' peninsula, B.S.] cannot influence the fate of the Sevastopol' defensive area, I request:

1. To confirm the mission of the troops of the Sevastopol' defensive area to fight to the end, thus supporting a possible evacuation from Sevastopol'.
2. To authorize the Black Sea Fleet's military council to fly to Novorossiisk. Major General comrade Petrov is to remain in place as senior officer.
3. To entrust Oktyabr'skii with the organization of an evacuation from Sevastopol', which is possible under current conditions, employing all of the fleet's means.
4. To cease supplying the Sevastopol' defensive area with reinforcements and food.
5. To continue the evacuation of the wounded by aircraft and combat ships.
6. I request that you immediately place at my disposal long-range bomber aviation (as much as possible) for destroying the enemy's aircraft on their airfields, thus easing the blockade of

Sevastopol' and the opportunity for the ships to break through to Sevastopol' and back.[18]

In all, 13 PS-84 aircraft managed to evacuate 222 chiefs, commanders and political workers and 49 wounded to the Caucasus.[19] Petrov, having heard of the horrors which accompanied the evacuation by air, when the admirals nearly became victims of a lynch mob by Red Army soldiers who had been left to their fate, decided that it was safer to leave Sevastopol' by submarine. On the evening of 29 June two submarines arrived in Sevastopol', having delivered munitions and fuel. During the unloading, the commander of one of the vessels received a written order from the Sevastopol' defensive area's chief of staff, Captain First Class Vasil'ev: 'Submarine Shch-209 is to remain in Sevastopol' under special orders. After unloading, you are to leave at dawn for the area of the 35th battery and lie on the bottom. Surface in the darkness and await orders.'

As soon as it grew dark, General Petrov and other commanders and commissars from the Maritime Army, hiding from their subordinates, reached the wharf through an underground passage. In the list for evacuation by submarine, which was confirmed by Oktyabr'skii and Kulakov, there were 139 men, of which 77 were from the Black Sea Fleet.

Submarine Shch-209 took on board the Maritime Army's military council, with its entire staff, of sixty-three men in all and at 02:59 on 1 July left for Novorossiisk, where it arrived following a difficult voyage at about 08:00 on 4 July. On 1 July Oktyabr'skii dispatched from Novorossiisk a report to the *Stavka*, with a copy for Budennyi:

> Proceeding from the existing situation as of 2400 on 30.06.42 and the condition of the troops, I believe that the remnants of the Sevastopol' defensive area's troops can hold out along a limited line one, or a maximum of two, days . . . Simultaneously, I report the following: Together with me about 600 men from the senior command of the army and fleet and civilian organizations were evacuated on the night of 1 July on all available means . . .

In all, they managed to evacuate 1,228 members of the higher command and political element, as well as party leaders. On the night of 30 June–1 July it was reported from fleet headquarters to Sevastopol' that Budennyi ordered the dispatch of all available vessels for evacuating 'wounded soldiers and commanders'. Major General Petr Novikov, who remained in Petrov's place, decided that the wounded didn't need to be evacuated and sent Budennyi this final telegram: '2045. 2,000 commanders are ready for transportation . . .'. But the ships never arrived. Novikov, along with seventy commanders, political workers and quartermasters, attempted to escape on launch no. 112, but were intercepted by German torpedo launches and captured.[20]

The Soviet command was obviously too late in evacuating Sevastopol'. The evacuation should have been begun no later than 17 June, when the Germans occupied positions enabling them to shell Sevastopol's northern bay and the Soviet anti-aircraft artillery ran out of munitions. Perhaps then it would have been possible to evacuate several dozen commanders and political workers. The conduct of the Soviet command echelon during the evacuation of Sevastopol' is in sharp contrast to that of the German generals and officers in the Stalingrad 'cauldron'. Soviet generals, admirals, and political workers ran away, leaving their subordinates to their fate. The German generals and officers did not attempt to run away, remaining with their soldiers to the end, even in a clearly hopeless situation.

At the same time German forces were pouring into the Caucasus and towards Stalingrad, the Soviet leadership nearly got into yet another fatal military escapade. In the spring of 1942 Stalin, significantly overestimating the successes of the Soviet counteroffensive, was preparing to attack Turkey, calculating that a war with that country would be the same sort of stroll in the park as the occupation of Iran in August 1941. In the first half of March the headquarters of the armies of the Trans-Caucasus Military District were sent plans for war games. According to their scenario, the 'Westerners' (Turks) had given passage to up to ten infantry divisions of the 'Blacks' (Germans) and 'under pressure and in alliance' with the latter had violated the border with the Soviet Union and Iran and had attacked along several axes: Batumi, Leninakan, Yerevan, Maku, Khvoy, and Rezaiyeh. The Soviet forces' countermeasures were seen as a decisive counteroffensive with the rout of the enemy on his own territory and the reaching of the line Trabzon–Erzurum. But just as in the case with the war games carried out during the preparations for an attack on Germany, only a Soviet offensive was to be played out, which would begin immediately after the Turks, 'following a series of provocative forays, violated our borders'. On 26 April the *Stavka* issued a directive to transfer a rifle and a cavalry divisions, a tank corps, 2 tank brigades, 6 air regiments, 6 artillery and rocket artillery regiments, 6 armoured trains, and 100 trucks to the Trans-Caucasus by the middle of May. On 1 May the Trans-Caucasus Military District was renamed a *front*. On 5 May a special martial regime was introduced into the border zone. In their training the Trans-Caucasus Front's troops prepared for an offensive in the mountainous conditions of Eastern Anatolia. It's a possibility that Stalin considered that Turkey would capitulate, that Soviet forces would establish control over the Straits and invade Bulgaria, and from there strike into Romania, leave the Germans without oil, and rout the entire southern wing of the German army on the Eastern Front.

However, the rout of the Soviet forces on the Kerch' peninsula in the middle of May and around Khar'kov in the middle and second half of May led to a situation in which the Trans-Caucasus Front did not receive the majority of its promised reinforcements, but rather had to turn over part of its forces to those *fronts* fighting against the Germans. On 7 June the *front* was also entrusted with covering the Makhachkala–Baku axis. Nonetheless, in the second half of June the 'Considerations on Planning the Trans-Caucasus Front's Operation' were drawn up, which called for, simultaneously with the defence of the Caucasus from the north and the covering of the Black Sea coast and without awaiting an attack from Turkey, 'to preempt the deployment and activity of the Turkish forces by routing them in the Trabzon–Bayburt–Erzurum–Kars–Artvin area,' and then be ready to encounter German forces in the foothills and passes of the Main Caucasian Range. But this time the attack on Turkey did not take place because of the *Wehrmacht's* too-rapid advance. One may say that the Germans saved the Turks from a Soviet invasion through their offensive toward the Caucasus. The Soviet plan's compilers assumed that the Germans would reach the foothills of the Caucasus within twenty-five to thirty days and that they could renew the offensive in the Caucasus within fifty to sixty days. Accordingly, they allotted forty to fifty days to the operation against Turkey, or ten to twenty days more than for the defeat of Germany according to the 1941 invasion plan. During this time the Soviet forces, consisting of 13 rifle and 2 cavalry divisions and 6 rifle and 3 tank brigades, were to advance 210 to 300km into Turkish territory. But the Southern and North Caucasus fronts' forces were routed far more decisively than they thought in Moscow and they were falling back to the foothills far faster than expected. As early as the beginning of August the Trans-Caucasus Front's forces were fighting the Germans in the area of Mineral'nye Vody and in the passes of the Main Caucasian Range. They were forced to give up the dream of a Turkish campaign, as it turned out, forever.[21]

This example show the adventuristic quality of Soviet military planning. Stalin and his generals and marshals, even following the very heavy defeats of 1941–2, colossally exaggerated the Red Army's combat capability and underestimated the combat capability of its enemies. Of course, the Turkish army had outdated armaments, few tanks, and aircraft and was poorly motorized. But the Turkish soldiers were highly motivated and trained in fighting in mountainous conditions, as opposed to the Soviet forces, as the battle for the Caucasus showed. In the mountains of Eastern Anatolia the

Soviet advantage in tanks, the motorization of troops and in aviation would have been annulled and the 13 rifle and 2 cavalry divisions, 6 rifle, and 3 tank brigades allotted for the invasion of Turkey would have got bogged down in extended fighting. If Soviet forces had invaded Turkey in July–August 1942 the Germans would have had a real chance to carry out a victorious march to Baku, even without the participation of German and Allied forces allotted for the Stalingrad direction. In the course of August alone the Trans-Caucasus Front was forced to send six rifle divisions and four rifle brigades and a significant part of its reinforcements to defend the Northern Caucasus. Without these forces it's doubtful whether they would have managed to slow down the Germans' advance, and in the event of a Soviet attack on Turkey they would have become tied down in Eastern Anatolia and the Germans could have made it to Baku.

Turkey, as opposed to the widespread opinion expressed in Soviet historiography, was not preparing to attack the Soviet Union. The Turkish army, which was not very mobile and almost completely lacking in tanks and aircraft was not capable of an offensive, particularly against such a serious opponent as the Red Army. Besides, Turkey was an ally of Great Britain and would not likely have risked attacking another mighty British ally. There was no place for the Germans to get the ten divisions, which the Soviet General Staff was dreaming about, for Turkey. For this they would have had to strip the entire Balkan peninsula, leaving it to the local partisans and quite likely Anglo-American landings. Beside this, all of these divisions would have had to be initially concentrated in Bulgaria and then thrown across the Straits and all of Asia Minor to the Soviet border. A Soviet embassy was operating in Bulgaria and there were a large number of Soviet agents, so that any such concentration of German troops would not have gone unnoticed. In practice, Turkey's abilities did not extend beyond occupying the territory immediately bordering on the Trans-Caucasus, but only in the event that the Red Army was completely defeated and the Soviet forces had left the Caucasus.

The dispersal of the German group of forces' efforts along two strategic directions – the Caucasus and Stalingrad – led to a worsening of the correlation of irreplaceable losses. At the same time, although the Caucasus direction remained the most important, from the strategic point of view, more and more forces were directed at Stalingrad. The real turning point in the correlation of irreplaceable losses took place in August 1942, when the German forces were attacking toward Stalingrad and the Caucasus, and the Soviet forces were attacking in the Rzhev area. And, as will be revealed, the worsening of the correlation of losses was observed precisely in the Caucasus, while around Stalingrad, Leningrad, and the Rzhev–Vyaz'ma axis it remained as before. In the Caucasus, where the Germans were nevertheless unable to break through to the Trans-Caucasus, the mountainous terrain limited the employment of tank and motorized troops, while the activities of the air force were also made more challenging, which made it difficult for the Germans to take advantage of their superiority in these areas. Here the Red Army could conduct a positional defence in a style closer to the conditions of the First World War, with the overwhelming role of artillery – the most powerful combat arm in the Red Army during that time.

Soviet losses in prisoners were significant and the undercounting of Soviet losses probably also played a role, but most likely it was not greater than in July. During August 1942 the German army in the East lost 160,294 men, including 31,713 killed and 7,443 missing in action. Soviet losses for this month were 385,000 killed and missing in action. This yields a correlation of 9.8:1, that is, by an order better for the Red Army than in the winter or spring of 1942.[22] Even taking into account the likely undercounting of Soviet losses in August, the change in the correlation of losses appears significant. All the more so, as the likely undercounting of Soviet losses was compensated by the significant increase in the losses among Germany's allies – the Romanian, Hungarian, and Italian troops which were actively taking part in the summer-autumn offensive. The correlation of losses improves not so much due to the lessening of Soviet losses (although it, in all probability, played a role) but the significant increase in German losses. It's no accident that it was precisely in August 1942 that Hitler, according to testimony by W. Schellenberg, for the first time admitted the possibility that Germany could lose the war, and in September there followed the notorious retirements of the chief of the army General Staff, F. Halder, and the commander of Army Group A, which was operating in the Caucasus, Field Marshal List.[23] Hitler began to realize that there was no way out of the dead end into which the German offensive in the Caucasus and on Stalingrad was drawing him and that the growing losses would reasonably quickly result in the *Wehrmacht's* exhaustion, but he could do nothing about it.

Halder's diary enables us to calculate the ground forces' losses only for the first ten days of September. They amounted to 48,198 men, including 9,558 killed and 3,637 missing in action.[24] Soviet losses were 473,000 killed and missing in action. These losses seem not only to not be understated but on the contrary, they more likely understate the true scope of Soviet losses in September by including earlier uncounted losses, insofar as in this month, compared with August, the index of those wounded in the fighting fell from 130 to 109. A third of 473,000 is 157,700. The correlation of Soviet and German irreplaceable losses in the first ten days of September 1942 is equal to 11.95:1, which proves that the August tendency for an improvement in the correlation of losses continued in September, particularly when taking into account the too-high increase in Soviet losses in this month.

During the German offensive on Stalingrad, as opposed to widespread opinion, Soviet losses were extremely high and exceeded by an order of magnitude those of the Germans by approximately the same proportion as in 1941. At the same time, Soviet losses were equally as great as during the Red Army's offensive operations north of Stalingrad in September and October and during the fighting immediately in the city.

For example, according to the combat journal, on 18 September 1942 the 258th Rifle Division (the future 96th Guards Rifle Division), which was attacking north of Stalingrad, alone lost 978 men killed and 2,030 wounded. There were probably missing in action as well, but insofar as this was only the first day of fighting they were not noted in the combat journal. Missing in action were included in the journal only following the end of the fighting, when at least some of them were found alive while some others could be confirmed as unquestionably killed.[25] In combat order No. 0060 of 19 September 1942, the 258th Rifle Division was to: 'Go over to a decisive attack and carry out the task assigned on 18 September 1942, without regard for anything or any resistance by the enemy.'[26] The entire German Sixth Army, which was attacking Stalingrad, lost irreplaceably during the second ten days of September just a little less than one Soviet division opposing it lost in one day of this ten-day period. The losses of Paulus's army during 11–20 September were 1,538 killed, 5,846 wounded ,and 223 missing in action.[27] If it is assumed that on 18 September the 258th Rifle Division also suffered some kind of losses in missing in action, then the division's and the army's losses could be equal to each other. It is necessary to stress that those irreplaceable losses, which were noted by name in the combat journal of regiments and divisions, exceeded in all cases the irreplaceable losses indicated in the combat report for the same day, according to the experience of researchers, while the difference could be as much as ten times.

At the same time, all of the Sixth Army's divisions during 11–20 September were involved in combat: on 11 and 12 and 18–20 September they repelled an offensive by more than twenty Soviet divisions and during all ten days attacked in Stalingrad.

I.Ya. Kuznetsov, the commander of an artillery regiment in the same 1st Guards Army, of which the 258th Rifle Division was a part, draws the same picture of heavy losses:

> A lot of disgraceful things along the road; about 200 of our killed have yet to be removed by anyone and this, of course, has a morale effect on the soldiers and commanders. The same picture exists for

the wounded: they walk along the road, asking for someone to give them a ride, but no one gives them a seat. They're bombing this ravine again, which is north of my command-observation post, although there's no longer anything there. The headquarters battery has a lot of casualties during these days, more than in the battalions, and not through work, but due to its own negligence; they wander around during a bombing attack with their mouths wide open, and so we have two killed and seven wounded, for a total of four killed and 15 wounded during these days, and all good guys; it's particularly sad about Sugantaev and Baklanov, the best soldiers in the headquarters battery.[28]

Russian official data on losses in the Battle of Stalingrad are understated several fold. For example, according to this data, during the course of the Stalingrad defensive operation, from 12 July to 18 November 1942, the Stalingrad Front (first and second formations), suffered 194,685 irreplaceable losses and the Southeastern Front, which was created on 7 August, lost 110,636 irreplaceably, while the losses of the Don Front, which was created on 30 September, were 18,028 men. Finally, the Volga Military Flotilla lost 507 men irreplaceably. During the Stalingrad offensive operation, which lasted from 19 November 1942 to 2 February 1943, the Southwestern Front lost up to the end of 1942 64,649 men irreplaceably. For the entire period of the operation, the Don Front lost 46,365 men and the Stalingrad Front lost 43,352 up to the end of the year. Besides this, during the period from 16–18 December 1942 the Voronezh Front's 6th Army and 16th Air Army lost 304 killed and missing in action, while the Volga Military Flotilla lost 15 men during the entire period.[29] However, if we take the data on losses by *fronts*, then the losses of the Stalingrad Front during its first formation and the Don Front, which inherited it, during the period from 12 July 1942 to 15 February 1943 were 116,130 killed and died from wounds during medical evacuation, 299,130 missing in action, and 13,783 deaths from non-combat causes. It should be noted that actually all of these losses were suffered in the period to 2 February 1943, because during the period from 3–15 February 1943 the Don Front suffered practically no losses. The Southeastern Front and the Stalingrad Front during its second formation, during the period from 7 August to 31 December 1942 lost 66,113 killed and died from wounds during medical evacuation, 104,490 missing in action, and 10,477 deaths from non-combat causes. The losses of the Southwestern Front during its second formation in 1942 were 32,265 killed and died from wounds, 6,543 missing in action ,and 3,790 who died from non-combat causes. The Volga Military Flotilla lost 272 men killed and died from wounds,

152 missing in action, and 198 who died from non-combat causes.[30] All the losses of the *fronts* and flotilla relate to the period of the Battle of Stalingrad. Total irreplaceable losses by the *fronts* are equal to 653,343 men or 653,647 if the losses of the 6th Army and the 16th Air Army are included. If the data on irreplaceable losses in the Stalingrad defensive and offensive operations is summarized, a figure of only 478,741 men, or 1.37 times less, is arrived at. At the same time, the *front* data is significantly higher than the data according to operations and is higher for all the *fronts*, with the exception of the Southwestern Front where, just the opposite, the data according to operations is 1.52 higher than the *front* data. If one assumes that in this case the data by operations is closer to the truth, then the Southwestern Front's losses should be increased by 22,051 men and the summary losses according to corrected *front* data is as many as 675,698 men, which is 1.41 times more than the data by operations. At the same time, there is no guarantee that there is not significant undercounting in the *front* data.

In both Soviet-Russian and Western historiography it is accepted that it was precisely in the street fighting in Stalingrad that Paulus's German Sixth Army suffered particularly heavy losses and was thus unable to seize the city. Actually, the situation was the exact opposite. If one looks at the data on the Sixth Army's losses, then it will become clear that in August, when the Germans had not yet entered Stalingrad and were still on the Don steppes, it shows 6,177 killed, 19,589 wounded, and 946 missing in action, for a total of 26,706 men. In September, when street fighting was already raging, Paulus lost 5,194 killed, 19,615 wounded, and 780 missing in action, for a total of 25,589 men, that is, 1,117 men fewer, while the decrease took place completely due to irreplaceable losses. Certainly, the Fourth Panzer Army's XLVIII Panzer Corps took part in the storming of the city, but it was operating in the southern part of the city, where the fighting was much less fierce than in the centre and in the north, in the factory area, and the Fourth Panzer Army's divisions operating in the city were later made part of the Sixth Army. The losses of the Fourth Panzer Army in August were 2,241 killed, 8,705 wounded, and 240 missing in action, for a total of 11,186 men. And these losses shrank in September, amounting to 1,619 killed, 5,982 wounded, and 152 missing in action, for a total of 7,753 men. There is no data for the last ten days of September for wounded and missing in action, but as the number of killed in comparison with the preceding ten-day period fell by almost four times, from 549 to 142, then there could not have been a lot of wounded and missing in action. In October the Sixth Army lost 4,055 men killed, 13,553 wounded, and 736 missing in action, for a total of 18,344 men, which is 7,245 men less than in September. In October the Fourth

Panzer Army had no losses. Finally, during the first 20 days of November the Sixth Army lost 1,207 killed, 4,658 wounded, and 199 missing in action, for a total of 6,064 men, which is 5,136 men less than the losses for the first 20 days of October. In November the Fourth Panzer Army suffered losses only in the first ten days and they were miniscule – one killed and eleven wounded.[31] Thus the Germans forces' losses from the beginning of the street fighting in Stalingrad did not increase, but went down. At the same time the strength of the Sixth Army was growing by the inclusion of formations from the Fourth Panzer Army. Most likely the correlation of losses in this fighting was less favourable for the Soviet forces than during the fighting on the Don steppes, including the heavy losses during the transfer of reinforcements across the Volga. The Germans had experience in street fighting and were the first to create storm groups, they had established much better coordination among the combat arms, and the level of training of soldiers and commanders was significantly higher. Street fighting is a more difficult form of combat and that army which is better trained has an additional advantage in it. On the other hand, it was much more difficult for the Germans to employ their advantage in mobility in the conditions of urban warfare. The *Luftwaffe's* opportunities were more limited, in that there was the risk of hitting one's own troops. But far more important was the fact that the German soldiers and officers were better trained and showed greater initiative in their actions and were better adapted to the conditions of urban warfare.

There may have been a grain of truth in the words of Marshal Rodion Malionvskii, who in 1965, during a meeting with the military and the intelligentsia, declared:

> I believe that we should not have defended Stalingrad. It would have been simpler to pull the troops back to the eastern bank of the Volga. The Volga was too much of a serious barrier for the Germans to force it. It would have been better to employ those forces, which were ground up in the fighting for the city, for counterblows against the enemy's flanks. Then our losses would have been far lower than those of the Germans, as they were several times more during the course of the defensive battle.[32]

It should also be noted that during the street fighting in September–November the German Sixth Army practically did not take prisoners.[33] This was due both to the ferocity of the fighting as well as to the specific character of the fighting, when the enemies' lines were mixed in with each other and it was difficult to evacuate prisoners from the battlefield. It was probably the memory of such cruelty that led to the situation in which, following the capitulation of the Sixth

Army, the Red Army soldiers were particularly cruel to the Stalingrad prisoners of war, of which only 5–6,000 were able to return to their homeland.

There exist differing estimates of Soviet losses during the Battle of Stalingrad. The former director of the Museum of the Defence of Tsaritsyn–Stalingrad, Andrei Mikhailovich Borodin, recalls the Red Army's losses:

> The first and last attempt to establish the scale of our losses in the Battle of Stalingrad was undertaken at the beginning of the 1960s. Yevgenii Vuchetich wanted to carve the names of all the soldiers and officers who fell during the Battle of Stalingrad on Mamaev Hill.[34] He thought this was possible, in principle, and asked me to draw up a complete list. I readily agreed to help and the oblast' committee relieved me of other work. I threw myself into the Podol'sk archive and the casualty office of the General Staff of the Ministry of Defence.[35] The major general who at the time headed the office told me that such a task had already been assigned to them by Central Committee secretary Kozlov.[36] Following a year of work he summoned the general and asked him about the results of his work. When he heard that they had already counted up two million killed and that there was still several months' work to be done, he said: 'That's enough!' and they stopped working. Then I asked this general: 'So, how many did we lose around Stalingrad, if only approximately?' 'I'm not going to tell you.' I see before me the reports by commanders of units abandoned during the course of the fighting. Nothing but tears. A combat load included 4–5 rounds per gun and not all the soldiers had rifles. There was nothing to eat. Regiments disappeared along with their headquarters and all their paperwork. There was no accounting of losses. This was just a meat grinder. Divisions would be destroyed in three days. No, not one researcher will be able to restore the picture of our losses. It is not given to us to understand this nightmare.[37]

In the offensive fighting against the German Sixth Army the 62nd Army's 196th Rifle Division lost 6,418 men during the period from 20 July to 1 August 1942.[38] During the period from 21–31 July the entire German Sixth Army lost only a few more – 1,565 killed, 6,413 wounded, and 475 missing in action, for a total of 8,453 men, or only 1.3 times more than the single Soviet 196th Rifle Division lost.[39] There is also data for this division on losses from 15 July to 1 August 1942. In all, during this time there were 7,412 losses, including 2,159 killed, 2,894, wounded and 2,359 missing in action.[40] During the period from 10–31 July the German Sixth Army lost 1,588 killed,

6,519 wounded, and 483 missing in action, for a total of 8,590 men. The army's overall losses are only 1.16 times the losses of a single Soviet division and as regards irreplaceable losses, the division somehow contrived to lose 2.18 times more than the German army opposing it and several tens more Soviet divisions. Typically, in the 196th Rifle Division the irreplaceable losses are greater than the medical ones by 1.56 times. Given that the division was attacking during this period, the majority of those missing in action were more likely to have been killed than captured.

During these days the losses of the Soviet forces directly defending Stalingrad were only a little smaller. According to a report by the NKVD's special section for the Stalingrad Front of 16 September 1942:

> during the day's fighting on 15 September the 13th Guards Rifle Division lost 400 men wounded and killed and expended all of its ammunition for automatic weapons, and during the night on 16 September the division did not receive munitions or artillery. The division is experiencing a critical shortage in artillery, which is necessary to destroy buildings where the enemy's automatic rifle-men have holed up.[41]

However, one should keep in mind that the main part of these losses were suffered by the 42nd Guards Rifle Regiment's 1st Battalion, under the command of Senior Lieutenant Z.P. Chervyakov, which had been reinforced with a company of automatic riflemen, artillery, and three tanks. It was precisely this battalion that carried the burden of the fighting on this day and won back the railroad station.[42] On 15 September only two of the 13th Guards Rifle Division's regiments (34th and 42nd guards) crossed the Volga into Stalingrad, while the remaining battalions took only a limited part in the fighting on 15 September. But the 258th Rifle Division attacked with all three regiments on 15 September. Thus in calculating by battalion the losses of the two divisions are comparable.

During the period from 14–20 September 1942 the German 71st Infantry Division lost 132 killed, 502 wounded, and 11 missing in action. On 21–2 September the same division lost 22 killed and 88 wounded. The German 295th Infantry Division, which fought together with it in Stalingrad lost 162 killed, 748 wounded, and 13 missing in action during the period from 14–20 September. On 21–2 September its losses were 54 killed, 217 wounded, and 5 missing in action.

The 13th Guards Rifle Division's irreplaceable losses for the period from 14–22 September 1942 have been calculated by the researcher Yegor Kobyakov, using data from the 'Memorial' electronic base, which, as is known, by no means reflects all irreplaceable losses. The division lost 910 men killed and 415 missing in action, as well as 19 who died from their wounds. On 14 September there were 11 killed and 8 missing in action. Evidently all of them perished while crossing the river on the night of 14–15 September. On 15 September 124 men died and 33 went missing in action, while 1 man died of his wounds. This tallies with the figure of overall losses of 400 men for 15 September from the report of the special section, particularly when taking into account that this may include the 19 killed and missing in action on 14 September. During the night of 14–15 September a military tribunal also sentenced two sailor-mechanics, who had refused to take their launch to the right bank, to death by shooting, but they obviously were not included in the division's rank and file. Then the overall number of wounded for 15 September in the 13th Guards Rifle Division may be estimated at 224 men, which exceeds only by a little bit the irreplaceable losses for this day, while the irreplaceable losses are somewhat understated.[43] Data on the losses by the two German divisions fully agrees with the ten-day data for losses by the German Sixth Army. The 71st and 295th infantry divisions account for 20.6 per cent of overall losses and 18.1 per cent of the Sixth Army's irreplaceable losses for the period from 11–20 September. These divisions suffered the greatest losses among all of the Sixth Army's divisions. But the 13th Guards Rifle Division alone irreplaceably lost (minus those who died of their wounds) 1,325 men during the period from 14–22 September, which exceeds the irreplaceable losses of the two above-named German divisions, which were 399 men, by 3.3 times. At the same time, one has to take into account not only the fact that on 14 September A.I. Rodimtsev's division had still not taken part in the fighting, but also that by no means did the 13th Guards Rifle Division fight alone against the 71st and 295th infantry divisions. The latter two also fought against the 10th NKVD Division, which by the start of the fighting numbered 8,615 men, only 988 fewer than in the 13th Guards Rifle Division, which had 9,603 men.[44] In addition, they also fought against the 91st Railroad Security Regiment, the 178th Critical Industrial Complexes Security Regiment, the 249th Convoy Regiment, a composite regiment from the 112th Rifle Division, the 244th Rifle Division (3,685 men by the start of the fighting in Stalingrad), the 137th Tank Brigade and the remains of the 133rd Tank Brigade, the 42nd Rifle Brigade (5,036 men), the 92nd Rifle Division (at full strength, numbering 6,000 men by the beginning of its participation in the fighting on 17 September, of which 5,000 fought directly in the city and another 1,000 remained beyond the Volga), the 6th Guards Tank Brigade, the full-strength 95th Rifle Division, and units from the people's militia.[45]

All of these formations, which were approximately equal in strength to three divisions, suffered losses no less, and probably even more, than the 13th Guards Rifle Division and by the end of the fighting had been completely decimated. By taking into account the fact that according to estimates there still remain 30.1 per cent of all killed and missing in action unaccounted for by 'Memorial', then the 13th Guards Rifle Division's true losses from 14–22 September 1942 may be estimated at approximately 1,896 killed and missing in action. This is 4.75 times greater than the *Wehrmacht's* 71st and 295th infantry divisions for the same period. Taking into account the irreplaceable losses of the other Soviet divisions which were fighting against the two above-named German divisions, the overall correlation of irreplaceable losses may prove to be close to 19:1 not in favour of the Red Army. The truth of the matter is that the 30 per cent undercounting of irreplaceable losses by 'Memorial' is due, in all likelihood, to, first of all, those called up directly into the units in place of those who were captured. Both of these factors in this case could not have played any kind of material role for the 13th Guards Rifle Division. Thus the actual correlation of irreplaceable losses for this division and the two German divisions lies between 3.3:1 and 4.75:1, or an average of 4:1. Accordingly, the average and most likely correlation of irreplaceable losses for the German 71st and 295th infantry divisions and all of the Soviet formations opposing them may be estimated at 16:1. But it seems that even this correlation is nevertheless at the very least just as unfavourable for the Soviet side as the correlation in losses in the fighting to the north of Stalingrad.

The ratio of losses along the front of the 64th Army, which was fighting at that time against the German Fourth Panzer Army, was not better. So, the 64th Army's 126th Rifle Division lost 10,336 killed and missing in August 1942.[46] The entire German Fourth Panzer Army suffered 11,186 casualties: 2,241 killed, 240 missing and 8,705 wounded in August 1942.[47] So the irreplaceable losses of one Soviet division were 4.17 times more than the irreplaceable losses of the whole German Fourth Panzer Army, despite the fact that the total casualties of this army exceeded the losses of the Soviet division only 1.08 times. It is also necessary to take into account that at least two other of the 64th Army's divisions, the 29th and 138th rifle divisions, were defeated at the end of August together with the 126th Rifle Division near Abganerovo and had suffered in August nearly as many losses as the losses of the 126th Rifle Division.[48] And the army's other four divisions and two brigades, together with the separate units under the army command, also suffered losses in August, although perhaps not as heavy as the losses of these two divisions. And the German Fourth Panzer Army also fought against some of the 51st and 57th armies' divisions in August 1942.

During the offensive north of Stalingrad, during the period from 24–9 October 1942, the 66th Army's 226th Rifle Division lost 3,509 men, including 954 killed.[49] During the period from 21–31 October the opposing German Sixth Army lost 1,542 killed, 338 missing in action, and 5,264 wounded, for a total of 7,144 men.[50] The correlation of overall losses is 2:1 and only 1.6:1 in killed. By this time the German Sixth Army already consisted of twenty divisions, which were engaged in intensive fighting throughout the last ten days of October. Thus the actual correlation of men killed along the Sixth Army's front during this period is probably not less than 50:1 in favour of the Germans, according to the most modest estimate. Once again, there is no basis for supposing that the 226th Rifle Division's losses were greatly different from the losses of the other Soviet divisions fighting in the Stalingrad area.

Soviet division were 4.17 times more

I. Nerodov writes:

> During the celebrations of the 60th anniversary of the victory in the Battle of Stalingrad, journalists from Germany visited the Rossoshki Military-Memorial Cemetery and our school museum. In answer to their question as to how many Russians died for Stalingrad, the well-known Volgograd television journalist, opening her notebook, replied: 'More than six million men!' Will that figure ever be confirmed?![51]

Let's examine this figure. Traditionally, in Soviet and Russian historiography, the duration of the Battle of Stalingrad is defined as from 17 July 1942 to 2 February 1943. For ease of calculation, the duration of the Battle of Stalingrad will be taken from 1 July 1942 to 31 January 1943. In July 1942 the irreplaceable losses of the German Sixth Army, which was attacking toward Stalingrad, were 3,181 killed and missing in action. In August the army lost irreplaceably 7,133 men. In this month the Sixth Army was joined by the Fourth Panzer Army, which lost in August 2,481 killed and missing in action, in the attack on Stalingrad. In September the Sixth Army's losses reached 5,974 killed and missing in action and those of the Fourth Panzer Army 1,773 men. In October the Sixth Army lost 4,791 killed and captured, while the losses of the XXIV Panzer and XXIX Army corps, which operated alternately in either the Fourth Panzer Army or the Sixth Army, were 151 killed and missing in action. In November the losses in Paulus's army were 2,319 killed and missing in action and 1 killed in the Fourth Panzer Army, while the XXIV Panzer and XXIX Army corps lost 98 men killed and missing in action. Let's assume that in the Stalingrad area during July–November 1942 the correlation of German and Soviet losses in killed was approximately the same as along the entire Soviet-German front and that the German forces in the Stalingrad area during this period lost almost no men captured. In July the correlation of losses killed was 21.7:1, in August 18.3:1, in September 19.5:1, in October 27.5:1, and in November 38.2:1. Such a high correlation in October and November in favour of the Germans was reached, probably, because of the fact that the Red Army suffered part of its losses in fighting against the Romanian forces. Accordingly, one may assume that the application of this correlation for determining Soviet losses in killed in the Stalingrad area will actually mean Soviet losses suffered in the fighting against Romanian forces will be included. Then the Soviet losses in killed in the Stalingrad area in July–November 1942 may be estimated at 624,400 (69,028 in July, 175,936 in August, 151,066 in September, 135,905 in October, and 92,368 in November).

It is known that the bodies of 42,754 city inhabitants, 171,170 Soviet soldiers, and 147,200 Germans, Romanians, and Croatians killed in Stalingrad and its suburbs were gathered up and buried after the end of the fighting.[52] The number of 171,170 killed Soviet military personnel may be accepted as approximately equal to the amount killed while eliminating the encircled Stalingrad group of forces after 23 November 1942 all the way up to 2 February 1943, although it must be borne in mind that some part of the Red Army soldiers died earlier. The losses incurred in fighting the German Fourth Panzer Army during December 1942 to January 1943 may also be apportioned to the losses at Stalingrad. In December 1942 the German army on the Eastern Front, minus the Sixth Army (it lost 6,914 killed and missing in action) lost irreplaceably 16,156 killed and missing in action. In January 1943 the German army in the East, excluding the Sixth Army (which lost 1,212 men in January), may be estimated at 20,764 killed and missing in action. Soviet losses in killed in December 1942 may be estimated at 615,000 men and 600,000 in January 1943. If those who died in the Stalingrad area are subtracted from this, then the overall number of Soviet military personnel who were killed on the remaining fronts in December 1942 to January 1943 may be estimated at 1,043,800 men, while among the German military personnel the figure was 36,920 men (assuming that all of the German prisoners taken during this time were captured only along the German Sixth Army's front). This yields a correlation of killed of 28.3:1 in favour of the German side. Such a large correlation of losses is also arrived at by the fact that the Soviet forces also suffered losses in the fighting against Romanian forces and the *Luftwaffe's* airfield divisions, which were not taken into account in the losses of the German ground forces. It must be emphasized that the airfield divisions and the Romanian forces suffered their chief losses during this period along the German Fourth Panzer Army's front.

Now the German Fourth Panzer Army's losses will be considered. In December 1942 it lost 621 men killed and missing in action and 1,061 men in

January 1943. The losses of the Soviet troops opposing it may be estimated at 53,000 men killed. Then the overall losses for the Soviet forces in the Stalingrad area in killed following the encirclement of the German Sixth Army may be estimated at 224,000 men and their overall losses in killed for the entire time of the Battle of Stalingrad at 848,400 men. It's possible that the overall number of those who died from illnesses and accidents or who were shot by sentences of tribunals, among the Soviet forces which took part in the fighting for Stalingrad, might have been several tens of thousands of men. Taking these losses into account, the overall number of Soviet soldiers who perished during the course of the Battle of Stalingrad may be around 900,000 men, but in no way 2 or 3 million. These latter estimates seem significantly inflated.

No less bitter fighting was going on along the other sectors of the Soviet-German front during the Battle of Stalingrad, along with a no less unfavourable correlation of irreplaceable losses for the Soviet side. For example, P.S. Rybalko's 3rd Tank Army, while conducting the Kozel'sk offensive operation from 21 August to 9 September 1943, lost 5,210 men killed, 13,880 wounded, and 7,282 missing in action, sick, or absent from the ranks due to other reasons.[53] It is clear that the overwhelming majority in this latter category may be ascribed to those missing in action. In all, the 3rd Tank Army lost 26,372 men. However, this number does not include the losses of the 3rd Tank Corps, the 342nd Rifle Division, and the 105th Rifle Brigade, which were committed into the fighting as part of Rybalko's army only on 24 August.[54] The German Second Panzer Army, which was opposing the Soviet 3rd Tank Army, lost 2,287 men killed, 10,027 wounded, and 552 missing in action, for a total of 12,866 men during the period from 21 August to 10 September.[55] However, only one of the Second Panzer Army's four corps – the LIII Army Corps – was fighting the 3rd Tank Army. Taking into account the fact that the 3rd Tank Corps, the 342nd Rifle Division, and the 105th Rifle Brigade comprised no less than one-third of the 3rd Tank Army's overall strength by 21 August, one may assume that their losses accounted for no less than a third of the losses of the 3rd Tank Army's other formations. On the other hand, taking into account the intensity of combat activities on various sectors of the German Second Panzer Army's front, it was unlikely that it suffered more than half of its overall losses for the period from 21 August to 10 September 1942 in fighting against the Soviet 3rd Tank Army. Then the 3rd Tank Army's overall losses, taking into account the losses of the 3rd Tank Corps, 342nd Rifle Division, and the 105th Rifle Brigade, which were included in the army during the course of the Kozel'sk operation, may be estimated at 35,100 men, including 6,900 killed, 18,500 wounded, and 9,700 missing in action or out of action due to other causes. The German Second Panzer Army's overall losses in the fighting against the Soviet 3rd Tank Army may be estimated at 6,400 men, including 1,100 killed, 5,000 wounded, and 300 missing in action. This yields a correlation of 5.5:1 in overall losses and 11.9:1 in irreplaceable losses in favour of the German side.

In 1943 the German army's losses on the Eastern Front were 255,257 killed, 976,827 wounded, and 332,649 missing in action.[56] Compared to 1942, the number of killed rose 1.13 times, the number of wounded 1.16 times, and the number of missing in action jumped 6.39 times, chiefly due to the killed and captured in the Stalingrad area. According to an estimate by the army's surgeon's division, the German Sixth Army lost 178,505 men missing in action after 12 January 1943.

The German army's overall irreplaceable losses in the East in 1941 were 209,595 men, 278,262 men in 1942, and 587,906 men in 1943, or 2.11 times more. Therefore, Soviet irreplaceable losses in 1941 were 5,500,000, 7,153,000 men in 1942, and 6,965,000 in 1943. In 1941 the correlation was 26.2:1, 25.7:1 in 1942, and 11.8:1 in 1943.

According to the estimate by the German Sixth Army's headquarters, its losses during the period from 13 September to 17 October 1942 were 343 officers and almost 13,000 enlisted men and NCOs killed, wounded, and missing in action. The losses from 21 August to 17 October were estimated at 1,068 officers and 39,000 enlisted men and NCOs. Paulus's headquarters estimated the Red Army's losses in the period from 13 September to 17 October at 17,900 killed, wounded, and captured, and for the period from 21 August to 17 October at 57,800.[57] Thus the headquarters of the German Sixth Army undercounted overall Soviet losses by 3–4 times. After all, during the period indicated the 258th Rifle Division alone lost 3,008 men in one day and the 13th Guards Rifle Division no less than 2,650 men in nine days, if you assume that the number of wounded in this division was at least no less than the number of killed and missing in action. No less than 9 per cent of the overall total of losses for Soviet forces which were facing the German Sixth Army during the period from 21 August to 17 October, according to the estimate by the latter's headquarters, can be apportioned to these two divisions alone. But no less than 93 divisions, 55 brigades, and 3 tank corps were fighting Paulus's army during this time.[58] But there's no way the remaining approximately 121.5 calculated divisions could be responsible for, on average, only 426 killed, wounded, and missing in action apiece in fifty-eight days of fighting, all the more so as during this time the majority of divisions managed to renew their strength.

Even according to clearly underestimated reports of the armies and of the entire Stalingrad Front from 1 to 20 September 1942, the Stalingrad Front's 1st Guards, 24th and 66th armies lost 88,715 killed, wounded and missing, including 28,404 irreplaceable losses. During the period from 20 to 26 September these armies' casualties amounted to 18,738, including 5,446 irreplaceable losses.[59] The casualties for the German Sixth Army amounted to 25,589, including 5,974 killed and missing.[60] But at this time the Sixth Army was fighting not only against these three armies, but also against the 62nd Army near and inside Stalingrad.

It's possible that the commander and headquarters of the German Sixth Army, knowing of the colossal Soviet losses in prisoners in 1941 and the spring of 1942, now seriously assumed that the Soviet commanders had finally wised up and had begun to conserve people. But it is equally possible that they ascribed to Stalin and his generals intentions which they never had all the way up to the end of the war.

There existed alternative scenarios for the German forces' actions around Stalingrad that could have prevented the encirclement of Paulus's Sixth Army. When these are analyzed it becomes clear just how much the Soviet counteroffensive's success depended on chance. From 10 October the Romanian Third Army, which had not a few draftees in its ranks and disposed of only forty-eight modern anti-tank guns, was already defending along the Don River from Kletskaya to Vyoshenskaya. The army's combat capability could have been increased by strengthening the defence with German troops. However, the German XLVIII Motorized Corps, which consisted of the Romanian 1st and German 22nd panzer divisions, was placed as a reserve behind the Romanian forces' front. If the German 6th Panzer Division, which played the main role in the attempt to relieve the encircled troops in Stalingrad in December, had arrived at the front from France about three weeks earlier then it could have formed a much-needed reserve along the Don. Hitler ordered this division and another two to three infantry divisions transferred from France to the Stalingrad area at the beginning of November in order to employ it as a reserve behind the positions of the Romanian Third and Italian Eighth armies.[61] If Hitler had ordered the dispatch of the 6th Panzer Division as late as 15 October, when an Allied landing in France was already impossible due to the weather conditions, then it would have arrived just in time for the start of the Soviet counteroffensive. The 6th Panzer Division, disposing of 200 tanks and assault guns, was stronger than the entire XLVIII Motorized Corps. The corps could then have been employed for thickening the Romanian defence.

But even without the 6th Panzer Division, Friedrich Paulus, the commander of the Sixth Army, Hermann Hoth, the commander of the Fourth Panzer Army, and Maximillian Weichs, the commander of Army Group B, had forces which, given a timely regrouping, could have averted the catastrophe.[62]

The Fourth Panzer Army included the 29th Motorized Division which had not taken part in the fighting in Stalingrad. It numbered fifty-nine tanks by the start of the Soviet counteroffensive. Given the will, this division could have been allotted to the reserve along the Don front and reinforced with at least one of the panzer divisions operating in Stalingrad; for example, the 14th Panzer (fifty-five tanks) or 24 Panzer (sixty tanks), which would not have seriously undermined the opportunities of the group of forces concentrated in Stalingrad.[63] Then two divisions could have formed the necessary reserve and the XLVIII Motorized Corps could have directly reinforced the Romanian Third Army's defence. With this scenario, the Romanians, together with the newly arrived reserves, could have delayed the Soviet offensive for a few days longer than was actually the case, thus giving the Sixth Army's main forces the opportunity to get out of Stalingrad. Incidentally, this would only have happened if Hitler had sanctioned a withdrawal from Stalingrad and he was unlikely to have done that. And after the encirclement of the Stalingrad group of forces had become a reality, the only sensible decision would have been an immediate breakthrough by the Sixth Army and the abandonment of Stalingrad, as Paulus and Weichs proposed. The surrounded forces still had enough fuel and munitions and held a bridgehead west of the Don and were perfectly capable of breaking through to the defensive line of the German and allied forces along the Don. In this case the *Wehrmacht* would have had an opportunity to avert the disaster that befell the Romanian, Hungarian, and Italian armies and to hold a front along the Don and Chir rivers. Then the 1942 campaign would not by any means have ended catastrophically for the Germans. They would not have achieved their strategic goals, would have abandoned Stalingrad, and would have halted quite far from Baku in the Caucasus. However, the correlation of losses would have remained quite acceptable for the German side, as both the German and allied forces on the southern wing of the Eastern Front would not have lost their combat capability and would have preserved a chance to launch a new campaign against Baku in the spring and summer of 1943. All of this would again have prolonged the war and made the American atomic bombardment of Germany inevitable. One may say that having left Paulus's army in Stalingrad, Hitler saved the German people from the horrors of nuclear war.

One of the key moments in the Battle of Stalingrad became the attempt to relieve the encircled troops by Hermann Hoth's Fourth Panzer Army in December 1942. One must take into account that the supply of the Sixth Army by air was only supposed to keep it alive in conditions of a relatively quiet situation along the front. The 'air bridge' was not calculated from the very beginning to support the waging by Paulus's army of heavy fighting in a major Soviet offensive for the purpose of eliminating the 'caludron'.

In Soviet and Russian historiography there is a discussion as to whether R.Ya. Malinovskii's 2nd Guards Army was employed correctly. As is known, at first it was planned to employ the army as part of the K.K. Rokossovskii's Don Front for the rapid elimination of the encircled group of forces, but the speedy advance by Hoth's divisions from Kotel'nikovo toward Stalingrad forced A.M. Vasilevskii, the chief of the General Staff, to insist that Malinovskii's army be turned against Hoth's group and then employed to eliminate the Kotel'nikovo bridgehead and for a further offensive on Rostov. As an alternative, Rokossovskii proposed either employing the 2nd Guards Army according to the original plan or to immediately move it on Rostov, which would have forced Manstein to instantly pull back Hoth's forces, as the threat of destruction hung over all of Army Group Don, the communications of which would have been cut off by the fall of Rostov.

Today, when the strength and plans of each side is known, the various options for the employment of the 2nd Guards Army can be realistically evaluated. One should begin with the fact that the variant that Rokossovskii, the commander of the Don Front, advocated more than anyone would have proved to be the most unfortunate one. Having received the 2nd Guards Army, the Don Front would have immediately begun an offensive in order to destroy the German Sixth Army. Paulus and his staff would have quickly understood that they could not withstand the Soviet pressure and, in all likelihood, would have been inclined to the single correct decision – the immediate breakthrough out of the cauldron. The commander of Army Group Don, Field Marshal Manstein, would also have understood the hopelessness of the Sixth Army's situation. In the developing situation, he would probably have issued Paulus a categorical order to immediately attempt a breakout. After all, Hoth's divisions were still 40–50km from the ring along the line of the Myshkova River and were even holding a small bridgehead along its right bank in the area of Vasil'evka. Of course, the entire Sixth Army would not have been able to break out, just as it would not have been able to remove a large part of its heavy weapons and equipment from the encirclement. However, most likely the army headquarters and the majority of the division and corps headquarters, with several dozen tanks and assault guns, as well as a significant part of the combat units, and possibly something from the rear establishments, would have got out. Then the Soviet victory would not have been as complete as it proved to be in February 1943. Hitler would not have declared a mourning period and the *Wehrmacht's* defeat at Stalingrad would not have made such a stunning impression on Germany, her allies, and the entire world.

However, in the event that Malinovskii's army had not been been thrown against the Kotel'nikovo group of forces, but into an offensive on Rostov,

Manstein's reaction might have been the very same as in the case of a major offensive by the Don Front against the Stalingrad group of forces. The commander of Army Group Don would have understood that he would not be able to hold the front along the Rostov axis and would have issued to Paulus an unambiguous order to attempt a breakthrough at any price in the immediate days ahead, while Hoth's divisions were in a condition to hold the line near the Myshkova. After Manstein was forced to remove the most powerful 6th Panzer Division, which before the beginning of the 'Winter Storm' relief operation had 160 tanks and 40 assault guns, on 23 December for repelling the Soviet offensive along the middle Don, Hoth was unable to continue the offensive toward Stalingrad. However, he was able for a certain time to continue defending the captured bridgehead. The Stalingrad Front's 51st and 5th Shock armies, which had been completely worn out in the previous fighting, were not in a condition to defeat the Kotel'nikovo group of forces. And as long as it was able to hold its positions near Stalingrad there remained the danger of a breakout by the encircled forces. At the same time, the offensive by the 2nd Guards Army on Rostov would not in and of itself have guaranteed rapid success and might not have led to a rapid withdrawal by Hoth's group of forces from the Myshkova. This is demonstrated by the fact that the Soviet forces needed almost two months to make it to Rostov, as well as by those heavy losses which the 2nd Guards Army suffered during the offensive.

In the 'Brief Military-Historical Digest on the 2nd Guards Army for 20 December,' which was graciously presented to the author by Natal'ya Rodionovna Malinovskaya, it states:

> By 18 February, during the fighting along the Mius River, the army no longer represented a powerful force capable of a further offensive. The army had lost its offensive and fire power.
>
> During the time of its offensive to the Mius River, the infantry had covered 600 kilometers in fighting, having captured the following: 1,300 prisoners, 14 tanks, 589 motor vehicles, 20 armoured cars, eight tractors, 32 motorcycles, 57 bicycles, 148 guns, 47 mortars, 105 heavy and 441 light machine guns, 68 rail cars, six automobile radios, 12 depots with munitions, six with clothes, eight with food, and 11 with weapons, 2,027 rifles, 1,077 horses, 1,725 carts, and 4,000 head of cattle.
>
> During this time the enemy suffered 32,500 soldiers and officers killed, 27 aircraft shot down, 352 tanks, 290 motor vehicles, 50 armoured cars, 148 guns, 636 carts, 77 mortars, and 150 heavy machine guns destroyed.

The German losses were significantly overstated.

And what were the 2nd Guards Army's losses? On 20 December it numbered 80,779 rank and file, and on 20 January only 39,110 men. It follows that even not counting possible reinforcement, the army's losses were 41,669 men. However, they were actually significantly greater.

By 25 November the 6 divisions of the 1st and 13th guards rifle corps had a combat strength of 21,077 men. By 3 December, when the order was received to load up the army, 'The combat strength was 80,779. The transfer was carried out in 165 trains.' However, it is beyond comprehension how the 2nd Guards Army's combat strength increased nearly fourfold in a week. After all, during this time the army's strength was augmented by the addition of the 2nd Mechanized Corps, which had an authorized strength of 13,559 men, as well as the 17th Guards Corps Artillery Regiment, the 54th Guards Independent Anti-Tank Artillery Battalion, the 408th Guards Independent Mortar Battalion, and the 355th Independent Engineer Battalion, which together probably did not number more than 3,000 men. Most likely, in this case the figure of 80,779 men does not represent the army's combat strength, but its overall numerical strength, particularly as how is it possible that 80,779 men could be transported by 165 trains?

After 20 December the army received as reinforcements 1 rifle division, 1 cavalry corps, 13 artillery and mortar regiments, 1 anti-aircraft artillery division, 1 mechanized corps, 1 tank corps, 4 independent tank regiments, 1 mine-engineer battalion, and 1 pontoon-bridge brigade. And by 20 December 1942 the 2nd Guards Army had 2 rifle and 1 mechanized corps, 1 artillery regiment, 1 artillery battalion, 1 mortar battalion, and 1 engineer battalion. And this does not take into account reinforcements. According to A.I. Yeremenko, only 2 of the 51st Army's mechanized corps received 3,000 reinforcements from the rear military districts during the final third of December.[64] It's hard to imagine that the 2nd Guards Army's 2 mechanized corps received less than 3,000 men in reinforcements during the month following 20 December 1942. A pontoon-bridge brigade had an authorized strength of 1,813 men and a mine-engineer battalion around 400. The mechanized, tank and cavalry corps, as well as the rifle division, even if their strength was lower than authorized at the point they entered the 2nd Guards Army, together would not likely have yielded an addition of less than 30,000 men. On 20 November the 4th Cavalry Corps numbered 10,284 men. However, at the time it was subordinated to R.Ya. Malinovskii's 2nd Guards Army it had already suffered heavy losses. Its 81st Cavalry Division lost 1,897 killed, wounded, and missing in action in the fighting on 4 December alone.[65] Thus the 4th Cavalry Corps arrived at Malinovskii's army most likely having no more than a third of its initial strength in rank and file. The authorized strength of a tank regiment was 339 men, so 4 regiments could increase the army's strength by 1,356 men. At the end of 1942 and beginning of 1943 artillery and mortar regiments had an authorized strength of 758–1,120 men, and an anti-aircraft artillery division 1,345 men. The strength of Malinovskii's army could have increased by approximately 13,500 men through additional artillery units. Besides this, there were reinforcements. Even if it is assumed that other combat units were reinforced to the same degree as the 2 mechanized corps, then they should have received by 20 January 1943 no less than 10,000 men in reinforcements. But it's entirely possible that both the mechanized corps and the other formations received even more reinforcements. One should assume that during the period from 20 December 1942 to 20 January 1943 the number of men who passed through the 2nd Guards Amy numbered not 80,779 men but, at a minimum, 140,900 men. Taking this into account, the army's losses were not 41,669 men but, at the least, 101,800 men.

The 2nd Guards Army was opposed by the Fourth Panzer Army. The latter lost 404 men killed, 1,216 wounded, and 53 missing in action during the last 10 days of December 1942. During the first 10 days of January 1943 the Fourth Panzer Army lost 135 men killed, 425 wounded, and 103 missing in action, and in the second 10 days of January 394 men killed, 1,117 wounded, and 50 missing in action. Overall losses for the Fourth Panzer Army during the period from 21 December 1942 to 20 January 1943 were 3,897 men, including 933 killed and 206 missing in action.[66] Even if these figures are compared with the losses of the 2nd Guards Army alone, then the correlation will be 26.1:1 in favour of the Germans. But at this time against the Germans' Fourth Panzer Army there were fighting, besides the 2nd Guards Army, the 51st and 5th Shock armies, the total losses of which were not likely to have been less than the 2nd Guards Army's. Beside this, the remnants of the Romanian 2nd and 18th divisions, as well as the 15th Airfield Division, also fought against the 2nd Guards Army, but their total losses were at least fewer than those of the Soviet 51st Army. Taking into account the fact that the share of irreplaceable losses in the Soviet losses was higher than in the *Wehrmacht's* losses, then the actual correlation of the Germans' Fourth Panzer Army's irreplaceable losses and that of the group of Soviet forces facing it was on the order of 35–40:1. The correlation of losses becomes more favourable for the Soviet side in 1943 only as a result of the enormous irreplaceable losses in the Stalingrad area, which comprise 30.3 per cent of all the Germans' irreplaceable losses in 1943.

Considering all of this data, it can be concluded that in December 1942 the 2nd Guards Army, which had been moved up against the German relief group, was optimally employed from the point of view of the Red Army's victory in the Battle of Stalingrad. All the other variants for utilizing it would have increased the chances of Paulus's army breaking out of the cauldron and threatened to reduce the scale of the Soviet victory.

As General Hermann Balck, the former commander of the German 11th Panzer Division, recalls, during the period from 7 December 1942 to 31 January 1943, during the retreat from the Chir River to Rostov-on-Don and during the fighting for Rostov, his division lost 215 men killed, including 15 officers, 1,019 wounded, including 47 officers, and 155 missing in action, including 3 officers.[67] The division's irreplaceable losses in equipment were 16 tanks, 4 reconnaissance armoured cars, and 12 anti-tank guns. Besides this, 745 motor vehicles (including 295 irreplaceably) and 280 motorcycles (180 irreplaceably) were lost. Balck estimated the Soviets' losses in the same fighting as 30,700 killed and dead from their wounds, as well as 225 tanks, 12 reconnaissance armoured cars, 35 artillery pieces, and 347 anti-tank guns. In Balck's opinion, such a high number of Russian losses 'was the result of Russian tactics and organization, which consisted of untrained human waves, supported by a large number of anti-tank guns, but almost without field artillery and other heavy weapons. Attacks were conducted in dense combat orders directly against our weapons and tanks.'[68]

One can assume that in estimating Soviet irreplaceable losses, Balck was counting the number of killed as approximately equal to the number of wounded, and the death toll from wounds approximately equal to 10 per cent, which was what it was in the *Wehrmacht*. In that case, he probably estimated the number of Red Army soldiers killed at 27,900. If it is assumed that all of the 11th Panzer Division's soldiers and officers missing in action were killed, then the correlation of losses in killed will be 75.4:1, which probably indicates that Soviet losses were overstated. Although the 11th Panzer Division was an elite unit in the *Wehrmacht* and the Red Army suffered relatively greater losses in engaging it than on average along the Soviet-German front, it's unlikely that this excess could have been so pronounced. It's possible that among the number of killed Balck included those Red Army soldiers who perished as early as during the German offensive in the summer and autumn of 1942.

Here is the only opporunity for comparing the losses of a single German division with the losses of an opposing Soviet army. And this took place right along the boundary of the two German army groups that were attacking towards Stalingrad and the Caucasus. The German 16th Motorized Division lost 48 men killed, 7 missing, and 119 wounded in the Kalmyk steppes in December 1942.[69] The opposing Soviet 28th Army numbered 44,000 men, which yielded a threefold numerical superiority for the Soviet side. According to far from complete data, which obviously understated irreplaceable losses, the 28th Army lost 2,180 men in the fighting in December, including 829 irreplaceably, which yields a correlation of irreplaceable losses of 15.1:1 and an overall correlation of 12.5:1.[70] Certainly, the 3 Turkestan battalions and 4 Kalmyk squadrons, which were attached to the 16th Motorized Division, also faced the 28th Army and lost in December up to 120 in killed, wounded, prisoners, and defectors. However, as Soviet and German documents show, almost all of the losses were suffered by the 28th Army in fighting against the Germans. Only a few dozen soldiers killed, wounded, and missing in action from the 28th Army can be attributed to fighting the Kalmyks and Turkestan troops. In the period from 1 September to 31 December 1942 the 28th Army's units lost 12,706 men, including 6,710 irreplaceably.[71] During this time the German 16th Motorized Division lost 406 killed, 32 missing in action, and 953 wounded, for a total of 1,391 men.[72] This yields a correlation of 9.1:1 for overall losses and 15.3:1 for irreplaceable ones. The 3 Turkestan battalions lost 400 men, while the 4 Kalmyk squadrons lost several dozen men killed, wounded, captured, and defected, but only an insignificant part of the Soviet losses were sustained in fighting against them.[73] They were mainly involved in fighting the partisans and reconnaissance-diversionary groups. On the whole, in four months of fighting the 16th Motorized Division, having lost approximately one-and-a-half motorized battalions in strength and having maintained its combat effectiveness, put one Soviet rifle division and one rifle regiment out of action. And this is when the estimate of Soviet losses is heavily understated. For example, the 248th Rifle Division's combat losses during the period from 1 October (it was not engaged in fighting earlier) to 31 December 1942 can be estimated at 1,332. At the same time, during this period its rank and file fell from 10,408 men to 7,333, that is, by 3,075 men.[74] It's hard to believe that the division's non-combat losses were 1,743 men and exceeded those due to combat. Most likely, in the book by the Astrakhan' local historian and socialist-inclined politician Oleg Shein, on which the author's estimates are based, by no means all of the 248th Rifle Division's losses were noted, due to the shortage of documents, as was the case with the 28th Army's other formations.[75]

Simultaneously with the Stalingrad cauldron, there existed along the northwestern sector of the front a 'mini-cauldron' in Velikie Luki, where the German 277th Infantry Regiment and the 83rd Infantry Division were surrounded. It's of interest to compare the existing data on the sides' losses during the siege and elimination of this 'cauldron'.

According to a report by the commissar of the Estonian 8th Rifle Corps, August Pusta, on 28 December 1942 250 soldiers from the Estonian 249th Division defected to the German relief group and their fate proved to be relatively positive. According to information from one of the leaders of the pro-German Estonian security police, Eduard Raig, during the battle for Velikie Luki a total of 1,887 Estonians either defected to the Germans or were captured, including 1,204 men along the external encirclement front and 683 in the 'cauldron'. The 1,204 prisoners taken outside the 'cauldron' were evacuated to the rear and released on 6 May 1943, having been granted a month's furlough with the obligation to serve in the German army, which, almost certainly, the overwhelming majority did not carry out, preferring to be hired as *ostarbeiters* or simply to escape into the woods or emigrate to Finland or Sweden.[76] The fate of those Estonians who ended up in the 'cauldron' was not so pleasant. One of the defectors, Ioann Saarniit, had the good fortune to defect to the Germans twice. The second time was in May 1943, near Smolensk. He said that the Estonians were in no way a welcome present for the Germans in Velikie Luki. They had no weapons, in that in defecting to the Germans with weapons they risked getting killed by German bullets and shells. Naturally, no one gave them any weapons in the 'cauldron' (there were not enough weapons for the much better trained Germans), while the defectors themselves evidently had no burning with desire to fight against their fellow Estonians. And the garrison's meagre food supplies had to be shared with the defectors. Saarniit maintained in his memoirs that there were about 900 defectors in Velikie Luki and when they once again fell into Soviet hands half of them were executed, while the other half were sent to punishment companies. However, judging from the documents, only 683 men deserted to the 'cauldron', while they shot no more than 54 men, according to data from the Estonian 8th Corps' special section – 41 sentenced by military tribunals and 13 directly by colleagues of the special section. At the same time, 29 men were officially sent to punishment companies, while another 147 men were sentenced to 5–10 years in camps, which in wartime conditions meant the same thing as a punishment company. One can assume that the remaining prisoners and defectors, who were freed in Velikie Luki, were enrolled back in their units. Data on the Estonian Corps' losses during the course of the fighting around Veliki Luki are very illustrative. According to a report by the commander of the Estonian 8th Corps, Major General Lembit Pern, on 20 January 1943, losses from 9 December 1942 to 19 January 1943 were 2,351 men killed and 9,560 wounded, for a total of 11,911 men (the general preferred to remain silent about those missing in action). According to a report by the chief of the corps' special section, Johannes Tipner, the corps' losses in the battle for Veliki Luki were 3,225 killed, 9,721 wounded, and 3,365 captured, deserted, and missing in action, for a total of 16,253 men.[77] If the Soviet forces' official losses during the Velikie Luki operation, which were based on reports by generals, are different from the actual ones in the same proportion as with the Estonian corps (1.4 times in overall losses and 2.28 times in irreplaceable losses), then the Red Army's true losses in the battle for Velikie Luki may be estimated at 145,600, including 88,700 irreplaceably.[78] In actuality, the irreplaceable losses were somewhat less, because part of those who were captured and defected and who were seized by the Velikie Luki garrison were freed during the elimination of the 'cauldron', and were once again enrolled in their units. German losses during this battle may be determined more or less exactly. The German Eleventh Army lost 36 men killed, 116 wounded, and 6 missing in action during the last 10 days of November 1942, while General Kurt von der Chevallerie's group, which was created in place of the Eleventh Army for relieving Velikie Luki, lost 1,938 killed, 8,711 wounded, and 225 missing in action from 1 December 1942 to 20 January 1943. Besides this, the 6th Airfield Division and *Luftwaffe* units, which were supplying and covering the 'cauldron', suffered losses, as did the 3rd Battalion/1st Parachute-Landing Regiment/7th Parachute Division, which lost from 17–20 January 1943 47 killed, 244 wounded, and 25 missing in action. A little more than 100 men broke out from the Velikie Luki garrison, which numbered approximately 7,500 men. Of this number, 3,944 men were captured (this figure may be inflated). Another 344 prisoners, as Zablotskii and Larintsev note, were captured in the fighting along the external encirclement front. Thus the garrison's losses in killed may be estimated at 3,450 men. Taking into account the losses by the 6th Airfield Division and the *Luftwaffe's* pilots and ground personnel, the Germans' overall losses in the battle for Velikie Luki may be estimated at 4,288 prisoners, about 5,500 killed and more than 9,000 wounded.[79] The correlation of overall losses is 7.7:1 and 8.9:1 in irreplaceable losses. The comparatively favourable correlation of irreplaceable losses for the Red Army is due to the prisoners in Velikie Luki.

In the event of an alternative scenario favourable to the Germans, with a German offensive only in the Caucasus, but not towards Stalingrad, with the capture of Baku by the end of 1942, the Soviet-German front would have run either along the territory of the Soviet Trans-Caucasus along the border with Iran, or along the border itself, along the steppes of the Northern Caucasus, then along the Don River, and then approximately along the front line as it existed before the start of the Soviet counteroffensive around Stalingrad in November. In the event of a version of this scenario unfavourable for the Germans, without the seizure of Baku, but also without the defeat at Stalingrad, the front in the Caucasus would have run either along the Main Caucasian Ridge, or in the Trans-Caucasus itself, but sufficiently far from Baku, so that the *Luftwaffe* could not yet bomb the Baku oil refineries and oil wells. The Germans and their allies would have had to hold significant forces there, because a Soviet breakthrough to Rostov would have threatened to cut off the entire Caucasian group of forces. Insofar as the front line from the beginning of the German summer offensive only increased in length and the Red Army had not been destroyed, Hitler would nevertheless have been unable to remove any kind of major forces from the Eastern Front. The most he could have hoped to send back to Germany for defending Italy against the inevitable Anglo-American invasion was the Italian Eighth Army, consisting of ten divisions, including one cavalry, three alpine, and three brigades of 'Black Shirts'.[80] In the actual course of combat operations, this army was almost completely destroyed in January 1943. The events along the Soviet-German front did not exert a serious influence on the North African theatre of military activities, where everything was determined by the Allies' overwhelming superiority on the sea and in the air. It's possible that because of the necessity of shifting part of Allied resources to aid the Soviet Union, the elimination of the Axis forces in Tunisia would have been pushed back one to three months, but they were nevertheless doomed. In May 1943 94,000–130,000 Germans and 120,000 Italians were taken prisoner.[81]

From June to December 1942 the *Luftwaffe* lost only 2,388 aircraft on the Eastern Front and 2,547 in the fighting against the Western Allies, while in the second half of 1941 only 20 to 25 per cent of the *Luftwaffe's* aircraft losses were due to Anglo-American air power.[82] Meanwhile, during these seven months in 1942 the *Wehrmacht* was carrying out a general offensive on the Eastern Front and at the end of November and in December the air bridge to Stalingrad, where the Luftwaffe suffered heavy losses, was active.

It should be noted that of the twenty divisions that were destroyed at Stalingrad, the Germans reformed nineteen. In all likelihood, had it not been for the Stalingrad disaster, the *Wehrmacht* would have been reinforced by nineteen new divisions. Most probably, all of them would have been sent to Italy or the West for repelling a landing by the Allies. In reality, seven of these divisions soon returned to the Eastern Front. It is likely, in the event of an alternative scenario for the war being realized, these divisions would have been employed against the Western Allies, probably in Italy. Taking into account the additional ten Italian divisions and three brigades transferred from Russia, this would have materially increased the Axis forces' strength in the fighting for Italy. Almost certainly, the Italian capitulation and the Allies' landing in the south of the Apennine peninsula would have been delayed by half a year. The Soviet Union would also have ended up in a much more restricted situation than following the Battle of Stalingrad. It would still have been dependent on the Western Allies for supplies of fuel and would have been forced to rely on Anglo-American troops along the Iranian front and would not have had the victory at Stalingrad behind it. However, one should not doubt that Germany, tied down by combat operations in the Mediterranean Sea and taking into account the losses incurred in the 1942 campaign, even without the catastrophe at Stalingrad, would not have had the strength for a general offensive in the East.

On 22 May 1942, replying to Molotov's question as to what would be the position of Great Britain if the USSR failed to withstand in 1942 the forthcoming German offensive, Churchill answered that

> if the Soviet military power was seriously reduced by the German onslaught, Hitler would in all probability move as many troops and air forces as possible back to the West, with the object of invading Great Britain. He might also strike down through Baku to the Caucasus and Persia. This latter thrust would expose us to the gravest dangers, and we should by no means feel satisfied that we had sufficient forces to ward it off. Therefore our fortunes were bound up with the resistance of the Soviet army. Nevertheless, if, contrary to expectation, they were defeated, and the worst came to the worst, we should fight on, and, with the help of the United States, hope to build up overwhelming air superiority . . . But what a tragedy for mankind would be this prolongation of the war, and how earnest was the hope for Russian victory, and how ardent the desire that we should take our share in conquering the evil foe![83]

In reality, the complete collapse of Soviet resistance would have been unachievable with any variation of actual development of events; thus in an alternative scenario the defence of Iran and the organization of the Red Army's supply with oil products was a quite realistic task.

If the German Sixth Army had not been routed at Stalingrad, the war might have lasted longer, but not likely for more than six months. Sooner or later, Stalin would have ground down the German defence with his soldiers' corpses and begun to liberate Soviet territory. The Red Army probably would have gone over to the offensive no later than the end of 1943. In the summer of 1944 the Allies, having created artificial ports and having accumulated a sufficient amount of landing craft would have landed in Normandy, where Hitler would have had to shift part of his forces from the Eastern Front. Nevertheless, the war would probably have continued into the summer of 1945 to the time of the first test of the American atomic bomb. Most likely, by that time the Western Allies would have liberated France and a large part of Belgium, but not yet invaded Germany, while in Italy they would still be south of Rome. Soviet forces more than likely would have been fighting at that moment along the Estonian border, in Belorussia and along the Ukrainian right bank, but would not yet have reached the border of Romania and the Curzon Line.[84] By that time the future defeat of Germany would not have been in doubt, although the Reich would still have been far from capitulating. It's possible that Finland would have already got out of the war, and it's possible that it could have done this without new territorial losses and retaining Petsamo, while Hungary and

Romania would still have remained German allies, although while searching hard for an opportunity to leave the Axis and conclude a separate peace.[85]

The alternative scenario proposed here, in the event of it being realized, could in no way have influenced the course and pace of the American and German atomic programmes. As is known, a controlled, self-sustained nuclear reaction, which was the key to creating an atomic bomb, had been carried out by Enrico Fermi in the USA in December 1942.[86] From this point to the testing of the first atomic bomb, employed as a realistic weapon, two years and eight-and-a-half months passed. The Germans attempted to carry out a similar reaction, unsuccessfully, only in March 1945.[87] Thus Hitler could not have produced an atomic bomb as a realistic weapon, which could be delivered to the enemy's territory with the aid of an airplane or rocket, earlier than the end of 1948. Taking into account the mass bombings which the Allied air forces subjected Germany to from 1943, the realization of a German atomic project would have been delayed even longer. However, the participants of the Manhattan Project did not know how far the Germans were behind them and they were making the atomic bomb against Hitler.[88] One shouldn't doubt that if the Germans had still been putting up resistance at the moment of the successful creation of atomic weapons, they would first of all have employed the atomic bomb against Germany, and not Japan, the situation of which in the summer of 1945 would have been completely hopeless following the loss of its air power, fleet, and sources of fuel. But taking into account the fact that the collapse of Germany would not yet have been obvious and that the fanatic Hitler would not likely have agreed to an unconditional capitulation, the Americans, in the case of Germany, would probably not have limited themselves to only two atomic bombs. Most likely, they would have accumulated at a minimum a dozen atomic bombs and then have thrown them all against Berlin and other major German cities, possibly immediately killing more than a million people. They would then have carried out the bombing not in August, as was the case with Japan, but probably in November 1945. In the actual war, the American command, on the eve of the Japanese capitulation, planned to drop a third bomb on Japan in August, three bombs in September, and another three in October. They no longer planned to drop new atomic bombs in November, as a major operation to seize the island of Kyushu was supposed to begin, which they assumed would end with the capitulation of Japan.[89] The Americans would probably have accumulated a dozen bombs in November. To all appearances, Hitler would not have surrendered and his generals and marshals would have carried out a military coup and capitulated in order to not expose the German people to total nuclear extermination. The example of Germany would have been sufficient in this case for Japan. The Allies would simply have said to Tokyo: 'Either capitulate, or else end up like Germany.'

It should be noted that the atomic bombing of Hiroshima and Nagasaki had a definite military significance, moving the capitulation forward and saving the lives of thousands of American and Japanese soldiers. This, of course, does not in any way justify the deaths of tens and hundreds of thousands of completely innocent inhabitants of the two Japanese cities. But in both the USA and in the entire civilized world, the bombing of Hiroshima and Nagasaki is seen first of all as one of the greatest tragedies of the Second World War. No one, of course, blamed the American pilots in any way for carrying it out, but no one made them national heroes either.

The role of the USSR in the capitulation of Japan was minimal. The Soviet declaration of war on Tokyo deprived the Japanese of any hope of the USSR's intercession in the search for a peace agreement with the USA distinguishable from unconditional surrender. But the rout of the Kwangtung Army did not play any kind of role, insofar as the Japanese command had written it off long ago. The majority of its divisions had been formed only in July and the beginning of August 1945 to replace those that had been sent long ago to the South Seas and southern China. Many of these divisions lacked artillery and were experiencing problems with fuel and munitions. Against the completely combat-capable 34 calculated rifle and mechanized divisions and the 18 calculated tank brigades of the Trans-Baikal Front, the Japanese could put up 9 infantry divisions, 5 composite brigades, and 2 tank brigades, whose sum total of combat worth the Japanese command estimated to be 3.85 infantry divisions. The combat capability of the newly formed tank brigades was not estimated, but taking into account that they did not enter the fighting, but instead retreated, while abandoning their equipment, their actual combat capability was close to zero. Against the Second Far Eastern Front's 18 calculated divisions the Japanese had 3 independent composite brigades and 3 infantry divisions, which taken together were equivalent in combat capability to 1.1 infantry divisions. Deployed against the First Far Eastern Front's 43 calculated divisions were 12 infantry divisions, 2 composite and 1 mobile brigades, and 1 border regiment, which were equivalent in combat capability to 2.8 infantry divisions.[90]

There was simply no good strategy for the Japanese in Manchuria. To meet the Soviet forces at the border or to move the main forces to central Manchuria were equal losers. In any event, there was no chance to repel the Soviet attack or to escape from pursuit, in that the Soviet mechanized forces would probably have caught up to the Japanese, who were deprived of fuel and transportation equipment. But even an immediate withdrawal to the seaports would not have saved the Kwangtung Army, as there were neither ships nor aircraft for its evacuation. In all instances, only the area of capitulation differed.

Obviously, in the case of the realization of an alternative scenario involving the atomic bombing of Germany, the geopolitical arrangement following the Second World War would have differed materially from that which actually arose. First of all, twelve Chernobyls would have arisen in the materially reduced but still heavily populated territory of Germany, and its industry would have been destroyed to an even greater degree than was actually the case by May 1945. As opposed to Japan, the atomic bombs would probably have destroyed all of the largest cities, such as Berlin, Hamburg, Munich, Cologne, Frankfurt-am-Main, Stuttgart, Dusseldorf, the Ruhr industrial area, and others. It's possible that Germany would not have recovered from such a blow, particularly had a harsh confrontation between the West and the USSR not arisen. Then the leading role in Europe would have been played by France, or maybe by Poland. So, the Germans should thank the Soviet soldiers who routed Paulus's army at Stalingrad and who thus spared Germany a nuclear Armageddon. The Soviet Union would have ended the war, given this development of events, weaker and more dependent on the Western Allies. It's quite possible then that Poland would have established a pro-Western democratic regime oriented on the basis of the government in exile in London. Most likely, all of East Prussia, along with Konigsberg, would have become Polish, and the Curzon Line might have gone according to Polish wishes, leaving Poland L'vov and Vil'nius. It was precisely that demarcation that the Polish government in London initially insisted on. The USSR could probably not have occupied the Baltic States and established a communist government in Poland and the other states of Eastern Europe. It's possible that in these conditions the centrifugal tendencies in Ukraine and the other republics would have brought about the break-up of the USSR and the democratization of Russia as early as the end of the 1940s or beginning of the 1950s. This would probably been more of a blessing than a misfortune for the Soviet people, and for the peoples of the entire world.

In reality, the Battle of Stalingrad became the first instance in which the Stalinist strategy of crushing the enemy with corpses brought about not only the failure of a German plan and the liberation of significant territory, but the destruction of major enemy groups of forces, including both German and allied forces. At the same time, the Germans' irreplaceable losses were greater than those of the Soviets only along the internal front of the 'cauldron'. However, the rout of two Romanian, one Hungarian, and one Italian army undermined Germany's ability to continue to seek a decisive victory on the Eastern Front.

Chapter 6

The Battle of Kursk – the *Wehrmacht's* Final Offensive on the Eastern Front

Why was 'Citadel' Halted?

Following the end of the fighting in Stalingrad, the Red Army, as at the beginning of 1942, continued the offensive along the entire front, during the course of which it managed to achieve only tactical successes, while losses were, as before, heavy. For example, during the fighting to expand the breakthrough of the Leningrad blockade, the 142nd Rifle Division lost from 3–26 February 1943 1,503 men irreplaceably and 5,142 wounded, for total losses of 6,645.[1] The German Eighteenth Army's irreplaceable losses for February 1943 were 6,767 men, with 17,226 wounded, for a total of 23,993 men.[2] This yields a correlation of overall losses of 3.6:1, and 4.5:1 for irreplaceable losses, which may indicate an undercounting of irreplaceable losses for the Soviet side. One must take into account that at the time the German Eighteenth Army had up to twenty-three divisions.

No fewer casualties were suffered by the Czechoslovak subunits allied with the Red Army, which were also trained according to Soviet standards. For example, on 8 March 1943 in an action in the village of Sokolovo, in the Khar'kov area, the 1st Reinforced Company of the 1st Independent Czechoslovak Battalion, which was commanded by Lieutenant Colonel Ludvik Svoboda, lost 200 men killed and missing in action and 60 men wounded out of 350.[3] The German Fourth Panzer Army, which was opposing it, lost 866 men killed, 2,564 wounded, and 159 missing in action in the period from 1–10 March 1943.[4] This comes to 102 irreplaceable losses by the Fourth Panzer Army per day, which is approximately 2 times less than the losses for 1 day by a single reinforced Czechoslovak company.

Soviet forces in the Khar'kov area suffered a major defeat at the hands of Field Marshal Manstein's Army Group South and were forced to abandon the recently captured cities of Khar'kov and Belgorod. This defeat could probably have been avoided if Stalin and his generals had not become dizzy from success following the Stalingrad victory. If a large part of the forces, which had been freed up following the elimination of the encircled Stalingrad group of forces, had been employed for developing the offensive in the south, where the Red Army was making its main attack, then it probably would have been possible to repel Manstein's counterblow and hold Khar'kov. However, Stalin ordered the dispatch of the Don Front's forces to the central sector, where Rokossovskii began to command the Central Front and undertook an unsuccessful offensive on Sevsk. If Rokossovskii's forces had been employed in the south and Khar'kov held, then the Kursk salient would not have formed. In this case, the German command would most likely have limited itself to an active defence on the Eastern Front with the broad employment of tank formations, while evacuating the Rzhev–Vyaz'ma and Demyansk salients, in order to have sufficient forces for defending the Orel salient. In this case, the Soviet forces would have been the first to undertake the offensive in the middle of May, following the end of the wet season. Most likely, they would have ultimately broken through the German defence, with heavy losses, and reached the Dnepr River, although this would have occurred a month or month-and-a-half earlier than actually happened. But this circumstance would hardly have materially changed the course of the fighting on the Eastern Front.

The 3rd Tank Army, which was unsuccessfully attempting to hold Khar'kov in March 1943, numbered by the start of the Ostrogozhsk–Rossosh' operation on 14 January 1943 69,933 men. During the course of the Ostrogozhsk–Rossosh' operation until the end of January it lost 3,016 men killed and died from wounds, 7,045 wounded and suffering from shell shock, 65 cases of frostbite, 707 missing in action and captured, and 1,069 men out of action for other reasons, yielding a total of 11,902 men.[5] During the period from 2–28 February, during the fighting to take Khar'kov, the 3rd Tank Army lost 5,804 men killed, 11,555 wounded, 111 cases of frostbite, and 1,788 missing in action and out of action due to other reasons (sickness, victims of accidents, suicides, etc.), for a total of 19,258 men.[6] During the period from 14 January until the end of February 1943 the 3rd Tank Army received 22,561 reinforcements, including 10,528 through the army reserve regiment, 2,574 from the *front's* own resources, 2,574 through city mobilization centres during the liberation of Khar'kov, and 6,017 men were mobilized directly by troop units.[7] It's probable that the number of mobilized into units was significantly higher. The Voronezh Front increased its strength by 29,886 men by calling up men directly into the units in February and March 1943, while it received only 20,838 men through central channels.[8] This means that the number of draftees from the occupied territories in 1943–5 often exceeded the central levy. However, even according to official data, by the beginning of March the Soviet 3rd Tank Army should have numbered

61,344 men. During the fighting to hold Khar'kov the army was reinforced by the 25th Guard Rifle Division which, while not very strong nevertheless probably did not number less than 5,000 men, as well as a brigade of NKVD troops, whose strength may be estimated at 5,000 men. Somewhat later new reinforcements arrived – three anti-tank artillery regiments, a battalion of rocket-propelled artillery, the 'numerically weak' 86th Tank Brigade, and the 19th Rifle Division. One may estimate their overall strength at no less than 10,000 men. Besides this, the 160th Rifle Division left the army, in place of which the 253rd Rifle Brigade arrived. As a result of this, the army's strength might have decreased by 2,000–3,000 men. Thus the 3rd Tank Army's overall strength during the defence of Khar'kov may be estimated at 79,000 men. According to the 3rd Tank Army command, approximately 8,500 men managed to break out of encirclement in the Khar'kov area by 20 March. At the same time, about 1,000 men remained in the 15th Tank Corps and about 3,000 in the 12th Tank Corps. Of this number, 85 per cent were draftees, as the report by the Third Tank Army headquarters states, 'from the liberated areas, without weapons, untrained and unclothed. The same percent of the rank and file were in the army's other authorized units and formations.'[9] This leads one to assume that the share of those drafted directly into the 3rd Tank Army's units was significantly greater than one might assume on the basis of the data cited above with regard to the number of reinforcements that arrived in the army in January and February and that the call-up directly into the units continued intensively in the 3rd Tank Army's units in March 1943 as well.

The Soviet 3rd Tank Army's irreplaceable losses for the period from 1–20 March may be estimated at 70,500 men. The 3rd Tank Army opposed the Fourth Panzer Army's SS II Panzer Corps. During the period of the second battle of Khar'kov, from 1 February to 20 March, the corps lost 11,519 men killed, wounded, and missing in action.[10] The entire German Fourth Panzer Army, which also included the XLVIII Panzer Corps, lost from 1–20 March 1,756 killed, 286 missing in action, and 5,499 wounded, for a total of 7,541 men.[11] If it is assumed that approximately two-thirds of these losses can be ascribed to Paul Hausser's SS II Panzer Corps, which was engaged in the more intensive fighting, then its losses may be estimated to be 1,171 killed, 191 missing in action, and 3,666 wounded, for a total of 5,028 men. The correlation of the Soviet 3rd Tank Army's irreplaceable losses in March may be estimated at an astronomical order of 50.4:1. Evidently, no small part of the Soviet irreplaceable losses during the defence of Khar'kov was due to prisoners of war, but there is as yet no reliable data on the number of Soviet prisoners taken by Army Group South in March 1943. They may be very approximately estimated at 17,477 men, if the number of prisoners captured by army groups A (2,801), Centre (9,980), and North (3,564) are subtracted from the overall number of Soviet prisoners for March 1943 (33,822).[12] Having assumed that all of the prisoners were taken in the Khar'kov area and that all of the missing in action were in Hausser's corps, then it can be determined that the number of killed on the Soviet side was 60,000 men, and that the correlation of losses killed between the Soviet 3rd Tank Army and the SS II Panzer Corps in March may be estimated at 36:1, which seems close to reality.

Because Hitler repeatedly postponed the beginning of Operation 'Citadel' from the middle of May to the beginning of July 1943, it was very difficult not to notice such a prolonged concentration of German troops. The German command knew just as well of the concentration of the Red Army's main forces in the area of the Kursk salient. It was difficult for the Soviet command to imagine that the Germans, following the rout at Stalingrad, would risk repeating their campaign in the Caucasus, if only from the line of the Mius River or from the Taman' peninsula.

The opinion has become entrenched in Soviet historiography that the tank battle at Prokhorovka on 12 July 1943, where the 5th Guards Tank and 5th Guards armies opposed the SS II Panzer Corps, played the main role in halting the German offensive along the southern flank of the Kursk bulge. However, research conducted by Russian and German historians, as was also the case with their foreign colleagues, following the collapse of the USSR, when the Soviet (Russian) archives became accessible for a period of time, showed that this was most definitely not the case. The Battle of Prokhorovka was unquestionably won by the German side, although this victory had no influence on the subsequent offensive by Army Group South along the southern flank of the Kursk salient. It was namely on 12 July that the Soviet offensive along the northern flank of the Kursk bulge began, while the Western Allies landed in Sicily. In these conditions, a continuation of the offensive on Kursk from the south made no sense and the SS corps was shifted to eliminate the local cauldron to the south of Ivanovka, into which a few of the Soviet 69th Army's divisions had fallen.

So, what were the sides' losses during the battle of Prokhorovka? According to a preliminary estimation by the German historian Karl-Heinz Frieser, by the beginning of the Battle of Prokhorovka the SS II Panzer Corps had a total of 273 tanks and assault guns remaining in line. The corps' losses in the fighting on 12–13 July amounted to 43 tanks and 12 assault guns, of which no more than 5 tanks (during the period from 10–13 July) were lost irreplaceably.[13] Subsequently, Frieser came to the conclusion that the Germans irreplaceably lost only three tanks in the Prokhorovka battle.[14] According to the 'Information on Irreplaceable Losses in Tanks During the Period of the Defensive Fighting of the Battle of Kursk', the 5th Guards Tank Army lost during 12–13 July 350 vehicles forever.[15] According to a report by the 5th Guards Tank Army's chief of staff, Guards Major General of Tank Troops Vladimir Baskakov, on 17 July, the army lost irreplaceably up to 16 July 334 tanks and self-propelled guns, including 222 T-34s, 89 T-70s, 12 British 'Churchills', and 11 self-propelled guns.[16] Practically all of these losses were incurred on 12 July, because during the remaining days Rotmistrov's defeated army only played a limited part in combat operations.[17] This data, by all appearances, is somewhat understated, because according to a report by the headquarters of the 29th Tank Corps, which suffered most heavily at Prokhorovka, on 12 July the corps lost 122 T-34s, including 75 irreplaceably, 36 of 70 T-70s, including 28 irreplaceably, and 19 of 20 self-propelled guns, including 14 irreplaceably.[18] Here the corps' irreplaceable losses in self-propelled guns are three times that of the entire 5th Guards Tank Army. Thus the estimation of the 5th Guards Tank Army's irreplaceable losses of 350 tanks and self-propelled guns on 12 July seems closer to the truth.

On the evening of 11 July, according to an estimate by the Swedish historians Niklas Zetterling and Anders Frankson, the SS II Panzer Corps had in line 294 tanks and assault guns. By the evening of 13 July this number had fallen to 251, chiefly due to a reduction in the number of combat-ready tanks and assault guns in the *Totenkopf* Division from 121 to 74.[19] At the same time, it's unlikely that the reduction happened as a result of the fighting around Prokhorovka, because the main burden of the fighting there was borne by the *Leibstandarte* Division.

The SS II Panzer Corps' losses for 12 July amounted to 842 killed, wounded, and missing in action. At the same time, the corps' three divisions announced the following destroyed tanks: during 11–12 July the *Leibstandarte* Division destroyed 192 enemy tanks, *Das Reich* and *Totenkopf* destroyed, respectively, 75 and 77 tanks, for a total of 344 tanks.[20] These figures are close to Soviet data on the 5th Guards Tank Army's irreplaceable losses of 350 tanks and self-propelled guns. In all, the SS Panzer Corps, during the period of Operation 'Citadel', lost from 5–16 July 8,095 killed, wounded, and missing in action, that is, an average of 675 men per day.[21] Thus the losses at the Battle of Prokhorovka were only 1.25 times less than the average for 'Citadel'. If one excludes the losses on 15–16 July, when the SS Panzer Corps was engaged in only limited combat operations and the losses were small (299 and 420 men), then the corps' average losses comprise only 738 men, which is even 1.14 times less than the losses during the Battle of Prokhorovka. It's not surprising that the SS Corps' commander, Paul Hausser, simply did not note in his memoirs the

Battle of Prokhorovka. For him and his subordinates, the day of 12 July was not distinguished from the other days of the Battle of Kursk. On the other days they lost more men and destroyed approximately the same number of Soviet tanks.

And this is how a German soldier saw the Prokhorovka battlefield:

> Wherever you look there lay killed Russian guards soldiers. Draped over their guns in their positions they appeared to be sleeping. Among them were those who had been blown to pieces and crushed in the communications trenches. Whoever survived an air attack fell victim to the attacking tanks, was shot, or was crushed and ground into the mud. Blondin had already seen some things in this war, but such mass death, such cruelty?
>
> 'It's strange' – he raised his upper lip to his nose – 'what were they thinking? The first and most important thing is that they were completely confident that the Germans would never pass through here. Here the Germans would break their last teeth. Besides this, they knew the time for the beginning of the offensive, their own numerical superiority in men, equipment and armaments, and all of a sudden this led to nothing! The Fritzes came not only on the ground, but in the air. And when the machine gun and anti-tank artillery crews and infantrymen saw the first attacking waves in the sky, they were very surprised at the absence of their own fighters. They had no time for anything else [. . .]'
>
> The Russians, who were being cut down with unusual rapidity by the machine gun bursts, tried to break through farther than their killed comrades. It was horrible and at the same time stunning to see with what stubbornness they continued to attack in order to fall victim to a German machine gun with inevitable exactitude. The picture repeated itself. The next wave leaped out. The attackers tried to leap ahead of their killed and wounded comrades who had been cut down and to win a few meters of space. The machine guns' staccato halted them, dropped them on each other and next to each other. The piles of bodies lying before the German grenadiers grew higher and wider.[22]

It should be noted that the German tanks had a material advantage over the Soviet ones in that the crew had a more comfortable environment, which enabled it to operate more effectively in battle. The tank was configured to the crew in the German army, while in the Soviet army the crew was configured to the tank, while the space for the crew was reduced in favour of a more powerful armament and weaponry.

At this time the Germans' 'Tigers' and 'Panthers' were superior to all the Soviet tanks in terms of combat qualities.[23] However, the 'Panthers', which were first employed in battle at Kursk, still had a number of undetected defects, and often broke down. Thus their irreplaceable losses were large. Of the 200 'Panthers' in Army Group South, 42 vehicles had been lost irreplaceably by 17 July.

But it was not so much a question of the Germans' qualitative superiority in armoured equipment as in the Germans' superiority in the level of training of the tank crews and tank commanders, just as it was in the level of training of infantrymen, pilots, the artillery troops, and combined-arms commanders, who were far more able than the Red Army commanders in establishing coordination on the battlefield. And the combination of Rotmistrov and Vatutin against Hausser and Manstein is not even the same as a carpenter against a joiner. So what were they thinking in deciding to launch their main attack in the direction of the Soviet anti-tank ditches?

According to reports, from 1–16 July 1943 the 48th Rifle Corps' 183rd Rifle Division lost 398 killed and 908 wounded (the missing in action were not taken into account). However, the strength of the division's rank and file, even without counting possible reinforcements, fell from the beginning of the fighting to 15 July from 7,981 men to 2,652, that is, its actual losses were not 1,300, but 5,329 soldiers and officers. Evidently, the difference of 4,029 men came about chiefly due to the uncounted missing in action. There was an enormous undercounting of losses in the 37th Rifle Division. During the fighting its strength fell from 8,647 to 3,526 men, which yields actual losses not of 236 but of 5,121 men.[24]

The situation was no better for the Red Army's losses during the fighting along the Kursk bulge. The official figures on losses are easily refuted by information contained in the collection *The Seal of Secrecy Removed* (in all of its editions). According to the collection's data, on 5 July 1943, by the start of the Battle of Kursk, the Central Front's forces numbered 738,000 men and, during the course of the defensive battle from 5–11 July inclusively it lost 18,561 in wounded and sick. At the same time, Army Group Centre took 6,647 prisoners in the first ten days of July and 5,079 in the second.[25] Almost all of these prisoners were taken before 12 July and almost all from the Central Front. Then the number of killed should amount to about 4,000 men, which is obviously too few for more than 18,000 wounded. By the time of the beginning of the Red Army's offensive on Orel on 12 July, the Central Front's strength was almost unchanged: one tank brigade had arrived and two rifle brigades had disappeared.

Actually, these two rifle brigades did not go anywhere. The 226th Rifle Division, which remained as part of the Central Front, was formed from the 42nd and 129th rifle brigades. And the number of divisions in Rokossovskii's front did not change, thanks to the fact that the 132nd Rifle Division, which had suffered heavy losses, was removed from the Central Front (and the active army) to be reformed.[26] Taking into account that the division's surviving rank and file was most likely employed for reinforcing the remaining divisions, one may assume that the Central Front's strength was practically unchanged. At the time a tank brigade had an authorized strength of 1,300 men and it was unlikely that significantly more than 1,300 soldiers remained in the 132nd Rifle Division, which had been pulled out. Taking this into account, by the beginning of the Orel operation the Central Front should have disposed of approximately 704,000 rank-and-file soldiers. However, as the authors of the book *The Seal of Secrecy Removed* maintain, at that moment Rokossovskii's forces numbered only 645,000 men. This means that the Central Front's true losses in the defensive battle around Kursk were, at a minimum, 58,700 men more than the official statistics aver, while the main mass of the undercounted are due to irreplaceable losses.

The Central Front's overall losses during the period from 5–11 July may be estimated at 92,600 men. If it is assumed that the undercounting of losses involved only irreplaceable losses, then the latter have been undercounted approximately by 4.8 times. And this is only on the basis that the Central Front's forces did not receive any reinforcements during the defensive operation. If such reinforcements did arrive, then the actual losses should be even higher (reinforcements did arrive at the neighbouring Voronezh Front during the course of the defensive operation).[27] It would be impossible for such a number of people to desert or to simply disappear without a trace, particularly during bitter fighting. Although it has been repeatedly pointed out to the authors of *The Seal of Secrecy Removed*, this obvious lack of correlation has not been rectified either in print or in direct conversations, and all of these figures remain unchanged in all editions of the book.[28]

The German Ninth Army's losses during the period from 5–11 July 1943 were 3,880 killed, 17,571 wounded, and 822 missing in action, for a total of 22,273 men.[29] The correlation of overall losses with the Soviet Central Front is 4.15:1. During the period from 1–20 July 11,726 prisoners were taken along Army Group Centre's front.[30] One may assume that practically all of them were taken during the period from 5–11 July. If it is assumed that among the Central Front's forces the number of wounded was approximately equal to the number of killed, then the number of killed may be estimated at 40,450 men. Then the correlation of irreplaceable losses with the German Ninth Army would be 11.1:1, and 10.4:1 in killed. However, the assumption that the number of killed among the Central Front's forces is equal to the number of wounded is hardly fair. Then it works out that the official data underestimates the number of wounded by 2.2 times, which seems unlikely. If it is assumed that the undercounting of the actual number of wounded was no more than 1.35 times (the proportion of the undercounting of losses in wounded established by the author for the defence of Odessa), then their true number did not exceed 25,100 men. Then the number of killed among the Central Front's forces may be estimated at 55,800 men. In this case, the Central Front's correlation of losses and the correlation of irreplaceable losses and those of the German Ninth Army will be 14.1:1, and in killed also 14.4:1.

This example destroys the old myth that in the defence around Kursk Rokossovskii's *front* operated significantly more effectively that Vatutin's Voronezh Front. However, it is not possible to so exactly count the correlation of human losses along the southern flank of the Kursk bulge.

The losses suffered by operational group 'Kempf' from 4–20 July were 1,271 killed, 6,994 wounded, and 224 missing in action, for a total of 8,489 men.[31] The Fourth Panzer Army's losses for the same period were 18,594 men.[32] This yields an overall total of 27,083 men. According to other data, group 'Kempf's' losses were 2,650 killed, 715 missing in action, and 14,404 wounded for 1–20 July. The Fourth Panzer Army lost 2,977 killed, 430 missing in action ,and 12,295 wounded. Overall, this amounts to 5,627 killed, 1,145 missing in action, and 26,699 wounded, for a total of 33,467 men.[33] This estimate seems the closest to reality. The Fourth Panzer Army's and group 'Kempf's losses in killed were 16.1 per cent and the losses in missing in action were 9 per cent of the losses of all the German forces in the East for July 1943.

In all, during the period from 5 July 1943 to 1 January 1944, Soviet forces took 40,730 prisoners.[34] During July–December 1943 the German eastern army lost 89,516 missing in action. It follows that during this period the share of prisoners among the missing in action among the German forces in the East is 45.5 per cent. One may assume that in the German armies which took part in the Battle of Kursk, the share of prisoners among the missing in action was approximately the same. Then the losses for group 'Kempf' and the Fourth Panzer Army in killed for 1–20 July may be estimated at 5,934 and 838 prisoners. The overall number of killed in the German army in the East may be estimated at 43,053, with 6,684 prisoners. Correspondingly, the share of killed for 1–20 July within group 'Kempf' and the Fourth Panzer Army comprised 13.8 per cent and the share of prisoners 12.5 per cent of the corresponding losses by the German army on the Soviet-German front.

One may determine Soviet losses along the southern flank of 'Citadel' in the following manner. Soviet losses in wounded in July and August 1943 were the highest for the entire war, primarily due to the losses in the Battle of Kursk. In July they were 144 per cent and in August 173 per cent of the average monthly loss for the war.[35] Correspondingly, the Red Army's losses in killed for these months may be estimated at 720,000 and 865,000 men respectively. One may assume that Soviet losses in killed during 1–20 July along the southern flank of the Kursk bulge were about 13.8 per cent of all killed in July, that is, 99,400 men. During 1–20 July Army Group South took 39,028 prisoners, practically all during 'Citadel'.[36] The correlation of irreplaceable losses along the southern flank of the Kursk bulge during the course of the German offensive may be estimated at 20.4:1 and the correlation of killed at 16.8:1. The better indices for the correlation of irreplaceable losses for Army Group South, compared with Army Group Centre, can be explained primarily by the large number of captured prisoners.

The situation in terms of losses for the Soviet forces along the southern flank of the Kursk bulge was even worse in the case of certain divisions. For example, the Soviet 5th Guards Army's 95th Guards Rifle Division lost 948 men killed, 1,649 wounded, and 729 missing in action, for a total of 3,326 men, on 12 July 1943 alone during the famous Battle of Prokhorovka. What is typical about this example is that the Soviet irreplaceable losses are 18 men more, or 1.01 times more than the losses in wounded. At the same time, the division's actions were considered successful and its commander, Guards Colonel A.N. Lyakhov, was awarded the Order of the Fatherland War First Class (he died on 19 September 1943) for the Battle of Prokhorovka.[37] At the same time, the German Fourth Panzer Army, which was fighting opposite the 95th Guards Rifle Division, lost 1,400 killed, 244 missing in action, and 4,081 wounded, for a total of 5,725 men, for the period of 11–20 July 1943.[38] If a German army's overall losses for the ten-day period are nevertheless greater than that of a Soviet division for one day, although this was only by 1.7 times, then the Soviet division comes out on top according to irreplaceable losses, insofar as its losses in killed and missing in action are 33 men more, or 1.02 times more than German losses. It should be added that on 11 July 1943, while repelling the German offensive, one of the battalions of the 290th Guards Rifle Regiment, which belonged to the same 95th Guards Rifle Division, lost 330 soldiers killed and wounded out of 600.[39] During July 1943 the Fourth Panzer Army numbered ten divisions, seven of which during the period from 11 through 20 July were engaged in practically non-stop fighting, while conducting an offensive within the confines of Operation 'Citadel' all the way up to 16 July, and then carrying out a withdrawal to their jumping-off positions through rearguard actions. They were opposed by the Soviet 69th, 5th, and

6th guards, 1st Tank and 5th Guards Tank armies, which numbered, not counting *front* reserves, twenty rifle and airborne divisions and nine mechanized corps. Only the LII Army Corps, which numbered three infantry divisions, did not participate in 'Citadel', but was only engaged in local fighting against the Soviet 40th Army, which consisted of seven rifle divisions. But even here the sides suffered significant losses. Thus it's possible that the actual correlation of irreplaceable losses along the front of the German Fourth Panzer Army during the period from 11–20 July 1943 could have exceeded 50:1 in favour of the Germans.

The situation of the German XLVIII Panzer Corps, which was operating against Mikhail Katukov's 1st Tank Army and which had a large number of unreliable 'Panthers', was at least in the Soviet tank troops' favour.[40] Thus the XLVIII Panzer Corps' irreplaceable losses reached seventy-eight tanks and seven assault guns by 16 July, which was twice that of the SS corps. Katukov's army irreplaceably lost 312 tanks and self-propelled guns in the defensive battle.[41] Mikhail Katukov nevertheless commanded more skillfully than the commander of the 5th Guards Tank Army, Pavel Rotmistrov.

Along the northern flank of the Kursk bulge the German Ninth Army's tank formations lost irreplaceably up to 14 July eighty-seven tanks and assault guns in the offensive on Kursk. During this same period the opposing Central Front lost approximately 400 vehicles. Army Group South's tank corps lost irreplaceably 161 tanks and 14 assault guns up until 16 July, while the opposing troops of the Voronezh Front lost about 1,200 tanks and self-propelled guns.[42]

During the Soviet offensive on Orel and Khar'kov during the second half of July and in August of 1943, the Soviet losses were just as large as they had been while repelling 'Citadel'. For example, during the offensive against the Orel salient on 18–20 July 1943 the 11th Guards Army's 108th Rifle Division lost 3,500 killed and wounded and 374 missing in action. During the period from 11–20 July the German Second Panzer Army, which was opposite it, lost 10,120 men killed and wounded and 375 missing in action. Taking into account that through these 10 days the Second Panzer Army was engaged in heavy fighting, one may assume that it lost about 3,000 men during the last 3 days, that is, possibly less than a single Soviet division.

The Soviet 3rd Guards Tank Army, in attacking on Orel during the period from 19–31 July 1943, lost 3,808 men killed and missing in action and 5,783 wounded, according to an army report.[43] However, on 10 July the 3rd Tank Army's rank and file numbered 39,344 men, while only 11,213 on 30 July.[44] This indicates a colossal undercounting of losses, particularly irreplaceable ones. The 3rd Guards Tank Army's actual losses may be estimated at 18,131 men, which is nearly twice as much as according to the command's report. During the period from 19–26 July Rybalko's army lost 2,484 killed, 5,241 wounded, burned and concussed, 912 missing in action, 55 fallen ill, and 131 out of action due to other causes, for a total of 8,823 men.[45] The German Second Panzer Army, which was facing the 3rd Guards Tank Army, lost during the period from 11–31 July 8,144 killed, 30,832 wounded, and 5,893 missing in action, for a total of 44,869 men.[46] However, as opposed to the 3rd Guards Tank Army, the German Second Panzer Army was fighting continuously from 11–31 July, and what was most important, only one of its three corps – Lothar Rendulich's XXXV Army Corps – which consisted of four infantry divisions, was fighting against the 3rd Guards Tank Army. And besides the 3rd Guards Tank Army, the German XXXV Army Corps was also attacked by the 61st and 3rd combined-arms armies, which numbered eight and six divisions, respectively, as well as the 63rd Army's right flank, consisting of three divisions, as well as one tank corps. All of these forces outnumbered the 3rd Guards Tank Army in strength by six times and took part in the fighting 2.5 times longer than Rybalko's army. Taking this into account, the 3rd Guards Tank Army probably accounts for no more than 1/36 of the German Second Panzer Army's irreplaceable losses for the period from 19–26 July, that is, about 390 men, which is 15.6 times less than the irreplaceable losses of Rybalko's army.

Also, the losses of the Soviet 11th Tank Corps during the battle for Orel, according to brigade reports, were no less than 804 killed and missing in action and no less than 1,619 wounded during the period from 26–8 July, for a total of 2,423 men. According to a corps report on losses, during the period from 20–9 July the 11th Tank Corps lost only 388 killed and missing in action and 792 wounded.[47] Thus even for a longer period of time the irreplaceable losses suddenly fell by 2.1 times and the losses in wounded by 2 times.

A threatening telegram by the deputy chief of the General Staff, A.I. Antonov to Rokossovskii, has been preserved: 'According to the General Staff's data, the 3rd Guards Tank Army's tank group, consisting of 110 tanks, lost 100 tanks on 10.8 in the fighting for height 264.6, that is, it was basically destroyed by the enemy.'[48] Rokossovskii attempted to hide this fact and, having pulled Rybalko's army into the reserve, that same evening of 10 August reported to the *Stavka* that the group would reenter the fighting on the morning of the 11th. However, someone, probably the General Staff's representative in the army, reported to Moscow that on 11 August Rybalko's army, having lost 100 tanks, was already in the reserve. As a result of this, by all appearances they decided to disperse the losses over 9–10 August, and not over 10–11 August. Thus, according to Soviet data, only sixty-five tanks were knocked out on 10 August.[49]

During the period from 3–8 August 1943, during the course of the Belgorod–Khar'kov operation, the 95th Guards Rifle Division lost 1,183 men killed and wounded.[50] During the first ten days of August the German Fourth Panzer Army lost 192 killed, 41 missing in action, and 969 wounded, for a total of 1,202 men, which is only 19 men, or 1.02 times more than the losses of a Soviet division in 6 days of fighting.

Things were no better for the correlation of losses during the course of the Soviet offensive on the Mius River, which continued from 17 July to 2 August 1943. For example, the 5th Shock Army alone lost during 16–17 July 1,607 killed and 4,770 wounded, for a total of 6,377 men, as well as 17 guns and 47 tanks.[51] During the period from 11–20 July, the German Sixth Army, which was facing it, lost 1,294 killed, 164 missing in action, and 5,920 wounded, for a total of 7,378 men, that is, only 1.2 times more than the 5th Shock Army lost over 2 days.[52] The 5th Shock Army lost 1.2 times more men killed than the German Sixth Army. Actually, the gap was even wider, because the Soviet forces probably suffered significant losses in missing in action. By factoring in the missing in action, the 5th Shock Army's overall losses for the two days most likely exceeded the German Sixth Army's losses for the ten-day period. But at this time the German Sixth Army was opposed not only by the 5th Shock Army, but also by the 28th, 44th, 51st and 2nd Guards armies. The 2nd Guards Army's 4th Guards Mechanized Corps alone lost from 21–3 July 914 killed and 3,915 wounded, for a total of 4,829 men and 128 out of 203 tanks.[53] During the period from 21–31 July the German Sixth Army lost 1,986 men killed, 8,034 wounded, and 1,275 missing in action.[54] The army's ten-day losses in killed were only 2.1 times more than the mechanized corps' losses over three days. During the offensive on the Mius from 17–25 July, the Soviet 28th Army lost 2,975 killed and 12,496 wounded.[55] Thus in killed and wounded, it suffered only 1.1 times fewer losses than the German Sixth Army during the last two ten-day periods of July. The Southern Front's overall losses during the period from 17–24 July of 43,000 killed, wounded, and missing in action seem heavily undercounted.[56] After all, only the losses by the armies and corps enumerated by the author for a shorter period of time yield no less than 26,677 men, while at the same time not counting the missing in action. And these figures concern less than half of the forces taking part in the offensive on the Mius during this period.

On 1 August the 1st Guards Mechanized Corps, which had been newly committed to the fighting, lost 189 killed, 360 wounded, and 160 missing in action.[57] During the period from 1–10 August the German Sixth Army lost 861 killed, 4,085 wounded, and 104 men missing in action.[58] This time the corps' losses in killed and missing in action for this day were only 1.8 times less than the German Sixth Army's ten-day losses. The practical equality of the numbers of wounded and the overall number of killed and missing in action leads one to assume that the losses were counted more or less precisely.

During the entire time of the Mius operation, from 17 July to 2 August the 28th Army lost 45 per cent of its rank and file.[59] From 17–28 July the 5th Shock Army lost 4,325 killed and 15,816 wounded. At the same time the army's 40th Guards Rifle Division alone, if one compares its strength at the beginning of the operation and at the end of the fighting, lost 4,640 killed, wounded, and missing in action, not counting possible reinforcements. As there were eight divisions and one brigade in the 5th Shock Army, it is highly unlikely that the remaining seven divisions and one brigade lost only twice as much as the 40th Guards Rifle Division. Evidently, there was in the 5th Shock Army, as in other armies, a colossal undercounting of losses due to missing in action, possibly by 1.5 times. From 18 July to 4 August the 4th Guards Mechanized Corps lost 5,400 killed, wounded, and missing. The 2nd Guards Mechanized Corps, according to incomplete data, lost during the Mius operation about 6,000 killed and wounded, while the remaining formations of the 2nd Guards Army lost about 20,000.[60] Clearly, all of these figures only take into account to an insignificant degree the losses incurred during the period from 30 July to 2 August, when the Southern Front's forces suffered their main losses, particularly in prisoners, as a result of the SS II Panzer Corps' counterblow. Overall, during the course of the Mius operation, the Germans captured 17,895 prisoners.[61] Thus the official figures for the losses by Soviet forces during the Mius operation of 61,070 men, including 15,303 irreplaceably, are significantly understated.[62] According to official figures, from 1–10 August the Southern Front's forces lost 6,249 killed, 4,258 missing in action, and 18,846 wounded.[63] The overwhelming majority of these losses were incurred on 1 and 2 August, when there was fighting on the bridgehead. Evidently, the losses in missing in action have been undercounted by several times, because the Germans took the main mass of prisoners in eliminating the bridgehead across the Mius on 1 and 2 August. However, even these undercounted figures are 5.8 times greater than the losses of the German Sixth Army for the same period. The correlation is even worse for the Soviet side in irreplaceable losses – 10.9:1. By taking into account uncounted losses in missing in action of 21,369 men, the actual correlation may exceed 20:1. The German Sixth Army lost 21,369 men during the period from 17 July to 2 August 1943, including 3,298 men killed, 2,254 missing in action, and 15,817 wounded.[64]

On 18–19 August, when the Soviet offensive along the Mius resumed, the Southern Front, according to a report by *front* headquarters, lost 2,468 men killed and 8,148 wounded, for a total of 10,616 men.[65] During the ten-day period from 11–20 August the German Sixth Army lost 218 men killed, 3 missing in action, and 1,462 wounded, for a total of 1,683 men.[66] As is already apparent, Soviet *front* reports on losses usually understate losses compared with the corresponding divisional reports, particularly in missing in action. But even these understated losses are greater than the German Sixth Army's losses for the entire ten-day period by 6.3 times. The correlation is even more favourable for the Germans in numbers killed – 11.3:1. During the period from 21–31 August the 248th Rifle Division alone lost 616 killed and 1,728 wounded.[67] During the period from 21–31 August the German Sixth Army lost 564 killed, 2,551 wounded, and 364 missing in action. Thus its losses for the last two ten-day periods in August were 5,162 men, including 782 killed, 4,013 wounded and 367, missing in action. Thus according to overall losses, a Soviet division lost 2.2 times less than a German army, and only 1.3 times according to those killed. But 20 rifle divisions, 2 mechanized, 1 tank, and 2 cavalry corps took part in the offensive.[68] For example, the 4th Guards Cavalry Corps alone lost 738 men from 26–9 August.[69] This leads one to assume that the losses of the Southern Front and the opposing German Sixth Army during the breakthrough of the Mius front during the second half of August 1943 were of different orders and that Soviet irreplaceable losses could have exceeded those of the Germans by 15–20 times.

Over counting the number of prisoners was a longstanding tradition in the Red Army. Moreover, this was done not only during 1944–5, when there were tens and hundreds of thousands, but in 1942 as well, when the numbers of prisoners were sometimes counted in tens and hundreds. For example, the deputy commander of the 4th Guards Kuban' Cossack Cavalry Corps, Colonel V.V. Bardadin, in a letter to the Central Committee of the VKP(b) of 28 October 1942, reported, in particular, that during a raid on Kushchevskaya stanitsa on 29 July 1942 units of the corps, which was commanded by Lieutenant General N.Ya. Kirichenko, took not 300 prisoners, as was written in the report, but only 13.[70] This is typical of the reports by the 4th Guards Cavalry Corps during the time N.Ya. Kirichenko commanded it; the number of prisoners taken was usually multiplied by 100. For example, during the breakthrough of the Mius front during the period from 26–30 August 100, 120, 150, and 200 prisoners were consecutively taken, for a total of 2,000 out of 5,100 prisoners, which were supposedly taken during the period from 18–30 August 1943 by the Southern Front.[71] Taking into account the fact that the German Sixth Army, which was opposite the Southern Front, lost during the final two ten-day periods in August 367 men missing in action, particularly as among them were both captured and killed, one may judge the degree of reality in the reports of both the 4th Guards Cavalry Corps and the

Southern Front as a whole.[72] It's likely that the correlation of the actual number of prisoners and those listed in the reports was approximately the same as during the fighting in Kushchevskaya stanitsa in July 1942.

During the operation to liberate Kiev, which was conducted by the forces of the First Ukrainian Front from 3–13 November 1943, the 3rd Guards Tank Army alone claimed to have captured 2,546 prisoners.[73] Meanwhile, the forces of the German Fourth Panzer Army, which were defending Kiev, lost 389 killed, 3,018 wounded and 432 missing during the period 1–20 November 1943.[74] Thus, the real number of prisoners taken by the Soviet side was overestimated by at least six times.

In July 1943 the losses of the German army in the East, by the author's estimates, were 43,053 killed and 6,684 captured. In this month 66,049 prisoners were taken.[75] The correlation of irreplaceable losses was 15.8:1 and in killed 16.7:1.

In August German losses may be estimated, taking the share of captured among the missing in action at 45.5 per cent, at 45,486 men, with 9,237 captured. In August the Germans captured 29,342 prisoners. The correlation of irreplaceable losses is 16.3:1 and the losses in killed are 19:1. A significant change in the data of the indices did not take place in comparison with July. The improvement in the correlation in killed for the Germans was almost totally compensated for by a worsening in the correlation of those taken prisoner, of which the Germans took in August 2.25 times fewer than in July. The fact that in July the Red Army was defending for a third of a month and only attacked in August resulted in a situation in which the correlation of killed worsened for it, while the losses in prisoners fell. Evidently, if the *Wehrmacht* had not attacked in July and only defended, it would have had approximately the same correlation of killed as the Red Army did in August, although it would have taken, as a minimum, twice as many prisoners less. The refusal to launch an offensive would not have changed the course of the struggle on the Eastern Front, or the time of the Soviet forces' arrival at the Dnepr.

In August the Red Army attacked not only along the Orel and Khar'kov axes, but along other sectors of the front, suffering equally heavy losses. The dispersion of force led to futile sacrifices. During the fighting in the area of the Sinyavin heights near Leningrad on 18–21 August 1943, the 67th Army's 196th Rifle Division lost 2,658 men, including 760 irreplaceably. At the same time, there was almost no fighting on 21 August.[76] The German Eighteenth Army opposite it lost 1,190 killed, 156 missing in action, and 4,600 wounded during the period from 11–20 August, for a total of 5,946 men.[77] This was 2.2 times greater than the losses of a Soviet division for four (actually, three) days. And the irreplaceable losses of a German army were only 1.8 times more than the losses of a Soviet division.

During the liberation of the Donbass and the Red Army's victorious advance to the Dnepr, the correlation of losses did not change principally. For example, in the fighting for the liberation of Kramatorsk during 6–8 September 1943, the 59th Guards Rifle Division lost 114 killed and 239 wounded (there is no data on the missing in action).[78] The opposing German First Panzer Army lost 624 killed, 3,146 wounded, and 384 missing in action for the 10-day period from 11–20 September.[79] Its losses could have amounted to about 187 in 3 day's fighting, which is comparable to the losses of a Soviet division.

As Sergei Pirozhkov, the former Ukrainian ambassador to Moldova and the current vice-president of the Ukrainian National Academy of Sciences, wrote, during the course of the battle for the Dnepr 'about 240,000 Soviet soldiers died on the Lyutezh bridgehead'.[80] The official Russian figure of Soviet irreplaceable losses in the Lyutezh operation during the period from 1 October to 2 November 1943 was 24,422 killed and missing in action, and 6,498 during the Bukrin operation during the period from 12–24 October 1943.[81] Even by taking into account the fact that significant losses were also suffered in the fighting from 26–30 September, as well as the period from 3–6 November, during the offensive on Kiev, the data is of a different magnitude. The First Ukrainian Front's losses in the Kiev operation from 3–13 November were 6,491 killed and 1,465 missing in action, and 14,758 wounded.[82] The German Fourth Panzer Army, which was opposite the First Ukrainian Front around Kiev during the period from 20 September to 10 November 1943, lost 1,548 killed, 1,465 missing in action, and 14,758 wounded.[83] During the period from 1 October to 1 November 1943 26 rifle and airborne divisions, 3 rifle and airborne brigades, 3 cavalry divisions, and 2 tank and 1 mechanized corps were added to the First Ukrainian (Voronezh) Front. During this same time 26 rifle and airborne divisions and 2 tank and 1 mechanized corps were removed from the *front*. In all, twenty-nine of fifty formations at the divisional level as of 1 October were removed.[84] The removed formations likely suffered the same kind of heavy losses that required the nearly completely replacement of the combat troops. Other 'old' divisions probably also suffered losses. Also, almost all of the new formations managed to take part in the October fighting, chiefly on the Bukrin bridgehead. If the figure of 240,000 irreplaceable losses is correct, then the First Ukrainian Front's overall losses should have amounted to, taking into account the wounded, no less than 480,000 men. Thus for each formation which made up a part of the First Ukrainian Front in October, there was an average of somewhat less than 6,000 killed, wounded, and missing in action, which is quite likely.

It should be noted that the member of the Southern Front's military council, the former deputy people's commissar for defence for personnel, Ye. A. Shchadenko, wrote on 6 October 1943 to GKO member G.M. Malenkov, that in September 1943 alone the *front* called up 115,000 men directly into the units, of which 18,675 (18 per cent) were draftees who had not previously served in the Red Army, and the remainder former Red Army soldiers who had stayed in occupied territory.[85] One may confidently assume that a significant part, if not the majority, of these who identified themselves as former servicemen, had not actually served in the Red Army, but preferred to call themselves former Red Army servicemen so as to avoid accusations of failing to be drafted and desertion in 1941.

According to a report by the headquarters of the Fourth Ukrainian Front for the period of the Melitopol' operation, which lasted from 26 September to 5 November 1943, the *front's* forces captured 22,207 enemy soldiers and officers.[86] One may be forgiven for doubting this figure. The Germans' Sixth Army's losses for the last ten days of September to the first ten days of November inclusively were 4,077 killed, 16,681 wounded, and only 3,591 missing in action.[87] Even if it is assumed that some portion of prisoners was due to the presence of a Romanian division as part of the Sixth Army, this is still a long way short of the figure of 22,207 prisoners. During September–November 1943 the Romanians on the Eastern Front lost 2,138 missing in action, of which the main part was due to the fighting along the Kerch' peninsula, which began on 31 October. Romanian losses in missing in action were only 89 men up to the end of October. As V.P. Galitskii notes, the Fourth Ukrainian Front captured only 10,687 men during the significantly greater period from 20 October 1943 to 1 March 1944.[88] The clearly exaggerated data on prisoners from the *front* command's combat report, where no less fantastical data for 85,000 Germans killed is found, was necessary in order to soften the impression of the Southern (Fourth Ukrainian) Front's heavy losses, which accounted for, according to the clearly undercounted data from the collection in *The Seal of Secrecy Removed*, 283,706 men, including 60,980 killed and missing in action.[89]

Soviet landings followed on the Kerch'peninsula, in the area of Kerch' and El'tigen, at the end of October and beginning of November 1943, which, on the whole, ended in failure, although the Soviets managed to hold a bridgehead in the Kerch'a area. On the eve of the landing, on 6 October, the *Luftwaffe* sank the Soviet flotilla leader *Khar'kov* and two destroyers, which were returning from a raiding operation against the Crimean ports. This was the last battle of major surface vessels in the history of the Soviet fleet. As a result, the *Stavka* forbade the employment of battleships, cruisers, and destroyers in combat operations without its permission, and they sat around in ports until the end of the war. As a result of this, the Kerch'–El'tigen landing operation was conducted only with the assistance of small vessels, which led to heavy losses. On the whole, the operation ended in a defeat. The Soviet forces were not only forced to renounce their initial plan for capturing the entire Crimea, but were not even able to liberate Kerch', and limited themselves to seizing a small beachhead along the Kerch' peninsula. The El'tigen landing was almost completely destroyed. As a result of this failure, the commander of the Independent Maritime Army, General Ivan Yefimovich Petrov, and the commander of the Black Sea Fleet, Vice Admiral Lev Anatol'evich Vladimirskii, were removed from their posts and reduced in rank.[90]

According to Andrei Kuznetsov's estimate, the Soviet side's irreplaceable losses in the Kerch'–El'tigen operation were about 9,500 men, including no less than 1,201 drowned and no fewer than 3,085 missing in action, with the wounded amounting to about 14,300 men.[91] However, this data is obviously undercounted. German Army Group A took 5,496 prisoners during the period from 1 November to 20 December.[92] The overwhelming majority of these prisoners were taken by the Seventeenth Army, which was fighting in the Crimea. If it is assumed that the army captured at least 5,000 prisoners and exclude the 1,200 drowned from the irreplaceable losses, then the share of killed alone remains at only 3,300 men. In this case, there are 4.3 wounded for each man killed. However, such a correlation of losses seems highly unlikely. After all, a significant portion of the wounded was captured and fell into the category of missing in action. Besides this, many landing groups were almost completely destroyed and had no opportunity to evacuate the wounded. The majority of the latter either died or was killed in the fighting. Thus the assumption that the number of killed is approximately equal to the number of wounded and accounts for about 14,300 men appears more realistic. Then the Soviet forces' overall irreplaceable losses may be estimated at 20,500 men. It should be noted that this is 2.9 times greater than the estimate of Soviet irreplaceable losses during the Kerch'–El'tigen operation of 6,985 made by G.F. Krivosheev and his colleagues.[93] And as has become clear, this source, on the average, undercounts Soviet irreplaceable losses by approximately three times. Thus overall Soviet combat losses may be estimated at 34,800 men.

The German Seventeenth Army's losses during the period from 1 November to 20 December 1943 were 1,577 killed, 796 missing in action, and 7,286 wounded.[94] According to A.Ya. Kuznetsov's estimate, the losses of the German forces, which had been combined with the V Mountain Rifle Corps, were about 1,655 killed and missing in action and 3,799 wounded in the fighting along the Kerch' peninsula.[95] If this calculation is true, then the loss of those units of the German Seventeenth Army that fought at Perekop may be estimated at 718 killed and missing in action and 3,487 wounded. It works out that at Perekop there were 4.9 wounded for every man killed or missing in action, while this was only 2.3 on the Kerch' peninsula. Such a material difference may have come about both by undercounting the wounded in A.Ya. Kuznetsov's estimate and, which seems more likely, by the fact that part of the Germans' irreplaceable losses on the Kerch' peninsula were due to those taken prisoner. If we assume that the actual correlation of wounded and killed on the Kerch' peninsula was at least the mean between 4.9 and 2.3, that is, 3.6:1, then the overall number of killed in the V Mountain Rifle Corps may be estimated at 1,055 men and the number of captured at 600 men, which seems quite close to the truth and does not contradict the data on the number of missing in action. The losses of the Romanian forces that took part in repelling the Soviet landings on the Kerch' peninsula were about 360 killed and missing in action and 1,510 wounded in the period from 1 November to 11 December.[96] The *Luftwaffe's* losses during this same period were 119 men killed, 6 missing in action, and 310 missing, while the *Kriegsmarine* lost 26 men killed, 32 missing in action, and 72 wounded.[97] In all, German and Romanian combat losses were 7,889 men, including 2,198 irreplaceably. This yields a correlation according to overall losses of 4.4:1 and 10.3:1 in irreplaceable losses. If one subtracts the irreplaceable losses by the Romanians, the *Kriegsmarine*, and the *Luftwafffe*, as well as the Red Army's losses in the fighting against them, as well as the losses in wounded, then the correlation of German and Soviet ground force losses in killed will be 13.9:1, which does not differ too much from the average correlation for the period from June 1941 to May 1944.

In December 1943 the Germans were able to launch a series of counterblows along the Ukrainian right bank that briefly halted the Soviet offensive. The German supreme command estimated the Soviet losses in the Radomyshl' area along the Fourth Panzer Army's front at 11,000 killed and 4,400 wounded, as well as 254 tanks and 927 guns from 1–20 December 1943.[98] The German Fourth Panzer Army's irreplaceable losses from 1–20 December 1943 were 1,582 killed and 633 missing in action.[99] The correlation in killed turns out to be 7:1 in favour of the Germans. But as the Fourth Panzer Army was engaged in heavy fighting during the period from 1–5 and from 14–20 December, the correlation of losses killed was actually even more favourable for the *Wehrmacht*.

Artillery divisions began to be formed in the Red Army as early as the end of 1942. At the beginning of 1943 brigades were organized within them. As a result, the heavy artillery regiments, which earlier were directly subordinated to the army and were supplied with shells, fuel, and spare parts from the army rear, were now forced to transmit the corresponding requests not directly through the army rear services, but first through the brigade, from which they arrived at the division, and only from there to the army, which tripled the documentary turnaround and sharply slowed down the supply of essentials. In reality, even a heavy artillery regiment had no operational importance, because it was employed, as a rule, by battalion, and sometimes even by battery. Artillery brigades and artillery divisions had even less operational significance. Thus only the number of generals' slots increased. The commander of the 1,100th Gun Artillery Regiment, Colonel Ivan Yakovlevich Kuznetsov, wrote in his diary on 7 January 1944 regarding this:

> Things are, as before, going poorly with the auto-tractor park; there are no tractors for an entire battalion and no one is taking any measures. The same thing with the vehicles; there are no spare parts, so you have to make repairs as best you can. I don't know what's ahead, but it would be better to disband the regiment, because that can be done now rather than keeping things in their present state. If an offensive should begin tomorrow the regiment will not be able to move and then correspondence will start all the way up to the prosecutor. When the regiment was an army one, it was another matter with supply of all kinds. We were never short of anything, but as soon as we became part of the artillery division interruptions and hardships began. Things have simply become shameful; for example, the division has its own rear establishment, a special group of workers, beginning with the deputy division commander for rear affairs, but instead of this apparatus supplying the units with the essentials, Kulagin sits and scribbles directives; the units themselves have to lay up all kinds of food supplies. This is simply a indignant fact, and when we begin to speak about this we are simply told 'Don't think, carry out your orders.' Thus we have to work for others.[100]

As a result, Soviet heavy artillery during 1943–5 was much more often stuck waiting for fuel, shells, and spare parts for vehicles than it actually participated in the fighting. Despite the turning point in the course of combat operations on the Soviet-German front, the new organizational forms, which had been introduced by the Red Army command, were purely bureaucratic innovations that did not ease but only made more difficult the carrying out of combat assignments.

From 1 July 1943, on the eve of the Battle of Kursk, all the way up to 1 May 1945, the strength of the German ground army on the Eastern Front fell steadily, according to the estimate by the German historian Rudiger Overmanns, from 3,100,000 to 1,500,000 men.[101] This took place due to the diversion of forces against the Western Allies and due to the impossibility of making good the constantly increasing losses through exhausted human resources. This increased the Red Army's numerical superiority and, accordingly, led to the further increase in German losses, putting the *Wehrmacht* in a hopeless situation. When the correlation of troop strength was 1:1 or 1.5:1 in favour of the Red Army (exactly as it was in 1941, taking into account that the Germans never had a numerical advantage), the *Wehrmacht* successfully attacked in all directions, created gigantic 'cauldrons', and captured millions of prisoners. When the Soviet numerical advantage rose to 2.5–3:1, as was the case during the Battle of Kursk and the subsequent battles during the second half of 1943, the Germans could only successfully conduct limited offensives involving the capture of tens of thousands of prisoners, after which, however, there inevitably followed Soviet offensives. As a result of these assaults, the Germans left large amounts of territory to the Red Army, but up until the middle of 1944 did not suffer large losses in prisoners. The exception was Stalingrad, but there the demise of the Sixth Army was the result of a political mistake by Hitler in not allowing Paulus's army to first fall back to the Don from the Volga trap and then forbidding him to break out in the first days following the encirclement. And following the Allied landings in Normandy and all the way up to the end of the war, when the Soviet numerical superiority was 4:1 and more, the Red Army attacked successfully, capturing tens and hundreds of thousands of prisoners, while the Germans could only launch limited counterblows, which often did not achieve their aim. At the same time, in 1941 and the first half of 1942 it made no great difference whether the Red Army attacked or defended, insofar as in all cases, excluding the Moscow counteroffensive in December 1941, it eventually suffered defeats and incurred irreplaceable losses tens of times exceeding those of the enemy. The defence and forced retreat in the south in the second half of 1942 may have saved the Soviet forces from an even greater defeat, but as early as September the Red Army was essentially attacking, attempting to cut off Paulus's army, which was not so difficult, because in the middle of November Romanian forces were chiefly defending its extremely elongated communications. In the Battle of Kursk, it was unlikely that the Red Army's striking first would have essentially hastened the end of the war. Such a development would only have increased the Red Army's losses in killed and reduced its losses in prisoners, particularly as both of these factors compensated each other to a great degree.

Such heavy casualties by the Red Army may be explained by the fact that its divisions actually represented poorly trained militia, which did not know how to attack or defend well. Stalin feared a professional army, in which he saw a threat to his own absolute power. In terms of combat capability, the Russian army was significantly inferior to the German army during the First World War, but by the beginning of the Great Patriotic War the gap between the two armies had grown even larger.

On the whole, in the second half of 1943 the Red Army, beginning with the Battle of Kursk, once again, as was the case at Stalingrad, was able, by crushing the enemy with corpses, to break the *Wehrmacht's* defensive front. But this time it broke the Germans not only with soldiers, but with a mass of armoured equipment. The number of Soviet tanks and self-propelled guns available on 30 June 1943 was 12,576 vehicles, of which 10,060 were combat-ready. By 31 December their number had fallen to 5,643, including 2,413 vehicles not ready for combat. On 30 June the Germans had 3,434 vehicles, including 3,060 considered combat-ready, and on 31 December 3,356, including 1,818 vehicles considered combat-ready.[102] Despite the USSR's two-fold superiority in the production of armoured equipment, the delivery of tanks through Lend-Lease and the necessity for Germany to dispatch part of its armoured equipment to the Italian front, during six months the gap between the overall strength of tanks and self-propelled guns fell from 3.7 to 1.7 times, and in the number of combat-ready tanks and self-propelled guns from 3.3 to 1.3 times. This was the result of the fact that Soviet irreplaceable losses in armoured equipment exceeded the Germans' by 4–5 times.

Victory at the Battle of Kursk enabled the Red Army to throw the *Wehrmacht* beyond the Dnepr, to liberate Smolensk, the entire Ukrainian left bank, and to create a broad bridgehead on the right bank. The next step was to arrive at the border of the USSR and to shift combat operations to the countries of Eastern Europe and German territory, where Stalin calculated on arriving before the Western Allies. There was as yet still human resources for making up the enormous losses. From 1943 employing draftees from the liberated territories was carried out extensively. These troops were most often called up directly into the units and thrown into the fighting completely without training and, in their overwhelming majority, without arms.

Following the Battle of Kursk, the German army had no opportunity to organize a full-scale offensive on the Eastern Front. The main part of the *Luftwaffe* had to be transferred to the West, in order to repel the Anglo-American strategic bombing campaign and for the struggle in the Mediterranean. The Italian collapse forced Hitler to transfer significant forces for holding the Italian front and the Balkans. Besides this, from January 1944 the German army and the *Luftwaffe* began to concentrate in France and Belgium for repelling the Allied landings, which were considered inevitable in the spring or summer of 1944. All of this deprived Germany of the opportunity of holding any kind of reserves on the Eastern Front, as well as to create a *Luftwaffe* group of forces sufficient if only for defensive purposes. All of this prevented the *Wehrmacht* from taking full advantage of the success of its counterblows in Ukraine at the end of 1943 and to attempt to at least restore the defence along the Dnepr.

Chapter 7

The Normandy Invasion and Soviet Successes in 1944–5

What Would Have Happened to the Red Army if the Normandy Invasion had Been Postponed Until June 1945? The Battle for the 'Alpine Redoubt'

Although the volume of Germany's efforts in the struggle against the Western Allies on the land fronts during 1941–5 is evaluated at 1,151 division-months, and at 7,510 division-months against the USSR, or 86 per cent of the overall volume of efforts, this index does not reflect the actual influence of the Western Allies on the course of the struggle on the Eastern Front.[1] As early as January 1944 the Germans began to concentrate forces for repelling the expected Anglo-American invasion of France and were deprived of the opportunity of holding sufficient planes and tanks in the East even for carrying out purely defensive actions.

At the beginning of 1944 Soviet forces continued the offensive, launching the main attack in Ukraine. However, the Soviet command sought to be strong everywhere and consecutively launched attacks along the entire front. On 6 November 1944 Stalin enumerated ten of these attacks in a report dedicated to the 27th anniversary of the October Revolution. Later, these began to be called the 'ten Stalinist blows'. The first attack was launched in January to break through the Leningrad blockade (Operation 'January Thunder'). But even before the beginning of the breakthrough of the Leningrad blockade, the Kirovograd operation began, and before the completion of Operation 'January Thunder' a large offensive began in the south for the purpose of encircling two German army corps in the Cherkassy area (this is called the Korsun'–Shevchenkovskaya group of forces in Soviet and Russian historiography). The Leningrad operation, a part of which was 'January Thunder', continued until 1 March, after which, without an operational pause, the Pskov operation began, and continued to the middle of April. The Western Front unsuccessfully continued to attack Army Group Centre during January–March in the area of Vitebsk, Orsha, and Bogushevsk.

In fact, in the first quarter of 1944, as in the succeeding months, as was the case earlier in 1942 and 1943, Soviet forces attacked simultaneously along several strategic directions. Towards the end of the year Stalin selected from this multitude of operations ten, which had been conducted consecutively in time and which, in his opinion, were the most successful and significant from the political and symbolic points of view, and declared them the ten main attacks of 1944. In this way he created the impression that he had a strategy, which he actually never possessed: the consecutive launching of attacks for the purpose of drawing away the enemy's forces, so that the next attack struck a sector that had been weakened by the transfer of reserves to the previous attack sector. It's more likely that such a strategy manifested itself only once – within twenty days after the start of Operation 'Bagration' when the rout of Army Group Centre's main forces took place in Belorussia, the First and Fourth Ukrainian fronts' L'vov–Sandomierz operation began on 13 July. But in practice this became the single exception, and not the rule, for Stalin's strategy. And it was conditioned by the concentration of all forces, including the supplies of munitions and fuel, for the elimination of the 'Belorussian balcony', which the Soviet forces had been unsuccessfully storming for half a year.

However, in practice, it would have been more rational at that moment to concentrate the Red Army's main forces in the south, which would probably have enabled it to destroy the group of forces in the Cherkassy area, when in reality it managed to break out of the 'cauldron' with small losses. This would have opened up great prospects for reaching Romania and later into the Balkans, as well as southern Poland. The operation in the Leningrad area was in no way able to weaken Army Group South, in that reinforcements for Army Group North, if they were sent at all, would have been sent from the neighbouring Army Group Centre. The Germans lacked reserves on the entire Eastern Front. If they had managed to destroy the forces surrounded near Cherkassy, and then the German First Panzer Army near Kamenets–Podol'skii, for which the Soviet command had every opportunity to concentrate sufficient forces against, had it not been distracted by the operation in the Crimea in April and May, then as early as April such a breach would have formed on the southern flank of the German Eastern Front that it is unlikely that the German command would have had a chance of holding Romania and would have been forced to restore the front at the expense of Army Group Centre's forces. The latter would have been extremely weakened and forced either to fall back to Poland, or to subject itself to a rout as early as April. Then the Soviet forces would have won decisive victories even before the landings in Normandy. But the dispersion of forces and the desire to consecutively liberate territory along the entire front prevented them from doing that.

1. Second Ukrainian Front command. Commander, Marshal of the Soviet Union Rodion Yakovlevich Malinovskii, member of the front military council Major General of Tank Troops Ivan Zakharovich Susaikov, and front chief of staff Colonel General Matvei Vasil' evich Zakharov, September 1944.

2. In liberated Rostov-na-Donu, 18 February 1943. In the first row: member of the Southern Front military council Major General Aleksei Ivanovich Kirichenko, member of the Southern Front military council member of the Politburo and first secretary of the Ukrainian Communist Party Lieutenant General Nikita Sergeevich Khrushchev, first secretary of the Rostov Oblast' Boris Aleksandrovich Dvinskii, commander of the Southern Front Colonel General Rodion Yakovlevich Malinovskii.

3. Commander of the Southern Front Lieutenant General Rodion Yakovlevich Malinovskii, and member of the front military council, Brigade Commissar Illarion Ivanovich Larin, December 1941.

4. The burial of the commander of the First Ukrainian Front General Nikolai Fedorovich Vatutin in the Mariinskii Park in Kiev, 17 April 1944. In the front row: member of the front military council and first secretary of the Ukrainian Communist Party N.S. Khrushchev.

5. Member of the Southwestern Direction military council, first secretary of the Ukrainian Communist Party N.S. Khrushchev, and the deputy chief of the Southern Front's political administration Brigade Commissar Leonid Il'ich Brezhnev, spring, 1942.

6. Commander-in-chief of Soviet Forces in the Far East, Marshal of the Soviet Union Aleksandr Mikhailovich Vasilevskii, commander of the Trans-Baikal Front, Marshal of the Soviet Union Rodion Yakovlevich Malinovskii, and commander of the First Far Eastern Front, Marshal of the Soviet Union Kirill Afanas'evich Meretskov, in Port Arthur.

7. Entering the Ul'yanovsk Flying School, second half of the 1930s.

8. An article from the newspaper *Poslednie Novosti* (*Latest News*), 1 February 1943.

9. Romanian prisoners of war in Stalingrad, February 1943.

10. Commander of the First Belorussian Front, Marshal of the Soviet Union Georgii Konstantinovich Zhukov, awarding the Order of Victory to the supreme commander-in-chief of Allied forces in Europe Dwight Eisenhower, Frankfurt-am-Main, 10 June 1945.

11. Commander of the First Belorussian Front, Marshal of the Soviet Union Georgii Konstantinovich Zhukov, awarding the Order of Victory to the commander-in-chief of British forces in Europe Field Marshal Bernard Montgomery.

12. Commander of the First Belorussian Front, Marshal of the Soviet Union Konstantin Konstantinovich Rokossovskii, July 1944.

13. Marshal of the Soviet Union Ivan Stepanovich Konev, 1945.

14. The Soviet T-34 tank – the most produced tank of the Second World War.

15. The German PzVI 'Tiger' tank – one of the most powerful tanks of the Second World War.

16. The La-7 – the best Soviet fighter of the Second World War.

17. The American Bell P-39 Airacobra fighter, delivered to the USSR through Lend-Lease.

18. The Focke-Wulf Fw-190 – the best German fighter of the Second World War.

19. The Soviet BM-13N 'Katyusha' system of field rocket-powered artillery, which was mounted on Studebaker automobiles delivered through Lend-Lease.

20. The grave of an unknown Soviet soldier. The writing on the cross reads in German: 'Here lies an unknown Russian soldier'.

21. Iosif Stalin, Harry Truman, and Winston Churchill at the Potsdam conference, July 1945.

22. Iosif Stalin and Franklin Roosevelt, Teheran, 1 December 1943.

24. Letter from the USSR People's Commissar of Foreign Affairs V.M. Molotov, to the American ambassador to the USSR William Standley, on the lack of Soviet interest in the exchange of information on Soviet prisoners of war and the prisoners of war of the Axis powers, 28 March 1943.

At the beginning of 1944, when the Red Army was only attacking, the situation with the correlation of losses remained essentially unchanged. For example, in January 1944 the 196th Rifle Division, which was operating as part of the Leningrad Front, lost 2,894 killed and wounded (possibly not including missing in action) of the 6,945 it numbered at the start of the fighting.[2] The German Eighteenth Army, which was facing the 196th Rifle Division, lost in January 1944 1.9 times more – 5,392 men.[3] But the correlation of losses in this case was in favour of the Red Army, not because Soviet losses fell and the Germans' rose, but because compared with the examples from 1941 and the beginning of 1942, the strength of a Soviet rifle division had fallen materially, while the number of such divisions grew, just as the number of tank and mechanized corps did. In all, by the start of the operation to lift the blockade of Leningrad, the Leningrad Front, which was opposing the German Eighteenth Army, had 30 rifle divisions, 3 rifle brigades, 4 independent tank brigades, and 3 fortified areas. Besides this, operating against the Eighteenth Army was the Volkhov Front, which numbered 22 rifle divisions, 6 rifle brigades, 4 independent tank brigades, and 2 fortified areas. It was also attacking, so that all of the German Eighteenth Army's divisions were engaged in heavy defensive fighting.[4] Only half of the Eighteenth Army's forces were operating against the Leningrad Front. Taking into account the losses of the Volkhov and Leningrad fronts' other formations, overall Soviet losses probably exceeded the German Eighteenth Army's losses by tens of times.

During the period from 5–15 January 1944, during the conduct of the Kirovograd offensive operation, the 95th Guards Rifle Division lost 250 men killed and 1,028 wounded.[5] The opposing German Eighth Army lost 2,256 men killed, 7,719 wounded, and 2,001 missing in action during the first 20 days of 1944.[6] The correlation in killed comes to 9:1, and in killed and wounded 7.8:1 in favour of the Soviet division. The uncharacteristic – for the Soviet side – correlation between the number of wounded and killed – 4.1:1 should be noted. This is most likely the result of an undercounting of irreplaceable losses by 3–4 times, as well as the lack of mention in the source of missing in action, as well as those killed not counted anywhere.

Six of the Second Ukrainian Front's armies – 52nd, 53rd, the 4th, 5th, and 7th guards, and 5th Guards Tank – were fighting against the German Eighth Army. These armies contained, taking into account *front* reserves employed, forty-five rifle and airborne divisions and three mechanized and two tank corps.[7] If it is assumed that all of these 50 formations at the divisional level suffered even the same losses as the 95th Guards Rifle Division, then the overall losses for Soviet forces in the Kirovograd operation (not counting the 5th Air Army, artillery, engineer, and other auxiliary units) should have been, as a minimum, in the area of 12,500 killed and 51,400 wounded. This exceeds the losses of the German Eighth Army in killed by 5.5 times and 6.7 times in wounded. One may assume that a significant part, if not the majority, of the German missing in action can be ascribed to prisoners, which were most likely captured during the next Korsun'–Shevchenkovskaya operation, which began on 24 January 1944. However, if the assumption that the 95th Guards Rifle Division's irreplaceable losses during the Kirovograd operation have been undercounted by no less than 3 times, then the overall number of the Second Ukrainian Front's soldiers killed during this operation may be estimated at 37,500. Then the correlation of irreplaceable losses (taking into account German missing in action) is 8.8:1, and by excluding from this number the German missing in action, then likely rises to 10:1. The correlation of overall losses will be 7.4:1 in favour of the Germans.

Such a correlation of losses in men killed, when the German losses were tens of times less than the Soviet ones, was maintained all the way up to the Allied landings in Normandy in June 1944. Then the Germans were forced to transfer to the West a significant part of their men and materiel from the Eastern Front. As a result, the Soviet superiority in men and equipment became overwhelming, which led to an improvement in the correlation of losses for the Red Army at the expense of German losses.

The value of conducting the Crimean operation, which diverted almost ½ million troops and a significant amount of combat equipment for more than a month, is not evident. It's possible that these forces could have been more effectively employed for augmenting the offensive in southern Ukraine and in Moldavia. It is possible then that the rout of the German forces in Romania and the latter's exit from the war could have taken place much earlier, not in August, but in June. Bulgaria would probably have followed Romania, and then the Germans would have had no place to which to evacuate their Crimean group of forces, which would have been forced to capitulate. If the Germans had begun evacuating their Crimean group of forces simultaneously with a Soviet offensive in Romania, then the main part of the Seventeenth Army would have been unable to take part in the decisive battles and would therefore have been forced to capitulate following Romania's leaving the war.

The fact that the Germans nevertheless managed to evacuate the greater part of the Seventeenth Army to Romania is explained by the passivity of the Soviet Black Sea Fleet. Following the loss of the three destroyers in October, there was not a sufficient number of destroyers in the fleet to escort the cruisers. The commander of the fleet, Admiral F.S. Oktyabr'skii, did not want to risk his large ships and assigned them to operations against the Romanian and German convoys that were evacuating troops from the Crimea. That the

Soviet command did not risk basing its aircraft in the Crimea, fearing strikes by the *Luftwaffe* against its airfields, also negatively affected operations by Soviet aviation. Moreover, due to the poor work of the transport services, Soviet aircraft, of which there were more than 1,000, experienced a fuel shortage.

About 16,000 Germans were captured in the Crimea, against a background of 31,700 losses in killed and missing in action, according to data by R.-D. Mueller.[8] At the same time, a significant part of the losses was suffered by the *Luftwaffe* and *Kriegsmarine*. In April–May 1944 the German Seventeenth Army lost 32,463 men missing in action, as well as 3,312 killed.[9] Taking into account the fact that the military personnel of the *Luftwaffe* and *Kriegsmarine*, also suffered irreplaceable losses, R.-D. Mueller's data seem understated. Of the 16,000 German prisoners, no less than 1,000 may be ascribed to the personnel of the *Luftwaffe* and *Kriegsmarine*.

The Allies, having landed in Sicily and southern Italy in July–September 1943 three to four times fewer troops and equipment than they landed in June 1944 in Normandy, were only able to supply them with the necessary means with great difficulty, by straining themselves to the limit. This became the chief reason behind the positional dead-end in Italy, which continued all the way up to the Normandy landings. One should not doubt that if Great Britain and the USA had preferred to invade France in the summer of 1943, and not Italy, then they would have had to transfer there, taking into account the existing German group of forces in the West, a minimum of three times more forces, including those from North Africa. This, by the way, would have helped Italy and Germany recover from the Tunisian disaster and strengthened the defence of Sicily. But by that time there would simply not have existed the necessary supplies and transport ships in the British Isles for supplying such a group of forces. They were able to create them only by May 1944. They also had to win the Battle of the Atlantic, involving a sharp drop in the tonnage of ships sunk by German submarines and an increase in the number of submarines sunk. It was only in July 1943 that the amount of commercial tonnage entering service exceeded that sunk. Great Britain and the USA were able to achieve this only in the middle of 1943 and to increase the necessary supplies in the British Isles only in the first quarter of 1944. This does not even take into account the fact that the artificial ports, which supported the success of the landings in Normandy during the first days before the capture and restoration work on the French ports, appeared only in 1944. If the landings in Normandy had occurred in 1943 they would probably have ended in a serious defeat of the Anglo-American forces. And this would have been felt most negatively on the strategic position of the anti-Hitler coalition as a whole, and in events on the Soviet-German front.

The land armies of Great Britain and the USA, as well as those of the British dominions, inflicted a quarter of the irreplaceable losses on the *Wehrmacht*. The destruction of the German-Italian forces in North Africa in May 1943 and the Allied landing in Sicily in July helped the Red Army to victory in the Battle of Kursk. But the most important event was the opening of the Second Front in Western Europe in Normandy on 6 June 1944; 156,000 men and up to 10,000 tanks and automobiles landed in the first echelon. This was a unique operation, in that for the first time a total of more than a million troops and an enormous amount of military equipment and other cargo necessary for supplying an expeditionary army had been moved across such a water barrier as the English Channel. The USSR admitted this during the war. On 11 June 1944 Stalin wrote Churchill:

> It appears that the landing, conceived on such a majestic scale, has been entirely successful. I and my colleagues cannot but admit that the history of warfare does not know of another similar undertaking from the point of view of its scale, the breadth of its conception and the brilliance of its conduct. As is known, in his time Napoleon suffered a shameful defeat in his plans to force the English Channel. The hysteric Hitler, who two years ago bragged that he would force the English Channel, did not even dare make a weak attempt to carry out his threat. Only our allies managed to carry out the grandiose plan of forcing the English Channel with honour. This will remain in history as an achievement of the highest order.[10]

The Germans were forced to transfer to the West, while still expecting a landing, more than twenty divisions from the Eastern Front and from Germany, including high-quality panzer divisions. Immediately following the Normandy landings, the SS Panzer Corps, which was stationed in Poland, was transferred to the Western Front. Of the *Wehrmacht's* twenty-six panzer divisions in June 1944, ten were operating against the Western Allies, and one (*Grossdeutschland*), was undergoing refitting in Germany. But a panzer regiment from the *Grossdeutschland* Division took part in the fighting in Normandy in the summer of 1944.[11]

Of 7 SS panzer divisions, 5 were operating in the West. Of the *Wehrmacht's* 9 motorized divisions, 5 were operating against the Western Allies, and of 6 SS motorized divisions, 4 were operating in the West and in the Mediterranean. Thus of 48 elite German divisions, 26 were operating against the Western Allies in June 1944, as well as a panzer regiment from another, while 15 of these divisions, including the panzer regiment, were directly along the invasion front in Normandy.[12] If only 12 of these 15 divisions had been in the East at that moment, and this would doubtlessly have happened if the Allies had not landed in France in June 1944, the outcome of the fighting on the Eastern Front would have been completely different.

A large number of fighters were also transferred to the West from the Eastern Front. There the front was far shorter than along the Eastern Front, and although there were fewer German divisions there, the density of the German defence was two to three times higher than in the East. Besides, in the West there were lines of permanent fortifications – the Atlantic Wall and the Siegfried Line – although these were unfinished. The diversion of 80–100 German divisions, including elite panzer and motorized ones, to the struggle against the Anglo-American forces, as well as the almost complete absence of German aviation in the East during the final period of the war, meant that during that year the Red Army was able to win its most significant victories from the point of view of prisoners taken and the irreplaceable losses suffered by the German side, which for the first time since the elimination of the Stalingrad group of forces, approached Soviet losses. Two army groups – Centre in Belorussia in June–July 1944, and North South Ukraine in Romania in August 1944 – were essentially destroyed.

As will be shown later, the average correlation of losses in killed between the Red Army and the *Wehrmacht* from 22 June 1941 to 10 May 1945, was 10:1 in favour of the *Wehrmacht*. During the period from 22 June 1941 to 31 May 1944 this correlation was 16.6:1, while from 1 June 1944 to 10 May 1945 it was 6.6:1. Thanks to the opening of the Second Front by the Allies in Normandy the correlation of losses in killed improved for the Red Army, at a minimum, by 2.5 times.

If the Western Allies had not landed in Normandy in June 1944, the Red Army would have been forced to halt its offensive and Soviet forces would even have been driven back along some sectors of the front. After all, in connection with the landing in Normandy the Germans transferred almost all of their aviation and more than half of their elite panzer and motorized divisions to the West. If all of these forces had remained in the East, the Red Army would not have managed to rout the enemy in Belorussia and Romania. As early as 1 January 1944 only 1,710 of 4,850 *Luftwaffe* first-line aircraft were in the East, or 35.3 per cent. On 1 April 1944 only 515 German single-engine fighters out of 1,675 were on the Eastern Front, or 30.7 per cent. This does not include night fighters, which operated almost exclusively against the Western Allies. There were 800 of these on 1 July 1944, of which 685 operated against British bombers, while the remainder flew against the Americans.[13] During the period from June to October 1944 the Luftwaffe lost exclusively on the Eastern Front 3,650 aircraft out of 14,832 losses on all fronts, which counted for 24.6 per cent.[14] If three times as many Luftwaffe aircraft had been on the Eastern Front in the summer of 1944, it's doubtful that the Red Army could have effectively realized its numerical superiority.

The Soviet air command adhered to the fallacious tactic of patrolling, when Soviet fighters 'ironed the air' along the entire front, which deprived them of the opportunity of concentrating fighters along those sectors where the Germans actually employed their aviation. Besides this, the guidance of aircraft to their targets from the ground by radio was poorly developed, while Soviet aviation was very inferior to the *Luftwaffe* in terms of radar. But by the middle of 1944 there was very little German aviation on the Eastern Front.

It was precisely from July 1944 that a sharp increase in irreplaceable losses in the German army took place, particularly in the number captured. In June the army's irreplaceable losses were 58,000 men and 369,000 in July and remained at this high level to the end of the war.[15] This is explained by the fact that Germany was forced to remove significant numbers of ground forces and the *Luftwaffe* from the Eastern Front, thanks to which the Soviet numerical superiority in men rose to seven and even eight times, which made any kind of effective defence impossible.

Typically, the German command employed its elite units, which included the German SS divisions, the *Grossdeutschland* Division, mountain-rifle divisions, and some parachute divisions, more actively than the other forces. The level of losses in the elite divisions was higher than on average in the *Wehrmacht*, but their correlation of losses against the enemy was more favourable for the Germans than for the German forces as a whole. The same principle was applied to the sea and air, where the main burden of the struggle was carried by the *Luftwaffe* aces and the submarine fleet, and it was they who suffered the greatest losses.

At a great stretch, one may consider the Red Army's guards units and formations elite. They were distinguished from ordinary divisions by a slightly larger strength and a larger amount of heavy weaponry, as well as by better food supply, but as opposed to the German elite units they barely exceeded the remaining forces regarding the level of combat training. Regarding Soviet aviation and navy, there were very few aces in the German sense of the word, and they were employed no more intensively than the other pilots and submariners.

On 18 April 1943 the *Stavka* of the Supreme High Command issued, over Stalin's signature, a directive entitled 'On the Employment of Guards Formations in Offensive and Defensive Operations.' There it stated:

The *Stavka* of the Supreme High Command orders that guards formations (guards rifle corps, guards armies), consisting of the most experienced and steady troops, are to be held, as a rule, in the reserve or in the second echelon and are to be employed in an offensive operation for the breakthrough along the axis of the main attack and in a defensive operation for a counterblow.

In accordance with this, it is necessary to gradually, and without harming the troops' combat readiness and the stability of the defence of the lines currently occupied, carry out a regrouping in the *fronts* and armies in order to pull the guards formations into the reserve or the second echelon.

While in the reserve, the guards formations are to be mainly trained for the offensive, for breaking through the enemy's defensive zone . . .

Following the breakthrough of the enemy's defensive zone, given the presence of powerful second echelons, the guards units that took part in this breakthrough are to be pulled into the reserve for rest and restoration and by no means are to be reduced to exhaustion.

The policy must be firmly put into practice of returning all wounded guards troops, following their recover, to their units. The regrouping of guards formations is not to be carried out without the *Stavka's* knowledge.

By their outward appearance, discipline, the speed and precision with which they carry out orders, and by their attention to the individual soldier, we should strive so that the guards units are a model and an example for all the Red Army's remaining units.[16]

In practice, a prolonged stay in the second echelon and being employed chiefly to develop the breakthrough, when the ordinary divisions had already 'gnawed through' the enemy defence, as well as the instruction not to allow the guards formations to become exhausted and to pull them into the rear at the first opportunity, led to a situation in which the guards units and formations were employed even less intensively than the remainder of the ground forces and suffered fewer, or at worse, approximately the same losses as the remaining divisions and brigades. In this fashion a relatively greater burden was laid on the worse-trained and supplied units, which made the correlation of irreplaceable losses even worse for the Soviet side. As regards the Germans, they, on the contrary, from time to time maintained their elite divisions on the front all the way up to complete exhaustion. For example, the SS *Das Reich* Division, at the time of its withdrawal from the Eastern Front in June 1942, numbered only about 1,000 men out of the 19,000 with which it had begun Operation 'Barbarossa', while the SS *Totenkopf* Division lost throughout the war 60,000 men killed, wounded, and missing in action, that is, three complete divisions.[17] For example, by 22 June 1941 the *Leibstandarte Adolph Hitler* Division, which numbered 11,535 men and had received by 6 March 1942 3,406 reinforcements, had lost by that time 1,247 killed, 2,620 wounded, 65 missing in action, and 1 dead in an accident, and 2,167 sick evacuated. By 6 March 1942 the *Leibstandarte* Division numbered 8,841 men.

The *Das Reich* Division numbered on 22 June 1941 19,026 men. By 7 March 1942 it had received 5,911 reinforcements, but numbered only 7,323 men. It had lost 3,027 killed, 9,622 wounded, 249 missing in action, and 4,716 sick evacuated.

By the start of the war against the USSR the SS *Totenkopf* Division numbered 17,265 men, and by 25 February 1942 there remained 9,669 men. During this time the division received 5,029 reinforcements and had lost 5,206 men killed, 8,521 wounded, 249 missing in action, and 1,649 sick evacuated.

During the period from 22 June 1941 to 10 March 1942 the SS *Wiking* Division fell in strength from 19,377 men to 13,115, having received 4,041 reinforcements. The *Wiking* Division's losses were 1,599 killed, 4,390 wounded, 203 missing in action, 150 dead as the result of accidents, and 3,961 sick evacuated.

On 22 June 1941 the SS *Nord* Mountain Rifle Division numbered 10,018 men. By 21 February 1942 it had received 2,576 reinforcements and was down in strength to 7,656 men. The *Nord* Division had lost 905 men killed, 3,321 wounded, 158 missing in action, 35 who died as the result of accidents, and 519 sick evacuated.

Finally, an SS police division on 22 June 1941 numbered 16,597 men, while by 3 March 1942 it had shrunk to 10,875 men. During this time it received 5,081 reinforcements and lost 1,687 men killed, 5,365 wounded, 168 missing in action, and 3,583 sick evacuated.[18]

At that moment the SS *Reich* and *Totenkopf* were the most combat-capable of all the SS divisions. And it was they which suffered the heaviest losses in relation to their initial strength. For *Das Reich* this index was 67.8 per cent and 80.1 per cent for *Totenkopf*. This index was equal to 43.5 per cent for the police division, 34.1 per cent for *Leibstandarte*, 32 per cent for *Wiking*, and 43.8 per cent for *Nord*. Beginning in 1942, *Leibstandarte* and *Wiking* became as elite as *Das Reich* and *Totenkopf*, which also resulted in their more active employment and the growth in the level of their losses.

Thanks to the exhaustion of the elite divisions, a more favourable correlation of losses was achieved and the less combat-capable divisions got time to gather combat experience.

Stalin preferred to save the Red Army's elite divisions, also because they were considered more politically reliable. The correlation of losses did not bother him and he was ready to sacrifice untrained conscripts without number. To be sure, the guards troops' external appearance likely stood out more in parades than in their level of combat ability, not being distinguished in this regard from ordinary divisions.

Immediately after victory, the Red Army, at least in its infantry units and formations, consisted chiefly of liberated prisoners of war and *ostarbeiters*, as well as of conscripts mobilized in those territories liberated during the last year of the war. Had the Allies not landed in France in June 1944 and the Germans managed to stabilize the Eastern Front approximately along the line where it had run at that moment, then all of these sources of reinforcements would not have been available for the Red Army. And insofar as its losses did not lessen all the way up to the end of the war, then as early as the end of 1944 there would have remained no infantry among the Soviet forces and it would have been necessary to end offensive operations.

In May 1944 the German army lost 24,400 men killed and 22,000 missing in action on all fronts. In June–November 1944 the German army's irreplaceable losses were 1,234,800 men.[19] If there had been no landings in Normandy in June 1944, one may assume that the German army's average monthly irreplaceable losses during June–November would have remained at the May level and would have then amounted to 278,000 men for the period in question, that is 956,400 fewer than was the case following the landings in Normandy. In Italy the German army lost 67,000 men irreplaceably from May 1943 to November 1944.[20] About 21,200 of these would have occurred during the period from June–November 1944. Then this should have been 257,200 men lost on the Eastern Front. The number of Red Army soldiers who perished during June–November 1944 may be estimated at 3,400,000 men.[21] If it is assumed that no less than 20 per cent of Germany's losses on the Eastern Front during June–November 1944, in the absence of a second front, would have consisted of prisoners, then the overall number of Germans killed may be estimated at 205,800 men. If one takes the average correlation of killed for June 1941 to May 1944 of 16.6:1, then there should have been precisely 3,400,000 Soviets for 205,800 Germans killed. In reality, the Germans took 65,700 prisoners on the Eastern Front during June–November 1944.[22] Without the second front, the number of prisoners could have tripled and accounted for approximately 197,100 men, that is, a number close to the actual number of prisoners in June–November 1943 of 172,300 men. Then the Red Army's overall irreplaceable losses in June–November 1944, in the absence of landings in Normandy, may be estimated at 3,600,000 men or 100,000 more than they were in reality.

In 1944 1,300,000 men were called up into the Red Army's ranks through the central authorities.[23] Approximately half of the Red Army's 1944 centralized draft contingent could have been inducted during June–November, that is, 650,000 men. If one assumes that in general the losses in wounded were compensated by the return of those who had recovered from their wounds, then in order to compensate for irreplaceable losses during June–November 1944, 2,750,000 men were called up, that is about 12 per cent of the prewar population from the territories liberated during this period, that is, from the greater part of Belorussia, Bessarabia, and Latvia, as well as from Eastern Galicia, the Trans-Carpathian area, part of Northern Bukovina, and Volhynia, Estonia, and Latvia, where 23,000,000 people lived before the war. In the absence of landings in Normandy, this deficit would have increased to 2,850,000 men.

The Red Army's strength would have decreased by approximately this number by the end of 1944 if the Allies had not landed in Normandy. At the same time, the German army's strength would have been greater by nearly a million men. Even if one assumes that the Germans would have thrown approximately half of this additional resource against the West in the beginning of 1945 in order to repel the Allies' expected landings, then a ½ million more German soldiers than was actually the case would have nevertheless been on the Eastern Front. And then the correlation in troop strength on the Soviet–German front would have been approximately the same as it was in the spring of 1942, when the *Wehrmacht* successfully attacked near Khar'kov and in the Crimea. Of course, under conditions in which the main part of the aviation and panzer divisions had been thrown against the West for repelling the Allied landings, the Germans would not have been able to undertake a general offensive on the Eastern Front, but would have been capable of a series of local counterblows.

By way of comparison, in January–May 1944 Soviet losses in wounded were 508 per cent of the average monthly figure for the entire war, which would correspond to approximately 2,540,000 killed. The Germans took 75,098 prisoners on the Eastern Front during this period.[24] The irreplaceable loss of approximately 2,600,000 men was fully covered by conscripts from the territories liberated during this period. The Red Army then took the Leningrad, Nikolaev, Vinnitsa, Zhitomir, Kamenets-Podol'sk, Kirovograd, Odessa, Rovno, and Tarnopol' oblasts and the Crimea, as well as a large part of the Volhynia and Chernovtsy oblasts, and part of the Kiev Oblast' and Moldavia. Approximately 21,000,000 people lived in these territories before the war. Taking into account the approximately 550,000 men from the centralized draft, in order to make good the losses, it was necessary to mobilize approximately 2,050,000 men from the liberated territories, or 9.8 per cent of the prewar population.

During the final months of the war German tanks and assault guns were delivered to the theatres of military operations as follows: 1,345 vehicles to the West and 288 to the East in November 1944, with correspondingly 952 and 31 in December, 343 and 1,264 in January 1945, 67 and 1,465 in February, and 134 and 367 in March.[25] During November and December the *Wehrmacht's* main efforts were concentrated in the West, where the German forces were holding back the Allies' efforts to invade Germany and carried out a counter-offensive in the Ardennes. But in January 1945, following the successful Soviet offensive from the Vistula to the Oder and all the way to the end of the war, the focus of the Germans' efforts shifted to the Eastern Front. The mass deliveries of tanks to the East during January 1945 can be explained by the transfer there of the SS Sixth Panzer Army and the conduct of counterblows in Hungary for the relief of Budapest. On 10 April there were 2,173 combat-capable German tanks and assault guns in the East and 226 in the West, with another 963 in the Balkans, Italy, Norway, Denmark, and the rear areas of the Reich.[26]

On 21 January 1945 there were 136 divisions on the Eastern Front, 73 on the Western Front, 24 in Italy, 9 in the Balkans, and 12 in Norway. On 1 February the number of divisions in the East rose to 140 and in the West fell to 68 and to 23 in Italy. By 31 March there were already 175 divisions in the East, 58 in the West, 22 in Italy, 7 in the Balkans, and 10 in Norway. Finally, on 12 April there remained 163 divisions in the East, 65 in the West, 19 in Italy, and 8 in the Balkans.[27] Thus from the end of January the German army's main efforts had been shifted to the Eastern Front.

In January–February 1945 alone the *Wehrmacht* in the East lost 606,000 men, including 77,000 killed and 195,000 missing in action.[28] According to other calculations, based on far from complete data, the German army's losses in the East from 1 January to 28 February 1945 were 411,873 men, including 60,108 killed and 72,494 missing in action.[29] The difference may be partially due to losses by the *Luftwaffe* and the *Kriegsmarine*, but these were likely not more than 10–15,000 men, including half irreplaceably. In all, from 1 January to the middle of April 1945 the German army lost 1,452,886 men, including 926,981 (63.8 per cent) irreplaceably.[30]

Without the Normandy landings, the Red Army's resources to continue to crush the enemy with corpses would simply have ended. There would have been nothing with which to defend the liberated territory and the *Wehrmacht* would have had the chance to win back part of the territory lost in the East. In this case, if the Allies had landed in France a year later, in June 1945, then the war would most likely have ended in the autumn of 1945 with a mass atomic bombardment of German cities. Insofar as at that moment Germany's situation would not have been so hopeless as Japan's actual situation in August 1945, it would have been necessary to drop on Berlin, Munich, Hamburg, Frankfurt-am-Main, and other German cities not two, as was the case with Japan, but a good dozen atomic bombs in order to force Germany to capitulate. Of course, then the geopolitical results of the war would have been somewhat different. It's quite possible that at the moment of surrender the Red Army would not yet have entered German territory. It's possible that Stalin would have been forced to satisfy himself with the 1939 boundaries and all of Eastern Europe would have come under the defence of the Western Allies. Given this scenario, it is not beyond the bounds of possiblity that Ukraine, the Caucasus, and other republics would have fallen away from the Soviet Union and that the Stalin regime would have been overthrown. Then the collapse of the Soviet Union and the fall of communism could have taken place significantly earlier than actually happened. In this case, Russia would likely have set out on the path of development that it started in 1991, nearly half a century earlier. And the place of Germany, which lay in radioactive ruins, in Central Europe might have been occupied in time by Poland, which, having maintained its eastern border, would have also acquired East Prussia, Pomerania, and Silesia. Then the USSR would have ended up in the role of a 'second-tier victor', something like Kuomintang China, and would have been forced to submit to the main victors – the USA and Great Britain. A similar scenario would be a good setting for a novel from the alternative history genre, but it was not actually realized, perhaps to the misfortune of Russia, which could have liberated itself from totalitarianism several decades earlier.

This example shows that Great Britain and the USA could have defeated Germany without such significant assistance from the USSR, but for this they would have had to employ atomic bombs. At the same time, the Western Allies would have won in any case, even if, for example, the Germans had, by adopting another strategy, managed to avoid the disaster at Stalingrad and had captured if not Stalingrad, then Baku. Then the Red Army's combat capability would have sharply fallen for a period due to the loss of its main source of oil, but the Western Allies would nonetheless have won, but only by employing nuclear weapons against Germany. Even given such an unfavorable outcome for the 1942 campaign for the Red Army, the USA and Great Britain would have gradually restored its combat-capability through additional deliveries of fuel and oil from Iran. But, of course, the USSR's dependence on the USA and Great Britain would have significantly increased. And in this case the war would have ended in the autumn of 1945, but with an even weaker Red Army and, correspondingly, with a postwar peace settlement even less favourable for Stalin.

If one compares Soviet losses in wounded for June, July, and August 1943 and 1944 then they, just as the proportional losses in killed, were almost unchanged. In 1943 the number of wounded was 365 per cent of the monthly average for the war, and for the same period in 1944, which saw the extremely successful Belorussian and Iasi-Kishinev operations, 360 per cent.[31] It's not that the Soviet forces learned to fight, but that there were materially fewer German forces on the Eastern Front due to the landings in Normandy. The Soviet superiority in men was overwhelming; there were almost no German fighter aircraft remaining in the East, and the best German panzer divisions were trying to repel the Allied landings. As a result, German losses rose, but Soviet losses practically did not fall. Quite the opposite, the Germans, while having materially fewer men and equipment, inflicted on the Red Army in 1944 the same losses as in 1943. This is hardly surprising. By the end of the war the Red Army consisted chiefly of those liberated from captivity, practically untrained conscripts from the occupied territories and mobilized *ostarbeiters*, while at the beginning of the war a significant proportion of the Red Army soldiers and commanders had served a year or more in the army and had the experience of the 'liberation campaigns' and the Finnish War.

As the Soviet superiority in men, tanks, artillery, and aircraft became overwhelming, because of the dispatch of a significant part of the German divisions and the overwhelming majority of the *Luftwaffe's* aircraft to the West, German losses on the Eastern Front, beginning in June 1944, increased sharply, including not just prisoners, but killed as well. It was not that the Red Army learned to fight, but that the *Wehrmacht* was deprived of the opportunity of holding sufficient forces in the East for any kind of successful defence.

In 1944 the German air force carried out 182,000 sorties along those fronts where the Western Allies were operating, and 342,500 sorties on the Eastern Front. But the correlation of losses was quite the opposite. In the West the *Luftwaffe*, according to the calculations of American researcher Don Caldwell, lost 9,768 combat aircraft in 1944, and only 2,406 in the East. The likelihood of being shot down for the *Luftwaffe* pilots in the West was almost eight times greater than in the East. And according to the calculations of German researcher Otto Grohler, the *Luftwaffe* had an average of 1,467 day fighters in September–December 1943 in the Western theatres of military operations, including the anti-aircraft defence of the Reich, while their losses were 2,614 planes. On the Eastern Front the number of day fighters was 412 planes, with losses of 445 planes, which were only 14.5 per cent of all losses among day fighters on the other fronts and the anti-aircraft defence of the Reich. If one takes aircraft of all types for this period, then the Germans had in the Western theatres 3,732 aircraft and lost 5,133, and correspondingly on the Eastern Front

2,888 and 1,736 planes, or 25.2 per cent of all losses. In January–May 1944 the number of day fighters in the western theaters was on average 1,491 planes and the losses were 5,694. In the East, the corresponding average strength was 411 aircraft, with losses of 784, or 12.1 per cent of all losses. The number of all aircraft in the Western theatres was 4,027, with losses of 10,745 aircraft. In the East there were 2,999 aircraft, with losses of 3,214, or 23.3 per cent of all losses. Finally, in June–October 1944, following the landing in Normandy, the Luftwaffe had an average of 1,135 day fighters in the West and lost 6,412 aircraft. There were 364 fighters in the East, while their losses were 1,065 aircraft. There were 3,387 aircraft of all types in the West, with losses of 11,182 planes. For the East, the corresponding figures were 2,948 and 3,650 aircraft, or 24.6 per cent of all losses. In all, from September 1943, following the beginning of the landings in Italy and with the beginning of the Western Allies' mass air offensive all the way up to October 1944, the Luftwaffe lost 27,060 combat aircraft of all types in the West, while losing only 8,600 aircraft in the East, or 24.1% per cent of all losses. The gap for day fighters is even sharper. In the West their losses for this period were 14,720 aircraft, with 2,294 in the East, or 13.5 per cent of all losses.[32] Thus as early as the end of 1943, the overwhelming majority of losses, in the order of three-quarters of the overall number, were suffered by the *Luftwaffe* in the struggle against the Western Allies. The difference in figures is due to the fact that Caldwell took only losses from combat reasons, and only irreplaceable ones. And this took place against the backdrop of the fact that in the East in 1944 it was mainly German pilots who had just graduated from flight school who fought, while the experienced pilots were concentrated in the West.

Following the Allied landings in Normandy Soviet losses did not decline at all, and even rose somewhat, although German losses in the East rose much more. For example, during the Iasi-Kishinev operation, which is considered exemplary and which lasted from 20–9 August 1944 and ended with the rout of Army Group South Ukraine, according to official data the losses of the Second Ukrainian Front, which numbered at the start of the operation 771,200 men, were 39,985 men, including 7,136 irreplaceably.[33] By 1 September the front's composition had changed insignificantly and had fallen by one rifle and one airborne division and one mechanized corps, while it grew by six cavalry divisions.[34] We can assume that these formations approximately balance each other in the strength of the rank and file. Then by the beginning of the Bucharest–Arad offensive operation on 30 August, the Second Ukrainian Front should have numbered, not counting possible reinforcements, about 731,200 men, while it actually numbered 681,556 men.[35] It follows that the Second Ukrainian Front's losses in the Iasi-Kishinev operation were undercounted by approximately 49,600 men, that is, more than twice. It is more than likely that the undercounting occurred primarily at the expense of irreplaceable losses.

The German command had been informed beforehand about Soviet plans for the summer 1944 campaign. At the end of April an unknown German agent, who had previously presented reliable data on plans for a Soviet offensive in the autumn of 1942, reported that in Moscow they were reviewing two alternatives. The first called for the launching of the main attack in the Kovel' and L'vov area, with a subsequent movement on Warsaw, where a Polish uprising was planned. It is possible that Soviet intelligence learned of the Home Army's plans to attempt to raise a rebellion in Warsaw, Vilnius, and other Polish cities upon the approach of the Red Army to them. It's quite feasible that there is another explanation: the *Stavka* hoped that pro-communist forces in Poland, whose influence was significantly exaggerated by Soviet intelligence organs, would raise a rebellion. The second alternative for conducting the summer campaign assumed that the main attack would be launched in the direction of the Baltic Sea through Belorussia and Poland, with a supporting attack in the south, while it was pointed out that Stalin had chosen the second option.[36]

Nonetheless, Hitler did not pull back Army Group Centre to the Western Bug River, which would have removed it from the expected Soviet attack but simultaneously would have put the Red Army more than 300km closer to the capital of the Reich. If this withdrawal had taken place, then the Soviet forces would have reached the Curzon Line in May, and not in July, as actually happened. One must also take into account here the expected Allied landings in France. Hitler counted on repelling these with a powerful tank counterblow and to win time was ready to sacrifice the German forces in Belorussia. If he had managed to throw the Anglo-American landings into the sea, then the tank and motorized divisions concentrated in Poland could be rapidly shifted to the East to save the remnants of Army Group Centre and Army Group North Ukraine (formerly Army Group South) from defeat. The führer rejected the proposal by the commander of Army Group Centre, Field Marshal Ernst Busch, to pull back his forces to the Berezina River and shorten the front by 240km.[37] He also took a panzer corps from Busch and transferred it to the commander of Army Group North Ukraine.

In the event of a timely withdrawal by Army Group Centre to the Western Bug River, the Red Army could have ended up as early as the beginning of June on the approaches to the German border. But Hitler was no longer fighting to win, but to gain time, while hoping either for a split in the enemy coalition or for the invention of some kind of 'miracle weapon', capable of radically altering the course of the war. From the point of view of gaining time, even the loss of significant German forces in Belorussia would have been justified, insofar as the Red Army's advance to the borders of the Reich would have been delayed if only for a month-and-a-half or two and there might have appeared some kind of chance of repelling the Allied landings. Thus Hitler forbade Army Group Centre to fall back, despite the risk of being encircled, and decided to fight along the previous lines.

On 1 June 1944 in Field Marshal Busch's Army Group Centre, not counting the Second Army, which was not subjected to attack in June, there were a total of 442,053 officers, NCOs, and soldiers, of which only 258,604 were serving in combat units. At the beginning of June the headquarters of Army Group Centre reported to the OKH that not one of the army group's divisions was capable of withstanding a major enemy offensive. The 6th, 12th, 18th, 25th, 35th, 102nd, 129th, 134th, 197th, 246th, 256th, 260th, 267th, 296th, 337th, and 383rd infantry and motorized divisions and also Corps Group 'D' were considered capable of limited offensive operations. The 5th, 14th, 45th, 95th, 206th, 252nd, 292nd, and 299th infantry divisions and the 4th and 6th airfield divisions were viewed as fully capable of conducting a defence. The 57th, 60th, and 707th infantry and motorized divisions were considered relatively capable of conducting a defence.[38]

Army Group Centre faced the forces of the First, Second, and Third Belorussian and First Baltic fronts, which numbered 2,331,700 men, and the Polish 1st Army, which had a strength of 79,000 men. From 23 June to 29 August the Soviet forces lost, according to official data, 178,507 men irreplaceably and 587,308 wounded and sick.[39] Because this source underestimates Soviet losses by on average three times, Soviet irreplaceable losses during the course of Operation 'Bagration' may be estimated at 525,500 men.

According to far from complete data, Army Group Centre's losses during the period from 21 June to 31 August 1944, were 20,780 killed, 28,254 missing in action, and 92,324 wounded.[40] But this is without counting the data from Army Group Centre's liquidation staff, which takes into account the losses of the units and formations which ended up in encirclement. The staff determined that of the 393,823 men who were encircled, 102,812 remained alive, 3,669 definitely died, 108,219 were missing in action, and the fate of 179,123 men as of 1 March 1945 could not be determined.[41] Practically all of them should be listed as killed and captured, just as the missing in action. Then Army Group Centre's overall irreplaceable losses for the period under consideration may be defined as 340,045 men. During the period from 1 March to 1 October 1944 the three Belorussian fronts and the First Baltic Front captured 153,770 prisoners.[42] Practically all of them were taken during

Operation 'Bagration'. Then the number of killed in Army Group Centre from 21 June to 31 August 1944 may be estimated at 186,275 men. Army Group Centre captured 9,756 prisoners.[43] Then the number of killed among the Soviet forces may be estimated at 515,700 men. The correlation of losses in killed during Bagration may be estimated at 2.8:1, 1.5:1 in irreplaceable losses and 2.6:1 in overall losses in favour of the Germans.

According to the level of losses, Operation 'Bagration' was the *Wehrmacht's* greatest defeat on the Eastern Front after Stalingrad.

Nonetheless, there were failures during the course of Bagration. On 6 July Lieutenant General N.I. Gusev's 47th Army occupied Kovel' and, together with Major General of Tank Troops F.N. Rudkin's 11th Tank Corps, began to pursue the enemy, without organizing reconnaissance.[44] The SS *Wiking* Division had consolidated along a well-outfitted anti-tank line and almost completely destroyed the 11th Tank Corps, which neither the infantry nor the artillery could intelligently support in the attack. On 16 July the following threatening order came from the *Stavka*:

> The commander of the First Belorussian Front, Marshal of the Soviet Union Rokossovskii, who was personally leading the troops' operations along the Kovel' axis, did not check the 11th Tank Corps' organization for battle. As a result of this extremely poor organization of the tank corps' commitment into the fighting, two tank brigades, which were thrown into the attack, irreplaceably lost 75 tanks.
>
> 'The *Stavka* of the Supreme High Command warns Marshal of the Soviet Union Rokossovskii about the necessity henceforth of the attentive and careful preparation of tank formations' commitment into the fighting . . .[45]

In the Iasi-Kishinev 'cauldron', according to data from the corresponding liquidation staff, German irreplaceable losses were about 240,000 men (minus the garrison on the island of Rhodes).[46] At the same time, during the period from 1 March to 1 October 1944 the forces of the Second and Third Ukrainian fronts captured 271,237 prisoners, of which approximately 130,000 were Romanians.[47] In this case, the Germans could not have lost in the Iasi-Kishinev cauldron more than 141,000 men, while at least 99,000 of those missing in action in the Iasi-Kishinev cauldron should be considered killed. The overwhelming majority of these were from the ground forces. The strength of all the German forces in Army Group South Ukraine was 337,000, according to reports. Approximately another 40,000 men may be classified as military personnel and civilian employees from the Luftwaffe and navy in Constanta, Bucharest, and Ploesti, and some other rear areas (including 25,000 in the Ploesti area and about 11,000 in the Bucharest area). The forces of the Second and Third Ukrainian fronts numbered 1,314,000 men and were approximately twice as strong as the German-Romanian group of forces and had six times the number of tanks and self-propelled guns. In order to avoid encirclement, Army Group South Ukraine would have had to fall back in a timely manner to Hungarian Transylvania. But this would have guaranteed Romania's exit from the war, because the Romanian soldiers would not have entered Hungarian territory and the oil-extraction and oil-refining facilities in Ploesti would have been lost. Thus at the moment of the encirclement of Army Group South Ukraine's main forces, even its successful breakout could not have prevented Romania's joining the anti-Hitler coalition. After all, those who broke out would nevertheless have had to fall back into Hungary.

During the second half of 1944 the Red Army was chiefly reinforced by conscripts from the recently liberated territories. Major General Petr Grigorenko, who served on the Fourth Ukrainian Front, recalled how the mobilization and draft of 'volunteers' directly into the units was carried out in Western Ukraine and the neighbouring Trans-Carpathian area in the autumn of 1944:

> They demanded that the Fourth Ukrainian Front seek out human resources on the ground–the mobilization of fighting-age cohorts in Western Ukraine, the hiring of volunteers in the Trans-Carpathian area [formally still a part of Czechoslovakia and thus not part of Soviet mobilization undertakings] and the return of recovered wounded and sick to their units. The shortage of people was so acute that they essentially turned the mobilization into a hunt for people, as slavers once captured Negroes in Africa.'[48]

The Warsaw uprising of 1944 is one of the most tragic and heroic events of Polish history. This incident occupies one of the central places in the historical memory of the Polish people about the Second World War. And the soldiers of the Home Army, its leadership, and the Polish government in exile in London, to which the Home Army was subordinated, understood that the chances of a successful uprising were small (if there were any at all). The Germans had a colossal superiority in numbers and weaponry so that the Home Army could not contend with them by itself. Hopes for Soviet help were ephemeral. After all, it had been more than a year since Moscow broke off relations with the Polish government in London, after the Germans unearthed the graves in Katyn', and had unleashed a campaign of repression against the leadership and members of the Home Army, which manifested itself especially during the liberation of Vilnius, during which the Home Army's soldiers rendered material aid to the Red Army. Nevertheless, the leadership of the Home Army decided upon an uprising, which became the meaning and essence of the Home Army's entire activity and was supposed to become a heroic example for current and future generations of Poles.

The Soviet 2nd Tank Army, which had arrived at the approaches to Warsaw, had been heavily battered as the result of a counterblow by four German panzer divisions, including the SS *Wiking* Division. According to German estimates, Soviet losses were 3,000 killed and 6,000 captured, as well as a significant amount of destroyed armoured equipment.[49] It's possible that the number of killed was undercounted here, because earlier it was clear that German estimates often undercounted Soviet losses, particularly those killed. However, this defeat was too small to by itself to force Stalin to renounce taking Warsaw.

The majority of Polish historians, as well as Polish officialdom, are convinced that the Red Army purposely failed to come to the aid of the Warsaw rebels, who were subordinated to the non-communist Polish government in London, and there existed some kind of halt order by Stalin forbidding Rokossovskii from taking Warsaw in August–September 1944, while the rebels were there. On the opposite side, the majority of Russian historians and Russian officialdom maintain that there was no halt order and that the Red Army was unable to help the Warsaw uprising due to objective reasons: its lengthy communications, the exhaustion of the troops following the month-and-a-half offensive in Belorussia, the absence of reserves, and the lack of coordination between the rebels' actions and those of the Soviet forces. Of course, a pause in the First Belorussian Front's offensive was required in order to bring up fuel and munitions. But this break could have lasted one, or a maximum of two, weeks, but instead lasted more than a month. And there were no military reasons for this, but political ones. An analysis of the development of events of the time shows that it's possible that there was not a specific halt order, but that Stalin's decision not to take Warsaw was politically motivated. As early as August, the German panzer divisions, which had severely battered the Soviet Second Tank Army beyond the Vistula, had been shifted to the shores of the Baltic Sea, in order to punch through a corridor to Army Group North, which had been cut off from Germany. At the same time, among the German soldiers, according to a report by *Einsatz* combat group 'Rasch' on 24 August 1944, the conviction reigned that 'we will not be able to hold Warsaw if the Russians are not stopped in the northeast and southeast of the city'.[50] If the Germans had not calculated on the Soviet forces in the Warsaw area behaving passively, it is unlikely that they would have decided to pull their panzer divisions out of there. After all, in the event that the German forces had fallen back from the Vistula to the Oder, they still would not have managed to evacuate Army Group North from the Baltic States along the land corridor. There was no need for Stalin to issue a halt order. It was sufficient to simply deprive Rokossovskii of reserves and force him to ask for permission to go over to the defence. Instead of attacking toward Warsaw and Berlin, Stalin preferred in the last third of August to begin an offensive in Romania. But who would have cared about Romania, even with its oil supplies, if the Soviet armies had stood along the Oder River, 60 miles from Berlin? If in August–September 1944 the Red Army could have liberated Warsaw, linked up with the rebels, and pushed the Germans back to the Oder, in all likelihood the war would have ended as early as the end of 1944. There would have been no German counteroffensives in the Ardennes and in Hungary, and there might not have been the bloody battle for Berlin, for the defence of which the Germans would simply have lacked the troops. However, Stalin on principle did not want to share Poland with the non-communist London government (it wasn't to share that he shot the Polish officers and other representatives of the Polish elites in Katyn' and other places). Thus he did not move to take Warsaw until the Germans had dealt with the rebels. In theory, it would have been worth it to the German command to enable the rebels to hold on as long as possible, perhaps even by secretly supplying them with food, in order to last out the winter. This would have served as a definite guarantee that the Soviet forces would not launch an offensive along the central sector of the front. After all, had the Red Army entered a Warsaw still controlled by the Home Army, it would have been highly inconvenient to arrest and disarm the rebels, which would have threatened a serious conflict with both the governments of Great Britain, the USA and, which was even more dangerous, with Western public opinion, which had earlier been quite favourable towards the Soviet Union. But the Germans did not risk endlessly drawing out the agony of the Warsaw uprising, either fearing that Stalin would change his mind or that an Anglo-American landing would take place in Warsaw, and forced the rebels to capitulate. It's likely that the Soviet forces' seizure of the right-bank Warsaw suburb of Praga in the middle of September pushed the Germans to complete the elimination of the uprising. Typically, this operation was not pursued. It's possible that its sole aim was to push the Germans into more rapidly dealing with the Polish rebels and in this way free Stalin's hands.

As a result of the Warsaw uprising, Stalin assured that the main and most combat-capable units of the Home Army were destroyed or captured by the Germans, which made the subsequent sovietization of Poland easier. The

Western Allies demonstrated that they were ready to sacrifice the interests of the Poles in order not to quarrel with Moscow. It was precisely then, in August–September 1944, and not at Yalta in February 1945, that the postwar fate of Poland was actually decided.

During the course of the Debrecen operation, which lasted from 6–28 October 1944, the Soviet cavalry-mechanized group (KMG) under General Issa Pliev, fell into an encirclement and suffered heavy losses.[51] On 3 October, by the beginning of the operation, the group numbered 56,847 men, and by 27 October only 31,185 remained.[52] However, on 19 October General Sergei Gorshkov's KMG was combined with Pliev's, which included a tank corps, a cavalry corps, and an airborne division.[53] Gorshkov's group was removed from Pliev's only on 31 October.[54] Gorshkov's group should have numbered no more than 40,000 men. Thus the losses by Pliev's group in the Debrecen operation were not 25,662 men, as it may appear from the KMG's reports, but about 65,700 men, that is, about 68 per cent of its actual strength. According to Soviet data, the Second Ukrainian Front's losses in the Debrecen operation were 84,010 men, including 19,713 irreplaceably.[55] This data seems colossally undercounted. More than likely, no less than half of the losses by Pliev's KMG were due to irreplaceable losses. In October German Army Group South captured 11,796 Soviet prisoners, of which 6,189 were taken in the last 10 days of October, mostly from Pliev's KMG.[56] It's likely that no less than half of the losses of Pliev's group, that is, about 32,800 men, were irreplaceable ones, of which no less than 26,600 were killed. But besides Pliev's and Gorshkov's KMGs, five combined-arms armies and one tank army took part in the Debrecen operation, as well as one tank corps, not counting Romanian forces, and it is highly unlikely that there were only 18,300 killed, wounded, and missing in action for 6 armies. Most likely, the sum of their losses exceeded the losses of Pliev's group. Even if one only takes them as being equal to the losses of Pliev's group, then the Soviet forces' overall losses, minus their Romanian allies, may be estimated at 131,400 men, including about 65,600 irreplaceably. The 4th Romanian Army's losses during the period from 21 September to 25 October 1944 were 24,630 men.[57] Of these, it's likely that no less than a third were irreplaceable losses. Army Group South's losses in October were only 1,643 killed, 2,264 missing in action, and 7,324 wounded.[58] Germany's Hungarian allies lost during this month 372 killed and missing in action and 2,519 wounded.[59] In this case the Hungarian losses seem highly understated, mostly at the expense of prisoners. The Romanian forces alone captured 19,820 prisoners from 1 September to 25 October, mostly Hungarians.[60] The correlation of Soviet and German losses in favour of the *Wehrmacht* in the Debrecen operation is 11.7:1 according to overall losses and 16.8:1 according to irreplaceable losses.

There is also other data on the losses by the *Wehrmacht* in the Battle of Debrecen, which were sent through the channel IIa – Department of Personnel Records, while the above data was sent through the channel IVc – Department of Chief Field Doctor of the *Wehrmacht*. According to the data of IIa, from 1–31 October 1944, Army Group South had lost 2,338 killed in action, 10,103 wounded in action, and 2,724 missing in action and only 15,165 in total. This is 3,934 more persons than the losses according to the IVc channel. The difference between the two numbers was probably formed at the expense of losses of separate units, which were under direct command of the headquarters of both Sixth and Eighth armies (911 persons), and also at the expense of miscellaneous individuals belonging to the concrete division or separate unit not established (1151 people) (in the second case double counting is possible).[61] The total number of losses, based on the data of channel IIa, exceeds the number of losses, based on the data of the channel IVc, by 1.35 times, and the number of the irreplaceable losses, based on the data of the channel IIa, exceeds the number of losses, based on the data of the channel IVc, by 1.30 times. Accordingly, the ratio of total Soviet and German losses in this case is 8.7:1, and irreplaceable losses 13.0:1 in favour of the Germans, which does not change the picture.

The correlation is approximately the same for irreplaceable losses as during the first three years of the war. This can be explained by the fact that during the last months of the war, particularly after the Germans could not manage to hold the Allies' offensive in Normandy and following the loss of Romania and its oil, Hitler carried out the 'strategy of the Alpine redoubt' on the Eastern Front. He concentrated his main forces along the southern wing for defending the remaining oil deposits and oil-processing plants in Hungary, Austria, and Slovakia and the last industrial areas in the Czech Republic and Slovakia that had not yet been destroyed by Allied bombings. That is why here, as well as in Courland, where the Germans were holding a very short defensive line and were able to create a sufficient operational density, the correlation of irreplaceable losses remained very unfavourable for the Red Army, just as in 1943 and the first five months of 1944. But in Poland, East Prussia, and eastern Germany, where the Red Army was planning to launch its main attack, its superiority in men and materiel was overwhelming. Thus here the correlation of losses for the Soviet side became significantly better in the final ten months of the war. Hitler was able to concentrate four panzer divisions, including one Hungarian, and one-and-a-half motorized divisions in Hungary. As the former commander of the German Sixth Army, Maximillian Fretter-Pico, maintained in the Debrecen operation:[62]

> our panzer divisions, which were full of fighting spirit, although they themselves suffered heavy losses, inflicted a destructive blow against the significantly more powerful Soviet forces. In these fierce battles, which ebbed back and forth, the troops and commanders of the Sixth Army manifested the highest combat capabilities, mobility and maneuverability, but most of all decisiveness. This was recognized in a *Wehrmacht* report of 30 October 1944. We might have been able to take advantage of the Soviet forces' defeat if we had had German infantry divisions at our disposal![63]

Germany did not have sufficient forces to take advantage of its final victory. This success enabled them only to safely pull the German-Hungarian group of forces out of Transylvania and to delay the Soviet encirclement of Budapest by a month-and-a-half.

In the Red Army the cavalry was viewed not as a palliative called upon to compensate for a shortage of motorized rifle units, but as an independent combat arm, with its advantages over the others in certain conditions. However, the cavalry's sole merit over motorized troops was the much smaller need for fuel, which was reduced to zero by the necessity of constantly supplying forage for the horses, which in encirclement definitely became a practically impossible task and naturally transformed the cavalry troops into infantry, as happened during the Debrecen operation. But even without encirclement, the problem of forage became the chief reason behind the cavalry's reduced advance. Unfed horses could not carry riders for long and complaints about the horses' tiredness are a constant refrain in reports by the cavalry commanders. The Red Army, as opposed to the *Wehrmacht*, employed cavalry corps directly at the front and even something like an army in the form of the cavalry-mechanized groups. The cavalry troops soon became a burden for the latter, in that they moved only a little more quickly than ordinary infantry.

The correlation of losses along the southern wing of the Soviet-German front remained the most unfavourable for the Red Army. For example, in October–November 1944, during the fighting in Yugoslavia, the 57th Army's (Third Ukrainian Front) 73rd Guards Rifle Division lost 3,538 men, including 676 killed (here, to all appearances, the missing in action were not counted).[64] The losses for the entire 'Southeast' command for the same period are slightly higher – 2,734 killed, 10,432 wounded, and 4,821 missing in action, for a total of 17,987 men.[65] This yields a correlation of 5.1:1 in favour of the Soviet division. Even if one adds the presumably uncounted among the Soviet losses in missing in action, the correlation of losses will not change in principle. It's unlikely that there were a large number of missing in action in the 73rd Guards Rifle Division. However, here the comparison is between the losses of a division and those of an army group, not an army. The 'Southeast' command in October–November 1944 included the Second Panzer Army, army group 'E', and a number of other units. The Third Ukrainian Front's 57th Army and the Second Ukrainian Front's 46th Army, which numbered nineteen rifle divisions, a mechanized corps, three rifle brigades, and an independent tank brigade, and a fortified area were fighting against it in October alone.[66] Besides this, German forces in the southeast faced the Yugoslav National People's Liberation Army, Bulgarian forces, and Greek partisans. In retreating from the Balkans, the troops of the 'Southeastern' command suffered significant losses in prisoners, while at the same time those German soldiers who were captured by the partisans were often shot on sight. If one takes the correlation of losses in wounded, which in this case is the most representative, then it is only 2.9:1 in favour of the Soviet division.

The fact that during the fighting in Yugoslavia there was a significant undercounting of the missing in action in the 73rd Guards Rifle Division proves that during the period from 13–26 November 1944 the division lost 385 men killed and 2,091 wounded.[67] Thus the correlation of killed and wounded is 5.4:1, which for the Red Army seems extremely unlikely. This correlation points to the fact that a significant number of those killed ended up in the category of missing in action, or were either not counted altogether. For purposes of comparison: in the second and third 10-day period in December the German forces in the 'Southeastern' command lost 861 killed, 3,539 wounded, and 1,963 missing in action, for a total of 6,363 men. The number of killed is only 2.2 times more than the Soviet division, with overall losses only 2.6 times more. And this in a situation in which a significant number of missing in action is not counted in Soviet losses.

During the period from 24 December 1944 to 10 February 1945 Soviet losses along the external front of the Budapest encirclement, according to the estimate by the command of army group Balck (German Sixth and Hungarian First and Third armies), were 6,532 killed and found on the battlefield, plus another 13,600 presumed killed, 5,138 captured, 1,981 tanks, 946 guns, 273 mortars, 1,700 anti-tank guns, and 63 aircraft destroyed. During this period group Balck lost 34,108 killed, wounded, and missing in action, including 1,111 officers, with insignificant losses in equipment.[68] According to other data, during the period from 21 December 1944 to 10 February 1945 this group lost 4,751 men killed, 6,339 missing in action (mostly Hungarians), and 24,756 wounded.[69]

This yields a correlation according to irreplaceable losses of 2.5:1 in favour of the Germans. However, Soviet losses in killed along all the fronts during the period from 21 December 1944 to 10 February 1945 may be estimated at 875,000 men.[70] The strength of F.I. Tolbukhin's Third Ukrainian Front, which was holding the external encirclement front around Budapest, by the close of the Budapest operation, was about 465,000 men, or about 7.6 per cent of the Soviet active army's strength (6,100,000) at that point.[71] If it is assumed that Tolbukhin's front suffered its losses killed in approximately the same proportion, then they may have amounted during this period to about 66,500 men, which is approximately 3 times the German estimate of 20,132 killed.

When Hitler returned the four elite panzer divisions to the SS Sixth Panzer Army on the Eastern Front in February–March 1945, the Soviet forces found the going very hard. In a battle near Lake Balaton during the final German offensive in the Second World War, the Third Ukrainian Front suffered very heavy losses, although the enemy was inferior to it in numbers of men by twofold, with an approximate equality in tanks. In 2001, in the book *Russia and the USSR in the Wars of the XX Century*, the strength of the Third Ukrainian Front at the start of the Balaton defensive operation, was given as 465,000 men. Here for the first time Soviet losses for the Balaton area were listed at 32,899 men, including 8,492 irreplaceably.[72] However, it should be kept in mind that also fighting on the Soviet side was the Bulgarian 1st Army, which numbered about 100,000 men, and 2 divisions from the Yugoslav People's Liberation Army, in which there may have been up to 30,000 men.

It's easy to prove that the data on Soviet losses has been undercounted by more than three times. By the start of the Vienna offensive operation on 16 March, the strength of the Third Ukrainian Front had increased to 536,700 men through the transfer to it of the 6th Guard Tank and 9th Guards armies.[73] The 9th Guards Army consisted of three guards corps and nine guards rifle divisions. These formations entered the fighting for the first time since the beginning of the war. They were fully up to authorized strength. Each division numbered 12,600 men. Besides this, the army also included 3 self-propelled artillery regiments, 6 artillery brigades, 3 mortar regiments, 3 independent anti-aircraft battalions, a communications regiment, an engineer brigade, and an independent flamethrower battalion. Together with corps and army units, the 9th Guards Army could not have numbered less than 135,000 men. From the beginning of February the 6th Guards Tank Army had been in the reserve and had been reinforced up to authorized strength. It included the 9th Guards Mechanized Corps, which numbered 16,318 men, and the 5th guards Tank Corps, which numbered 12,010 men. Besides this, the army included the three-regiment 202nd Light Artillery Brigade, the 51st Guards and 207th self-propelled artillery brigades, the 49th Guards Heavy Tank Regiment, the 364th Guards Heavy Self-Propelled Artillery Regiment, the 4th Guards Motorcycle Regiment, the 207th Guards Army Communications Regiment, and the 22nd Motorized Engineer Brigade. According to the 1945 strength table, a light artillery brigade numbered about 3,000 men, and the 207th Self-Propelled Artillery Brigade, which took part in the Lake Balaton fighting, numbered 1,492 men, and the 51st Guards Self-Propelled Artillery Brigade numbered 1,804 men.

The motorcycle regiment had an authorized strength of 1,188 men. The heavy self-propelled artillery regiment had 420 men, the heavy tank regiment 374 men, the motorized engineer brigade 1,180 men, and the army communications regiment 525 men. In all, the 6th Guards Tank Army numbered about 40,000 men and 406 tanks and self-propelled guns, taking into account rear elements. Besides this, the Third Ukrainian Front had transferred to it the 209th Self-Propelled Artillery Brigade as early as the Lake Balaton fighting.

Thus the strength of the Third Ukrainian Front increased by approximately 176,500 men by the addition of new armies, and had it not been for the losses in the Lake Balaton fighting the *front's* strength would have been about 641,500 men, while only 536,700 remained. This means that the losses for the period 6–15 March were at a minimum 104,800 men, not counting possible reinforcements. On 10 March the Third Ukrainian Front received a significant reinforcement of armoured equipment.[74] In addition, in all likelihood the *front* received rank-and-file reinforcements, the number of which could certainly not have been less than 10,000 men (they simply would not have dispatched less to a *front*). Taking this into account, the Third Ukrainian Front's losses in the Lake Balaton fighting could have been about 113,000 men killed, wounded, and captured. In March 1945 the forces of Army Group South took 2,980 prisoners.[75] It's likely that practically all of them were captured during the course of the Lake Balaton fighting. As the main undercounting in the Red Army was done at the expense of irreplaceable losses, one may assume that in the Lake Balaton fighting the number of killed was approximately equal to the number of wounded. Then the Third Ukrainian Front's losses in killed may be estimated at 55,000 men, with all irreplaceable losses at 58,000 men, which is 6.8 times higher than the official data on irreplaceable losses.

Soviet losses in armoured equipment during the Lake Balaton fighting, according to a report by the Third Ukrainian Front command, were 165 tanks and self-propelled guns, including 84 T-34s and 48 SU-100s.[76] But the actual losses were 2.5 times as high.

By the close of 5 March 1945 there were 157 T-34-85s (another 4 vehicles were undergoing repairs), 13 IS tanks, 95 SU-76s, 12 SU-85s, 80 SU-100s (another 2 vehicles were undergoing repairs), 23 ISU-122s (1 vehicle was undergoing repairs), 10 ISU-152s, (1 vehicle was undergoing repairs), 47 M4A2 'Shermans', (1 vehicle was undergoing repairs), 3 M3A1 'Stuarts', and 7 T-70s, 1 captured tank, and 3 captured assault guns, for a total of 479 combat-ready tanks and self-propelled guns, with 10 undergoing repairs.[77] By the evening of 16 March the forces of the Third Ukrainian Front (minus the 6th Guards Tank Army, but taking into account the armoured equipment of the 9th Guards Army) had 99 T-34s (with another 11 undergoing repairs), 4 ISs, 227 SU-76s (with 1 undergoing repairs), 2 SU-85s, 142 SU-100s (with another 9 undergoing repairs), 18 ISU-122s, 10 ISU-152s, 60 'Shermans' (with 1 undergoing repairs), 1 'Stuart', as well as 5 SU-57s, 9 captured tanks, and 12 captured assault guns, for a total of 589 combat-ready tanks and self-propelled guns.[78] Another 22 vehicles were undergoing repairs.

During the March fighting around Lake Balaton the 22nd Tank Regiment, the 207th and 209th self-propelled artillery brigades, the 1094th and 1922nd self-propelled artillery regiments, and the 27th Army's independent self-propelled artillery battalion were also committed into the fighting. The armoured equipment of the 854th, 1891st, and 1201st self-propelled artillery regiments, the 3rd Guards, 58th, 72nd, and 432nd independent self-propelled artillery battalions, the 32nd Guards Motorized Rifle Brigade, and the 249th Tank Regiment were completely put out of action, or 75 SU-76s, 20 'Shermans', and 20 T-34s. At the same time only the 23rd Tank Corps received T-34s, while only the 1896th, 1891st, and 1202nd regiments, the 18th Tank Corps, and units of the 4th Guards Army received self-propelled artillery.[79]

If this information is correct, then the irreplaceable losses among the different types of armoured equipment can be determined approximately: 82 T-34s, 75 SU-76s, and 7 'Shermans'. Besides this, one can assume that as a minimum 1 SU-57 in the 29th Brigade, 2 'Stuarts', 10 SU-85s, 164 SU-100s, 1 KV, 6 T-70s, 9 ISs, 17 ISU-122s, 7 ISU-152s, 11 captured tanks, and 19 captured assault guns were destroyed. In all, the forces of the Third Ukrainian Front lost no less than 411 tanks and self-propelled guns irreplaceably. Insofar as, according to a report by the *front* command, 84 T-34s were irreparably lost, it can be assumed that 2 of the T-34s were from the 22nd Tank Regiment, which were compensated by the delivery of no less than 3 new vehicles. Taking this into account, as well as, at a minimum, 1 SU-85, which reinforced the 22nd Regiment, the overall number of irreplaceably lost armoured equipment increases to 414 tanks and self-propelled guns. Besides this, the 1094th and 1922nd self-propelled artillery regiments, which were committed during the course of the fighting, numbered on 16 March correspondingly 21 SU-100s (with 1 vehicle undergoing repairs) and 16 SU-100s (with 1 vehicle undergoing repairs). A regiment had an authorized strength of 21 SU-100s, so it may be assumed that the 1922nd Regiment lost irreplaceably 4 self-propelled guns, which increases the overall irreplaceable losses to 418 tanks and self-propelled guns, including 118 tanks.[80] According to the estimate of German historians, the Soviet side's irreplaceable losses in the Lake Balaton fighting were 152 tanks.[81]

The following formations fought on the German side during the Balaton operation. The Sixth Army (Balck's army group) included the III Panzer Corps (1st, 3rd, and, from 12 March, the 6th panzer divisions, and the 356th Infantry Division). The SS Sixth Panzer Army consisted of the SS I Panzer Corps (1st and 12th SS panzer divisions and the 44th '*Reichsgrenadier*' Division) and the I Cavalry Corps (3rd and 4th cavalry divisions and, from 10 March, the Hungarian 25th Infantry Division). These formations were supposed to attempt to carry out on their own Operation 'Spring Awakening' (*Fruhlingserwachen*). The Second Panzer Army from Army Group South was to carry out a supporting operation, code named 'Icebreaker' (*Eisbrecher*). It included the LXVIII Army Corps (SS 16th Motorized Division and 71st Infantry Division) and the XXII Mountain Rifle Corps (118th Jaeger and 1st People's Grenadier divisions). The XCI Army Corps (104th Jaeger, 297th Infantry, 11th Air Field, and 1st Cossack Cavalry divisions), which was subordinated to Army Group Southeast ('E'), was to carry out yet another supporting operation, code named 'Forest Devil' (*Waldteuffel*).

The strength of the German forces which took part in 'Spring Awakening' was 25 divisions, including 1 Hungarian, which numbered 297,903 men, with 595 tanks and assault guns and 600 field guns. The strength of the Hungarian 25th Division probably did not exceed 10,000 men. Thus the Germans probably were approximately half as strong in numbers as the forces of the Third Ukrainian Front, which numbered 465,000 men, 407 tanks and self-propelled guns, and 2,600 field guns. It should be noted that the paper strength increased the strength of the German divisions, in that it included wounded and missing in action for the last month. For example, according to testimony by the former chief of staff of the SS *Hitlerjugend* Division, Hubert Meyer, on 1 February 1945 this division had a paper strength of 20,102 men, against an authorized strength of 18,548. However, the paper strength in this case included 4,266 wounded and evacuated sick for the previous six weeks, so that the division's actual strength was only 15,836 men. As the division was being transferred from the Western Front to the Eastern Front, those missing in action were evidently not included in the paper strength.[82]

The SS Sixth Panzer Army's losses during the period from 6–13 March were 5,919 men, including 963 killed, 4,328 wounded, and 658 missing in action.

The Second Panzer Army lost 3,562 men, including 508 killed, 2,897 wounded, and 157 missing in action. Army group Balck (Sixth Army) lost 2,877 men, including 474 killed, 2,093 wounded, and 310 missing in action. In all, Army Group South lost 12,358 men, including 1,945 killed, 9,318 wounded, and 1,095 missing in action.[83] Army Group Southeast ('E') lost during the same period 2,460 men, including 506 killed, 1,798 wounded, and 156 missing in action.[84]

In all, during the period from 6–13 March the forces which took part in Operation 'Spring Awakening' lost 14,818 men, including 2,451 killed, 11,116 wounded, and 1,251 missing in action. By taking into account losses in the fighting on 14–15 March and the losses of the Hungarian division, overall losses may have reached 16–17,000 men, taking into account the much less-intensive fighting during the final 2 days of Operation 'Spring Awakening'. The Hungarian 25th Division's losses, taking into account the short time it took part in the fighting, probably did not exceed 500 men. The SS *Hitlerjugend* Division, which was on the Eastern Front from 10 February to 8 May 1945, lost 4,376 men, including 1,498 killed; 32 PzIVs and 35 'Panthers' were irreplaceably lost.[85]

The Germans' irreplaceable losses in armoured equipment in the March fighting around Lake Balaton in the SS Sixth Panzer Army were 31 tanks, 11 assault guns, and 1 armoured transport, including 12 tanks and 1 assault gun in the 1st SS Division, 5 tanks and 2 assault guns in the 12th Division and 4 tanks and 5 assault guns in the SS 2nd Division, 4 tanks in the SS 9th Division, and 6 tanks, 3 assault guns and 1 armoured transport in the 23rd Panzer Division. If it is assumed that the level of irreplaceable losses in armoured equipment in the Sixth Army and Second Panzer Army was approximately the same as in the SS Sixth Panzer Army, then these armies might have irreplaceably lost twenty tanks and assault guns.[86]

According to the estimate by the Russian historians A. Isaev and M. Kolomiets, in falling back the German forces left about 250 tanks and assault guns. These included both damaged tanks and working vehicles, which had to be abandoned due to a severe shortage of fuel, with some of them having been blown up beforehand.[87]

It should be stated that in the middle of March 1945 Anglo-American aviation launched a series of air strikes against strategic targets in southern Austria, western Hungary, and southern Slovakia. A number of airfields, railroad junctions, bridges, and industrial sites were subjected to bombing. The main target was oil-processing factories, which by the admission of the German command, led to a sharp drop in the production of fuel. The following was written on 15 March in the war diary of the *Wehrmacht* high command: 'As a result of the air strikes against the oil refineries in Komarno, the production of oil here . . . has decreased by 70% . . . Due to the fact that army groups South and Centre have heretofore been supplied with fuel from Komarno, the consequences of the air strikes will influence operational decisions as well.'[88] One of the reasons for halting Operation 'Spring Awakening' was namely a shortage of fuel.

It makes sense to compare the Third Ukrainian Front's losses and the formations of Army Group South, which were fighting against it, because the forces of the XCI Corps were fighting almost exclusively against Bulgarian and Yugoslav forces, the losses among which are unknown. It can be estimated that the losses of the formations of Army Group South which took part in the Lake Balaton fighting at 14,000 men, including losses by the Hungarians, including 3,400 irreplaceably. The correlation of overall losses is 7.5:1 and 15.4:1 among irreplaceable losses in favour of the Germans. The correlation of irreplaceable losses in tanks and self-propelled guns is also in their favour – 6.5:1, if one counts only German irreplaceable losses directly as a result of the Lake Balaton fighting, and 1.7:1 if one also takes into account the armoured equipment abandoned during the retreat at the beginning of the Vienna operation.

Thus the Germans tactically won the Lake Balaton fighting, but lost strategically, having proved unable to restore a defence along the Danube River and thus predetermined the collapse of the idea of the 'Alpine Redoubt'.

It's of interest to compare the losses of German forces on the Western and Eastern fronts. The SS Sixth Panzer Army will be used to illustrate this. During the period from 11–31 January 1945 Sepp Dietrich's army lost on the Western Front 2,081 killed, 6,895 wounded, and 5,891 missing in action, for a total of 14,867 men.[89] During the period from 11–31 March 1945, but already on the Eastern Front, the SS Sixth Panzer Army lost 1,313 killed, 6,529 wounded, and 779 missing in action, for a total of 8,621 men.[90] Overall losses on the Western Front are higher by 1.7 times, with irreplaceable losses higher by 3.8 times. On the Eastern Front another 4 divisions were added to the SS Sixth Panzer Army, thanks to which its strength grew from 81,400 to 122,400 men. Thus, by calculating the 'old' divisions that had fought on the Western Front as well, the army's losses in Hungary were even less.

In carrying out the Vienna operation, it was initially planned to employ the 6th Guards Tank Army, which on 16 March numbered 426 combat-ready tanks and self-propelled guns (not counting the 207th Self-Propelled Artillery Brigade, which was transferred to it later) in the Second Ukrainian Front's 46th Army's zone, as *front* commander Marshal Malinovskii had proposed. However, on 16 March, the day the operation began, the 6th Guards Tank Army was transferred to Marshal Tolbukhin's Third Ukrainian Front for commitment into the fighting in the 9th Army's sector. This was motivated by the fact that the Third Ukrainian Front's shock group, the 4th and 9th guards armies, had only 200 armoured vehicles, while the enemy along their sector had 270.

Actually, it would have been expedient to commit the 6th Guards Tank Army into the offensive zone of the Third Ukrainian Front's 46th Army, as Malinovskii had suggested. There a significant part of the defenders was made up by Hungarian divisions, which were of little combat value, as well as the *Wehrmacht's* infantry divisions, but without German panzer formations. Here, as early as 18 March, on the offensive's second day, the main defensive zone was penetrated there where the Hungarians were defending and the shock group's forces were forcing the Altal River. As early as 19 March the 2nd Guards Tank Corps was committed to the breakthrough. By the close of 19 March the 46th Army had broken through two of the enemy's defensive zones along a 16km front to a depth of 30km. Along the offensive sector of the 9th Guards Army, where on 19 March the 6th Guards Tank Army was committed into the fighting, the German defence had not yet been pierced and the tank crews suffered heavy losses, having been unable to develop a high offensive pace. It should be noted that the attempts by the 6th Guards Tank Army to block the SS Sixth Panzer Army's withdrawal collapsed completely, although the former disposed of 425 combat-ready tanks and self-propelled guns and had fought initially only against the SS I Panzer Corps, which disposed of only 82 combat-ready tanks and assault guns.[91]

They could have reinforced the Third Ukrainian Front's shock group by taking a part of the 360 armoured vehicles in the *front's* other armies. The 9th Guards Army's slow offensive may be explained to a great extent by the fact that all of this army's divisions had gone into fighting for the first time. Of course, there were a certain percentage of soldiers and commander with combat experience, but the commanders had never yet lead their units and subunits in combat, which had a negative imapct on cooperation and the subunits' combat viability. The *Stavka* plan was to encircle the SS Sixth Panzer Army with the aid of Kravchenko's tank crews.[92] However, they were unable to do this and Dietrich's army fell back to the west through the narrow 2.5km corridor in the Fuzfo area, while the Soviet tank crews suffered heavy losses, and as early as 2 April it was necessary to pull the 6th Guards Tank Army out of the fighting for reinforcement. For example, on 20 March alone the SS I Panzer Corps reported destroying sixty-six Soviet tanks.[93] Overall Soviet irreplaceable losses in armoured equipment in the Vienna operation, according to official data, were 603 tanks and self-propelled guns.[94] At the same time, if the 6th Guards Tank Army had been committed into the 46th Army's offensive sector immediately following the breakthrough of the enemy's defence, as had been initially planned, then the Soviet forces along this axis, having three times as many tanks and self-propelled guns, would have advanced even more rapidly and would have achieved greater successes, advancing directly on Vienna. In this case, the SS Sixth Panzer Army would have had to hurriedly retreat, while abandoning a large part of its armoured equipment because of lack of fuel. Then it's likely that the 6th Guards Tank Army's losses and those of the Third Ukrainian Front's other armies would have been less and Vienna could have been taken several days earlier.

The idea of 'Spring Awakening' somewhat resembles that for 'Citadel'. It was planned to encircle and press to the Danube and destroy part of the Third Ukrainian Front's forces. Only this time the attacks were launched not along converging but along diverging axes. But if the SS Sixth Panzer Army's group of forces, many soldiers and officers of which had taken part in the Battle of Kursk, had managed to advance sufficiently far, the Sixth Army's group of forces would have been halted quite quickly. The correlation of forces was just as unfavourable for the Germans as during Operation 'Citadel', which also predetermined the failure of 'Spring Awakening'.

As is well known, Operation 'Citadel' was halted after the forces of the Western and Bryansk fronts attacked the Orel salient. Evidently, following the Battle of Kursk, Stalin decided to operate according to the same template in repelling major German offensives: first wear out the attackers, and then launch a counterblow. In the Lake Balaton fighting the same principle was applied: first wear out the enemy, and then begin a general offensive on Vienna. At the same time, they failed to take into account the fact that the situation in Central Europe in March 1945 was completely different from that along the Kursk salient in July 1943. One should begin with the fact that not one, but many roads led to Vienna, the main strategic point and a very important railroad junction along the southern part of the Soviet-German front, and that the Germans simply lacked the forces to cover even the majority of them. By no means did all the roads run through western Hungary, and an offensive in the area of Lake Balaton could have forced the Soviet command to renounce a movement on Vienna for a time only along this route. And following the beginning of 'Spring Awakening' the most powerful reply from the Soviet side would have been the beginning of an offensive on Vienna through the territory of Slovakia, not immediately upon the completion of the German offensive near Lake Balaton, but within four to five days of 'Spring Awakening', say 9 or 10 March. If during these days Malinovskii's Second Ukrainian Front had begun the Vienna offensive operation through Gron and (or) the Bratislava-Brno operation, but with the main effort not toward Brno, but also toward Vienna, and also by employing the two armies in the reserve – 9th Guards and 6th Guards Tank – the German defence would have simply collapsed. In these conditions, Operation 'Spring Awakening' would have lost all meaning. Most likely, Hitler would have then ordered the end of the offensive in Hungary and the immediate dispatch of either the entire SS Sixth Panzer Army for the defence of Vienna, or at least one of its corps consisting of three panzer divisions. One recalls it took nine days just to transfer the SS I Panzer Corps from the Esztergom (Gran) area to the offensive area near Lake Balaton. Now, in order to carry out a reverse transfer towards Gran, actually now towards Vienna, insofar as it would nevertheless been impossible to hold Gran, would have probably required no less than twelve days, in that the corps still had to be pulled out of the fighting. One should take into account the fact that at that moment Anglo-American aviation reigned supreme along all of the German Eastern Front's rear communications and that the Germans could have carried out the transfer only at night. At Kursk in July 1943 the German command was able to rapidly transfer forces from the shock group of forces and, thanks to this, to materially slow down the Soviet offensive against the Orel salient. But in March 1945, such a rapid regrouping was in principle impossible, and in all likelihood would have led to a situation in which a large part of three German panzer divisions would have travelled in rail cars, deprived of any opportunity of entering the fighting. To all appearances, in this case the Red Army would have occupied all of Austria. After all, in the middle of March the Anglo-American forces had not yet broken through the German front in northern Italy, while in the West the Allies had only just seized the Remagen bridgehead over the Rhine and had not yet begun the offensive for the purpose of encircling the Ruhr group of forces.[95] In any event, given such circumstances, the Third Ukrainian Front's losses, which it suffered while repelling the German offensive, would have been significantly reduced. It's possible that the end of the war could have been shortened by two to three weeks and thus hundreds of thousands of Soviet soldiers' lives saved. But Stalin preferred to act according to a template.

During the Vienna operation, which lasted from 16 March to 15 April 1945, the Third Ukrainian Front, according to official data, lost 32,846 men irreplaceably, while the Second Ukrainian Front's 46th Army and 2nd Guards Mechanized Corps lost another 5,815 men.[96] One should not doubt that as in the Berlin and other operations the irreplaceable losses in the Vienna operation have been lowered three to four times by official sources. Combat operations during the Vienna operation were waged primarily on Austrian territory and Soviet forces actively received reinforcements from liberated prisoners and *ostarbeiters*, which enabled them to conceal their irreplaceable losses in their reports. The Second and Third Ukrainian fronts' irreplaceable losses in the Vienna operation may be estimated at 116,000–154,000 men, while the irreplaceable losses of the Soviet forces fighting the German SS Sixth Panzer Army, the Second Panzer, and the Sixth armies (Balck's group) from 1 March to 30 April 1945 may be estimated at 174,000–212,600 men, of which no more than 3,000 were prisoners. The author consciously excluded from these calculations the Hungarian Third and Bulgarian 1st armies, which were fighting, correspondingly, on the German and Soviet sides, as these armies' losses in killed were insignificant. The losses of the three indicated German armies during the period from 1 March to 20 April 1945 were 6,284 killed and 8,240 missing in action, for a total of 14,524 irreplaceable losses.[97] Almost no one from the three German armies got into an encirclement, so that the ten-day reports on losses should be sufficiently accurate. Only the report on the SS Sixth Panzer Army's losses from the period 1–10 April is missing, but one can assume that the data for this period was included in the final reports sent for 11–20 April, in which the number of missing in action rose sharply – from 237 in the last 10 days of March to 2,533. The correlation of irreplaceable losses is 12.0:1 to 14.6:1 in favour of the German side. In killed, the advantage is in favour of the Germans to an even greater degree, in that a significant part of their losses in missing in action (probably no less than half and, possibly, more) are due to prisoners, while among the Soviet irreplaceable losses prisoners comprise an insignificant amount. Such an unfavourable correlation of irreplaceable losses for the Soviet side is a result of the fact that elite divisions of the SS Sixth Panzer Army and the SS IV Panzer Corps were fighting on the German side.

The idea of the 'Alpine Redoubt' suffered its final collapse following the fall of Vienna, which was captured by the Red Army on 13 April 1945. On the territory of the 'Alpine Redoubt', which theoretically included Bavaria, Austria, the Czech Republic, Slovakia, and western Hungary, as well as the South Tyrol and other Italian territory bordering on Austria, there were practically no supplies of munitions and fuel sufficient for prolonged resistance in conditions of intensive combat operations. Moreover, the picture was the same in almost all of the territories still under the control of Nazi Germany. In the best case, there might have been enough munitions to last for the first ten days of May. Besides this, the 'Alpine Redoubt' contained a numerically significant non-German population which was hostile to Germany, which was confirmed by the May uprising in Czech Prague. This would have excluded the successful waging of a partisan struggle in a significant part of the 'Alpine Redoubt's' territory, with the exception of Bavaria, Austria, and the Sudetenland, but there had been no preparations made for a partisan war in the form of the prior creation of partisan bases with supplies of arms, munitions, and food. And Hitler would have considered it personally humiliating and pointless to hide in some Alpine village. Thus following the beginning of the Soviet offensive on Berlin he abandoned the idea of the 'Alpine Redoubt' and remained in the capital of the Reich.

Chapter 8

The Battle of Berlin

Was There a Race Between the Red Army and the Allied Armies?

On 12 January 1945 the Red Army's general offensive on the Vistula and against East Prussia began. Simultaneously, the Second and Fourth Ukrainian fronts began an offensive in Slovakia and southern Poland. The German group of forces in the East had been weakened by the transfer of the most combat-capable divisions for the Ardennes offensive. According to an estimate by the then chief of the German General Staff, Heinz Guderian, the Soviet superiority was 11:1 in infantry, 7:1 in tanks and 20:1 in artillery and aircraft. German intelligence had previously and accurately determined the date for the start of the Soviet offensive – 12 January, as well as the launching of the main attacks along the Vistula and in East Prussia, but the lack of reserves prevented them from offering any kind of effective counter to the Soviet plans.[1]

The German front along the Vistula was easily pierced. As early as 22 January the forces of the First Belorussian Front had begun the siege of Poznan. By the start of February the *front* had reached the Oder River and seized a bridgehead in the Kustrin area. On 31 January Zhukov sent a report to the *Stavka*, in which he requested that the Second Belorussian Front be ordered to immediately begin an offensive to the west to eliminate the gap with the First Belorussian Front, and for the First Ukrainian Front to reach the Oder as quickly as possible.

In 1965 the former commander of the 8th Guards Army, Marshal V.I. Chuikov, maintained that 'Berlin could have been captured as early as February. And this, naturally, would have brought the end of the war nearer.'[2] On 17 January 1966 Vasilii Ivanovich was summoned for criticism to the chief of the GlavPUR, A.A. Yepishev, along with other military leaders.[3] Chuikov declared that:

> Soviet forces, having covered 500 kilometers and halted in February 60 kilometers from Berlin . . . Who was stopping us? The enemy or the command? There were more than enough forces for an offensive on Berlin. The two and a half months respite that we gave the enemy along the western direction helped him to prepare to defend Berlin.

The other marshals did not support him. Yepishev, summing up the results of the discussion, declared: 'We must not blacken our history; otherwise on what will we raise our youth?'[4]

In his memoirs, Chuikov related how the February offensive on Berlin was called off:

> On 4 February the commander of the First Belorussian Front gathered commanders Berzarin, Kolpakchi, Katukov, Bogdanov, and me for a meeting at the headquarters of the 69th Army, to which he had himself arrived.[5] We . . . discussed the plan for the offensive on Berlin, when the high frequency telephone rang. I was sitting almost right by it and could hear the telephone conversation well. Stalin called. He asked Zhukov where he was and what he was doing. The marshal replied that he had gathered the commanders in the headquarters of Kolpakchi's army and was engaged with them in planning the offensive on Berlin. Having heard the report, Stalin suddenly and completely unexpectedly, as I understood it, for the *front* commander, demanded that he cease this planning and instead work out an operation for defeating the Hitlerite forces of Army Group Vistula, which were in Pomerania.

Zhukov, in his *Memoirs and Reminiscences*, sought to dispute Chuikov:

> There was no such meeting in the headquarters of the 69th Army. Thus there was also no conversation on the high frequency telephone, about which Chuikov writes, with Stalin. On 4–5 February I was in the headquarters of the 61st Army, which was being deployed along the *front's* right flank in Pomerania for operations against the enemy's Pomeranian group of forces. Nor could the commander of the 1st Guards Tank Army have been at this mythical meeting, because according to a *front* directive of 2 February 1945 . . . he had been carrying out the regrouping of his army's forces from the morning of 3 February from the Oder to the Friedberg–Berlichen–Landsberg area. The commander of the 2nd Guards Tank Army, Gen. Bogdanov, also could not have been at the meeting due to illness (at this time his duties were being carried out by the army commander, Gen. A.I. Radzievskii[6]). And Chuikov himself was in the city of Poznan on 3 February, from where he reported to me on the course of the fighting for the city. Chuikov's memory has evidently betrayed him.[7]

On 4 February there really was no meeting between Zhukov and the army commanders, because it took place on 10 February. On this day the plan for the First Belorussian Front's Berlin offensive operation was drawn up and reported by Zhukov to Stalin by high frequency telephone at 1515. The marshal asserted:

> The enemy is carrying out a regrouping of Army Group Vistula's forces for the purpose of organizing a firm defence along the approaches to Stettin and along the line of the Oder River. Striving to prevent the arrival of our forces at Stettin and the isolation of his Pomeranian group of forces, the enemy is reinforcing Army Group Vistula's left wing, transferring formations from the Courland bridgehead and from East Prussia. He is simultaneously reinforcing the Ninth Army, which is covering Germany from the east, moving up new divisions to the first line: the 21st Panzer Division, the 25th Motorized Division, the SS 15th Panzer Division, the 212th Panzer Division, and the *Doberitz* Infantry Division for developing and strengthening the defence along the western bank of the Oder and along the lake system east of Berlin. Besides this, he is hurriedly transferring the SS Sixth Panzer Army, with an overall strength of up to six panzer and six infantry divisions, from the Western Front to the Berlin direction. The purpose of the operation is to foil the enemy's operational concentration, to break through his defence along the western bank of the Oder River and to capture Berlin.

Further on the marshal recounted the tasks of the *front's* armies by the days and stages of the operation. On the whole, this was the same plan that the First Belorussian Front carried out in April, when Stalin finally sanctioned the offensive on Berlin. It was planned to outflank the capital of the Reich from the northwest and southwest and then to destroy the encircled group of forces through concentrated attacks from all directions. Five combined-arms and two tank armies, reinforced by two independent tank corps, were to attack Berlin. Due to the lagging behind of the Second Belorussian Front's forces, in order to repel a possible counterblow from the north, out of Pomerania, Zhukov was to leave behind the 3rd Shock, 61st, and Polish 1st armies, reinforced by two cavalry and one rifle corps and two fortified areas. These forces were to subsequently reinforce the shock group of forces. In conclusion, Zhukov reported:

> I can begin the regrouping of men and materiel from the *front's* right flank to the Oder River only with the Second Belorussian Front's assumption of the offensive, that is, from 10.2.45, and complete it on 18.2.45. In this regard, the troops designated for operations

against Berlin, will be prepared to go over to the offensive only on 19–20.2.45. It is necessary before this time to carry out a regrouping of the *front's* men and materiel, repair the combat vehicles' equipment, bring up supplies, and to organize the battle.[8]

Zhukov's proposal was quite sensible from the military strategic point of view. The Germans had almost no forces east of Berlin. They would have been hopelessly late in transferring formations from the Western Front and there is no way they could have concentrated them on the Oder by the start of the First Belorussian Front's planned offensive. Zhukov sought to justify his refusal of an immediate offensive on Berlin by citing the threat from the group of German forces in Pomerania, which was significantly inferior in men and materiel to the First and Second Belorussian fronts' armies facing them. As early as 25 January Guderian told Ribbentrop: 'What will you say if the Russians are standing before Berlin in two to three weeks?' The Reichminister exclaimed in horror: 'Do you believe that's possible?' The chief of the General Staff assured him that such a development of events was not only possible, but more than likely; taking into account the German Eastern Front's unenviable situation, and proposed that together they convince Hitler to attempt to achieve a separate peace in the West.[9]

As early as 20 January the *Stavka*, that is, Stalin, turned the Second Belorussian Front's main forces into East Prussia, instead of Pomerania. In the same way the First Belorussian Front's turn into Pomerania on 10 February was brought about primarily for political reasons. Stalin did not want to take Berlin too rapidly. He assumed that the fall of the capital would bring about the end of German resistance. Stalin seriously feared that in the event of Berlin's fall the *Wehrmacht's* remaining groups of forces in Pomerania, East Prussia, and Courland would capitulate to the Western Allies, and then Anglo-American forces would appear in these territories and following the end of the war would attempt to establish their control over Poland and the Baltic States, confirming the power there of anti-Soviet governments. Actually, neither Washington nor London had any such plans. But Stalin preferred to occupy all the territories that were supposed to become a part of the USSR or fall in the Soviet sphere of influence before the general capitulation of Germany. Thus all the way up to the end of March Soviet forces were engaged in useless and bloody operations in Courland and, before the end of the war, just as bloody an offensive in eastern Pomerania and East Prussia, which had long before been cut off from the main territory of the Reich. These battles not only did not bring the end of the war closer, but quite the opposite; they pushed it back, insofar as they delayed the fall of Berlin and the occupation of central Germany by the Red Army. Thanks to the respite that was granted them, the Germans had time to construct a defence of Berlin from the east, which significantly increased the Red Army's losses during the offensive on Berlin in the second half of April.

During the final offensive operations of the Great Patriotic War, the Soviet generals and also lower level commanders continued to colossally inflate the enemy's losses and undercount their own losses. In attempting to combat this, the *Stavka* and the General Staff demanded that the armies and *fronts* not only report on the number of enemy military personnel killed and taken prisoner, but that they also gave a precise breakdown of just how many generals, staff officers, junior officers, NCOs, and privates were killed and taken prisoner. If, regarding prisoners, this sort of demand made at least some sense, then it was simply outright humiliation for those killed. Imagine a Soviet officer feverishly trying to determine by collar tabs and epaulets whether the man killed was a junior officer or NCO. In practice, these demands in no way limited the creativity of Soviet generals and officers. They lied not only about the killed and captured generals – the *Stavka* carefully investigated them and demanded that the reporting be accurate – giving their surnames, ranks, and positions. As regards the rest, one could, as before report made-up data about how many enemy troops were captured and killed. You just had to make sure that in the report the number of staff officers did not exceed the number of junior officers and that the number of NCOs did not exceed the number of privates.

The same was true of captured equipment, as with prisoners. Speaking at a scientific conference on studying the First Belorussian Front's Berlin operation, Lieutenant General K.F. Telegin declared:[10]

> During the January 1945 fighting the headquarters of the armies and independent corps of the First Belorussian Front reported destroying 1,749 and capturing 599 enemy tanks and assault guns, which corresponded to 2,348, the number needed to outfit 14 German panzer divisions. In reality, in January 1945 two panzer divisions, three brigades of assault guns, two motorized divisions, and independent panzer units and subunits were facing the *front*, with an overall number of 920 vehicles, and here we had already destroyed 2,348 . . .

God himself ordered the number of prisoners to be over counted. Telegin complained:

> Following the Warsaw-Lodz-Poznan operation, we began to total up how many prisoners had been taken and how many actually reached the collection-transfer stations for the camps. A striking

picture emerged. For example, from 14 January through 12 March the 8th Guards Army showed us in a report 28,149 men, and according to the army's ten-day reports 40,000 had been captured, while according to the army's reports, only 27,953 men were turned over to the front stations, while 5,221 were actually delivered from the 8th Guards Army. Five thousand remained out of 40,000. Why did they report that the *front* stations had received 28,000? The 47th Army reported that 4,497 men had been turned over to the 61st Army's processing stations, while the 61st Army does not confirm this with any documents.[11]

Taking into account this admission, one must approach official Soviet data very carefully to the effect that during the Vistula–Oder operation (this was the Warsaw–Lodz–Poznan operation) the Red Army supposedly took 150,000 prisoners. In his order of 23 February 1945, Stalin maintained that in 40 days of the Soviet winter offensive along the Vistula–Oder and East Prussian directions, 350,000 prisoners had been taken.[12] Undoubtedly, taking into account the examples put forward by General Telegin, these figures should be reduced by 5–8 times. In all, from 1–20 January 1045 67,776 prisoners were taken in, some portion of which from the Hungarian garrison of Budapest and other Hungarian forces.[13] Taking into account the fact that the main mass of prisoners was captured during the first week of the Vistula–Oder and East Prussia operation, the overall number of German prisoners probably accounted for 50,000–60,000 men, and in no way 350,000.

The Soviet forces' losses were significant in the fighting for the bridgeheads over the Oder in February 1945. In these battles the 5th Guards Army's 95th Guards Rifle Division lost during the period from 1–15 February 1945 203 killed and 494 wounded.[14] The opposing German Seventeenth Army lost during the first twenty days of February 1,766 men killed, 2,524 missing in action, and 7,452 wounded.[15] Besides the 5th Guards Army, the 6th, 52nd, and 3rd Guards Tank armies were operating against the Seventeenth Army at that time. They numbered 23 rifle and airborne divisions, 1 fortified area, 2 tank and 1 mechanized corps.[16] If it is assumed that all 27 division-level formations suffered approximately the same losses during the first 20 days of February as did the 95th Guards Rifle Division, then the overall losses for the Soviet forces operating against the German Seventeenth Army during this period may be estimated at 5,500 killed and 13,300 wounded. The correlation in numbers killed is 3.1:1 in favour of the Germans, which appears likely. It's probably the case that the majority of the German missing in action in this case were prisoners. Probably the number of killed among the Soviet forces operating against the Seventeenth Army was higher, in that they suffered some unknown losses among the missing in action, the majority of which were actually killed. The correlation of losses in wounded may be estimated at 1.8:1, also in favour of the Germans.

On the territory of East Prussia, according to the data supplied by the authors of the book *The Seal of Secrecy Removed*, the Red Army irreplaceably lost 16,819 men in the Gumbinnen–Goldap operation from 16–30 October 1944, 403 during the capture of Memel (Klaipeda) during the period from 25 January to 4 February 1945, and 126,464 men during the East Prussian offensive operation from 13 January to 25 April 1945.[17] This amounted to 143,686 men overall. At the same time, according to data from the working group for preparing the Kalingrad Oblast's book of remembrance, *Let's Call Them by Name*, by 2005 it had been established that more than 137,000 Red Army soldiers died on the territory of the oblast' during October 1944 to May 1945, and that the work was still far from finished. And the territory of the Kalingrad Oblast' comprises only a third of the territory of East Prussia.[18] If one assumes that the level of losses for the Soviet forces in the fighting for that part of the territory of East Prussia that now belongs to Poland is approximately the same as in the fighting on the territory of what is now the Kalingrad Oblast', then overall Soviet losses in the struggle for East Prussia may amount to about 411,000 men killed. Besides this, Army Group Centre, which was defending in East Prussia, captured from 11–31 October 1944 3,443 prisoners and from 11–31 January 1945 another 1,892 prisoners. The same army group, which was renamed Army Group North, captured from the beginning of February up to the end of March 1945 3,444 prisoners, for a total of 8,779 prisoners.[19] Thus the Red Army's overall irreplaceable losses in the fighting for East Prussia may be estimated at 419,779 men. In all likelihood the Red Army's official irreplaceable losses in East Prussia have been undercounted by 2.9 times.

Karl Knoblauch, the former adjutant (chief of staff) of the 1st Parachute-Panzer Division's fusilier battalion, recalled, on the basis of diary entries, the fighting in East Prussia during 19–22 January 1945, about how great both sides' losses were and how bitter was the fighting in which prisoners were not taken:

> The commander returned within two hours: 'Knoblauch, the 1st Company no longer exists. The trenches which I managed to view are full of dead men, Russians and Germans. There's no more firing. Evidently the Russian infantry's losses were so high that there was nothing left for the next attack. Temporarily, at least . . .'
>
> The fusilier who had fallen at the door of the building was dead. An automatic rifle burst had shot him through the chest. No one

survived among the Russians. At about 0300 the firing died down in front of all the positions. The Russians had evidently suffered heavy losses. Before dawn they attacked again, but fell down under our fire. There were five men killed in the battalion. The time dragged by very slowly. Each man understood that our situation was hopeless. But no one spoke of this. I thought of what to do if we run out of ammunition and the Russians come. I didn't even have the courage to think of the word 'captivity'.[20]

The German troops fought desperately during the final months of the war, despite the hopelessness of the situation.

A number of riveting and believable accounts have been preserved as regards what went on at that time in East Prussia, as well as in other parts of Germany being occupied by the Red Army. Aleksandr Solzhenitsyn, who fought in East Prussia in the beginning of 1945, recalled: 'The war had been going on in Germany for three weeks and all of us well knew: should any German girls turn up, then they could be raped and then shot, and this would almost be considered a combat feat; should Polish girls or our forced-labour girls turn up, then they could be driven through the garden naked and have their thighs slapped, as if they were an amusing toy, and nothing more.[21]

And this is what the artist Leonid Rabichev wrote in his memoirs:

On carriages and automobiles, and on foot, old men, women and children, large patriarchal families were moving west along all the country's roads and highways.

Our tank crews, infantrymen, artillery troops, and communications troops drove them on, and in order to clear a path were tossing their carriages with furniture, handbags, suitcases, and horses into the ditches along the shoulders of the roads, and pushed the old men and children to one side and, having forgotten their duty and honour and about the German subunits that were retreating without a fight, threw themselves by the thousands on the women and young girls.

Women, mothers and their daughters, are lying to the right and left along the road and in front of each stands a laughing armada of men with their pants down.

Bleeding and losing consciousness, they are dragged off to the side and the children who rush to help them are shot. There are guffaws, snarling, laughter, cries, and moans. And their commanders, their majors and colonels are standing on the road, some chuckle to themselves, while some are conducting it, or, rather, are regulating matters. No, this is not a mutual guarantee, and certainly not revenge against the cursed occupiers – this is hellish group sex. Everything is allowed, nothing is punished, no one is responsible, and the cruel logical of a mindless mob . . .

And a colonel, the one who was directing, couldn't hold out any longer and takes his place in line, while a major shoots any witnesses, the hysterically struggling children and old men.

'Wrap it up. Everybody back in the trucks!'

And another subunit is already behind them.

And the director-colonel? Was a single command sufficient? After all, the commander of the Third Belorussian Front, Gen. Chernyakhovskii, had travelled in his jeep along this same road.[22] Did he see, did he see all of this and went into buildings where women lay on beds with bottles? Was a single command sufficient? So, who was the guiltiest: the soldier from the ranks, the director-major, the laughing colonels and generals, or me who observed all of this, or on those who said that 'War writes off everything . . .?'

A crazy thought tormented me: Stalin summons Chernyakhovskii and whispers in his ear 'Shouldn't we just destroy all of those East Prussian imperialists at the very root; after all, according to international agreements, this territory will be our Soviet territory?' And Chernyakhovskii says to Stalin: 'It will be done, comrade general secretary!'[23]

During the preparatory period for the stillborn February offensive against Berlin, a tragicomic incident took place. Here is Zhukov's note to the commander of the 1st Guards Tank Army, M.Ye. Katukov, dated 1 February 1945:

> Directly into the hands of comrades Katukov and Popel' [member of the military council of Katukov's army, B.S.]
>
> I have a report from highly responsible personages to the effect that comrade Katukov is manifesting a complete lack of responsibility, does not command the army, and is sitting snug at home with some broad, and that this girl who has shacked up with him is interfering with his work. Right now Katukov enjoys no authority in the corps and even Shalin [the army's chief of staff, B.S.] and the staff officers around Katukov are saying the most awful things.
>
> Katukov doesn't seem to visit the units. He does not organize the corps' and army's combat, as a result of which the army has lately been suffering reverses.

I demand:

1. That each of you gives me a truthful personal explanation of this matter.
2. Immediately remove the woman from Katukov's presence. If this is not done, I will order that she be removed by SMERSH.
3. Katukov should get down to business.

If Katukov does not draw the necessary conclusions for himself, he will be replaced by another commander.[24]

The piquancy of the situation was further heightened by the fact that Mikhail Yefimovich became a widower before the war, so one could not even accuse him of cheating on his wife.

Imagine the Field Marshal Kluge writes a note to General Guderian: 'If you do not immediately get rid of the girl you're living with, I will order the secret field police to remove her.' Or imagine the American general Eisenhower, who had his own campaign wife in the person of his driver, kindly informing General Patton: 'Dear George! If you do not end relations with the woman in question, I will be forced to insist that members of the military police remove her from the army.' What would have been the reaction of the subordinate generals to such an unceremonious invasion by the leadership into their private lives? Would they have punched their chiefs out or challenged them to a duel? This is because in the Western armies the institution of 'campaign-field wives' as a mass phenomenon, which blossomed in the Red Army during the war years, was absent. And there was no natural base for it in the Western armies in the form of a large number of women serving directly in the combat units or the nearby rear. Both Hitler and the Western Allies kept women far from the front. Bachelor soldiers and junior officers from the German, American, and British armies satisfied their sexual needs with the aid of prostitutes and even received additional payments for treating venereal diseases. As for senior officers and generals, sex on the side was condemned and had unpleasant consequences, and those few who, like Eisenhower, had 'campaign-field wives' carefully hid them. Hitler sent into retirement the war minister, Field Marshal Blomberg, when it transpired that in her youth his wife had for a short time been a prostitute.[25] A divorce or living openly with a mistress, if it did not mean an end to one's career, would then make very difficult the career of any officer or general in the Western armies.

The very institution of 'campaign-field wives' arose in the Red Army as there were quite a lot of women in the Red Army – about 1 million. Another reason was that the women, nurses, and communications employees were completely dependent on their commanders and did not dare reject their solicitations. The Soviet soldiers did not have the money and extra rations for prostitutes, and they themselves often went hungry. This was one of the reasons for the waves of rapes which swept over the European countries after the Red Army's entrance there.

Zhukov, as did many others, had a 'campaign-field wife'. It's interesting how he would have viewed a note or an oral reprimand from the supreme commander-in-chief with the following content: 'Comrade Zhukov, immediately remove this girl, or I will order the chief of SMERSH, comrade Abakumov, to immediately remove her as a harmful element.[26] Do you understand that you're living with some broad and have let the control of the offensive on Berlin slip . . .!' Katukov is also a good example. Since Zhukov awarded him a second Hero of the Soviet Union medal (the order is dated 6 April), it meant that Katukov humbly bore the humiliation, although he did not send away his mistress, who later became his wife.

The East Pomeranian operation, which the First Belorussian Front was forced to carry out with the Second Belorussian Front instead of an immediate offensive on Berlin, was also distinguished by heavy Soviet losses.

In the East Pomeranian operation, which lasted from 10 February to 4 April 1945, the Soviet forces' irreplaceable losses totalled 52,740 men, with sanitary losses 172,952. In the same operation the Polish 1st Army lost, according to official Russian data, 2,575 men killed and missing in action.[27] However, according to Polish data, the army's losses were 5,400 killed and 2,800 missing in action.[28] This yields 8,200 irreplaceable losses, which is 3.2 times greater that the official Russian accounting of Polish losses in the East Pomeranian operation. Accordingly, the overall Russian estimate of Soviet and Polish irreplaceable losses in this operation should be increased by 3.2 times, from 55,315 to 176,149 men.

Stalin viewed the capture of Berlin by the Red Army as one of the main goals of the war. From his point of view, the capture of the capital of the Reich by Soviet forces was supposed to underscore the decisive role of the USSR in the victory over Nazi Germany and have an important propaganda influence on public opinion in the Allied countries. As early as September 1944 the occupation zones in Germany were finally defined, according to which the state of Brandenburg, along with Berlin, was to be part of the Soviet occupation zone. This was according to the principle that the historically based German lands should not be divided by the boundaries of the occupation zones. It was also established that Berlin, which was part of the Soviet occupation zone, would be under joint control of the four victorious powers. Germany itself was to be confined to the territory between the Oder and the Rhine rivers. If Berlin had been included in the British or American occupation zone, the Soviet occupation zone would have been reduced to a small amount of territory east of Berlin, where the largest city would have been Dresden. In this case, the Soviet occupation zone would have been smaller than each of the western occupation zones. Such a distribution of occupation zones would have fixed the secondary position of the Soviet side in the matter of the future joint control of Germany, which was proclaimed as one of the foundations for a future stable peace in Europe. Stalin would never have agreed to such a humiliation and his Western partners in the negotiations understood this perfectly well. They seriously counted on cooperating with Stalin in the matter of governing Germany, at least in the first postwar years. Thus they were ready to observe the principle of equality of the sides in the distribution of the occupation zones. Moreover, the Western Allies had no effective means of pressuring Stalin. Neither Roosevelt nor Churchill, nor their replacements Truman and Attlee, were prepared to begin a war or even a new military confrontation in the centre of Europe with an ally from the anti-Hitler coalition. There were not sufficient forces for this nor, what is even more important, support from public opinion. To be sure, there were certain fears regarding 'Uncle Joe', especially on the part of Churchill. He was afraid that the Soviet advance westwards might continue even after the achievement of victory over Germany. Thus immediately following the German capitulation on 8 May 1945, Churchill issued an order to the British General Staff to draw up plans for possible military resistance, if the Soviet Union should try by force to seize that part of the Soviet occupation zone occupied by the Western Allies, and to also give some thought to means allowing them 'to impose the will of the United States and the British Empire on Russia', in order to secure 'a just resolution of the Polish question'. However, all calculations showed that the Western Allies would not be able to rapidly defeat the Red Army either through an offensive or through a defence, and that it would be necessary to wage a prolonged total war. Consideration was even given, despite the fantastic nature of such an assumption, to the idea that the USSR would enter into an alliance with Japan.[29]

Returning to the final weeks of the Second World War, the definition of the demarcation lines between the occupation zones at Yalta by no means signified that the Soviet and Anglo-American forces would meet precisely along the zonal boundaries. Stalin most feared that the Western Allies might enter Berlin ahead of the Red Army. He viewed such a variant of the development of events as a serious blow to Soviet prestige.

On 28 March 1945, following the encirclement of a large German group of forces in the Ruhr, the supreme commander-in-chief of Allied forces in Europe, the American general Dwight Eisenhower, addressed Stalin in a personal communication, in which he proposed that the Allied and Soviet forces link up along the line Erfurt–Leipzig–Dresden and Vienna–Linz–Regensburg. Eisenhower wanted to direct his main forces to the south of Berlin, assuming that the most powerful group of German forces was concentrated in southern Germany, Austria, and Czechoslovakia. In a telegram on 1 April, Stalin replied, consciously misleading Eisenhower by declaring that he was in agreement with his estimate of the situation and that 'Berlin has lost its former strategic significance and thus the Soviet High Command is thinking about allotting secondary forces toward Berlin.' At the same time, Stalin maintained that the Soviet forces' main attack would be launched only in the second half of May.[30] He himself was hurriedly preparing an offensive on Berlin, set to begin on 16 April.

But was Eisenhower really wrong in his assessment of the situation? After all, the most powerful German group of forces – Army Group Centre – really was operating in Czechoslovakia. Besides this, German forces in Austria and southern Germany, which were fighting both the Red Army and the Western Allies, were more numerous than the forces fighting in the Berlin area and in the north. Army Group Vistula, which was defending Berlin and northern Germany against Soviet forces, numbered about twenty-two divisions and was far from being up to strength in both men and materiel. At the same time, Army Group Centre numbered up to forty-five divisions, which were much better outfitted, and Army Group South (subsequently, Army Group Austria), which had up to thirty-five divisions, was also outfitted better than Army Group Vistula's formations. If one takes those German forces fighting against the Anglo-American forces, then the forces of the commander-in-chief West, which were operating along the southern wing of the Western Front, numbered fifty-one divisions, while the forces of Army Group Northwest, which were defending the northern wing of the Western Front, numbered only seventeen divisions (another three divisions were located in Denmark). Besides this, Army Group C, which was operating in Italy and which numbered up to twenty-four divisions, could fall back into Austria.

This disposition of the *Wehrmacht* can be explained by Hitler's intention to defend against both the Red Army and against the Western Allies in the Alpine Redoubt. This was true even when the Soviet general offensive on Berlin had begun. The evacuation of government institutions and archives southwards continued. It was only on 21 April, the day after American forces took Nurnberg, that Hitler made his final decision to remain in Berlin, realizing that death in the capital of the Reich would look better in the eyes of history than an unknown death in some god-forsaken Alpine village. This decision was made when he had lost all hope for the outbreak of an armed conflict between the USSR and the Western Allies. This hope had flared up briefly following the death on 12 April of American president Franklin Roosevelt. The American forces that had reached the Elbe River and seized bridgeheads along its eastern bank had not begun an offensive on Berlin from there. This must have been viewed by Hitler as evidence of the fact that there must exist among the Allies some kind of preliminary agreement on the demarcation lines in Germany. This is why he removed Walther Wenck's Twelfth Army from the Elbe and threw it towards Berlin in order to prolong the capital's agony.[31]

If the Americans had not halted on 13 April along the bridgeheads over the Elbe, 85km the German capital, and had continued their offensive with their main forces on Berlin, the German Twelfth Army would not only not have been able to launch a successful counterblow against one of the American bridgeheads over the Elbe, but it simply could not have held out more than a day. Eisenhower and Bradley, the commander of the Twelfth Army Group, maintained that an offensive on Berlin might cost American forces losses of 100,000 killed and wounded.[32] It's possible that they significantly overestimated these losses, perhaps in order to hide from their subordinates through purely military considerations the predominantly political component of Roosevelt's and Truman's decision not to take Berlin, in order not to aggravate Stalin, who considered the capital of the Reich his lawful booty. Bradley's insistence that supposedly 'the approaches to Berlin from the east were incomparably more convenient for the movement of troops than the approaches from the west, because a marshy area lay to the west of Berlin' looks like an attempt to justify through natural reasons the political decision not to try and take Berlin.[33] In reality, the terrain to the east of Berlin is just as cut by lakes and marshy areas as to the west of the city. The main thing is that the fortified area of the Seelow Heights lies to the east of Berlin, while to the west of Berlin, including along the Elbe, there were no fortifications, which is why Simpson calculated on reaching Berlin within 24 hours.[34] The American military historian Steven T. Ross writes:

> On 12 April the 9th Army seized two bridgeheads over the Elbe. A German counter-attack eliminated one foothold but the other held. Lead elements of the 9th Army were fifty miles from Berlin [80km, B.S.]. The Soviets were about thirty-five miles from the city [56km, B.S.]. If the Allies had decided to advance on Berlin, 9th Army's leading elements would, nevertheless, need to be

resupplied and reinforced before advancing any further, but any thought of a quick strike for the city was precluded by the start of a massive Soviet offensive on 16 April. The Americans had been willing to contemplate a drive on Berlin if circumstances permitted. Churchill raised the issue again in mid-April, but Eisenhower flew to London and convinced the Prime Minister on 17 April that his forces could not in fact beat the Russians into the German capital.[35]

Ross continues, 'Moreover, it was unclear to Eisenhower and others what the Anglo-American coalition would accomplish if they took Berlin . . . Thus even if American or British forces reached Berlin first, they would have to relinquish their conquest or risk a major confrontation with the USSR before the conclusion of the war with Japan.'[36]

Actually, if the main forces of the Ninth Army had crossed the Elbe and units of the American First Army had reached the Elbe, throwing back the Twelfth Army's two opposing divisions, it would have gone bad for Wenck. What could he have accomplished with his forces, in numbers not exceeding an army corps and nearly deprived of tanks, against a full-strength American army? However, the Americans retained only one bridgehead over the Elbe, but gave up on an offensive on Berlin. As early as 15 April the commander of the American Ninth Army, General Simpson, received an order not to attack Berlin but to stand on the Elbe, which greatly upset him and his subordinates. He had counted on being in Berlin in two or three days, even before the start of the Soviet offensive.

If the American command had planned a campaign beyond the Elbe, towards Berlin, it could have easily succeeded. For this, it would have been necessary to concentrate beforehand all efforts to seize the single convenient bridgehead at Barby, putting into the fight not only the 84th Infantry but also the 2nd Tank divisions, as well as to concentrate the efforts of American assault aviation in this area, in order to paralyze counterattacks by the small number of German tanks and assault guns. The Barby bridgehead was seized by the 83rd Infantry Division on the evening of 13 April. On 14 April the division successfully repelled a German counterattack by the *Scharnhorst* Division. If the 2nd Tank Division had been immediately dispatched here, instead of being distracted by the seizure of the less convenient bridgehead to the south of Magdeburg, which was eliminated on 14 April by a counterattack by the German *Burg* combat group (the future *Ferdinand von Schill* Division), then they could have begun an offensive on Berlin as early as 14 April, by defeating the *Scharnhorst* Division in a meeting engagement. General Simpson, the commander of the American Ninth Army, had drawn up a plan, according to which following the concentration of the necessary forces of two divisions over the course of two days on the Barby bridgehead, the American forces would reach Berlin. This was the 'Plan for Broadening the Bridgehead on the Elbe River by Including in it Potsdam (a Suburb of Berlin)'. But on 15 April army group commander Omar Bradley and the supreme commander-in-chief Eisenhower finally rejected this scheme.[37]

However, the plan was quite realistic and attainable without great losses. At that moment only the *Scharnhorst* Division (5,000 men) and the *Burg* combat group (at 8,000–10,000 men, the strongest one in the Twelfth Army) were able to oppose the Ninth Army's divisions.[38] The two American divisions numbered up to 40,000 men. In order to inflict losses of 100,000 men, each soldier of the 2 German divisions would have had to kill or wound no less than 7 Americans. In reality, when on 27 April the Americans undertook a demonstration attack to the east of the Elbe, in order to distract German forces from the Eastern Front, they advanced 20km without any problem and defeated and captured a German reserve infantry regiment.[39]

And if the American offensive on Berlin had continued, then dramatic changes might have taken place in Hitler's strategy. Seeing how the American tanks were so rapidly moving on Berlin from the west and that in the east the Soviet forces were already making a reconnaissance in force, Hitler might have nevertheless followed his initial plan and left for the south, for the Alpine Redoubt. The führer might have hoped that a combat collision would take place between Soviet and American forces in the Berlin area and that this would save Germany from collapse. Of course, such calculations were built upon sand, but if Hitler had left for the south, in the hopes of freeing the battlefield for his enemies to work out their relations in the Berlin area, then it's unlikely that the war would have dragged out as the Germans' munitions were running out. Then it simply would have been a case of the final and most bitter battles taking place not in Berlin, but in Bavaria, in the area of Hitler's Berchtesgaden residence. At the same time, the losses of the Soviet forces attacking Berlin would have probably been reduced.

The forces of the three Soviet *fronts* directly taking part in the Berlin operation numbered 2,100,000 men, with the 2 Polish armies numbering another 155,900 men.[40] Neither Stalin nor Zhukov was troubled by the fact that they would have to attack through the Germans' fortified positions along the Seelow Heights. They were probably hoping that their overwhelming superiority in men and materiel would enable them to quickly crush the German resistance, particularly as the Germans were already experiencing a shortage of munitions. Besides, the enemy had very few tanks and assault guns. Zhukov's front alone had more than 3,000 tanks and self-propelled guns, against which the Germans along the Seelow Heights could oppose with 587 tanks and assault guns. On 7 June 1945, while addressing a press conference in Berlin, Zhukov declared that 'More than 500,000 German soldiers and officers took part in the Berlin operation. Of this number, more than 300,000 were taken prisoner by us and no less than 150,000 were killed, while the rest ran away.'[41]

The strength of the German forces facing the three Soviet *fronts* in the Berlin operation, cited by Zhukov, would appear realistic, although the data on German losses, as was the custom among Soviet generals and marshals, had been increased several fold. The German Twelfth Army numbered no more than 35,000 men at the time of its approach to Berlin. The Berlin garrison, which consisted of the LVI Panzer Corps and independent units, numbered 50,000–60,000 men. Other formations of the Ninth Army, numbering up to 50,000 men, were encircled south of Berlin. The 11 German divisions operating north of Berlin did not number more than 100,000 men. Even taking into account the losses suffered by the Germans during the Soviet forces' breakthrough of the defence along the Oder and Neisse rivers (these could have numbered as many as 50,000 killed, wounded, and captured), the overall strength of Army Group Vistula before the start of the Soviet offensive likely did not exceed 250,000 men, and by taking into account the Twelfth Army and the *Volkssturm*, then the overall strength of the German forces that took part in the Berlin operation may be estimated at 300,000 men.[42] The First Belorussian Front, which numbered about 1 million men, was opposed by little more than 100,000 German soldiers and officers. Besides this, 5 divisions from the Fourth Panzer Army, which numbered 10 divisions and 6 combat groups (3 divisions and 2 combat groups were later transferred to the Ninth Army), were opposite the First Ukrainian Front's left wing. They could have contained up to 160,000 men.

Actually, the optimal variation for conducting the Berlin operation would have been the launching of the main attack south of Berlin, in order to bypass the fortifications along the Seelow Heights. It would have been much more difficult to bypass the heights from the north, as here was the serious obstacle of the lower course of the Oder River. However, the shifting of the main attack south of Berlin would have made not Zhukov, but Konev, the main player in the operation. Of course, they could have 'castled' the commanders, put Zhukov in Konev's place and vice versa. However, Stalin had already carried out one such 'castling' quite recently, before the Vistula–Oder operation, having sent the Pole Rokossovskii to command the Second Belorussian Front instead of the First Belorussian Front, and appointing Zhukov commander of the First Belorussian Front. It was then assumed that it was namely this *front* that would take Berlin. A new castling before the last major operation of the

Great Patriotic War was undesirable and could have sowed some confusion and made command and control more difficult. Stalin hoped a little bit that the Seelow Heights would not become a serious obstacle for Zhukov. But he was mistaken.

Only after a breakthrough had been achieved south of Berlin and the Germans had thrown in their forces defending against the First Belorussian Front to eliminate it, then that *front's* forces should have gone over to the offensive against the capital of the Reich. And only then, when the Germans had sent in troops from the north for the defence of Berlin, should the Second Belorussian Front have gone over to the offensive. The Red Army's overwhelming numerical superiority enabled it to allot sufficient forces for flank cover. Berlin should have been encircled and taken by siege. Such a form of operations would have enabled the Soviets to minimize losses. But Stalin did not think of this. He and Zhukov probably calculated that they would be able to break through the German defence on the Seelow Heights, where the Soviet forces had an overwhelming superiority in men, artillery, tanks, and aircraft.

In the Berlin operation, which lasted from 16 April to 8 May 1945, the Soviet forces' irreplaceable losses are officially placed at 81,116 men, including the losses of the Polish 1st and 2nd armies. At the same time, the irreplaceable losses of the two Polish armies supposedly accounted for only 2,825 men. However, official Polish data shows that the two Polish armies' irreplaceable losses in the Berlin operation were 7,200 killed and 3,800 missing in action, which yields irreplaceable losses of 11,000 men, that is, 3.9 times more than the official Russian data maintains.[43] One may assume that the irreplaceable losses of the remaining forces that took part in the Berlin operation were understated by the same proportion. In that case, they must number 304,800 men.

Here is evidence of the mobilization of units in Berlin itself: 'The 79th Soviet Corps, which was moving a little to the west of the flak tower, through the sluices of the Plotzensee, crossed the Hohenzollern Canal north of the Spree River and entered the Moabit District. Here is seized the notorious Moabit prison complex, freeing thousands of Soviet prisoners, who were armed on the spot and enrolled in the rifle battalions.[44]

As strange as it seems, from the point of view of reconnoitring the enemy's positions and troop cooperation for the offensive, the Berlin operation was prepared quite poorly. Soviet aviation had almost complete air superiority and was able to make uninhibited observations of the German positions. After the war, Marshal Konev criticized Marshal G.K. Zhukov for the fact that the latter, while commanding the First Belorussian Front, during the Berlin operation underestimated the existing data on the purposeful withdrawal of the enemy's forces to the Seelow Heights, which were 6–8 kilometers from the forward edge. As a result of the incorrect evaluation of the situation, the *front's* forces, upon reaching the heavily fortified Seelow Heights, were forced to storm them without sufficient preparation, which resulted in . . . the slow pace of the breakthrough of the enemy's defence in the First Belorussian Front's attack zone.[45]

As a result, the powerful artillery preparation fell practically on an empty space. However, along the First Ukrainian Front, commanded by Konev, the same mistake was made as on Zhukov's front. As Vladimir R. Kabo, an artilleryman-gun layer in the units of D.D. Lelyushenko's 4th Guards Tank Army/First Ukrainian Front testifies:[46]

On the night of 15–16 April we received orders to move up to the jumping-off point and occupied a sector of the woods along the high bank of the river. The Germans had dug into the ground on the other side of the river. Upon seeing the rocket signal, our guns and rocket mortars opened up and the artillery preparation began. I had never been witness to such a thing – this was total howling and din, in which it was impossible to distinguish individual rounds, the air shook and the glow of the fire hung over the river valley, and all of this continued, as it seemed to me, several hours. My gun crew fired and fired, emptying one ammunition case after another. When it had barely dawned our forces went over to the attack and forced the river. The first ones to leave were the tanks, and then they laid down a bridge and a stream of vehicles, artillery and infantry moved over it. The opposite bank had been plowed up by shell holes from the explosions. It seemed as if not a single square meter of earth remained which the hellish tornado of fire and metal had not passed over. There was no sign of life and there no killed to be seen. The Germans had left.[47]

Even in the final operation of the Second World War, the Soviet forces, despite an overwhelming superiority in men and materiel, lost tactically to the *Wehrmacht*, although this could no longer have any kind of strategic consequences.

According to the estimates by the authors of the official German history of the Second World War, German losses during the Berlin operation were about 100,000 killed and captured, including 92,000 in the area of the Seelow Heights, Halbe, and in Berlin itself, and 8,000 in other areas, predominantly in Pomerania.[48] This yields a correlation of irreplaceable losses of 3.2:1 in favour of the Germans. Such a correlation must have been even more favourable for the German side in numbers killed, as the Soviet side suffered almost no losses in men captured. If it is assumed that the understating of losses was the same for all three Soviet *fronts*, then the losses of the Second Belorussian Front may be estimated at approximately 51,000 men and the losses of the German forces opposite at 8,000 men, which yield a correlation of 6.4:1 in favour of the Germans. The fact that this correlation proved to be significantly worse than for the other two *fronts* may be explained by the fact that in the Second Belorussian Front's zone the Germans were defending only along previously prepared positions and covered by the lower course of the Oder, and fell back, but did not engage in street fighting in the towns in light of the enemy's colossal superiority in tanks and artillery, and did not break out of encirclement. At the same time, in the First Belorussian and First Ukrainian fronts' attack zone the Germans troops often waged street fighting and tried to break out of encirclement, and it was precisely in such fighting that they suffered disproportionately heavy losses.

As the American historian and journalist Cornelius Ryan wrote, 'Marshal Konev told me that his forces alone lost "in all the fighting from the Oder to Berlin, including the southern flank, which was moving on the Elbe . . . 150,000 killed".[49] This means that on the whole, Zhukov's and Konev's forces lost at least 100,000 men killed in storming Berlin. It's of interest that the English-language edition of this book came out in 1966, when Marshal I.S. Konev was still alive.[50] But all the way up to his death in 1973, he never went back on his words quoted to Ryan, which enables us to treat reliably the figures quoted in Ryan's book. But as these figures are rounded off, they are most likely approximate ones. Incidentally, General A.V. Gorbatov, who commanded the 3rd Army in the Berlin operation, told the critic V.Ya. Lakshin, that during the street fighting in Berlin alone no less than 100,000 Soviet soldiers and officers died, which coincides with Ryan's estimate.[51] It's possible that Konev also included among the 150,000 killed the First Ukrainian Front's irreplaceable losses in the Prague offensive operation, which, according to official data, were 6,384 men.[52] If it is assumed that they have been lowered by the same proportion as those of the Poles during the Berlin operation, then the First Ukrainian Front's actual losses in the Prague operation may be estimated at approximately 25,000 men. Then the losses of Konev's *front* in the Berlin operation would be 125,000 killed. Then the official irreplaceable losses of all the *fronts* in the Berlin operation should be increased by 4.5 times, which would yield 354,800 men. If 150,000 of these losses were killed in the First Ukrainian Front in the Berlin operation alone, then the actual losses of all three Soviet *fronts* in the Berlin operation may be estimated at 425,800 men, a figure which strikes one as obviously overly high. It seems that the estimate of Soviet irreplaceable losses in the Berlin operation of 304,800 men is the closest to reality, and together with Polish losses, comes to 315,800 men. This was the cost to the Red Army of the halt of the American offensive on the Elbe on Stalin's ambiguous request.

As early as before the Berlin operation, during the period from 1 February to 20 May 1945, the First Ukrainian Front's forces received 40,000 reinforcements from 'Soviet citizens of draft age liberated from German captivity'. At the same time, *ostarbeiters* predominated among those liberated and not former military personnel. As the chief of the First Ukrainian Front's political administration, Major General F.V. Yashechkin, reported on 7 April 1945, 'Among the 3,870 men who arrived to reinforce the formation's units, where Maj. Gen. Voronov was chief of the political section [that is, the 13th Army, B.S.], there were 873 former servicemen and 2,997 called up for the first time, including 784 women.[53] Thus the share of former military personnel was no more than 23 per cent of the new intake. Also, the fact that 20 per cent of those conscripted were female *ostarbeiters* proved that the Red Army's human resources were close to exhaustion. They would send the women to the rear establishments in order to free up 'active bayonets' for the final battles.

They called up *ostarbeiters* in the same way directly into the Second Belorussian Front's units operating in Pomerania. L.Ye. Rubinchik, who ended the war as a sergeant, recalled that his company, which was part of the 10th Guards Rifle Division's 24th Guards Rifle Division, was staffed 'chiefly with soldiers freed from captivity and boys, who had been driven to Germany to work. By the way, these boys, who had barely reached the age of 17–18 years, according to their stories, didn't live so badly among their German masters. They worked a lot, but the fed them well.' Many of them died in the company's last battle on 5 May 1945 near Schneidemuhl. According to L.Ye. Rubinchik:

> An enemy machine gun suddenly opened up and in an instant cut down all of those who were on the knoll. Thus perished almost all of the draftees, boys born in 1927, who had been sent to Germany and called up into the army here on territory occupied by us. These boys had received no military training and did not know how to crawl and make short sprints. 25–30 men died in this battle, about ten were wounded, and few survived.[54]

Those conscripted *ostarbeiters* who were called up for the first time and who died in the fighting for Berlin probably did not make it into the Russian Defence Ministry's database of irreplaceable losses because they were called up directly into the units. In working with the OBD 'Memorial', the author only on one occasion came across a soldier killed or missing in action where it was indicated that he had been called up directly into the unit, and this after reviewing several tens of thousands of such pieces of information. These people were most likely included among civilian losses in the postwar calculations, which is incorrect, or they did not include them at all among the irreplaceable losses.

The opinion that the German troops' main forces, which were defending Berlin, were destroyed along the Seelow Heights, and only their pitiful remnants fell back on Berlin, is also untrue. Marshal Zhukov defended this view very stubbornly, in order to justify the head-on storming of the Seelow Heights. Actually, everything was different.

During the period from 11–20 April 1945, which includes the beginning of the Red Army's Berlin operation, the losses of the German Ninth Army, which was opposing Soviet forces along the Berlin direction, according to the ten-day casualty reports, were 336 were killed, 1,218 wounded, and 7,502 missing in action? To judge from this, prisoners predominated among the missing in action. Practically all of these losses were suffered during the First Belorussian Front's breakthrough of the defence along the Seelow Heights. There is no data on the Third Panzer Army's losses for this period, but they were probably not significant, insofar as the Second Belorussian Front began its offensive against the Third Panzer Army only on 20 April. The losses of the Fourth Panzer Army, the main part of whose formations came under attack from the First Ukrainian Front, while one corps fought against the First Belorussian Front, were 537 killed, 2,549 wounded, and 281 missing in action.[55] We should note that the commander of the LVI Panzer Corps, K. Weidling, whose corps defended the Seelow Heights and then Berlin, reported during an interrogation on 3 May 1945 that on 16 April the 9th Parachute Division numbered up to 12,000 men, the 18th Motorized Division up to 9,000 men, the SS *Nordland* 11th Motorized Division up to 11,000 men, the 20th Motorized Division up to 8,000 men, and the *Munchenberg* Panzer Division up to 6,000 men, while the entire LVI Corps, together with five battalions of corps artillery, numbered up to 50,000 men. At the same time, according to Weidling, by 23 April, when the corps had fallen back to the outskirts of Berlin, there remained in the 18th Motorized Division as many as 4,000 men, up to 200 men in the *Munchenberg* Panzer Division, 3,500–4,000 men in the SS *Nordland* Division, 800–1,200 men in the 20th Motorized Division, and up to 500 men in the 9th Parachute Division, although in Berlin it was reinforced with up to 4,000 men. The entire corps numbered only 13–15,000 men.[56] This data contradicts the data on German losses. If it is assumed that the LVI Panzer Corps, which bore the brunt of the Soviet attack, accounted for 80 per cent of the Ninth Army's losses, then its losses may be estimated at 7,250 men. The corps suffered some losses during 21–3 April, but they were probably less than during the fighting along the Seelow Heights. If one allows that the losses for these days accounted for approximately half of the losses suffered during 15–20 April, then the corps' overall losses by the time of its arrival in Berlin would have been about 11,000 men. If the LVI Panzer Corps' strength on 16 April was really 50,000 men, then approximately 39,000 men must have made it to Berlin and not 13–15,000 men as Weidling maintained. The difference of 24–26,000 men may have arisen due to 3 factors: the underreporting of losses in the 10-day report for 11–20 April; Weidling's inflated reporting of the LVI Panzer Corps' strength on 16 April; and the understating of the corps' strength when it arrived in Berlin. It should be noted that Weidling, while testifying to his recent enemies, was interested both in overstating the corps' strength by the beginning of the battle and in understating its strength by the time it reached Berlin. The German general could have been given to understand that the Russian generals interrogating him were interested in confirming their reports about the tens of thousands Germans killed and captured, and because of this it was desirable to overstate the strength of the LVI Panzer Corps. On the other hand, Weidling himself and the other officers of the corps' headquarters could have been interested in understating the strength of their troops that arrived in Berlin in order that they might try as long as possible to pass themselves off as unarmed *Volkssturm* soldiers or civilians and attempt to avoid captivity. It should also be noted that in the document that contains data on the German army's losses for 11–20 April 1945 there is no provision made for the possible incomplete data for the Ninth Army, although in a number of other cases there are such allowances. The author's estimate of the LVI Panzer Corps' strength at the time it arrived in Berlin of 39,000 men is confirmed by the testimony of Major Siegfried Knappe, the former chief of the LVI Panzer Corps' staff's operational section. According to his calculations, the corps' strength when it arrived in Berlin was about 40,000 men, while other units of the Berlin garrison that took part in the fighting numbered about 20,000 men. He put forward these figures in his memoirs, which were written following his liberation from captivity, when it was no longer necessary to try and mislead anyone, all the more so as he refers to a report in his possession.[57] Thus the LVI Panzer Corps' main losses were suffered in Berlin itself and during the attempt to break out of the encirclement.

Official Soviet sources put the number of prisoners taken by the Red Army in Berlin at 134,700 men, of which 100,700 were taken by the First Belorussian Front.[58] And this is despite the fact that the actual strength of the Berlin garrison was 50,000–60,000 men, of which several thousand broke out to the west. According to the conclusion reached by the office which was attached to the headquarters of the Group of Soviet Forces in Germany, which based its findings upon the interrogation of prisoners, in all 15,000–17,000 German military personnel and 80–90 armoured vehicles broke out of Berlin, although by no means did all of these reach the American and British lines.[59] Evidently all of the adult male population, including firemen, policemen, and employees of ministries and departments located in Berlin, were included in the number of prisoners. The overall figure of 480,000 prisoners taken in the Berlin operation cannot be reached even by including civilian prisoners.[60] Probably many of the prisoners of war, which were supposedly taken during the Berlin operation, existed only on paper. After all, the figure of 480,000 prisoners exceeds the overall strength of the German forces in the Berlin operation. There exists an estimate of German losses during the fighting in Berlin itself of 22,000 civilians killed and the same number of military personnel killed, although it is not clear what this is based on.[61] This estimate seems to be overstated as regards the numbers of military personnel. There is another estimate of 18,320 German military personnel killed in Berlin.[62] It's possible that this includes all of the LVI Panzer Corps' losses killed during the period from 16 April to 2 May. If so, then this data seems far more realistic.

During the Ninth Army's breakout from the encirclement in the area of Frankfurt an der Oder during the period from 24 April to 1 May 1945, which is otherwise known as the Battle of Halbe, about 30,000 military personnel escaped. No less than 25,000 German soldiers became prisoners. About 15,000 German military personnel perished in this battle and are buried in a cemetery in Halbe, alhough only a third of them have been identified. About 30,000 Soviet soldiers also died and are buried in a cemetery near the Baruth–Zossen road. But, aside from these 30,000, there remain thousands of unburied Soviet soldiers in this area.[63]

On the whole, one may enumerate the following chief reasons for the Soviet Union's victory in the Great Patriotic War: a significantly large population, which exceeded by 2.5 times the population of the Reich; an enormous territory; aid from the Western Allies in the form of Lend-Lease and the diversion of the main forces of the German *Luftwaffe* and *Kriegsmarineto* their fronts, as well as up to a quarter of the German army; the presence in the USSR of a sufficiently developed military industry capable of producing modern weaponry and military equipment; the presence of a large Red Army capable of waging modern war by employing the latest types of weapons and combat equipment; the presence of a totalitarian system capable of holding out in the face of defeat; and Hitler's veto of proposals to create anti-communist Russian (or) Ukrainian governments and armies. Clearly all of these factors cannot be rated individually in terms of importance because the absence of only one of them would have guaranteed the defeat of the USSR. For example, if the territory of the USSR had been only four times larger than that of 1939 Poland, then the country would have been completely occupied as early as two months into the war. If the USSR's population had been smaller than that of the Reich, its human resources would have been exhausted as early as the end of 1941. If the Red Army had not been capable of waging modern war, it would have turned into an army like Chiang Kai-shek's, capable of waging only a limited semi-partisan war. If a totalitarian system had not been in place in the Soviet Union, but an authoritarian one, similar to what actually existed in the Russian Empire in 1914, the war would have ended in the defeat of Russia and a revolution. If there had been a democracy in the USSR in 1939, the Second World War would not have broken out at all in those circumstances in which it actually did. And if Hitler had created an anti-Bolshevik Russian government and army at the very beginning of the war, Stalin would have lacked the human resources for victory.

The Red Army's crimes were primarily the mass rape, murder, and looting of the civilian population of Germany, Austria, Hungary, Poland, Czechoslovakia, Serbia, and the Baltic States. There are almost no documents on the conviction of Red Army soldiers for such crimes, or they have not been published. However, it is known that some marauders and rapists were shot without trial. The main mass of evidence are the materials of investigations which the German authorities conducted in several towns in East Prussia and in the Lower Silesian town of Lauban, the same from investigations by the Hungarian authorities in several towns in Hungary, as well as the recollections of the numerous victims who survived, and the diaries and reminiscences of those Soviet soldiers and officers who were witness to these crimes. It is disputed precisely how many people were killed and raped by Red Army soldiers (among whom there were officers). But even the most minimal estimates point to tens of thousands killed and hundreds of thousands raped. To be fair, one should note that Soviet allies in the anti-Hitler coalition were not innocent in this regard. Soldiers from the French colonial units – Senegalese and Moroccans – particularly distinguished themselves in raping and looting. At the same time, their countries were never occupied by the Axis powers. More than sixty death sentences were carried out in the American army for murders and rapes among the civilian population. Nevertheless, the Western Allies carried out crimes against the civilian population on at least an entire order less than the Red Army. It's no accident that in the spring of 1945 millions of German refugees ran to the Western occupation zones, while a stream the other way was not observed.

Some evidence has been preserved by Stalin's allies in Eastern Europe. In October 1944 Soviet soldiers in Serbia raped 121 women and killed 111 of them. In connection with this, a delegation from Tito left for Moscow, and included the future famous dissident and the then partisan general Milovan Djilas.[64] According to his words, the assertions by the members of the delegation that the Red Army was looting, killing, and raping while British military personnel, representatives of a bourgeois army on Yugoslav territory, weren't doing anything similar, was not accepted by Stalin. He accused Djilas and his comrades of insulting the Red Army and condescendingly observed that soldiers who had carried out a fighting advance from Stalingrad to the Balkans deserved a little break. Probably, following the adoption of a law, Djilas's memoirs, where this episode is detailed, will be banned, while documents on the Yugoslav delegation's stay in Moscow will remain 'secret' in the Russian archives. As a result it will be necessary to ban the book by Joachim Hoffman, *Stalin's War of Extermination*, Antony Beevor's book on the fall of Berlin, the war stories of Vasil' Bykov, the works of Aleksandr Solzhenitsyn, particularly his poem 'Prussian Nights', the war memoirs of Lev Kopelev, as well as a great number of other books, films, and shows. And also the author's friend Leonid Rabichev, a front soldier, artist, and poet, who in his memoirs *The War Will Write Everything Off* painted a vivid picture of the brutalities carried out by Soviet soldiers in East Prussia. To the author's great regret, Leonid Nikolaevich passed away on 20 September 2017 at the age of 94.

Rabichev's hypothesis that the Soviet command shut its eyes to the excesses of its subordinates, while they took place on those German territories which following the war were supposed to be awarded to Poland and the USSR, seems quite plausible. After all, these crimes forced the Germans to abandon these territories as quickly as possible. But when Soviet forces crossed the Oder and invaded territory which was supposed to remain German after the war, on 20 April 1945 appeared Stalin's order, which was read to the troops fighting in Germany:

> Demand that the troops change their attitude toward the Germans, both military and civilian, and to treat the Germans better. Cruel treatment arouses among them fear and forces them to stubbornly resist and not surrender. The civilian population, fearing retribution, is organizing into bands. This is not a favorable situation for us. A more humane attitude toward the Germans will make it easier to wage combat activities and lower the Germans' stubbornness in defence. A German administration must be created in the German lands and burgomasters appointed in the liberated towns. Rank and file members of the National Socialist Party should not be touched if they have a loyal attitude to the Red Army, and only the leaders should be detained if they have not yet had time to run away.[65]

Following the appearance of this order, Soviet commanders began to shoot their subordinates more often for murders, rapes, and looting of the civilian population. But they only managed to put a stop to such excesses several months after the end of the war.

A document concerning the Red Army's conduct in Hungary, which was produced by Hungarian communists, is of relevance here. The Hungarian historian Krisztian Ungvary published it in his book *Battle for Budapest. 100 Days in World War II.* In February 1945 the communists of the town of Kobanya, now the tenth district of Budapest, adopted an appeal to the Soviet command:

> Over the course of decades the toiling people of the entire world have looked to Moscow just as the illiterate toilers looked at Christ. It was precisely from there that they awaited liberation from fascist barbarism. After long and torturous persecutions the glorious and long-awaited Red Army has arrived, but what did it prove to be!
>
> The Red Army liberated Kobanya on 2 January, following a stubborn struggle for each building and left behind it destruction and devastation. And this was not because among the mounds of furniture of people who were slaves for decades one could find fascists. Among the workers of Kobanya there were very few who sympathized with the Germans, and the majority hate the fascists. But suddenly there was an explosion of insane and frenzied hatred. Drunken soldiers raped mothers before their children and husbands. They took 12-year-old girls from their fathers and mothers to be raped by groups of 10–15 soldiers, among whom there were many who were infected with venereal diseases. After the first group, others would come and who followed the example of their predecessors. Several of our comrades were killed when they tried to defend their wives and daughters . . .
>
> The situation in the factories is horrible. The Russian officers have created intolerable conditions for work, ignoring the worker's committees in which there are many communists. The workers toil for three pengos an hour on an empty stomach, with the opportunity only once a day at lunch to each peas or beans . . . They are far more respectful of the former fascist directors than of the worker's committees, insofar as the directors deliver women to the Russian officers . . . Marauding by the Russian soldiers is still going on . . . We know that the most intelligent representatives of the army are communists, but when we approach them for assistance they fly into a rage and threaten to shoot us, declaring: 'And what did you

do in the Soviet Union? Did you really not rape our wives in front of our eyes and then kill them together with the children, burn our villages and destroy our cities to their foundations?' We know that Hungarian capitalism carried out its own sadistic acts of cruelty . . . But we don't understand why soldiers from Siberia say these things . . . when the fascist attacks did not even reach the Urals, the dream of the German fascists, not to mention Siberia . . .

It's not right to extol the Red Army on banners, in the party, the factories, and anywhere else, when at the same time people who lived through the Szalasi tyranny are now being driven like cattle by Russian soldiers, leaving dead bodies behind them . . .[66] The peasants rained questions down on those comrades who were sent to the village for carrying out the redistribution of the land: what's the good of the land if we have nothing to plow it with? The Russians took our horses. We can't plow with our own noses. If such things are halted, then it will neutralize all of the enemy's propaganda and the Hungarian workers will regard the Russian soldiers as gods.[67]

It is clear from this document that revenge was not the reason for the violence, as it was not those soldiers whose relatives might have suffered from the actions of the Hungarian army in the USSR who came to Hungary.

If one compares the Red Army's crimes with those of the *Wehrmacht*, it may be concluded that they were not less than the Germans' in scale and sometimes even exceeded them. The reasons for these crimes should be sought in the nature of the Stalinist system, which was no less criminal than the Nazi one, as well as in the fact that Soviet soldiers, feeling that they were cannon fodder that the command did not bother to spare, vented their hatred, both of the command and the enemy who began this war, on the civilian population and prisoners.

The scale of Soviet and Anglo-American-Franco crimes in occupied Germany (and the French in Italy) was incomparable, if only because the German population en masse ran away from the Soviet to the Western occupation zones, and not the other way around. The Soviet soldiers not only raped but also killed Germans en masse, which the Western Allies rarely did. Besides this, Soviet crimes covered not only Germany, but practically all of Eastern Europe, from the Baltic States to Serbia. Of what offence were the Polish or Russian female *ostarbeiters*, about whom Solzhenitsyn wrote, guilty of before the Red Army? One cannot speak of any kind of revenge against them. And when Milovan Djilas, sent by Iosip Broz Tito as part of a delegation to Moscow, raised at Tito's request the question of punishing Soviet soldiers who had committed on the territory of Serbia and the Vojvodina 121 rapes,

111 victims of which were killed, and 1,204 robberies and pointed out that this discredited the Red Army in the eyes of local residents, when at the same time the British soldiers did nothing similar, Stalin replied that it was not worth attaching too much importance to the Red Army soldiers' crimes because the Red Army was hitting the Germans very hard.[68] After all, the Serbs had never fought on Soviet territory and there was nothing the Soviet soldiers could take revenge for. All the more so the Chinese, Koreans, and Japanese who became victims of exactly the same sort of crimes on the part of the soldiers and commanders of the Red Army during the Manchurian operation in August 1945 and during the subsequent Soviet occupation of northeastern China and northern Korea had not attacked the USSR. Just as in Hungary along with the mass removal of industrial equipment to the USSR from Manchuria brought about protests from the local communists, to which the Red Army command paid no attention.[69]

In August 1945 Eisenhower visited the Soviet Union. During his stay in Moscow and flight to Leningrad, Zhukov and Eisenhower spoke a good deal about the recent war. Eisenhower was interested in how the Red Army overcame minefields. In his *Crusade in Europe*, he relates his conversation with Zhukov on this question:

> Highly illuminating to me was his description of the Russian method of attacking through mine fields. The German mine fields, covered by defensive fire, were tactical obstacles that caused us many casualties and delays. It was always a laborious business to break through them, even though our technicians invented every conceivable kind of mechanical appliance to destroy mines safely. Marshal Zhukov gave me a matter-of-fact statement of his practice, which was, roughly, . . . 'When we come to a mine field our infantry attacks exactly as if it were not there. The losses we get from personnel mines we consider only equal to those we would have gotten from machine guns and artillery if the Germans had chosen to defend that particular area with strong bodies of troops instead of with mine fields. The attacking infantry does not set off the vehicular mines, so after they have penetrated to the far side of the field they form a bridgehead, after which the engineers come up and dig out channels through which our vehicles can go.'
> I had a vivid picture of what would happen to any American or British commander if he pursued such tactics, and I had an even more vivid picture of what the men in any one of our divisions would have had to say about the matter had we attempted to make

such a practice part of our tactical doctrine. Americans assess the cost of war in terms of human lives, the Russians in the overall drain on the nation. The Russians clearly understood the value of morale, but for its development and maintenance they apparently depended upon overall success, upon patriotism, possibly fanaticism.

As far as I could see, Zhukov had given little concern to methods that we considered vitally important to the maintenance of morale among American troops: systematic rotation of units, facilities for recreation, short leaves and furloughs, and, above all, the development of techniques to avoid exposure of men to unnecessary battlefield risks, all of which although common practices in our Army, seemed to be largely unknown in his.[70]

Eisenhower testifies that the other Soviet marshals, such as Budennyi, adhered to the same views as Zhukov. On14 August, when the Japanese government and emperor announced their capitulation, and on the eve of Eisenhower's departure from Moscow, the American ambassador gave a reception in the general's honour:

But I noted that old Marshal Budenny, who was stading at my side, did not seem to exhibit any great enthusiasm. I asked him whether he was not glad the war was over and he replied, 'Oh yes, but we should have kept going until we had killed a lot more of those insolent Japanese.' The marshal seemed to be a most congenial, humane and hospitable type but at the same time he seemed to have no concern that even one day's continuance of the war meant death or wounds for additional hundreds of Russian citizens.[71]

General John R. Deane, the head of the American military mission in Moscow, who was present at this reception, recalled that having had a drink and following this with food, Zhukov and Eisenhower got into a friendly argument about freedom of the press:[72]

This was quite revealing of fundamental differences in our thinking. Eisenhower stated our position extremely well but made no impression whatever on Zhukov. He was the product of generations that had never known individual freedom of any sort, and to him no argument could justify an individual expressing sentiments or thoughts either in writing or orally that were opposed to the interests of the state.[73]

The basic difference in Zhukov's and Eisenhower's thinking also manifested itself in the problem of prisoners of war. Eisenhower recalled:

> I mentioned the difficult problem that was imposed upon us at various periods of the war by the need to care for so many German prisoners. I remarked that they were fed the same rations as were our own soldiers. In the greatest astonishment he asked, 'Why did you do that?' I said, 'Well, in the first place my country was required to do so by the terms of the Geneva Convention. In the second place the Germans had some thousands of American and British prisoners and I did not want to give Hitler the excuse or justification for treating our prisoners more harshly than he was already doing.' Again the Russian seemed astounded at my attitude and he said, 'But what did you care about men the Germans had captured? They had surrendered and could not fight any more.'[74]

The American general did not know that Zhukov had been among those who signed the draconian Order No. 270, regarding the fate of Soviet prisoners of war and their families.

Eisenhower could still understand why the Russians harshly treated German prisoners of war. By this time American soldiers had freed many prisoners from the German concentration camps and saw the dreadful state these living corpses were in. But Eisenhower could not understand why the fate of captured Red Army soldiers did not concern Zhukov.

Eisenhower and Zhukov belonged to different worlds and operated in completely different political systems. In the American army, just as in the British and German, commanders were obliged to concern themselves with sparing the lives of their subordinates; otherwise they would be immediately removed from their posts and turned over for trial. In the Red Army the most terrible crime was the failure to carry out even an obviously impossible and sometimes criminal order from higher up. The offender was threatened with immediate execution or being sent to a punishment battalion, which was almost the same thing, even if they later arrested the commander who issued the order. In the Western armies the soldiers and officers would have refused to carry out an order to attack over uncleared minefields and as a consequence there would probably have been a judicial investigation resulting in the removal of the commander. Just the opposite, Soviet soldiers and commanders well knew that complaining about the leadership was a hopeless cause. Not only their own experience but that of their fathers and grandfathers convinced them of this.

In general, the main task of the Soviet commanders and chiefs at all levels was to deceive their superiors and to put themselves in the most favourable light. Only the second most important task was deceiving the enemy, as well as an ally (since an ally was considered as a possible enemy in the near future). This is the reason for the large degree of unreliability in Soviet reports, especially about their own losses and the enemy's losses and equipment captured.

For orders tantamount to suicide for the troops to appear, there must not only be commanders ready to issue them, but also subordinates capable of uncomplainingly carrying them out. If Eisenhower or, say, Manstein had been in Zhukov's place they would very soon have shared the sad fate of General D.G. Pavlov. And the Red Army under Eisenhower's command would have fought even worse than under the command of Zhukov. The American general would have assigned the troops missions that they would in any event have been incapable of carrying out due to their insufficient training and would only have suffered losses in vain. According to observations by German generals, Soviet aviation very rarely operated at a depth of more than 30km from the front line. If Eisenhower had demanded that it carry out bombings on an operational and strategic scale, there would have been not only a shortage of trained pilots, but an insufficient number of appropriate aircraft.

The result would have been no better if Zhukov had headed the Western Allies in Europe. It's likely the marshal would very quickly have been court-martialled for demanding that the German defence be crushed with British and American corpses. There was no time for Eisenhower and Zhukov to reeducate themselves. No, only Zhukov or a military leader like him could be a worthy deputy of Stalin in the Great Patriotic War and the leader of the Red Army's largest operations. It seems that Eisenhower understood that it made no sense to arrive at an evaluation of Zhukov according to Western standards, so he accepted the marshal as he was.

Chapter 9

If Not for the Allies . . .

The Soviet Economy and Lend-Lease

Aid from the USA, Britain and Canada, as represented in the confines of the American Lend-Lease programme, that is, the delivery of munitions, combat equipment, industrial equipment, raw goods, and food for rent without immediate repayment to countries whose security was important to the USA, played a critical role in Soviet military efforts. Lend-Lease covered the major 'narrow places' in the Soviet economy – the production of gasoline, explosives, aluminum, ferrous metals, radios, and trucks, etc. Without Lend-Lease deliveries, the Soviet economy would have produced significantly fewer tanks and aircraft, bombs, mines, and shells than was actually the case and it would have been far more difficult to employ all of this equipment due to a shortage of fuel, transportation equipment, and communications equipment, etc. In a hypothetical one-on-one clash between the USSR and Germany, without the assistance of Lend-Lease, as well as the diversion of the *Luftwaffe's* and *Kriegsmarine's* main forces, as well as more than a quarter of the army for the struggle against Britain and the USA, Stalin could not have defeated Hitler. In 1940 the USA's gross domestic product was estimated to be 101.4 billion dollars.[1] Overall, American Lend-Lease deliveries were 50.1 billion dollars, of which the Soviet Union's share was 11.36 billion, with 31.4 billion for Great Britain. Besides this, Canada had its own Lend-Lease programme, which delivered materials to Great Britain and the USSR, valued at 4.7 billion dollars. Lend-Lease deliveries were also carried out from Great Britain, but these were thanks mainly to American Lend-Lease deliveries to Britain. According to M.N. Suprun's data, all of the deliveries to the USSR, including those which did not make it to their destination, were valued at 13.253 billion dollars, while deliveries from the USA amounted to 11.36 billion, 1.693 billion from Great Britain (420 million pounds sterling), and 200 million dollars from Canada.[2] The Americans estimated reverse Lend-Lease from the USSR at a miserly 2.1 million dollars, which was several times less than the aid to the Soviet Union alone from the American Red Cross, which in 1941 alone amounted to 5 million dollars.[3] According to the author's estimate, the USSR's actual gross domestic product in 1984 was only one-sixth that of the USA.[4] If it is assumed that in 1940 the correlation of the gross domestic product of the two countries was approximately the same, then the volume of the Soviet gross domestic product at that time may be estimated at 16.9 billion dollars. In this case, the overall volume of Lend-Lease deliveries to the USSR amounted to 78.4 per cent of the Soviet yearly gross domestic product.

Even before the war the Soviet Union depended on the Western countries for borrowing advanced models of combat equipment. For example, M.V. Zefirov and D.M. Degtev justly note that:

> American "Wright-Cyclones" and French "Gnome et Rhone" engines and other kinds of old motors from the mid-1920s in the Soviet Union had completely exhausted their resources and there was no prospect of modernizing them. And the country might have begun a war with hopelessly outdated aircraft, such as in Romania and Hungary. But in 1939–1940 the production of the M-103, which was actually the French "Hispano Suiza" 12Ybs aviation motor, bought up in the mid-1930s, was finally mastered by our industry. It was this that saved the Soviet aviation industry from complete collapse.[5]

American aircraft and tanks were not as bad as was maintained by postwar Soviet propaganda. But they were significantly more complex to control and sensitive to the observance of all technical norms. Meanwhile, the level of training for Soviet pilots and tank crews was on the average appreciably lower than for the British or American colleagues, and they experienced difficulties in mastering American equipment. Aces had no problem with this. It's sufficient to recall that three-times Hero of the Soviet Union Aleksandr Ivanovich Pokryshkin scored his victories in an 'Airacobra'.[6] The Red Army's armoured and mechanized forces and deputy defence commissar, Marshal of Armoured Forces Ya.N. Fedorenko gives a good account of American tanks, writing in March 1946:

> Of the models of tank equipment currently in the Red Army's armament, one should single out the American 'Sherman' M4A2 medium tank, armed with a powerful 76.2mm gun, and the Canadian 'Valentine' MK-9 light tank with a 57mm gun with a limited recoil...[7] The above-named tank models are distinguished from the domestic ones by ease of control, a significantly increased service time between repairs, and the simplicity of maintenance and ongoing repairs, while their weaponry, armour and mobility enable them to resolve the entire set of tasks entrusted to the armoured forces...

Such a difference between domestic tanks and the tanks received through Lend-Lease can be explained by the fact that Soviet tanks were made, as they say, in haste, as it was already assumed that they would not last long. No one thought about the comfort of the crew or the length of time between repairs, just as no one considered the ease of control and simplicity of repair. Neither the generals nor the designers gave any thought to the fact that these indices also influenced the viability of the tank and its crew and how many attacks on the enemy it could take part in, and what damage it could inflict on the enemy before it was destroyed. Everyone was pursuing quantity over quality. The tank designer L. Gorlitskii recalled:

> When the war ended in 1945 we discovered that all our tanks which we had made during the war were unfit for service in peacetime. During the war a medium tank and self-propelled artillery survived on the front from three days to a week (rarely longer), at most managing during this time to take part in two to three attacks and to fire from its gun at best from half to a whole combat load . . . It's understandable that the life of these vehicles was short. Following the war, a tank was supposed to run not for a week, but for up to five years. Thus all of the wartime tanks had to be refined in order to eliminate these shortcomings.[8]

The main significance of Lend-Lease was in the fact that without American and British deliveries the Soviet economy would not have been able to produce the quantity of tanks and aircraft that it did during the war years. In order to produce armour, it was extremely important to have alloyed additives, which arrived almost completely through Lend-Lease. More than a third of all explosives used in the Soviet Union during the war arrived from Great Britain, the USA, and Canada. More than 55 per cent of all aluminum employed in Soviet industry arrived from the USA and the countries of the British Empire.

Of the overall volume of the production of aviation fuel in the USSR during the war, 57.8 per cent was delivered from the USA, Great Britain, and Canada to the Soviet Union. Actually, Lend-Lease deliveries were included in the Soviet production of fuel, as they were used almost exclusively for diluting Soviet aviation fuel for the purpose of raising its octane level. Suffice it to say that before the war the overwhelming number of aviation fuels in the USSR had an octane level no higher than 74, which was not suitable for the latest aircraft, while 97 per cent of the aviation fuel received through Lend-Lease had an octane level no less than 99. It is clear that without Lend-Lease deliveries Soviet aviation would have been left without fuel.

And it was not only deliveries of strategic raw materials from the USA and the British Empire that were vitally important for the Red Army's victory. For example, 35,800 radio sets, 5,899 receivers, and 348 locators were delivered to the USSR through Lend-Lease, which satisfied the Red Army's basic needs. Also, 32,200 motorcycles arrived from the USA, which exceeded by 1.2 times the total Soviet production of motorcycles during 1941–5, as well as 409,500 automobiles, which exceeded Soviet production during the war years by 1.5 times, On 1 May 1945 32.8 per cent of the Red Army's automobile park consisted of vehicles delivered through Lend-Lease (58.1 per cent consisted of domestic models and 9.1 per cent of captured motor vehicles). Taking into account their increased carrying capacity and higher quality, the role of American motor vehicles was even greater. 'Studebakers' were particularly employed as artillery tows. Besides this, the Soviet 'Katyusha' rocket mortars were mounted almost exclusively on 'Studebaker' chassis (20,000 platforms), while only 600 'Katyushas' were mounted on the chassis of Soviet ZIS-6 trucks.[9] Also, the functioning of Soviet railroad transportation would have been impossible without Lend-Lease. American deliveries accounted for about 93 per cent of the overall volume of the Soviet production of railroad rails. Even more noticeable was the role of Lend-Lease deliveries in maintaining at the necessary level the numbers of the Soviet locomotive and rail car park. The production of main-line steam engines and diesel locomotives in the USSR was practically halted during the war years. Through Lend-Lease, 1,900 steam engines and 66 diesel electric locomotives were delivered to the USSR, which exceeded the overall Soviet production of steam engines by 2.4 times and electric locomotives by 11 times. In addition, 10.2 times more rail cars were delivered through Lend-Lease than produced by the Soviets during 1942–5. It is worth remembering that in many ways during the First World War the transportation crisis at the turn of 1916–17 which provoked the February Revolution, was caused by the insufficient production of railroad rails, steam engines, and rail cars, as the efforts of industry and production were converted to the production of munitions.[10] During the Great Patriotic War only Lend-Lease deliveries prevented the paralysis of the USSR's railroad transportation.

One should also not forget the delivery of complex machine tools and industrial equipment from the USA. The Americans sent 38,100 metal cutting machines Great Britain 6,500 machines and 104 presses. During 1941–5, 115,400 metal cutting machines were produced in the Soviet Union, that is, 2.6 times more than the Lend-Lease deliveries. However, in reality, if one takes into account cost indices, then the role of Western machines will be far more significant – they were more complex and expensive than the Soviet ones.

Machines and equipment for industry worth 607 million dollars was delivered from the USA alone in 1941–5 through Lend-Lease to the USSR.

During the war years 1.5 times as many automobiles were delivered from the USA than were produced in the USSR. Almost half of the rails used in the USSR arrived through Lend-Lease. Lend-Lease deliveries exceeded the overall Soviet production of steam engines by 2.4 times, that of electric engines by 11 times, and the number of rail cars by 10.2 times. It's clear that only Lend-Lease enabled the USSR to avoid a transportation crisis, which in its time became one of the reasons for the February Revolution. Deliveries of explosives from the USA and Great Britain were 53 per cent of overall Soviet production. For copper, this percentage was 82.5 per cent of Soviet production, and 125 per cent for aluminum. Thus without Western deliveries 2.25 time fewer aircraft would have been produced, which would in any event have been unable to fly due to a lack of fuel . It's superfluous to explain how this would have influenced the outcome of the war.[11]

Stalinist modernization, which was built on blood, did not in any way reduce the gap between the USSR and the leading Western powers. The USSR had to pay for its backwardness with tens of millions of lives. Economically, the Soviet Union was not in a condition to wage war with Germany one-on-one without economic assistance from the Western Allies.

During the war years Stalin very highly rated the role of Lend-Lease. On 30 November 1943, while speaking in Teheran at a celebratory luncheon in honour of Churchill's birthday, he made the following toast:

> I want to tell you, from the Russian point of view, what the president and the United States have done for victory in the war. The most important things in this war are machines. The United States has proven that it can produce from 8,000 to 10,000 aircraft per month. Russia can produce, at most, 3,000 aircraft per month. England produces 3,000–3,500 per month, mostly heavy bombers. Thus the United States is a country of machines. Without these machines received through Lend-Lease, we would have lost this war.[12]

Nikita Khrushchev recalled conversions with Stalin about

> when we 'spoke freely' among ourselves. He stated openly that if the USA had not helped us, then we would not have won the war: one-on-one with Germany, we would not have been able to withstand her pressure and would have lost the war. No one among us officially touched on this point and nowhere did Stalin, I think, leave

any written traces of his opinion, but I declare here that he pointed out this circumstance several times in conversations with me.[13]

Let one imagine that none of this took place and that the USSR had been forced to fight Nazi Germany one-on-one, without any kind of deliveries from abroad. Then 2 times fewer Soviet tanks and aircraft would have been produced and 3 times less munitions. The national economy and the army would have experienced continuous breakdowns in automobile transport and fuel, and the railroads would have been periodically paralyzed. It's unlikely that the Russians could have defeated the Germans under such conditions and Hitler could have reached the Urals. H. Hopkins, President F.D. Roosevelt's special envoy, who had been in Moscow, reported in a message on 31 July 1941 that Stalin believed that it was impossible for the USSR to hold out against the materiel might of Germany, which disposed of the resources of occupied Europe, without aid from Great Britain and the USA.[14]

Of course, Lend-Lease was in no way charity on the part of the USA and Great Britain. Munitions, equipment, and strategic materials were delivered on credit and without any hope of being fully repaid only because Soviet soldiers were dying on the battlefields and not only for their motherland, but also for American and British interests, in this way reducing the human and materiel losses of the democratic powers.

However, the contribution of the Western Allies to the Soviet victory was in no way limited to Lend-Lease deliveries. One should not forget that the American and British armed forces carried the main burden of the struggle with the *Luftwaffe* and the *Kriegsmarine*. Germany lost 60 per cent of its aircraft and more than 95 per cent of its fleet in the struggle against the Western Allies. Let one once again hypothetically imagine that Germany had the opportunity to fight against the Soviet Union one-on-one and employ against the USSR 2 to 3 times as more aircraft than was actually the case. Would Soviet aviation have then been able at any time to win air superiority? The answer to that question seems obvious. It's not even about how much the strategic bombing of Germany, which was carried out by Anglo-American aviation, slowed down the growth of the Reich's military production and, correspondingly, reduced the quantity of weaponry and combat equipment which might have reached the Soviet-German front. From March–September 1944 alone the production of aviation fuel in Germany, which was carried out almost exclusively in synthetic fuel factories – the chief target of Allied bombings during this period, fell from 181,000 tons to 10,000 tons and, following a small increase in November to 49,000 tons, and in March 1945 collapsed completely. And this was the chief reason the Luftwaffe was grounded in the final months of the war.[15] And the fact that Germany was forced to build hundreds of submarines for the struggle with

Great Britain, diverting significant resources for this, prevented it from sending additional thousands of tanks and aircraft to the Eastern Front. Had it not been for the Anglo-American air force and navy, the Soviet Union could not have held out against the German advance. And there would have been no 'economic victory by socialism over capitalism', about which Soviet propaganda tirelessly repeated, pointing out that the USSR produced far more armaments and combat equipment than Germany. Quite the opposite, then the *Wehrmacht* would have had no difficulty in crushing the Red Army with armadas of tanks and aircraft, which were superior not only in quality, but in quantity as well. And, of course, the USA played the decisive role in the victory over Japan, which, had it not been for the military conflict with the USA, in which the navy and air force played the main role, could have attacked the Soviet Union in the Far East.

It's clear that on its own the Soviet Union would have been unable to deal with Germany. And could Great Britain and the USA have done this without Soviet help? This is the question Molotov put to Churchill on 22 May 1942 in London: 'What will Great Britain's position be in 1942 if the USSR does not hold out against the pressure in the forthcoming fighting, which Hitler will probably attempt to make as strong as possible?' Churchill replied:

> If the Russians are defeated or Soviet military power is seriously undermined by the Germans, Hitler, in all likelihood, will move as many troops and aircraft to the West for the purpose of invading Great Britain. He may also attack through Baku to the Caucasus and Persia. This would put us in very serious danger and we would in no way feel confident that we dispose of a sufficient amount of forces for repelling this attack. Thus our well being depends upon the Soviet army's resistance. Nonetheless, if against all expectations the Soviet army is defeated and the worst comes to pass, we will fight and hope with aid from the United States to achieve overwhelming air superiority, which in the course of the next 18 months or two years will allow us the opportunity for subject German cities and industry to destructive attacks. Moreover, we will support the blockade and make landings on the continent in growing numbers. In the end, Great Britain and the United States will win. One should not ignore the fact that following the fall of France, Great Britain alone faced over the course of an entire year Hitler's numerous and victorious divisions, having itself only poorly armed troops.

> But such a continuation of the war would be a tragedy for mankind and our sincere hope is for a Russian victory and our passionate wish to take upon ourselves our share in the defeat of these devilish forces.[16]

Chapter 10

Life Under German Occupation

Soviet Partisans and Collaborationists

Life in the German-occupied territories was by no means pleasant. The main thing the overwhelming part of the population was worried about was physical survival. People could at any moment become victims of the occupation authorities and the local partisans, and could also die from hunger. Besides this, they risked becoming the victims of combat operations if the front moved into their territory. All of these risk factors were present in those Soviet territories which were not subjected to German occupation. Thus, for example, it has been impossible to this day to establish where excess mortality was higher – in the occupied or unoccupied territories of the USSR. For example, in the opinion of the German historian Rolf-Dieter Muller, the scientific director of the German ministry of defence's Military-History Institute in Potsdam, 'the partisans killed more Soviet citizens in the occupied territories than did German soldiers'.[1]

But there were two categories of people who were threatened with certain death in the occupied territories. These were Jews, who were being completely destroyed by the Nazis within the confines of the 'final solution of the Jewish problem', and Gypsies. The latter were destroyed for their 'non-Aryan origin' (they were actually the true Aryans) and for their nomadic way of life. Settled Gypsies, as opposed to those who roamed, were not subjected to repressions and could legally live in the occupied territories. In all, the Nazis destroyed about 30,000 Gypsies in the Soviet Union, including 2,000 on Latvian territory.[2] Victims among the Jews were of a much greater order.

In Kiev on 29–30 September 1941 one of the largest mass executions in the history of mankind took place. During this time, according to the account by *Brigadeführer* of *Einsatzgruppe* C, Dr Otto Rasch, in the gulley of Babii Yar, within the confines of Kiev, 33,771 Jews were shot. As the men had been mobilized into the Red Army, the victims were mostly women, children, and old men. This crime was also typical in that the most active part in it was played by the *Wehrmacht* and that the initiator of this massacre was not Himmler's department, but the military commandant of Kiev, Major General Kurt Eberhard. The executions were directly carried out by *Sonderkommando*

4A, headed by *Standartenführer* Paul Blobel and Operational Group 5, under the command of SS *Obersturmbahnführer* August Meyer.[3] They killed almost 17,000 people a day in one place. For the sake of comparison: in order to shoot from 22,000–25,000 Polish officers and civilians, the Soviet NKVD required a month-and-a-half (April and the first half of May 1940), while the executions were carried out in more than five places – in Katyn', Khar'kov, and Mednoye, as well as in the prisons of Western Ukraine and Western Belorussia. Evidently at Babii Yar at the end of September 1941 each of the executioners killed several tens of victims apiece.

What served as the excuse for such a large-scale and quick massacre? There is yet another tragedy, only far smaller in size. Units of the Soviet 37th Army, which abandoned Kiev on 19 September (they were commanded by, incidentally, the well-known general Andrei Vlasov, who later went over to the Germans and headed the ROA – the Russian Liberation Army), mined a number of buildings in the centre of Kiev, in which, as they assumed, German headquarters would be stationed following the occupation of the city. On 24 September from territory still under Soviet control, signals were sent out to radio-controlled detonators. Explosions erupted in the centre of Kiev, on the Kreshchatik, followed by a firestorm.[4] The explosions and fires continued until 28 September. The centre of Kiev was completely burned out and was not restored during the war; 940 buildings were destroyed and about 50,000 people remained without shelter. The exact number of victims among the residents of Kiev was not established, nor was the number of German military personnel who suffered as the result of the explosions and fires. If during the period from 11–20 September the German Sixth Army, which occupied Kiev, lost 210 missing in action, then during the period from 21–30 September, which covers the time of the Kiev explosions, this number rose to 810.[5] This is what the Germans were enraged at! Several times more residents of Kiev probably died than Germans. Essentially, this act purposely doomed to death and suffering civilians deprived of a place to live. They probably did not guess in the Soviet headquarters that the explosions would serve as an excuse for destroying Kiev's Jews.

The Germans blamed the Jews for the explosions and arson, although no evidence for this was found. The explosions only served as a pretext for speeding up the elimination of Kiev's Jews and brought their demise closer by at least a few weeks. In any event, within the confines of the 'final solution' they were not supposed to remain alive. During a meeting on 26 September, as a member of *Sonderkommande* 4A, SS *Obersturmführer* August Hefner, recalled, Eberhard ordered us 'to shoot all the Jews in Kiev. He then asked whether I had the authority to shoot Jews. I replied in the affirmative, which was true. To his question of how many Jews were in Kiev, I answered that

I had no idea, but perhaps about 5,000. He then ordered me to shoot all the Jews.' Hefner declared that Blobel's imprimatur would be required, which immediately followed. As early as 27 September they began to paste up leaflets, ordering 'all the Yids in Kiev' under threat of death to gather on the morning of 29 September with their valuables, money, documents, undergarments, and warm clothing at the corner of Mel'nikova and Dokterivskaya streets, near Babii Yar. The commandant explained to the rabbis of Kiev that following sanitary procedures all of the Jews would be evacuated to a safe place and the rabbis made a corresponding appeal to their flocks. And then there was the gully, which became a giant common grave.⁶

Who carried out the execution? *Wehrmacht* units convoyed the Jews to the place of execution. The 303rd Police Battalion from Hamburg, under the command of SS *Sturmbahnführer* Heinrich Hannibal, cordoned off the area. The local auxiliary police did not yet exist in Kiev. It began to be formed only on 3 October, when the recruitment of volunteers into the 'Ukrainian People's Police' was announced. Thus the Ukrainians, whether they wanted to or not, could not have taken part in the shooting of the Jews in Babii Yar. The shooting itself was carried out by members of *Sonderkommande* 4A and Operational Group 5, as well as a company from a special designation SS battalion under the command of *Sturmbahnführer* Bernhard Grafhorst and members of the 45th Reserve Police Battalion under SS *Sturmbahnführer* Martin Besser. This is how Hefner described the method of the execution:

> The first Jews were led off into the ditch by SS soldiers. They were to get down on their knees and in such a way as they bent their backs toward their knees, bowed their heads and crossed their hands. The shooter would stand behind them and from a short distance shoot them from an automatic rifle either in the back of the head or in the cerebellum. After the first Jews had been shot, other Jews would arrive in single file. They had to get down on their knees in the empty spaces left by those who had been shot and were shot in the same manner . . . After the bottom of the hollow had been filled, the shooting continued further so that they dead lay in layers one on top of the other. The shooters stood on the corpses.⁷

There it is, German precision in action!

The population of Kiev, stirred up by the explosions in the centre of the city and thanks to ancient anti-Semitic prejudices and easily believing the Nazi propaganda regarding Jewish involvement in the explosions, did not, by a large majority, sympathize with the victims of Babii Yar. The local inhabitants enriched themselves on the things the unfortunates were carrying. It may also be possible that there were isolated instances of cruel murders of Jews by residents of Kiev. However, the Ukrainian police could not have taken part in the shootings of 29–30 September 1941 in Babii Yar. This does not mean, of course, that the local police did not take part in later executions in Babii Yar. In all, according to various estimates, during the period of the Nazi occupation of Kiev, from 19 September 1941 to 6 November 1943, 100,000–150,000 people were shot here, including Jews, Gypsies, Soviet military personnel, and members of the underground, as well as more than 600 Ukrainian nationalists, among which were, in particular, the famous poet and publicist Yelena Teliga. In all, 1.5 million local civilian Jews became victims of the Holocaust, and approximately another 500,000 Western European Jews were deported and then destroyed on Soviet territory.[8]

And what fate befell the Babii Yar executioners? SS *Obergruppenführer* Friedrich Echeln, the SS and police commander in the rear of Army Group South in September 1941, who sanctioned the shooting in Babii Yar, was hanged in Riga on 3 February 1946, according to the sentence of the military tribunal of the Baltic Military District. Kurt Eberhard committed suicide on 8 September 1947 in the American prison in Stuttgart. Otto Rasch was brought to trial by the Americans on the matter of the *einsatzgruppen*, but his prosecution was halted due to his health. Rasch was found to be suffering from Parkinson's disease and was released. The former chief of the *Einsatzgruppe* C died on 1 November 1948 in Bad Salzburg. Paul Bobel was condemned to death by an American military tribunal on the matter of the *einsatzgruppen* in 1948 and was hanged in Landsberg on 7 June 1951. August Meyer committed suicide on 13 May 1960, not long after he had been arrested by the West German authorities on charges relating to the *einsatzgruppen*. Bernhard Grafhorst, who condemned the execution in Babii Yar, served to the rank of SS *hauptsturmführer* and died on the Eastern Front on 2 September 1943, while commanding the 'Narva' Battalion. Martin Besser was brought to trial by the West German government on charges relating to the *einsatzgruppen*, but due to his health the case against him was dropped. August Hefner was condemned at a trial in Darmstadt in 1967–8 and sentenced to nine years behind bars. He died in 1999. SS *Brigadeführer* Heinrich Hannibal was not held responsible and died in 1971.[9]

The tragedy of Babii Yar was not publicized in the USSR, insofar as the chief victims there were Jews, and following the war anti-Semitism essentially became the state policy of the USSR.

In the Soviet Union they hid to an even greater degree the fact that danger threatened the Jews not only from the Germans and collaborationists, but also from Soviet partisans to the same extent as from the local population, including those who did not cooperate directly with the Germans. It should be noted that Soviet influence in the occupied territories remained in the form of the Soviet partisan movement and the underground structures of the VKP(b), VLKSM, and NKVD. There were only no partisans in the territories occupied by the USSR in 1939–40. The Soviet partisan movement was absent in Bessarabia, Western Ukraine, Western Belorussia, and in the Baltic States. UPA detachments predominated in Western Ukraine and fought not so much against the Germans as with Polish partisans from the Home Army and carried out 'ethnic cleansings' of the Polish population in Volhynia and Eastern Galicia.[10] Soviet partisan detachments here were small in number and, as a rule, only carried out raids from that part of Ukrainian territory which had been Soviet prior to 1939. Units of the Home Army predominated in Western Belorussia and Southern Lithuania, and in Southern Lithuania faced detachments of the Lithuanian Freedom Army.[11] From the end of 1943 the Home Army periodically got into fights with Soviet partisan detachments which would arrive from Eastern Belorussia and attack them. Due to the broad support of the Home Army by the local Catholic Belorussians, the Soviet partisans were not able to consolidate in Western Belorussia all the way up to the liberation of this territory by the Red Army in the summer of 1944.

Kazimir Mette, the head of the underground NKVD in Mogilev, testified that:

> The Germans physically destroyed all the Jews in the first months of the occupation. This fact brought forth a lot of different judgments. The most reactionary part of the population, comparatively small in number, fully justified this beastliness and aided them in this matter. The main man-in-the-street contingent did not agree with such a cruel massacre, but maintained that the Jews were themselves to blame for the fact that everyone hated them, although it would have been sufficient to limit them economically and politically, while shooting only a few occupying responsible positions. The remaining pro-Soviet part of the population, sympathized and helped the Jews in many ways, but were very indignant at the Jews' passivity, because they gave themselves up to be slaughtered without making any kind of even elemental attempt to rise up against the Germans in the city or by joining the partisans en masse. Besides this, pro-Soviet people noticed that before the war a lot of Jews tried to set themselves up in the most profitable and good positions [as if the Russians or Belorussians did not try to do the same, B.S.], set up mutual guarantees between themselves and often allowed themselves a tactless attitude toward Russians, threatening to take them to court for the slightest remark against the Jews, etc. 'And now the

Jews also expect help from the Russian Ivans and don't do anything themselves,' they would say.

The overall judgment of the population was thus: lest the German deal with everyone the way he deals with the Jews. And this forced many to think on it and undermined faith in the Germans.[12]

And this is what Lientenant Colonel of State Security, Hero of the Soviet Union Kirill Prokof'evich Orlovskii, said about partisan mores to the Commission on the Patriotic War of the Central Committee of the Belorussian Communist Party:

I organized a detachment named after Kirov exclusively from Jews who had escaped from Hitler's executioners.[13] I knew that I was facing incredible difficulties, but did not fear these difficulties and undertook this only because all of the partisan detachments and the partisan formation around us from the Baranovichi and Pinsk oblasts had turned their back on these people. There were instances of murdering them. For example, the 'partisan' anti-Semites from Tsygankov's detachment killed 11 Jews and the peasants from the village of Radzhalovichi in Pinsk Oblast' killed 17 Jews, while the 'partisans' from the Shchors detachment killed seven Jews.[14] When I first came to these people I found them unarmed, barefoot and hungry. They declared to me: 'We want to get revenge on Hitler, but we don't have the opportunity.'

After this I spared neither myself nor my time in order to teach these people the tactics of partisan struggle with our common sworn enemy. I want to say that the energy spent by me was not wasted. What seemed at first sight to be people completely incapable of armed struggle, former speculators, petty salesmen, tradesmen, and others, desiring to get revenge on the German monsters for the people's blood spilled, under my leadership carried out no less than 15 combat operations in 2.5 months, and every day destroyed the enemy's telegraph and telephone communications, killed Hitlerites, policemen and traitors to our motherland. They gradually became not only disciplined, but also brave, both in carrying out diversions and in night movements from one area to another.

Alongside diversionary, organizational and intelligence work, I was daily involved in a ruthless struggle with bandit-like attitudes toward the local population on the part of some bandit 'partisan' groups in the Baranovichi and Pinsk oblasts. I could not but devote attention to this problem, because in each village there were instances of drunkenness, marauding, rapes of women, murders, and the arson of individual farms and villages by the bandit groups, which under the guise of partisans systematically terrorized the local population and thus tried to compromise the people's avengers-partisans, frightened off and pushed the peasants away from helping the partisans in their struggle . . . The local Belorussian population, seeing in the Beria partisan detachment their defenders not only against the German occupiers, but also against the bandit elements, which were hiding in the woods in the guise of partisans, remained very satisfied with this.[15]

And some of the partisan commanders managed to take part in the 'final solution of the Jewish problem' before they became partisans. On 1 October 1942 Ye.A. Kozlov, the commissar of a partisan brigade, wrote a denunciation to the chief of the Central Staff of the Partisan Movement, P.K. Ponomarenko against his brigade commander, Col. Marchenko:[16]

> Astreiko [the commander of one of the detachments in the brigad, B.S.], the assistant chief of police in Trudy (in the winter), according to reliable sources, was shot Jews (confirmed by T. Lapenko, the brigade commissar, and Capt. Keshcheryakov, the commander of one of the detachments of our brigade who, lived exclusively underground during the winter and who remained faithful to the motherland to the end), but nevertheless enjoyed enormous authority with Marchenko. This is obvious by the way Marchenko twice appointed Astreiko commander of partisan brigades, both of Stankevich's and his own, when Marchenko himself left for the post of commander of the Polotsk zone. Thanks to intervention in this matter by the oblast' committee (Vitebsk) and headquarters, Astreiko was not allowed to become commander of the brigade. The word 'shooting' has burrowed deeply into the consciousness of the majority of the brigade's fighters. It has been inculcated by Marchenko and Astreiko.

However, Kozlov perished in an airplane crash soon after this and Senior Lieutenant Aleksandr Aleksandrovich Astreiko (Avstreiko) and Colonel Arkadii Yakovlevich Marchenko, who commanded the 3rd Belorussian Partisan Brigade, fought safely until the end of the war.[17] In October 1944 Astreiko, being the commander of a company belonging to the 539th Rifle Regiment/ 108th Rifle Division/65th Army, was even recommended for the title of Hero of the Soviet Union for bravery exhibited in holding the bridgehead over the

Narew River, but in the end received only the Order of Suvorov Third Class. He had earlier been awarded the Order of the Patriotic War Second Class.

The partisans also dreamed up a story that the Germans supposedly sent Jews to the partisan detachments as their spies, believing that there was no way the partisans would suspect that Jews could be helping the Nazis. And partisans in all of the occupied territories, in Belorussia, in the Crimea, and in the Bryansk area, regularly forced Jews who had the misfortune to wind up in the ranks of the Soviet partisans to admit under torture that they were 'agents of the Gestapo, after which they shot them with a clean conscience. In fact, the Germans never sent Jews to join the partisans as agents, as it was impossible to rely upon such an agent for whom the return through the front line to his masters threatened greater danger than working among those whom he was supposed to work against. Anti-Semitism manifested itself in the shooting of Jews accused of collaborating with the Nazis, an anti-Semitism that was endemic to many Soviet partisans.[18]

But this revealed itself not only against Jews, but also against Poles. But if in the case of the Jews the behaviour is not a manifestation of USSR state policy, but only the anti-Semitism of a significant part of the soldiers and commanders, then in the case of the Poles Stalin's purposeful policy surely comes into play.

Following the Jews and the Gypsies, the Germans' treatment of the Poles was the worst. By a tragic coincidence, Soviet power treated them just as bad. Although before the break in diplomatic relations with the Sikorski government, the Soviet partisans sometimes cooperated with the Home Army in the fight against the Germans. The former assistant and chief of operations staff of the 229th Rifle Division's 804th Rifle Regiment, S.I. Kozlov, who escaped from a prisoner of war camp on Polish territory, testified about the attitude of the Polish population of Poles'ye:[19]

> After the German authorities applied crueler measures against the Poles than even against the Russians, Ukrainians, Belorussians, and Lithuanians, the attitude of the Polish population sharply changed in favour of Soviet power. Sikorski's arrival in Moscow was met with especial passion. In connection with this, commentary among the Polish population became particularly agitated: Sikorski concluded an agreement in Moscow with the Soviets, he received money and weapons and now Poland will be reconstituted.
>
> In February a general strike, which lasted an entire week, erupted at the Gainov sawmill (Brest Oblast'). The workers' main demands were 'Bread and food.' In each building and on each pole in the entire worker's settlement, the following slogans were pasted up:

'Down with Hitler!' and 'Help Sikorski and the Red Army defeat Hitler!' 'Long live Sikorski!' 'Long live Poland!' and an entire series of other slogans appealing to the Polish population to a fight against the occupiers.

Actually, the Poles began to treat Soviet power with more tolerance and the Soviet Union as a state, once the Sikorski government concluded an agreement with it. The fact that before 1943 the Poles did not undertake any kind of hostile actions against the Soviet partisans is confirmed in the report by the commander of a partisan detachment that operated in the Braslav District in Vileya Oblast', N.I. Petrov:

> A large number of Polish defence detachments are located in the Augustow woods, numbering up to 3,000 men and operating in a number of areas of the western oblasts. These detachments organized a raid on the town of Postavy, Vileya Oblast', where they destroyed up to 400 Germans and policemen, as well as a number of warehouses.
>
> In July 1942 the Germans, in strength up to 3,000 men, undertook offensive operations against Polish defence detachments. The Germans, having lost about 1,500 men, fell back.
>
> The Polish population of the Vileya Oblast' in its overall mass has a good attitude toward the partisans and is awaiting the Red Army's arrival. But it is simultaneously interested in Sikorski and the political system following the Red Army's arrival. The population of the villages inhabited by Poles actively supports the partisans, passes on information to the partisans about traitors and informs them about the arrival of police detachments, etc. Couriers who arrived at Petrov's detachment from Polish defence detachments, declared: 'The Polish defence detachments are fighting against the Germans and police for an independent Poland. They accept Poles and Russians (mostly prisoners of war) into their detachments. The attitude of the members of the Polish defence toward the partisans is quite friendly. Each detachment member in the Polish defence wears on his left sleeve an armband with the letters PO'.

These reports show that contrary to the claims of Soviet propaganda, detachments of the Home Army in the western districts of Ukraine and Belorussia by no means sat on their hands in the forests, but were engaged in an active and successful struggle against the Germans and the police.

But immediately following the victory at Stalingrad a shift occurred in Moscow's attitude toward the Poles. Now it was no longer necessary to continue to play the game of ally with the Polish government in exile. Stalin had no doubt that the Red Army would manage to seize Poland and set up a friendly regime. Thus as early as February 1943, two-and-a-half months before the graves in Katyn' were uncovered, the Central Committee of the Belorussian Communist Party sent out a secret letter to the commanders of the partisan formations and the leaders of the underground party organizations, where, in particular, it was stated:

> In those areas where there are already Polish nationalist detachments, created by Polish reactionary circles, they should, first of all, be stubbornly pushed out by the creation of our partisan detachments and groups, and, secondly, to adopt measures for insinuating their agents into them, studying their ties, tasks, organization, and methods of work, and to expose the real representatives of the Polish nationalists or German intelligence.
>
> These groups should be demoralized through the sending of reliable Poles from our side, while laboring Poles should be brought over to our side . . .
>
> We must by all means bring over to the active armed struggle with the Germans all the laboring Poles residing in the western districts of Belorussia. Their duty, as Soviet citizens, is to be in the same ranks alongside all the other peoples of our country in the struggle against the Hitlerite fascist hordes.
>
> The organizers and leaders of the movement must bring in working Poles into both existing partisan detachments and to newly formed ones.
>
> In certain cases, when this is necessary according to the specific situation and providing we can secure our full influence, we may organize partisan detachments in which the majority of the troops are Poles. Such detachments, as do all Soviet partisan detachments in the enemy rear, should wage the struggle in the interests of the Soviet Union.
>
> In those areas where our partisan detachments and underground centers already enjoy influence, the activities of groups of nationalistic Polish reactionary circles are not to be allowed. Their leaders are to be removed without being noticed. These detachments are to be broken up and their weapons bases gathered up, or, if it appears possible, the detachments should be placed under our reliable influence and employed, directing them toward an active struggle with the Germans, while correspondingly moving them and making them larger so as to deprive them of significance as independent

combat units, attach them to other large detachments, and conduct a corresponding and secret purge of hostile elements.[20]

At the same time, Ponomarenko was forced to admit that the soldiers of the Home Army were actively fighting the Germans. At the end of June 1943 he wrote to Stalin:

> In my report of 10 June 1943, I informed you about the appearance of Lieutenant Milaszewski's Polish detachment of in the Stolbtsy area.
>
> On 26 June of this year the assistant plenipotentiary of the Central Committee of the VKP(b) for the Baranovichi Oblast', comrade, Sidorok, informed me that: 'on 12.6.43 this latter detachment, while returning to the district center of Ivanets, Baranovichi Oblast', killed 40 Germans and 106 policemen and that all of the young people had gone over to the detachment.
>
> The detachment burned down three of the gendarmes' buildings, a depot with munitions, and destroyed one gun, ten motor vehicles, and 5,000 grenades, and other weapons. 806 rifles, three automatic rifles and 18 horses, were seized.'

On 22 November 1943 Ponomarenko scared Stalin once again with the Polish threat in Western Belorussia, sending him a corresponding note in which he laid out the circumstances of the destruction of Kmitec's Polish detachment near Lake Naroch':

> One of the most maliciously nationalistic bands is that of the Polish legion under Lieutenant Kmitec (300 men), which broke off relations with comrade Markov's (the deputy chairman of the Vileya Oblast' executive committee) partisan brigade, which is operating the Vileya Oblast'. [Fedor Grigor'evich Markov, a former functionary of the western Belorussian Communist Party did not suffer any punishment for his crime, but, quite the opposite, was awarded the medal of Hero of the Soviet Union on 1 January 1944. On New Year's eve in 1942 partisans from Markov's detachment attacked an estate in Shemetovo, Myadel' District, Minsk Oblast', and burned it down, killed 19 civilians, mostly Poles, including the mistress, Gabriela Skirmunt, her daughter Lidia Gabriela Karibut-Dashkevich, Prince Jozef Drutskii-Lyubetskii, and the overseer Bochkovskii. It was impossible to justify this crime by any military considerations, but Markov was not punished for this either. Antonii Chekhovich, had

been a fellow classmate of Markov's, which did not keep the latter from settling scores with him, B.S.].[21]

While conducting negotiations, at the same time the legion was preparing to destroy the brigade's command element and to disarm the brigade. Comrade Markov, received a warning about this from his people who had previously been dispatched to the legion and as a result of countermeasures taken he arrested the legion's leadership, disarmed the legion, and shot 80 people among the officers and sergeants, including Kmitec and his staff, while the remainder were disarmed and released to their homes and small groups were attached to our detachments.

The episode involving the destruction of Lieutenant Kmitec and his comrades was made up out of whole cloth. Would the unhappy lieutenant really have thought to kill the commander of one of the partisan brigades, which outnumbered his legion by more than 3 times, in order to gain a dangerous enemy? Moreover, the Poles would nonetheless have been unable to destroy the command of individual detachments of Markov's brigade, as those would have waged a war of extermination against Kmitec's legion. There was evidently something else going on here. Poor Kmitec was really preparing to cooperate with the Soviet partisans in the struggle against the Germans; the partisans simply lured him into a trap and destroyed him. In order to justify the murder of eighty people, Markov made up the story of a supposed Polish plot.

In the same letter, Ponomarenko proposed to Stalin: 'to destroy the Polish detachments and groups which are operating in western Belorussia and attacking Soviet partisans. All the other groups occupying a wait-and-see attitude should be discredited, disarmed and scattered. Their command element should be destroyed.'

The commander of a partisan brigade, Viktor Aleksandrovich Manokhin (his mother was a Pole) and commissar Petr Mironovich Masherov, the future leader of the Belorussian communists, made similar proposals in December 1943: 'to conduct an outwardly friendly policy toward the legionnaires and their command, while at the same time to prepare such a blow that will eliminate not only their armed forces, but also the roots of their deep underground, remembering the lessons near Lake Naroch', where they only "scared" the White Poles, while their organization remained'.

Here it was admitted that the Poles' accusations that the Soviet partisans killed, raped, and robbed the local population, both Polish and Belorussian, were well founded:

Taking into account the significant authority that the Polish partisans enjoy among the local population of the oblast's western districts, it is necessary for us to change our behavior with iron firmness among the local population and to decisively put a stop to the constant drunkenness and marauding among our partisans and in this fashion deliver a blow against the Polish partisans among a significant portion of Catholics; that is to say, by a correction and skillful approach to the population.

All of the proposals put forth by Ponomarenko, Manokhin, and Masherov were adopted. This is precisely how the Soviet partisans began to operate against the Poles in Belorussia and Ukraine. With the arrival of the Red Army in Belorussia and Western Ukraine, the detachments of the Home Army operating there were destroyed or captured. A part of them was able to break out into Poland, where they were able to wage an armed struggle for another few years against the communist government of Wladyslaw Berut and Soviet forces.[22]

And before long, following the end of the war, a most famous crime was committed by the army's SMERSH, aided by units of the Red Army. This was the 'little Katyn', the shooting without trial and investigation of 592 Poles in the Augustow woods, which was carried out by the chief of the GUKR SMERSH, Major General Gorgonov, with a group of counterintelligence personnel in July 1945. The report by the chief of SMERH, Viktor Abakumov, to Beria about how the general was commandeered with a team of SMERSH men for 'carrying out the eliminating of bandits arrested in the Augustow woods' has been preserved. Operational groups and a battalion of troops from the SMERSH directorate for the Third Belorussian Front (Abakumov was also the NKVD plenipotentiary for this *front*) also took part in the shooting. It was not a battalion of NKVD troops, but an ordinary army rifle battalion, which had been placed at the disposal of SMERSH. This is apropos the question about the Red Army's units taking part in war crimes. All 592 were accused of being soldiers of the Home Army, which had been disbanded by this time. But of this number only 69 had weapons and among those shot were 27 women and 15 teenagers.[23]

Stalin attached particular importance to the sovietization of Poland. Poland was supposed to guarantee the establishment of his control over Eastern Europe. Thus of all the Eastern European countries it was namely in Poland that Soviet structures of state security and their communist allies applied the greatest mass repressions against the numerous soldiers of the Home Army and other allies of the government in exile. And, all the way up to 1956, out of all the Eastern European countries, it was in Poland, whose minister of defence was the Soviet marshal Konstantin Rokossovskii, where the USSR was able to completely control the Polish armed forces, along with the assistance of Soviet generals and officers there.

Turning to the problem of Vlasov and the Vlasovites, in order to objectively evaluate this phenomenon it is useful to compare them with collaborationists in other countries. For example, in the countries of South and Southeast Asia that were occupied by Japan. Here Sukarno, the father of Indonesian independence, quite successfully collaborated with the Japanese up until the Japanese capitulation and was even awarded a medal from Emperor Hirohito, which did not prevent him from later serving for two decades as the president of independent Indonesia.[24] The same thing may be fairly said of the leader of the Vietnamese communists, Ho Chi Minh.[25] And the prominent activist of the Indian Congress Party, Subhas Bose, headed the Indian National Army, which fought on the side of Japan, a fact that has not hindered the Indians in honouring him as one of the heroes of the struggle for independence.[26] An attempt by the British after the war to try officers of the INA for treason collapsed, insofar as it brought about dissatisfaction in the Indian army. But what is important here is not the resemblance to Vlasov, but the difference. Sukarno, Bose, and Ho Chi Minh began their struggle against, respectively, the Dutch, British, and French colonial authorities long before their countries encountered the Japanese occupation, which they attempted to take advantage of (not unsuccessfully at all, in the case of Sukarno and Ho Chi Minh, although in the war's final months Ho Chi Minh, understanding Japan's inevitable collapse, took up the struggle against the Japanese) in the interests of this struggle. Vlasov and the overwhelming majority of the ROA's leadership became leaders of the anti-Stalin movement only because they had ended up in German captivity.[27] The very same Vlasov was well regarded by Stalin and had he not been captured he would have ended the war a general of the army or marshal. On the other hand, he much more resembled General Walther Seydlitz, who in Soviet captivity agreed to head the Union of German Officers.[28] He, for his part, had had a successful career and was valued by Hitler, and had it not been for being captured he could easily have become a field marshal. Evidently the nature of collaborationism and the fate of the collaborationists from totalitarian and non-totalitarian states were materially distinct.

The captured Soviet generals had a much greater chance of surviving captivity than a rank-and-file Red Army soldier. But this only proves that the motives for collaboration were different for different people. For many rank-and-file Red Army soldiers and junior officers cooperation with the enemy was simply a way of saving themselves from death by hunger in the camps. Ambition and careerism were the prime factors for the senior officers and generals, including Vlasov. Of course, there were exceptions. For example, the former commander of the ROA Air Force, former RKKA Colonel Viktor Ivanovich Mal'tsev, who was arrested in 1938 and then rehabilitated, but cashiered from the army, appeared at German headquarters immediately following the German capture of Yalta and proposed forming a volunteer anti-Bolshevik unit. One may see the same ideological motives among the creators of the Lokot' Republic, Konstantin Pavlovich Voskoboinik, and Bronislav Vladislavovich Kaminskii, although one should not idealize them either (before going over to the Germans, this same Kaminskii was a secret collaborator with the NKVD).[29] Of course, the White émigrés who served in the ROA and other collaboration structures were ideological warriors against bolshevism. After all, they were not threatened with death by starvation and they voluntarily signed up to serve the Germans in order to continue the struggle with communism that they had lost during the civil war. However, the émigrés were not influential in Vlasov's army and were quickly pushed aside by the Soviet generals and colonels. The Germans did not interfere with this process, evidently and not without foundation, supposing that it would be easier for former Soviet generals to command the captured Red Army soldiers who joined the ranks of Vlasov's army than veterans of the White movement.

Vlasov began to cooperate with the Germans only because he was captured and when Germany's victory seemed quite likely. If he had been able to get out of encirclement in the summer of 1942, as some of the senior commanders of the 2nd Shock Army managed to do, he would most likely have ended the Great Patriotic War a general of the army or a marshal, a Hero of the Soviet Union, and a *front* commander. After all, Andrei Andreevich was thought highly of in the Red Army and enjoyed Stalin's protection. And Vlasov was not at fault in the disaster of the 2nd Shock Army. He also refused to be evacuated to the rear when the 2nd Shock Army was completely surrounded and preferred to remain with his troops. So, Vlasov was no shrinking violet and, as opposed to what he said at his trial, he was not driven by cowardice to serve the Germans, but by ambition. Andrei Andreevich very much wanted to become a Russian Charles de Gaulle. Having been captured, he understood that his career in the Red Army was over. Even if the Soviet Union won the war and he were to be liberated following the end of the war, he could at best hope for some kind of unimportant posting, for example, as head of a department in a military academy, and in the worst case he could be repressed.

Vlasov was not the first Soviet general to have expressed a desire to collaborate with the Germans. For example, the former commander of the 19th Army, Lieutenant General Mikhail Fedorovich Lukin, having been in captivity since December 1941, proposed to the commander of Army Group Centre, Field Marshal Fedor von Bock, the formation of an anti-Bolshevik

Russian government and army. Lukin tried to convince von Bock: 'The people will be faced with an unusual situation: the Russians have taken the side of the so-called enemy, which means that going over to them does not constitute treason, but only abandoning a system ... Even well-known Soviet personages will probably think on this. After all, not all the leaders are fanatical followers of bolshevism.'[30] His proposal was not accepted because of Hitler's opposition, and Lukin later refused to join the ROA, by which means he saved his life.[31] The protocol of his interrogation in von Bock's headquarters was unearthed only many years later following Mikhail Fedorovich's death. Even Major General Vasilii Fedorovich Malyshkin, the former chief of staff of the 19th Army, who, like Lukin, had also been captured as a result of the Vyaz'ma disaster, began to cooperate with the Germans much earlier than Vlasov. But it was Vlasov, as the most famous of all the captured generals in the USSR, who the Germans preferred to make the head of the ROA.

However, by no means did all of the Soviet prisoners of war join the ROA just to save themselves from death by starvation or to forge a career. Among them were officers who were captured after Stalingrad, when hardly anyone doubted Germany's final defeat. However, the one thing they realistically hoped for was to offer their service in Vlasov's army to the Western Allies, or, at worst, to surrender to them. Vlasov himself, and the other leaders of the ROA, it seems, maintained these illusions to the end. For the sake of this goal, they sought to pull all of the ROA's formations to the south, to the Prague area, in order to present a liberated Prague to the approaching American forces and thus earn themselves an amnesty for their previous service with the Germans. They didn't know about either the agreements in Yalta, which called for the forced repatriation of former Soviet citizens from the Western occupation zones, or that according to the demarcation lines established between Soviet and Anglo-American forces the Red Army was supposed to liberate Prague.

If Hitler as early as 1941, immediately following the beginning of the war with Stalin, had sanctioned the formation of a Russian anti-Bolshevik government and army, then it's possible that this could have prolonged the war, while at the same time saving the lives of a significant number of Soviet prisoners who actually died in the winter of 1941–2. In an alternative scenario to the actual events, they would have been enrolled in the ROA as early as 1941. But it's doubtful that the ROA divisions would have been more combat-capable than the two divisions of Vlasov's army created in 1945, and would have been good for, at best, as was the case with all the other Russian and Belorussian collaborationist formations, the anti-partisan struggle. The Vlasovites had no ideology and the majority of them saw in German service only a means of physically surviving, while any kind of political organization inside the USSR, on which they might have relied, was absent.

The extent of Vlasov's 'ideology' showed itself well in his behaviour at trial. Understanding that there was no way to avoid the death penalty, Andrei Andreevich, in his final arguments, declared in a servile way: 'I not only fully recanted, late, to be sure, but during the trial and investigation tried to expose as clearly as possible the entire gang. I expect an extremely cruel punishment.'[32]

The proposal for creating a Ukrainian state, a partisan of which was the minister for the eastern territories, Alfred Rosenberg, perhaps had a greater chance.[33] The Organization of Ukrainian Nationalists (OUN) actively operated and was popular in Polish Ukraine, and the most influential faction in it was that of Stepan Bandera, which, just like the faction of Andrei Mel'nyk, cooperated with Germany in 1939–41.[34] Before long, following the occupation of L'vov by the Germans, the Banderovites created there on 30 June the government of Yaroslav Stets'ko and proclaimed the restoration of the Ukrainian state. However, as early as 5 July the Stets'ko government was disbanded by the Germans and before long Bandera and other leaders of OUN-B were arrested.[35] Had a Ukrainian government been recognized by the Germans, then the OUN could have formed no less than 10 divisions out of the more than 8 million Ukrainians living in Poland, including captured Red Army soldiers, which being armed and trained by the Germans would not have been inferior in combat-capability to the Baltic SS divisions and would have been superior to the Red Army. But in the beginning of the war the OUN had practically no influence, just as it did not have its own cells in that part of Ukraine which had been Soviet since 1920. The formation of Ukrainian divisions in Eastern Ukraine would have been problematic and their combat-capability doubtful. Ten Western Ukrainian divisions, with a strength of 150,000–200,000 men (the maximum strength of the OUN-B UPA Ukrainian Rebel Army) would not have been influential and would have only slightly increased the *Wehrmacht's* combat capabilities and just as slightly decreased the Red Army's mobilization capabilities.

However, because of the position of Hitler, who viewed Ukraine as a German colony and who was preparing to throw Russia back, at a minimum, to the Volga and leave it under the power of Stalin or his successors, neither a Russian nor a Ukrainian anti-communist army was created in 1941. And part of the SS 14th 'Galicia' Division, which was formed in 1943 from inhabitants of Western Ukraine, was captured by the Soviets in the Brody 'cauldron' in 1944, while the greater part of it filled out the ranks of the UPA. The ROA, all the way up to the autumn of 1944, when its two divisions began to be formed, remained a purely propaganda project, directed at demoralizing the Red Army. In the final half-year of the war, when its outcome was no longer in doubt, neither two nor even a larger number of Vlasovite divisions were any longer able to play any kind of role.

Chapter 11

Life in the Soviet Rear

The life of the civilian population in those parts of the USSR's territory that were not subjected to occupation was just as much a struggle for survival as in the occupied territories. It was particularly difficult for those who had been evacuated from territories occupied by the enemy, who at the same time did not receive a 'worker's ration card', but were registered as dependents. They often did not have relatives who could have helped them or apartments or homes where they could live, with gardens to grow vegetables in order not to die from hunger. Thus the death rate among those evacuated was especially high.

It is still impossible to determine whether the death rate in the unoccupied territories was higher among the rural or urban population. There are no reliable statistics for this comparison. Urban dwellers received food according to ration cards, while at the same time working for 12 hours in plants and factories without practically no days off, so that there only remained time for eating and sleeping. Rural dwellers did not receive ration cards, although they had their own garden plots, while at the same time they worked intensively during the sowing and harvesting periods. Which model was more favourable for survival – the chance to obtain food with ration cards with intensive labour, or the absence of ration cards with no less intensive labour and the opportunity to growing food on one's one plot – is now impossible to determine.

It was particularly difficult for the residents of blockaded Leningrad. Here were seen both examples of the greatest human failing, cannibalism, as well as the highest manifestations of the human spirit, when mothers who were dying of hunger gave their last crumbs of food to their children and working sons and daughters set aside bread from their meagre ration for their elderly parents, who were issued with only 125g of blockade bread during the most difficult blockade winter of 1941–2. At the same time, Andrei Zhdanov and the other representatives of the party *nomenklatura* who remained in the city did not deny themselves anything and ate just as bountifully as in peacetime. But it was not only high-ranking party bosses who did not go hungry in the conditions of the blockade, but the middle and lower *nomenklatura* as well. This is what Nikolai Ribkovskii, an instructor in the personnel section of the city party committee, wrote in his diary on 9 December 1941:

> I have no particular food needs now. In the morning I have macaroni or noodles, or oatmeal with butter, and two glasses of sweet tea for breakfast. During the day I have lunch, of which the first course is cabbage or beet soup, with some meat every day for the second course. Yesterday, for example, I had for starters cabbage soup with sour cream, and for the second course a cutlet with vermicelli, and today I started with soup with vermicelli, and then pork with stewed cabbage. The quality of lunches in the Smolny's lunchroom is significantly better than in those lunchrooms in which I had to lunch while I was idle and waiting.[1]

Evidently the weak groans of those dying from hunger did not reach the inhabitants of the Smolny. And this same Ribkovskii, if he had shared his breakfasts, lunches and dinners, might have saved about five people from death by starvation.

The single serious threat from political demonstrations in the unoccupied territories arose in the middle of October 1941, when Soviet forces were routed at the approaches to Moscow and the real propspect of the capital falling arose.

The 'evacuation' of the leading workers from Moscow occurred in terrible haste. The Central Committee VKP(b) apparatus, which called upon the people to fight to the last man and to selflessly labour in the rear under the slogan 'Everything for the front. Everything for victory!', ran away faster than anyone. Firefighting equipment and gas masks littered the corridors of the Central Committee's abandoned building on Old Square, while secret papers, directives, and telegrams lay about the offices. More than 100 typewriters, 128 pairs of felt boots, greatcoats, 22 bags of shoes, several tons of meat and potatoes, and several barrels of herring, etc., were abandoned in the panic.[2]

In the courtyard of the 'Precise Measurement' Factory a crowd of workers waiting to be paid saw motor vehicles loaded up with the personal effects of the workers of the People's Commissariat of the Aviation Industry. The indignant workers began to throw things off and take them themselves 'in lieu of a salary'. They practically lynched the factory director. And the workers of the Moscow Mikoyan Meat Factory grabbed 5 tons of sausages from the storehouse.[3] The workers of the 'Storm Petrel' factory in the Sokol'niki District, who had not been paid, cleaned out a storehouse of ready prepared food.[4]

Pogroms of food and appliance stores and warehouses began in Moscow, which had been abandoned by the authorities. The journalist Nikolai Verbitskii wrote in his diary:

Yes, 16 October will go into history as the most shameful day, a day of cowardice, panic and treason in the history of Moscow. These are people who were the first to go on about heroism, unbending will, duty, and honor. The Highway of Enthusiasts, along which on this day the automobiles of yesterday's 'enthusiasts' sped along, loaded down with polished beds, leather suitcases, rugs, boxes, and greasy meat of the owners of these odds and ends, has been disgraced.[5]

Anti-soviet and anti-communist slogans were heard among the workers.

There was disorder and looting, just like the abandonment of Moscow by the party-economic *nomenklatura* (only it disposed of transportation) among the broad masses of Muscovites, who were trying to get out of the capital on foot and bicycles. From time to time they would stop the bosses' cars, loot them and then throw them into the ditch. Disorders also broke out in the Moscow area and in the neighbouring oblasts – Ivanovo and Yaroslavl' and others. But the Germans nevertheless failed to reach Moscow and after 18 October the authorities gradually got the situation under control. In any case, all of these outbreaks were elemental and had no organized centre. It was easy to suppress them with the aid of the militia and NKVD troops, when the authorities recovered from the shock and understood that the Germans would not take Moscow within the next few days. On 19 October by a decree by the State Defence Committee (GKO), a state of siege was proclaimed in Moscow, allowing the authorities to shoot on sight and to bring to trial, or even without trial, robbers and other violators of public order, as well as people carrying out anti-soviet agitation and suspected of espionage. During the period from 15–28 October alone 760 deserters and 933 'anti-soviet elements' were arrested. On 30 October a prohibition against alcohol was introduced in Moscow.[6]

A decree by the Supreme Soviet of the USSR of 26 June 1941 'On the Work Regime of Workers and Employees during Wartime' authorized directors to establish mandatory overtime work of 3 hours every day. In practice, such overtime work basically became compulsory for all workers until the end of the war. On 26 December 1941 the state 'delighted' the workers with a new decree 'On the Responsibility of Workers and Employees of Military Industry for Voluntarily Leaving the Workplace'. From now on a worker who voluntarily left the factory, to which he was assigned, was to be declared a 'labour deserter' and be subject to repressions.

Milling machine operator Anatolii Korovin, who in November 1941 was a 15-year-old student at the plant-factory school (FZU), was dispatched to the Stalin Machine Construction Factory No. 92 in Gor'kii. He recalled:

Before long an order arrived to immediately transfer me on 26.11.1941 to factory work and together with six friends I was assigned to the Stalin Artillery Factory, from where I was sent to mechanical shop no. 18. My first machine tool was called No. 67, 'Dzerzhinets'. This was the German machine tool 'Franz Werner'. Insofar as I was not very tall, they made a special plank for me. My first work day was 12 hours long. They immediately explained to me that it was forbidden to be late for work, and 25% of one's salary would be deducted for six months for being 20 minutes late. And this is how I worked until the very end of the war! And there weren't any kind of days off or holidays. I had two days off during the entire war. The shift was increased once a month. Then I had to work from 1300 to 0730, that is, 18 hours straight.

Taking into account the fact that people sometimes had to get to the factory on foot, and that not everyone was lucky enough to squeeze into an overcrowded trolley car or to jump into the back of a truck, many workers, having made their way to their dormitories, only had time to sleep before once again getting to the factory on time. As Anatolii Korovin testified, during the hard winter of 1942, in - 40 degree weather:

workers did not go home, but went to hot shops and slept there. But there were dangers waiting here. One worker crawled into a container for molten metal and burned to death in the oven in the kiln. A terrible accident! We workers from shop no. 18 did not go into the hot shops, but slept next to the heating batteries in the accounting office.

At the same time, the average salary at a military factory was 800 rubles per month and by the end of the war this had risen to 1,000 rubles, but it did not keep up with the pace of inflation. A loaf of bread cost 400 rubles in the market. The factories held on to their workers through food cards, with which one could get 800g of bread per day, a little bit of meat, some fish, and other products for a token price. Besides this, violators of labour discipline who were of draft age were threatened with losing their factory 'deferment' and being sent to the front, where the chances of surviving were significantly less than in the rear.

Ration cards and food coupons became the main focus of counterfeiting and thievery, since forging them was much easier than currency notes. D.V. Pavlov, the GKO plenipotentiary for supplying Leningrad with food, recalled: 'If a person had an extra ration card, then he enjoyed an incomparable advantage with it over others. Thus self-centered people and rogues strove in all dishonest ways to acquire two, and if possible, even more ration cards. They tried to get all sorts of coupons in all manner of ways for the sake of their stomach . . .'[7] And the situation with the ration cards existed not only in blockaded Leningrad, but throughout the entire country.

In order to get enough to eat, city dwellers grew potatoes and vegetables on their own plots and other small plots of land in the city and suburbs, which were rented for a token amount, including collective and state farms on the edge of the cities. It was particularly difficult for dependents, that is, people who didn't work and who received only 400g of bread per day through their ration cards. This allocation sometimes fell to as low as 125g in blockaded Leningrad during the critical days of autumn and winter 1941–2.

The situation was somewhat better in the countryside than in the cities. The working day during the sowing season began at 4 in the morning and ended late in the evening. And then one's own garden still had to be tended. Almost all of the draft-age men, the agricultural equipment, and a significant number of the horses had been mobilized into the army. Almost all of the work had to be done by hand. A refusal to work on the collective farm's fields was punishable by several years in the camps. V.Ye. Ped'ev, the Party Control Committee plenipotentiary with the Central Committee of the VKP(b) for the Gor'kii Oblast', wrote on 31 May 1944 to Central Committee secretary G.M. Malenkov:

> There are numerous reports of collective farm women harnessing themselves 5–6 people at a time to the plow and plowing their personal plots. The local party and soviet organizations reconcile themselves to this politically harmful phenomenon and are not stopping them and are not mobilizing the masses of collective farm workers for digging of their personal plots by hand and using livestock for this purpose.'[8]

Before the war, the minimum of workdays, when the collective farmer had to work essentially without pay on the collective farm's field, was sixty, and although this coincided with the sowing and harvesting, it was still bearable. But on 13 April 1942 a government decree appeared 'On Increasing the Minimum of Workdays for Collective Farmers'. Now each collective farmer over 16 years was supposed to work 100 days, and teenagers 50 days. They raised this minimum to 150 days in the cotton-growing areas. Failure to fulfill the quota was punishable by corrective-labour work, that is, an additional work commitment.[9] Besides this, the peasants were saddled with further obligations during the winter, such as digging trenches, the construction of fortifications, or the procurement of firewood.

The situation of those who had been evacuated was particularly hard. For example, at the end of 1942 in the 'Twelfth Year of October' Collective Farm in the Saratov Oblast's Bezymyannoe District, where evacuees accounted for a quarter of the population, the family of the Selishcheva woman, who had been evacuated from Voroshilovgrad Oblast', four sons of whom were fighting at the front, received only 36kg of bread that year for work on the collective farm, and she had no personal plot of land. The woman and the members of her family were swollen with hunger. According to a report by the oblast' administration of the NKVD, the family of collective farm member Semyonova, also from the Voroshilovgrad Oblast', was also starving. And the local collective farmers were at times unable to work due to exhaustion. In the winter of 1942–3 there were a number of incidents of cannibalism in Saratov Oblast'.[10]

D.A. Volkogonov painted a similar picture:

> Kharchenko, the people's commissar of internal affairs for the Tadzhik SSR reported: 'In Leninabad Oblast' . . . 20 people were discovered to have died of exhaustion and 500 have swollen up from a lack of food. In the Stalinabad Oblast', in the Ramit, Pakhtaabad, Obigarm and other districts, more than 70 people have died from exhaustion. There are also incidents of exhaustion and swelling from hunger. There are similar cases in the Kurgan-Tyube, Kulob and Gharm oblasts. The assistance that has been rendered to these areas on the ground is insignificant . . .' In the Chita Oblast' there were incidents 'of eating dead animals, trees and tree bark. A terrible incident was reported when one peasant woman and her sons killed her young daughter and used her for food . . . And there's another such incident . . .'[11]

Most cases of cannibalism were recorded in blockaded Leningrad in the winter of 1941–2. In December 1941 26 people were arrested for eating human meat, 366 in January 1942, and nearly 500 during the first 15 days of February. Certainly the majority of these were not cannibals, that is, those who killed people in order to eat them, but ate the corpses of those who had died recently. They acted alone and in bands and sold human remains on the market. There were no articles for cannibalism in the RSFSR criminal code and of the other union republics. Thus they arrested cannibals and consumers of corpses according to article 59–3, 'banditry', and, as a rule, they were shot. In all, 332 men and 564 women were detained for cannibalism in Leningrad.

Among them were 11 party members and 4 Komsomol members, with male and female workers predominating according to social category.[12]

On the collective farms a significant amount of the grain harvested, at times up to 50 per cent of the crop, was embezzled by both the work supervisors and the rank-and-file collective farm members, as well as those evacuees who were working on the collective farm. For collective farm labourers and especially for those who had been evacuated and did not have their own personal plots, thievery was at times the sole means of survival, because they received too little food for their working days on the collective farms. And for the *nomenklatura* even at the district level, which was not threatened with hunger, the embezzlement of food was a means of improving one's living conditions. M.I. Rodionov, the first secretary of the Gor'kii Oblast' Committee of the VKP(b), speaking at the oblast' committee's XVII plenum, declared:

> We must clip the hands of those district workers who get into col-
> lective farm property to which they have no right . . . Nonetheless,
> many try to get into the collective farm. While looking at the district
> worker, the collective farm chairmen are stealing, while looking at
> him, the storekeepers are stealing, as well as the heads of farms, etc.
> The secretaries of the district committees and the chairmen of the
> district executive committees must relentlessly take upon them-
> selves the security of collective farm property, while communists
> most display an example first of all.[13]

They caught and punished rank-and-file collective farm members for stealing by sentencing them to several years in a labour camp camp, but not the party bureaucrats.

In November 1943, as a result of mass air attacks by the *Luftwaffe* on the cities of the Volga River area, the shipment of grain to the liberated areas and the poor harvest necessitated a lowering of the bread ration. For workers and first category engineer-technical workers the quota fell from 800g to 600g per day. This provoked mass agitation among the population. As the Gor'kii Oblast' administration of the NKVD reported, the workers and employees expressed their feelings about the food situation at the end of 1943 in the following manner:

> Of course it's understandable, they've stolen it and now it's nec-
> essary to bring up the reserves at the expense of the workers, and
> we've fought to the very end'; 'Comrade Stalin said that the war will
> soon be over, so they're reducing the norms, which means that the
> war will continue for a long time, while the people are already going

hungry, and now they're taking bread away, and many people are going to swell up and die'; 'We receive as much as Hitler hands out in the occupied areas'.[14]

As opposed to the occupied territories, where the German occupation authorities did not hinder but often supported the migration of urban dwellers to the countryside, which helped them to survive, such a migration in the unoccupied territories was reduced to a minimum by the existing ration card system and the attachment of workers and employees to their plants and offices. 'Labour desertion' was usually carried out within the confines of a single city.

However, the severity of these laws was mitigated by their not being carried out. The same Korovin recalled that 'the norms for making parts were artificially raised. The new norms allowed five to ten minutes for doing what could be done in two minutes. All you had to do was press a little and the norm would be fulfilled by 50–70%.'[15]

Not being able to bear the hard-labour conditions of work, people ran away in droves from a number of factories where the regime was particularly harsh and sought to establish themselves in other plants where management looked the other way at such 'deserters' because of the chronic labour shortage. Some young people even tried running away to the front, not imagining the tragic fate of the Red Army soldiers. There was no possibility for the deserters to hide legally, as this was equivalent to death by starvation. People in the rear could not survive without their ration. In all, during 1941–5 12,865,706 people were charged with 'labour desertion' while 70 per cent of them were tried *in absentia*. It was only on 29 June 1944 that the default persecution of 'labour deserters' was revoked. Actually, many 'deserters' were drafted into the Red Army, without telling the management of their factories and thus remained at large. And all the other uncaught 'deserters', with rare exceptions, laboured at other plants and factories. The NKVD could only catch a 'deserter' while the scent was fresh, while as a rule he was not looked for further. On 30 December 1944 the USSR Supreme Soviet had to issue a decree 'On the Granting of Amnesty to Those who Left Factories of the Military Industry and Voluntarily Without Authorization and who Voluntarily Returned to these Factories'. Now it was sufficient for the 'deserter', following his arrest, to express a readiness to return to the factory, and he was released from responsibility for 'desertion'.[16]

On the whole, enthusiasm for labour in the unoccupied territories, which was summed up by the slogan 'Everything for the front, everything for victory!', had to be constantly maintained through repressions. And mass thievery and 'labour desertion' became phenomena that the authorities were unable to contain until the end of the war.

In the USSR the level of criminality in 1942 grew by 22 per cent, by 21 per cent in 1943, and by 8.6 per cent in 1944. In the first six months of 1945 alone the number of crimes fell by 10 per cent. During the second half of 1941 3,317 murders were registered in the unoccupied territories alone, while in 1944 there were 8,369 murders, and the number of armed attacks and robberies increased correspondingly, from 7,449 to 20,124. The number of thefts rose from 252,588 to 444,906 and the cases of of livestock being stolen from 8,714 to 36,285.[17] It was mostly deserters and criminals who committed serious crimes, taking advantage of the weakening of the militia due to the war, while thefts were sometimes a means of survival for average citizens. There were a large number of teenagers among the criminals. Many of them had become orphans, while for others their mothers, who were occupied the entire day at the factory and their fathers were away at the front, did not have the opportunity of looking after them properly.

During the war years 376,300 people were condemned for 'desertion', and 212,400 deserters were never found.[18] It is possible that many of them were drafted a second time into the Red Army or were able to legalize themselves as workers in defence plants.

Chapter 12

The Price of Victory

Soviet Losses During the Second World War

The official figure for the Red Army's losses in killed and died of 8,868,000 is a political one, which has been used to prove that it fought no worse than the *Wehrmacht*. The authors of the book *The Seal of Secrecy Removed* now maintain that the correlation of irreplaceable losses for the Soviet forces and the *Wehrmacht* and their allies is only 1.3:1 in favour of the Germans. This is supposed to cheer up the military personnel of the Russian army, who consider it the Red Army's heir, and on the other hand to justify the Stalin period of the country's history.[1] The preceding chapters have repeatedly demonstrated the absurdity of these figures.

D.A. Volkogonov first made public the data on the Red Army's irreplaceable losses in 1993, which was before the publication of the collection *The Seal of Secrecy Removed*. It's most likely that the calculation of the irreplaceable losses for 1942 was done at the beginning of 1943. D.A. Volkogonov puts forward the breakdown of losses by month. For comparison there is the monthly fluctuation of the Red Army by those who suffered in the fighting during the period from July 1941 to April 1945 inclusively. The corresponding table was reproduced in a book by Ye.I. Smirnov, *War and Military Medicine*, by the former chief of the Red Army's Main Military-Medical Administration. The monthly loss figures for the Soviet armed forces for 1942 are shown in the following table.

The Red Army's Losses in 1942[2]

Month	Irreplaceable Losses (in thousands of men)	Losses of Those in Battle (as a percentage of the average monthly level for the war = 100)
January	628	112
February	523	98
March	625	120

April	435	81
May	422	78
June	519	61
July	330	83
August	385	130
September	473	109
October	819	80
November	413	83
December	318	123
Total for the Year	5,889	1,158

It is obvious to the naked eye that D.A. Volkogonov's data significantly understates the true size of the irreplaceable losses. For example, in May 1942 the Soviet forces' irreplaceable losses supposedly amounted to 422,000 men and had even fallen in comparison with the April figures by 13,000 men. At the same time, German forces in May captured about 150,000 Red Army soldiers on the Kerch' peninsula and about 240,000 in the Khar'kov area.[3] In April Soviet losses in captured were insignificant. It turns out that in May the losses in killed and those who died from wounds, disease, and accidents did not exceed 32,000 men, while in April they reached nearly 430,000, while the index of the number of losses in the fighting from April to May fell by only 3 points, or less than 4 per cent. It's clear that there has been a colossal undercounting of irreplaceable losses during the general retreat of Soviet forces from May to September inclusively. After all, it was just at that time that the overwhelming majority of the 1,653,000 Soviet prisoners captured by the Germans in 1942 were taken.[4] According to D.A. Volkogonov, during that time irreplaceable losses reached 2,129,000, as opposed to 2,211,000 for the four preceding months, when the losses in prisoners were insignificant. It's not by accident that in October the Red Army's irreplaceable losses suddenly increased by 346,000 in comparison with September, with a sharp decline in the index of those who suffered in the fighting by an entire 29 points and the absence at this time of any kind of major encirclements of Soviet troops. It's likely that the undercounted losses of the preceding months were partially included in the October losses.

It seems that the most reliable data on irreplaceable losses comes from November, when the Red Army suffered almost no losses in prisoners and when the front line was stable all the way up to 19 November, when Soviet forces launched a counteroffensive at Stalingrad. Thus one may consider that the losses in killed in this month are more complete than in the preceding and succeeding months, when the rapid movement of the front and headquarters made accounting difficult and that irreplaceable losses in November are due almost exclusively to those killed, as Soviet forces suffered almost no losses in men captured. In this case, the 413,000 men who were killed or died from their wounds is 83 per cent of those losses suffered in the fighting, which means that 5,000 who were killed and died from their wounds is equal to 1 per cent of the average monthly number of those who suffered in battle.

Data from the German archives confirms that the number of Soviet prisoners captured in November was minimal for all of 1942 and came to 22,241 men.[5] Strictly speaking, one should subtract 22,000 prisoners from the figure of 413,000 killed and missing in action and use the figure of 390,000 killed in November. However, it is preferable to retain the figure of 413,000, keeping in mind the likely undercounting of killed in the final 11 days of November and assuming that the figure of 22,000 in some way compensates for this.

The correlation for November established between the number of losses suffered in the fighting and those who were killed and died from their wounds seems close to the average for the war as a whole. Then the Red Army's irreplaceable losses (minus prisoners and non-combat losses) in the war with Germany may be estimated at, multiplying 5,000 men by 4,656 (4,600 is the sum, in percentages, of the losses suffered in the fighting during the period from July 1941 to April 1945, and 17, which was the figure for those losses suffered in the fighting during June 1941, and 39, which was the figure for those losses suffered in the fighting in May 1945, adopted by the author as one-third of the losses correspondingly for July 1941 and April 1945). As a result, the figure arrived at is 23,280,000 killed. One should subtract from this number the 939,700 military personnel who were listed as missing in action but who, following the liberation of the corresponding territories, were once again conscripted into the army. The majority of these were not prisoners, although some of them escaped from captivity.[6] Thus the overall number of those who died falls to 22,340,000 men. According to the latest estimate by the authors of the book *The Seal of Secrecy Removed*, the Red Army's non-combat losses were 555,500 men.[7] Then the Soviet armed forces' overall irreplaceable losses (not counting those who died in captivity) may be estimated at 22,900,000 men.

In order to arrive at a summary figure for military losses, it is also necessary to estimate the number of Soviet prisoners of war who died in captivity. According to various German documents, 5,754,000 prisoners of war were taken on the Eastern Front, including 3,355,000 in 1941, while at the same time the authors of the documents, which were presented to the Western Allies in May 1945, made the caveat that the accounting of prisoners for 1944–5 was incomplete. At the same time, the number of those who died in captivity was estimated at 3,300,000 men.[8] However, according to early data from the OKW, during the period from 22 June to 1 December 1941 3,806,861 prisoners were taken on the Eastern Front, and according to a declaration made by Mansfeld, a government bureaucrat, to the Reich Economic Chamber on 19 February 1942, the number of Soviet prisoners of war numbered 3,900,000 men (almost all of them were captured in 1941).[9] The number of 3,800,000 prisoners in 1941 probably includes approximately 200,000 prisoners from the occupied territories who were released from camps as early as 1941. One must take into account approximately 450,000 prisoners who were not counted in 1941, as well as the prisoners taken by Germany's allies (Finland captured 64,188 prisoners, of which 19,276, or 30 per cent, died; Romania about 160,000 prisoners, of which 5,200 died).[10] Then the overall number of Soviet prisoners of war can be estimated at 6,300,000 men. About 220,000 of this number come from Germany's allies, while 1,836,000 men returned to the motherland from German (as well as from Finnish and Romanian) captivity, and approximately another 250,000, according to an estimate by the USSR Ministry of Foreign Affairs in 1956, remained in the West after the war.[11] It can be estimated that the overall number of those who died in captivity, adding to this the 19,700 Red Army soldiers who died in Finnish captivity and the 5,200 who died in Romanian captivity, is approximately 4,000,000 men. This accounts for 63.5 per cent of the overall number of prisoners.

Such a high incidence of mortality among Soviet prisoners of war was due to the fact that the conditions of the Geneva Convention were not adhered to, Jews and political workers were consciously exterminated, and for objective reasons, particularly the severe shortage of food. The number of Soviet prisoners taken in 1941 exceeded by ½ million the strength of the German army in the East, which numbered 3,300,000 men and itself was experiencing a shortage of food. Thus the Germans, even had they wanted, could not feed such a number of prisoners, which doomed the majority of them to death in the winter of 1941–2. It was also impossible to rapidly move them to the deep rear in Poland due to the shortage of rail cars and the railroads' low capacity.

However, the mortality rate in Soviet camps for prisoners of war for the *Wehrmacht* and its allies during the war was also extremely high, chiefly because of the shortage of food, which was critically low for the Red Army and the civilian population as well. Before 1945 the number of prisoners in the USSR was significantly less than in Germany. The existing food ration in

1942–3 did not provide the minimum energy even for non-working prisoners. From the start of the war up to 1 May 1943 196,944 out of 292,630 prisoners died, or 67.3 per cent, which was even higher than the mortality rate among Soviet prisoners in German camps. And it is correct to compare precisely these indices because the repatriation of prisoners was impossible for Germany. Besides, in Germany there were millions of French and Polish prisoners. Only at the end of 1944 did the food quotas for prisoners of war in the USSR provide the physiological minimum, but it was often not achieved due to theft and the shortage of food. The quotas once again fell sharply in 1946, due to the hunger which gripped the country.[12] It is known, for example, that of the approximately 110,000 Germans captured at Stalingrad only 5,000 men, or 2.6 per cent of all prisoners, returned home from captivity.[13]

Following the conclusion of the war, the mortality among prisoners in the USSR fell because the weak and ill prisoners were repatriated first of all. According to official data, of the 3,576,300 German prisoners, 442,100 died, or 12.4 per cent.[14]

The murder of German and other prisoners of war was practised no less rarely than in the *Wehrmacht*. For example, on 5 January 1942 the Black Sea Fleet carried out a landing in the port of Yevpatoria. The landing party broke into the city hospital, where at that time a German hospital was housed. A. Kornienko, one of the few survivors of the landing party, recalled: 'We broke into the hospital . . . and destroyed the Germans with knives, bayonets and rifle butts and threw them out of the window and onto the street . . .' The same thing took place in Feodosiya and Kerch', which were captured by the main landing. The Germans then also killed the wounded from the landing party in revenge. This is how the historian Vsevolod Abramov wrote about his meeting with the writer Konstantin Simonov:

> During the course of our meeting Konstantin Mikhailovich told me much that was new about Mekhlis that I did not know. It turns out that the *Stavka* representative, during breaks from his main work, loved to interrogate captured German officers. These were most often pilots who had been shot down. If the prisoner was not inclined to answer questions, then Mekhlis would summon his adjutant and the fascist would be shot near the building of the *Stavka* represent-ative. It is interesting that this fact was to a certain degree fixed in document fashion in the *Stavka* representative's papers. I saw in the Ministry of Defence archives several official death sentences. At the same time, the crime of the captured German officer was formulated as 'treason against the motherland.' Only it's not clear which moth-erland they're talking about.[15] And Mekhlis immediately wrote his

son with pleasure: 'In the city of Kerch' there are up to 7,000 corpses of civilians (including children), all of whom were shot by the fascist monsters. The blood runs cold from rage and the thirst for vengeance. I order that fascist prisoners be finished off. And Fisunov [the chief of Mekhlis's secretariat and his adjutant] does a good job. He destroys the villains with particular pleasure.[16]

But the murder of prisoners took place not only along those sectors of the front where Mekhlis was in command. For example, on 30 June 1941, in the area of the village of Bronniki, near Rovno, a battalion from the 25th Motorized Infantry Division's (First Panzer Group) 35th Infantry Regiment was counterattacked by Colonel M.Ye. Katukov's 20th Tank Division from Major General K.K. Rokossovskii's 9th Mechanized Corps. Having been surrounded and having expended their ammunition, 180 soldiers from the battalion, the majority of them wounded, were captured and 153 of them were killed, including by bayonet.[17]

The same thing happened along the other fronts. For example, P.K. Ponamarenko, a member of the Northwestern Front's military council, in March 1942 reported to Stalin: 'Of course, few will surrender, if A) we do not approach them with comprehensible leaflets, and B) if we are going to shoot prisoners in full view of the Germans (near Kholm we slaughtered a group which was leaving the town toward our units with their hands raised).'[18]

The majority of the cases of Soviet reprisals of prisoners occurred in 1941–2. At that time these were encouraged by the Soviet command, as it hoped that the murder of prisoners would invite retaliatory repressions on the part of the Germans, which would teach the Red Army soldiers not to surrender.

Taking deceased prisoners into consideration, the overall losses of the Soviet armed forces may be estimated at 26,900,000 men. One should take into account that the difference between 4 million and 3.3 million dead prisoners, counted by the Germans, is about 700,000 men. This includes both prisoners who died following their capture but without being registered by the Germans, as well as prisoners who escaped from the camps and who died later, either in partisan detachments, or simply in the village where they were hiding from the Germans. The figure of 700,000 also includes those prisoners of war who served in the *Wehrmacht*, the SS, and auxiliary police formations and who later died fighting the Red Army or the partisans.

S.A. Il'enkov, based on the card catalogue of losses at the Ministry of Defence, estimates losses among the Soviet forces at no less than 13,850,000 killed and died.[19] I.I. Ivlev, who used the same card file of losses for the rank and file and officers, believes that the Soviet armed forces' losses in killed and died could not be less than 15.5 million men, but that this could also be 16.5 million, or even as high as 20–1 million men.[20] The latter figure was arrived at in the following manner. The overall number of notices from the military commissariats about those killed and missing in action that reached families in Archangel Oblast' exceeds 150,000. According to Ivlev's estimate, approximately 25 per cent of these notices did not reach the military commissariats. At the same time, there were 12,400,900 notices in the Russian Federation's military commissariats, including 61,400 for those border troops who died or went missing in action, and 97,700 for the USSR NKVD's internal troops. Thus 12,241,800 notices were sent from the units of the People's Commissariat for Defence and the People's Commissariat for the Navy. According to Ivlev's estimate, of this number about 200,000 were repeats, concerning people who remained alive, as well as for people who served in civilian bureaus. By subtracting them, the figure of 12,041,800 unique notices is arrived at. If the proportion of notices that did not reach the military commissariats for all of Russia is approximately the same as was defined for the Archangel Oblast', then the overall number of unique notices within the confines of the Russian Federation should be estimated at no less than 15,042,000. In order to estimate the number of unique notices which should be located in the remaining former union republics, Ivlev assumes that the share of killed inhabitants of Russia among all of the irreplaceable losses of the Red Army and Red Navy is approximately equal to the share of Russians in irreplaceable losses set forth in the books of G.F. Krivosheev's group – 72 per cent. In this case, the remaining republics account for approximately 5,854,000 notices, so that their overall number within the confines of the USSR may be estimated at 20,905,900 men. By taking into account the losses among the NKVD's border and internal troops, the number of unique notices, according to Ivlev, exceeds 21 million men.[21]

However, it seems incorrect to estimate the share of notices located beyond the confines of the Russian Federation, basing it upon an estimate of the share of the non-Russian population among the irreplaceable losses. Not only Russians live and lived in Russia. And they lived not only in the RSFSR, but in all the remaining union republics. And for Krivosheev the share of Russians among those military personnel who were killed and died is estimated not at 72 per cent, but at 66.4 per cent, particularly as this was taken not from a document on irreplaceable losses, but calculated on the basis of data on the national composition in the Red Army's muster strength in 1943–5. If one adds here an estimate of the losses of the nationalities who resided primarily in the RSFSR based on today's boundaries: Tatars, Mordvins, Chuvash, Bashkirs, Udmurts, Mari, Buryats, Komi, the peoples of Dagestan, Ossetians,

Kabardins, Karelians, Finns, Balkars, Chechens, Ingush, and Kalmyks, then the Russian Federation's share of losses will increase by another 5.274 per cent. It is possible that Ivlev added on to this half of the Jews' losses 0.822 per cent, and then the losses of the peoples of the RSFSR will increase to 72.5 per cent.[22] Ivlev, probably rounding off this number, arrived at 72 per cent. Thus, in order to estimate the number of unique notices beyond the confines of the Russian Federation, it is necessary to employ data on the share of the population of the RSFSR in the USSR as of 1 January 1941. It was 56.2 per cent, and by subtracting the population of the Crimea, which was transferred to Ukraine in 1954, and by adding the population of the Karelo-Finnish SSR, which was included within the RSFSR in 1956, it is 55.8 per cent.[23] Then the overall number of unique notices may be estimated at 26.96 million, and by counting the notices for the border and internal troops, 27.24 million. By subtracting from this figure the military personnel who remained in emigration, the overall number of killed and died will be 26.99 million men.

This figure practically coincides with the estimate of the Soviet armed forces' losses in killed and dead of 26.9 million men. The USSR's overall losses in the war, including losses among the civilian population, are estimated at 40.1–40.9 million killed and dead.[24] As the historian Nikita P. Sokolov notes, 'according to the testimony of Col. Fedor Setin, who worked in the middle of the 1960s in the Ministry of Defence's central archives, the first group estimated the Red Army's irreplaceable losses at 30 million men, but these figures "were not accepted upstairs".[25] He stresses that G.F. Krivosheev and his comrades did not take into account 'the mobilization carried out directly by the units of the active army on the territory of the oblasts occupied by the Germans following their liberation, the so-called unorganized reinforcements. Krivosheev indirectly admits this when he writes that 'during the war years the following percentage capable of labour was taken from the population: in Russia 22.2%, 11.7% in Belorussia, and 12.2% in Ukraine'. Of course, in Belorussia and Ukraine no less of the 'labour-capable population' was called up than in the whole in Russia, only here a smaller part was conscripted through the military commissariats, and a larger part directly into the units.[26]

In the German army the number of wounded was approximately triple the number killed, while in the Red Army the numbers of killed and wounded were approximately equal. This was due to the huge number of Soviet losses and the poorly conducted evacuation of the wounded from the battlefield. In the German army tanks and other armoured equipment were extensively employed for evacuating the wounded – tank troops, infantrymen, and artillery troops, while Soviet tank troops have no memory of this sort of thing.[27]

The wonderful Belorussian writer and war veteran Vasil' Bykov, the author of truly honest books about the war, testifies in his memoirs that:

> Our losses in the offensive were monstrous, and of course their greatest number was at the expense of the wounded. The lightly wounded left the battlefield under their own power; the badly wounded often lay in the firing zone for long periods of time, getting new wounds and sometimes dying. Only specially designated soldiers – orderlies and orderly instructors – had the right to carry the wounded from the battlefield. No one else was allowed to accompany the wounded to the rear and attempts to do so were seen as shirking. Of course, the female instructors tried as best they could, but one orderly instructor was assigned to each company, and there were always tens of wounded on the battlefield. As much as you might like, how could you have the time? And they didn't have time; the wounded were forced to wait a long time for assistance and, while bleeding, died on the field or on the way to a medical battalion.
>
> We still don't know exactly who had the 'brilliant' idea of employing women in the war. It seems that this was a purely Soviet innovation, as nothing similar was observed in the German army before the end of the war. Given the obvious surplus of human (male) material in the war, what was the reason behind sending young girls who were poorly adapted for the peculiarities of combat life under fire? What use were they? Just to brighten up the spare time and daily life of the senior commanders and political workers who were temporarily deprived of their wives and rear-area girlfriends.[28]

Because in the Red Army it was not hefty male orderlies who dragged the wounded from the battlefield, as the Germans did, but slight girls, yesterday's schoolgirls, just the same as there were several times more wounded in the fighting (that is, those who did not die immediately as soon as they were struck by a bullet or shell fragment) in the Red Army than in the *Wehrmacht*, the chances of a wounded Soviet soldier being carried off the battlefield and delivered to a hospital was on an order less than their German counterparts in similar circumstances. Thus among the Soviet wounded there was a far higher share of those who died on the battlefield before they could receive aid. Thanks to these two factors, there were far more wounded to one dead in the *Wehrmacht* than in the Red Army. As a result of this, the Red Army's irreplaceable losses, which by an order of magnitude exceeded the *Wehrmacht's* losses, rose sharply.

The Red Army's overall irreplaceable losses by year are as follows: 5,500,000 in 1941, 7,153,000 in 1942, 6,965,000 in 1943, 6,547,000 in 1944, and 2,534,000 in 1945. For the sake of comparison, let's take the German army's irreplaceable losses by year, based on data by Mueller-Gillebrand, at the same time subtracting from the final figures those losses suffered away from the Eastern Front, roughly dispersing them over the years. Thus one arrives at the following figures for the Eastern Front (the figure for the army's overall irreplaceable losses for the year is in parentheses): 1941 (from June)–301,000 (307,000), 1942–519,000 (538,000), 1943–668,000 (793,000), 1944–(for this year the losses in December are taken as being equal to those in January) 1,129,000 (1,629,000), and 1945–(up to 1 May) 550,000 (1,250,000).[29] The correlation in all cases is in favour of the *Wehrmacht*: 1941–18.1:1, 1942–13.7:1, 1943–10.4:1, 1944–5.8:1, and 1945–4.6:1. These correlations should be close to the true correlations of irreplaceable losses of the armies of the USSR and Germany on the Soviet-German front, insofar as the losses of the army accounted for the lion's and by far the greater share of all Soviet military losses than for the *Wehrmacht*, while the German air force and navy suffered their main irreplaceable losses during the war beyond the confines of the Eastern Front. As regards the losses among Germany's allies in the East, the undercounting of which somewhat worsens the Red Army's indices, it should be taken into account that in fighting them the Red Army suffered relatively far fewer losses than in the struggle against the *Wehrmacht* and that Germany's allies were far from actively operating throughout the entire war and suffered their greatest losses in prisoners due to general capitulations (Romania and Hungary). Besides this, the losses of those Polish, Czechoslovak, Romanian, and Bulgarian units that fought with the Red Army have not been taken into account on the Soviet side. Thus, on the whole, the correlations put forward here should be sufficiently objective. They show that the improvement in the correlation of irreplaceable losses for the Red Army takes place only from 1944, when the Allies landed in the West and Lend-Lease assistance rendered its maximum effect, both in terms of direct deliveries of munitions and equipment and in the expansion of Soviet military production. The *Wehrmacht* was forced to shift its reserves to the West and could no longer, as had been the case in 1943, carry out active operations in the East.

The German military historian R. Overmans estimates the losses of the German armed forces during the Second World War at 5,318,000 killed, including those who died in captivity. This figure appears exaggerated. It was arrived at in the following manner. Overmans took a representative sample of 7,619 cards from the German investigative service's (*Deutschen Dienstellle*) card catalogue of those personnel of the German armed forces, who were believed to have remained alive following the war. According to his estimate, there were about 15,200,000 cards in the card catalogue of the living. Overmans explained that of the 7,619 people upon whom he based his research, it is possible that 1,100 people (14.4 per cent) died during the course of the war or in captivity, as there was no information that they were alive. These people were declared as having died by the courts or by a decision of the authorities. Having applied this proportion to the whole, Overmans came to the conclusion that approximately 2,200,000 men of the number of those military personnel who were listed as having survived the war should actually be included in the category of those who died during the war, including in this definition postwar captivity. Overmans added to these 1,100 cards 3,051 cards from the card catalogue of those 'reliably killed ,that is, those military personnel whose death was either verified by combat reports or by the testimony of eyewitnesses. Typically, Overmans does not show that women were included among the 10,670 cards researched by him.

According to the estimate by Overamans, there are about 3,100,000 cards (to be exact, 3,078,735 cards at the end of 1994) in this card catalogue and with the rare exception there are no duplicates.[30] On the basis of this sample he determined the structure of those who perished by the years in which they were drafted, the years in which they died, the theatres of military activities, the years of birth, and the areas in which they were drafted, as well as by the service arms. Overmans did not exclude from the card catalogue the likely double counting among the living (possibly equal to the repeat conscription at the end of the war of those previously demobilized) and operates with the overall estimate of 18.2 million mobilized people. At the same time, he broke down according to the year of birth or the areas in which they were drafted only those military personnel from the army, air force and navy, excluding the SS troops, among whom there were many foreigners. Overmans estimated the strength of the SS troops at 900,000 men. It should be noted that there may be double counting among the 'reliably killed' of 3.1 million people, but Overmans believes that very little has been overlooked in this category. Actually, Overmans did not investigate the fate of each of the 1,100 'conditionally killed' studied by him, that is, he was not able to ascertain the time, place, and circumstances of their deaths. The study of this question evidently requires time that goes beyond the life of a single investigator and in a number of cases the task is impossible in principle. Thus Overmans evidently established only the absence of facts in the card catalogues available to him that point to whether a person was alive after the war, although this is probably insufficient to unconditionally assign these people to the category of killed.

At the same time, the sample made by Overmans is not completely correct. According to his assumption, the cards for 3.1 million killed are in the card catalogue of those who died (*Totenkartei*), which, according to his estimate, account for 58 per cent of all those killed. At the same time, the cards for 2.2 million people, whom Overmans considers to have perished, should be in the general card catalogue for the *Wehrmacht's* military personnel (*Allgemeine Kartei*) and should account for 52 per cent of all who perished. However, in his sample Overmans took 3,051 cards from the card catalogue of those who died, which account for 74 per cent of the sample, while only 1,100 cards were taken from the general card catalogue of *Wehrmacht* military personnel, or 26 per cent of the entire sample. Thus that part of the sample which deals with 'conditionally killed' is less precise and may by itself inflate the number of conditionally killed by 100–200,000 people.[31]

Some of the 'conditionally killed', particularly from the number of wounded and invalids, could very likely have died after the war due to natural causes, while others could have gone missing due to a change of address or migration to other countries. One must also take into account the fact that they first of all released from Soviet captivity invalids and those suffering from dystrophy, who had a greater chance of dying in the first months or years following their return to their homeland and before they were able to establish contact with their relatives. Under conditions in which as a result of the war almost half of the population of Germany and Austria was forced to either change their place of residence, while these countries themselves were divided into occupation zones, and while Germany did not have its own government until the end of 1949, the search for relatives and acquaintances was a difficult and prolonged process. The entire German army ended up in captivity following the capitulation, which more than doubled the number of irreplaceable losses and eliminated the structure which was supposed to count losses.

One should also bear in mind that no less than 2 million prisoners of war were released by the Soviet, American, and British occupation authorities in the first weeks and months following the end of the war. They were not registered as prisoners and therefore did not go into the existing databases. People from the youngest and oldest draft cohorts predominated among the released prisoners, as well as the wounded and invalids. It is probable that it was particularly difficult for these people to establish contact with their relatives in the postwar confusion; while on the other hand, they had a high likelihood of dying as early as the first postwar years. Many of these could have ended up among the 2.2 million 'conditionally killed'.

In 1963 the number of reliably killed military personnel was 2,960,923 men. By the end of 1994 this number had grown to 3,078,735 men.[32] Of 2.2 conditionally killed the death of 1,095,787 was recognized by the courts through the declaration of relatives, who had not had any contact with them following the war. Another 1,154,744 people are considered to be missing in action and are registered as having perished by the authorities, as there has been no information about them for an extended period of time to say that they are alive.[33] The decision to recognize them as dead was adopted on the initiative of the interested parties – relatives trying to get inheritances, to dissolve a marriage, and so forth, or bureaucrats trying to exclude them from the unified system of social security. All of these decisions could only have been adopted after 1956, when the process of returning the German prisoners was completed.

Of the 5,318,000 who perished and went missing in action, 4,737,000 of these were on the territory of the Reich, including Austria, the Sudetenland, and the Protectorate of Bohemia and Moravia. A total of 610,000 who perished and went missing in action are foreigners who served in the *Wehrmacht*, as well as conscripts and volunteers from the territories of Poland, France (Alsace and Lorraine), Luxembourg, Denmark, and Belgium, annexed during the course of the war. Besides this, the figure of 5,318,000 includes a significant number of soldiers from the *Volkssturm* (78,000), as well as persons not differentiated by branch of service (154,000, including 63,500 policemen, a number of whom did not take part in combat operations).[34] The number who perished and went missing in action among those born between 1873 and 1889 is 36,332 people, while 142,482 were called up from these years.[35] This means that a quarter of all of those of these ages who were called up perished, which is a little more than the index for all who perished – 29.1 per cent, if you attach the number of 5,318,00 to the entire call-up of 18.3 million people, without counting those called back into the national economy. Such a high percentage of perished and dead for aged persons seems unlikely, taking into account the fact that they only took part in the fighting in rare cases, even if one factors in the increased mortality of this cohort from diseases. If one takes the overall number of those persons mobilized who were born in 1900 and older – 1,472,000 people, then the number of those who perished and went missing is equal to 288,310 people, which is 19.6 per cent. This index seems too high.

If the figure of 5.3 million who perished is accurate, then according to the calcualations by Overmans, it works out that during the final 10 months of the war almost as many German military personnel perished as during the preceding 4½ years, primarily due to the mass murder of prisoners in the final months of the war and soon after the capitulation, chiefly on the Eastern Front. In all, according to the estimate by Overmans, during 1944 and 1945 respectively 1.8 and 1.54 million men perished, including those who died in captivity.[36] At the same time, he assigns 135,000 of those who perished to 1946 and later. As Overmans supposes, during the final three months of the war about a million German military personnel perished, including those who died in captivity. However, it is known that the *Wehrmacht* suffered its chief losses in the final year of the war in prisoners, and not killed or wounded, while the strength of the German army was irreversibly shrinking, so that there's no place for millions of perished. Also, the quantity of those who died, particularly in the West, where the overwhelming majority of prisoners were released during the first two postwar years, could not have been so great.

What is also striking is that the 'conditionally dead' are mainly from the Eastern Front (there their share is 41.4 per cent, while it is 15.0 per cent in the West), as well as the battles of the last five months of the war, when the share of 'conditionally dead' reaches 56.7 per cent. But this is from that front and that period when it is most difficult to establish the fate of German military personnel, which in no way means that they perished.

A significant number of the foreigners listed among the irreplaceable losses did not actually die and did not enter prisoner of war camps. For example, a large part of the SS 14th Division ('Galicia') (up to 10,000 men), which ended up in the Brody 'cauldron' in July 1944, went over to the Ukrainian Insurrection Army (UPA). The same was true of the main part of the SS 19th Latvian Division, which ended the war in Courland and which did not capitulate, but left for their homes and to a significant degree subsequently made up the core of the 'forest brothers'.[37] Of approximately 14,000 military personnel, only 1,477 capitulated.[38] Actually, a significant part of the foreigners listed among the 2.2 million who conditionally perished could have remained alive.

According to the estimate by R. Overmans, which is based on the card catalogue in the German search service, 22,000 people died in American captivity, 34,000 in French, 21,000 in British, 11,000 in Yugoslav, and 363,343 in Soviet captivity. Besides this, another 8,100 persons died in captivity, but it is not known whose.[39] The overall number of those who died in captivity will then amount to 459,500, which is significantly less than the search service's estimate, which relates to the beginning of the 1950s. However, this data concerns only those military personnel whose death was reliably established, and thus may significantly understate the number of those who died in captivity, particularly in the West. Overmans estimates the overall number of prisoners in the USA at 3.1 million, 3.64 million in Great Britain, 940,000 in France, 3.060 million in the USSR, 190,000 in Yugoslavia, and 170,000 men in other countries.[40]

One should bear in mind that despite a ban there was illegal immigration from Germany during the first postwar year, which became legal after 1950. For example, during 1941–50 14,400 people of 'German extraction' entered

Canada.[41] Evidently practically all of them entered after 1945 and a significant part of them consisted of former military personnel. There probably also existed emigration to the USA and the countries of Latin America, as well as to the Scandinavian countries and the Iberian peninsula. In all, the number of emigrants among the former military personnel could have exceeded 100,000 people. Besides this, hundreds of thousands, if not millions, of German prisoners were transported to the USA and Canada. It's quite possible that many of them managed to remain in these countries and began a new life, preferring not to return to Germany or Austria, especially if they had no hope of finding their families or came from regions from which the German population had been deported.

The centralized draft into the Red Army, taking into account the peacetime army, amounted to 34,476,700 people.[42] Of course, it wasn't every month that 40,000 or 100,000 and more people were called up, but something on the order of 10 *fronts* were operating simultaneously, and conscription en masse directly into the units began from the time of the counteroffensive around Rostov-on-Don in November and around Moscow in December 1941 and continued all the way up to the victory in May 1945. Millions of men were conscripted directly into the units throughout the war. In order that the estimate of losses is as accurate as possible, it is sufficient that the number of those conscripted directly into their units be in the order of 7 million men, or, taking the period from December 1941 to May 1945 inclusively, an average of about 170,000 per month. As became clear earlier, in some months even one of the *fronts* had an index sufficiently close to this figure.

The correlation of irreplaceable losses speaks best about the level of the combat-capability of the Red Army and *Wehrmacht*. According to the author's research, which was conducted by using various methods of calculation and the entire accessible database, the Soviet Union's losses in the Great Patriotic War ranged from 40.1 to 40.9 million who died, of which the Red Army accounted for 26.9 million. The correlation of losses in killed and perished with the *Wehrmacht* for the entire war is 10:1 in favour of the German side.

During the period from 22 June 1941 to 31 May 1944 the German army on the Eastern Front lost 763,313 killed, 543,275 missing in action, and 2,869,956 wounded. Total irreplaceable losses were 1,306,588 people. During the period from 1 June 1944 to 20 April 1945 German losses in the East were 258,473 killed, 832,750 missing in action, and 1,182,525 wounded. Total irreplaceable losses for this period were 1,091,223 men. However, a colossal undercounting was observed in the ongoing reports of irreplaceable losses in the encircled groups of forces during this period. In particular, summary figures from the Iasi–Kishinev operation (predominantly prisoners) were not included among the irreplaceable losses, as well as a significant part of the losses suffered during the Red Army's offensive between the Vistula and Oder rivers in January to February 1945. The counted irreplaceable losses for June 1944 to April 1945 proved to be less than the irreplaceable losses for the three preceding years of the war in the East by only 1.2 times. But the correlation of losses in wounded and killed in the first three years of the war is 3.8:1, which is sufficiently close to the actual correlation of killed and wounded in the German army and proves that the overwhelming majority of those missing in action during this period ended up in captivity. And during the war's last year there were already 4.6 prisoners for each man killed. This proves that a significant number of those killed actually were among those killed, even taking into account the fact that many wounded ended up in captivity. If one assumes that the average correlation of killed and wounded in the *Wehrmacht* was close to 1:3, then the number of those killed who ended up among those missing in action in the first three years of the war may be estimated at 193,400 men, and 135,700 men during the final year of the war. Then the overall number of killed may be correspondingly estimated at 956,700 and 394,200 men respectively. If one assumes that German losses in killed during the last ten days of April and the first ten days of May were approximately equally and were approximately equal to the losses for the first ten days of April, when losses were counted more or less completely and amounted to 5,818 killed and consider all 4,781 missing in action to have been prisoners, then the German army's losses in the final 20 days of the war may be estimated at approximately 12,000 men. However, the actual number of killed among the missing in action was significantly higher due to uncounted losses, including those in the Iasi–Kishinev 'cauldron'. If one assumes that among all of the remaining uncounted missing in action during the period from June 1944 to May 1945 the overall number of killed accounted for at least half of the overall number killed in the Iasi–Kishinev 'cauldron', that is, about 50,000 men, then the overall number of killed for this period may be estimated at a minimum at 555,000 men. This proves to be only 1.7 times less than during the first three years of the war. Having taken Soviet losses in killed for the period from June 1944 to 10 May 1945 at 1.260 per cent of the average monthly for the war (it turns out that they even rose somewhat during the final months in comparison with the first three years of the Great Patriotic War), and for the first three years of the war at 3.395 per cent of the average monthly figure for the war, and the average for the period from 22 June 1941 through 10 May 1945, then the correlation of losses in killed between the Red Army and the *Wehrmacht* was 10:1 in favour of the *Wehrmacht*, this means that during the period from 22 June 1941 to 31 May 1944 this correlation was equal to 16.6:1, and from 1 June 1944 to 10 May 1945 it was 6.6:1. Thus thanks to the opening of the second front by the Allies in Normandy the correlation of losses killed improved for the Red Army at a minimum of 2.5 times.[43] And 13.2 to 14 million civilians perished.

These estimates can be substantiated by comparing data from the censuses of the population in 1939 and 1959, as there is reason to assume that in 1939 there was a very significant undercounting of men in the draft-age cohorts. This is, in particular, indicated by the significant female preponderance, as fixed by the 1939 census, in the 10–19 age bracket, when for purely biological reasons it should be the other way around, with a preponderance of men, while the preponderance of females cannot be the result of any kind of war. This undercounting gradually fell all the way to the census of 1979, which was the most exact of all Soviet censuses, when the female predominance began at 30 years of age, which is as it should be if just biological factors are at work.[44]

In the work 'The Book of Memory. Kimry', in which all the residents of the town of Kimry who perished in the ranks of the Red Army during the Great Patriotic War are listed, there are 12,814 persons.[45] Among these people there is one repeat – on p. 570 the name of Vasilii Dmitrievich Solonev, born in 1921, appears twice. This evidently was the result of a printer's mistake. Besides this, among those listed are 177 civilians (rear area labourers) and 252 military personnel who survived the war. Among them are those who also survived captivity. By subtracting all of these categories, 12,384 military personnel remain from the number of inhabitants of Kimry and the Kimry District of Kalinin (now Tver') Oblast', who perished during the course of the Great Patriotic War. It should also be noted that all of the Red Army soldiers from the Kimry District were incontestably Soviet citizens before 1939 and among those who became prisoners there was almost no chance of remaining in the West following the war.

According to the USSR population census of 1939, the population of the Kalinin Oblast' at the beginning of the year was 3,213,139 people, and the population of the Kimry District, including the town of Kimry, was 93,858 people.[46]

By the beginning of 1940 the population of the Kalinin Oblast' was estimated at 3,221,200 people, and the entire population of the USSR (in the borders at the end of 1940) at 195,954,300 people.[47] The losses of Soviet military personnel, killed and died, estimated by the author at 26.9 million account for 13.7 per cent of the population of the USSR at the beginning of 1940. The number of those who perished and those missing in action military personnel who did not return from the war of the number of inhabitants of the Kalinin Oblast's Kimry District out of the population of the district at the beginning of 1940 is 13.2 per cent, which more or less coincides with the estimate and proves its reliability. One must also take into account the fact that the urban population of the Kimry District, along with the town of Kimry, was 48 per cent in 1939, according to the census data, while in the country as a whole it was only 32.9 per cent.[48] While in 1940, within the new boundaries, the share of the urban population was estimated at 32.3 per cent.[49] The percentage of the urban inhabitants mobilized was lower than in the rural areas as many of them had factory work deferments. Correspondingly, the chance of the inhabitants of the Kimry District dying at the front was a little less than in the country as a whole. It's possible that this difference amounted to 0.5 per cent of the population. Such a small difference also suggests that those who are listed as having perished in the Kimry book have been counted accurately. It is likely that the creation of district books of memory both in Russia and in the other post-Soviet states is the most efficacious means of finally determining the Soviet armed forces' irreplaceable losses during the Great Patriotic War and creating a database of all Soviet military personnel who perished.

Here is another example. Among the population of the Kalinin Oblast's Loknya District, with a 100 per cent rural population, 4,142 inhabitants perished at the front.[50] This is from a population of about 60,700 people at the beginning of 1940, which is only 6.8 per cent. However, one must take into account the fact that 15,576 residents of the Loknya District were sent to Germany as forced labour, of which 6,171 people did not return, which is 10.2 per cent of the district's population. One can assume that the majority of these were mobilized into the Red Army in the final year of the war and perished in its ranks.

If one assumes that the true share of military personnel who perished among the population of the Loknya District at the beginning of 1940 was at least the average nationwide, that is, 13.7 per cent, then the overall number of Red Army men who perished may be estimated at 8,316 men. In this case, the number of 4,174 comes from those who were driven into German territory or other occupied territories and who, following their liberation, were mobilized into the Red Army and perished in its ranks. This amounts to 67.6 per cent of the overall number of those who perished among the *ostarbeiters* and other forced labourers, which seems to be a perfectly realistic number.

In the Gork'ii Oblast's Voznesenskoe District, of the 7,713 men who left for the front, 3,870 perished, or 50.2 per cent. Among them, 1,831 men, or 47.3 per cent of those who perished, went missing in action.[51] According to the 1939 census the district's population was 38,336 people, which by the beginning of 1940 could have grown to 38,830.[52] Then the number of those who perished will be 10 per cent of the district's population in 1940. Even though this data was taken from the 'Book of Memory', which was published in 1994, one may assume here that there was undercounting. The district is completely rural, although it is possible that part of the population could have worked in the factories in Gor'kii and received a deferment.

The Vologda researcher Pavel Shabanov notes that the population of the Vologda Oblast's Nikol'skoe District, according to the 1939 census, was 55,085 people. According to data from the district military commissariat a total of 11,066 people were mobilized in the district, that is, 20 per cent of the population, while 5,146 perished on the Great Patriotic War's fronts, while noting that at the beginning of his research there were only 3,447 cards for those who perished in the district military commissariat.

According to data from the 'Book of Memory' for the Vologda Oblast', which appeared in 1993, 7,175 (7,169 according to the electronic version) from the Nikol'skoe District perished –13 per cent of the population and 65 per cent of those conscripted. In all, as of 4 May 2015, there are 170,699 entries for those military personnel who perished and were missing in action in the Vologda Oblast's electronic book of memory. At the same time, the printed version of the book, which appeared in 1992, lists 178,711 who perished. P.N. Shabanov is amazed: 'During these years the search detachments returned hundred and thousands of names from obscurity, and the list of those who fell became shorter?' In the Nikol'skoe District, besides the 7,175 who perished, there are 3,181 who went missing in action. But to all appearances this is a case of double counting. Otherwise it works out that even when counting those who served in the peacetime army, almost no one returned from the front in the Nikol'skoe District.

The population of the Vologda Oblast's Kichmengskii Gorodok District was 51,512 people in 1941. Of these, 10,500 people took part in the Great Patriotic War, or 20.3 per cent of the population and 7,126 people did not return from the war, meaning 13.8 per cent of the district's population perished, or 67 per cent of those conscripted. And in Cherepovets, with a population of 30,000 prewar residents, 4,097 people perished, or 13.7 per cent. In P.N. Shabanov's opinion, these statistics can be applied to the population of the USSR at the beginning of the war, or 200 million people, which yields approximately 27 million military personnel who perished; and if one takes the average index for the three districts of the Vologda Oblast' then the share of those who perished is 13 per cent of the overall population; 9,271 people from the Vologda District returned from the war, while 11,632 did not return.[53]

Data from the book of memory for the Altai Krai shows that in all 243,284 military personnel called up from this region perished. The overall number of draftees was about 500,000 people.[54] In this case the mortality rate among the conscripts is about 48.7 per cent, which is less than the overall average for the country. This may be partially explained by the fact that part of the conscripts from the Altai Krai served in the forces stationed in the Far East and suffered almost no combat losses.

However, it is more likely this is a definite case of undercounting of losses. The compilers of the book of memory based their work on data from the military commissariats and, as has become clear through the example cited by I.I. Ivlev for the Archangel Oblast', approximately a quarter of all death and missing in action notifications did not reach the military commissariats. If approximately the same situation existed in the Altai Krai and if one allows that the number of those who perished, as presented in the book of memory, reflects for the most part data from the military commissariats, then the true number of those who perished out of the number of conscripts from the Altai Krai may be estimated at 324,400 people, or 64.9 per cent. It's most likely that the share of those who perished is somewhat lower, as the actual number of those conscripted was, in all likelihood, more than 500,000 people.

It is known that of 22,000 communists conscripted for the front from the Altai Krai, more than 16,000 did not return home.[55] Thus the share of those who perished among the Altai communists, whom they counted more accurately than all the other conscripts, is 72 per cent, which is even higher than the author's calculations. But it should be kept in mind that the overwhelming majority of communists were called up to the front in the first months of the war, thus the likelihood of them perishing was higher than for all the conscripts as a whole. After all, many non-party men were called up only in 1943 or 1944.

The volume of German conscription during the Second World War proved to be quite comparable to the Soviets'. In all (taking into account the peace-time army) 17.9 million people were drafted into the *Wehrmacht*, of which about 2 million were recalled for work in the national economy. Thus a pure draft of 15.9 million people accounted for 19.7 per cent of Germany's population of 80.6 million in 1939 (including the population of Austria and the Protectorate of Bohemia and Moravia).[56] The mobilization capability of the USSR and Germany proved to be practically equal as regards the overall size of the population. The Soviet Union was able to mobilize a somewhat larger population thanks to the assistance of the Western Allies in the form of Lend-Lease, which enabled it to free up additional manpower from industry to meet the needs of the front, as well as the fact that any kind of civilian production more or less ceased as early as 1941, while as late as 1943 in Germany a significant part of industry was producing goods to satisfy the civilian population's needs. Besides this, in the USSR women, the elderly, and teenagers were employed for work in the national economy to a much greater degree. In Germany the mobilization capability grew thanks to the employment of foreign workers and prisoners of war (5,655,000 people in September 1944).[57]

Up until November 1944 the *Wehrmacht's* irreplaceable losses were sufficiently accurately counted according to data from the personal (by name) counting produced by Germany's military-accounting institutions. During the period from 1 September 1939 to 31 December 1944 the army lost 1,750,000 men killed on the battlefield, as well as those who died from wounds, disease, accidents, and other causes, with 1,609,700 missing in action. During this same period the navy lost 60,000 men killed and 100,300 missing in action, and the air force 155,000 killed and 148,500 missing in action. Losses for the period from 1 January to 30 April 1945 were estimated by the central accounting bodies at 250,000 for the army and 1 million missing in action, 5,000 killed, and 5,000 missing in action for the navy, and 10,000 killed and 7,000 missing in action for the air force.[58] According to the type of calculations, all of the army's missing in action during the period from 1 January to 30 April 1945 may be assigned to the category of prisoners. Also, the majority of those who went missing in action during this period from the navy and air forces may also be considered prisoners. Taking into account data on the number of prisoners on different fronts, it can be estimated that the number of those who perished in the German army from the beginning of the war until the end of 1944 was 2,496,000 men. The overall number of those who perished among the German armed forces, including the *Luftwaffe* and *Kriegsmarine*, may be estimated at 4 million men, of which 0.8 million died in captivity, including 0.45–0.50 million in the USSR, and 0.3–0.35 million in the West.[59] In all, approximately 11.6 million German military personnel became prisoners, including more than 8 million in the West.[60] Of this number, according to the author's estimate, about 2.6 million German military personnel perished in the East, of which about 100,000 were from the *Luftwaffe* and Kriegsmarine.[61]

One may allow that up to half of the 2.2 million German military personnel who were not found remained alive. In this case, the estimate of General Muller-Gillebrand of the number of victims for the German armed forces as 4 million men can be seen as the most realistic.

It's impossible today to estimate Germany's overall irreplaceable losses, just as it is impossible to estimate the civilian population's losses. Estimates of civilian losses of 2–2.5 million civilians who perished during the Second

World War, which are encountered from time to time, are conditional and not reinforced by any kind of reliable statistics or demographic balances.[62] The latter are almost impossible to compile due to the significant changes in boundaries and the migrations of the population after the war.

During the Soviet-Finnish War of 1939–40 the correlation of killed and died was 7.2:1 not in favour of the Red Army.[63] One may assume that the same correlation held true during 1941–4. Then in the fighting with the Finnish forces the Red Army could have lost up to 408,000 killed and dead from wounds. One must also take into account the fact that the Red Army's irreplaceable losses in the war with Japan numbered 12,000 men.[64] It may be assumed that the Red Army's losses in the fighting with Germany's remaining allies were approximately equal to that of the enemy. Then in this fighting the Red Army could have lost up to 284,000 men. In the battles against the *Wehrmacht* the Red Army's losses in those who died should number about 22.2 million killed and those who died from their wounds versus approximately 2.1 killed and died on the German side. This yields a correlation of losses of 10.6:1.

Such an unfavourable correlation of losses for Russia (USSR) in two world wars is explained first of all by Russia's overall economic and cultural backwardness in comparison with Germany and the Western Allies. In the case of the Second World War, the situation was exacerbated as a result of the peculiarities of Stalinist totalitarianism, which had destroyed the army as an effective instrument for waging war. Stalin was not able to overcome this backwardness in twenty years, but at the same time remained firmly in the late-imperial tradition and preferred to win not through skill, but through the loss of a great deal of blood, in that he saw a potential threat to the regime in the creation of a highly professional army. But nevertheless the Soviet Union was forced to pay in tens of millions of human lives not so much for Stalinist totalitarianism in and of itself, as for the desire to preserve and expand the empire.

The totalitarian system guaranteed the state's solidity during the period of the heaviest defeats. The defeats did not result in a revolution, and the Soviet Union was able to win the final victory. But the fact that Germany attacked the USSR during the actual absence of a second front in Europe led to a situation in which the German army's main ground forces, as opposed to the First World War, fought against the Red Army during 1941–5 (while the *Luftwaffe's* and the *Kriegsmarine's* main forces fought against the Western Allies throughout the war). This led to a situation in which the Red Army's irreplaceable losses in the Great Patriotic War exceeded significantly the Russian army's losses during the First World War. The losses of the Anglo-American forces in killed were equal to or even less than German losses on those fronts of the Second World War where the *Wehrmacht* had to fight against the Western Allies.[65]

In all, in the war against the USSR the German armed forces lost during the period from 22 June 1941 through 20 April 1945 1,021,786 killed (including 1,373 in Norway and northern Finland), 4,052,481 wounded (including 60,419 in Norway and northern Finland), and 1,376,025 missing in action (including 6,851 in Norway and northern Finland). Overall losses are 6,450,392 (including 83,643 in Norway and northern Finland). It should also be noted that the German forces suffered some small losses in the fighting against the Red Army in the Balkans during 1944–5, but their number is still impossible to establish. At the same time, the German army lost from 1 September 1939 to 20 April 1945 1,211,222 killed, 4,708,977 wounded, and 2,394,751 missing in action. Overall losses for this period were 8,314,950 men.[66] Of these, 84.4 per cent of the killed, 86.1 per cent of the wounded, and 57.5 per cent of the missing in action were incurred on the Soviet-German front. The sum share of the Soviet-German front in irreplaceable losses is 66.5 per cent and 77.6 per cent in overall losses. The Eastern Front's reduced share in irreplaceable losses compared to overall losses is explained by the large number of prisoners taken by the Anglo-American allies in the West.

A German soldier who fought in the Leningrad area recalled:

> We were witnesses to how they threw unarmed soldiers into the attack along the Volkhov River and how they picked up the rifles of their fallen comrades, and how the NKVD troops aimed the barrels of their machine guns at the backs of the attackers so that they would not even think about retreating. Having no choice, they went into the attack against our well defended positions and were either killed, just as in a slaughterhouse, or captured.[67]

And Hermann Neidermeyer from the 1st SS Panzer Division *Leibstandarte* thus described the fighting around Millerovo on 27 December 1942:

> We laid in our foxholes and saw how the masses of Red Army soldiers, thousands of black dots against the background of the boundless snowy desert, threw themselves against us with cries of 'hurrah'. Our commanders gave the command to open fire. The bursts of our machine guns gathered a bloody harvest from the shortest distance. Cartridge belt followed cartridge belt. When we were finished with the first wave of attackers a new one burst upon us, which the same fate awaited. In very short order our unit was surrounded by an enormous number of killed and wounded Red Army

soldiers, the groans of which we could distinctly hear. The snow was no longer visible, as if it had become black. Our own losses were insignificant.[68]

Evidently all of the quoted figures for the sides are of different orders. Such a monstrous correlation of irreplaceable losses for the Soviet side was due to the extremely low level of combat training of the overwhelming majority of the Red Army's soldiers and commanders. This can be explained by the following circumstance. One could convince a German, American, British, Polish, or some other soldier from the Western armies that the zealous study of military affairs in peacetime could significantly increase his chances of survival in an actual battle. There is no possibility of convincing a Soviet soldier, and perhaps a modern Russian one, of this, as he well understands that the last thing his commanders are going to worry about in conditions of actual combat is saving his life and thus treats military training in a slipshod manner. This is explained by the very low price placed on human life in the USSR, particular in the Stalin era. That Stalin preferred to deal with a militia army, because he saw in a highly professional army the threat of a new 'Bonaparte' appearing, was a significant factor. Fear of Bonapartism following, as Stalin hoped, a Soviet victory in the Second World War explains the repressions of 1937–8 against the higher command element, which deprived the Red Army of many independently thinking commanders in which Stalin saw potential candidates for a 'Bonaparte'. The repressions also negatively influenced the Red Army in the sense that they strengthened the commanders' fear of making independent decisions. This also led to a rise in losses. The relative backwardness of the Russian imperial army in comparison with the German army, which manifested itself during the First World War, also played its part. Then the correlation of killed was 7:1 in favour of the Germans.[69] This gap increased further during the interwar period. As regards those killed in the Russian and German armies in the First World War, it is more appropriate to compare not the overall correlation of killed and dead between the Red Army and the *Wehrmacht* in 1941–5 (10:1), but the correlation from June 1941 to May 1944 (16.6:1). After all, the presence of the second front exerted a decisive influence on the correlation of losses between the German and Soviet sides during the last ten months of the war. Actually, the correlation of the number of killed between the *Wehrmacht* and the Red Army was the same as in the wars of the metropolitan countries against the militias of the colonial peoples.

In the First World War Russia collapsed as early as February 1917 and its army fell apart. The USSR was victorious in the Great Patriotic War and the relatively weaker, in comparison with the czarist army, Red Army entered Berlin. The super totalitarian Stalinist system ruled out a revolution even during the period of the heaviest defeats, the scope of which the majority of the population had no idea about. The enormous losses led to a situation in which the surviving soldiers and officers were constantly removed from the front line for reforming and the period of their uninterrupted service at the front rarely exceeded a month. Therefore the Red Army did not suffer that demoralization throughout the entire war that began in the czarist army as early as the end of 1916 and beginning of 1917 due to the troops' prolonged occupation of the trenches.

Stalin did not know of the true magnitude of Soviet losses, nor did he strive to know them, although it is possible that he guessed that they significantly exceeded the Germans'. But the dictator did not overly trouble himself with this. The price of victory did not concern him. The main thing was that he achieved, if not all, then many geopolitical goals – he revived the Russian Empire and created enormous spheres of Soviet influence in Eastern Europe and eastern Asia.

This is how the writer K.M. Simonov, who often met with Stalin and who dreamed of writing an artistic-documentary chronicle of the Great Patriotic War, evaluated Stalin's attitude toward losses:

> It would be foolish, of course, to assume that Stalin, as the supreme commander-in-chief, did not want to avoid the heaviest losses in each case.
>
> But the fact of the matter is that the style of leadership from above, which issued from Stalin, and first of all that feature of this leadership style, was linked to the systematic and constant lateness in switching from offensive to defence, in the desire to squeeze everything out of the troops, the final kilometers, in which they lost most of all, and to halt as late as possible, against the proposals and reports of the army and *front* commanders – this leadership style objectively led to a wasting of forces, to unjustifiably heavy losses at the end of each operation and thus, in the final analysis – to a delay in the beginning of the following operation, or to a reduction in the time for its planning and preparation. This, in its turn, led once again to excessive losses.
>
> In a word, this feature of the style of leadership inevitably led to heavier losses than might have been given another leadership style.
>
> Try to psychologically unearth why he acted this way. What spoke in him, aside from ruthlessness toward people and an indifference to losses? The desire to squeeze out of people everything of which they were capable? To mobilize internal resources?[70]

Simonov accurately noted Stalin's complete indifference to losses among the Soviet troops, as well as the desire to always attack without fail, and to attack for as long as possible, until the troops were completely exhausted and all resources, human and materiel, had been spent. But in this sense he was no different to his generals and officers of lower rank. Aleksei Pivovarov's film, *The Second Shock Army. Vlasov's Betrayed Army*, quotes a story by Aleksandr Orlov, a battlefield searcher, about how in retreat Soviet soldiers blew up medical vehicles containing the wounded so that they would not be captured, and the battlefield searchers managed to find such vehicles. And in another source, the recollections of a veteran of the 2nd Shock Army describe how the commander ordered them to focus on preserving the equipment, as people could always be found.

Stalin considered heavy losses not only inevitable, but in some ways even useful. On the one hand, the soldiers often attacked, while on the other hand, due to heavy losses, they were at the front a comparatively short time. Divisions that had lost the main part of their combat element were sometimes pulled back into the rear for reforming within a few days after of being at the front. Thus there did not arise the demoralization among the troops, including the rear units, which arose in the Russian imperial army at the end of 1916 and the beginning of 1917 in the conditions of a prolonged positional war, which became one of the reasons behind the February revolution.

One Soviet historian wrote with pride:

> Thanks to the all-round assistance from the local party and soviet organizations, the army had received more than 400 new divisions by the end of 1941. In the extremely difficult conditions of the war the country created in half a year an armed force exceeding that which it disposed of before the attack by Hitler's Germany, which enabled us to halt the offensive by the enemy forces. Such a mobilization of human and materiel resources in such a short time could only be accomplished by the Soviet state. The USA needed two years (from January 1941 through December 1942) to form 36 new divisions, given the absence of military operations on its territory.[71]

Strictly speaking, the USA was formally outside the war for almost all of 1941 and was not able to create divisions with the kind of intensity as the belligerent powers did. But the chief reason for the yawning gap in the number of divisions formed lay elsewhere. The Americans established exactly as many divisions at that moment as they required for the landing in North Africa and for the struggle in the Pacific Ocean, where maritime battles were unfolding initially. On the other hand, these divisions were well trained and the

400 newly created Soviet divisions were several times inferior to them in this regard. Actually, the Soviet divisions were only poorly trained militia.

In explaining the huge Soviet human losses, German generals usually point to the indifference to the lives of their soldiers on the part of the high command, the poor tactical training of the middle and lower command element, the hackneyed forms employed during the attack, and the inability of both the commanders and soldiers to make independent decisions.[72] One could consider such assertions a simple attempt to lessen the virtues of an enemy who nevertheless won the war, were it not for numerous analogous statements from the Soviet side. For example, Zhores Medvedev, recalls the fighting around Novorossiisk in 1943:[73]

> The Germans had two defensive lines around Novorossiisk, which were well fortified to a depth of approximately three kilometers. It was believed that the artillery preparation had been effective, but it seemed to me that the Germans adapted themselves to it quite rapidly. Having noticed that the equipment was being concentrated and that a powerful fire was beginning, they would fall back to the second line, leaving only a few machine gunners on the front line. They would fall back and observe with the same interest as we did all of the noise and smoke. Then we were ordered to move forward. We moved and set off mines and occupied the trenches, which were already almost empty, with only two or three corpses lying there. Then a second order would be issued – attack the second line. Here up to 80% of the attackers died, as the Germans were sitting in their excellently fortified structures and shot at us at almost point blank range.[74]

The American diplomat, A. Harriman, passed on Stalin's words about how 'in the Soviet Army you have to have more courage to retreat than to attack,' and comments on it thus:[75]

> This phrase by Stalin well shows how aware he was of the situation in the army. We were shocked, but we understood that this is forcing the Red Army to fight . . . Our military men who consulted with the Germans following the war, told me that the most destructive thing in a Russian offensive was its mass character. The Russians came on wave after wave. The Germans literally mowed them down, but as the result of such pressure, one wave would break through.[76]

And here is testimony about the fighting in December 1943 in Belorussia by a former platoon commander from the headquarters of the 273rd Rifle

Division's 812th Artillery Regiment (11th Guards Army), Valentin Potapovich Dyatlov (1923–99), who ended his service in the Red Army as a lieutenant colonel, but who then held the rank of junior lieutenant.[77]

> A line of people in civilian dress passed by me in the communications trench, with huge 'packs' on their backs. 'Brothers, who are you and where are you going,' I asked. 'We're from the Orel region, we're reinforcements.' 'What kind of reinforcements are you when you're in civilian clothes and without rifles?' 'They told us we'd get all that in battle . . .'
>
> The artillery fire against the enemy last five minutes. The artillery regiment's 36 guns 'banged away' at the Germans' front line. The visibility became worse due to the explosions of the shells . . .
>
> And now the attack. The line rose up, weaving like a back and crooked snake. And behind it a second line. And these black, winding and moving snakes looked so ridiculous and unnatural against the gray and white earth! Black against the snow – a perfect target. And the German 'watered' these lines with dense lead. Many firing points sprang into life. Large-caliber machine guns fired from the second trench line. The lines hit the dirt. The battalion commander howled: 'Forward, . . . you mother fuckers! Forward! Into battle! Forward, or I'll shoot you!' But it was impossible to get up. Just try and tear yourself from the ground under artillery, machine gun and automatic rifle fire . . .
>
> The commanders nevertheless tried several times to raise up the 'black' village infantry. But it was all in vain. The enemy fire was so dense that upon running a few steps people would fall as if cut down. We, the artillery men, also were unable to help reliably – there was no visibility, the Germans had masked their firing points well, and, what was most likely, the main machine gun fire came from pillboxes, and thus fire from our guns did not yield the necessary results.

The same individual very eloquently describes the reconnaissance in force, which was so praised by many among the marshals and generals, carried out by a punishment battalion:

> Two battalions from our regiment took part in the fire assault, and that's all. There was silence for a few seconds following our fire. Then the battalion commander leaped up from the trench onto the parapet: 'Laaaaaaaads! For the motherland! For Stalin! After me!

Hurraaaaah!' The punishment soldiers slowly crawled out of the trench and, as if waiting for the last ones, with their rifles held horizontally, ran forward. A groan or a cry with a prolonged 'aaaaaaah', sounded from left to right and then left again, first quieting and then growing stronger. We also leaped out of the trench and ran forward. The Germans launched a series of red rockets toward the attackers and immediately opened a powerful mortar-artillery fire. The lines hit the dirt, and we a little behind them in a longitudinal furrow. It was impossible to raise one's head. How and who could locate the enemy's targets in this hell? His artillery was firing from covered positions and far away from the flanks. Heavy guns were firing as well. Several tanks were firing directly at us and their shells flew whistling over our heads . . .

The punishment soldiers lay before the German trench, on the open field and a small group of bushes, while the German 'threshed' this field, plowing up the earth, the bushes and the bodies of people . . . Only seven men fell back with the punishment battalion, and together there had been 306.[78]

There was actually, so to speak, no attack along this sector. And of the 299 who did not return from the attack, the overwhelming majority perished, although, it's likely that some of the lightly wounded managed to crawl off the battlefield with the onset of darkness.

Accounts of similar senseless and bloody attacks feature in the memoirs and letters of German soldiers and junior officers. One nameless witness describes an attack by units of A.A. Vlasov's Soviet 37th Army against a height occupied by the Germans near Kiev in August 1941, and his description coincides in its details with the story by the Soviet officer cited above. Here are the useless artillery preparation, which missed the Germans' positions, an attack in thick waves which died under the German machine guns, and the unknown commander unsuccessfully trying to raise his people and dying from a German bullet. Similar attacks against a not very important height continued three days in a row. The German soldiers were more struck by the fact that when the entire line died individual soldiers would nevertheless continue to run forward (the Germans were incapable of similar senseless actions). These unsuccessful attacks nevertheless wore out the Germans physically. As one German soldier recalled, he and his comrades were most shaken and depressed by the methodical manner and scale of these attacks: 'If the Soviets can allow themselves to waste so many people in trying to eliminate such insignificant results of our advance, then how often and in what strength will they attack if the target is actually very important?'[79]

And in a letter from a German soldier home during the retreat from Kursk during the second half of 1943, there is described, just as in V. Dyatlov's quoted letter, an attack by almost unarmed and unclothed reinforcements from the recently liberated territories (the very same Orel area), in which the overwhelming majority of participants perished (according to accounts by a witness, even women were among the conscripts). Prisoners told how the authorities suspected the inhabitants of cooperating with the occupation authorities and that the mobilization served as sort of a punishment for them. The very same letter describes an attack by Soviet punishment troops through a German minefield in order to set off mines at the cost of their own lives. And once again the German soldier was struck by the submissiveness of the conscripts and the punishment troops. The captured punishment soldiers 'with rare exceptions, never complained about this sort of treatment', saying that life is hard and that 'one must pay for one's mistakes'.[80] Such submissiveness on the part of the Soviet soldiers clearly shows that the Soviet regime raised not only commanders capable of issuing such inhuman orders, but also soldiers capable of carrying out such orders unquestioningly.

There is testimony from high-ranking Soviet military leaders on the Red Army's inability to fight in a way other than that which incurred a high price in blood. For example, Marshal A.I. Yeremenko, describes in the following manner the peculiarities of the 'military art' of the celebrated (did he really deserve it?) 'marshal of victory', G.K. Zhukov: 'One should say that Zhukov's operational art is a 5–6-fold superiority of force; otherwise he won't take the matter on, and he did not fight with skill, but with quantity, and built his entire career on blood'.[81] By the way, in another case this is how the same A.I. Yeremenko passed on his impressions from his acquaintance with memoirs by German generals: 'The question arises by itself, how is it that the German "heroes," who "defeated" our squad with two men and five men an entire platoon, were unable to carry out their goals during the first period of the war, in which the unarguable numerical and technical advantage was on their side?'[82] It turns out that the irony was just for show, for A.I. Yeremenko actually knew quite well that the German commanders did not exaggerate the correlation of forces in favour of the Red Army. After all, G.K. Zhukov directed the main operations along the important directions and had an overwhelming superiority in men and materiel. It's another matter that the other Soviet generals and marshals did not likely know how to fight in another way to that of G.K. Zhukov, and A.I. Yeremenko himself was not an exception in this matter.

It's possible that had the population of Germany in 1939 been approximately the same as the population of the USA, then the Soviet tactics of 'burying with corpses' would not have worked and, even in the case where Germany fought against a coalition of the USSR, Great Britain and the USA, the Red Army's strength on the Eastern Front would have been exhausted before that of the *Wehrmacht*. However, in reality the population of Germany, even together with the annexed territories, from which conscription into the *Wehrmacht* was carried out (about 80 million people), was 1.7 times less than the population of the USA (131,669,000 people, according to the population census of 1 April 1940, in continental America, with another 2,477,000 in Alaska, Hawaii, Puerto Rico, American Samoa, Guam, the American Virgin Islands, and the Panama Canal Zone[83]) and 2.5 times less than the population of the USSR in its 1941 boundaries.

It should also be noted that the Red Army's enormous irreplaceable losses did not allow it, to the same degree as in the *Wehrmacht* and the armies of the Western Allies, to preserve experienced soldiers and junior officers, which decreased the cohesion and stability of the units and did not allow the reinforcement troops to acquire combat experience from the veterans, which only further increased losses.

As Ye.I. Malashenko, the former scout and officer who after the war served to the rank of lieutenant general, recalled, even in 1945 Soviet forces often operated very ineffectively:

> On 10 March, a few hours before our division's offensive, the reconnaissance group . . . seized a prisoner. He testified that his regiment's main forces had been pulled back 8–10 kilometers into the depth . . . I reported this information to the division commander by telephone, and he reported it to the army commander. The division commander gave us his car to deliver the prisoner to army headquarters. While driving up to the command post, we heard the roar of the beginning artillery preparation. Unfortunately, it was carried out against unoccupied positions. Thousands of shells, which had been delivered with great difficulty over the Carpathians [this took place on the Fourth Ukrainian Front, B.S.], proved to have been expended in vain. The surviving enemy halted our forces' advance with his stubborn resistance.

The same author offers a comparative evaluation of the combat qualities of the German and Soviet soldiers and officers – and not in favour of the Red Army:

> The German soldiers and officers didn't fight badly. The rank and file was well trained, operated skillfully in the offensive and on the defensive. Well-trained NCOs played a more noticeable role in battle

than our sergeants, many of which were almost indistinguishable from privates. The enemy infantry constantly laid down an intensive fire, operated persistently and vigorously in the offensive, defended stubbornly and carried out rapid counterattacks, usually with artillery support and sometimes from air strikes. The tank troops also attacked energetically, fired on the move and with brief halts, maneuvered skillfully and carried out reconnaissance. In the event of failure, they would quickly concentrate their forces along a different axis and often launched attacks along the boundaries and flanks of our units. The artillery opened fire efficiently and sometimes fired very precisely. The artillery disposed of a large quantity of shells. The German officers skillfully organized the battle and directed the actions of their subunits and units, while skillfully taking advantage of the terrain, and carried out manoeuvre along a promising axis in a timely manner. Under the threat of encirclement or defeat, the German units and subunits would carry out an organized withdrawal into the depth, usually in order to occupy a new line. The enemy's soldiers and offices were frightened by rumors about repressions against prisoners, and would surrender without a fight extremely rarely . . .

Our infantry was trained more poorly than the German. However, it fought bravely. Of course, there were cases of panic and untimely withdrawal, particularly in the beginning of the war. The artillery very much helped the infantry, while the most effective was the fire from 'katyushas' in repelling the enemy's counterattacks and in launching strikes against areas where his troops were gathering and concentrating. However, the artillery had few shells in the beginning of the war. I must admit that the tank subunits did not always operate skillfully in attacks. At the same time, they displayed themselves brilliantly in the operational depth while developing the offensive.[84]

Some Soviet generals admitted to the inordinately large losses by the Soviet armed forces during the Great Patriotic War, although this was in no way not risky. For example, Lieutenant General S.A. Kalinin, who earlier commanded an army and an operational group during the Battle of Smolensk and who later prepared reserves, was so careless as to write in his diary that the supreme high command 'does not concern itself with preserving human reserves and allows heavy losses in individual operations'. This one, along with other 'anti-Soviet' remarks, earned the general a twenty-five-year sentence in the camps.[85] Incidentally, as early as the first months of the war, in a report to the military council of the Western Front entitled 'Some Conclusions from the Experience of the First Three Months of War and the Nature of the Close Battle' which was dated 25 September 1941, the very same S.A. Kalinin placed the fear of losses as one of the weaknesses of the enemy, that is, of the Germans. He maintained:

> The main thing that determines all of the combat arms, especially the infantry, is the fear of losses. This phenomenon is sharply expressed and forced the German command to renounce the classical forms of waging the operation and battle [. . .] The inability to attack against a prepared defence. This, evidently, is linked to a shortage of artillery. The fear of night operations, the fear of the bayonet and, as a result, they do not carry out counterattacks. There is sloppiness in the support services, which is evidently the result of conceit.[86]

It's quite typical that a Soviet general attributed the Germans' drive to minimize their losses to the *Wehrmacht's* weaknesses. Evidently Kalinin also ascribed the Red Army's ability to attack without regard to losses to its strengths. And it's probable that Stepan Andrianovich was not alone among the Soviet generals and marshals. Kalinin woke up only towards the end of the war and he suffered cruelly for this. In a denunciation of Kalinin, who in 1944 was the commander of the Khar'kov Military District, the member of the military district military council, Major General P.I. Krainev, noted that Kalinin, in speaking of the Red Army's victories during the course of the war, raised doubts as to the truthfulness of the communications in the domestic press as to the Germans' losses on the Soviet-German front. In his opinion, 'the Red Army loses ten men for every German killed, and that he himself became convinced of this during the defeat of the Germans at Stalingrad'. At the end of April 1944, S.A. Kalinin, while conducting a meeting with the officer element of the 144th and 168th regiments of the 6th Reserve Rifle Brigade, declared: 'It's possible that we will defeat Germany, but there are different kinds of victories.'[87] According to the author's estimate, the correlation of 10:1 in killed between the Red Army and the *Wehrmacht* in favour of the latter is the average for the war.

Such an unfavourable correlation of losses for Russia (USSR) in two world wars in the realm of losses is explained first of all by Russia's overall economic and cultural backwardness in comparison with Germany and the Western Allies. In the case of the Second World War, the situation was exacerbated as a result of the peculiarities of Stalinist totalitarianism, which had destroyed the army as an effective instrument for waging war. Stalin was not able to overcome, as he had urged, in ten years this lag behind the leading capitalist countries, which he determined to be 50–100 years.[88] But at the same time he remained firmly in the late-imperial tradition and preferred to win not through skill, but through a great deal of blood as he saw a potential threat to the regime in the creation of a highly professional army.

It's interesting that as opposed to the First World War, the Red Army in the Great Patriotic War expended more munitions that did the German army and its allies on the Eastern Front – 8 million tons versus 5.6 million tons.[89] This is due to the circumstance that the German artillery mostly employed aimed fire, while the Soviet artillery fired over areas. As opposed to widespread opinion, the Soviet forces' much better provisioning with munitions, compared to that of the Russian army in the First World War, did not result in a reduction in the Red Army's human losses.

The USSR's relative military weakness in comparison to Germany, as paradoxical as it may sound, helped Stalin to win the war. In choosing between the two totalitarian regimes, the Western democracies inevitably had to end up on the side of the weaker party, who presented less of a threat to them, and thus guaranteed him victory.

Chapter 13

Epilogue: Soviet Heroic Myths and Real Feats

Soviet heroic myths from the time of the Great Patriotic War, as a rule, have little in common with reality. They had a purely propaganda significance and, in the main, were invented by political workers and military journalists, and after the war continued to be printed uncritically by Soviet propagandadists. Myths about heroes were most often called upon to mask the Red Army's actual failures.

One of the most famous myths is the myth of the five Red Fleet sailors, who at the cost of their lives halted German tanks around Sevastopol' on 7 November 1941, on the twenty-fourth anniversary of the October revolution. These sailors became the heroes of Andrei Platonov's story, 'Inspired People'.[1]

But what actually happened? In the official citation for awarding the title of Hero of the Soviet Union to Nikolai Fil'chenkov, Vasilii Tsibul'ko, Daniil Odintsov, Ivan Krasnosel'skii, and Yurii Parshin, it was stated that on 7 November 1941 in the area of the village of Duvankoi:

> The enemy, with seven tanks and up to two companies of infantry, began an attack against height 103.4. Comrade Shikaev [the secretary of the party bureau of the 18th Independent Battalion and senior political officer, B.S.] organized a tank destruction group headed by senior political officer [actually, officer] Fil'chenkov [in the document on awarding the title of Hero of the Soviet Union, he was mistakenly identified as Fil'chenko, B.S.] . . . With a heavy machine gun and two soldiers, he advanced to the firing position and began to cut off the enemy infantry . . . In this uneven battle five sailors, led by Fil'chenkov, destroyed three fascist tanks and the remainder, unable to withstand the sailors' pressure, turned back. The Hitlerites resumed the attack, this time with the support of 15 tanks . . . The wounded sailors did not abandon the battlefield, while destroying and putting out of action the fascist vehicles. The valiant machine gunner V.G. Tsibul'ko was mortally wounded and I.M. Krasnosel'skii died the death of a hero. The bullets and the bottles with

flammable liquid ran out. Then N.D. Fil'chenkov, having strapped grenades to himself, threw himself under the treads of an approaching tank. Yu.K. Parshin and D.S. Odintsov followed his example. The hero-sailors destroyed up to 10 enemy tanks in this battle. The enemy was halted.[2]

L.N. Yefimenko, the former commissar of the 8th Independent Naval Infantry Brigade, which was next to the 18th Independent Battalion, tells in greater detail in his memoirs about the fighting on 7 November:

Soon the main theme of conversation in the trenches became the feat that had been accomplished . . . along the sector of the 18th Independent Naval Infantry Battalion . . . The first reports of this feat reached us through messengers and instantaneously spread throughout the brigade. However, at first no one knew the surnames of the heroes, and the details of everything that had happened were related in different ways.

On the evening of 8 November I got in touch with my neighbors by telephone and asked the commissar of the 18th Battalion, Senior Political Officer Mel'nik, if he could come to the command post of the nearest battalion of our brigade to him – the second. We met within about forty minutes, and this is what I heard . . .

'Fil'chenkov let us know at the command post that tanks had appeared and that he and his fellow sailors would try to delay them. Seven tanks were moving and Fil'chenkov's group lay down across their path with grenades and bottles. They knocked out three scout tanks. The remainder turned back and the Germans, evidently from fear, did not understand that there were only five of our people . . . And then there appeared fifteen tanks. We had already prepared to meet them on the front line. But Fil'chenkov decided not to allow them as far as the battalion line. And he did not. Five sailors destroyed another several tanks. They had a good number of grenades, but, as you can understand, there weren't enough for such a fight. The grenades are running low and the tanks are crawling forward . . . In order to somehow delay them, our boys began to throw themselves under the treads with grenades. First Fil'chenkov, then two sailors after him, who, it seems, were already wounded . . . The entire five perished. The last one, Vasilii Tsibul'ko, died in the arms of our corpsman, Petrenko. Most of what is known came from him. We're clarifying the details, as someone saw the fight from a distance. The other three sailors were named Ivan Krasnosel'skii, Yurii

Parshin and Daniil Odintsov, but I don't know anything more about
them . . . The battalion is new and everyone is a stranger . . .[3]

In a leaflet from 1942 it was maintained that the red sailors burned three
tanks out of seven with grenades and bottles of flammable liquid. Within
approximately 2 hours another fifteen tanks arrived to relieve them and the
main battle was joined:

Again Tsibul'ko fires on the viewing apertures and with his first
burst knocks out one tank. But now the bullets have run out; and
Tsibul'ko grabs some grenades, crawls toward the tank approaching him, tosses two grenades, and a second tank is knocked out!
He throws himself against a third one and throws his last grenades
. . . The third tank began to spin around with a broken tread, but
Tsibul'ko himself was mortally wounded. Then Krasnosel'skii ran
out with four bottles and with a sure throw he set one tank afire,
then another, and then fell dead, shot by the enemy. Three remained
– Fil'chenkov, Parshin and Odintsov. Five German tanks were
already within fifty meters. And then Fil'chenkov decided on something unheard of – to halt the tanks with his own chest. He parts
with his comrades and ties the grenades to his belt . . . Fil'chenkov
jumps up and runs toward the forward tank, toward death. The tank
approaches closer and the hero throws himself under the tracks. An
explosion erupts and the tank lists heavily to one side. Parshin and
Odintsov, following the example of their hero commander, throw
themselves under the tanks with grenades. These two tanks also
blow up. And then the incredible happened: the remaining eight
German tanks swiftly turned around [such an 'incredible thing' is a
common feature of a myth; this was the official myth regarding the
death of a Russian landing company around Ulus-Kert in Chechnya
in March 2000, where it is maintained that the Chechens, having
destroyed the landing party, were frightened of their valour and fell
back, although there was no one in their path, B.S.] . . . At the cost
of their lives the heroes destroyed up to ten tanks and on that day
blocked the enemy's path to Sevastopol' with their own bodies . . .[4]

The leaflet also contained this happy finale: their comrades from the battalion
came to the aid of the five and pushed the Germans back from the battlefield,
where they found the bleeding Tsibul'ko. The latter was able to tell about his
comrades' death before his own. The lack of credibility of the episode with
the five Sevastopol' sailors is obvious, as they say, to the naked eye. What was

the sense of throwing oneself under tanks with batches of grenades? Only to then weaken the force of the explosion with one's own body? After all, if they managed to make it almost all the way to the tank, it's far simpler to throw a grenade or a bottle of flammable liquid under its tread. But propaganda specifically required a sacrifice. The heroes were supposed to destroy the enemy at the price of their own lives. This is how the myth evolved of the sailors who threw themselves under the enemy tanks.

The episode with political officer Fil'chenkov's five sailors likely lacks any kind of real foundation. The fact of the matter is that on 7 November 1941 the Sevastopol' sailors, whatever their desire, could not have destroyed ten German tanks as at that time the German-Romanian Eleventh Army, which was operating in the Crimea, did not dispose of a single tank or assault gun around Sevastopol'. This is what the former commander, Field Marshal Erich von Manstein, states, and on this score contemporary Russian historians completely agree with him, insofar as in the autumn of 1941 'everywhere in our documents the offensive by Manstein's forces was invariably supported by 30–70 tanks, which simply did not exist . . . Manstein complains that he did not have a single tank, and proceeding from the overall operational situation on the Eastern Front and the structure of the German armed forces, one cannot but believe this.'[5]

In the German-Romanian Eleventh Army there was only the 190th Assault Gun Battalion, which by the start of the fighting had 18 Stug-III guns.[6] As part of Ziegler's motorized brigade, which was formed by Manstein, the battalion was sent to Sevastopol'; however it came under fire from the heavy guns of the Soviet shore and anti-aircraft batteries, and the army command, fearing losses, as early as 6 November pulled it back to Bakhchisarai. Thus on 7 November Fil'chenkov and his comrades, whatever their wishes, could not have met up with German assault guns. Ziegler's brigade could also have contained two Romanian mechanized scout squadrons from the 5th Cavalry Brigade's 6th Motorized Regiment and the 6th Cavalry Brigade's 10th Motorized Regiment, each of which had an authorized strength of six R-1 light tanks made in Czechoslovakia.[7] However, by November these squadrons had already been fighting for five months and there is no information that by the time of the first offensive on Sevastopol' there remained any kind of armoured equipment in the line. Manstein, in any event, does not confirm the presence of armoured equipment in Ziegler's brigade. All the more so, as this brigade was disbanded on 6 November, as Manstein would not risk continuing the offensive on Sevastopol' because of the increased resistance and instead concentrated on the destruction of the Soviet forces along the Kerch' peninsula. The Romanian tankettes, even if they were available, could not have attacked Sevastopol' on 7 November.

Grigorii Yefimovich Zamikhovskii, a former sailor with the Black Sea Fleet, testifies as follows:

> I don't recall the 'famous' feat of political officer Fil'chenkov's group! Please forgive me, but I was at Duvankoi on 7 November and our company immediately behind the 18th Naval Infantry Battalion under the command of Chernousov. There were no German tanks there! The tanks attacked a composite battalion of cadets from the shore defence school in honor of the Leninist Komsomol. The battalion occupied positions near Bakhchisarai. Just try and find in Russia two former cadets, Roitburg and Israilevich. They're still alive. Let them tell you how 1,200 sailors from this battalion defended Sevastopol' with training rifles and almost all of them laid down their lives.

In reality, the 190th Assault Gun Battalion fell back on Bakhchisarai and the cadets could have encountered German armoured equipment there.[8]

The mythical German tanks were required by Soviet commanders only in order to justify their own inglorious defeat in the Crimea at the end of October and beginning of November 1941, when the remnants of the 51st Independent Army were evacuated in complete disorder and with heavy losses and units of the Independent Maritime Army, unable to render them assistance, fell back to Sevastopol'.

The author has attempted to unearth data on political officer Fil'chenkov and his comrades in the Ministry of Defence's and the 'Memorial' society's unified database.[9] In the card catalogue of irreplaceable losses among the command element, which was compiled on 5 April 1945, it states that Nikolai Dmitrievich Fil'chenkov, political officer and head of the 18th Naval Infantry Battalion's club, 'perished in November 1941', and that his relatives are in Gor'kii (without a specific address). But that same N.D. Fil'chenkov is listed in the 'List of the Black Sea Fleet's Political Workers, who Perished in the Fighting with German Fascism in December 1941', which was compiled on 2 January 1942. Here he is shown to have died in December during the defence of Sevastopol'. December is also listed in later reports. It was only in reports compiled on 21 June 1944 and 12 March 1945 that the time of death is listed as November. And in the report compiled on 28 January 1944, the date of his death is even listed as 16 February 1942.

In the thirteenth volume of the 'Nizhnii Novgorod Book of Memory', Fil'chenkov's year of birth is listed as 1907 and his place of birth the village of Kurilovo, in the Dal'nee Konstantinovo District, and his place of burial the village of Verkhnesadovoe, in Sevastopol'. In the same 'Book of Memory's' sixth volume his year of birth is listed as 1912 and place of burial simply Sevastopol'.[10]

The situation is even worse regarding Fil'chenkov's comrades. In a report of 23 April 1943, addressed to the chief of the second section of the Black Sea Fleet's political administration, Colonel Kornienko, which is contained in the 'Memorial' unified database, it states directly:

> Heroes of the Soviet Union who died the death of the valiant in November 1941 around Sevastopol' are the Red Fleet sailors: 1. Krasnosel'skii, Ivan Mikhailovich; 2. Odintsov, Daniil Sidorovich; 3. Parshin, Yurii Konstantinovich; 4. Tsibul'ko, Vasilii Grigor'evich.
>
> According to registration data of the Black Sea Fleet's Organizational Combat Directorate, the names and patronymics of those listed in the decree by the Presidium of the USSR Supreme Soviet are not listed.
>
> According to the register, up to 70 people have the same surnames, but the names and patronymics do not coincide.

In the seventh volume of the 'Krasnodar Krai Book of Memory', there is listed as having died from his wounds a Vasilii Grigor'evich Tsibul'ko, born in 1901, but he is buried in the village of Ozhiduvo, in Western Ukraine and has no connection to Sevastopol'. In another report an infantryman Vasilii Grigor'evich Tsibul'ko, born in 1921, is listed as having perished on 15 July 1944 in Western Ukraine and buried in the village of Ozyutichi, Volhynia Oblast'. This is more than likely the same man, only the date of birth of 1901 is recorded incorrectly. However, this man had no connection to Sevastopol'.

Yurii Konstantinovich Parshin was more fortunate. He is listed on a card in the card catalogue of irreplaceable losses from 7 January 1946 as having perished in the Duvankoi area near Sevastopol'. At the same time, his year of birth is shown as 1924 and his place of birth the town of Orekhovo-Zuevo, in the Moscow Oblast', and the year he was drafted as 1941. Information was later added that Parshin is permanently listed as belonging to the Black Sea Fleet's 410th Independent Landing Rifle Regiment. However, there are no earlier reports indicating the data and place of his death. In the 'Roll of the Black Sea Fleet's Irreplaceable Losses of Ships and Units for November–December 1941', on 23 December 1945 Parshin is listed as having perished in the Duvankoi area on 7 November 1941, alongside Vasilii Grigor'evich Tsybul'ko (this is probably the correct spelling of his surname) and Daniil Sidorovich Odintsov, although the report was written after the appearance of the decree.

Yurii Konstantinovich Parshin also appears in the second part of volume 18 of the 'Moscow and Moscow Oblast' Book of Memory', where it is reported that he was born in 1924 in Orekhovo-Zuevo and was called up in 1942 by the Orekhovo-Zuevo military commissariat and went missing in action in April 1943. This undoubtedly is one and the same man. April 1943, as the date when Yu.K. Parshin went missing in action, possibly goes back to the April report, which stated that they were unable to discover Fil'chenkov's fellow sailors in the Black Sea Fleet. It's possible that the time of his drafting, 1942, is assumed, as they were then only calling up 18-year-olds. However, it is possible that Parshin somehow got into the army (or in the navy) as early as 1941 and ended up in Sevastopol' at the end of the year. His repeat call-up could have followed in 1942, for example, following his wounding, as in the book of memory he is listed as a guards sergeant in the 38th Guards Rifle Division, which was never in Sevastopol'. The division was formed only in August 1942 and sent to Stalingrad. Then in April 1943 Parshin could actually have gone missing in action or a little bit later in the area of the Northern Donets River, where the division was then operating. He evidently had no idea that he had become a Hero of the Soviet Union.

However, the cadre officers doubted that Yu.K. Parshin, who fought against German tanks at Sevastopol' in November and Yu.K. Parshin, who was called up by the Orekhovo-Zuevo military commissariat, were one and the same man. Thus data on the call-up by the Orekhovo-Zuevo military commissariat was crossed out in his card in the card catalogue of irreplaceable losses and it was added that he had been drafted into the army in 1941. The address of his father, Konstantin Sidorovich Parshin, Orekhovo-Zuevo, Bugrov St, bldg No. 195, was also crossed out. All of this data was taken from the report of 23 December 1941. On 7 January 1946 a new card was compiled on Parshin, where it was only indicated that he perished on 7 November 1941 near Duvankoi and that he is a Hero of the Soviet Union.

A card was compiled on Odintsov the same day as Parshin – 7 January 1946, and there the date of his death – 7 November 1941, near Duvankoi – is also detailed. He's also listed in the report from 23 December 1945. There is no doubt that the report of 23 December served as the basis for entering data on Tsybul'ko, Odintsov, and Parshin in the card catalogue of irreplaceable losses.

It's likely that the real surname of the Hero of the Soviet Union was Tsybul'ko He also features with this surname in the seventh volume of the 'Krasnoyarsk Krai Book of Memory', as having been a private and born in 1921 and called up by the Otradnoye District military commissariat and who died from wounds in 1941. He is buried in the village of Ozyubychi, in Volhynia Oblast', which makes it more likely that he died in 1944. There is a

Vasilii Grigor'evich Tsybul'kko in the irreplaceable losses card catalogue. His card is dated 7 January 1946 and there it says that he perished on 7 November 1941 in the Duvankoi area.

It's quite likely that V.G. Tsybul'ko and V.G. Tsibul'ko are one and the same man and that Ozyubychi, Ozhiduvo, and Ozyutichi are one and the same village in the Lokachi District, the correct spelling of which is Ozyutichi, and that the legend of Tsibul'ko as the last survivor of the fighting near Duvankoi and who managed to tell people the story of this feat before his death through wounds has some foundation. It's possible that V.G. Tsybul'ko was born in 1921 and that he really was seriously wounded in the November or December fighting around Sevastopol' and was evacuated from the Crimea. The leadership, considering him to be dead, included him in the recommendation for the title of hero as one of Fil'chenkov's comrades in arms. But Vasilii Grigor'evich survived and continued fighting and perished only in July 1944 in Volhynia, never having learned that he had been awarded the Hero of the Soviet Union. Now he has been reburied in a common grave in the village of Zaturtsy, in the Volhynia Oblast's Lokachi District. In the burial documentation his date of birth is shown as 1921.

The situation is the same for Ivan Mikhailovich Krasnosel'skii. The dates of his death appear in documents only after the publication of the decree. In the seventh volume of the 'Krasnodar Krai Book of Memory' it is reported that Ivan Mikhailovich Krasnosel'skii was born in 1913 in Sharypovo District and that he perished in 1942 near Sevastopol'. It should be noted that in 1942 he could have perished either at the very beginning of January, as following the landing in Kerch' Manstein halted the storming of Sevastopol', or in June–July, during the final German storming of the fortress city. And in the electronic book of memory for the Archangel Oblast', Ivan Mikhailovich Krasnosel'skii, born in 1913, is listed as a native of the village of Yevlashevka, in the Chernigov Oblast's Borzna District, and perished on 7 November 1941 near Duvankoi. However, here the text of the decree of 7 November 1942 evidently served as the source for this information. The very same Krasnosel'skii is in the card catalogue of irreplaceable losses. His card is dated 15 February 1945, and it is far more detailed than those of his comrades. The year and place of his birth are reported – 1913, in the village of Yevlashevka, in the Chernigov Oblast's Komarov District, and that he was called up by the Crimea's Kirov District military commissariat, and that he was a Ukrainian and member of the VKP(b). The address of his wife, Fedora Ivanovna Krasnosel'skaya, Kirov District, Crimean ASSR, Islan-Terek station, 124 Chkalov St, apartment 1 is given. It should be noted that to judge by her name Krasnosel'skii's wife was Greek, which means that in the event she had remained in the Crimea for the arrival of Soviet forces, then she could have easily have been deported. This information is also contained in a report of 9 February 1945. One may assume that in all cases this is the same person and that Hero of the Soviet Union I.M. Krasnosel'skii was born in the village of Yevlashevka, Chernigov Oblast'. It certainly remains unclear how he was connected to the Krasnodar Krai's Sharypovo District and the Archangel Oblast'. It's possible that there were identical namesakes, whose years of birth also coincided.

Of the real Nikolai Dmitrievich Fil'chenkov it is known only that he perished either in November or December 1941, although it was most likely in December. However, the incident required that this be November – the day of the anniversary of the October revolution. And just as in the case of Klochkov at Dubosekovo, they added four surnames of Red Navy sailors to Fil'chenkov at Sevastopol' (and perhaps not sailors) taken at random, who supposedly perished (and two were actually still alive at the time when they were awarded the title of hero, and as to the other two it is impossible to state with confidence when they perished at all and, as regards D.S. Odintsov, it's impossible to state with confidence whether such a person existed at all). It will never be known where these five names came from. Not long after Fil'chenkov's feat became widely known, Sevsastopol' fell into German hands.

The undertaking of Fil'chenkov's five first began to be widely publicized when the Soviet forces' operation on the Kerch' peninsula ended in disaster. On 19 May 1942, in the Sevastopol' newspaper *the Commune's Lighthouse*, there appeared a feature story by Meer Kogut, 'The Feat of the Five Black Sea Fleet Sailors', in which the surnames and names of all five were listed, and it was precisely from this source that they were taken for the decree of 23 October 1942, by which all five were awarded the title of Hero of the Soviet Union. Only in the decree Fil'chenkov somehow was transformed into Fil'chenko. During the days of the Kerch' disaster it was necessary to buck up the fighting spirit of the defenders of Sevastopol', who had lost hope of rapid liberation. It was then that Kogut's story about the five hero sailors appeared. And soon after the fall of Sevastopol' a heroic subject, linked with the city of Russian glory, was even more needed. Kogut's story was reprinted in *Red Fleet* and *Red Sailor of the Black Sea Fleet* and other newspapers. It ended with a great deal of pathos:

> The five heroic knight-errant Black Sea Fleet sailors placed their lives on the altar of the Fatherland. The sailors knew what they were dying for. They fulfilled their military duty, they blocked the enemy's path to their beloved city . . . Let the feat of the five Black Sea Fleet knights, their glorious names and their bright visages forever stand before the eyes of our warriors. Their feat calls us to the fateful battle with the enemy, to the final defeat of the German aggressors.

Senior political officer Meer Naumovich Kogut, chief of the agitation and propaganda section of the *Red Sailor of the Black Sea Fleet* newspaper, himself went missing in action at the beginning of July 1942, during the final days of the defence of Sevastopol'. The chances of him, a Jew, surviving in captivity were very slim. Thus it was impossible to find out from where he took the surnames of Fil'chenkov's comrades in arms in the immediate weeks following the story's publication.

An even better known feat was that of the twenty-eight hero Panfilov soldiers at Dubosekovo station near Moscow on 16 November 1941.[11] This incident was almost transformed into the chief feat of the Great Patriotic War and was repeatedly propagandized, including in works of art. The latest example is the film *The Twenty Eight Panfilov Soldiers* by Andrei Shal'opa and Kim Druzhinin, the premiere of which took place on 16 November 2016. Here the Soviet-era legend was carefully repeated: 28 soldiers from the 316th Rifle Division destroyed 18 German tanks out of 54 and all of them perished, but they did not let the enemy break through.

The true story of the battle of the twenty-eight guards-Panfilov soldiers was deconstructed quite a while ago and has nothing to do with the heroic myth. During the course of the investigation conducted by the main military prosecutor in 1948, it transpired that no '28 hero Panfilov soldiers' existed at all. As early as August 1942 the Kalinin Front's military prosecutor, while conducting a verification of the declarations of a number of soldiers who were claiming their qualifications for the gold stars of hero of the Soviet Union for the fighting at the station, discovered:

> On 16 November 1941 the enemy, having forestalled our units' offensive, attacked at about 0800 with a large force of tanks and infantry.
>
> As a result of the fighting and under pressure from superior enemy forces, the 1075th Rifle Regiment suffered heavy losses and fell back on a new defensive line.
>
> For this withdrawal, the regimental commander Kaprov and the military commissar Mukhomed'yarov were removed from their posts and restored to command after the division had gotten out of the fighting and was resting and reforming. [Actually, they were temporarily relieved because on 24 November the regiment had fallen back without orders, B.S.]
>
> No one knew anything about the feat of the 28 at either during the fighting or immediately afterwards, and they were not popularized among the mass of soldiers.[12]

A correspondent for *Red Star*, Vasilii Koroteev, told the investigator about his conversation with the paper's editor: 'Ortenberg asked me how many people had been in the company . . . I replied that the company was evidently under strength and had about 30–40 men. I also said that two of these people proved to be traitors . . .'[13] Evidently both David Ortenberg and Koroteev himself understood perfectly that no one would allow them to write about the death of an entire company with less than 120 men. And to immediately decorate more than 100 men was too much by the standards of 1941.

The commander of the 1075th Rifle Regiment, Colonel Il'ya Vasil'evich Kaprov, testified:

> There was no battle involving 28 Panfilov soldiers with German tanks at Dubosekovo station on 16 November 1941 – this is a complete fabrication. On this day the 2nd Battalion's fourth company really did fight heroically against German tanks near Dubosekovo station. More than 100 men out of the company died, and not 28, as they wrote about in the newspapers. None of the correspondents approached me during this period; I didn't tell anyone about a battle involving the 28 Panfilov soldiers, and could not have done so, because there had been no such battle. I did not write any kind of political report on this account. I don't know on the basis of what materials they wrote in the newspapers, particularly in *Red Star*, about the fight of the 28 guards troops from the Panfilov division.

Wartime documents found by the investigator paint the true picture of the events of 16 November. That same Kaprov reported:

> By 16 November the division was preparing for an offensive battle, but the Germans preempted us. Early in the morning of 16 November 1941 the Germans carried out a large air raid, and then a powerful artillery preparation, which hit the 2nd Battalion's position particularly hard. At approximately 1100 small groups of enemy tanks appeared along the battalion's sector. There were about 10–12 enemy tanks along the battalion's sector. I don't know how many tanks were heading to the 4th company's sector, and it's likely I can't determine that. This German tank attack was beaten back with the regiment's weapons and the 2nd Battalion's efforts. The regiment destroyed 5–6 German tanks in the fighting and the Germans fell back . . . At about 1400–1500 the Germans opened a powerful artillery fire against all the regiment's positions and the German tanks moved once more into the attack. They were deployed along

the front in waves, with approximately 15–20 in a group. More than 50 tanks were attacking the regiment's sector, with the main attack directed at the 2nd Battalion's positions because this sector was the most accessible for the enemy's tanks. During the course of approximately 40–45 minutes the enemy tanks crushed the 2nd Battalion's position, including the 4th company's sector, and one tank even reached the regiment's command post and set fire to some straw and a cabin, so that it was only by accident that I was able to get out of the dugout; a railroad embankment saved me. When I made it past the railroad embankment, people who had served following the German tank attack began to gather around me. The 4th company suffered the most from the attack; 20–25 people, led by company commander Gundilovich, survived, while the rest perished. The remaining companies suffered less . . .[14]

According to the political report by the commissar of the 1075th Rifle Regiment, Akhmedzhan Latypovich Mukhamed'yarov, of 18 November 1941, the regiment lost 400 men killed during the 2 preceding days, 100 men wounded, and 600 missing in action.[15] Overall, as was the custom, this was another case of covering up a serious defeat with a heroic legend.

From the German side, the fighting on 16 November is viewed as follows. Two of the German 2nd Panzer Division's 3 combat groups, which had 1 tank battalion and 1 tank company (a maximum of 60 tanks, although there were probably significantly fewer, as there had been 90 tanks in 2 battalions at the beginning of October) attacked the 1075th Rifle Regiment. Kaprov's troops had 7 anti-tank rifles and the regiment's artillery had 20 armour-piercing shells. The German attacked began 2½ hours before the planned Soviet offensive and proved to be a complete surprise. The 16th Army's forces had been provided with 2 tank brigades, numbering by 28 October no less than 71 combat-ready tanks, for the offensive. But it is not known how many of these had been attached to Kaprov's regiment. There were no combat activities of any kind near Dubosekovo mentioned in the German division's reports. Only in a report by the first combat group is there mention of the enemy's bitter resistance in Dubosekovo and neighboring Shiryaevo, where another company of approximately the same strength as Gundilovich's company was defending. The first group had no more than 45 tanks, so, accordingly, no more than 20–5 tanks could have attacked Dubosekovo, and it is more likely that there were 10–15. The 2nd Panzer Division's headquarters evaluated the fighting on 16 November as 'resistance by a weak but stubborn enemy, who is taking advantage of the superiority of the broken terrain', while noting that at the same time the enemy was suffering from 'a shortage of fighting spirit'. The 2nd Battalion's positions had been broken through by the middle of the day and both German combat groups carried out their mission for the day, occupying the villages of Lushchevo and Rozhdestvenno 8km north of Dubosekovo. More stubborn resistance was put up during the following days, when the element of surprise had been lost. By 20 November 700 men remained in the 1077th Regiment, 200 in the 1073rd, 120 in the 1075th, and 180 in the 690th. Taking into account the fact that the authorized strength of a regiment in October 1941 was 2,723 men, the division's losses in 4 days of fighting could have amounted to something in the order of 10,000 men, not counting division artillery and independent units. According to Kaprov's testimony, the regiment's companies had been at full authorized strength. The 1075th Regiment maintained that it had destroyed 4 tanks. According to an evaluation by the Western Front's artillery headquarters, the 1075th Regiment destroyed 2 tanks with its anti-tank rifles. At best, Gundilovich's company could have destroyed 1 tank.[16] The Fourth Panzer Group, which included among its units the 2nd Panzer Division, lost 5,168 men (975 killed, 539 missing in action, and 3,654 wounded) during 11–20 November, that is, 2 times less than Panfilov's division facing the panzer group.[17]

The conclusion of the prosecutor's investigation was categorical:

> It has been established by the investigation's materials that the feat of the 28 guards Panfilov soldiers, which has been highlighted in the press, is an invention by correspondent Koroteev and the editor of *Red Star*, Ortenberg, and especially the paper's literary secretary Krivitskii. This invention was repeated in works by the writers N. Tikhonov, V. Stavskii, A. Bek, N. Kuznetsov, V. Lipko, M. Svetlov, and others and has been widely popularized among the population of the Soviet Union.[18]

What actually did happen? This was a quiet military engagement by hundreds and thousands of soldiers and commanders of the 318th Rifle Division, who gave their lives for the motherland and clearly lost the battle near Dubosekovo station and along other sectors of the front on the approaches to Moscow. Such battles were a quite common thing for the *Wehrmacht* in 1941–2, which is why the battle at Dubosekovo was not in any way reflected in German documents.

On 29 November 1941, in the village of Petrishchevo, near Moscow, the Germans hanged the 18-year-old partisan Zoya Kosmodem'yanskaya. They had caught her the previous evening, after she had attempted to burn down a hut that the Germans had turned into a stable. Before her death, Zoya, whom the local residents knew by the name of 'Tanya', appealed to everyone who had gathered on the square:

> Hey, comrades! Why are you looking so sad; be braver, fight, attack the Germans, burn and hunt them down! . . . I'm not afraid of dying, comrades. It is happiness to die for one's people . . . You are going to hang me now, but I'm not alone. There are two hundred million of us and you can't hang all of us. They will wreak their revenge on you for me. Soldiers! Surrender before it's too late, because victory will nevertheless be ours!

This quote is from a sketch by the *Pravda* correspondent Petr Aleksandrovich Lidov, 'Tanya', which was published in *Pravda* on 27 January 1942.[19] The correspondent had been in Petrishchevo and talked to the local residents. This sketch revealed Zoya Kosmodem'yanskaya to the world, although at the time her real name wasn't yet known. Then this episode became one of the chief heroic myths of the Great Patriotic War, and was widely circulated during the war years and during the postwar period. And this was precisely the case when a real event lay behind the myth. In this case the creators of the myth did not make anything up, as was the case with the twenty-eight heroic Panfilov soldiers, but simply did not mention some of the actual circumstances. For example, during Soviet times it was not acceptable to write that Zoya had essentially been a 'torch bearer'. She and her comrades were carrying out Stalin's (formally, the *Stavka* of the Supreme High Command) order of 17 November 1941 on carrying out 'scorched earth' tactics, which demanded that they:

> Destroy and burn to the ground all inhabited locales in the rear of the German troops to a distance of 40–60 kilometers in depth from the front line and 20–30 kilometers to the right and left of roads . . . Create in each regiment teams of hunters of 20–30 people apiece, each for blowing up and burning down inhabited locales in which the enemy's troops are quartered.[20]

Naturally, the inhabitants of Petrishchevo were not thrilled with the fact that partisans dispatched from Moscow were burning their homes. The women whose hut Zoya and her comrades had tried to burn down detained and beat Zoya and even poured a bucket of slops over her. One of the victims, Agrafena Smirnova, beat Zoya about the legs with a stick before her execution, crying 'Whom did you harm! You burned down my home and didn't do anything to the Germans . . .' After the liberation of Petrishchevo, Soviet troops shot Smirnova and Fedos'ya Solina, who also beat Zoya, following the verdict of a military tribunal. Naturally, they didn't write about that in Soviet times. But one can sympathize with the victims of the house burnings. After all, to be without a roof over one's head in the bitter cold threatened them with death.[21]

Not everything is clear regarding the circumstances of Zoya's detention. Lidov wrote in the sketch mentioned above:

> Having walked up to the stable, the man put a 'Nagan' in his bosom, got a bottle with gasoline from a bag, poured it and then bent down so as to light the match.[22] At that moment the guard snuck up on him and grabbed his hands from behind. The partisan was able to push the German away and seize his revolver, but did not have time to fire. The soldier knocked the weapon from his hand and raised the alarm. They took the partisan into the building and determined there that it was a girl, quite young, tall and swarthy, with black eyebrows, lively dark eyes and short dark hair.

Subsequently, when researchers were able to access to the archives, a version arose that the guard was a local resident.

But Lidov very soon published an alternative version of Zoya's detention, in the sketch 'What's New About Tanya', which appeared on 5 May 1942 in the jubilee issue of large circulation newspaper *Pravdist*, for internal use of the *Pravda* staff. There he maintained:

> The circumstances of Zoya's death are now viewed differently. The Germans themselves did not catch the partisan girl; she was betrayed by her comrade of the same age, who went with her on the fateful night of 26 November and who was supposed to simultaneously throw with her his incendiary bottle. He chickened out at the last moment because he was afraid of being hanged by the Germans, but he was shot by the Russians.
>
> Vasilii Klubkov chickened out and was caught. Zoya did not chicken out and completed her mission and went back to the agreed-upon place. She could have gone further into the woods, but she didn't want to abandon her comrade in danger. Zoya trustingly waited for Klubkov, but instead of him German troops dispatched by him came to the edge of the woods.
>
> They interrogated Zoya in Klubkov's presence. She refused to identify herself, refused to answer where she had come from and why she had come. She said that she didn't know Klubkov and was seeing him for the first time.

Then an officer looked at Klubkov. Klubkov said: 'She's lying; we're from the same detachment. We were carrying out a mission together. Her name is Zoya Kosmodem'yanskaya, and there was a Boris Krainov with us . . .'

They completely undressed Zoya in front of Klubkov and beat her with rubber sticks, after which she said: 'Kill me, but I won't tell you anything.'

After some time, Klubkov returned to Moscow, to that very unit which he had joined a few months before as a soldier-volunteer. This time he came as a German spy.

Here the narration of the plot about Tanya gets more complicated. The story of her charming soul had to be filled out with a story about the lowlife and traitorous rat Vasilii Klubkov. One would think that new circumstances would feature, which would illuminate that which still seems mysterious about Tanya's story.

The following picture emerges from Klubkov's testimony. On the night of 27 November Boris Krainov, Vasilii Klubkov, and Zoya Kosmodem'yanskaya set fire to three buildings in the village of Petrishchevo and destroyed twenty horses. Klubkov was captured and showed the place where he was supposed to meet up with his comrades. Zoya was captured there and Krainov, who was late to the rendezvous and did not wait for his comrades, returned safe and sound to his comrades. On 28 January 1942 Klubkov was sent through the front line as a German agent and he was found out in Moscow. His captors did not believe his account that following his detention the Germans had taken him somewhere and he managed to escape from their vehicle. He admitted the following during his interrogation:

> The officer asked me if she was the one and what I knew about her. I said that this was actually Zoya Kosmodem'yanskaya, who had arrived with me at the village for carrying out diversionary acts and that she had set fire to the southern outskirts of the village. After this Kosmodem'yanskaya did not reply to the officer's questions. Seeing that she was being stubbornly silent, several officers undressed her completely and for 2–3 hours beat her with rubber sticks, trying to get information from her. Kosmodem'yanskaya said: 'Kill me, but I won't tell you anything.' After this they took her away and I didn't see her anymore.[23]

After all, it was well known that the Germans shot partisans and diversionists caught with the goods on the spot. Vasilii Klubkov admitted that he had betrayed Zoya and become a German agent. He was shot on 16 April 1942.

It should be noted that in order for the Germans not to shoot a partisan caught in the act and to attempt to employ him as their agent, he would have to have done something to earn their trust. And the betrayal of Zoya was probably sufficient for that.

It turns out that the Germans never found out 'Tanya's' real name. However, this was not particularly important for them. It was all the same to the Germans who had attempted to burn down the stable – Tanya, Masha, or Zoya and what her real surname was – Ivanova, Petrova, or Kosmodem'yanskaya. A rapid death sentence was preordained. And it transpires that they, having learned everything they needed from Klubkov, beat Zoya out of sheer sadism, wreaking their vengeance for the slaughtered horses. After all, this was her second trip to Petrishchevo. The first time Zoya and her comrades were able to burn down a pair of huts and some horses.

After all, Zoya's feat was not that she burned down a pair of huts and some horses. This was hardly a palpable loss for the *Wehrmacht*. And if the group of partisans, of which Zoya was a member, burned down two or three buildings in Petrishchevo and then returned home safe and sound, no one in the world today would remember the name of Kosmodem'yanskaya. No, Zoya's achievement was a strictly moral one and lay in her strength of character in the face of torture and in her call to the people to rise up which she made standing under the gallows. Here, as opposed to the case of the twenty-eight Panfilov soldiers, the journalist did not have to make anything up. The investigation, which was conducted immediately after the event, established that approximately the same words quoted by Lidov were actually pronounced by Zoya before her death. And it was with this that one could educate the Red Army's soldiers and commanders and inculcate them with hatred for the enemy.

Petr Lidov was unable to discover which of the versions of Zoya's capture was closer to the truth. On 22 June 1944 he and his combat comrade, the photo correspondent Sergei Strunnikov, who took the famous picture of the dead Zoya, perished during a *Luftwaffe* raid on the airfield at Poltava. American 'flying fortresses' would land there following raids on Germany. The journalists could have remained in the shelter, but they wanted to leave a memory of a real battle, even at the risk of their own lives. Lidov and Strunnikov were real front-line journalists.

Zoya Kosmodem'yanskaya's deed was that rare case in which the myth does not significantly differ from the real circumstances. It's just that the story told by the journalist Lidov was very useful for propaganda purposes, describing the heroic self-sacrifice and brave behaviour of the Komsomol girl before her execution.

Sergeant Pavlov's house is the oblast' consumer union's four-story building in the centre of Stalingrad on the 9th of January Square (the address then was Penza Street, 61). It became a symbol of the stalwartness and heroism of the Red Army's soldiers during the Battle of Stalingrad. On 28 September 1942 a scouting party of four men, led by Sergeant Yakov Fedotovich Pavlov, from the 42nd Guards Rifle Regiment of General Aleksandr Il'ich Rodimtsev's 13th Guards Rifle Division, occupied this building. There were no Germans present at that time, although in his memoirs Pavlov himself later maintained the opposite. As Pavlov's group was the first to go into the building, it was later noted on maps as 'Pavlov's house'. On the night of 1 October a machine-gun platoon from the 42nd Guards Regiment's seventh company, under Senior Lieutenant Ivan Filippovich Afanas'ev, who took over command, was sent to reinforce the building's defenders. However, Afanas'ev's role remained in the shade.

In all, twenty-nine soldiers defended Pavlov's house. Of these no one was killed before the close of the defence, which speaks of the high level of leadership of the garrison by Afanas'ev, and that as 'Pavlov's house' did not create any particular problems for the Germans they did not attempt to seize it.

Up to ten men from the garrison were wounded. Besides the soldiers, one nurse and two female orderlies from among the local inhabitants were always in the building. Afanas'ev also mentioned in his memoirs two cowards whom he was forced to send back to the company, lest they demoralized the garrison. Up to thirty civilians remained in the building for a month, including a young mother with her newborn daughter, hiding there from the bombing. The defenders of Pavlov's house shared the last bits of their meagre rations with the women, children, and old men. After all, one could only deliver food and munitions to the building under cover of darkness, and not every night. According to Afanas'ev's memoirs, 'we mostly ate wheat, which we cooked whole, or which we crushed', until they dug a communications trench at the end of October to the windmill, where the 7th Company was defending.

A cement gas reservoir, to which they had dug an underground passage, was located in front of the building. Yet another convenient position had been outfitted about 30m behind the building, where there was a hatch for a water tunnel, to which an underground passage had also been dug. When a bombardment would begin, the soldiers would immediately go into the shelter. Their small losses can be explained by these circumstances. The Germans preferred to shell Pavlov's house and not attack it.[24]

In 1965 a memorial wall was created alongside Pavlov's house. A memorial plaque was set up two buildings from it, in the building where Ivan Afanas'ev lived and died. But the fact that Sergeant Pavlov was chosen for the role of hero and not Lieutenant Afanas'ev may be explained not only by the accidental circumstance that the famous building was noted on maps as 'Pavlov's house', in honour of the commander of the subunit which first entered the building, but even more importantly by the fact that propaganda required a hero from among the number of soldiers defending Stalingrad, thus Sergeant Pavlov's candidacy was more preferable to that of Lieutenant Afanas'ev.

Having successfully withstood a fifty-eight-day siege, many of the defenders of Pavlov's house perished or were wounded during the unsuccessful attempt on 25–6 November to seize the 'dairy building', called thus because of its colour, which stood opposite. It was necessary for the attack to force the 9th of January Square, which had been well registered by the Germans. Moreover, the 'dairy house' did not have any basements and it was difficult to hold. Afanas'ev was seriously concussed and Pavlov was wounded in this battle. More than 100 soldiers from the 7th Company attacked the 'dairy building' and literally 3–4 remained unharmed by the close of this unsuccessful fight.

It was accurately established that Senior Lieutenant Ivan Ivanovich Naumov, the commander of the 7th Company, Lieutenant Kubati Batirbekovich Tukov, the company's political deputy, platoon commander Junior Lieutenant Nikolai Yepifanovich Zabolotnyi, and privates I.L. Shkuratov, Faizullin, P.D. Demchenko, Davydov, and Karnaukhov died in this battle.

Among the defenders of Pavlov's house who died in this battle were Junior Lieutenant Aleksei Nikiforovich Chernyshenko, the commander of a mortar platoon, Sergeant Idel' Yakovlevich Khait, a section commander, and Private Andrei Sabgaida. In all, more than 1,800 men rest in a common grave on the 9th of January Square.

Ivan Timofeevich Svirin, whom they often number among the killed in defending Pavlov's house, actually died much later, on 19 January 1943, when Soviet forces had already gone over to the offensive against the encircled German group of forces. He was wounded on this day and died in the hospital.

Following his wounding, Pavlov served as a gun layer and commander of a scouting section in artillery units. On 15 and 30 May 1945 he was awarded two orders of the Red Star and he had earlier been awarded the medal 'For Valour'. On 17 June 1945 Yakov Fedotovich was awarded the title of Hero of the Soviet Union. Before long Master Sergeant Pavlov was promoted to Junior Lieutenant, at which rank he was discharged into the reserves in 1946. In the citation to Pavlov's hero medal, which was signed on 30 November 1944 by the commander of the 42nd Guards Rifle Regiment, Lieutenant Colonel Ivan Kuz'mich Polovets, also a hero of the Soviet Union, it stated, in part: 'In honour of the heroic feat of Pavlov, a labourer of Stalingrad who was one of the first to build "Pavlov's house" and who set up a memorial plaque on it.' It was also mentioned that 'the writers I. Ehrenburg and V. Grossman describe "Pavlov's house", and that it occupies a noted place in the film *Stalingrad*.[25] By that time both Pavlov and Afanas'ev had long ceased serving in the 13th Guards Rifle Division. The citation was obviously dictated from on high. They made Pavlov an official hero. He subsequently completed the higher party school and served at *nomenklatura* posts. Afanas'ev was not recongised by those on high.

Afanas'ev received his first Order of the Red Star on 22 February 1943 not for Stalingrad, but for the fighting on 17 January 1943 in which he was wounded. The citation stated: 'He distinguished himself in the fighting for the city of Stalingrad in the area of the Red October village, where on 17.1.43 he and his machine gun platoon destroyed 150 enemy soldiers and he personally killed 18 enemy soldiers and blocked four enemy dugouts, which enabled the infantry subunits to advance, while comrade Afanas'ev himself was wounded in this battle.' We should note that in the hospital in Saratov Ivan Filippovich miraculously met his bride, Katya, with whom he had parted when he left for the front.

The figure of Pavlov, who was also a hero, was canonized by propaganda as early as the days of the Battle of Stalingrad obliterating the figure of the one who actually commanded the garrison of the legendary building – Lieutenant Afanas'ev. Ivan Filippovich survived the war but did not receive the Hero of the Soviet Union. In 1951 Pavlov published his memoirs, *In Stalingrad*, in which there is not a single word about Afanas'ev.

In that same year of 1951 Ivan Filippovich could see almost nothing (the consequences of a concussion and a wound made themselves felt) and was discharged from the army into retirement with the rank of captain. In February 1964 he managed to restore his sight as a result of a successful operation, which Professor Aleksandr Mikhailovich Vodovozov, from the Volgograd Medical Institute, performed.

In 1970 he also published his memoirs, *The House of Soldier's Glory*, which was written in a clear and accessible style, where he does homage to the bravery of all the defenders, including Pavlov, and in no way focuses on his own role. Afanas'ev settled in Stalingrad in 1958. Here Ivan Filippovich passed away on 17 August 1975, at the age of 59, due to the effects of his wound and concussion. He was buried in the central cemetery of Volgograd. Afanas'ev searched for the surviving defenders of Pavlov's house to the end of his days and in his correspondence with them tried to establish the true circumstances of the fighting.[26]

The myth of Aleksandr Matrosov's feat lies in the statement that Matrosov covered the embrasure of a German pillbox with his chest and thus secured the success of his subunit's attack. Also mythological is the date of the feat – 23 February 1943, Red Army Day.

Hero of the Soviet Union Aleksandr Matveevich Matrosov was born on 6 February 1924 in Dnepropetrovsk. The date and place of his birth are unconfirmed, as Sasha lost his parents in early childhood and was raised in the Ivanovo and Melekesskii District's children's homes in Ul'yanov Oblast'. He was sentenced for some sort of criminal act (according to the official version, for voluntarily leaving his work place, for which at the time people could be sentenced) and ended up in the Ufa labour colony for minors, where he was among the activists and following his release he worked in the same colony as an assistant teacher. In September 1942 Matrosov was assigned to the Krasnyi Kholm Infantry School, but by January 1943 had already been sent to the Kalinin Front.

There is no confirmation that Matrosov was in a punishment company. Quite the opposite, Matrosov was a soldier in the elite 6th Siberian Volunteer Rifle Corps named after Stalin. It is possible that the hero's service in a formation named in honour of the leader was an additional factor for his achievements becoming known to the entire country.[27]

According to the official version, on 23 February 1943, on the twenty-fifth anniversary of the Red Army, Private Aleksandr Matrosov, from the 91st Siberian Volunteer Rifle Brigade's 2nd Battalion, covered with his chest the embrasure of a German pillbox in fighting near the village of Chernushki, near Velikie Luki in Pskov Oblast', which secured the forward advance of his subunit. In a report by an agitator from the 91st Siberian Volunteer Rifle Brigade's political section, Senior Lieuenant Volkov, it states: 'In the fighting for the village of Chernushki, Komsomol member Matrosov, born in 1924, carried out a heroic act – he covered the embrasure of a pillbox with his body, which enabled our troops to move forward. Chernushki has been taken. The offensive continues. I will report the details when I get back.' However, Volkov perished in the evening of that same day and the details of what happened thus remained unknown. In a report by the brigade's political section to the political section of the 6th Siberian Volunteer Rifle Corps it was noted:

> Red Army soldier and Komsomol member Matrosov, from the 2nd Battalion, displayed extreme bravery and heroism. The enemy opened powerful machine gun fire from a pillbox and prevented our infantry from advancing. Comrade Matrosov received orders to destroy the enemy's fortified firing point. With contempt for death, he covered the embrasure with his body. The enemy's machine gun fell silent. Our infantry moved forward and a pillbox was captured.

Comrade Matrosov died the death of the brave for the Soviet motherland.[28]

On 19 June 1943 Aleksandr Matrosov was posthumously awarded the title of Hero of the Soviet Union. According to one version, the initiator of the move to permanently inscribe Matrosov into the unit's roster and to award the regiment his name was the commander of the Kalinin Front, Andrei Yeremenko, who in August 1943 met with Stalin during the latter's trip to the front and convinced the Supreme Commander-in-Chief to make Matrosov's feat known to the entire country. In an order by the people's defence commissar of 8 September 1943 the 254th Guards Rifle Regiment, which included the 91st Independent Brigade's 2nd Battalion, was awarded the title of the '254th Guards Rifle Regiment named after Aleksandr Matrosov', while the hero himself was permanently inscribed in the rolls of the regiment's first company. He became one of the first heroes permanently inscribed in the rolls of a military unit.

In the report on the 91st Independent Rifle Brigade's irreplaceable losses for the period from 24 February through 30 March 1943, it shows that Red Army soldier Matrosov, born in 1924 and member of the VLKSM, was killed on 27 February and buried in the area of the village of Chernushki. Here it was mentioned to whom and to what address the news of his death should be sent: Ufa, NKVD Children's Labour Colony, barracks No. 19, to Matrosov's wife.[29] To judge from this note, the hero had a family. But for a heroic myth, a young orphan, who had no one in the world aside from his motherland, was more appropriate. Incidentally, Volkov's political report was dated 27 February, and the date of 23 February in the award citation was chosen purely for propaganda considerations.

However, it's simply impossible to block an embrasure with one's body. Even a single rifle bullet that hits a man in the hand is enough to knock him off his feet. And a burst from a machine gun at point-blank range will probably throw aside even the heaviest body from an embrasure. This is how Lieutenant L. Korolev, the commander of the platoon in which Matrosov fought, described his subordinate's feat in the *front* newspaper:

> He ran up to the pillbox and fell on the embrasure. The machine gun became clogged with the hero's blood and fell silent.
>
> I didn't need to give the order. The soldiers, who were lying up front, heard how Sasha, in falling on the embrasure, had shouted: 'Forward!' And the entire platoon, as one man, rose up and threw itself toward the pillbox. Sergeant Kuznetsov was the first to reach the entrance. Soldiers from his section ran up behind him. The silent clash in the pillbox lasted no more than a minute. When

I went inside there lay, among the spent rounds and ammo belts, six dead German soldiers and two machine guns.

And there, in front of the embrasure, in the snow, covered with soot and blood, lay Sasha Matrosov. The last machine gun burst cut short his young life. He was dead, but the battalion had already crossed the hollow and broken into the village of Chernushki. The order had been carried out. Sasha Matrosov sacrificed himself in to clear the battalion's way to victory.[30]

Here Korolev changes a metaphor into reality, forcing the machine gun 'to get clogged with the hero's blood'. To be sure, it is determined that there was not one machine gun in the pillbox, but two. The lieutenant could not explain how it came about that both barrels immediately became clogged with blood. However, one should approach with caution the number of machine guns, as with the information about the corpses of the six Germans, who supposedly remained in the pillbox. Nothing is said about them in any other source. If the press mentioned the heroic death of one Soviet soldier or officer, then it was mandatory to claim for him several killed enemy soldiers.

But in one thing Korolev did not deviate from the truth. As he maintained, Matrosov's corpse lay not across the embrasure, but in the snow in front of the pillbox. Due to this fact, however, it becomes simply impossible to believe how the slain automatic rifleman could silence the enemy machine gun.

It's mostly likely that Matrosov was cut down next to the pillbox and Korolev, who saw his corpse, dreamed up the rest.

In the case of Matrosov he undoubtedly was a real living person, only one who died not on 23, but on 27 February, and was simply cut down by a machine-gun burst from a pillbox, but who did not cover the embrasure with his chest.

In order to find out the real feats of Soviet soldiers, and not the ones dreamed up by propagandists, one must first of all consult the German documents and memoirs. There was no need for the Germans to make up Soviet achievements. Here the most worthy of attention is the feat of a KV-1 crew near the Lithuanian village of Raseiniai. The author learned of this from the memoirs of a former brigade commander in the German 6th Panzer Division, Colonel General Erhard Raus (he ended the war as commander of the Third Panzer Army). On 24–5 June 1941 a heavy Soviet KV-1 tank from the 2nd Tank Division's 4th Tank Regiment successfully held a crossroads, blocking the supply of the combat group commanded by Raus. They were unable to put out the tank with a 50mm anti-tank gun. The shells bounced off the armour and two guns were destroyed by return fire, with another two damaged. An 88mm anti-aircraft gun, which they attempted to use against the tank, was also damaged. The engineers were only able to damage the KV's treads. It was only when, under the cover of a tank attack, that they were able to bring up another 88mm anti-aircraft gun and shoot it at point-blank range that the tank fell silent. Then they threw a grenade into a shell hole in the turret, which killed the crew. The Germans buried six dead tank troops with military honours.[31] Upon exhuming the grave in 1965, they were able to establish the names of two of the tank troops from the surviving documents – Pavel Yegorovich Yershov and V.A. Smirnov, and the initials of a third, Sh.A.[32]

What is noteworthy in this case is that the Soviet tank troops not only sacrificed their lives, but in the course of nearly an entire day controlled an important road junction, blocking the movement of a German panzer division's combat group. Here the fact that in the beginning of the war KV tank crews were made up almost exclusively of re-enlisted commanders and sergeants certainly played a role.

Yet another heroic episode is found in the memoirs of another German panzer general, Hermann Balck, who at the end of 1943 and beginning of 1944 commanded the XLVIII Panzer Corps on the Ukrainian right bank. Balck recalled:

> On 16 January we captured a radio relay station. The station chief cooperated willingly and told us everything we wanted to know. Two of the captured radio operators were women. One of them, named Masha, was gravely wounded and later died. We intercepted a radio transmission from a higher-level Russian General Staff officer asking about Masha. He was very concerned about her. [She was probably either a relative or a 'campaign field wife' of one of the senior officers or generals, B.S.]. The other female radio operator told us, 'I am a communist. I will not say anything. I am not such a disgraceful wimp, like that one,' she said pointing at the station chief. And she stuck to it, earning our respect. We treated her accordingly – we let her escape.[33]

The famous Belorussian writer Vasil' Bykov fought in the same areas. He could have heard the story about the brave radio operator who was let go by the Germans. In any event, a similar story was described in his novel *The Dead Don't Hurt* and in his novella *The Trap*.

Notes

Preface

1. K. Benyumov, 'Ves' vash pravyashchii klass schitayet sebya naslednikom sovetskoi sistemy', Interv'yu Enn Epplbaum, poluchivshei pulitserovskuyu premiyu za knigu o GULAGe//Meduza, 2017, 29 iyulya (https://meduza.io/feature/2017/07/29/ves-vash-pra-vyashchiy-klass-schitaet-sebya-naslednikom-sovetskoy-sistemy?utm_source=facebook. com&utm_medium=social&utm_campaign=ves-vash-pravyashchiy-klass-schitaet-sebya-na&utm_content=8440485).

2. Editor's note. The *Wehrmacht* ('defence force') was the German term for the unified armed forces (army, navy, and air force) and existed from 1935 to the end of the war.

3. Editor's note. The *Luftwaffe* was the name of the German air force from 1933–45.

4. Editor's note. The Molotov-Ribbentrop Pact, better known as the Nazi-Soviet Non-Aggression Pact, was signed by Soviet people's commissar for foreign affairs V.M. Molotov, and German foreign minister, Joachim von Ribbentrop, in Moscow on 23 August 1939. A secret protocol to the pact divided Eastern Europe between the Soviet Union and Germany.

5. Editor's note. The Soviet-Japanese War lasted from 9 August to 2 September 1945. During the campaign the Red Army defeated the Japanese Kwangtung Army and conquered Manchuria, the southern part of Sakhalin Island and the Kurile Islands.

6. Editor's note. The *Stavka* of the Supreme Commander-in-Chief (*Stavka Verkhovnogo Glav-nokomanduyushchego*), also known as the *Stavka* of the VGK, was the Soviet Union's highest military body during the Second World War. The *Stavka* comprised high-ranking civilian and military personnel and functioned as Stalin's military secretariat. Stalin, as supreme command-er-in-chief, was the chairman of this body and the General Staff its executive organ. A *front* is a higher Russian-Soviet military formation organizationally similar to an army group. The *Stavka* representatives were high-ranking officers dispatched by the *Stavka* to particularly crit-ical *fronts*, for the purpose of assisting the *front* commanders or coordinating the activities of two or more *fronts*.

7. Editor's note. SMERSH (*Smert' shpionam*) was the name for Soviet wartime counterintelli-gence. The phrase means 'death to spies'.

8. Editor's note. 'Chekist' refers to the first Soviet secret police organization, the Extraordinary Commission, known colloquially as the *CheKa*. Even after the organization was repeatedly renamed, its functionaries continued to be popularly referred to as 'chekists' (*chekisty*).

9. Editor's note. The FSB, or Federal Security Service (*Federal'naya Sluzhba Bezopastnosti*), is the post-Soviet successor to the various pre-1991 secret police organizations.

10. Editor's note. The GKO, or State Defence Committee (*Gosudarstvennyi Komitet Oborony*), was organized shortly after the start of the German invasion in June 1941. Chaired by Stalin, the GKO was the country's highest wartime body and supreme decision-making organ.

11. Editor's note. Vyacheslav Mikhailovich Molotov (Skryabin) (1890–1986) joined the Russian Social Democratic Labour Party in 1906 and aligned with its Bolshevik faction. Following the Soviet victory during the civil war, he rose quickly through the party's ranks as an unwavering supporter of Stalin in the intra-party struggles that followed Lenin's death. Molotov served as chairman of the Council of People's Commissars from 1930 to 1941, and people's commissar of foreign affairs/minster of foreign affairs from 1939–49 and 1953–6, and was also a wartime member of the GKO and the *Stavka*. Implicated in a plot to overthrow N.S. Khrushchev in 1957, Molotov was relieved of his posts and later expelled from the Communist Party. Georgii Maksimilianovich Malenkov (1902–88) joined the Red Army in 1918 and the Communist Party two years later. Following the civil war, Malenkov rose quickly in the party's ranks as a staunch Stalinist and took an active role in the purges of the late 1930s. During the Sec-ond World War Malenkov was a member of the GKO and also visited the front as Stalin's representative. Following Stalin's death, Malenkov replaced him as chairman of the Council of

Ministers during 1953–5. Malenkov was implicated in the plot to overthrow Khrushchev and deprived of his government posts. The Battle of Prokhorovka took place on 12 July 1943, during the German offensive against the Kursk salient (Operation 'Citadel'). Although the Soviets lost large numbers of tanks, they did succeed in blunting the German advance.

Chapter 1

1. Winston S. Churchill, *The Second World War*, vol. 1. (Boston: Houghton Mifflin Co., 1985), pp. 351–2.
2. Editor's note. The term 'Winter War' refers to the Soviet-Finnish War of 1939–40. After talks between the two sides failed to satisfy the Soviet Union's territorial demands, the Red Army attacked Finland in November 1939. Despite serious defeats, the Red Army was eventually able to overpower the Finns, who concluded peace in March 1940, ceding sizeable tracts of territory to the USSR.
3. Editor's note. Bessarabia is the territory lying between the Prut and Dnestr rivers. It was annexed by Russia in 1812 and seized by Romania in 1918. The Soviet Union annexed the area in 1940 and won it back in 1944. Most of this area is now the independent country of Moldova. Northern Bukovina is the northern half of the former Austro-Hungarian province of Bukovina. Romania gained control of this area after the First World War and the Soviet Union annexed the northern portion in 1940. This area is now part of independent Ukraine.
4. B. Bonvech and Yu. Galaktionov (eds), *Istoriya Germanii* (Moscow: KDU, 2008), vol. II, p. 266. Characteristically, not a word is spoken in this edition about the Red Army's crimes against the civilian population of Germany.
5. Editor's note. The term 'rootless cosmopolitans' was applied to individuals, usually Jews, in the Soviet Union following the Second World War. These people were charged with displaying in their writings and art too little grounding in the traditions of the Russian people and for kowtowing to foreign, usually Western, countries. The NKVD (*Narodnyi Komissariat Vnutrennykh Del*), or People's Commissariat for Internal Affairs, was the name of the Soviet secret police between 1934 and 1946. This agency had the task of carrying out repressions against the regime's domestic and foreign enemies. These 'national operations' were campaigns of repression carried out by the NKVD against national minorities within the USSR.
6. Editor's note. Nuremberg refers to the series of trials for war crimes and crimes against humanity conducted in the city of Nuremberg during 1945–6.
7. Editor's note. Collectivization refers to the Soviet policy of expropriating private agricultural lands and forcing the rural population into large farming units controlled by the state.
8. Editor's note. Nikita Sergeevich Khrushchev (1894–1971) joined the Communist Party in 1918 and served as a political commissar during the civil war and rose through the ranks of the Communist Party under Stalin's patronage. He was head of the party's Ukrainian branch during 1937–49 and served as a political commissar at the front during the Second World War. Following Stalin's death in 1953, Khrushchev outmanoeuvred his rivals for control of the party and state apparatus. Khrushchev was himself overthrown by his lieutenants in 1964 and forced into retirement.
9. Editor's note. The term kulak ('fist' in Russian) referred to those independent farmers in the late Russian Empire and afterwards who had achieved some measure of prosperity. During Stalin's collectivization campaign of the late 1920s and early 1930s the term was attached to anyone who balked at joining the collective farms then being established in the Soviet Union. The Iron Guard, also known as the Legion of the Archangel Michael, was a nationalist, anti-semitic and anti-communist movement founded in Romania in 1927. The movement was suppressed by the dictator Ion Antonescu in 1941.
10. The documents are cited as follows: Russian State Archive of Socio-Political History (hereafter, RGASPI), f. 558, op. 11 (I.V. Stalin fond), d. 59, pp. 5–7.

11. Editor's note. The *Reichswehr* was the name of the German armed forces from 1919–35, when it was renamed the *Wehrmacht*.
12. Editor's note. Ieronim Petrovich Uborevich (1896–1937) joined the imperial Russian army in 1916 and the Red Army in 1918, in which he fought in the civil war. Following the war, he rose rapidly in the army's ranks and commanded several military districts. Uborevich was arrested and executed in June 1937.
13. L.N. Lopukhovskii and B.K. Kavalerchik, *Zaprogramirovannoe Porazhenie* (Moscow: Yauza; EKSMO, 2010), p. 49. Editor's note. The RKKA (*Raboch'e-Krest'yanskaya Krasnaya Armiya*), or Worker's-Peasant's Red Army, was the official name of the Red Army from 1918 to 1946.
14. Editor's note. The Treaty of Versailles refers to the peace treaty between Germany and the Allied powers signed at Versailles in 1919. The treaty provided for Germany to pay reparations and make territorial concessions and also sharply limited the size of the German army.
15. Lopukhovskii and Kavalerchik, *Zaprogramirovannoe*, pp. 71–2.
16. *Ibid.*, p. 97.
17. Editor's note. Vladimir Kiriakovich Triandafillov (1894–1931) joined the imperial army in 1914 and the Red Army in 1918 and fought in the civil war. Following the war, Triandafillov held a number of posts in the general staff apparatus and was a leading theoretician in the field of operational art. He was killed in a plane crash. Konstantin Bronislavovich Kalinovskii (1897–1931) joined the Red Army in 1918 and fought in the civil war. Following the war, he commanded an experimental mechanized regiment and was chief of the army's mechanization and motorization administration. He died in the same plane crash that killed Triandafillov.
18. Editor's note. Emil Dominik Josef Hacha (1872–1945) became prominent in Czechoslovak legal circles and politics following the country's independence in 1918. Hacha was named president of Czechoslovakia in 1938, following the Munich Agreement that awarded the Sudeten region to Germany. However, Hacha was forced to agree to the occupation of the country by German forces in March 1939, although he retained his title under the Nazi Proctectorate. Hacha was imprisoned after the war and died there under mysterious circumstances.
19. P. Aptekar', 'Vystrelov ne Bylo', *Rodina* (1995), no. 12, pp. 56–7.
20. Editor's note. Otto Wilhelm Kuusinen (1881–1964) joined the Finnish Social Democratic Party as a young man but was driven from the country following the collapse of the Finnish Socialist Workers' Republic in 1918. He was appointed head of the Finnish Democratic Republic at the beginning of the Soviet-Finnish War in 1939, but it was forgotten in the ensuing fighting. Kuusinen continued to occupy high posts in the Soviet Communist Party until his death. The Comintern (Communist International), or Third International, was established by a number of communist parties in 1919 to promote a world revolution and to replace the discredited Second International, which had collapsed three years earlier during the First World War. Stalin abolished the Comintern in 1943 as a gesture to the Western Allies.
21. Editor's note. Jozef Klemens Pilsudski (1867–1935) was a Polish nationalist leader who joined the Polish Socialist Party in 1893. In 1914 he organized Polish forces to fight for the Central Powers against Russia. At the end of the First World War he led Polish forces against Ukraine, the Soviet Union, Lithuania, and Germany. After retiring from politics, Pilsudski led a coup and became the dominant power in the government until his death.
22. Editor's note. This refers to the massacre of approximately 22,000 captured Polish officers, policemen, and members of the prewar Polish intelligentsia near the village of Katyn' and other locales in the western Soviet Union in April–May 1940 at the hands of the NKVD.
23. Editor's note. Wladyslaw Eugeniusz Sikorski (1881–1943) was a Polish nationalist who fought for his country's independence following the First World War. He was active in Polish postwar politics and served as prime minister. He also served as prime minister of the Polish government in exile during 1939–43 until his death in a plane crash. Stanislaw Mikolajczyk (1901–66) joined the Polish army in 1920 and later became involved in politics. He served as prime minister of the Polish government in exile during 1943–4, when he returned to Poland

as deputy prime minister of a coalition government. He fled abroad in 1948 following rigged elections and the establishment of a communist government and died in exile.

24. Editor's note. The Mannerheim Line was the popular name for the complex of fortifications during the interwar period along the Karelian Isthmus. The fortifications were named in honour of Carl Gustaf Emil Mannerheim (1867–1951), who served as commander-in-chief of the Finnish armed forces and later as president. The Red Army broke through the Mannerheim Line during the 1939–40 'Winter War'.

25. A.A. Smirnov, *Krakh 1941–Repressii ni pri Chyom* (Moscow: Yauza; EKSMO, 2011).

26. Editor's note. Mikhail Nikolaevich Tukhachevskii (1893–1937) joined the imperial Russian army in 1914 and the Red Army in 1918 and fought in the civil war. Following the war, Tukhachevskii put down internal rebellions against Bolshevik rule and served as chief of staff, commanded military districts and directed the Red Army's rearmament programme. He was arrested and executed along with several other high-ranking officers in June 1937. Iona Emmanuilovich Yakir (1896–1937) joined the Red Army in 1918 and fought in the civil war. Following the war, he commanded the Kiev Military District for over a decade before being arrested and shot in June 1937, along with Tukhachevskii and Uborevich.

27. Editor's note. Semyon Mikhailovich Budennyi (1883–1973) was drafted into the Russian imperial army in 1903 and fought in the Russo-Japanese War and the First World War. He joined the Red Army in 1918 and commanded cavalry forces during the civil war. Following the war, Budennyi allied himself with the Stalin clique and rose to high rank. He commanded large forces during the Second World War, but was eventually relieved for incompetence, although he never suffered for his mistakes.

28. Editor's note. Boris Sergeevich Gorbachev (1892–1937) joined the Red Army in 1918 and fought in the civil war. He eventually rose to the rank of military district commander until his arrest and execution in July 1937.

29. Editor's note. The *Komsomol* was the popular acronym for the Soviet-era *Vsesoyuznyi Leninskii Kommunisticheskii Soyuz Molodezhi* (All-Union Leninist Communist Union of Youth), or VLKSM, which was the Communist Party's youth auxiliary. Founded in 1918, the organization was dissolved in 1991.

30. A.A. Smirnov, *Boevaya Vyuchka Krasnoi Armii Nakanune Repressii* (Moscow: Rodina Media, 2014) vol. I, p. 416; vol. 2, p. 568. For an abbreviated version of this book, see 'Mental'nost' Protiv Taktiki', *Voenno-Promyshlennyi Kur'yer (BPK)*, 2015, 13 maya, no. 17, p. 11, https://vpk-news.ru/articles/25171; 'Armiya-Nedouchka. Komandiry Predrepressionnoi RKKA veli Voiska na Uboi', *VPK*, 2015, 3 iyunya, no. 20, p. 11, https://vpk-news.ru/articles/25471; 'Part-kanonada. Ideologicheskie Ustanovki Razvalivali RKKA Gorazdo Effektivnee Vrazheskoi Agentury', *VPK*, 2015, 17 iyunya, no. 22, p. 11, https://vpk-news.ru/articles/25675; 'Rozygrysh Voenachal'nikov–Chast' I. Kievskie Manevry 1935 Goda byli Grandioznoi Pokazukhoi//', *VPK*, 2015, 1 iyulya, no. 24, p. 11, https://vpk-news.ru/articles/25866; 'Rozygrysh Voenachal'nikov–Chast' II. Kievskie manevry 1935 goda byli Grandioznoi Pokazukhoi', *VPK*, 2015, 8 iyulya, no. 25, p. 11, https://vpk-news.ru/articles/25982.

31. Editor's note. The SS (*Schutzstaffel*) was founded in 1923 to provide security for Nazi Party gatherings and later evolved into a large military organization in its own right under its leader Heinrich Himmler (1900–45). During the Second World War the SS was responsible for carrying out the Holocaust and other crimes against humanity. The national units referred to here were raised among the citizens of the occupied countries.

32. I. Butulis and A. Zunka, *Istoriya Latvii* (Riga: Jumava, 2010), p. 167.

33. Editor's note. The Moscow Peace Treaty, signed in Moscow on 12 March 1940, ended the Soviet-Finnish War.

34. Editor's note. Chiang Kai-shek (1887–1975) joined the Chinese army in 1906. Following the overthrow of the imperial dynasty in 1911, he gradually rose to head the Chinese Republic as head of the Kuomintang, or Chinese Nationalist Party. Chiang fought the Japanese during

1937–45 and a twenty-year civil war with the Chinese Communists until the latter's victory in 1949. Chiang and his followers then fled to the island of Taiwan, where he ruled as president until his death.

35. Editor's note. Hermann Wilhelm Goring (1893–1946) joined the imperial German army in 1912 and became a decorated fighter pilot during the First World War. Following the war, Goring joined the Nazi Party and became one of Hitler's trusted lieutenants and designated successor. He commanded the Luftwaffe before and after the Second World War until relieved by Hitler during the war's closing days. Goring was sentenced to death during the Nuremberg war crimes trials, but committed suicide before the sentence could be carried out.

36. Editor's note. Berthold Konrad Hermann Albert Speer (1905–81) trained as an architect and joined the Nazi Party in 1931 and became Hitler's personal architect. Hitler appointed Speer armaments minister in 1942, after which German armaments production improved greatly, although this involved the large-scale employment of forced labour. Speer was tried at Nuremberg and sentenced to twenty years in prison for war crimes. He was released in 1966. Walter Friedrich Schellenberg (1910–52) joined the SS in 1933 and was one of the architects of the Holocaust. He became head of foreign intelligence in 1944, but was imprisoned and convicted by the Allies of war crimes. He was released from prison in 1951 and died in Italy.

37. Editor's note. Leonid Il'ich Brezhnev (1906–82) joined the Communist Party in 1929 and also served as a military commissar during the Second World War. He replaced Nikita Khrushchev as party chief in 1964 and ruled the Soviet Union until his death. His years in power are now widely derided as a period of 'stagnation'.

38. Editor's note. The British Expeditionary Force (BEF) was dispatched to France upon the outbreak of war in 1939 and evacuated back to the United Kingdom from Dunkirk in May–June 1940.

39. Editor's note. 'I' tank refers to the British MK1 ('Matilda') light tank which appeared briefly during the Second World War. One model weighed 11 tons and carried a crew of two. It was armed with a 7.7mm or 12.7mm machine gun.

40. Editor's note. Karl Rudolph Gerd von Rundstedt (1875–1953) joined the imperial German army and served during the First World War and in the postwar *Reichswehr*. During the Second World War he commanded army groups in Poland, the West, and the Soviet Union, and was commander-in-chief of German forces in the West during 1942–5. Following the war, he was charged with war crimes, but was later released.

41. Editor's note. Charles Andre Joseph Marie de Gaulle (1890–1970) joined the French army in 1912 and fought in and was captured during the First World War. During the interwar period he was an advocate of armoured warfare and commanded an armoured division during the Second World War. Following the defeat of France, de Gaulle fled to Great Britain and organized the 'Free French' forces. Following the liberation of France, de Gaulle headed the provisional government until his resignation in 1946. De Gaulle continued to remain politically active, however, and returned to power as president of the Fifth Republic in 1958, in which post he remained until his resignation in 1969.

42. J. Fuller, *Vtoraya Mirovaya Voina, 1939–1945. Strategicheskii i Takticheskii Obzor*, trans. from English (Moscow: Innostrannaya Literatura, 1956), pp. 102–3. Editor's note. Lord Gort, John Standish Surtees Prendergast Vereker (1886–1946), was commissioned in the British army in 1905 and fought in the First World War. During the Second World War he commanded the British Expeditionary Force (BEF) in France until its evacuation from Dunkirk. Although not blamed for the debacle, Gort was relegated to secondary assignments for the duration of the war.

43. Editor's note. Heinz Wilhelm Guderian (1888–1954) joined the German imperial army in 1907 and fought in the First World War and served in the interwar *Reichswehr*. He was the army's most prominent advocate of mechanized warfare and commanded armoured formations in Poland, the West, and the Soviet Union. Guderian also served as chief of the army general staff

during 1944–5. He was arrested and held after the war, but was never charged with a crime before his release in 1948.

44. Editor's note. Albert Kesselring (1885–1960) joined the imperial German army in 1904 and fought in the First World War and served in the interwar *Reichswehr*. During the Second World War Kesselring commanded German air forces in Poland, the West, the Battle of Britain, and in the Soviet Union and later commanded German forces in the Mediterranean and the West. Following the war, Kesselring was convicted of war crimes and sentenced to death, but he was freed in 1952.

45. A. Kesselring, *Luftwaffe. Triumf i Porazhenie. Vospominaniya Fel'dmarshala Tret'ego Reikha, 1933–1947*, trans. from English (Moscow: Tsentropoligraf, 2003), p. 88.

46. Editor's note. The Siebel ferry (*Siebelfahre*) was a shallow-draft landing craft invented by aircraft designer Fritz Siebel in preparation for Operation 'Sea Lion' and used by the German army during the Second World War.

47. Kesselring, *Luftwaffe*, p. 87.

48. Editor's note. Operation 'Sea Lion' was the code name for the German invasion of the British Isles. Following the *Luftwaffe's* failure to gain air superiority during the Battle of Britain, Operation 'Sea Lion' was shelved.

Chapter 2

1. Editor's note. The Maginot Line was an extensive system of concrete fortifications built along the Franco-German border during the 1930s and named after the defence minister Andre Maginot. The Germans bypassed the Maginot Line in 1940 and it has since become a metaphor for expensive failure.

2. V.F. Tributs, *Baltiitsy Vstupayut v Boi* (Kaliningrad: Knizhnoye Izdatel'stvo, 1972), p. 29; N.G. Kuznetsov, *Krutye Povoroty: Iz Zapisok Admirala* (Moscow: Molodaya Gvardiya, 1995), p. 209.

3. 'Akt o Priyome Narkomata Oborony Soyuza SSR tov. Timoshenko S.K. ot tov. Voroshilova K.Ye.', *Voenno-Istoricheskii Zhurnal* (hereafter *V-IZh*) (1992), no. 1, p. 14.

4. Editor's note. The *Einsatzgruppen* ('task forces') were special SS death squads, which were responsible for carrying out mass murders in German-occupied territory during the Second World War.

5. Ye. Aronov, 'Zachem SShA Khranili Sekrety Katyni?'. Radio 'Svoboda', 11 September 2012, https://www.svoboda.org/a/24704433.html.

6. Editor's note. Lend-Lease was an American aid programme that delivered food, military equipment, and raw materials to the Allies during the Second World War. In all 50.1 billion dollars of aid was delivered, including 11.3 billion dollars to the USSR.

7. Editor's note. The Warsaw uprising was an armed insurrection by the Polish Home Army to liberate Warsaw from German occupation before the city could be captured by the Red Army. The uprising began on 1 August and ended with the Polish forces' surrender on 2 October 1944.

8. Editor's note. Mikhail Sergeevich Gorbachev (1931–) joined the Communist Party as a young man and rose rapidly through its ranks, becoming General Secretary in 1985. He then embarked upon a campaign to reform the inflexible Soviet system, but his efforts were unsuccessful and the country fell apart in 1991.

9. 'The Katyn' Forest Massacre', repr. House Report No. 2505, 82nd Congress, 2nd Session (22 December 1952) (Washington, US Government Printing Office, 1988); J.K. Zawodny, *Death in the Forest: The Story of the Katyn Forest Massacre* (University of Notre Dame, 1962), p. 91ff.; US House of Representatives, Select Committee on the Katyn Forest Massacre. The Katyn Forest Massacre. Hearings Before the Select Committee to Conduct an Investigation of the Facts. Evidence and Circumstances of the Katyn Forest Massacre. 82nd Congress, 1st and

2nd Sessions, 1951-2 (Washington, US Government Printing Office, 1952), 7 pts, 2,362 pp.; part 6, Exhibit 32, pp. 1795-6.

10. Editor's note. Paul Joseph Goebbels (1893-1945) joined the Nazi Party in 1924 and soon entered Hitler's inner circle. Upon the Nazi assumption of power in 1933, Hitler named Goebbels minister of propaganda. He kept this post throughout the war and was also in charge of the country's total mobilization drive from 1943 on. Hitler appointed Goebbels as chancellor, but he survived Hitler by only one day. He and his wife poisoned their children and then killed themselves.

11. M.A. Gareev, *Neodnoznachnye Stranitsy Voiny (Ocherki o Problemnykh Voprosakh Velikoi Otechestvennoi Voiny* (Moscow: RFM, 1995), p. 93. Editor's note. Nikolai Fyodorovich Vatutin (1901-44) joined the Red Army in 1920 and afterwards rose through the ranks, primarily in staff positions. During the Second World War Vatutin was deputy chief of the General Staff and commanded various *fronts*. He was ambushed by Ukrainian partisans and later died of his wounds.

12. *Na Priyome u Stalina. Tetradi (Zhurnaly) Zapisei Lits, Prinyatykh I.V. Stalinym (1924-1953 gg.)* (Moscow: Novyi Khronograf, 2008), p. 582.

13. *Ibid.*, pp. 327-8, 311.

14. VS. Parsadanova, 'Stalin, Beria i Sud'ba Armii Andersa v 1941-1942 gg. (Iz Rassekrechennykh Arkhivov)', *Novaya i Noveishaya Istoriya* (1993), no. 2, p. 62. Editor's note. The Politburo (full title, Political Bureau of the Central Committee of the Communist Party of the Soviet Union) was founded in 1917 as the highest political body in the Bolshevik Party. It was reestablished in 1919 and continued operating until its dissolution in 1991. The Politburo was also known as the Presidium during 1952-66.

15. Additions to excerpts from the materials of the American 'Special Commission . . .', 18 July 1953. In O.B. Mazokhin(ed.), *Politburo i Delo Beria. Sbornik Dokumentov* (Moscow: Kuchkovo Pole, 2012), p. 122. An anonymous witness told the American Congress's commission about this, citing a conversation with Colonel Gorczynski. Editor's note. Lavrentii Pavlovich Beria (1899-1953) joined the Bolshevik Party in 1917 and afterwards began his career in the state security apparatus. After a political and secret police career in Georgia, Stalin appointed Beria head of the NKVD in 1938. During the Second World War Beria was responsible for such delicate operations as the Katyn' massacre as well as the Soviet atom-bomb project. Beria was arrested shortly after Stalin's death and executed. Berling is probably Zigmunt Henryk Berling (1896-1980), who joined the Polish army in 1918. The Soviets captured Berling in 1939, but he evidently agreed to collaborate with them. He joined the Soviet-sponsored Polish army in 1943 and the following year he was made deputy commander. He was recalled to Moscow in 1944 and returned to Poland only in 1947 and retired from the service in 1953. He spent the rest of his career in non-military positions.

16. Editor's note. Kliment Yefremovich Voroshilov (1881-1969) joined the Bolshevik faction of the Russian Social Democratic Labour Party in 1905. During the civil war he commanded a *front* and was a political commissar. He aligned himself with the Stalin faction and served as defence commissar from 1925-40, when he was relieved due to the Finnish debacle. Voroshilov commanded Soviet forces during the Second World War, but was relieved for incompetence, although he continued to occupy ceremonial posts in the state and party until his death.

17. P. Aptekar', 'Neizvestnoe Voisko Nesushchestvuyushchei Strany', *Nezavisimaya Gazeta*, 1994, 25 November, p. 4.

18. Editor's note. This was the code name, picked by Hitler, for the plan for the invasion of Russia. Its application is generally confined to the period June–December 1941.

19. Editor's note. *Blitzkrieg*, or 'lightning war', was the term popularly employed to describe the German strategy of quick and sudden military victories over individual opponents, with the widespread employment of tanks and aircraft.

20. V.N. Kisilev, 'Upryamye Fakty Nachala Voiny', *V-IZh* (1992), No. 2, pp. 17-18.

21. Editor's note. Aleksandr Mikhailovich Vasilevskii (1895–1977) joined the imperial army in 1915 and the Red Army in 1918. During the Second World War he served primarily in the General Staff apparatus and was chief of the General Staff during 1942–5. He was also a *Stavka* representative to several *fronts* and commanded troops in Europe and the Far East. Following the war he again served as chief of the General Staff and was later minister of the armed forces. Vasilevskii's career went into decline after Stalin's death and he was forced to retire in 1957. Semyon Konstantinovich Timoshenko (1895–1970) was drafted into the imperial Russian army in 1914 and the Red Army in 1918. He later commanded Soviet forces in Finland and was appointed defence commissar in 1940. During the Second World War he commanded several *fronts* and high commands, but his lack of success led to his eventual eclipse and he never held an important command after 1942. Georgii Konstantinovich Zhukov (1896–1974) was drafted into the Russian imperial army in 1915 and joined the Red Army in 1918. During the Second World War Zhukov served as chief of the General Staff, commanded several *fronts* and was a *Stavka* representative to others. He was unceremoniously demoted by Stalin after the war but returned to power under his successors. Nikita S. Khrushchev removed Zhukov from his post of defence minister in 1957.
22. For the text to the 15 May plan see V.P. Naumov (ed.), *1941 God. Dokumenty* (Moscow: Mezhdunarodnyi Fond 'Demokratiya', 1998), vol. II, pp. 215–20.
23. V.D. Danilov, 'Hat der Generalstab der Roten Armee einen Praventivschlag gegen Deutschland vorbereitet?', *Osterreichische Militarische Zeitschrift*, XXXI, Jg., H. 1, (1993), pp. 41–51. V.D. Danilov first published this article, with excerpts from the document, at the start of 1992 as 'Gotovil li Stalin Napadenie na Germaniyu? Kommentarii V. Danilova', *Komsomol'skaya Pravda*, 1992, 4 January, p. 5.
24. Editor's note. Mikhail Petrovich Kirponos (1892–1941) was drafted into the Russian imperial army and joined the Red Army in 1918. He later commanded a division in the war with Finland. During the Second World War Kirponos commanded the Southwestern Front, but his forces were surrounded east of Kiev and he was killed trying to break out. Dmitrii Grigor'evich Pavlov (1897–1941) fought in the First World War and joined the Red Army in 1919. During the interwar period he commanded armoured forces in Spain. During the Second World War he commanded the Western Front until he was blamed for the disaster of the opening days and relieved of command. Pavlov was executed a month later.
25. Editor's note. The Balkan campaign began with the abortive Italian invasion of Greece in October 1940, after which a stalemate ensued. German forces invaded Yugoslavia and Greece in April 1941 and quickly overwhelmed the native and British forces in the area.
26. M. Solonin, 'Igry 41-go Goda—Chast' II', *VPK*, 2012, 21 Noyabrya, no. 46, pp. 10–11, https://vpk-news.ru/articles/13223.
27. M. Solonin, 'Igry 41-go Goda—Chast' I', *VPK*, 2012, 14 Noyabrya, no. 45, pp. 10–11, https://vpk-news.ru/articles/13123.
28. Editor's note. As a result of the Reds' opponents during the Russian Civil War being known as the Whites, for sometime afterwards the adjective 'White' was automatically attached to any movement or regimen deemed unfriendly by the Soviets. The words 'noble fury' and 'boil up like a wave' are from a wartime song, 'The Sacred War' by A. Aleksandrov and V. Lebedev-Kumach. M. Solonin, 'Neizvestnaya "Igra" Maya 41-go', *VPK*, 2012, 22 Fevrelya, no. 7, pp. 10–11, http://vpk-news.ru/articles/8636.
29. Naumov, *1941 God*, vol. II, pp. 216–18.
30. Editor's note. Paul Ludwig Ewald von Kleist (1881–1954) commanded armoured troops in Poland, the West, the Balkans, and the Soviet Union. Hitler relieved him of command in 1944. The Americans extradited von Kleist to the Soviet Union, where he was imprisoned until his death.

31. Danilov, V.D., 'Zabyvchivost' ili Obman? O Nekotorykh Nestykovkakh v Osveshchenii Preddverii Velikoi Otechestvennoi Voiny', *Nezavisimoye Voennoye Obozreniye*, 2001, 22 Iyunya, no. 22, p. 5. See also Kisilev, 'Upryamye', pp. 14–15.

32. Editor's note. The OKW (*Oberkommando der Wehrmacht*) was established in 1938 to coordinate army, navy and air force operations. As the war progressed, the OKW came increasingly to operate as Hitler's military staff in opposition to the army high command (OKH). Wilhelm Keitel (1882–1946) joined the imperial army in 1901 and fought in the First World War and served in the interwar *Reichswehr*. Hitler appointed Keitel chief of the armed forces high command (OKW) in 1938 and he held this post to the end of the war. Keitel signed the German surrender in Berlin. He was tried for war crimes in Nuremberg and executed. Alfred Josef Ferdinand Jodl (1890–1946) joined the imperial army in 1910 and fought in the First World War and served in the interwar *Reichswehr*. In 1939 he was appointed chief of the armed forces high command (OKW) operations staff. Jodl signed the German surrender at Reims on 7 May 1945. He was convicted of war crimes at Nuremberg and executed.

33. V.A. Lebedev, 'Priznaniya bez Pokayaniya (iz Protokolov Pervykh Doprosov Natsistskikh Prestupnikov', *V-IZh* (1993), no. 8, p. 83.

34. V. Schellenberg, *Labirint*, trans. from the English (Moscow: Dom Biruni, 1991), p. 192. Editor's note. Reinhard Tristan Eugen Heydrich (1904–42) joined the German navy in 1922 and the SS in 1931. He rose rapidly in the organization and was one of the prime authors of the Holocaust. He was killed by Czech partisans.

35. 'Kratkaya Zapis' Rezul'tatov Oprosa V. Keitelya', *Rasplata: Tretii Reikh: Padenie v Propast'*, compiled by Ye.Ye. Shemeleva-Stenina (Moscow: Respublika, 1994), pp. 116–17.

36. Editor's note. Gunther Alois Friedrich Blumentritt (1892–1967) joined the imperial army in 1911 and served in the First World War. During the Second World War he served in a variety of increasingly more responsible staff positions and also commanded corps and an army. Following the war, Blumetritt helped to organize the new West German army.

37. G. Blyumentrit, *Fel'dmarshal fon Rundshtedt*, trans. from English (Moscow: Tsentrpoligraf, 2005), p. 100.

38. G.K. Zhukov, *Vospominaniya i Razmyshleniya*, 12th edn (Moscow: Novosti, 1995), vol. I, p. 373.

39. Editor's note. This refers to the visit by V.M. Molotov, then chairman of the Council of People's Commissars and commissar for foreign affairs.

40. H. Guderian, *Panzer Leader* (Cambridge, MA: Da Capo Press (the Perseus Book Group), 2002), p. 141. H. Guderian, *Erinnerungen Eines Soldaten* (Neckargemuend: Kurt Vowinkel Verlag, 1960), IV Aufl., p. 127. In the Russian translation of 1954, which was uncritically reproduced in subsequent editions, this passage was shortened and tendentiously distorted. Only the following text remained: 'From Molotov's visit and the course of the negotiations, Hitler came to the conclusion that war with the Soviet Union could not be avoided. More than once he drew for me the course of the Berlin negotiations in the very same way in which I presented them above [an obvious trace of the shortening]. To be sure, he spoke to me about this matter for the first time in 1943, but he subsequently and repeated to me the same thing, evaluating in the same way the negotiations unalterably. I doubt [in the original it is 'I don't doubt', *Ich zweifle nicht*] that he relayed to me exactly that point of view which he maintained at that time'. G. Guderian, *Vospominaniya Soldata* (Smolensk: Rusich, 1999), p. 190.

41. A.M. Vasilevskii, 'Nakanune Voiny (Interv'yu 1965 g.)', *Novaya i Noveishaya Istoriya* (1992), no. 6, p. 8.

42. 'Direktivy I.V. Stalina V.M. Molotovu pered Poezdkoi v Berlin v Noyabre 1940 g', *Novaya i Noveishaya Istoriya* (1995), no. 4, pp. 77–9.

43. RGASPI, f. 558, op. 11, d. 208. TASS communiqués with Stalin's notations.

44. Editor's note. Aleksandr Nikolaevich Poskryobyshev (1891–1965) joined the Bolshevik Party in 1917 and quickly rose through the party's administrative ranks, becoming the head of Stalin's personal secretariat in 1928, where he served a quarter of a century. Stalin removed

Poskryobyshev in 1952, but he was reinstated following the dictator's death. Poskryobyshev was retired in 1956. TASS (*Telegrafnoye Agenstvo Sovetskogo Soyuza*), or Telegraph Agency of the Soviet Union, was the Soviet official news agency from 1925 to 1992.

45. Editor's note. Vichy is a reference to the French government in non-occupied France during 1940–2, its capital situated in the provincial town of Vichy. The government pursued a policy of collaboration with Nazi Germany.

46. RGASPI, f. 558, op. 11, d. 208, pp. 65–6.

47. Editor's note. This was a German light tank which saw brief service during the Second World War. One model weighed 5.4 tons, carried a crew of two and mounted two 7.92mm machine guns.

48. RGASPI, f. 558, op. 11, d. 206 (see V.A. Nevezhin, *Esli Zavtra v Pokhod . . .* (Moscow: Yauza; EKSMO, 2007), pp. 280–1.

49. Editor's note. Nikolai Gerasimovich Kuznetsov (1904–74) joined the Red Navy in 1919 and rose rapidly through the ranks and was appointed people's commissar for naval affairs in 1939. During the Second World War he commanded the Soviet navy and was a member of the *Stavka*. Kuznetsov was tried and demoted in 1948, but returned to favour in 1951 as naval minister. Kuznetsov was relieved of his post and demoted in 1956 and was not fully rehabilitated until after his death.

50. N.G. Kuznetsov, *Nakanune* (Moscow: Voennoe Izdatel'stvo, 1966), pp. 323–4. In subsequent editions of his memoirs this place was cut by the censor.

51. N.G. Kuznetsov, *Krutye Povoroty*, compiled and ed. by V.N. Kuznetsova and R.V. Kuznetsova (Moscow: Molodaya Gvardiya, 1995), pp. 76–7, 47–8.

52. Lopukhovskii, et al., *Zaprogramirovannoe*, p. 468.

53. *Ibid.*, p. 553.

54. Naumov, *1941*, vol. II, p. 216.

55. Editor's note. The Tripartite Pact was signed on 27 September 1940 by representatives of Germany, Italy, and Japan and seen as directed chiefly against the USA. Hungary, Romania, Bulgaria, and Yugoslavia later signed the agreement, as well as the German client state of Slovakia and the German-occupied territory of Croatia.

56. 'Kratkaya Zapis', p. 117.

57. Naumov, *1941*, vol. II, p. 219.

58. O.V. Vishlev, 'Pochemu zhe Medlil Stalin in 1941 g.?', *Novaya i Noveishaya Istoriya* (1992), no. 2, pp. 78, 82–3.

59. See P.N. Bobylev, 'K Kakoi Voine Gotovilsya General'nyi Shtab RKKA v 1941 Godu?', *Otechestvennaya Istoriya* (1995), no. 5, pp. 3–20. See also his 'Repetitsiya Katastrofy', *V-IZh* (1993), no. 6, pp. 10–16; no. 7, pp. 14–21; no. 8, pp. 28–35. See also his 'V Yanvarye Sorok Pervogo Krasnaya Armiya Nastupala na Kenigsberg', *Izvestiya*, 1993, 22 Iyunya, pp. 4–5.

60. B. Myuller-Gillebrand, *Sukhoputnaya Armiya Germanii, 1933–1945*, trans. from the German (Moscow: Izografus; EKSMO, 2003), pp. 663–5. Editor's note. Citadel was the German code name for the offensive against the Kursk salient in July 1943.

61. Yu.A. Gor'kov and Yu.N. Semin, 'O Kharaktere Voenno-Operativnykh Planov SSSR Nakanune Velikoi Otechestvennoi Voiny. Novye Arkhivnye Dokumenty', *Voina i Politika, 1939–1941* (Moscow: Nauka, 1999), p. 291. The plans for the covering of the western border military districts were published in Yu.A. Gor'kov and Yu.N. Semin, 'Konets Global'noi Lzhi', *V-IZh* (1996), no. 2, pp. 2–14; no. 3, pp. 4–17; no. 4, pp. 2–17; no. 5, pp. 2–15; no. 6, pp. 2–7.

62. Lopukhovskii et al., *Zaprogramirovannoe*, p. 412.

63. E. Manshtein, *Uteryannye Pobedy*, trans. from German (Moscow: AST; St Petersburg: Terra Fantastica, 1999), pp. 185–6. Editor's note. Erich von Manstein (1887–1973) joined the German imperial army in 1906 and fought in the First World War. During the Second World War he served as chief of staff of an army group and commanded corps, an army, and an army group. He was relieved by Hitler in early 1944 and never held a command afterward. Follow-

ing the war, Manstein was convicted of war crimes, but served only a few years before being released.

64. Lopukhovskii et al., *Zaprogramirovannoe*, pp. 428, 430.

65. *Ibid.*, pp. 441–5.

66. Kavalerchik et al., *Zaprogramirovannoe*, p. 506. Editor's note. Yakov Nikolaevich Fedorenko (1896–1947) was drafted into the Russian imperial navy in 1915 and he joined the Red Army in 1918. During the Second World War he headed the Main Armoured Administration and was simultaneously chief of the Red Army's mechanized and armoured forces.

Chapter 3

1. Editor's note. Walther Hewell (1904–45) joined the Nazi Party at an early age and was a close personal friend of Hitler and served as personal liaison between the dictator and the Ministry of Foreign Affairs. Hewell committed suicide after the fall of Berlin.

2. R. Ribbentrop, *Moi Otets Ioakhim fon Ribbentrop: 'Nikogda Protiv Rossii'* (Moscow: Yauza, 2015), p. 251.

3. Editor's note. Stepan Andriyonovich Bandera (1909–59) became involved in Ukrainian nationalist politics as a student. Following the invasion of the Soviet Union he was arrested by the Germans, who later freed him in the hopes of stemming the Soviet advance. Bandera was killed in Munich by a Soviet agent. Yaroslav Stetsko (1912–86) was born in Austria-Hungary and became active in Ukrainian nationalist politics in interwar Poland. He was a follower of Stepan Bandera and imprisoned with the latter by the Germans. Stetsko was the leader of the OUN from 1968 until his death.

4. Editor's note. The *Armia Krajowa* (Home Army) was the armed force of the Polish government in exile. Organized in 1942, it was disbanded in 1945 under the threat of civil war and increasing Soviet repression against its members.

5. D.B. Khazanov, *1941. Voina v Vozdukhe. Gor'kie Uroki* (Moscow: Yauza; EKSMO, 2006), p. 159, table 2.5.

6. D.B. Khazanov, 'Nad Kurskoi Dugoi'//STsBIST (Elektronnyi Resurs), 2012, 13 Avgusta, http://scbist.com/blogs/admin/499-d-hazanov-nad-kurskoi-dugoi.html. Vitalii Gorbach calculates the German Sixth Air Fleet's combat and non-combat irreplaceable losses along the northern flank of the Kursk salient on 5 July at 21 aircraft, assigning to this group aircraft that suffered damage of 40 per cent and more (V. Gorbach, *Nad Ognennoi Dugoi. Sovetskaya Aviatsiya v Kurskoi Bitve* (Moscow: Yauza; EKSMO, 2007), p. 60).

7. C. Hanser, 'German and Soviet Losses as an Indicator of the Length and Intensity of the Battle for the Brest Fortress (1941)', *The Journal of Slavic Military Studies*, 2014, vol. 27, no. 3, pp. 449–66; C. Hartmann, *Wehrmacht im Ostkrieg. Front und Hinterland, 1941–42* (Munchen, 2010), p. 263.

8. Editor's note. The T-34 was the Red Army's premier medium tank of the Second World War. It first appeared in 1940 and weighed 26.5 tons. The early model carried a crew of four and was armed with a 76mm gun and two 7.62mm machine guns. A later model mounted an 85mm gun and carried a crew of four.

9. A. Gurov, 'Boevye Deistviya Sovetskikh Voisk na Yugo-Zapadnom Napravlenii v Nachal'nom Periode Voiny', *V-IZh* (1988), no. 8, p. 310. Editor's note. The Stalin Line refers to the fortifications along the Soviet Union's pre-1939 frontier.

10. Guderian, *Vospominaniya*, pp. 255–71.

11. Editor's note. The OKH (*Oberkommando des Heeres*) was the abbreviation for the German army high command.

12. Editor's note. Operation 'Typhoon' is the code name given to the German offensive operation to capture Moscow.

13. V.G. Krivosheev (ed.), *Rossiya i SSSR v Voinakh XX Veka* (Moscow: Olma-Press, 2001), p. 310.

14. M. Axworthy, C. Scafes, C. Craciunoiu, *Third Axis, Fourth Ally. Romanian Armed Forces in the European War, 1941–1945* (London: Arms and Armour Press, 1995), p. 58. The figure of 16,000 representing prisoners captured by the Romanians in the fighting for Odessa is confirmed by the fact that when in 1943 Romania officially annexed Transnistria (Odessa oblast'), 13,682 natives of Transnistria were freed (A. Shneer, *Plen* (Jerusalem: author's publication, 2003), vol. I, pp. 222–3). There is no doubt that the majority of these were captured during the fighting for Odessa. Besides this, 3,331 Soviet military personnel, mainly natives of Transnistria, escaped from Romanian captivity. (Axworthy et al., *Third Axis*, p. 217).

15. A.S. Yunovidov, *Oborona Odessy. 1941. Pervaya Bitva za Chernoye Morye* (Moscow: Veche, 2011), p. 406.

16. Axworthy et al., *Third Axis*, p. 58.

17. *Khronika Velikoi Otechestvennoi Voiny Sovetskogo Soyuza na Chernomorskom Teatre* (Moscow: 1945), Vypusk 1, p. 83 (cited according to Khazanov, *1941*, pp. 371–2). Editor's note. Filipp Sergeevich Oktyabr'skii (nee Ivanov) (1899–1969) joined the Red Navy in 1918 and fought in the civil war. During the Great Patriotic War he commanded the Black Sea Fleet and Amur River Flotilla. Following the war, Oktyabr'skii continued to command the Black Sea Fleet and also served in the navy's scientific research and educational apparatus.

18. K.M. Simonov, *100 Sutok Voiny* (Smolensk: Rusich, 1996), p. 496. Editor's note. Konstantin Mikhailovich Simonov (1915–79) was a noted Soviet author, playwright, and war correspondent. Following the war, Simonov held a number of high-ranking posts in the Soviet literary establishment.

19. Axworthy, et al., *Third Axis*, p. 58.

20. Yunovidov, *Oborona*, p. 405.

21. *Ibid.*, pp. 404–6, 416.

22. 9may.od.ua-Odessa v Velikoi Otechestvennoi Voine. 421-ya strelkovaya diviziya//may.od.ua/history/oborona/11–421-ya-strelkovaya-diviziya.html.

23. Yunovidov, *Oborona*, p. 139.

24. Editor's note. Lev Zakharovich Mekhlis (1889–1953) joined the Russian army in 1911 and the Red Army in 1918. During the Second World War he headed the armed forces Main Political Directorate (GlavPUR) during 1941–2, until he was relieved. He also served as a political commissar on several fronts. Following the war Mekhlis served in the government apparatus. GlavPUR was the Soviet-era acronym for the armed forces' Main Political Directorate, responsible for the armed forces' political loyalty.

25. Yunovidov, *Oborona*, pp. 416, 139.

26. 'Razvitie Organizatsionnoi-Shtatnoi Struktury Strelkovoi Divizii RKKA (http://rkka.ru./iorg.htm).

27. K.A. Kalashnikov, V.I. Fes'kov, A.Yu. Chmykhalo, V.I. Golikov, *Krasnaya Armiya v Iyune 1941 Goda (Statisticheskii Sbornik)* (Novosibirsk: Sibirskii Khronograf, 2003), p. 62.

28. Axworthy et al., *Third Axis*, p. 58.

29. 'Voiinskie Soedineniya, Istoriya Kotorykh Svyazana s Novorossiiskom', //http://novorosforum.ru/threads/Voinskie-soedineniya-istoriya-kotorykh-svyazana-s-Novorossiiskom. 2087/. Editor's note. The Perekop isthmus connects the Crimean peninsula with the mainland.

30. B.V. Sokolov, *Tsena Voiny. Lyudskie Poteri Rossii/SSSR v Voinakh XX-XXI vv.* (Moscow: AIRO-XXI, 2017), pp. 514–19, 521.

31. TsGA SPb, f. 8357, op. 6, d. 1108, pp. 46–7. This data has been published in the Wikipedia article 'Blokada Leningrada'.

32. Human Losses in World War II. Heeresarzt 10-Day Casualty Reports per Army/ Army Group, 1941 [BA/MA RW 6/556, 6/558] (http://web.archive.org/web/20161102103505/http://ww2stats.com:80/cas_ger_okh_dec41.html).

33. Yu.A. Syakov, *Neizvestnye Soldaty. Srazheniya na Vneshnem Fronte Blokady Leningrada* (St Petersburg: Znanie, 2004), p. 74. Editor's note. Grigorii Ivanovich Kulik (1890–1950) served in

the Russian imperial army during the First World War and joined the Red Army in 1918. He served as head of the Main Artillery Directorate from 1937–41. During the Second World War Kulik commanded armies, but his incompetence caused him to be demoted from the rank of marshal to major general. Kulik was arrested in 1947 on charges of treason and later executed.

34. Human Losses in World War II. Heeresarzt 10-Day Casualty Reports per Army/Army Group, 1941, [BA/MA/RW 6/556, 6/558] (http://web.archive.org/web20161102103505/http://ww2stats.com:80/cas_ger_okh_dec41.html)

35. V. Lyubbeke, *U Vorot Leningrada. Istoriya Soldata Gruppy Armii 'Sever,' 1941–1945* (Moscow: Tsentrpoligraf, 2017), p. 124.

36. Human Losses in World War II. Heeresarzt 10-Day Casualty Reports per Army/Army Group, 1941, [BA/MA RS 6/556, 6/558] (http://web.archive.org/web/20161102103505/http://ww2stats.com:80/cas_ger_okh_dec41.hhtml).

37. V. Antonov, 'Shturmmann Khristen Protiv Polkovnika Rotmistrova'//Warspot, 2016, 1 Dekabrya, http://warspot.ru/7665-shturmmann-hristen-protiv-polkovnika-rotmistrova.

38. Human Losses in World War II. Heeresarzt 10-Day Casualty Reports per Army/Army Group, 1941, [BA/MA RS 6/556, 6/558] (http://web.archive.org/web/20161102103505/http://ww2stats.com:80/cas_ger_okh_dec41.html).

39. Antonov, 'Shturmmann Khristen protiv Polkovnika Rotmistrova.

40. *Ibid.* See the commentary by Aleksandr Poleshchuk.

41. Editor's note. Ivan Vasil'evich Rogov (1899–1949) joined the Red Army in 1919 and fought in the civil war as a political officer. During the Second World War he headed the navy's political administration. He was removed from this post in 1946 and sent as political commissar to a military district. *Vsesoyuznaya Kommunisticheskaya Partiya (Bol'shevikov)*, or the All-Union Communist Party (Bolsheviks), was the official name of the ruling party in the Soviet Union from 1925–52.

42. Editor's note. Order No. 270 was drawn up by I.V. Stalin as chairman of the State Defence Committee on 16 August 1941. The order forbade Red Army personnel to surrender and that they fight to the last man. All those who surrendered were to be regarded as 'deserters' and they and their families would be subject to harsh reprisals.

43. RGASPI, f. 83, op. 1, d. 18, pp. 18–19.

44. *Sovershenno Sekretno! Tol'ko dlya Komandovaniya!* , trans. from German (Moscow: Nauka, 1967), pp. 339–40.

45. Editor's note. Karl Donitz (1891–1980) joined the German imperial navy and fought in the First World War. During the Second World War he served as commander of the German submarine fleet and from 1943 he was commander-in-chief of the navy. He became head of state of Germany following Hitler's suicide. Donitz was convicted of war crimes in 1946 and served ten years before his release.

46. Editor's note. Aleksandr Ivanovich Marinesko (1913–63) joined the Soviet navy in 1933. During the Second World War he commanded submarines and was responsible for sinking the German transport *Wilhelm Gustloff*, causing the single greatest loss of life in maritime history. Marinesko was demoted and dishonourably discharged in 1945 for alcohol problems, but was reinstated in 1960.

47. Editor's note. Ivan Ivanovich Fedyuninskii (1900–77) joined the Red Army in 1919 and fought in the civil war. During the Second World War he commanded a corps and armies and was briefly commander of the Leningrad Front. Following the war he commanded forces abroad and military districts. Andrei Aleksandrovich Zhdanov (1896–1948) joined the Bolshevik faction of the Russian Social Democratic Labour Party in 1915 and rose swiftly through its ranks following the revolution. During the Second World War he was head of the Leningrad party apparatus and the political commissar for the Leningrad Front. Following the war, Zhdanov spearheaded Stalin's cultural retrenchment policies. Aleksei Aleksandrovich Kuznetsov (1905–50) joined the Communist Party in 1925. During the Second World War he

was Zhdanov's deputy during the defence of Leningrad. Kuznetsov was promoted to a higher post in Moscow after the war, but was arrested in 1949 and executed the following year.

48. RGASPI, f. 558, op. 11, d. 488, pp. 12–13.

49. S.N. Borshchev, *Ot Nevy do El'by* (Leningrad: Lenizdat, 1973), p. 117.

50. Heeresarzt 10-Day Casualty Reports per Army/Army Group, 1941 [BA/MA RW 6/556, 6/558]//Human Losses in World War II. German Statistics and Documents, (http://www.ww2stats.com/cas_ger_okh_dec41.html).

51. Editor's note. Andrei Andreevich Vlasov (1901–46) joined the Red Army in 1919 and fought in the civil war. During the Second World War he commanded a corps and armies until his capture in 1942. He later joined the Germans and commanded the Russian Liberation Army (ROA), made up of captured Soviet soldiers and other volunteers. Vlasov was captured at the end of the war and executed.

Chapter 4

1. L.N. Lopukhovskii, *Vyazemskaya Katastrofa 41-go Goda* (Moscow: Yauza, 2007), p. 536.

2. *Ibid.*, p.604.

3. F. Von Bock, *Voennyi Dnevnik, 1939–1945* (Smolensk: Rusich, 2006), p. 312. Editor's note. Fedor von Bock (1880–1945) joined the German imperial army in 1898 and fought in the First World War. During the Second World War he commanded army groups in Poland, France, and the Soviet Union until relieved by Hitler in 1942. Von Bock was killed in an Allied air attack at the end of the war.

4. F. Gal'der, *Voennyi Dnevnik* (Moscow: Voennoe Izdatel'stvo, 1971), vol. III, book 1, p. 371. Editor's note. Franz Halder (1884–1972) joined the German imperial army in 1902 and fought in the First World War. He was named chief of the army (OKH) staff in 1938 and served in this position until relieved by Hitler in 1942. Halder spent two years in prison following the war and worked for the US army historical branch.

5. M. Khodorenok and B. Nevzorov, 'Chernyi Oktyabr' 41-go. Pod Vyaz'moi i Bryanskom Krasnaya Armiya Poteryala Sotni Tysyach Boitsov', *Nezavisimoe Voennoe Obozrenie*, 2002, 21–7 Iyunya, no. 20, p. 5.

6. L.M. Sandalov, *Na Moskovskom Napravlenii* (Moscow: Veche, 2006), p. 207. Editor's note. Leonid Mikhailovich Sandalov (1900–87) joined the Red Army in 1919 and fought in the civil war. During the Second World War he served as chief of staff of various armies and fronts. Following the war, he served in a variety of staff positions. Sandalov retired in 1955.

7. A.I. Yeremenko, *V Nachale Voiny* (Moscow: Nauka, 1965), p. 329. Editor's note. Andrei Ivanovich Yeremenko (1892–1970) was drafted into the Russian imperial army in 1913 and joined the Red Army in 1918. During the Second World War he commanded armies and *fronts*. Following the war he commanded a number of military districts. Yeremenko retired in 1958.

8. *Ibid.*, p. 340.

9. Gal'der, *Voennyi*, vol. III, book 1, p. 375.

10. Editor's note. Ivan Stepanovich Konev (1897–1973) was drafted into the Russian imperial army in 1916 and he joined the Red Army in 1919 and fought in the civil war. During the Second World War he commanded an army and several *fronts*. Following the war, Konev commanded Soviet occupation forces in Germany twice, headed the ground forces, and commanded the suppression of the Hungarian revolution in 1956.

11. M.Yu. Myagkov, *Vermakht u Vorot Moskvy, 1941–1942* (Moscow: RAN, 1999), p. 67. Editor's note. Boris Mikhailovich Shaposhnikov (1882–1945) joined the Russian imperial army in 1901 and fought in the First World War and later joined the Red Army in 1918. During the interwar period he twice headed the General Staff and commanded military districts. During the Second World War he again headed the General Staff until poor health forced his retirement in 1942.

12. K. Reingardt, *Povorot pod Moskvoi. Krakh Gitlerovskoi Strategii Zimoi 1941/42 Goda. Istoricheskii Ocherk* (Moscow: Voennoe Izdatel'stvo, 1980), p. 83; N. Zetterling, and A. Frankson, *The Drive on Moscow, 1941: Operation Taifun and Germany's First Great Crisis of World War II* (Havertown, PA: Casemate Publishers, 2012), p. 253.
13. Reingardt, *Povorot*, p. 76.
14. Khodorenok and Nevzorov, 'Chernyi Oktyabr', p. 5.
15. D.B. Khazanov, *Aviatsiya v Bitve za Moskvu* (Moscow: Izdatel'stvo GBU 'TsGA Moskvy', 2013), p. 246.
16. *Velikaya Otechestvennaya Voina. Entsiklopediya* (Moscow: Sovetskaya Entsiklopediya, 1985), p. 198.
17. O. Groelhler, *Krieg im Westen* (Berlin: Deutscher Militaerverlag, 1968), p. 166.
18. Gal'der, *Voennyi*, vol. III, book 1, p. 373. Editor's note. Walther von Brauchitsch (1881–1948) joined the imperial army in 1900 and fought in the First World War. He was appointed commander-in-chief of the army in 1938 and oversaw the campaigns in Poland, the West, the Balkans, and the Soviet Union. He was relieved by Hitler during the Battle of Moscow and took no further part in the war. Following the war, Brauchitsch was imprisoned on suspicion of war crimes, but died before he could be tried.
19. Bock, *Voennyi*, p. 314. Editor's note. Hermann Hoth (1885–1971) joined the German imperial army in 1903 and served during the First World War. During the Second World War he commanded a mechanized corps, a panzer army, and a field army. Hitler relieved him of command at the end of 1943. Following the war, Hoth was convicted of war crimes, but was released from prison in 1954.
20. Gal'der, *Voennyi*, vol. III, book 2, p. 11.
21. Editor's note. Erich Hoepner (1886–1944) joined the imperial army in 1906 and served in the First World War. During the Second World War he commanded a corps in the West and a panzer group in the Soviet Union until relieved by Hitler in early 1942. Hoepner was implicated in the 20 July 1944 plot against Hitler and executed.
22. Gal'der, *Voennyi*, vol. III, book 2, p. 14.
23. Khodorenok and Nevzorov, 'Chernyi Oktyabr', p. 5.
24. *Mirovaya Voina 1939–1945: Sbornik Statei* (Moscow: Izdatel'stvo Inostrannoi Literatury, 1957), p. 179.
25. Khodorenok and Nevzorov, 'Chernyi Oktyabr', p. 5.
26. Heeresarzt 10-Day Casualty Reports per Army//Army Group, 1941 [BA/MA RW 6/556, 6/558]//Human Losses in World War II. German Statistics and Documents, (http://www.ww2stats.com/cas_ger_okh_dec41.html).
27. M. Khodorenok, 'Prolog Vyazemskoi Katastrofy', *Nezavisimoe Voennoe Obozrenie* (2001), no. 43, p. 5, http://nvo.ng.ru/history/2001-11-23/5_prologue.html.
28. Editor's note. Mikhail Fedorovich Lukin (1892–1970) joined the Russian imperial army in 1913 and fought in the First World War. He joined the Red Army in 1918 and fought in the civil war. During the Second World War he commanded armies, but was captured in October 1941. Lukin was liberated in 1945 and retired the following year.
29. F. von Bock, *Ya Stoyal u Vorot Moskvy* (Moscow: Yauza; EKSMO, 2006), p. 187.
30. Editor's note. Gunther Hans von Kluge (1882–1944) joined the imperial army in 1901 and served during the First World War. During the Second World War he commanded an army and an army group and was briefly commander-in-chief of German forces in the West. Kluge was implicated in the 1944 plot to assassinate Hitler and committed suicide.
31. Bock, *Ya Stoyal*, p. 189.
32. *Ibid.*, p. 191.
33. *Ibid.*, pp. 192–3.
34. *Ibid.*, p. 197.
35. *Ibid.*, p. 200.

36. *Ibid.*, p. 201.
37. *Ibid.*, p. 202.
38. *Ibid.*, pp. 203–4.
39. *Ibid.*, p. 204.
40. *Ibid.*, p. 204.
41. *Ibid.*, p. 209.
42. P. Hausser, *Vaffen-SS v Boyu*; K. Zalesskii, *Chernaya Gvardiya Gitlera* (Moscow: Izdatel' Bystrov, 2007), pp. 409–10.
43. *Ibid.*, p. 409.
44. K.-Kh. Kaufman, "Provyv Mozhaiskoi Linii Oborony 40-m Tankovym Korpusom v Oktyabre 1941 g. (po Dokumentam Voennogo Arkhiva Vermakhta i Voisk SS)", in *Boi za Moskvu na Mozhaiskom Napravlenii. Issledovaniya, Dokumenty, Vospominaniya* (Moscow: Poligraf-Servis, 2007), pp. 109–11.
45. G. Got, *Tankovye Operatsii* (Moscow: Voennoe Izdatel'stvo, 1961), pp. 160–1.
46. Gal'der, *Voennyi*, vol. III, book 2, p. 33.
47. Got, *Tankovye*, p. 162.
48. Gal'der, *Voennyi*, vol. III, book 2, p. 53.
49. Z. Vestfal', V. Kreipe, G. Blyumentrit, F. Baierlein, K. Tseitsler, B. Tsimmerman and Kh. Manteifel', *Rokovye Resheniya* (Moscow: Voennoe Izdatel'stvo, 1958), p. 93.
50. Kesselring, *Luftwaffe*, pp. 140–1.
51. *Ibid.*, p. 141.
52. G. Guderian, *Vospominaniya Nemetskogo Generala*, trans. from English (Moscow: Tsentropoligraf, 2010), pp. 102–4.
53. See B.V. Sokolov, *Kto Voeval Chislom, a Kto Umeniem* (Moscow: Yauza-Press, 2011), pp. 94–5. Calculations based on D.A. Volkogonov, 'My Pobedili Vopreki Beschelovechnoi Sisteme', *Izvestiya*, 1993, 8 Maya, p. 5; Gal'der, *Voennyi*, vol. III, book 2, pp. 161–240.
54. Gal'der, *Voennyi*, vol. III, book 2, pp. 80–1.
55. Editor's note. Konstantin Konstantinovich Rokossovskii (1896–1968) joined the imperial army in 1914 and fought in the First World War. He joined the Red Army in 1918 and fought in the civil war. Rokossovskii was arrested in 1937 during Stalin's purge, but survived and was released in 1940. During the Second World War he commanded a corps, armies, and *fronts*. Following the war, Rokossovskii commanded Soviet forces in Poland and during 1949–56 he served as Polish minister of defence. Rokossovskii retired in 1962.
56. K.K. Rokossovskii, *Soldatskii Dolg* (Moscow: Voennoe Izdatel'stvo, 1988), pp. 163–6.
57. Reingardt, *Povorot*, p. 381, supplement 5.
58. V. Khaupt, *Srazheniya Gruppy Armii 'Tsentr'* (Moscow: Yauza; EKSMO, 2006), p. 349, supplement 4.
59. TsAMO, f. 500, op. 12479, d. 1335, pp. 81–3.
60. Boevoi Sostav Sovetskoi Armii na 1 Aprelya 1942 g.//Boevye Deistviya Krasnoi Armii v Velikoi Otechestvenoi Voine, http://bdsa.ru/-sostav-voisk-(pomesyachnyi)/3751-1-1942-1863).
61. Human Losses in World War II. Heeresarzt 10-Day Casualty Reports per Army//Army Group, 1941 [BA/MA RW 6/556, 6/558] (http://www.ww2stats.com/cas_ger_okh_dec41.html); Human Losses in World War II. Heeresarzt 10-Day Casualty Reports per Army//Army Group, 1941 [BA/MA RW 6/556, 6/558] (http://www.ww2stats.com/cas_ger_okh_dec42.html).
62. See Khodorenok, 'Prolog', p. 5.
63. Volkogonov, 'My Pobedili', p. 5.
64. M.D. Vorob'ev, *V Serdtse i v Pamyati* (Chelyabinsk: Yuzhno-Ural'skoe Knizhnoe Izdatel'stvo, 1984), p. 160.
65. Heeresarzt 10-Day Casualty Reports per Army//Army Group, 1941 [BA/MA RW 6/556, 6/558]//Human Losses in World War II. German Statistics and Documents], (http://www.ww2stats.com/cas_ger_okh_dec41.html)

66. Ye.S. Yumaev (ed.), *95-ya Gvardeiskaya Poltavskaya* (Moscow: Sputnik, 2016), p. 24.
67. Heeresarzt 10-Day Casualty Reports per Army//Army Group, 1941 [BA/Ma RW 6/556, 6/558]// Human Losses in World War II. German Statistic and Documents] (http://www.ww2stats. com/cas_ger_okh_dec41.html).
68. Yumaev, *95-ya Gvardeiskaya*, p. 24.
69. Heeresarzt 10-Day Casualty Reports per Army//Army Group, 1941 [BA/MA RW 6/556, 6/558]// Human Losses in World War II. German Statistic and Documents, (http://www.ww2stats.com/ cas_ger_okh_dec42.html).
70. Yumaev, *95-ya Gvardeiskaya*, p. 28.
71. Human Losses in World War II. Heeresarzt 10-Day Casualty Reports per Army//Army Group, 1942 [BA/MA RW 6/556, 6/558]//Human Losses in World War II. German Statistic and Documents, http://www.ww2stats.com/cas_ger_okh_dec42.html.
72. A.I. Shumilin, 'Ne Otpravlennoe Pis'mo A. Shumilina k B. Polyakovu' (http://nik-shumilin. narod.ru/dok/per/r_nepis.html).
73. H. Haape, *Oskal Smerti. 1941 God na Vostochnom Fronte*, trans. from English by A. Myasnikov (Moscow: Yauza-Press, 2009), p. 392.
74. P.N. Knyshevskii (ed.), *Skrytaya Pravda Voiny: 1941 God* (Moscow: Russkaya Kniga, 1992), p. 222. The totaling up of the final figures in the report yields 4,138 killed, wounded, missing in action, and sick. It is possible that the increase occurred at the expense of those whom they had not distributed by category of losses.
75. Heeresarzt 10-Day Casualty Reports per Army//Army Group, 1941 [BA/MA RS 6/556, 6/558]// Human Lossses in World War II. German Statistic and Documents, http://www.ww2stats.com/ cas_ger-okh_dec41.html.
76. F.I. Golikov, *V Moskovskoi Bitve* (Moscow: Nauka, 1967), pp. 70–1, 94–5.
77. Knyshevskii, *Skrytaya Pravda*, p. 222.
78. Calculation done according to Ssylki na Doneseniya o Poteryakh Divizii, Vylozhennye na Saite OBD-Memorial. Strelkovye Divizii. Chast' 4 (http://www.teatrskazka.com/Raznoe/DivDocs/ DivDocs01-4.html).
79. A.I. Shumilin, 'Van'ka-Rotnyi. Glava 11. Peredovaya i Tyl' (http://nik-shumilin.narod. ru/41/r_11.html).
80. Human Losses in World War II. Heeresarzt 10-Day Casualty Reports per Army//Army Group, 1941, [BA/MA RW 6/556, 6/558] (http://web.archive.org/web/20161102103505/http:// ww2stats.com:80/cas_ger_okh_dec41.html).
81. A.N. Lepekhin, compiler, 'Na Dedilovskom Napravlenii' (Dedilovo, 2011 (http://iknigi.net/ avtor-aleksandr-lepehin/125999-na-dedilovskom-napravlenii-velikaya-otechestvennaya-voy- na-na-territorii-kireevskogo-rayona-aleksandr-lepehin/read/page-6.html).
82. Human Losses in World War II. Heeresarzt 10-Day Casualty Reports per Army//Army Group, 1941, [BA/MA RW 6/556, 6/558] (http://web.archive.org/web/20161102103505/http:// ww2stats.com:80/cas_ger_okh_dec41.html).
83. Na Dedilovskom Napravlenii (Dedilovo, 2011 (http://iknigi.net/avtor-aleksandr-lepehin/125999-na- dedilovskom-napravlenii-velikaya-otechestvennaya-voyna-na-territorii-kireevskogo-rayo- na-aleksandr-lepehin/read/page-12.html).
84. Human Losses in World War II. Heeresarzt 10-Day Casualty Reports per Army//Army Group, 1941, [BA/MA RW 6/5Il56, 6/558] (http://web.archive.org/web/20161102103505/http:// ww2stats.com:80/cas_ger_okh_dec41.html).
85. Na Dedilovskom Napravlenii (Dedilovo, 2011 (http: //iknigi. net/avtor- aleksandr-lepe- hin/ 125999- na-dedilovskom-napravlenii- velikaya- otechestvennaya-voyna-na- territorii- kireevskogo-rayona- aleksandr-lepehin/read/page-23.html).
86. Human Losses in World War II. Heeresarzt 10-Day Casualty Reports per Army//Army Group, 1941, [BA/MA RW 6/556, 6/558] (http://web.archive.org/web/20161102103505/http:// ww2stats.com:80/cas_ger_okh_dec41.html).

87. A.A. Il'yushechkin and M.N. Mosyagin, *Varshavskoe Shosse-Lyuboi Tsenoi.Tragediya Zait-sevoi Gory. 1942–1943* (Moscow: Tsentrpoligraf, 2014), p. 52.

88. Human Losses in World War II. Heeresarzt 10-Day Casualty Reports per Army//Army Group, 1941, [BA/MA RW 6/556, 6/558] (http://web.archive.org/web/20161109212513/http://ww2stats.com:80/cas_ger_okh_dec42.html).

89. Il'yushechkin, et al., *Varshavskoe*, p. 54.

90. Human Losses in World War II. Heeresarzt 10-Day Casualty Reports per Army//Army Group, 1942, [BA/MA RW 6/556, 6/558] (http://web.archive.org/web/20161109212513/http://ww2stats.com:80/cas_ger_okh_dec42.html).

91. Il'yushechkin et al., *Varshavskoe*, p. 74.

92. Human Losses in World War II. Heeresarzt 10-Day Casualty Reports per Army//Army Group, 1941, [BA/MA RW 6/556, 6/558] (http://web.archive.org/web/20161109212513/http://ww2stats.com:80/cas_ger_okh_dec42.html).

93. Il'yushechkin et al., *Varshavskoe*, p. 92.

94. Human Losses in World War II. Heeresarzt 10-Day Casualty Reports per Army//Army Group, 1941, [BA/MA RW 6/556, 6/558] (http://web.archive.org/web/20161109212513/http://ww2stats.com:80/cas_ger_okh_dec42.html)

95. Krivosheev, *Rossiya i SSSR*, p. 277.

96. Human Losses in World War II. Heeresarzt 10-Day Casualty Reports per Army//Army Group, 1942 [BA/MA RW 6/556, 6/558] (http://web.archive.org/web20161109212513/http://ww2stats.com:80/cas_ger_okh_dec42.html).

97. G.K. Puzhaev, *Krov' i Slava Miusa* (Taganrog: BANNERplyus, 2008), p. 179. 'Human Losses in World War II. Heeresarzt 10-Day Casualty Reports per Army//Army Group, 1941' [BA/MA RW 6/556, 6/558], http://ww2stats.com:80/cas_ger_okh_dec42.html.

98. Knyshevskii, *Skrytaya Pravda*, p. 225. The authorized strength of a rifle division was established in August 1941 at 11,447 men, of which there remained 10,530 by 1 January 1942. The losses materially exceeded the division's authorized strength. On 1 February 1942 there remained a total of 3,190 men in the 376th Rifle Division, which forces us to assume that the division's actual losses were approximately 5,000 men more.

99. Human Losses in World War II. Heeresarzt 10-Day Casualty Reports per Army//Army Group, 1942, [BA/MA RW 6/556, 6/558] (http://ww2stats.com:80/cas_ger_okh_dec42.html); Human Losses in World War II. Heeresarzt 10-Day Casualty Reports per Army//Army Group, 1941, [BA/MA RW 6/556, 6/558] (http://web.archive.org/web/20161102103505/http://ww2stats.com:80/cas_ger_okh_dec41.html).

100. Puzhaev, *Krov' i Slava*, p. 33.

101. Human Losses in World War II. Heeresarzt 10-Day Casualty Reports per Army//Army Group, 1941, [BA/MA RW 6/556, 6/558] (http://ww2stats.com:80/cas_ger_okh_dec42.html)

102. Puzhaev, *Krov' i Slava*, p. 36.

103. *Ibid.*, pp. 38–9.

104. G.T. Zavizion (ed.), *Boevoi Sostav Sovetskoi Armii* (Moscow: Voennoe Izdatel'stvo, 1966), vol. II, p. 48.

105. *Ibid.*, p. 66.

106. Puzhaev, *Krov' i Slava*, p. 32. The 102nd Rifle Brigade entered the fighting only on 26 March. From 26–9 March it lost 1,519 men killed, wounded, and missing in action. In all, during the period from 9 March to 2 April 1942, it lost, according to incomplete data, 1,734 men, including 321 killed, 131 missing in action, 1,225 wounded, and 57 cases of frostbite out of 4,479 men in the brigade at the beginning of March. (Khronologiya 102-oi Otdel'noi Strelkovoi Brigady v Sostave 3-go Gvardeiskogo Strelkovogo Korpusa 56-oi Armii Yugo-Zapadnogo Fronta//Poiskovyi Otryad Pobeda', http://www.poisk-pobeda.ru/forum/index.php?topic-5792.0). According to other data, the brigade lost 1,571 men on 26 March alone. See V.I. Afanasenko, *Chernye Bushlaty na Belom Snegu* (Rostov-na-Donu: Molot), p. 12.

107. Puzhaev, *Krov' I Slava*, p. 49.
108. Editor's note. The KV tanks were a series of heavy armored vehicles named in honour of Soviet defence commissar Kliment Voroshilov. The most common models were the KV-1 (45 tons, a crew of five, a 76.2mm gun, and four 7.62mm machine guns) and the KV-2 (53.1 tons, a crew of six, a 152mm gun, and two 7.62mm machine guns). Other models were produced as well, although in small amounts.
109. Khronologiya 102-oi Otdel'noi Strelkovoi Brigady v Sostave 3-go Gvardeiskogo Strelkovogo Korpusa 56-oi Armii Yugo-Zapadnogo Fronta//Poiskovyi Otryad Pobeda, http://www.poisk-pobeda.ru/forum/index.php?topic-5792.0.
110. Puzhaev, *Krov' i Slava*, p. 67.
111. Afanasenko, *Chernye*, p. 12.
112. Puzhaev, *Krov' i Slava*, p. 97.
113. Heeresarzt 10-Day Casualty Reports per Army//Army Group, 1942 [BA/MA RW 6/556, 6/558]//Human Losses in World War II. German Statistics and Documents], (http://www.ww2stats.com/cas_ger_okh_dec42.html).
114. L.G. Ivanov, *Pravda o SMERShe. Voennyi Kontrrazvedchik Rasskazyvaet* (Moscow: EKSMO; Yauza, 2015), p. 90.
115. Heeresarzt 10-Day Casualty Reports per Army//Army Group, 1942 [BA/MA RW 6/556, 6/558]//Human Losses in World War II. German Statistics and Documents], (http://www.ww2stats.com/cas_ger_okh_dec42.html).
116. Knyshevskii, *Skrytaya Pravda*, pp. 241–2.
117. Reinhardt, *Povorot*, p. 381.
118. C. Bergstrom and An. Mikhailov, *Black Cross/Red Star. Vol. I, Operation Barbarossa, 1941* (London: Pacifica Military History with Classic Publications, 2000), pp. 254–5.
119. Krivosheev, *Rossiya i SSSR*, p. 475.
120. *Ibid.*, p. 484.
121. Khazanov, *Aviatsiya*, pp. 630–48.
122. Editor's note. Henri Philippe Benoni Omer Joseph Petain (1856–1951) joined the army in 1876. During the First World War he rose rapidly from the command of a brigade to commander-in-chief of French forces and distinguished himself at the defence of Verdun. During the interwar period he served in a variety of military and government posts. Petain was appointed prime minister during the Battle of France and agreed to an armistice with Germany. He later became head of the successor government in Vichy. Following the war, he was tried for treason and sentenced to death, but this was commuted to a life sentence. Petain died in prison.
123. Editor's note. Erwin Rommel (1891–1944) joined the army in 1910 and served in the First World War. During the Second World War he commanded a division and German forces in North Africa (Afrika Corps). He later commanded German forces in Greece and Italy before being appointed to command an army group in France. Rommel was implicated in the 1944 plot to kill Hitler and he committed suicide.

Chapter 5

1. Editor's note. Friedrich Wilhelm Ernst Paulus (1890–1957) joined the imperial army in 1910 and fought in the First World War. During the Second World War he served in senior staff positions until his appointment as commander of the German Sixth Army in early 1942. Paulus and his army were encircled at Stalingrad and forced to surrender in early 1943. While in captivity, Paulus became a critic of Hitler and joined the National Committee for a Free Germany. He was freed and returned to East Germany in 1953.
2. Editor's note. Rodion Yakovlevich Malinovskii (1898–1967) joined the Russian imperial army in 1914 and fought in the First World War in Russia and France, before returning home to join the Red Army. During the Second World War he commanded a corps, armies,

and *fronts* in Europe and the Far East. Following the war, Malinovskii remained in the Far East before returning to Moscow to command the ground forces and serve as defence minister from 1957 until his death. Order No. 227 ('Not a Step Backward') was issued by people's commissar of defence, I.V. Stalin, on 28 July 1942, following a string of Red Army defeats in Ukraine and southern Russia. The order forbade any withdrawal without orders and called for the formation of punishment units for transgressors.

3. C.E. Kirkpatrick, *An Unknown Future and a Doubtful Present: Writing the Victory Plan of 1941* (Washington, DC: US Army Center of Military History, 1992), p. 82.

4. D. Havlat, *Western Aid for the Soviet Union During World War II* (Vienna: Universitaet Wien, 2015), p. 77.

5. *Narodnoe KhozyaistvoSSSR v Velikoi Otechestvennoi Voine 1941–1945 gg. Statisticheskii Sbornik* (Moscow: IITs, Goskomstata SSSR, 1993), p. 55; B.H. Jones, *The Roads to Russia: United States Lend-Lease to the Soviet Union* (Norman, OK: Oklahoma University Press, 1969), appendices.

6. O. Nuzhdin and S. Ruzaev, *Sevastopol' v Iyune 1942 Goda: Khronika Osazhdennogo Goroda* (Yekaterinburg: Izdatel'stvo Ural'skogo Universiteta, 2013), p. 589.

7. Human Losses in World War II. Heeresarzt 10-Day Casualty Reports per Army/Army Group, 1942, [BA/MA RW 6/556, 6/558] http://web.archive.org/web/20161109212513/http://ww2stats.com:80/cas_ger_okh_dec42.html.

8. *Ibid.*

9. Editor's note. The *nomenklatura* was the list of people in the Soviet Union and the former Eastern Bloc countries who held important positions in the government bureaucracy, subject to Communist Party approval.

10. A. Melenberg, 'Vzorvany i Zabyty', *Novaya Gazeta*, 2005, 3 March, no. 16, p. 5. 11. Editor's note. Nikolai Mikhailovich Kulakov (1908–76) joined the navy in 1932 and served in its political branch. During the Second World War he was the political commissar of the Black Sea Fleet before being relieved of his post and demoted in 1944. Following the war Kulakov had a roller coaster career, which included more demotions and rehabilitations until his retirement in 1971.

11. Nuzhdin et al., *Sevastopol'*, p. 589.

12. Ye.I. Kel'ner, 'Trudyashchiesya Sevastopolya v Bor'be s Gitlerovskimi Zakhvatchikami (1941–1942 gg)', *Voprosy Istorii*, 1956, no. 9, pp. 105, 108.

13. Nuzhdin et al., *Sevastopol'*, pp. 61–2, 68.

14. *Ibid.*, p. 588.

15. Editor's note. Ivan Yefimovich Petrov (1896–1958) joined the Red Army in 1918 and fought in the civil war. During the Second World War he commanded armies and *fronts*. Following the war, Petrov commanded a military district and served in the central military apparatus. Dmitrii Timofeevich Kozlov (1896–1967) joined the imperial army in 1915 and the Red Army in 1918. During the Second World War he commanded a military district and *fronts*. He commanded the disastrous Soviet landing on the Kerch' peninsula, for which he was demoted and consigned to secondary posts for the remainder of the war. Following the war, Kozlov was deputy commander of a military district until his retirement in 1954.

16. Editor's note. Ivan Stepanovich Isakov (1894–1967) joined the imperial navy in 1917 and the Red Navy the following year. During the Second World War he commanded a fleet and oversaw the landing of Soviet troops at Kerch'. He was severely wounded in 1942, but continued to serve in high-ranking positions. Following the war, Isakov continued to serve in high-ranking posts and to engage in scholarly work.

17. Editor's note. 'Douglas' was the popular Soviet nickname for the Douglas C-47 transport aircraft, which was widely used by American and Allied forces during the Second World War.

18. Melenberg, 'Vzorvany i Zabyty', p. 5.

19. S. Taratukhin, 'Broshennyi Garnizon', *Zerkalo Nedeli*, 2012, 6 Iyulya, https://zn.ua/SOCIETY/broshennyy_garnizon.html. Editor's note. The PS-84 (or Li-2) was a Soviet licensed version of the American-made Douglas DC-3 transport aircraft.

20. *Ibid.*

21. A.Yu. Bezugol'nyi, 'Upredit' Razvertyvanie i Aktivnost' Turetskikh Voisk, Putem Razgroma ikh ...: Turetskaya Problema v 1942 g. v Dokumentakh Zakavzskogo Fronta', *Velikaya Otechestvennaya Voina 1941–1945 gg: Opyt Izucheniya i Prepodavaniya. Materialy Mezhvuzovskoi Nauchnoi Konferentsii, Posvyashchennoi 60-Letiyu Pobedy v Velikoi Otechestvennoi Voine, 17 Maya 2005 g.* (Moscow: RGGU, 2005), pp. 71–6.

22. Calculations made according to Halder, *Voennyi*, vol. III, book 2, pp. 161, 188, 207, 225, 240, 263, 284, 315, 337, 343 (entries for 5 January, 4 February, 5 March, 6 April, 5 May, 14 June, 5 July, 5 August, and 15 September 1942).

23. Editor's note. Wilhelm List (1880–1971) joined the imperial army in 1898 and fought in the First World War. During the Second World War he commanded armies in Poland, France, and the Balkans. He also commanded an army group in the USSR, but was relieved by Hitler in late 1942 and was never recalled to active duty. List was sentenced to life in prison for war crimes, but was released in 1952.

24. Halder, *Voennyi*, vol. III, book, 2, pp. 337, 343 (entries for 4 and 15 September 1942).

25. TsAMO RF, fond 96-i Gvardeiskoi Strelkovoi Divizii, op. 1, d. 23. Zhurnal Boevykh Deistvii, p. 42. (Cited in I. Derodov, 'Tsena Pobedy. Pochemu tak Mnogo Poter'? Stalingrad 1942–43 gg', *Stalingradskaya Bitva v Istorii Rosii. Iz Materialov VIII Yunosheskikh Chtenii, Provedennykh 29.03.2003 g. Fakul'tetom Istorii i Mezhdunarodnykh Otnoshenii VolGU i NII Ekonomicheskoi Istorii XX Veka VolGu*, ed. M.M. Zagorul'ko (Volgograd: Nauchnoe Izdatel'stvo, 2004, p. 46. http://forum.vgd.ru/106/18610).

26. *Ibid.*

27. Heeresarzt 10-Day Casualty Reports per Army//Army Group, 1942 [BA/MA RW 6/556, 6/558]//Human Losses in World War II. German Statistics and Documents], (http://www.ww2stats.com/cas_ger_okh_dec42.html)

28. 'Dnevnik Polkovnika E.Ya. Kuznetsova', *My vse Voiny Shal'nye Deti . . . Dnevniki Perioda Velikoi Otechestvennoi Voiny 1941–1945* (Saratov: Upravlenie po Delam Arkhivov Upravleniya Delami Pravitel'stva Saratovskoi Oblasti, 2010), p. 152.

29. *Velikaya Otechestvennaya Voina bez Grifa Sekretnosti, Kniga Poter'* (Moscow: Veche, 2010), pp. 109, 114.

30. *Ibid.*, pp. 221, 223, 225, 262.

31. Human Losses in World War II. Heeresarzt 10-Day Casualty Reports per Army/Army Group, 1942, [BA/MA RW 6/556, 6/558] http://ww2stats.com/cas_ger_okh_dec43.html

32. As told to the author by Anatolii Ivanovich Utkin.

33. Human Losses in World War II. AOK/Ic POW Summary Reports [BA/MA RH 2/2087, 2/2621, 2/2622K, 2/2633K, 2/2635K, 2/2636-2642, 2/2707, 2/2773, IfZ ED 48] (http://ww2stats.com/pow_ger_okh_aok.html).

34. Editor's note. Yevgenii Viktorovich Vuchetich (1908–74) was a Soviet sculptor and artist whose works came to exemplify the 'gigantist' approach to memorializing the Red Army's victories during the Second World War.

35. Editor's note. The Ministry of Defence Archive is located in the small town of Podol'sk, south of Moscow.

36. Editor's note. Frol Romanovich Kozlov (1908–65) joined the Communist Party in 1926 and gradually rose through its ranks in the provinces, in Leningrad, and then at the national level. He was widely viewed as N.S. Khrushchev's successor, but a stroke incapacitated him from 1963 until his death.

37. PP. Popov, A.B. Kozlov and B.G. Usik, *Perelom* (Volgograd: Izdatel', 2000), p. 249.

38. Kuropatkov, Ye.P., Sukhenko, I.P., Frolov, S.S., Ivanov, B.P., *Boevoi Put' 196-i Gatchinskoi Krasnoznamennoi Strelkovoi Divizii (Ot Batal'ona do Armii. Boevoi Put'.* (Moscow: Akademiya Istoricheskikh Nauk, 2007), vol. I, p. 90.

39. Heeresarzt 10-Day Casualty Reports per Army//Army Group, 1942 [BA/MA RW 6/556, 6/558]// Human Losses in World War II. German Statistics and Documents], (http://www.ww2stats.com/cas_ger_okh_dec42.html)

40. Kuropatkov et al., *Boevoi Put'*, p. 101. The calculations are the author's. In this source the incorrect figure of 6,414 is cited.

41. *Stalingradskaya Epopeya: Materialy NKVD SSSR i Voennoi Tsenzury iz Tsentral'nogo Arkhiva FSB RF* (Moscow: Zvonnitsa-MG, 2000), p. 204.

42. A.I. Rodimtsev, '13-ya Gvardeiskaya Strelkovaya Diviziya v Boyakh za Stalingrad', in *Stalingradskaya Epopeya* (Moscow: Nauka, 1968), pp. 321–2.

43. Ye. Kobyakov, 'Neizvestnyi Stalingrad: Grenada, Grenada, Grenada Moya . . . 2015, 16 September', http://warspot.ru/3227-neizvestnyy-stalingrad-grenada-grenada-grenada-moya.

44. A.V. Isaev, *Stalingrad. Za Volgoi dlya nas Zemli net* (Moscow: Yauza; EKSMO, 2008), p. 162, table 6; 171. Certainly, having cited on p. 171 data that 'according to the report on the strength of the 13th Guards Rifle Division on 13 September 1942, the formation numbered 9,603 men', A.V. Isaev here, on p. 172, maintains that 'according to the report on the combat and numerical strength on 15 September the 13th Guards Rifle Division numbered 8,009 men'. As neither on 13 or 14 September was the division engaged in combat one may only assume that it numbered 8,009 by the evening of 15 September, following the end of the fighting. Then the losses during the crossing and the fighting on this day may be estimated at 1,594 men, and by no means 400 men, as is maintained in the report from the special section. Insofar as A.V. Isaev on these pages puts forward data to the effect that the number of rifles in A.I. Rodimtsev's division from 13–15 September fell from 7,745 to 5,616, that is, fell by 2,129 units, even more than the division's assumed human losses. On the other hand, the division received an additional 20 heavy machine guns, 295 light machine guns, 550 Shpagin and Degtyaryov automatic rifles and 140 anti-tank rifles. Some kind of additional human reinforcements were probably fed into the division along with new weaponry during 14–15 September. Taking this into account, the actual losses for 15 September could have been closer to 2,129 killed and wounded, judging by the number of lost rifles. Incidentally, this is the maximum possible estimation of losses for the 13th Guards Rifle Division for 15 September 1942. Probably the figure of 8,009 men may reflect the division's strength, minus rear elements, and in the morning, rather than the end of the day of 15 September. Then the division's actual losses for 15 September are close to 400 killed and wounded. One can only assume that by 15 September it had been reinforced by several hundred soldiers and by the time of its entrance into the fighting numbered no less than 10,000 men.

45. In all, during the period from 18–26 September, the 92nd Rifle Brigade lost about 4,800 men, while there remained 214 men of those who crossed into Stalingrad. According to the estimate by the brigade's chief of staff, N.F. Yemel'yanenko, the brigade's total losses were about 2,000 killed and missing in action (300 sailors were captured, according to German data) and about 3,000 wounded, that is, its irreplaceable losses even exceeded the irreplaceable losses of Rodimtsev's division, which exceeded by more than 1.5 times the strength of the brigade. At the same time, one must take into account that the brigade was formed from sailors from the Baltic and Northern fleets, who were almost untrained for fighting on land (their training lasted only two weeks). Besides this, the brigade operated almost without artillery support. One should also take into account that the 92nd Rifle Brigade fought against both the *Wehrmacht's* 71st and 94th infantry divisions. (Boevye Deistviya v Tsentre Stalingrada Sentyabr' 42-Fevral' 43gg.//Voennyi Al'bom, 2015, 12 Oktyabr', http://waralbum.ru/bb/viewtopic.php?id=554&p=22. Lieutenant Colonel Aleksandr D, the author of the publication, cites the book N.F. Yemel'yanenko and A.A. Rukavtsov, *Moryaki Verny Traditsiyam. 92-ya Otdel'naya*

Strelkovaya Brigada (Volgograd: Nizhnevolzhskoe Knigoizdatel'stvo, 1979). The very same data, with a reference to Aleksandr D's publication and the book by N.F. Yemel'yanenko and A.A. Rukavtsov, are put forward in the following article: Ye. Kobyakov, 'Neizvestnyi Stalingrad', *Elevator*, 2015, 3 Noyabrya, http://warspot.ru/3511-neizvestnyy -stalingrad-elevator).

46. *'Ty nasha bol - pigshaja divizija'. Geroicheskaja Dal'nevostochnaja strelkovaja divizija #126 ('You are our pain - the lost division'. The Heroic Far Eastern 126th Rifle Division)* (Oktjabrskij village, Volgograd Region: Regional Public Organization 'Poisk', 2009), p. 27.

47. Human Losses in World War II. Heeresarzt 10-Day Casualty Reports per Army/Army Group, 1942 [BA/MA RW 6/556, 6/558] (http://web.archive.org/web/20160304172106://ww2stats. com/cas ger okh dec42.html).

48. A. Panin, *Stalingrad: Zabytoe Srazhenie (Stalingrad: The Forgotten Battle)* (Moscow: AST; St Petersburg: Terra Fantastica, 2005), p. 116.

49. Yumaev, *95-ya Gvardeiskaya*, p. 33.

50. Human Losses in World War II. Heeresarzt 10-Day Casualty Reports per Army/Army Group, 1942, [BA/MA RW 6/556, 6/558] http:// Human Losses in World War II. German Statistics and Documents, http.ww2stats.com/cas_ger_okh_dec42.html

51. Nerodov, *Tsena Pobedy*, p. 46.

52. Yu.N. Panchenko, *163 Dnya na Ulitsakh Stalingrada* (Volgograd: Printerra, 2006), p. 317.

53. Editor's note. Pavel Semyonovich Rybalko (1892–1948) joined the imperial army in 1914 and the Red Army four years later. During the Second World War he commanded a tank army in several of the war's major operations on the Eastern Front. Following the war, Rybalko was appointed head of the army's mechanized forces.

54. D.V. Shein, *Tanki Vedet Rybalko. Boevoi Put' 3-i Gvardeiskoi Tankovoi Armii* (Moscow: Yau-za-EKSMO, 2007), p. 23.

55. Human Losses in World War II. Heeresarzt 10-Day Casualty Reports per Army/Army Group, 1942, [BA/MA RW 6/556, 6/558] http:// Human Losses in World War II. German Statistics and Documents, http.ww2stats.com/cas_ger_okh_dec42.html.

56. Human Losses in World War II. Heeresarzt 10-Day Casualty Reports per Army/Army Group, 1943, [BA/MA RW 6/556, 6/558] http:// Human Losses in World War II. German Statistics and Documents, http.ww2stats.com/cas_ger_okh_dec43.html.

57. E.F. Ziemke and M.E. Bauer, *Moscow to Stalingrad: Decision in the East* (Washington, DC: US Army Center of Military History, 1987), p. 462.

58. Krivosheev, *Rossiya i SSSR*, p. 279.

59. A.V. Isaev, *Za Volgoi dlya nas Zemli net (There is no Land for us on the Left Bank of the Volga)* (Moscow: Yauza, 2017), pp. 194, 198.

60. Human Losses in World War II. Heeresarzt 10-Day Casualty Reports per Army/Army Group, 1942 [BA/MA RW 6/556, 6/558] (http://web.archive.org/web/20160304172106/http://ww2stats. com/cas ger okh dec42html).

61. M. Kerig, '6-ya Armiya v Stalingradsom Kotle', in *Stalingrad. Sobytie. Vozdeistvie. Simvol* (Moscow: Progress-Akademiya, 1994), p. 83.

62. Editor's note. Maximillian von Weichs (1881–1954) joined the imperial army in 1914 and fougth in the First World War. During the Second World War he commanded a corps, armies, and army groups in Poland, the West, the Soviet Union, and the Balkans. Following the war, von Weichs was arrested for war crimes but was later released.

63. Isaev, *Stalingrad*, p. 295, table 19.

64. A.I. Yeremenko, *Stalingrad. Zapiski Komanduyushchego Frontom* (Moscow: Voennoe Izdatel'stvo, 1961), p. 417.

65. A.V. Isaev, *Antisuvorov. Desyat' Mifov Vtoroi Mirovoi* (Moscow: EKSMO; Yauza, 2004), p. 163, table 3, p. 171.

66. Human Losses in World War II. Heeresarzt 10-Day Casualty Reports per Army/Army Group, 1942, [BA/MA RW 6/556, 6/558] (http://web.archive.org/web/20161109212513/http://

ww2stats.com:80/cas_germ_okh_dec42.html); Human Losses in World War II. Heeresarzt 10-Day Casualty Reports per Army/Army Group, 1943, [BA/MA RW 6/556, 6/558] (http://ww2stats.com:80/cas_germ_okh_dec43.html).

67. Editor's note. Hermann Balck (1897–1982) joined the army in 1913 and fought in the First World War in France, Russia, Italy, and the Balkans. During World War II he commanded a tank regiment, division, corps, and army in the East and later commanded an army group in the West. He was convicted of war crimes, but released in 1950.

68. H. Balck, *Order in Chaos*, ed. and trans. D.T. Zabecki and D.J. Biedekarken (Lexington, KY: The University Press of Kentucky, 2015), p. 292.

69. Human Losses in World War II. Heeresarzt 10-Day Casualty Reports per Army/Army Group, 1942, [BA/MA RW 6/556, 6/558] (http://web.archive.org/web/20161109212513/http://ww2stats.com:80/cas_germ_okh_dec42.html).

70. Calculated according to Shein, O.V., *Neizvestnyi Front Velikoi Otechestvennoi Voiny. Krovavaya Banya v Kalmytskikh Stepyakh* (Moscow: Yauza; EKSMO, 2009), pp. 208–44. On reading Oleg Shein's books and those of other local searchers, one get the impression that beginning roughly from December 1942 accurate data, which approximates the truth, stops being available to researchers. Before this date a significant number of missing in action, including in offensive fighting, when the overwhelming majority of those missing in action are evidently killed, shows up. But starting in December 1942 only killed and wounded, including those in fighting where there were obviously a lot of missing in action, appear in the reports cited. For example, during the forcing of the Manych River on 9 January 1943 by units of the same 28th Army and the forced withdrawal from the captured bridgehead to the eastern bank by fording under enemy artillery fire, the losses were supposedly only 107 killed and 187 wounded. (See Shein, *Neizvestnyi*, pp. 248–9). However, as some of the troops probably drowned while crossing and some were killed on the enemy bank or taken prisoner, their fate would not have been known to the command. One gets the impression that the most complete reports on losses, beginning in December 1942, are still classified and are not open to researchers.

71. *Ibid.*, pp. 89–244. The losses of air force units, reconnaissance-diversionary groups, and partisan detachments, as well as those of the Astrakhan' garrison and non-combat losses, are not counted.

72. Human Losses in World War II. Heeresarzt 10-Day Casualty Reports per Army/Army Group, 1942, [BA/MA RW 6/556, 6/558] (http://web.archive.org/web/20161109212513/http://ww2stats.com:80/cas_germ_okh_dec42.html).

73. Shein, *Neizvestnyi*, pp. 129, 250.

74. U.B. Ochirov, '248-ya Strelkovaya Diviziya v Boyakh na Territorii Kalmykii v 1942–1943 gg.', *Vestnik Kalmytskogo Instituta Gumanitarnykh Issledovanii* (Moscow: RAN, 2010, no. 1, pp. 35–6) (http://knigilib.net/book/313-vestnik-kaklmyckogo-instituta-gumanitarnyx-issledovanij-ran/8-248-ya strelkovaya-diviziya-v-boyakh-na-territorii-kalmykii-v-1942-1943-gg.html).

75. Oleg Shein notes only one case of the 248th Rifle Division's large number of non-combat losses – 200 hospitalized sick people as a result of exhaustion and colds, of which 31 men died in the period from 11–15 November. Besides this, on 15 November the commander of the 899th Rifle Regiment, Daniil Shcherbak, was killed in an accident. See Shein, *Neizvestnyi*, pp. 145–6. However, by the end of December the overwhelming majority of those sick should already have recovered.

76. Editor's note. *Ostarbeiters* refers to 'Eastern worker', and here specifically Soviet prisoners of war or other inhabitants in the German-occupied territories who signed up to work for the Germans.

77. P. Kaasik, *The 8th Estonian Rifle Corps in Northwestern Russia, 1942–1944. Estonia 1940–1945* (Tallinn: Raamatutruekikoda, 2006), pp. 914, 918.

78. Krivosheev, *Rossiya i SSSR*, p. 312.

79. Human Losses in World War II. Heeresarzt 10-Day Casualty Reports per Army/Army Group, 1942, [BA/MA RW 6/556, 6/558] (http://web.archive.org/web/20161109212513/http://ww2stats.com:80/cas_germ_okh_dec42.html); Human Losses in World War II. Heeresarzt 10-Day Casualty Reports per Army/Army Group, 1943, [BA/MA RW 6/556, 6/558] (http://ww2stats.com:80/cas_ger_okh_dec43.html); A. Zablotskii and R. Larintsev, 'V Teni Grandioznoi Bitvy. Snabzhenie Germanskoi Transportnoi Aviatsiei Chastei, Okruzhennykh v Velikikh Lukakh Zimoi 1942/43 gg'. This is the author's version of the article 'Vdali ot Stalingrada. Aviatsiya v Bitve za Velikie Luki', published in the journal *Aviamaster*, 2005, no. 2, Voenno-patrioticheskii sait 'Otvaga', 2013, 26 Maya, http://otvaga2004.ru/boyevoe-primenenie/boyevoe-primeninie09/v-velikikh-lukax-zimoj-1942-43/.

80. Editor's note. The Black Shirts (Voluntary Militia for National Security) began as the paramilitary arm of Benito Mussolini's fascist party after the First World War and served as the model for the German SA and SS. The Black Shirts also took part in fighting during the Second World War, but were disbanded in 1945.

81. J. Piekalkiewicz, *Die Schlacht von Monte Cassino: Zwanzig Volker ringen meinen berg* (Gustav LubbeVerlag GmbH, 1980), p. 65.

82. W. Murray, *Strategy for Defeat: The Luftwaffe, 1933–1945* (Montgomery, AL: Air University Press, 1983), p. 114; Havlat, *Western Aid*, p. 34.

83. Cherchill, *Vtoraya Mirovaya Voina*, book 2. (Moscow: Voennoe Izdatel'stvo, 1991, p. 461.

84. Editor's note. The Curzon Line was proposed as the eastern border of Poland by British foreign secretary Lord George Curzon (1859–1925) during the negotiations at Versailles in 1919. Although the proposal was never implemented, the current eastern boundary of Poland roughly follows its contours.

85. Editor's note. A port on the Barents Sea, Petsamo was originally founded as the Pechenga Monastery in 1533. The city was ceded to Finland in 1920, but was recaptured by Soviet forces in 1944 and renamed Pechenga.

86. Editor's note. Enrico Fermi (1901–54) was an Italian-American physicist who won the Nobel Prize in 1938. He left Italy that same year for the USA, where he supervised the construction of the first nuclear reactor in 1942, which led to the development of the atomic bomb.

87. See D. Irving, *Istoriya Germanskogo Atomnogo Proekta: Atomnaya Bomba Adol'fa Gitlera*, trans. from English (Moscow: Yauza; EKSMO, 2004),

88. Editor's note. The Manhattan Project was the popular name for a research project (1939–47) which produced the first atomic bomb in 1945.

89. Telephone conversation transcript, General Hull and Colonel Seaman, 13 August 1945, 13.25? Doc. 87//The National Security Archives, The George Washington University, http://nsarchive.gwu.edu/NSAEBB/NSAEBB162/72.pdf.

90. Calculated according to D.M. Glantz, *August Storm: The Soviet 1945 Strategic Offensive in Manchuria*, Leavenworth Papers no. 7. (Ft Leavenworth, KS: Combat Studies Institute, 1983).

Chapter 6

1. A.V. Marchukov, *Ot Leningrada do Berlina. Vospominaniya Artillerista o Voine i Odnopolchanakh. 1941–1945* (Moscow: Tsentrpoligraf, 2015), p. 346.

2. Human Losses in World War II. Heeresarzt 10-Day Casualty Reports per Army/Army Group, 1943, [BA/MA RW 6/556, 6/558] (http://ww2stats.com:80/cas_ger_okh_dec43.html).

3. A.P. Dikan', *Gvardeitsy Dvadtsat' Pyatoi* (Moscow: Voennoe Izdatel'stvo, 1984), p. 66. Editor's note. Ludvik Svoboda (1895–1979) was drafted into the Austro-Hungarian army in 1915 and captured on the Eastern Front and later served in the Czechoslovak Legion in Russia. He later served in Czechoslovak army, but eventually ended up in the Soviet Union where he came to head Czechoslovak forces during the Second World War. Following the communist takeover, he headed the armed forces and was in charge of a military academy. Svoboda served as president of Czechoslovakia during 1968–75, when he was forced out of office.

4. Human Losses in World War II. Heeresarzt 10-Day Casualty Reports per Army/Army Group, 1943, [BA/MA RW 6/556, 6/558] (http://ww2stats.com:80/cas_ger_okh_dec43.html).
5. Shein, *Tanki*, p. 54.
6. *Ibid.*, p.76.
7. *Ibid.*, pp. 76-7.
8. A.V. Isaev, *Osvobozhdenie 1943. 'Ot Kurska i Orla Voina nas Dovela . . . '* (Moscow: Yauza: EKSMO, 2013), p. 147.
9. *Ibid.*, pp. 87, 92–4.
10. Hausser, *Voiska SS*, p. 109.
11. Human Losses in World War II. Heeresarzt 10-Day Casualty Reports per Army/Army Group, 1943, [BA/MA RW 6/556, 6/558] (http://ww2stats.com/cas_ger_okh_dec43.html).
12. Human Losses in World War II. OKH/Gen/Qu POW Figures [BA/MA RW 6/543-548, 19/1387–1393, RH 2/2623, 2/2773] (http:web.archive.org/web/20160304112058/http://ww2stats.com/pow_ger_okh_gen.html); Human Losses in World War II. AOK/Ic POW Summary Reports, [BA/MA RH 2/2087, 2/2621, 2/2622K, 2/2633K, 2/2635K, 2/2636–2642, 2/2707, 2/2773, IfZ ED 48] (http://web.archive.org/web/20160304195737/http://ww2stats.com/pow_ger_okh_aok.html).
13. K.-H. Frieser, 'Schlagen aus der Nachhand-Schlagen aus der Vorhand. Die Schlachten von Char'kov und Kursk 1943', *Gezeitenweschsel im Zweiten Weltkrieg?* (Hamburg-Berlin-Bonn: Verlag E.S. Mittler & Sohn, 1996), pp. 120, 130.
14. S.F. Kellerhof, *Unternehmen Zitadelle*, 'Stalins Panzer fuhren einen Kamikaze-Angriff' [Interview mit Karl-Heinz Frieser], *Die Welt*, 2013, 15 Juli, https://www.welt.de/geschichte/zweiter-weltkrieg/article117992840/Stalins-Panzer-fuhren-einen-Kamikaze-Angriff.html.
15. *Ibid.*, pp. 121–2.
16. Editor's note. Churchill was the popular name of the British-made Mk IV (A22) heavy tank during the Second World War. One model weighed 40.7 tons and carried a crew of five. It was armed with a 75mm gun and two 7.92mm machine guns.
17. Kellerhof, *Unternehmen Zitadelle*, p. 121, fn. 34. Editor's note. Pavel Alekseevich Rotmistrov (1901–82) joined the Red Army in 1919 and fought in the civil war and later took part in the 1939–40 war against Finland. During the Second World War he served as chief of staff of a mechanized corps and later commanded a tank brigade, tank corps, and tank army before being relieved in 1944. Following the war, Rotmistrov commanded Soviet tank forces in Germany and later was chief of the army's armoured academy.
18. *Ibid.*, p. 122.
19. N. Zetterling and A. Frankson, *Kursk 1943. A Statistical Analysis* (London: Frank Cass Publishers, 2006), table 7.2, p. 103. https://books.google.ru/books?id=IZb7AQAAQBAJ&pg=PT113&hl=ru&source-gbs_toc_r&cad=2#v=onepage&q&f=false.
20. *Ibid.*, p. 105, table 7.3.
21. *Ibid.*, p. 105.
22. K. Pfyoch, *Esesovtsy pod Prokhorovkoi. 1-ya Diviziya yeyo 'Leibstandart Adol'f Gitler' v Boyu*, trans. from German (Moscow: Yauza-Press, 2010), pp. 135–6, 211.
23. Editor's note. Tiger was the popular name for the PzKpfw VI German heavy tank, which served during 1942–5. One model weighed 54 tons and carried a crew of five. It was armed with an 88mm gun and two 7.92mm machine guns. Panther was the popular name for the PzKpfw V German medium tank, which served during 1943–5. One model weighted 44.8 tons and carried a crew of five. It was armed with a 75mm gun and two 7.92mm machine guns.
24. V.N. Zamulin and L.N. Lopukhovskii, 'Prokhorovskoe Srazhenie. Mify i Real'nost'', *Voenno-Istoricheskii Arkhiv* (2003), no. 3, p. 101; L.N. Lopukhovskii, 'Prokhorovka—bez Grifa Sekretnosti', *Voenno-Istoricheskii Arkhiv* (2004), no. 2, p. 73.

25. Krivosheev, *Rossiya i SSSR*, pp. 285–6; Human Losses in World War II. AOK/Ic POW Summary Reports [BA/MA RH 2/2087, 2/2621, 2/2622K, 2/2633K, 2/2635K, 2/2636–2642, 2/2707, 2/2773, IfZ ED 48] (http://ww2stats.com/pow_ger_okh_aok.html).

26. Zavizion, *Boevoi Sostav*, vol. III, pp. 162–3, 191–2.

27. See, for example, S. Ivanov, 'Oboronitel'naya Operatsiya Voronezhskogo Fronta', *V-IZh* (1973), no. 8, p. 22.

28. See B. Sokolov, 'Skol'ko my Poteryali v Velikoi Otechestvennoi Voine i kak Fal'sifitsiruyut Istoriyu', *Novaya Gazeta*, 2009, 22 June, pp. 8–9.

29. Zetterling et al., *Kursk 1943*, table 8.1, p. 113. https://books.google.ru/books?id=IZb7AQA-AQBAJ&pg=PT113&hl=ru&source=gbs_toc_r&cad=2#v=onepage&q&f=false.

30. Human Losses in World War II. AOK/Ic POW Summary Reports, [BA/MA RH 2/2087, 2/2621, 2/2622K, 2/2633K, 2/2635K, 2/2636–2642, 2/2707, 2/2773, IfZ ED 48] (http:web.archive.org/web/20160304195737//http://ww2stats.com/pow_ger_okh_aok.html).

31. Zetterling et al., *Kursk 1943*, table 8.2, p. 114. Editor's note. Kempf was the shorthand name for Army Detachment Kempf, which was commanded at this time by General Werner Kempf (1886–1964). During the Battle of Kursk the group included the III Panzer Corps and the XI and XLII army corps. The group was later redesignated as the Eighth Army.

32. *Ibid.*, table 8.3, p. 115.

33. Human Losses in World War II. Heeresarzt 10-Day Casualty Reports per Army/Army Group, 1943, [BA/MA RW 6/556, 6/558] (http://ww2stats.com/cas_ger_okh_dec43.html)

34. V.P. Galitskii, 'Vrazheskie Voennoplennye v SSSR (1941–1945 gg.)', *V–IZh*, no. 9 (1990), p. 41, table 2.

35. Ye.I. Smirnov, *Voina i Voennaya Meditsina*, 2nd edn (Moscow: Meditsina, 1979) p. 188.

36. Human Losses in World War II. AOK/Ic POW Summary Reports, [BA/MA RH 2/2087, 2/2621, 2/2622K, 2/2633K, 2/2635K, 2/2636-2642, 2/2707, 2/2773, IfZ ED 48] (http:web.archive.org/web/20160304195737//http://ww2stats.com/pow_ger_okh_aok.html).

37. Yumaev, *95-ya Gvardeiskaya*, p. 47.

38. Human Losses in World War II. Heeresarzt 10-Day Casualty Reports per Army/Army Group, 1943, [BA/MA RW 6/556, 6/558] (http://ww2stats.com/cas_ger_okh_dec43.html).

39. Yumaev, *95-ya Gvardeiskaya*, p. 188.

40. Editor's note. Mikhail Yefimovich Katukov (1900–76) joined the Red Army in 1919 and fought in the civil war. During the Second World War he commanded a tank brigade, a tank corps, and a tank army in several major operations. Following the war, Katukov commanded the Soviet army's mechanized forces in Germany and served in the central military apparatus.

41. Frieser, 'Schlagen', p. 130; N.G. Andronikov, 'Gitlerovskii "Fakel" Byl Pogashen na "Ognennoi Duge"', *V-IZh* (1993), no. 8, p. 2.

42. Frieser, 'Schlagen', pp. 120–9.

43. Ye.Ye. Shchekotikhin, *Krupneishee Tankovoe Srazhenie Velikoi Otechestvennoi. Bitva za Orel* (Moscow: Yauza; EKSMO, 2009), p. 118.

44. *Ibid.*, p. 127.

45. Shein, *Tanki*, pp. 114–15.

46. Human Losses in World War II. Heeresarzt 10-Day Casualty Reports per Army/Army Group, 1943, [BA/MA RW 6/556, 6/558] (http://ww2stats.com/cas_ger_okh_dec43.html).

47. Shchekotikhin, *Krupneishee*, pp. 216, 251.

48. Editor's note. Aleksei Innokent'evich Antonov (1896–1962) was drafted into the imperial army in 1916 and he joined the Red Army in 1919. During the Second World War Antonov served as chief of staff of a number of *fronts* and in 1942 was summoned to Moscow to serve as chief of the General Staff's operational directorate and in 1945 he was appointed chief of the General Staff. Following the war, Antonov commanded a military district and was chief of staff of the Warsaw Pact forces.

49. *Russkii Arkhiv. Velikaya Otechestvennaya. General'nyi Shtab v Gody Velikoi Otechestvennoi Voiny. Dokumenty i Materialy. 1943 God*, vol. XXIII (12–3) (Moscow: TERRA, 1999), p. 257.
50. Yumaev, *95-ya Gvardeiskaya*, p. 49.
51. Puzhaev, *Krov' i Slava*, p. 220.
52. Human Losses in World War II. Heeresarzt 10-Day Casualty Reports per Army/Army Group, 1943, [BA/MA RW 6/556, 6/558] (http://ww2stats.com/cas_ger_okh_dec43.html).
53. Puzhaev, *Krov' i Slava*, p. 236.
54. Human Losses in World War II. Heeresarzt 10-Day Casualty Reports per Army/Army Group, 1943, [BA/MA RW 6/556, 6/558] (http://ww2stats.com/cas_ger_okh_dec43.html).
55. Puzhaev, *Krov' i Slava*, p. 241.
56. *Ibid.*, p. 242.
57. *Ibid.*, p. 249.
58. Human Losses in World War II. Heeresarzt 10-Day Casualty Reports per Army/Army Group, 1943, [BA/MA RW 6/556, 6/558] (http://ww2stats.com/cas_ger_okh_dec43.html).
59. Puzhaev, *Krov' i Slava*, p. 252.
60. *Ibid.*, p. 256.
61. *Ibid.*, p. 253.
62. Krivosheev, *Rossiya i SSSR*, p. 313, table 142.
63. A. Isaev, 'Proryv Mius-Fronta', *Frontovaya Illustratsiya*, 2006, no. 3, p. 56.
64. *Ibid.*, p. 56.
65. Puzhaev, *Krov' i Slava*, pp. 270–1.
66. Human Losses in World War II. Heeresarzt 10-Day Casualty Reports per Army/Army Group, 1943, [BA/MA RW 6/556, 6/558] (http://ww2stats.com/cas_ger_okh_dec43.html).
67. Puzhaev, *Krov' i Slava*, p. 282.
68. Zavizion, *Boevoi Sostav*, vol. III, p. 197; A. Isaev, 'Provyv', p. 58.
69. Puzhaev, *Krov' i Slava*, p. 302.
70. See B.V. Sokolov, *Razvedka. Tainy Vtoroi Mirovoi Voiny* (Moscow: AST-Press, 2001), p. 112. Editor's note. A *stanitsa* is the name for a village in the Cossack-inhabited areas.
71. Puzhaev, *Krov' i Slava*, pp. 294, 298, 302, 305, 313.
72. Human Losses in World War II. Heeresarzt 10-Day Casualty Reports per Army/Army Group, 1943, [BA/MA RW 6/556, 6/558] (http://ww2stats.com/cas_ger_okh_dec43.html).
73. Osvobozhdenie Kieva ot Fashistkikh Zakhvatchikov. Spravka (The Liberation of Kiev from the Nazi Invaders. Information)//RIA Novosti Ukraina, 2015, 6 November (https://rian.com.ua/dissier/20151106/376476994.html).
74. Human Losses in World War II. Heeresarzt 10-Day Casualty Reports per Army/Army Group, 1943 [BA/MA RW 6/556, 6/558] (http://web.archive.Org/web/20160305195605/http://ww2stats.com/cas ger okh dec43.html)
75. Human Losses in World War II. AOK/Ic POW Summary Reports, [BA/MA RH 2/2087, 2/2621, 2/2622K, 2/2633K, 2/2635K, 2/2636-2642, 2/2707, 2/2773, IfZ ED 48] (http://web.archive.org/web/20160304195737/http://ww2stats.com/pow_ger_okh_aok.html).
76. Kuropatkov et al., *Boevoi Put'*, vol. I, p. 273.
77. Human Losses in World War II. Heeresarzt 10-Day Casualty Reports per Army/Army Group, 1943 [BA/MA RW 6/556, 6/558] (http://ww2stats.com/cas_ger_okh_dec43.html).
78. A.M. Chmerev, *Proshla s Boyami . . .* (Kishinev: Kartya Moldovenyaske, 1983), p. 49.
79. Human Losses in World War II. Heeresarzt 10-Day Casualty Reports per Army/Army Group, 1943, [BA/MA RW 6/556, 6/558] (http://ww2stats.com/cas_ger_okh_dec43.html).
80. S.I. Pirozhkov, *Prazdnik Stoikosti i Geroizma. Velikaya Pobeda i Sovremennost'*, p. 28. Here it is pointed out that during the fighting for the Bukrin bridgehead, of more than 800 men in a battalion of the 136th Rifle Division's 342nd Rifle Regiment only 5 remained alive. See also, '70 Let Nazad Osvobozhdena Stolitsa Sovetskoi Ukraini—Gorod Geroi Kiev', *Voennyi Obozrevatel'*, 2013, 7 Noyabrya (http://warsonline.info/velikaya-otechestvennaya-voyna/6-november-1943-osvobo-

zhdenie-kieva-wwii.html/). On the other hand, the figure of 240,000 dead also includes the fighting for the Bukrin bridgehead, including 7,000 airborne troops. See M. Marchenko, 'Bitva za Denpr: Platsdarm Lozhnyi, a Smert' Nastoyashchaya', *Ukraina Kriminal'naya*, 2008. 7 Noyabrya (http:cripo.com.ua/?aid=62031&sect_id=9). It is possible that the figure of 240,000 killed and missing in action refers to the losses on both bridgeheads during the period from 22 September to 6 November 1943.

81. Krivosheev, *Rossiya i SSSR*, p. 314.

82. *Ibid.*, p. 291.

83. Human Losses in World War II. Heeresarzt 10-Day Casualty Reports per Army/Army Group, 1943, [BA/MA RW 6/556, 6/558] (http://web.archive.org/web/20161113221248/http://ww2stats.com/cas_ger_okh_dec43.html).

84. Zavizion, *Boevoi Sostav*, vol. III, pp. 222–3, 250–1.

85. RGASPI, f. 83, op. 1, d. 29, pp. 75–7. Editor's note. Yefim Afanas'evich Shchadenko (1885–1951) joined the Russian Social-Democratic Labour Party in 1904 and adhered to its Bolshevik faction. During the civil war he served as a political commissar with armies and *fronts*. During the Second World War he headed the army's directorate for forming and outfitting units and also served as political commissar with *fronts*. His increasing mental instability evidently was the cause for his recall from the front in 1944 and afterwards he was not employed.

86. A.V. Isaev, *Osvobozhdenie*, p. 534.

87. Human Losses in World War II. Heeresarzt 10-Day Casualty Reports per Army/Army Group, 1943, [BA/MA RW 6/556, 6/558] (http://ww2stats.com/cas_ger_okh_dec43.html).

88. Galitskii, 'Vrazheskie', p. 41, table 2.

89. Krivosheev, *Rossiya i SSSR*, p. 291.

90. Editor's note. Lev Anatol'evich Vladimirskii (1903–73) joined the Red Army in 1921 and was transferred to the navy the following year. During the Second World War he commanded a squadron and the Black Sea Fleet during 1943–4, but was relieved following a failed raiding operation. Following the war, Vladimirskii held a number of administrative posts and took part in scientific expeditions until his retirement in 1970.

91. A.Ya. Kuznetsov, *Bol'shoi Desant. Kerchensko-El'tigenskaya Operatsiya* (Moscow: Veche, 2011), pp. 380–2.

92. Human Losses in World War II. AOK/Ic POW Summary Reports, [BA/MA RH 2/2087, 2/2621, 2/2622K, 2/2633K, 2/2635K, 2/2636-2642, 2/2707, 2/2773, IfZ ED 48] (http://web.archive.org/web/20160304195737/http://ww2stats.com/pow_ger_okh_aok.html).

93. Krivosheev, *Rossiya i SSSR*, p. 314.

94. Human Losses in World War II. Heeresarzt 10-Day Casualty Reports per Army/Army Group, 1943, [BA/MA RW 6/556, 6/558] (http://web.archive./web/20160305185605/http://ww2stats.com/cas_ger_okh_dec43.html).

95. Kuznetsov, *Bol'shoi Desant*, p. 385.

96. *Ibid.*, p. 384.

97. *Ibid.*, p. 385.

98. H. Balck, *Order from Chaos*, p. 321.

99. Human Losses in World War II. Heeresarzt 10-Day Casualty Reports per Army/Army Group, 1943, [BA/MA RW 6/556, 6/558] (http://web.archive./web/20160305185605/http://ww2stats.com/cas_ger_okh_dec43.html).

100. 'Dnevnik Polkovnika I.Ya. Kuznetsov, *My Vse Voiny Shal'nye Deti*, pp. 228–9.

101. From the graph, 'Gesamtstaerke und blutige Verluste des Ostheeres', which was compiled by director Rudiger Oversmans and graciously put at the author's disposal.

102. 'Operation Citadel. An Analysis of its Critical Aspects', *Kursk. The German View. Eyewitness Reports of Operation Citadel by the German Commanders*, trans., ed. and annotated by Steven H. Newton (Cambridge, MA: Da Capo Press, 2002), pp. 413–14.

Chapter 7

1. Havlat, *Western Aid*, p. 60.
2. Kuropatkov et al., *Boevoi Put'*, vol. I, p. 373.
3. Heeresarzt 10-Day Casualty Reports per Army/Army Group, 1944, [BA/MA RW 6/559]// Human Losses in World War II. German Statistics and Documents, (http://ww2stats.com/ cas_ger_okh_dec44.html).
4. Krivosheev, *Rossiya v Voinakh*, p. 293.
5. Yumaev, *95-ya Gvardeiskaya*, p. 67.
6. Human Losses in World War II. Heeresarzt 10-Day Casualty Reports per Army/Army Group, 1944, [BA/MA RW 6/559] (http://ww2stats.com/cas_ger_okh_dec44.html).
7. Zavizion, *Boevoi Sostav*, vol. IV, pp. 46–7.
8. R.-D. Mueller, *Der letzte deutsche Krieg 1939–1945* (Stutttgart: Klett-Cotta, 2005), p. 290.
9. Human Losses in World War II. Heeresarzt 10-Day Casualty Reports per Army/Army Group, 1944, [BA/MA RW 6/559] (http://ww2stats.com/cas_ger_okh_dec44.html).
10. *Perepiska Predsedatelya Soveta Ministrov SSSR s Prezidentami SShA i Prem'er-Ministrami Velikobritanii vo Vremya Velikoi Otechestvennoi Voiny, 1941–1945 gg.; Preepiska s U. Cherchillem i K. Ettli (Iyul' 1941 g.–Noyabr' 1945 g.), Perepiska s F. Ruzvel'tom i G. Trumenom (Avgust 1941 g.–Dekabr' 1945g.)* (Moscow: Voskresen'e, 2005), no. 279, p. 216.
11. G. Uil'yamson and R. Bukheiro, *Elitnye Chasti Vermakhta 1939–1945 gg.*, trans. from English (Moscow: AST, 2003), p. 216.
12. Calculated according to Myueller-Gillebrand, *Sukhoputnaya Armiya*, pp. 747–812.
13. *Podlinnaya Istoriya Lyuftvaffe. Vzlet i Padenie Detishcha Geringa*, trans. from English (Moscow: Yauza; EKSMO, 2006), pp. 434, 500, 520.
14. G.A. Litvin, *Slomannye Kryl'ya Lyuftvaffe// . . . Para Bellum! Sbornik Statei* (Moscow: Duel', 1998), table 19 (http://malchish.org/lib/history/parabellum/pril_1html).
15. Myueller-Gillebrand, *Sukhoputnaya Armiya*, pp. 716–17.
16. *Sbornik Boevykh Dokumentov Velikoi Otechestvennoi Voiny*, Vypusk 5 (Moscow: Voennoe Izdatel'stvo, 1947), p. 17.
17. R. Ponomarenko, K. Zalesskii and K. Semenov, *Voiska SS bez Grifa Sekretnosti* (Moscow: Veche, 2010), p. 29.
18. Human Losses in World War II. SS Losses. Strengths, Replacements, and Losses of Waffen-SS Units, [BA NS 19/1520] (http://www.ww2stats.com/cas_ger_var_ssl.html).
19. *Ibid.*, p. 733.
20. *Ibid.*, p. 732.
21. Smirnov, *Voina i Voennaya*, p. 188.
22. Human Losses in World War II. AOK/Ic POW Summary Reports, [BA/MA RH 2/2087, 2/2621, 2/2622K, 2/2633K, 2/2635K, 2/2636-2642, 2/2707, 2/2773, IfZ ED 48] (http://web.archive.org/ web/20160304195737/http://.ww2stats.com/pow_ger_okh_aok.html).
23. S. Zaloga, *Downfall 1945. The Fall of Hitler's Third Reich* (Oxford: Osprey Publishing, Ltd, 2016), p. 25.
24. Human Losses in World War II. AOK/Ic POW Summary Reports, [BA/MA RH 2/2087, 2/2621, 2/2622K, 2/2633K, 2/2635K, 2/2636-2642, 2/2707, 2/2773, IfZ ED 48] (http://web.archive.org/ web/20160304195737/http://.ww2stats.com/pow_ger_okh_aok.html).
25. *Ibid.*, p. 11.
26. *Ibid.*, p. 23.
27. *Ibid.*, p. 22.
28. *Ibid.*, p. 13.
29. Human Losses in World War II. Heeresarzt 10-Day Casualty Reports per Army/Army Group, 1945, [BA/MA RW 6/559, RH 2/1355, 2/2623] (http://web.archive.org/web/20160303231601/ http://ww2stats.com/cas_ger_okh_dec45.html).
30. Zaloga, *Downfall*, p. 23.

31. Smirnov, *Voina i Voennaya*, p. 188.
32. O. Grohler, 'Starke, Verteilung und Verluste der deutschen Luftwaffe im zweiten Weltkrieg', *Militargeschichte*, no. 17 (1978), pp. 316–36; D. Caldwell, *Luftwaffe Aircraft Losses by Theater, September 1943–October 1944* (http://don-caldwell.be.bs/jg26/thtrlosses.htm).
33. Krivosheev, *Rossiya i SSSR*, p. 298.
34. Zavizion, *Boevoi Sostav*, vol. IV, p. 261.
35. Krivosheev, *Rossiya i SSSR*, p. 316.
36. J. Erickson, *The Road to Berlin* (Boulder, CO: Westview Press, 1983), p. 200.
37. Editor's note. Ernst Bernhard Wilhelm Busch (1885–1945) joined the imperial army in 1904 and fought in the First World War. During the Second World War he commanded a corps, an army and army groups. Busch was captured by the British and died in captivity.
38. V. Haupt, *Srazhenie Gruppy Armii 'Tsentr'. Vzglyad Ofitera Vermakhta*, trans. from German (Moscow: Yauza; EKSMO, 2006), p. 305.
39. Krivosheev, *Rossiya i SSSR*, p. 296.
40. Human Losses in World War II. Heeresarzt 10-Day Casualty Reports per Army/Army Group, 1944, [BA/MA RW 6/559] (http://web,archive.org/web/20160304175048/http://ww2stats.com/cas_ger_okh_dec44.html).
41. Human Losses in World War II. Abwicklungsstab, Group C (A.Gr.Center), [BA/MA RH 15/290] (http://web.archive.org/web/20160411222116/http://ww2stats.com/cas_ger_var_abwc.html).
42. Galitskii, 'Vrazheskie', p. 41, table 2.
43. Human Losses in World War II. AOK/Ic POW Summary Reports [BA/MA RH 2/2087, 2/2621, 2/2622K, 2/2633K, 2/2635K, 2/2636-2642, 2/2707, 2/2773, IfZ ED 48] (http://web.archive.org/web/20160304195737/http://.ww2stats.com/pow_ger_okh_aok.html).
44. Editor's note. Nikolai Ivanovich Gusev (1897–1962) joined the imperial army in 1916 and the Red Army two years later. During the Second World War he commanded a division, a corps, and several armies. Following the war, Gusev commanded armies, served abroad as a military adviser and attaché, and worked in the central military apparatus.
45. *Russkii Arkhiv. Velikaya Otechestvennaya*, vol. XVI (5–4), pp. 47–8.
46. Human Losses in World War II. Abwicklungsstab, Group F (A.Gr.South-Ukraine), [BA/MA RH 15/290] (http://www.ww2stats.com/cas_ger_var_abwf.html).
47. Galitskii, 'Vrazheskie', p. 41, table 2.
48. P. Grigorenko, *V Podpol'e Mozhno Vstretit' Tol'ko Krys . . .* (Moscow: Zven'ya, 1997), pp. 245–6.
49. *5th Waffen SS Panzer 'Division Viking,' 1940–1945. Illustrated* (Potsdam: German Army Centre of Military History, 2015), p. 26.
50. V. Khristoforov, P. Meretskii et al., *Warshavskoe Vosstanie 1944 v Dokumentakh iz Arkhivov Spetssluzhb/Powstanie Warszawskie 1944 w Dochumentack z Archiwow Sluzb Specialnych* (Moscow-Warsaw: Tyrsa, 2007), p. 92. Editor's note. This is a reference to Emil Otto Rasch (1891–1948), who served in the First World War and held two doctoral degrees and who later worked as an attorney. He joined the Nazi Party in 1931and the SS two years later. He was responsible for killing Polish prisoners and in 1941 headed *Einsatzgruppe* C in the Soviet Union, where he carried out the massacre at Babii Yar. Rasch was later discharged and spent the rest of the war as director of an oil company. He was indicted for war crimes, but the case was dropped due to his poor health.
51. Editor's note. A KMG (*konno-mekhanizirovannaya gruppa*), or cavalry-mechanized group, was a temporary operational-tactical formation employed by the Red Army during the Second World War during the exploitation phase of offensive operations. These groups generally consisted of a tank or mechanized corps and a cavalry corps, plus other, smaller units. Issa Aleksandrovich Pliev (1903–79) joined the Red Army in 1922. During the Great Patriotic War he commanded a cavalry division and corps and later a cavalry-mechanized group in Europe and the Far East. Following the Great Patriotic War he commanded armies and a military district and was the commander of Soviet forces in Cuba during the Missile Crisis.

52. Yu.V. Mikhailik, *Istoriya Boevykh Deistvii Krasnoi Armii na Territorii Vengrii (Sentyabr' 1945– Aprel' 1945 gg. Dissertatsiya na Soiskanie Uchenoi Stepeni Doktora Istoricheskikh Nauk* (Voronezh: Voronezhskii Gosudarstvennyi Pedagogicheskii Universitet, 2016), pp. 98–9. It's interesting, reading from a report by the KMG, at that time it was demanded of Soviet generals that they report the exact number of enemy captured and killed with their precise division into the following categories: general, staff officer, officer, NCO, soldier. Naturally, the figures of enemy losses in Soviet reports were fantastically inflated, and not only as regards those killed, but those captured as well, and that they arbitrarily divided up the prisoners, making sure that there were not more staff officers than NCOs, etc. Pliev estimated enemy losses at 4,655 captured and 16,078 killed.

53. Editor's note. Sergei Il'ich Gorshkov (1902–93) joined the Red Army in 1920 and put down domestic uprisings following the civil war. During the Second World War he commanded a cavalry division, a cavalry corps, and temporarily commanded a cavalry-mechanized group. Gorshkov retired in 1946.

54. I.A. Pliev, *Dorogami Voiny* (Moscow: Veche, 2015), pp. 161, 166, 169.

55. Krivosheev, *Rossiya i SSSR*, p. 316.

56. Human Losses in World War II. AOK/Ic POW Summary Reports, [BA/MA RH 2/2087, 2/2621, 2/2622K, 2/2633K, 2/2635K, 2/2636-2642, 2/2707, 2/2773, IfZ ED 48] (http://web.archive.org/web/20161113070518/http://.ww2stats.com:80/pow_ger_okh_aok.html).

57. Axworthy et al., *Third Axis*, p. 201.

58. Human Losses in World War II. Heeresarzt 10-Day Casualty Reports per Army/Army Group, 1944, [BA/MA RW 6/559] (http://web,archive.org/web/20160304175048/http://ww2stats.com/cas_ger_okh_dec44.html).

59. Human Losses in World War II. Losses of German Allies (Heer and Luftwaffe, as reported by Heeresarzt), [BA/MA RW 6/553, 6/554, RH 2/1355] (http://web.archive.org/web/20161113072715/http://ww2stats.com/cas_ger_var_all.html).

60. Axworthy et al., *Third Axis*, p. 202.

61. Perry Moore, *Panzerschlacht. Armoured operations on the Hungarian plains September – November 1944* (Solihull (West Midlands): Helion & Company, 2008), p. 184–5.

62. Editor's note. Maximilian Ludwign Julius Franz Fretter-Pico (1892–1984) joined the army in 1910 and fought in the First World War. During the Second World War he commanded a division, corps, and an army. Fretter-Pico was captured and interned at the end of the war, but released in 1947.

63. M. Fretter-Pico, *Nemetskaya Pekhota. Strategicheskie Oshibki Vermakhta. Pekhotnye Divizii v Voine Protiv Sovetskogo Soyuza, 1941–1944*, trans. from German by A.T. Kuprin (Moscow: Tsentropoligraf, 2013), p. 187.

64. V.I. Davidenko and N.I. Yashchenko (eds), *73-ya Gvardeiskaya. Sbornik Vospominanii, Dokumentov i Materialov o Boevom Puti 73-i Gvardeiskoi Strelkovoi Stalingradsko-Dunaiskoi Krasnoznamennoi Divizii* (Alma-Ata: 1986), p. 17.

65. Human Losses in World War II. Heeresarzt 10-Day Casualty Reports per Army/Army Group, 1944, [BA/MA RW 6/559] (http://www.ww2stats.com/cas_ger_okh_dec44.html).

66. Krivosheev, *Rossiya i SSSR*, p. 300.

67. Davidenko et al., *73-ya Gvardeiskaya*, p. 201.

68. Balck, *Order in Chaos*, p. 414.

69. Human Losses in World War II. Heeresarzt 10-Day Casualty Reports per Army/Army Group, 1944, [BA/MA RW 6/559] (http://www.w2stats.com/cas_ger_okh_dec44.html); Human Losses in World War II. Heeresarzt 10-Day Casualty Reports per Army/Army Group, 1945, [BA/MA RW 6/559] (http://www.ww2stats.com/cas_ger_okh_dec45.html).

70. Smirnov, *Voina i Voennaya*, p. 188.

71. Krivosheev, *Rossiya i SSSR*, p. 317, table 142; Zaloga, *Downfall*, p. 25. Editor's note. Fedor Ivanovich Tolbukhin (1894–1949) joined the imperial army in 1914 and the Red Army in 1918.

During the Great Patriotic War he served as a front chief of staff, and army commander and a *front* commander. Following the war, Tolbukhin served as commander-in-chief of the Southern Group of Forces and commanded a military district.

72. Krivosheev, *Rossiya i SSSR*, p. 317, table 142.

73. *Ibid.*, p. 306.

74. A.V. Isaev and M.V. Kolomiets, *Agoniya Pantservaffe. Razgrom Tankovoi Armii SS* (Moscow: Yauza; EKSMO, 2012), p. 155.

75. Human Losses in World War II. AOK/Ic POW Summary Reports, [BA/MA RH 2/2087, 2/2621, 2/2622K, 2/2633K, 2/2635K, 2/2636-2642, 2/2707, 2/2773, IfZ ED 48] (http://ww2stats.com/pow_ger_okh_aok.html).

76. Editor's note. The SU-100 was a self-propelled gun that first appeared in 1944. It contained a crew of four and had a maximum weight of 31.6 tons. It was armed with a 100mm gun.

77. Editor's note. IS tanks refer to a series of heavy tanks produced for the Soviet army during the Second World War and afterwards. These included the IS-1, IS-2, IS-3, IS-4, IS-6, IS-7, and IS-10. The SU-76 was a self-propelled gun that first appeared in 1942. It contained a crew of four and had a maximum weight of slightly over 11 tons. It was armed with a 76mm gun. The SU-85 was a Soviet self-propelled gun which first appeared in 1943. One model weighed 29.6 tons and carried a crew of four. It was armed with an 85mm gun. The ISU-122 was a self-propelled gun that first appeared in 1943. Depending on the model, it carried a crew of four or five men and had a maximum weight of 45.5 tons. It was armed with a 122mm gun and a 12.7mm machine gun. The ISU-152 was a self-propelled gun that first appeared in 1943. Depending on the model, it carried a crew of four or five men and had a maximum weight of 45.5 tons. It was armed with a 122mm gun and a 12.7mm machine gun. The M-4 'Sherman' was a US-made medium tank which first appeared in 1942. One model weighed 30.3 tons and carried a crew of five. It was armed with a 75mm gun, a 50-calibre machine gun and two 30.06 machine guns. The 'Stuart' M3 was an American-made light tank produced during the Second World War. One model weighed 15.2 tons and had a crew of four. It was armed with a 37mm gun and three 7.62mm machine guns. The T-70 was the Red Army's most common light tank, introduced in 1942. It weighed 9.2 tons, carried a crew of two, and was armed with a 45mm gun and a 7.62mm machine gun.

78. Editor's note. The SU-57 was the Soviet designation for the US-built T48 gun motor carriage, which the Red Army received through Lend-Lease during the latter half of the war. The SU-57 carried a crew of five and was armed with a 57mm gun.

79. Estimate from Isaev et al., *Agoniya Pantservaffe*, pp. 127, 155.

80. M. Svirin, O. Baronov, M. Kolomiets and D. Nedogonov, *Boi u Ozera Balaton. Yanvar'–Mart 1945 g.* (Moscow: EksPrint NV, 1999), p. 79.

81. K.-H. Frieser, K. Schmider, K. Schonherr, G. Schreiber, K. Ungvary and B. Wegner, *Das Deutsches Reich und der Zweite Weltkrieg* (Munchen: Deutsche Verlags-Anstalt, 2007), vol. VIII, p. 930.

82. H. Meyer, *The 12th SS: The History of the Hitler Youth Panzer Division* (Mechanicsburg, PA: Stackpole Books, 2005), vol. II, p. 283 (electronic version).

83. *Ibid.*, p. 941.

84. *Ibid.*, p. 941.

85. *Ibid.*, p. 366. Editor's note. The Panzer IV was a German medium tank that first appeared in 1939. One model weighed 25 tons and had a crew of five. It was armed with a 75mm gun and two 7.92 machine guns.

86. Isaev et al., *Agoniya Pantservaffe*, p. 155; Frieser et al., *Das Deutsche Reich*, vol. VIII, pp. 941–2.

87. Isaev et al., *Agoniya Pantservaffe*, p. 158.

88. H. Greinert and P.E. Schramm, *Kriegstagebuch des Oberkommandos der Wehrmacht (Wehrmachtfuhrungsstab) (KVT/OKW)* (Frankfurt am Main: Bernadr & Graefe Verlag fur Wehrwesen, 1961), book IV, p. 1,173.

89. Editor's note. Josef 'Sepp' Dietrich (1892–1966) joined the Bavarian army in 1911 and fought in the First World War. He joined the Nazi Party in 1928 and rose rapidly through the ranks of the SS. During the Second World War he commanded a division and a panzer corps. He later commanded the SS Sixth Panzer Army on the Western and Eastern fronts. Following the war, Dietrich spent several years in prison for war crimes.

90. Human Losses in World War II. Heeresarzt 10-Day Casualty Reports per Army/Army Group, 1945, [BA/MA RW 6/559, RH 2/1355, 2/2623] (http://www.ww2stats.com/cas_ger_okh_dec45.html).

91. Meyer, *The 12th SS*, vol. II, p. 320 (electronic version).

92. Editor's note. Andrei Grigor'evich Kravchenko (1899–1963) joined the Red Army in 1918 and fought in the civil war and the Soviet-Finnish War. During the Great Patriotic War he commanded a tank brigade and a tank corps, and then a tank army in Europe and the Far East. Following the war, Kravchenko commanded an army and retired in 1955.

93. T. Miller, *Agoniya 1-go Tankovogo Korpusa SS. Ot Ardenn do Budapeshta* (Moscow: Yauza-Press, 2009), p. 321. (This book is a translation into Russian of M. Reynolds's *Men of Steel: 1st SS Panzer Corps, the Ardennes and Eastern Front 1944–5* (London: Pen and Sword,1999).)

94. Krivosheev, *Rossiya i SSSR*, p. 487.

95. Editor's note. This refers to the encirclement of German Army Group B by US forces in the Ruhr industrial area in April 1945; 325,000 prisoners eventually fell into Allied hands. Remagen refers to the capture of the Ludendorff Bridge over the Rhine River by US forces on 7 March 1945. This coup enabled Allied forces to cross the last natural barrier to the German interior.

96. Krivosheev, *Rossiya i SSSR*, p. 306.

97. Human Losses in World War II. Heeresarzt 10-Day Casualty Reports per Army/Army Group, 1945, [BA/MA RW 6/559, RH 2/1355, 2/2623] (http://www.ww2stats.com/cas_ger_okh_dec45.html).

Chapter 8

1. Guderian, *Vospominaniya*, pp. 523, 530.

2. Editor's note. Vasilii Ivanovich Chuikov (1900–82) joined the Red Army in 1918 and fought in the Russian Civil War. During the interwar period he commanded an army during the 1939–40 war with Finland and was the Soviet military advisor to Chinese leader Chiang Kai-shek. During the Second World War Chuikov commanded an army in the defence of Stalingrad and held this post until the end of the war. Following the war, Chuikov commanded Soviet occupation troops in Germany, served as commander-in-chief of the Ground Forces, and was chief of national civil defence.

3. Editor's note. Aleksei Alekseevich Yepishev (1908–85) joined the Communist Party in 1929 and the Red Army a year later. During the Second World War he held various government and party posts and was a political commissar with an army. Following the war, Yepishev continued his state and party career. He was appointed chief of the Main Political Administration of the Soviet Armed Forces and served in that capacity until 1985.

4. A.N. Gordienko, *Marshal Zhukov* (Minsk: Literatura, 1998), pp. 163–4.

5. Editor's note. Nikolai Erastovich Berzarin (1904–45) joined the Red Army in 1918 and fought the Japanese in the Far East in 1938. He commanded several armies during the Great Patriotic War and was appointed commandant of Berlin following the city's capture. He was killed in a motorcycle accident in June 1945. Vladimir Yakovlevich Kolpakchi (1899–1961) joined the Red Army in 1918 and fought in the civil war. During the Second World War he served in higher staff positions and commanded a number of armies. Following the war, Kolpakchi commanded a number of military districts and served in the central military apparatus. He died in an airplane crash. Semyon Il'ich Bogdanov (1894–1960) joined the Red Army in 1918 and fought in the civil war. During the Second World War he commanded tank divisions and tank

and mechanized corps and a tank army in several of the war's major operations. Following the war, Bogdanov commanded the army's armoured forces and was chief of the army's armoured academy.

6. Editor's note. Aleksei Ivanovich Radzievskii (1911–79) joined the Red Army in 1929. During the Second World War he served in a variety of staff positions at various levels and commanded a tank army. Following the war, Radzievskii served in the central military apparatus and in the army's military-educational system.

7. Zhukov, *Vospominaniya*, vol. III, pp. 201–10. For Chuikov's version, see *Novaya i Noveishaya Istoriya* (1965), no. 2, pp. 6–7; *Oktyabr'*, (1964), no. 4, pp. 128–9.

8. Yu.M Komarov, '. . . Nastuplenie na Berlin Mogu Nachat' 19-20.45', *V-IZh* (1995), no. 2, pp. 4–6.

9. Guderian, *Vospominaniya*, p. 557.

10. Editor's note. Konstantin Fedorovich Telegin (1899–1981) joined the Red Army in 1918 and the Communist Party a year later. During the Second World War he served as political commissar on various fronts. He was dismissed from the army in 1947and arrested the following year and sentenced to a lengthy prison term in an effort to compromise Zhukov, with whom he had served. Telegin was freed following Stalin's death in 1953 and retired in 1956.

11. *Russkii Arkhiv: Velikaya Otechestvennaya*, vol. 15 (4–5), pp. 498–9.

12. *Pravda*, 1945, 23 February, p. 1.

13. Galitskii, 'Vrazheskie', p. 40.

14. Yumaev, *95-ya Gvardeiskaya*, p. 90.

15. Human Losses in World War II. Heeresarzt 10-Day Casualty Reports per Army/Army Group, 1945, [BA/MA RW 6/559, RH 2/1355, 2/2623] (http://www.ww2stats.com/cas_ger_okh_dec45.html).

16. Zavizion, *Boevoi Sostav*, vol. V, pp. 54–5.

17. Krivosheev, *Rossiya i SSSR*, pp. 316, 304.

18. S. Gol'chikov, *Posle Boya—Prussiya* (Kalingrad: Tipografiya 'Umnozhenie', 2005), p. 10.

19. Human Losses in World War II. AOK/Ic POW Summary Reports, [BA/MA RH 2/2087, 2/2621, 2/2622K, 2/2633K, 2/2635K, 2/2636-2642, 2/2707, 2/2773, IfZ ED 48] (http://web.archive.org/web/20160304195737/http://www.ww2stats.com/pow_ger_okh_aok.html).

20. K. Knoblaukh, *Krovavyi Koshmar Vostochnogo Fronta. Otkroveniya Ofitersa Parashyutno-Tankovoi Divizii 'German Gering'*, trans. from German by S. Lipatov (Moscow: Yauza-Press, 2010), pp. 97, 108.

21. A. Solzhenitsyn, *Arkipelag GULAG*, vol. I, part 1, chapter 1. 'Arrest', http://e-libra.ru./read/179801-arxipelag-gulag.-1918-1956-opyt-xudozhestvennogo-issledovaniya.-t.-1.html. Editor's note. Aleksandr Isaevich Solzhenitsyn (1918–2008) served during the Second World War as an artillery officer in the Red Army, but was arrested in 1945 and sentenced to eight years in labour camps. Following his relief, he worked as a school teacher and began his writing career, which eventually earned him the Nobel Prize for Literature in 1970. Solzhenitsyn was expelled from the Soviet Union in 1974, but he returned to Russia in 1994.

22. Editor's note. Ivan Danilovich Chernyakhovskii (1906–45) joined the Red Army in 1924 and served in various command capacities before the war. During the Great Patriotic War he advanced from the command of a division to that of a corps and army, and in 1944 was appointed to command the Third Belorussian Front. He was killed during the East Prussian operation in February 1945.

23. L.N. Rabichev, 'Voina vse Spishet', *Znamya* (2005), no. 2, http://magazine.russ.ru/znamia/2005/2/ga8.html.

24. V.V. Karpov, *Marshal Zhukov* (Moscow: Veche, 1999), pp. 376–7.

25. Editor's note. Werner Eduard Fritz von Blomberg (1878–1946) joined the imperial army in 1897 and served in the First World War. In 1933 Hitler appointed him minister of defence and he was made minister of war and commander-in-chief of the armed forces in 1935. He was

implicated in a scandal in 1938 and forced to resign, which enabled Hitler to declare himself commander-in-chief. Blomberg took no part in the war and died in captivity.

26. Editor's note. Viktor Semyonovich Abakumov (1908–54) joined the Red Army in 1922 and the OGPU in 1932. During the Second World War he headed the army's counterintelligence service (SMERSH). He was appointed head of the Ministry of State Security in 1946 and carried out purges of party and military officials under Stalin's orders. He was arrested in 1951 and later executed.

27. Krivosheev, *Rossiya i SSSR*, p. 305.

28. *Vklad Pol'shi i Polyakov v Pobedu Soyuznikov vo II Mirovoi Voine* (Varshava: MID Pol'shi, 2005), p. 34.

29. M. Hastings, 'Operation Unthinkable: How Churchill Wanted to Recruit Defeated Nazi Troops and Drive Russia out of Eastern Europe', *Daily Mail*, 26 August 2009, http://www.dailymail. co.uk/debate/article-1209041/Operation-unthinkable-How-Churchill-wanted-recruit-defeated-Nazi-troops-drive-Russia-Eastern-Europe.html#xzz52GibFOV5.

30. D. Eizenkhauer, *Krestovyi Pokhod v Yevropu* (Moscow: Voennoe Izdatel'stvo, 1980), pp. 446–58; Cherchill', *Vtoraya Mirovaya*, vol. VI, pp. 262–9.

31. Editor's note. Walther Wenck (1900–82) joined the *Freikorps* in 1919 and the *Reichswehr* the following year. During the Second World War he served as chief of staff in a corps, army, and army groups. He later led the unsuccessful attempt to relieve Berlin in April 1945. Following the war, Wenck was released from captivity in 1947 and became an industrial manager. He died in a car crash.

32. O. Bredli, *Istoriya Soldata*, trans. from English (Moscow: EKSMO; Izografus, 2002), p. 640. Editor's note. Omar Nelson Bradley (1893–1981) graduated from West Point in 1915, but took no active part in the First World War. During the Second World War he commanded a corps, army, and an army group. Following the war, Bradley headed the Veteran's Administration and served as chairman of the Joint Chiefs of Staff until his retirement in 1953.

33. *Ibid.*, p. 642.

34. Editor's note. William Hood Simpson (1888–1980) graduated from West Point in 1909 and fought in the First World War. During World War II he commanded a division, a corps, and armies. He retired in 1946.

35. S.T. Ross, *American War Plans, 1941–1945: The Test of Battle* (London: Frank Cass, 1997), p. 149.

36. *Ibid.*, pp. 147–8.

37. C.B. MacDonald, *Tyazheloe Ispytanie. Amerikanskie Vooruzhennye Sily na YevropeiskomTeatre vo Vremya Vtoroi Mirovoi Voiny*, trans. from English (Moscow: Voennoe Izdatel'stvo, 1979), pp. 307–8.

38. G.W. Gellerman, *Die Armee Wenck. Hitlers letzte Hoffnung. Aufstellung, Einsatz und Ende der 12. Deutschen Armee im Fruhjar 1945* (Koblenz: Bernard U. Graefe Verlag, 1984), p. 39.

39. *Ibid.*, p. 107.

40. Krivosheev, *Rossiya i SSSR*, p. 307.

41. *Marshal Pobedy. K 100-Letiyu G.K. Zhukova. Sbornik* (Moscow: Voennoe Izdatel'stvo, 1996), p. 208.

42. Editor's note. The *Volkssturm* (people's storm) units were organized by the Nazi Party as a national militia during the final months of the Second World War, embracing males between the ages of 16 and 60 who were not otherwise serving. Due to poor training and lack of weapons, these units were of negligible value.

43. Krivosheev, *Rossiya i SSSR*, p. 307; *Vklad Pol'shi*, p. 34.

44. *Entsiklopediya Vtoroi Mirovoi Voiny. Krakh Tret'yego Reikha (Vesna–Leto 1945)*,trans. from English by V.D. Tarasova (Moscow: 000 TD 'Izdatel'stvo Mir Knigi', 2007), p. 109.

45. I.S. Konev, 'Sila Sovetskoi Armii i Flota v Rukovodstve Partii, v Nerazryvnoi Svyazi s Narodom', *Pravda*, 1957, 3 Noyabrya, p. 1.

46. Editor's note. Dmitrii Danilovich Lelyushenko (1901–87) joined the Red Army in 1919 and fought in the civil war. During the Second World War he commanded a mechanized corps and several armies. Following the war, Lelyushenko commanded military districts and served in the central military apparatus.

47. V.R. Kabo, *Doroga v Avstraliyu. Vospominaniya* (New York: Effect Publishing, 1995), http://aboriginals.narod.ru/doroga_v_Avstraliyu9.htm.

48. *Das Deutsche Reich und der Zweite Weltkrieg, Band X (1)*, Hrsg. Von Rolf-Dieter Muller (Stuttgart: Deutsche Verlags-Anstalt, 2008), p. 673.

49. K. Raian, *Poslesdnyaya Bitva*, trans. from English (Moscow: Tsentropoligraf, 2003), p. 418.

50. C. Ryan, *The Last Battle* (New York: Simon & Schuster, 1966).

51. V. Ya. Lakshin, *Otkrytaya Dver'* (Moscow: Moskovskii Rabochii, 1989), pp. 327–30. Editor's note. Aleksandr Vasil'evich Gorbatov (1891–1973) joined the Red Army in 1919 and fought in the civil war. He was arrested during Stalin's purge and sent into exile, but survived. During the Second World War he commanded a division, corps, and army. Following the war, Gorbatov commanded the airborne troops, and a military district, among other duties.

52. Krivosheev, *Rossiya i SSSR*, p. 308.

53. *Russkii Arkhiv: Velikaya Otechestvennaya*, vol. 15 (4–5), p. 148.

54. L,Ye. Rubinchik, 'Vospominaniya i Razmyshleniya Serzhanta ob Otdel'nykh Sobytiyakh Otechestvennoi Voiny 1941–1945 Godov', //*Ya Pomnyu.Veterany VOV.Vospomaniniya Veteranov Velikoi Otechestvennoi Voiny*, Opublikovano 28 Avgusta 2007 Goda, http://iremember.ru/memoirs/pekhontintsi/rubinchik-lazar-evseevich/.

55. Human Losses in World War II. Heeresarzt 10-Day Casualty Reports per Army/Army Group, 1945, [BA/MA RW 6/559, RH 2/1355, 2/2623] (http://www.ww2stats.com/cas_ger_okh_dec45.html).

56. *Russkii Arkhiv: Velikaya Otechestvennaya*, vol. 15 (4–5), doc. No. 204, pp. 302–6.

57. S. Knappe and T. Brusaw, *Soldat. Reflections of a German Soldier, 1936–1949* (Shrewsbury: Airlife, 1993), chap. 16, pp. 178–206. For the Russian translation of the fragment of Knappe's memoirs dedicated to the battle for Berlin, see *Bitva za Berlin. Vospominayaet Zigfrid Knappe*//Parabellum (http://www.vn-parabellum.com/battles/berlin-knappe.html).

58. F.D. Vorob'ev, I.V. Parot'kin and A.N. Shimanskii, *Poslednii Shturm* (Moscow: Voennoe Izdatel'stvo), p. 370.

59. *Russkii Arkhiv: Velikaya Otechestvennaya*, vol. 15 (4–5), p. 508.

60. Vorob'ev et al., *Poslednii Shturm*, p. 415.

61. P.D. Antill, *Berlin 1945. End of the Thousand Year Reich* (Oxford: Osprey Publishing Ltd, 2005), p. 85.

62. Zh. Bernazh, *Berlin. 1945. Agoniya 'Tysyacheletnego' Reikha*, trans. from French (Moscow: EKSMO, 2007), p. 175.

63. N. Sennerteg, *Nionde Armens Undergang: Kampen om Berlin 1945* (Historiskt Media, Lund, 2007), p. 378. The British historian Antony Beevor estimates the number of civilian victims in the Ninth Army's breakout at 10,000. See A. Beevor *Padenie Berlina. 1945*, trans. from English (Moscow: AST;Tranzitkniga, 2004), p. 436.

64. Editor's note. Iosip Broz (Tito) (1892–1980) was drafted into the Austro-Hungarian army in 1913 and was later captured on the Eastern Front, where he became a convert to communism. Returning home after the civil war, he helped organize and lead the Yugoslav Communist Party. During the Second World War he led the communist Partisans against the Nazis and Yugoslav royalists and took control of the country in 1945. In 1948 Stalin expelled him from the international communist movement, but Tito survived and adopted a somewhat more independent line between East and West.

65. N.V. Petrov (ed. and compiler), *SVAG i Nemetskie Organy Samoupravleniya, 1945–1949* (Moscow: ROSSPEN, 2006), document No. 57.

66. Editor's note. Ferenc Szalasi (1897–1946) joined the Austro-Hungarian army and fought in the First World War. He left the Hungarian army in 1935 and became involved in politics and later helped found the fascist Arrow Cross Party. Following Horthy's removal in October 1944, the Germans installed Szalasi as head of the government. During his brief tenure in power, he increased the persecution of Hungary's Jewish population and helped the German effort under Adolf Eichmann. Szalasi was captured by US forces in 1945 and was returned to Hungary, where he was tried and executed in 1946.

67. K. Ungvary, *Battle for Budapest. One Hundred Days in World War II*, trans. from Hungarian (London: I.B. Tauris & Co., Ltd, 2003), p. 287.

68. M. Dzhilas, *Litso Totalitarizma* (Moscow: 'Novosti,' 1992), pp. 310–11, 320–1.

69. R.H. Spector, *In the Ruins of Empire: The Japanese Surrender and the Battle for Postwar Asia* (New York: Random House, 2008), pp. 34–5, 144–5.

70. D. Eisenhower, *Crusade in Europe* (New York: Da Capo Press, 1977), pp. 465–8. This episode is missing from the Russian translation of Eisenhower's memoirs, which appeared in 1980.

71. *Ibid.*, p. 465.

72. Editor's note. John Russell Deane (1896–1982) served as head of the US military mission to the Soviet Union during the Second World War.

73. J.R. Deane, *The Strange Alliance. The Story of American Efforts at Wartime Cooperation with Russia* (London: John Murray, 1947), p. 219.

74. Eisenhower, *Crusade*, pp. 468–9.

Chapter 9

1. Chart of US Gross Domestic Product, 1929–2004, http://economics-charts.com/gdp/gdp-1929-2004.html.

2. M.N. Suprun, *Lend-Liz i Severnye Konvoi, 1941–1945 gg.* (Moscow: Andreevskii Flag, 1997), pp. 350, 352.

3. *Ibid.*, p. 352; *Sovetsko-Amerikanskie Otnosheniya vo Vremya Velikoi Otechestvennoi Voiny 1941–1945. Dokumenty i Materialy*, 2 vols (Moscow: Politizdat, 1984), vol. I, p. 137.

4. B.V. Sokolov, 'Sovetskaya Ekonomika: Pravda i Mif', *Pravda o Velikoi Otechestvennoi Voine (Sbornik Statei)* (St Petersburg: Aleteiya, 1998), pp. 336–48; B.V. Sokolov, 'Soviet Economy. Truth and Myth', in *The Role of the Soviet Union in the Second World War: A Re-Examination* (Solihull, UK: Helion & Co., 2013), pp. 137–42.

5. M. Zefirov and D. Degtev, *Vse dlya Fronta? Kak na Samom Dele Kovalas' Pobeda* (Moscow: AST, 2009). See the chapter 'Motornyi Tupik, ili Konets Tsiklona', http://www.e-reading.club/chapter.php/143024/45/Degtev%2C_Zefirov_Vse_dlya_fronta_Kak_na_samom_dele_kovalas%27_pobeda.html.

6. Editor's note. Alesandr Ivanovich Pokryshkin (1913–85) joined the Red Army in 1932 and became a pilot in 1939. During the Second World War he was the highest-scoring Soviet ace and is officially credited with sixty-five victories and was awarded the Hero of the Soviet Union medal three times. Following the war, Pokryshkin served in a variety of command slots, including a stint as deputy chief of the National Air Defence Forces. The Bell-39 Airacobra was a single-seat American-built fighter used by American and Allied forces, including the Soviets, during the Second World War. One model had a maximum speed of 626km per hour and was armed with four 12.7mm machine guns and one 37mm cannon. It could also carry up to 230kg of bombs.

7. M.N. Svirin, *Tankovaya Moshch' SSSR. Chast' III Zolotoi Vek* (Moscow: EKSMO, 2009), chap. XXI, 'Perekuem Mechi na Orala', http://www.nnre.ru/transport_i_aviasija/tankovaja_mosh_sssr_chast_ iii_zolotoi_vek/p8.php. Editor's note. The MkIII 'Valentine' was an infantry tank produced by Great Britain during the Second World War. One model weighed 16 tons and carried a crew of four. It was armed with a 40mm gun and a 7.92mm machine gun.

8. *Ibid.*

9. Editor's note. 'Katyusha' was the popular name for the various Soviet multiple-rocket launcher systems employed during the Second World War.

10. Editor's note. The February Revolution (Old Style, 24–8 February 1917; New Style 8–12 March 1917) overthrew the Romanov dynasty in Russia and paved the way for the proclamation of a republic.

11. For the methodology of and sources for the calculations, see B.V. Sokolov, 'The Role of Lend-Lease in Soviet Military Efforts', *Journal of Slavic Military Studies* (1994), vol. 7, No. 4, repr. in B.V. Sokolov, *The Role*, pp. 48–63. For the Russian text of the article, see B.V. Sokolov, *Vtoraya Mirovaya. Fakty i Versii* (Moscow: AST-Press, 2005), pp. 284–306. The main sources of information are: R.H. Jones, *The Roads to Russia: United States Lend-Lease to the Soviet Union* (Norman, OK: Oklahoma University Press, 1969), appendices; *Tyl Sovetskoi Armii v Velikoi Otechestvennoi Voine, 1941–1945*, chasti I–VI (Leningrad: Akademiya Tyla i Transporta, 1963), chast' I, p. 46; chasti II and III, pp. 147–8; chasti IV, V, VI, pp. 51, 100.

12. *Foreign Relations of the United States: Diplomatic Papers, the Conferences at Cairo and Tehran, 1943* (Washington, DC: United States Government Printing Office, 1961), p. 469.

13. N.K. Khrushchev, *Vremya. Lyudi. Vlast'. (Vospominaniya)* (Moscow: IIK 'Moskovskie Novosti', 1999), book I, p. 598.

14. E.M. Bennett, *Franklin Roosevelt and the Search for Victory: American-Soviet Relations, 1939–1945* (Wilmington, DE: Scholarly Resources, 1990), p. 31. Editor's note. Harry Lloyd Hopkins (1890–1946) was an American social worker who later became one of the architects of Roosevelt's New Deal and secretary of commerce. During the Second World War Hopkins was also a close advisor of the president's on such wartime measures as relations with the Soviet Union.

15. *Promyshlennost' Germanii v Period Voiny*, trans. from German (Moscow: Izdatinlit, 1956), pp. 149–50.

16. O.A. Rzheshevskii, *Stalin i Cherchill'. Vstrechi. Besedy. Diskussii. Dokumenty, Kommentarii. 1941–1945* (Moscow: Nauka, 2004), p. 115.

Chapter 10

1. R.-D. Muller, *The Unknown Eastern Front. The Wehrmacht and Hitler's Foreign Soldiers*, trans. from German by D. Burnett (London; New York: I.B. Taurus, 2012), p. xxvii.

2. D. Kendrick, *The Destiny of Europe's Gypsies* (New York: Basic Books, 1972), p. 183. According to an estimate by Latvian historians, 2,000 Gypsies became victims of genocide. See I. Freibergi and I. Fel'dmanisa, *Istoriya Latvii. XX Vek*, trans. from Latvian (Riga: J.L.V., 2005), p. 269.

3. Editor's note. The *sonderkommandos* were special ad hoc SS subunits formed for carrying out special tasks, such as murder. Paul Blobel (1894–1951) fought in the German army during the First World War. Following the war, he worked as an architect before joining the Nazi Party and the SS in 1931. During the war he and his *sonderkommando* comrades carried out mass murders in various parts of Eastern Europe. Following the war, Blobel was arrested for war crimes and executed in 1951.

4. Editor's note. Kreshchatik is the main street of Kiev, Ukraine.

5. Human Losses in World War II. Heeresarzt 10-Day Casualty Reports per Army/Army Group, 1941, [BA/MA RW 6/556, 6/558] (http://web,archive.org/web/20161102103505/http://ww2stats.com:80/cas_ger_okh_dec41.html).

6. See A. Kruglov, *Tragediya Babego Yara v Nemetskikh Dokumentakh* (Dnepropetrovsk: Tkuma, 2011), pp. 16–17.

7. *Ibid.*, pp. 32–3.

8. R. Ryurupa (ed.), *Voina Germanii Protiv Sovetskogo Soyuza 1941–1945. Dokumental'naya Ekspozitsiya Goroda Berlina k 50-Letiyu so Dnya Napadeniya Germanii na Sovetskii Soyuz* (Berlin: Argon, 1992), p. 117ff.; Sokolov, *Tsena Voiny*, p. 282.

9. Kruglov, *Tragediya*, pp. 118–39.

10. Editor's note. The UPA was the abbreviation of the Ukrainian Insurgent Army, which was formed in 1942 and fought the Germans and Soviets and the nationalist and communist Poles during and after the war. The army was finally suppressed by the Soviets in 1949.
11. Editor's note. The Lithuanian Freedom Army (*Lietuvos laisves armija*) was established in 1941 to free the country from Nazi and Soviet domination. The army fought against the Red Army from 1944 until its suppression in 1946, although partisan activities continued until 1953.
12. B.V. Sokolov, *Okkupatsiya: Pravda i Mify* (Moscow: AST-Press, 2002), pp. 135–6.
13. Editor's note. Sergei Mironovich Kirov (Kostrikov) (1886–1934) joined the Russian Social Democratic Labour Party in 1904 and sided with its Bolshevik faction. During the civil war he was active in the Trans-Caucasus. He was a loyal supporter of Stalin during the latter's climb to power and was made head of the Leningrad party organization. Kirov was assassinated on 1 December 1934, although the circumstances of his death remain vague.
14. Editor's note. Nikolai Aleksandrovich Shchors (1895–1919) fought in the First World War and joined the Red Army and Communist Party in 1918. During the civil war he fought against the Germans and White forces and died in battle.
15. B.V. Sokolov, *Front za Liniei Fronta. Partizanskoe Dvizhenie, 1939–1945 gg.* (Moscow: Veche, 2008), pp. 416–18.
16. Editor's note. Panteleimon Kondrat'evich Ponomarenko (1902–84) joined the Communist Party in 1925 and gradually worked his way through the ranks. He served as head of the Belorussian party organization during the war and was a member of the military council on several *fronts*, and during 1942–4 was head of the Soviet partisan organization. Ponomarenko's career went into eclipse following Stalin's death and he retired in 1978.
17. Sokolov, *Front za Liniei*, p. 141.
18. *Ibid.*, pp. 341–60.
19. Editor's note. The Poles'ye is a large (240,000km²) area of forest and marsh on either side of the Pripyat' River in modern Belarus and Ukraine. It has traditionally divided the western frontier of Russia into northern and southern halves.
20. RGASPI, f. 625, op. 1, d. 8, pp. 63–6; Sokolov, *Front za Liniei*, p. 382–9.
21. On Markov's crime and that of his partisans, see D. Gienek, *Sovetskie Partizany: Galereya Anti-geroev//*Westki.info,2011,8 maya,http://westki.info/blogs/11497/sovetskiie-partizany-halierie-ia-antihieroiev.
22. B.V. Sokolov, *Front za Liniei*, pp. 392–401, 409. Editor's note. Boleslaw Beirut (1892–1956) joined the Polish Communist Party at an early age and spent the interwar years in Poland and the Soviet Union. He was instrumental in establishing communist rule in postwar Poland and served variously as president, prime minister, and head of the Communist Party.
23. See N.V. Petrov, *Po Tsenariyu Stalina: Rol' Organov NKVD-MGB SSSR v Sovetizatsii Stran Tsentral'noi i Vostochnoi Evropy. 1945–1953 gg.* (Moscow: ROSSPEN, 2011), pp. 164–6, 269–70.
24. Editor's note. Sukarno (1901–70) was an Indonesian nationalist leader who fought against Dutch colonial rule, at one time cooperating with the Japanese. Following the Second World War, he resumed the struggle against the Dutch, which led to the country's independence in 1949. Sukarno ruled as an autocrat until 1965, when he was removed by a military coup. He died under house arrest. Hirohito (1901–89) was the 124th emperor of Japan, from 1926 until his death. His reign saw Japanese aggression against China and the Western colonial powers, culminating in the Second World War. Following the war, Hirohito ruled as a constitutional monarch.
25. Editor's note. Ho Chi Minh (1890–1969) was a Vietnamese communist leader who fought the French colonial administration and later the Americans. He proclaimed the Democratic Republic of Vietnam in 1945 and was the head of the ruling communist party and government until his death.
26. Editor's note. Subhas Chandra Bose (1897–1945) was a radical Indian nationalist leader who collaborated with both the Germans and Japanese in order to gain independence from British

colonial rule. Bose also headed the pro-Axis Indian National Army (INA) from 1943 to the end of the war. He was killed in a plane crash.

27. Editor's note. The ROA was the acronym for the Russian Liberation Army (*Russkaya Osvoboditel'naya Armiya*), which was formed from captured Soviet soldiers and White émigrés under German command from 1944 to the end of the war. General A.A. Vlasov hoped to make this an independent force, but was not trusted by the Germans and ROA units eventually turned against the Nazis. Following the war, the top leaders of the movement were executed and the rank and file imprisoned.

28. Editor's note. Walther Kurt von Seydlitz-Kurzbach (1888–1976) joined the imperial army in 1908 and fought during the First World War. During the Second World War he commanded a division and corps on the Eastern Front until he surrendered at Stalingrad. He later collaborated with the Soviets against Hitler. The Soviets sentenced him for war crimes, but released him back to West Germany in 1955. The League of German Officers (*Bund Deutscher Offiziere*) was founded in 1943 and comprised captured German officers who had become disillusioned with Hitler. The organization was headed by von Seydlitz and took an increasingly pro-Soviet line as the war progressed.

29. Editor's note. Lokot'Republic refers to the 'Lokot' self-government' (*Lokotskoe samoupravlenie*), which was organized by the Germans along the contiguous territories of the Bryansk, Orel, and Kursk oblasts' in late 1941. The area had nominal control over its own affairs and pursued a policy of eliminating communists and the collective farms. This territory was lost to the Red Army during the latter half of 1943. Konstantin Pavlovich Voskoboinik (1895–1942) joined the imperial army in 1916 and fought with the Reds during the civil war, although he later took part in anti-Soviet peasant rebellions. The Germans appointed him head of the Lokot' self government, but partisans killed Voskoboinik shortly afterwards. Bronislav Vladislavovich Kaminskii (1899–1944) joined the Red Army and Communist Party, but was later arrested, although he became an NKVD agent. He replaced Voskoboinik as chief of the Lokot' self government and later headed anti-partisan activities for the Germans. Kaminskii was executed by the Germans when they learned of his NKVD ties.

30. I. Hoffman, *Istoriya Vlasovskoi Armii*, trans. from German (Paris: YMCA Press, 1990), pp. 118–19.

31. V.K. Shtrik-Shtrikfeldt, *Protiv Stalin I Gitler: General Vlasov i Russkoe Osvoboditel'noe Dvizhenie*, 3rd edn (Moscow: Posev, 1993), pp. 33–4.

32. A.N. Kolesnik, *ROA—Vlasovskaya Armiya. Sudebnoe Delo A.A. Vlasova* (Khar'kov: Prostor, 1990), p. 76.

33. Editor's note. Alfred Ernst Rosenberg (1893–1946) was born in the Russian Empire of German parents, but he emigrated to Germany in 1918 and joined the Nazi Party the following year. He later became one of the party's chief ideologists and racial theoreticians. In 1941 he was appointed Reich Minister for the Occupied Eastern Territories, but had little real power. Rosenberg was later convicted of war crimes and executed.

34. Editor's note. Andrei Melnyk (1890–1964) was born in Austria-Hungary and fought in its army during the First World War. He was captured by the Russians and later gravitated to Ukrainian nationalist politics. He helped found the Organization of Ukrainian Nationalists (OUN) in 1929 and later headed its more conservative branch, the OUN-M. He cooperated with the Germans during the Second World War, but escaped to the West following the war and died in Luxembourg.

35. The OUN-B was a more radical offshoot of the more established Organization of Ukrainian Nationalists (OUN), the letter B standing for Stepan Bandera, its leader. The OUN-B established the Ukrainian Insurgent Army (UPA) in 1942.

Chapter 11

1. N.N. Kozlova, 'Stseny iz Zhizni 'Osvobozhdennogo Rabotnika', *Sotsiolologicheskie Issledovaniya*, 1998, no. 2, p. 111. Editor's note. 'Smolny's' is a reference to the Smol'nyi Institute, which was built in the early nineteenth century as a school for young noble women. The Bolsheviks commandeered the institute in 1971 and it afterwards served as the headquarters of the city party organization. The Smol'nyi now houses the city and provincial administration.

2. N.Ya. Komarov and G.A. Kumanev, *Bitva pod Moskvoi. Prolog k Velikoi Pobede. Istoricheskii Dnevnik. Kommentarii* (Moscow: Molodaya Gvardiya, 2005), p. 123.

3. Editor's note. The Moscow Mikoyan Meat Factory was named after Anastas Ivanovich Mikoyan (1895–1978), an Armenian-born revolutionary who joined the Bolshevik faction of the Russian Social Democratic Labour Party in 1915. As one of Stalin's early and ardent supporters, he rose quickly through the party's ranks, although Stalin was evidently planning to have him arrested at the time of his death. Mikoyan held high posts in the Soviet state and party apparatus for forty years until forced to retire in 1965.

4. Komarov et al., *Bitva pod Moskvoi*, p. 119.

5. *Ibid.*, p. 119.

6. *Ibid.*, p. 128.

7. D.V. Pavlov, *Leningrad v Blokade* (Leningrad: Lenizdat, 1985), pp. 107–8.

8. Zefirov, et al, *Vse dlya Fronta?* Glava 'Stalinskaya Barshchina', http://www.e-reading.club/chapter.php/1430224/69/Degtev%2C_Zefirov_-Vse_dlya_fronta_Kak   na_samom_dele_kovalas%27_pobeda.html.

9. V.A. Somov, *Po Zakonam Voennogo Vremeni. Ocherki Istorii Trudovoi Politiki SSSR v Gody Velikoi Otechestvennoi Voiny (1941–1945 gg.)* (Izdatel'stvo Nizhegorodskogo Universiteta, 2001), p. 33.

10. V.M. Soima, *Sovetskaya Kontrrazvedka v Gody Velikoi Otechestvennoi Voiny* (Moscow: Kraft+, 2005), pp. 114–15.

11. D.A. Volkogonov, *Stalin. Politicheskii Portret*, 4th edn (Moscow: Novosti, 1997), book 2, pp. 114–15.

12. Zefirov et al., *Vse dlya Fronta?* Glava 'Ukaz, sem'-vosem', sh'esh', nachal'nik', http://www.e-reading.club/chapter.php/143024/75/Degtev%2C_Zefirov_-Vse_dlya_fronta_Kak_na_samom_dele_kovalas%27_pobeda.html.

13. Zefirov et al., *Vse dlya Fronta?* Glava iVorovskoi Khleb, http://www.e-reading.club/chapter.php/143024/68/Degtev%2Zefirov_Vse_dlya_fronta_Kak_na_samom_delekovalas%27_pobeda.html.

14. *Ibid.*

15. *Ibid.*, Chapter 'Na zavode kak v kontslagere', http://www.e-reading.club/chapter.php/143024/61/Degtev%2C_Zefirov_-Vse_dlya _fronta_Kak_na_samom_dele_kovalas%27_pobeda.html.

16. *Ibid.*, Chapter 'Za progul—sem' let lisheniya svobody', http://www.e-reading.club/chapter.php/143024/64/Degtev%2C_Zefirov_-Vse_dlya _fronta_Kak_na_samom_dele_kovalas%27_pobeda.html.

17. *Ibid.*, Chapter 'Kriminal'noe Povolzh'e', http://www.e-reading.club/chapter.php/143024/72/Degtev%2C_Zefirov_-Vse_dlya _fronta_Kak_na_samom_dele_kovalas%27_pobeda.html.

18. *Ibid.*

Chapter 12

1. See Krivosheev, *Rossiya i SSSR*, pp. 500–20. The correlation of 1/3:1 is on p. 518.

2. Smirnov, *Voina i Voennaya*, p. 188; D.A. Volkogonov, 'My Pobedili', p. 5.

3. Gal'der, *Voennyi Dnevnik*, vol. III, book 2, p. 250. *Mirovaya Voina 1939–1945*, trans. from German (Moscow: Izdatel'stvo Innostrannoi Literatury, 1957), p. 189. N.S. Khrushchev, who at the time was a member of the Southwestern Front's and southwestern direction's military council confirmed the German data on the number of prisoners around Khar'kov in his memoirs (see

Ogonyok, 1989, no. 31, p. 22). The data on losses at Khar'kov of 266,927 men, including 13,556 killed, 46,314 wounded/evacuated, and 207,047 missing in action (K.V. Bykov, *Poslednii Triumf Vermakhta: Khar'kovskii 'Kotel'* (Moscow: EKSMO; Yauza-Press, 2009, p. 452), which features in Soviet documents, and in all probability significantly understates losses at the expense of irreplaceable losses among those who were drafted directly into their units. As a contemporary Khar'kov local expert notes, 'the so-called "jackets wearers," or "black coat wearers," as they were known colloquially, first appeared in the history of warfare during the offensive on Khar'kov. Men from 17 to 55 years old, and who for various reasons were not drafted into the army before the occupation, were hurriedly conscripted into the army in the villages occupied by the RKKA. They were not put in military uniforms and, having been quickly distributed throughout the subunits, were thrown into the fighting without any kind of training, often even without weapons. Thus the term "jackets wearers." This phenomenon was widely employed in 1943 during the battle for the Dnepr from the Chernigov region to Tavriya.' (V. Dzhuvaga, 'Segodnya 69-ya Godovshchina Nachala Khar'kovskoi Katastrofy Sovetskikh Voisk//Sait goroda Khar'kova', 2011, 12 maya, http://wwe.057.ua/article/53735). The fate of the 'jacket wearers', including women, was tragic. A German captain, the commander of a battalion in the 294th Infantry Division, which was defending the village of Peschanoe on 16 April 1942, wrote in his diary: 'I saw here a battlefield that one can only encounter in this campaign. Hundreds of killed Russians, and among them German soldiers. The majority of them are half-dressed, without boots, and with horrible wounds and stiffened extremities. Among them are Russian civilians, women.' (*Stalingradskaya Epopeya* (Moscow: Lada IKTTs, Zvonnitsa-MG, 2000), p. 28). Actually, the first 'jacket wearers' appeared as early as the Soviet counteroffensive around Moscow in December 1941. But it is possible that the conscription of people directly into units was in practice even earlier, during the Soviet forces' retreat.

4. A. Dallin, *German Rule in Russia, 1941–1945* (London, New York: St Martin's Press, 1957), p. 427.

5. Human Losses in World War II. AOK/Ic POW Summary Reports, [BA/MA RH 2/2087, 2/2621, 2/2622K, 2/2633K, 2/2635K, 2/2636-2642, 2/2707, 2/2773, IfZ ED 48] (http://web.archive.org/web/20160304195737/http:///.ww2stats.com/pow_ger_okh_aok.html).

6. Krivosheev, *Grif Sekretnosti*, p. 129.

7. Krivosheev, *Rossiya i SSSR*, p. 237.

8. Dallin, *German Rule*, p. 427.

9. *Nyurnbergskii Protsess* (Moscow Gosudarstvennoe Yuridicheskoe Izdatel'stvo, 1960), vol. III, pp. 29–30.

10. E. Pietola, 'Voennoplennye v Finlyandii 1941–1944', *Sever* (1990), no. 12. The mortality rate among Soviet prisoners in Romania was not high. At the time Romania left the war in August 1944, there were 59,856 prisoners in the camps. 5,221 prisoners of war died before this, while another 3,331 escaped from captivity. In 1943 the Romanian authorities freed from captivity 13,682 people born in Transnistria, on territory annexed by Romania, and as early as 1941 about 80,000 natives of Bessarabia and Northern Bukovina were freed (A. Shneer, *Plen*, pp. 222–3.). In all, the Romanians captured more than 160,000 prisoners. The Hungarian and Italian units turned over their prisoners to the Germans, so they were not counted among the Soviet prisoners taken by the Germans.

11. M. Gareev, 'O Mifakh Starykh i Novykh', *V-IZh* (1991), no. 4, p. 47.

12. See S.G. Sidorov, 'Organizatsiya Pitaniya Voennoplennykh v SSSR v 1941-1955 gg', *Vestnik Volgogradskogo Gosudarstvennogo Universiteta* (Seriya 4: Istoriya. Filosofiya. Vypusk 1, 1996), pp. 71–82; S.G. Sidorov, *Stalingradskaya Bitva v Istorii Rossii* (Sankt Peterburg: Izdatel'stvo Sankt-Peterburgskogo Gosuniversiteta, 1997), pp. 85–105.

13. R. Overmans, 'Drugoi Lik Voiny: Zhizn' I Gibel' 6-I Armii', in J. Furster (ed.), *Stalingrad: Sobytie. Vozdeistvie. Simvol*, trans. from German (Moscow: Progress-Akademiya, 1994), p. 469, table 3.

14. Krivosheev, *Rossiya i SSSR*, p. 515, table 201.
15. V. Abramov, *Kerchenskaya Katastrofa 1942* (Moscow: Yauza; EKSMO, 2006), p. 19.
16. Yu.V. Rubtsov, *Mekhlis. Ten' Vozhdya* (Moscow: Veche, 2011), p. 259.
17. Rasstrel nemetskikh voennoplennykh v Bronnikakh. 30 iyunya-1 iyulya 1941 g.//http://allin777.livejournal.com/138875.html.
18. Sokolov, *Okkupatsiya*, pp. 269–70.
19. S.A. Il'enkov, 'Pamyat' o Millionakh Pavshikh Zashchitnikov Otechestva Nel'zya Predavat' Zabveniyu', *Voenno-Istoricheskii Arkhiv*, 2000, no. 7(22), pp. 77–8. This author may be grouped with the national-democratic sub-tendency of the liberal-democratic movement.
20. I.I. Ivlev, '. . . A v Otvet Tishina—on Vchera ne Vernulsya iz Boya!', *Voennaya Arkheologiya*, 2011, nos 1–4. These articles are also located at the site of I.I. Ivlev, a noted Archangel searcher, 'Soldat.ru.' (http://www.soldat.ru/news/865.html; http://www.soldat.ru/news/866.html; http://www.soldat.ru/news878.html; http://www.soldat.ru/news/880.html). This author may be grouped with the representatives of the right-nationalist movement.
21. *Ibid.*, http://www.soldat.ru/news/880.html.
22. Krivosheev, *Rossiya i SSSR*, p. 238, table 121.
23. Calculation according to V.S. Kozhurin, 'O Chislennosti Naseleniya SSSR Nakanune Velikoi Otechestvennoi Voiiny', *V-IZh* (1991), no. 2, p. 26.
24. B.V. Sokolov, *Tsena Voiny*, p. 280.
25. N. Sokolov, (Redaktsiya 'Vokrug Sveta'), 'Svedenie schetov. Ob"yasnenie s Chitatelyami po sluchayu spornykh tsifr sootnosheniya poter' Krasnoi armii i vermakhta v gody Vtoroi mirovoi voiny', *Telegraf. Vokrug Sveta* 30 June 2011 (http://www.vokrugsveta.ru/telegraph/history/1339/); F. Setin, 'Skol'ko zhe my Poteryali v Voine?', *Russkaya Zhizn'*, 1991, 25 Maya.
26. N. Sokolov (Redaktsiya 'Vokrug Sveta'), 'Svedenie schetov'; *Rossiya i SSSR*, p. 245.
27. See V. Fei, *Tankovye Srazheniya Voisk SS.*, trans. from English (Moscow: Yauza Press, 2009), pp. 109–11, 140, 146, 168–99, 254, 264, 296, 309, 327, 337–40, 352–4, 358, 362, 373; A.V. Drabkin, *Ya Dralsya na T-34* (Moscow: Yauza; EKSMO, 2010).
28. V. Bykov, '"Za Rodunu! Za Stalina!" Tsena Proshedshikh Boev', *Rodina* (1995), no. 5, pp. 32–3.
29. Estimated according to Myueller-Gillebrand, *Sukoputnaya Armiya*, vol. III, pp. 338–44; Dzh. Erman, *Bol'shaya Strategiya: Oktyabr' 1944–Avgust 1945* (Moscow: Inostrannaya Literatura, 1958), pp. 119, 121.
30. R. Overmans, *Deutsche militaerische Verluste im Zweiten Weltkrieg* (3 Aufl.-Muenchen: R. Oldenbourg Verlag, 2004) p. 195, table 14.
31. See N. Zetterling, 'Comments on "Deutsche Militarische Verluste: by Rudger Overmanns', http://web.archive.org/web/20060219111518/http://web.telia.com/u18313395/overmans.pdf.
32. Overmans, *Deutsche militaerische*, p. 194, table 14.
33. *Ibid.*, p. 336, table 73f.
34. *Ibid.*, p. 260, table 49; p. 335, tables-73b-73d.
35. *Ibid.*, p. 332, table 72; p. 334, table 73.
36. *Ibid.*, p. 242, table 40.
37. Editor's note. This was the colloquial name given to the anti-communist Estonian, Latvian, and Lithuanian guerillas that waged a partisan struggle against Soviet forces for several years during and after the Second World War.
38. S. Akhonen, 'Stranitsy Slavy Latyshskogo Legiona SS'//Informatsionnoe Agentstvo InfoRos, 2005, 22 aprelya (http://www.inforos.ru/?id=5862).
39. R. Overmans, *Deutsche militaerische*, p. 336, table 73e.
40. *Ibid.*, p. 286, table 65. This estimate is based on data from the commission of the historian Erich Maschke, which was created by the Federal Republic of Germany for determining the fate of German prisoners of war. In 1974 the commission published an account, according to which about 25,000 Germans died in French captivity, about 5,000 in American captivity, and about 2,700 in British captivity. (P. Buttar, *Battleground Prussia. The Assault on Germany's Eastern*

Front 1944–45 (Oxford: Osprey Publishing Ltd, 2010, p. 421). Evidently the data presented above on the mortality of prisoners of war relates only to those whose death in captivity was reliably established through the exact determination by name and surname, when the actual mortality was probably significantly higher.

41. Calculation made by M.Ya. Berzina on the basis of the yearly *Canada Yearbook* for different years. See M.Ya. Berzina, *Formirovanie Etnicheskogo Sostava Naseleniya Kanady (Etnostatis-ticheskoe Issledovanie)* (Moscow: Nauka, 1971), p. 70, table 5.

42. Krivosheev, *Rossiya i SSSR*, p. 245.

43. B.V. Sokolov, *Tsena Voiny*, pp. 353–4.

44. *Ibid.*, pp. 256–73; B.V. Sokolov, 'Estimating Soviet War Losses', *The Role*, pp. 116–36.

45. D.I. Stupin (ed.), *Kniga Pamyati. Kimry* (Moscow: ANO 'Redaktsiya gazety 'Kimry Segodnya', 2016.

46. *Vsesoyuznaya Perepis' Naseleniya 1939 g. Chislennost' Nalichnogo Naseleniya SSSR po Raionam i Gorodam*//http://www.demoscope.ru/weekly/ssp/rus_pop_39_2.php.

47. V.S. Kozhurin, 'O Chislennosti Naseleniya', p. 24.

48. *Vsesoyuznaya Perepis'*//http://www.demoscope.ru/weekly/ssp/rus_pop_39_2.php.

49. Kozhurin, 'O Chislennosti', p. 24.

50. A. Mikhailova and Ye. Khrenova, 'Oni Srazhalis' za Moyu Rodinu', //http://wiki.pskovedu.ru/index.php/Oni_srazhalis'_za_moyu_rodinu.

51. 'Analiz Poter' Voznesenskogo Raiona v Velikoi Otechestvennoi Voine', GBU Tsentr Sotsial'nogo Obsluzhivaniya Grazhdan Pozhilogo Vozrasta i Invalidov Voznesenskogo Raiona, 2015, 16 Aprelya, http://cso.vzn.ru/k-70-letiyu-pobedy/410-analiz-poter-voznesenskogo-rajona-v-ve-likoj-otechestvennoj-vojne.html (Elektronnyi Resurs). Based on *Kniga Pamyati Nizhegorodtsev, Pavshikh v Velikoi Otechestvennoi Voine 1941–1945 Godov. Bol'shemurashinskii, Buturulinskii, Varnavinskii, Voznesenskii, Volodarskii, Vyksunskii Raiony* (Nizhnii Novgorod: Nizhepoligraf, 1994), vol. V, pp. 302–411, 629–31.

52. *Vsesoyuznaya Perepis'*//http://www.demoscope.ru/weekly/ssp/rus_pop_39_2.php; V.S. Kozhurin, 'O Chislennosti', p. 24.

53. P.N. Shabanov, *Tsena Pobedy. Popytka Novogo Vzglyada na Poteri RKKA. Ch. 1*//belorizec.livejournal.com/,29 marta 2015; http://belorized.livejournal.com/119139.html; See his *Tsena Pobedy. Popytka Novogo Vzglyada na Poteri RKKA. Ch. 2*//belorizec.livejournal.com/5 maya 2015://belorizec.livejournal.com/121791.html; P.N. Shabanov's letter to the author of 29 April 2015.

54. V.S. Usatykh (ed.), *Altaiskii Krai 1941–1945 gg. Kniga Pamyati* (Barnaul: Altaiskoe Knizhnoe Izdatel'stvo, 1996), vol. IX, pp. 597, 3.

55. N.S. Gavrilov, *Altai v Velikoi Otechestvennoi Voine* (Barnaul: Altaiskoe Knizhnoe Izdatel'stvo, 1990), p. 236.

56. Myuller-Gillebrand, *Sukhoputnaya Armiya*, vol. III, pp. 323, 328.

57. *Ibid.*, vol. III, p. 327.

58. *Ibid.*, vol. III, p. 338.

59. According to official data, 442,100 former military personnel of the German army died in captivity in the USSR (Krivosheev, *Rossiya i SSSR*, p. 515, table 201). Earlier, the authors of *The Seal of Secrecy Removed* adhered to a higher estimate of the number of those who died in captivity – 450,600 (Krivosheev, *Grif Sekretnosti*, pp. 391–2.)

60. V. Erlikhman, *Poteri Narodonaseleniya v XX Veke. Spravochnik* (Moscow: Russkaya Panorama, 2004), p. 133.

61. Estimate according to Myuller-Gillebrand, *Sukhoputnaya Armiya*, vol. III, pp. 323–44. For more detail, see B.V. Sokolov, 'The Cost of War: Human Losses for the USSR and Germany,

1939–1945', *Journal of Slavic Military Studies*, March 1996; B.V. Sokolov, *Tainy Vtoroi Mirovoi* (Moscow: Veche, 2001), pp. 247–50.

62. See R. Overmans, 'Chelovecheskie Zhertvy Vtoroi Mirovoi Voiny v Germanii', *Vtoraya Mirovaya Voina. Diskussii. Tendentsii. Rezul'taty Issledovanii*, trans. from German (Moscow: Ves' Mir, 1997), p. 682, table 1. Here are also lower estimates of 1.5 million, as well as higher ones of up to 3 million.

63. B.V. Sokolov, *Tainy Finskoi Voiny* (Moscow: Veche, 2000), p. 346.

64. Krivosheev, *Poteri Rossii i SSSR*, p. 309.

65. According to our estimate, the correlation of losses in Italy between the German forces and the Anglo-American troops was approximately equal, and in the northwestern theatre of military operations the correlation of killed following the landings in Normandy was approximately 1.6:1 in favour of the Western Allies, chiefly due to the losses in 1945. Estimate according to B.Ts. Urlanis, *Voiny i Narodonaselenie Evropy* (Moscow: Sotsekgiz, 1960), pp. 221–35; Myuller-Gillebrand, *Sukhoputnaya Armiya*, vol. III, pp. 338–44; V.I. Dashichev, *Bankrotstvo Strategii Germanskogo Fashizma* (M: Nauka, 1973), vol. II, pp. 637–8; Makdonal'd, *Tyazheloe Ispytanie*, p. 346.

66. Human Losses in World War II. Heeresarzt 10-Day Casualty Reports per Army/Army Group, 1945, [BA/MA RW 6/559, RH 2/1355, 2/2623] (http://web.archive.org/web/20160303231601/ http://ww2stats.com/cas_ger_okh_dec45.html).

67. V. Lyubekke, *U Vorot Leningrada. Istoriya Soldata Gruppy Armii 'Sever.' 1941–1945*, trans. from German (Moscow: Tsentropoligraf, 2017), p. 167.

68. G. Neidermeyer, 'Na Vraga s Diviziei "Leibshtandart"'. H. Neidermeyer and I. Walters, *Esesovskaya 'Gvardiya' v Boyu: Frontovye Memuary Veteranov 1-i Tankovoi Divizii SS 'Leibshtandart Adol'f Hitler'* (Moscow: Yauza; Press, 2011), p. 69.

69. B.M. Sokolov, *Tsena Voiny*, pp. 22–3.

70. K.M. Simonov, 'Nashe Vremya eshche Zanesut na Skrizhali . . . Zapisi v Rabochikh Tetradyakh: Besedy i Razmyshleniya', *Druzhba Narodov*, 2015, no. 12, http://magazines.russ.ru/druzhba/2015/12/12s.html.

71. N.S. Gavrilov, *Altai v Velikoi*, p. 18.

72. See *Mirovaya Voina 1939–1945*, pp. 153–4; F. Mellentin, *Tankovye Srazheniya 1939–1945 gg.*, trans. from English (Moscow: Izdatel'stvo Inostrannoi Literatury, 1957), pp. 148, 244–6, 252.

73. Editor's note. Zhores Aleksandrovich Medvedev (1925–) was trained as a biologist, but later became a dissident historian and was even confined to a mental hospital. He was later stripped of his Soviet citizenship. He continues to engage in polemics with the new regime.

74. Zh. Medvedev, 'Monolog o Svoei Zhizni Zhoresa Medvedeva, Byvshego Sovetskogo Sumashedshego, Literaturnaya Deyatel'nost' Kotorogo Vyzyvala Nedovol'stvo KGB i TsRU, Nyne Izvestnogo Angliiskogo Uchenogo', *Zvezda* (1990), no. 3, pp. 140–1.

75. Editor's note. William Averell Harriman (1891–1986) was the son of a wealthy businessman and who became active in Democratic Party politics and later served in a variety of posts at the state and national level. During the Second World War he was Roosevelt's personal envoy in Great Britain and the Soviet and was later appointed ambassador to the latter country.

76. 'Russkie shli Volna za Volnoi. Beseda Amerikanskogo Professora Urbana s Byvshim Poslom v SSSR Garrimanom (1979 g.)', *Rodina* (1991), nos 6–7, p. 49.

77. See information on V.P. Dyatlov in the database 'Podvig Naroda', http://podvignaroda.mil.ru/?#id=39414751&tab=navDetailManAward.

78. *Komsomol'skaya Pravda*, 1993, 24 Iyunya, p. 3.

79. J. Lucas, *War on the Eastern Front; the German Soldier in Russia* (London: Greenhill Publishers, 1991), pp. 31–3.

80. *Ibid.*, pp. 35–6; Eisenhower, *Crusade*, pp. 465–8.

81. A.I. Yeremenko, *Stalingrad* (Moscow: Veche, 2013), p. 352

82. A.I. Yeremenko, *Protiv Fal'sifikatsii Istorii Vtoroi Mirovoi Voiny* (Moscow: Izdatel'stvo Inostrannoi Literatury, 1958), p. 93.
83. About the 1940 Census//Official 1940 Census website (http://1940 census.archives.gov/about/).
84. Ye.I. Malashenko, 'Ya v Razvedke s Sorok Pervogo . . ', *V-IZh* (1995), no. 3, pp. 77–8.
85. A.I. Muranov and V.Ye. Zvyagintsev, *Dos'e na Marshala: Iz Istorii Zakrytykh Sudebnykh Protsessov* (Moscow: Andreevskii Flag, 1996), p. 200.
86. M. Myagkov, 'Osen' 41-go. Pervye Uroki Voiny', *Krasnaya Zvezda*, 2001, 24 November.
87. V.S. Khristoforov, 'Snyat' s Dolzhnosti . . . i Otdat' pod Sud', *V-IZh* (2001), no. 11, pp. 49–50. During one of his interrogations in 1944, S.A. Kalinin admitted that according to his calculations the USSR's losses in the war with Germany would amount to no less than 20 million people, while at the same time the Germans' losses would be twice as few. In all likelihood, he had in mind only those killed and significantly overstated the Germans' losses. In his diary the general stressed that the high command of the Red Army did not concern itself with preserving human resources, allowing large losses in individual operations and that not a single state expends its people so uneconomically as the Soviet Union. S.A. Kalinin also wrote in his diary that the arrests of 1937–8 terrorized the command element of the RKKA and made it lacking in initiative and independence (*ibid.*, pp. 50–1).
88. 'My Otstali ot Peredovykh Stran na 50–100 Let. My Dolzhny Probezhat' eto Rasstoyanie v Desyat' Let. Libo my Sdelaem eto, Libo nas Somnut'. (I.V. Stalin, 'O Zadachakh Khozyaistvennikov. Rech' na Pervoi Vsesoyuznoi Konferentsii Rabotnikov Sotsialisticheskoi Promyshlennosti 4 Fevralya 1931 g', I.V. Stalin, *Sobranie Sochinenii* (Moscow: OGIZ, 1951), vol. XIII, p. 39.)
89. V.N. Novikov (ed.), *Oruzhie Pobedy*, 2nd edn (Moscow: Mashinostroenie, 1987), p. 447.

Chapter 13

1. Editor's note. Andrei Platonov was the literary pseudonym of Andrei Platonovich Klimentov (1899–1951), an early Soviet writer whose works often ran foul of the official line. Platonov also served as a war correspondent.
2. *Geroi Sovetskogo Soyuza Voenno-Morskogo Flota* (Moscow: Voennoe Izdatel'stvo, 1977), p. 488.
3. L.N. Yefimenko, 'Vos'maya Morskaya', *U Chernomorskikh Tverdyn'* (Moscow: Voennoe Izdatel'stvo, 1967), pp. 287–8.
4. The text of the leaflet is cited according to Ye.L. Yagodinskii, *Zolotye Zvezdy Rechnikov* (Moscow; DOSAAF, 1979), vypusk 3, pp. 89–90.
5. B. Pereslegin, Kommentarii to E. Manstein *Uteryannye Pobedy*, p. 307.
6. Editor's note. The Stug III (*Sturmgeschutz III*) was a mobile assault gun widely used by the Germans as a tank destroyer during the Second World War. One model weighed 23.9 tons and had a crew of four. It was armed with a 75mm gun and one 7.92mm machine gun.
7. Editor's note. The R-1 was a Romanian licensed version of the Czechoslovak-made AH-IV light tank. One model weighed 3.9 tons and carried a crew of two. It was armed with two 7.92mm machine guns.
8. 'Zamikhovskii, Grigorii Yefimovich—Matros Chernomorskogo Flota. Interv'yu Grigoriya Koifmana', *Voennoe Obozrenie*, 2013, 18 Yanvarya.
9. http://www.obd-memorial.ru/html/index.html.
10. V.I. Lysov et al. (eds), *Kniga Pamyati Nizhegorodtsev, Pavshikh v Velikoi Otechestvennoi Voine 1941–1945 Godov* (Nizhnii Novgorod: Nizhpoligraf, 1995), vol. VI, p. 478, http://nipol.ucoz.ru/load/nezhegorodskaja_oblast/kniga_pamjati_nizhegorodskoj_oblasti/kniga-pamjati_nizhegorodcev_pavshikh_v_veliloj_otechestvennoj_vojne_1941_1945_godov_tom_6/9-1-0-37.
11. Editor's note. The name for those soldiers (Russ., *Panfilovtsy*) who served in Major General Ivan Vasil'evich Panfilov's 316th Rifle Division during the Battle of Moscow.

12. Spravka-doklad glavnogo voennogo prokurora N. Afanas'eva 'O 28 Panfilovtsakh"//Gosudarst-vennyi arkhiv Rossiiskoi Federatsii, http://statearchive.ru/607

13. *Ibid.* Editor's note. *Red Star* (*Krasnaya Zvezda*) was the official organ of the Soviet armed forces from its founding in 1924. It now serves the same purpose for the Russian armed forces. David Iosifovich Ortenberg (1904–98) joined the Communist Party in 1921 and the Red Army in 1938. During 1941–3 he was editor of *Red Star* and later served as political commissar in an army. Following the war, Ortenberg continued to serve in military-political posts

14. *Ibid.*

15. A.F. Katusev, 'Chuzhaya Slava', *V-IZh* (1990), no. 9, pp. 74–5.

16. A. Statiev, 'La Garde meurt mais ne se rrend pas! Once again on the 28 Panfilov Heroes', *Kritika: Explorations in Russian and Eurasian History*, 13.4. Fall 2012, pp. 769–98.

17. Human Losses in World War II. Heeresarzt 10-Day Casualty Reports per Army/Army Group, 1945, [BA/MA RW 6/556, 6/558 (http://web.archive.org/web/20161102103505/http://www.ww2stats.com:80/cas_ger_okh_dec41.html).

18. Spravka-doklad glavnogo voennogo prokurora N. Afanas'eva 'O 28 Panfilovtsakh"//Gosudarst-vennyi arkhiv Rossiiskoi Federatsii, http://statearchive.ru/607.

19. Editor's note. *Pravda* was the official organ of the Soviet Communist Party Central Committee from 1912–91. It has since been revived as the organ of the Communist Party of the Russian Federation.

20. *G.K. Zhukov v Bitve pod Moskvoi. Sbornik Dokumentov* (Moscow: Mosgorarkhiv, 1994), pp. 47–8.

21. A. Krechetnikov, 'Russkaya Zhanna d'ark: kak Zoya Kosmodem'yanskaya Stala Geroinei Voiny'//Russkaya Sluzhba Bi-Bi-Si, 2016, 29 Noyabrya, http://www.bbc.com/russian/features-37950999.

22. Editor's note. 'Nagan' was the Russian pronunciation for the Nagant M11895 seven-shot revolver, which was originally designed and produced by Leon Nagant, a Belgian manufacturer, for the Russian Empire. The revolver also saw service well into the Soviet era.

23. M. Gridneva, 'Agent Reabilitatsii ne Podlezhit', *Moskovskii Komsomolets*, 2002, 9 Oktyabrya, p. 5.

24. See I.F. Afanas'ev, *Dom Soldatskoi Slavy* (Moscow: DOSAAF, 1970).

25. Editor's note. Il'ya Grigor'evich Ehrenburg (1891–1967) was a Soviet-era author and journalist who first achieved fame as a correspondent during the First World War. He returned to Russia after the revolution and became a vocal supporter of the regime, particularly abroad. Vasilii Semyonovich Grossman (1905–64) was trained as a chemist, but later became a journalist and author. His later works dealing with the Second World War were banned by the regime.

26. The fate of the defenders of 'Pavlov's house' were tracked down according to: Yu.N. Panchenko, *163 Dnya na Ulitsakh Stalingrada* (Volgograd: Printerra, 2006); Ye. Platunov, 'Odin iz 24-kh'//http://www.amic.ru/article/95726/,2008,25 Noyabrya.

27. For A.M. Matrosov's biography, see 'Brosok v Bessmertie', *Eto Bylo na Kalininskom Fronte* (Moscow: Moskovskii Rabochii, 1985), p. 73; A.P. Kovalenko, *Vershiny Muzhestva* (Moscow: MOF 'Pobeda', 1995) p. 38.

28. 'Brosok', pp. 72–3.

29. https://www.obd-memorial.ru/html/info.htm?id=55053408.

30. Kovalenko, *Vershiny*, p. 40.

31. E. Raus, *Panzer Operations. The Eastern Front Memoir of General Raus, 1941–1945*, compiled and trans. by Steven H. Newton (Boston: Da Capo Press, 2003), pp. 26–34.

32. V.M. Kolomiets, 'Istoriya Boya KV c Nemetskimi Chastyami v Iyune 1941 g.'//Feldgrau.Info. Voenno-istoricheskii sait, 2016, 29 marta, http://feldgrau.info/other/14467-istoriya-boya-kv-s-nemetskimi-chastyami-v-iyune-1941g.

33. Balck, *Order in Chaos*, pp. 333–4.